The Korean Government:

Policies and Administration

1948~2013

The Korean Government:
Policies and Administration
1948~2013

The Korea Institute of Public Administration

The Korean Government:
Policies and Administration
1948~2013

ISBN 978-89-7644-543-8
Published by Choon Hwan Lim
Daeyoung Moonhwasa Publishing Co.
5, Cheongpa-ro 61-gil, Yongsan-gu, Seoul, 04308, Korea
TEL (02) 716-3883, (02) 714-3062
FAX (02) 703-3839
Published on 31 December, 2015

Price ₩30,000

Foreword

This year marks the 67th anniversary of the inauguration of the first administration of the Republic of Korea. The country has since grown remarkably to become the world's 10th biggest economy. The world marveled at the astonishing growth of the country, with many developing countries striving to learn from the experience of the Republic of Korea.

The government of the Republic of Korea has always been in the center stage of the country's rapid development. Numerous administrations have come and gone since the inauguration of the Syngman Rhee administration in 1948, each of them pushing forward with its own policy initiatives and national projects. Thanks to such governmental policy initiatives and national projects, the country was able to erase the scars of the Korean War that broke out in 1950 while accomplishing unprecedented economic growth and democratization of its political system at the same time.

Not all policy initiatives were successful, though; some of them disappointed the people by failing to meet the promised goals set for national development and the uplifting of the living standards of the people.

Success or failure notwithstanding, all the policy initiatives that were pushed forward and implemented by the governments of the Republic of Korea are the legacy of the country's modern history as well as precious references worth consulting by the future administrations when they establish and implement their own policy packages. Furthermore, the key policy initiatives of the past governments of the Republic of Korea are the object of attention of many countries the world over, including many developing countries. Therefore, an analysis of the factors that contributed to the success or failure of the policies that were pushed forward by the past governments of the Republic of Korea, and the utilization of those analysis results as reference points for the policy planning and implementation of the future administrations, would be absolutely required.

The Korea Institute of Public Administration (KIPA), a government-affiliated national research and development institute within the jurisdiction of the Prime Ministerial Office, has embarked on a publishing project with the aim of identifying the key policies that were implemented by the past governments of the Republic of Korea as well as the background of each policy initiative and its execution. The endeavor materialized in the form of Key Policies and Administration of the Governments of the Republic of Korea, an eight-volume book that deals with the related issues comprehensively.

The project of compiling and publishing the Korean edition, which had been planned and implemented since the latter part of 2013 with the participation of 80 scholars from the Korea Institute of Public Administration and other institutions, covers the development of the key policy initiatives and administration of the past governments of the Republic of Korea, from the Syngman Rhee administration to the Lee Myung Bak administration, from an objective and comprehensive perspective. The key sub-topics were selected by the Korea Institute of Public Administration, but the direction and contents of each selected subtopic were left to the discretion of each writer.

This book was completed by summarizing and editing the eight-volume Korean version published in 2014 and then translating the result into English. The book is made up of eight chapters, starting from Chapter 1: The Syngman Rhee/Jang Myeon Administration to Chapter 8: The Lee Myung Bak Administration. With the exception of the Heo Jeong Cabinet, which was an interim government, and the incumbency of President Choi Kyu Ha, the book covers the key policy initiatives and national projects of the past governments of the Republic of Korea as well as their efforts to reform the government. The introduction to this research can be found in the front section of Chapter 1, and the conclusion, in the concluding section of Chapter 8.

Each government was covered in three major sections, with the exception of the short-lived Jang Myeon administration, with section 1 focusing on explaining the inauguration of each administration as well as the basis of the respective government administrations. Section 1 contains a general introduction of each administration as well as an analysis of the key goals and directions of the respective government administrations, and section 2 of each chapter contains an analysis of the key policy initiatives and national projects that were pushed forward by each administration.

The key policy initiatives and national projects that were included in section 2 of each chapter were selected by identifying the key policies that each administration made its priority as well as those that were the objects of national controversy, and section 3 of each chapter deals with the government reforms implemented by each administration.

The publication of this book was the brainchild of Prof. Lee Eun Jae. She is the former president of the Korea Institute of Public Administration who was at the helm of planning and execution of the project before her retirement in September 2015. Without her relentless effort and enthusiasm, this book would not have seen the light of day. I am sincerely grateful to Prof. Lee for the unwavering support and dedication she has given to this endeavor.

Finally, I would like to extend my sincere gratitude to all the writers, editorial committee members, and advisory committee members who made valuable contributions to this work. I genuinely hope that the achievements contained in this marvelous endeavor would provide valuable insight to the researchers of the Republic of Korea as well as to the world's policymakers.

Thank you.

December 2015
Dr. Yoon-Soo Jung
President of KIPA

TABLE OF CONTENTS

Chapter 2 The Park Jung Hee Administration

Chapter 3 The Chun Doo Hwan Administration

Chapter 4 The Roh Tae Woo Administration

Chapter 5 The Kim Young Sam Administration

Chapter 6 The Kim Dae Jung Administration

Chapter 8 The Lee Myung Bak Administration

Conclusion: Foundation of the Republic of Korea, Miraculous Industrialization and Democratization, and Strategy of Government Administration

Introduction

1. Objective of Study

2015 marks the 70th anniversary of the country's liberation from the iron grip of Japan. The country has since been governed by 10 administrations, each having had to grapple with its share of historical burden, including a war, a student revolution, a military coup, and a democratic uprising. The government of the Republic of Korea has always been at the center stage in the country's turbulent modern history, which is riddled with innumerable political ups and downs despite its relative shortness. Meanwhile, within that short period, what was once one of the poorest countries in the world that largely depended on an agrarian economy has dramatically evolved and has joined the club of the advanced economies of the world. The South Korean government has also been in the middle of a case of astounding economic growth that stunned the whole world. For all the gaffes and misjudgments that it had made while formulating its policy initiatives, it would be fair to say that the government of the Republic of Korea has played a decisive role in making the country what it is today.

The Korea Institute of Public Administration has embarked on a project to identify and to analyze the key policies from those implemented by the successive administrations for decades. These assessment results are to be used as reference materials for the formulation and implementation of future government policies. The endeavor is significant because it is a monumental step towards the establishment of the legitimate history of the governments of the Republic of Korea. In the introduction, the roles played by each successive government — from the Syngman Rhee administration to the Lee Myung Bak administration — in building the country up to its current state shall be examined.

Each administration shall be analyzed for the role that it played from the perspective of national development. Specifically, the Syngman Rhee administration shall be analyzed for its contribution to the foundation of the country, followed by an analysis of the modernization and economic development. Then, an analysis of the still-ongoing democratization process that was implemented in earnest by following administrations in the wake of the democratic civil uprising in 1989. Furthermore, analyses of major financial upheavals that took place during the process of nation's ongoing economic advancement, including the 1997 Asian financial crisis, in which the country was ruled by the rigorous regime outlined by the International Monetary Fund, as well as the two successive financial crises triggered by the fiscal blunders committed by the advanced economies.

2. Nation Building

The most pressing task faced by the fledgling new country that was born in 1948 was nation building. The country was liberated from the Japanese colonial rule, with the northern half of the peninsula occupied by the Soviet army and the southern half by the U.S. forces.

During the three years of military administration following the liberation, the country struggled through an extreme political quagmire marked by a fierce rivalry among the different political camps, in which the left, right, and moderate groups vied for political supremacy in the liberated Korea. In the Interim Meeting of Foreign Ministers of the United States, Soviet Union, and United Kingdom (a.k.a. the Moscow Tripartite Summit), which was held in Moscow in December 1945, the participants agreed to establish a four-power trusteeship for the Korean Peninsula involving the United States and the Soviet Union.[1] The meeting led to the installation of the Joint U.S. - U.S.S.R. Commission on Korea, in which the U.S. forces occupied the southern part of the Korean Peninsula to oversee the establishment of an interim governance system.

However, the two national leaders, Syngman Rhee and Kim Koo, joined forces and opposed the trusteeship, demanding the immediate transition of the country to a fully independent state. The North Korean group led by Kim Il Sung expressed its support for the trusteeship while the U.S. military government showed its uneasiness towards the opposition to the trusteeship. Syngman Rhee went further by arguing for the need for the inevitable establishment of a single government (a single government by the South) in June 1946.[2] His argument for the establishment of a single government was largely based on his deep-seated distrust of the Soviet Union and its communist sympathizers as well as a possible suspicion that the United States would eventually leave Korea.

The U.S. military government, which did not find Rhee's argument particularly attractive, tried to resolve this issue on the table of the Joint U.S. - U.S.S.R. Commission on Korea. Having failed to reach any agreement, however, the Commission eventually passed the jurisdiction over the Korean Peninsula to the United Nations General Assembly on September 17, 1947. The UN General Assembly decided with a majority vote on November 14 that a free election, observed by the United Nations, should be held, with the number of representatives allocated in proportion to the populations of the North and South. The Soviet Union completely rejected this resolution, and as such, an election was held only in the southern half of the peninsula.

As such, Rhee's proposition involving the establishment of a single government in the South became a reality. Naturally, the conservative group headed by Rhee himself became the front stage of the political arena and pushed forward the nation building.

First, Rhee having been elected as chairman of the National Assembly with a landslide vote, played a leading role in the establishment of the country's constitution. The name of the country (Republic of Korea) and the key governing structure under the central leadership of the president were passed down to the present, albeit the numerous constitutional amendments that have been

1) The Joint U.S. - U.S.S.R. Commission on Korea, which was established in accordance with the agreement made on the table of the Moscow Tripartite Summit, specified that an agreement on the four-power (United States, United Kingdom, Soviet Union, and China) trusteeship should be drafted and submitted in close consultation with the Interim Government of Chosun within the period of up to 5 years.

2) While visiting various parts of South Korea, Syngman Rhee stressed in the speech that he delivered in Jeongeup on June 3, 1946 that "South Korea alone should form an interim government or some form of committee," which suggested his political preference for a single government that he made clear in the later days.

made. On July 17, 1948, the constitution of the Republic of Korea, which was founded on the spirit of liberal democracy and free market economy, was promulgated, followed by the election on July 20 of Syngman Rhee as the first president of the country in the National Assembly. The government of the Republic of Korea was officially inaugurated on August 15.

Despite the seemingly flawless advancement of the nation building process, the early journey of the government of the fledgling new country was not without some unexpected impediments. In April 1948, hundreds of armed militias from the Workers Party of South Korea stormed 12 police stations in Jeju Island in protest against the May 10 general election. The attack triggered a series of armed crackdowns by the police forces under the U.S. military government as well as uncontrolled counterattacks on civilians by the vigilante corps known as West-North Youth Association.[3] The armed conflict grew in scale and continued well into the Korean War, eventually claiming tens of thousands of lives.

Meanwhile, just two months after the inauguration of the new government, hundreds of servicemen secretly allegiant to the Workers Party of South Korea joined forces with anti-government groups to start an armed uprising in the Yeosu - Suncheon region. Likewise, faced with series of violent clashes throughout the country, the Syngman Rhee administration had to endure an extreme level of restlessness since its birth.

In the middle of such deteriorating situation, leaving only the military advisory group in the peninsula, Washington pulled out all the U.S. forces in South Korea after a brief suspension of the evacuation operation in 1949 in the wake of the Yeosu - Suncheon Rebellion. The decision left the peninsula in an extremely precarious state in terms of balance of power, in which the lightly armed South Korean army had to confront the 200,000-strong North Korean armed forces. Such unnatural imbalance in military power between the South and the North led to the eventual outbreak of the Korean War in the next year. As such, President Syngman Rhee had to confront the overwhelming onslaught of the North Korean army without being prepared at all in terms of internal security and defense capabilities.

The worst civil war in the history of Korea lasted for three years until the ceasefire in 1953, leaving an enormous scar in its wake.[4] A total of 15 UN member states led by the U.S. entered the war to render a helping hand to the country. Even after the conclusion of the war, the

3) The total human cost of the Jeju April 3 Incident amounted to 14,032 deaths (number of deaths during the crackdown by the counter-insurgency force: 10,955; number of deaths caused by the armed insurgents: 1,764). In January 2000, the "Special Act on the Investigation of the Jeju April 3 Incident and on Regaining the Tarnished Reputation of the Victims," which dealt mostly with the government-led investigation of the Jeju April 3 Incident and with regaining the tarnished reputation of the victims, was legislated. A host of associated projects were implemented in accordance with the Act, including the Jeju April 3 Incident Memorial Service, the construction of the April 3 Peace Park, Memorial Hall, and Peace Foundation, and the provision of support to the people who had been disabled during the incident. See the "Progress Report on the Implementation of Key Tasks" by the National Committee for the Investigation of the Jeju April 3 Incident (http://www.jeju43.go.kr).

4) The Korean War inflicted the most devastating and enormous damages to peninsula among all the wars in the history of country. About 1.5 million soldiers hailing from 25 countries, the biggest ever in the history of the world, came to the country to engage in the international war. The aftermath of the Korean War was far-reaching: the war casualties included 620,000 deaths among the South Korean troops, 160,000 deaths among the UN troops, 930,000 deaths among the North Korean troops, about 1 million deaths among the Communist Chinese Army, and 2.5 million civilian casualties (including deaths, POWs, and missing persons). The number of civilian war victims reached 3.7 million, and in addition, 300,000 war widows, 100,000 war orphans, and about 10 million members of separated families were recorded.

Syngman Rhee administration, still unprepared for postwar restoration, was in desperate need of aid from the U.S. both for postwar recovery and for national security. The administration succeeded in making the U.S. sign the U.S. - ROK Mutual Defense Treaty in October 1953. With the treaty taking effect in November of the succeeding year,[5] the administration, with the assistance of the U.S, was able to run the country by implementing diverse policy initiatives ranging from internal security to defense, postwar recovery, and economic rehabilitation.

The Syngman Rhee administration pronounced the country as a democratic republic. In reality, however, it failed to run the government in accordance with the democratic processes befitting a democratic republic. The biggest reason was that President Syngman Rhee understood the significance of democracy more than anyone else but failed to actually apply what he understood. He pushed forward with two consecutive constitutional amendments, including the "rounding off" constitutional amendment in 1954 in an attempt to consolidate his power,[6] used the Anti-Communist Law, which was intended to deter North Korean intervention in the South Korean society, for his own political ends by using it to eliminate his political rivals[7]; and laid the groundwork for perpetuating his power as president by rigging the election. His attempt at rigging the March 15 presidential/vice presidential election in his favor triggered the April 19 Student Revolution in 1960, which led to the forced resignation of the president.[8]

Seen from this perspective, even though the Syngman Rhee administration was the country's first administration since the foundation of the republic, it failed to solicit sufficient support to be considered as a legitimate government. Specifically, the administration left precedents that are unacceptable as a democratic government, such as the perpetration of illegal acts, the manipulation of laws, and the increasingly autocratic enforcement of power.

Meanwhile, in North Korea, a powerful state system led by Kim Il Sung emerged under the systematic support of the Soviet forces after the liberation. However, the U.S. military government

---

5) Under the treaty, the U.S. can engage in any war in Korea without needing to undergo a deliberation or voting process in the UN in the event of an armed clash in the Korean Peninsula.

6) The first constitutional amendment pronounced on July 7, 1952 was a selected amendment of the constitution. The government threatened the members of the National Assembly to pass the bill for a constitutional amendment with a standing vote by orchestrating a series of government-sponsored protests behind the scenes. The bill dealt mostly with the direct election of the president. the second constitutional amendment, which was proclaimed on November 29, 1954. was a rounded-off constitutional amendment. The proposed bill for the constitutional amendment was voted down with 135 "yes" votes, 60 "no" votes, and 7 blank ballots among the 203 enrolled members. The Liberal Party, however, came up with a preposterous idea based on the rounding off theory to justify the ballots, and still passed the bill (two-thirds of the 203 enrolled members is 135-3... to be exact, but as the integer nearest this number 135; when the number is rounded off, they argued, it can be assumed that the bill has been passed).

7) As Cho Bong Am, the leader of the Progressive Party, rose quickly as the political rival of the president in the wake of the presidential election, the administration arrested him for having violated the National Security Law. He was sentenced to death in the Supreme Court in February 1959, and was then executed in July of the same year. The entire panel of Supreme Court judges reviewed the case in the retrial held in 2011 and ruled on January 20 that he was not guilty.

8) The Liberal Party did not hesitate to engage in every dirty trick imaginable for the successful election of Lee Ki Poong, who ran for vice president, including lining up illegal slush funds for the campaign, manufacturing advanced and open ballots, expelling the election observers sent by the opposition party, and rigging the ballot counting by employing hired thugs. Stunned by the downright violation of the election laws and other dirty tricks involved in the election, protestors went to the streets all over the county, starting in Masan, denouncing the rigged election and demanding the immediate withdrawal of the totalitarian government, which again triggered the April 19 Student Revolution.

did not consider it a looming threat and, instead, focused on negotiating with the Soviet Union, while South Korea was divided into multiple factions squabbling in a prolonged political quagmire. Therefore, it is undeniable that President Syngman Rhee laid the foundation of the Republic of Korea by proposing the country's adoption of the "One People Principle" (a philosophical idea claiming that united, a people can survive)[9] in the midst of such quagmire. Such proclamation, thereby, opened the door for establishing a single government in the South and built the basic framework of liberal democracy and a free market economy rather than the communist system.

3. Modernization

After the eradication of the Syngman Rhee administration as a result of the April 19 Student Revolution and the establishment and eventual dismantling of an interim government headed by Heo Jeong, a government based on the parliamentary cabinet system, which was headed by Prime Minister Jang Myeon and President Yoon Bo Seon, was inaugurated in July 1960. The Jang Myeon administration was launched with two key missions: realization of the democratic political system and economic development. The administration, however, soon stumbled upon a series of roadblocks that the people behind it had not anticipated. The first limitation of the new administration was the fact that its birth was the result of the April 19 Revolution rather than of its own political struggle. The Jang Myeon administration failed to handle the huge civil demand for democratization and unification led by student groups and only exacerbated the political and social confusion. Making matters worse, the confrontation between the old group in the Democratic Party, led by Yoon Bo Seon, and the new group led by Jang Myeon further escalated; in the absence of a political agreement between the two, the old group eventually broke off from the party and formed the New Democratic Party.[10] In such difficult political situation, Jang Myeon succeeded in forming an image as a clean cabinet leader who advocated democracy but largely failed to show decisive leadership in managing the aftermath of the democratic revolution. The Jang Myeon administration was inaugurated in August 1960 and ruled the country for nine months until May 16 of the succeeding year, when Park Jung Hee seized power through a military revolution.

The Jang Myeon administration's efforts to democratize the country were not inherited by the military government, but the Five-Year Economic Development Plan that it drafted during its short incumbency laid the foundations for the 1st Five-Year Economic Development Plan established by the military government. The Park Jung Hee administration justified the coup d'état as an effort to modernize the country, and it focused on economic advancement in modernizing the country. Given that the per-capita national income of South Korea then was less than $ 83, which was close to that of the poorest country in the world at that time, the first Five-Year Economic Development Plan centered on the labor-intensive light industries. It was also the period when the

9) The "One People Principle" is the political ideology proclaimed by President Syngman Rhee in May 1949, in which he proposed that the country commit itself to democracy as "one people" while eschewing communism.

10) The old group in the Democratic Party declared its plan to form a new party on October 13, 1960 and inaugurated the New Democratic Party, the country's largest opposition party, by holding an inauguration ceremony on February 20, 1961, thereby entirely severing its relations with the Democratic Party.

country strove for economic development under slogans such as "Let's Live Better" and "We Can Do It." Following the light industries, the steel and machine industries were added when the 2nd Five-Year Economic Plan (1967～1971) was drafted. Then, the 3rd Five-Year Economic Development Plan (1972～1976) concentrated on the heavy industries, including the steel, automotive, shipbuilding, and chemical industries, and The 4th Five-Year Economic Development Plan (1977～1981) put emphasis on technological innovation and productivity improvement on top of the heavy industries.

Such massive economic development plan required an enormous amount of fiscal support to turn the country's economic system from one based on an agrarian economy to another based on industrial infrastructure. With an insufficient amount of natural as well as financial resources, the country had to rely on overseas capital. The economic aid and loans provided by the U.S. made up the country's early financial resources, the compensation and loans provided by the 1965 Korea-Japan Agreement,[11] the additional economic boost created by the dispatch of the country's armed forces to Vietnam,[12] and the surging demand for new construction projects in the Middle East in the wake of the oil shock provided the much-needed resources required to turn the goals laid out in the economic plans into reality.

Meanwhile, the Saemaul Movement, which proposed the adoption of diligence, self-help, and collaboration as key spirits, was implemented by the government throughout the 1970s in an attempt to narrow the widening income gap, which was triggered by the country's rapid urbanization, between the urban and rural areas.

The ambitious drive for economic growth became a huge success. In 1979, near the end of the Park Jung Hee regime, the country's per-capita gross domestic income rose to over $1,600, and the host of modern infrastructures that were built in line with the rapid urbanization, such as Gyeongbu Expressway, the Seoul Metros, Greenbelt, and the afforestation of the country's mountains symbolized the rapid economic-development process and the remarkable modernization of the country. If modernization can be defined as a process in which the lifestyle of each individual assumes a modern form through industrialization, urbanization, and other social changes, it will be fair to say that the Park Jung Hee administration achieved this objective to a level sufficient to convince the Organization for Economic Cooperation and Development (OECD) to classify South Korea as a newly industrialized country (NIC) along with Hong Kong, Taiwan, and Singapore.

The modernization of South Korea that was pushed forward under the Park Jung Hee regime was achieved, however, by sacrificing the democratic progress of South Korean society. Park Jung Hee's governance style was a typical example of what is known as "developmental dictatorship" in the academic circle. In 1967, President Park extended his term forcefully by pushing forward with a constitutional amendment that would allow him a third-term presidency, and in 1972, he laid the foundation for his permanent presidency by establishing the Yushin Constitution. His

11) South Korea and Japan closed the deal on the right to demand compensation by agreeing on the following amount: $ 300 million in free loans, $ 200 million in paid loans, and $ 100 million in private commercial loans.

12) The total revenue in foreign currency that the country received by dispatching its troops to the Vietnam War added up to roughly $ 5 billion if the military aid provided by the U.S. and the effect of the economic boom from the war would be included. The total amount of the country's exports in 1963 was barely less than $ 100 million, which was a substantial amount for the country during that time.

iron-fist rule resulted in the outbreak of popular uprisings in Busan and Masan in 1979, and was concluded with the assassination of President Park by his close aid Kim Jae Kyu, who was then the head of the Korea Central Intelligence Agency.

The Chun Doo Hwan administration, which succeeded the Park Jung Hee regime, was built on the ashes that had been left after the brutal crackdown on the Gwangju Democratic Movement by the new military elites led by General Chun Doo Hwan, who came to the center of the political stage after the December 12 military coup d'état in 1980. Due to difficult situations created by the 1979 political upheaval and the global economic contraction in the wake of the second oil shock,[13)] the administration had to endure unprecedented inflation and economic decline in its early years in the 1980s. To overcome such challenges, the Chun Doo Hwan administration came up with a modified economic-development plan that focused on stabilization rather than growth, and renamed it as 5th Economic and Social Development Plan (1982～1986), with the same policy directions also applied to the 6th Economic and Social Development Plan (1987～1991).

The Chun Doo Hwan administration relegated a substantial part of its leadership to the implementation of the economic policy on the free market economy. Coupled with the "three lows" (low interest rate, low oil price, and low dollar exchange rate), the administration enjoyed an unprecedented economic boom during its term. Also, with its successful bid for the 1986 Asian Games and the 1988 Seoul Olympic Games, the administration secured a platform on which it can raise the global profile and overall prestige of the Republic of Korea.

The Chun Doo Hwan administration, however, failed to accommodate the heightened democratic awareness that the South Korean people developed along with the country's modernization, including the people's immense desire for political participation. It, however, pushed ahead with its iron-fist rule only to crack down on such irreversible trends. Such efforts were all futile against the flow of history; the monopolization of the power by a few members of the army elite veterans ended with the citizens' June 1987 Democratic Uprising.

4. Democratization

The popular uprising of the democratic citizens in June 1987 against the totalitarian regime of Chun Doo Hwan was a struggle for the democratization of South Korea, with its rallying point distilled in the two key slogans "Down with Dictatorship" and "Constitutional Amendment for Direct Presidential Election."

Signaled by the proclamation on June 10 of the fight for constitutional amendment by the "People's Movement Headquarters for Democratic Constitution," tens of thousands of citizens and university students took to the streets en masse to join the nationwide protest.[14)] The movement

---

13) The Bank of Korea announced that the country recorded a -5.98% growth in the 2nd quarter, and a -4% growth in the first half of the year.

14) The opposition leaders and civil groups outside the political institution, led by Kim Young Sam and Kim Dae Jung, rallied the people by establishing the "People's Movement Headquarters for a Democratic Constitution," and the death of Park Jong Cheol (a student activist) after being tortured by police investigators, and the subsequent cover-up and fabrication of lies regarding the incident, triggered a nation-wide outbreak of popular angst against the totalitarian regime. The university students' protest grew more violent with the death of Lee Han Yeol, who was killed by a tear bomb fired by riot police. The March for Democratization held on June 10

grew increasingly larger in scale and gave more pressure on the regime until Roh Tae Woo, the ruling party presidential candidate, conceded to the people's request by announcing his acceptance of the direct presidential election and the local self-governing system in his June 29 Declaration.[15) It was the inflection point from which the country's political system began to be democratized in earnest.

In December of the same year, a presidential election was held in accordance with the new constitution, which was established based on the agreement between the ruling and opposition parties. Roh Tae Woo, the ruling party presidential candidate, won the election without much difficulty as Kim Young Sam and Kim Dae Jung, the two leading opposition presidential candidates, failed to unify their candidacy. The opposition, however, overwhelmed the ruling party in the general election that was held in the following April, for the first time in the history of the Republic of Korea. Riding the crest of their much stronger presence in the National Assembly, scores of opposition lawmakers scrambled together to create the "Special Committee to Investigate the Acts of Fraud Committed by the 5th Republic," which soon started the hearing process.[16) In the process, former president Chun Doo Hwan issued a special statement in which he apologized to the people, before moving to Baekdamsa Temple to live in seclusion. However, he could not avoid taking the stand in the hearing; when he finally took to the stand, he simply read the statement he had prepared in advance, but its political ramifications were far and wide.

With the power of the military elites shrinking slowly, President Roh Tae Woo, instead of dominating the political stage by exercising his power throughout his presidency, had to rely on his political wit and on his ability to compromise, with the most compelling example being his establishment of a three-party merger. The merger of the Unified Democratic Party led by Kim Young Sam and the New Republican Party led by Kim Jong Phil with the ruling Democratic Justice Party, each with completely different political roots, resulted in the creation of the Democratic Liberal Party, which had come to enjoy majority seats in the National Assembly.

In conclusion, the Roh Tae Woo administration played the role as a stepping stone in the transition from military rule to civilian rule, and from authoritarian to democratic politics. Also, Roh Tae Woo's successor was not selected from the military but was handpicked: Kim Young Sam, a seasoned politician with a civilian background.

The economy continued to prosper thanks to the surging demands created by the 1988 Seoul

---

and 26 showed that the protest had grown in size and scales as hundreds of thousands of citizens in the major cities joined the pretest. The People's Movement Headquarters for a Democratic Constitution announced that a total of 240,000 people participated in the June 10 rally, and nearly half a million people turned up for the June 18 rally to eliminate tear bombs while a record 1.3 million protestors turned up for the June 26 peaceful people's march.

15) The key points of the June 29 Declaration were: (1) immediate constitutional amendment to allow direct presidential election; (2) fair amendment of the Act on Presidential Election; (3) amnesty for and reinstatement of Kim Dae Jung and comprehensive release of political prisoners; (4) strengthening of the basic rights of the people in the new constitution; (5) guaranteeing the autonomy of the press; (6) implementation of the local self-governing system and autonomous education system; (7) guaranteeing the right for political parties to carry out acceptable activities; and (8) preparation of measures to purge the society.

16) The deliberation on the 5th Republic consisted of a series of hearings held in the National Assembly by the "Special Committee to Investigate the Acts of Fraud Committed by the 5th Republic." As all the hearings were broadcasted live on TV, revealing in the process the explicit details of the acts of fraud perpetrated by the 5th Republic as well as those of the Gwangju Incident and the infringement of the freedom or press, the outpouring of public angst grew larger.

Olympics and the continuation of the "three lows." Likewise, the nation observed further expansion of housing, road, airport, and subway network. The economy briefly contracted in the days leading up to the presidential election, but the ruling party candidate, Kim Young Sam, defeated the opposition candidate, Kim Dae Jung, by campaigning for reformation based on stability.

Full-fledged democratization started in earnest with the inauguration of the Kim Young Sam administration. President Kim Young Sam billed his administration as a "Civilian Government" and also emphasized that the administration was in line with the May 18 Gwangju Democratization Movement by pushing ahead with a campaign to rectify the country's twisted history. Beginning with the replacement of the Army Chief of Staff and the Defense Security Commander barely on the 11th day after President Kim Young Sam's inauguration, his administration dismantled Hana Group, a private army group led by Chun Doo Hwan and Roh Tae Woo.

Meanwhile, right after his inauguration as president, President Kim Young Sam disclosed the full details of the property owned by him and his family members on February 27 and put pressure on other high-ranking officials, including the key members of the administration, the National Assembly, and the Supreme Court, to follow suit. With the conclusion of the disclosure, the real-name financial transaction system, which had been secretly prepared under presidential order, was immediately implemented by emergency economic/financial order.[17)] The swift implementation of the real-name financial transaction system provided a turning point for the country, an opportunity to root out the fraudulent practices in the past while also laying the foundation for building a transitional economic order on which the democracy can take root in the daily lives of the people.

The move also provided a legitimate ground to investigate the slush funds raised by the former presidents, and to bring them to court. Pursuant to the Special Act on May 18 enacted in December 1995, judicial action was taken on the two former presidents. Specifically, Chun Doo Hwan was sentenced to life imprisonment, and 220.5 billion KRW was additionally collected from him, and Roh Tae Woo was sentenced to 17-year imprisonment, and 262.8 billion KRW was additionally collected from him. Moreover, all those who had participated in the military coup d'état were punished through a due judicial process, thereby making it impossible for the military elites to meddle in politics.

Furthermore, the Kim Young Sam administration decreed that the heads of the local governments should be elected through direct popular vote, thereby fulfilling its mission as the country's first civilian government. Kim Young Sam's capability to manage the economy, however, seemed to have failed to match his political wit and acumen. The financial crisis that hit the economy by the end of the term pushed the country's economy on the brink of sovereign crisis, forcing the government to seek emergency bailout loans from the International Monetary Fund, hence putting the country's economy under the stewardship of the IMF.

---

17) The most important and decisive action that was pushed forward in the early days of the Kim Young Sam administration along the path of economic reformation was the real-name financial transaction system. Although it was a simple measure that made it mandatory to perform financial transactions under one's real name, it has since been considered on of the key reforms of the civilian government because it had a huge impact on politics and the economy.

Kim Dae Jung, the opposition candidate, won the presidential election that was held towards the end of 1997, thereby making history with regard to the country's democracy: the peaceful change of government through an election. It was also a monumental event that lifted the country's democracy to the next stage. The new administration was named "People's Government" to reflect such historical significance. President Kim Dae Jung started his presidency with two imperatives: to reform the country's economic system so that it would be comparable to other advanced economies by successfully graduating from its stewardship by the International Monetary Fund and to ensure the evolution of the country into a fully mature democracy.

With only $ 3.9 billion in foreign reserves and suffocating under its massive foreign debt, which amounted to a whopping $ 159.2 billion, the new administration had to deal with the most urgent imperative: to spur the recovery of the country's economy. The first step in a series of such nationwide efforts was to collect gold. The Gold Collection Campaign, which lasted from January 5, 1998 until the end of April of the same year, was a phenomenal success, with the entire country participating in the campaign, and ended up with mountains of collected gold.[18] Thanks to such popular support to the government's policy initiative, the administration was able to push forward with its restructuring drive on the following key areas: businesses, the financial sector, the government, and the labor force.

After announcing the "Five Principles of Corporate Restructuring" to the country's major business leaders, the administration enforced the restriction on unfair internal transactions and mutual investment, banned the conglomerates' dominance over the financial industry, and restricted inheritance of corporate assets through evasive and manipulative tactics. It pushed ahead with not only a substantial reduction of the number of affiliated companies of the country's five major conglomerates but also what was known in the popular circle as the "Big Deal": an industry-wide cross-restructuring of business portfolio so that conglomerates would be able to focus on their respective areas of strength.[19]

Meanwhile, by injecting 157 trillion KRW of public funds on strengthening the financial structure of insolvent financial institutions and on protecting the depositors of the now-liquidated financial institutions, the administration ensured the healthiness of such financial institutions and contributed significantly to the recovery of the real economy. Moreover, the formation of the Korea Tripartite Commission, which is composed of representatives from the labor, the management and the government, allowed the administration to push forward with the drive to restructure the labor market. The administration also reformed the government organization while

---

18) The Gold Collection Campaign was a voluntary people's movement to collect gold in the wake of the Asian financial crisis. The campaign lasted from early January 1998 to the end of April of the same year and managed to collect 227 tons of gold (KRW .25 trillion) from a total of 3.51 million participants. The export of the collected gold helped the country boost its foreign currency reserve by $ 2.2 billion.

19) The automotive businesses were consolidated into Hyundai Group, the semiconductor businesses to Samsung Group, and the petrochemical businesses to LG, and the same practice was also applied to other industries, with the leading company in each industry being merged with the marginalized industry competitors. The remarkable results of such restructuring of the key industrial sectors were obvious in the four major conglomerates, with the exception of Daewoo Group, compared to the period before the restructuring. As of the end of 2000, the major conglomerates recorded impressive improvement in their consolidated financial performances: a KRW 3.2 trillion increase in the combined assets (15.1% improvement), an additional employment of 2,600 workers (13.8% improvement), KRW 7.9 trillion in reduced liabilities (25.8% improvement), and a 401% improvement in the debt ratio of the consolidated corporation.

privatizing scores of public enterprises in an attempt to improve the government's efficiency.

Such series of efforts resulted in a number of positive outcome: the country was given a suitable-for-investment sovereign credit rating in 1999, after a reassessment of its economy, and fully graduated from its stewardship by the IMF in 2001, three years ahead of the targeted schedule. The middle- and working-class people, however, emerged as the biggest victims of such extensive restructuring process. In an effort to address such problem, the Kim Dae Jung administration introduced the concept of "productive welfare,"[20] which provided a policy framework for a series of efforts to improve the people's welfare level, including the consolidation of the diverse medical insurance systems, the expanded application of the national pension benefits to individual proprietors in the urban area, and the implementation of the National Basic Living Security Act.

In addition, the Kim Dae Jung administration pushed forward with the so-called "Sunshine Policy" in an effort to open the new era of reconciliation and collaboration with North Korea. The Sunshine Policy achieved some successes, including the Mt. Kumgang Tourism project and the construction of the Kaesung Industrial Complex, but still failed to stop Pyongyang from perpetrating armed provocations or nuclear experiments.

Moreover, the administration also strove to improve the poor human rights conditions in the country by promulgating the Act on Human Rights and raised the transparency and reliability of the administration through the legislation of the Corruption Prevention Act. The administration played the role of upgrading the country's democracy to the next level by promoting the autonomy and the check-and-balance function of the National Assembly. For all its achievements, however, the administration suffered from a series of setbacks and publicity disasters near the end of its term, with the revelation of countless acts of fraud committed by the president's close aides. Making matters worse, the second and third sons of the president were both brought to justice for their alleged acts of fraud and bribery, and were later imprisoned. Roh Moo Hyun, however, the ruling party presidential candidate who succeeded in unifying his candidacy with Jung Mong Joon, who was then enjoying popularity due to his successful hosting and management of the 2002 World Cup, won the presidential election and inherited the administration.

The Participatory Government headed by President Roh started its administration by focusing on substantiating the contents of the country's fledgling democracy through citizen participation, promoting the regionally balanced development of the country, and opening the Era of Peace and Prosperity in Northeast Asia as its policy initiatives.

In March 2004, by expanding the applicability of the public-financed electoral management, the National Assembly ensured that no capable talent should be prevented from running for office due to the massive costs associated with the election campaign. The National Assembly also made it mandatory to keep the election budget transparent while also stipulating that any voter who received entertainment or other favors from a candidate should be required to turn in 50 times the value he/she received. In addition, the modified Political Fund Law banned the act of donation by a corporation or an organization, but instead fostered micro-donation by many and succeeded in

20) The key contents of "proactive welfare" are guaranteeing the people's basic living security, active job placement of unemployed workers through extensive job training and lifelong education, and strengthened implementation of the medical, unemployment, and occupational health and safety insurance and the National Pension Fund.

rooting out the so-called "election tarnished by slush funds or governmental meddling."[21)]

Meanwhile, the administration pushed forward with an ambitious project involving the construction of the New Administrative Capital in an effort to promote the balanced development of the country. Driven by the vision of accelerating the integration of the Greater Seoul Area and other local areas, the policy took its form when the National Assembly enacted the "Special Act on the Construction of a New Administrative Capital" on December 29, 2003. The relocation project of the administrative capital floundered, however, when the Constitutional Court ruled that the act was unconstitutional. The administration responded to the ruling by coming up with a proposal to build a complex city centered on the administrative function, which was supported by the successful passing of the Special Act on Administrative Cities. The project went through another round of political squabbling in the Lee Myung Bak administration before the complex city, Sejong City, was finally built.

In the diplomatic front, the Roh Moo Hyun administration laid out its plan to play the role of a balancer in Northeast Asia, in which it would strive to adjust the conflicts among the four powers surrounding the peninsula.[22)] The realization of such ambitious policy goal would certainly require the implementation of equidistance diplomacy towards the country's powerful neighbors, but it was impossible in practice to overcome the close diplomatic ties between Seoul and Washington. The administration played a certain role in the Six-Party Talks, which included North Korea, but still could not overcome the limitations in playing the leading role.

The South Korean economy during the Roh Moo Hyun administration enjoyed moderate growth as the country escaped the economic gloom in the aftermath of the Asian financial crisis, and the global economy was enjoying a relative economic boom before the onset of the international financial crisis in 2008. In such favorable economic climate, the country's per-capita gross domestic income briefly rose over the $ 20,000 mark in 2007.

The administration of the state affairs during the Roh Moo Hyun administration, however, was not without its own stumbling blocks. The characteristically peculiar manner of the president's speech involving election intervention resulted in the impeachment of the president, a first in the history of the Republic of Korea. A pandemonium ensued in the aftermath of the president's impeachment. The administration hailed the people's participation in politics as one of the country's most cherished values, but the smooth government operation by the administration was often hindered by excessive participation in the political process. The series of suspensions or renouncements of the government initiatives, such as the Plan to Strengthen the USFK, the Saemangeum Project, and the Seoul - Incheon Canal, sent out a clear signal to the various interest groups that they can have their own way in the end provided they put enough pressure on the government.

Furthermore, some of the closest aides of President Roh were also accused of being involved

---

21) The Act on Election for Public Office and Prevention of Election Fraud, the Political Party Act, and the Political Fund Act, which were modified during the Roh Moo Hyun administration, were the results of the bipartisan efforts to right the election environment muddled with corrupt practices.

22) In the State of the Nation address delivered in the National Assembly on February 25, 2005 to mark the 2nd anniversary of his presidency, President Roh said, "The Republic of Korea's armed forces, which stands as an independent army complete with its own operation right, will ensure peace in Northeast Asia as a balancer in the region." The proponents of "Balancer in Northeast Asia" suggested that South Korea should play the role of balancing the weight in Northeast Asia.

in fraudulent acts near the end of his presidency, and after his presidency, the president himself was embroiled in a scandal involving his relatives. Such scandals eventually forced him to present himself to the attorney's office for a thorough investigation, which led to the president's tragic ending, concluding his life by killing himself.

5. Advancement

In the past, South Korea was always classified in the international stage as a fledgling or developing/underdeveloped nation, and it indeed used to be one of the poorest countries in the world. However, thanks to the modernization policy implemented during the Park Jung Hee administration, the country was able to escape poverty, and near the end of the administration, it started to be classified as an emerging industrialized nation and was referred to as one of the "Four Dragons" in Asia.

The country's per-capita income passed the $ 10,000 mark in 1996, and the Kim Young Sam administration successfully joined OECD, which is composed mostly of advanced nations, as a member state. The euphoria did not last that long, however, as the country's economy nosedived in the wake of the Asian financial crisis. Thereby, the country's road to become a member of advanced economies further lengthened. Having overcome the economic crisis, thanks to the efforts made during the Kim Dae Jung administration, by the end of the Roh Moo Hyun administration, the country had opened the era of the $ 20,000 per-capita gross income. It was still early to conclude, however, that the country had attained the status of an advanced nation in terms of the practical state of the economy or the quality of life of the people.

By effectively running the campaign with the slogan "Advancement," The opposition presidential candidate, Lee Myung Bak, defeated the ruling party candidate, Jeong Dong Yeong, who ran for presidency with the slogan "Democratization," with the largest margin in the history of the country's presidential election. The global financial crisis triggered by the financial meltdown in the U.S., however, contracted the global economy in the early days of the Lee Myung Bak presidency, casting a thick cloud of gloom over the country's economy. The global fiscal crisis triggered by Greece's fiscal deficit sent another crippling blow to the global economy, enough to lower the sovereign credit ratings of virtually all advanced economies.

The Lee Myung Bak administration, which billed its mission as the "construction of an advanced, first-rate country," had to struggle with a series of popular protests in its early days on account of its poor handling of the import of foreign beef as well as the global financial crisis that followed. The president held a weekly crisis management meeting in the emergency economic-situation room installed in the underground bunker at Cheongwadae (the presidential office), a practice that persisted until the end of the presidency.[23] Entrepreneurs and various other groups in the South

23) President Lee Myung Bak announced his plan to launch an "emergency economy government" in his State of the Nation address in January 2009. He chaired a total of 245 emergency economy meetings, which handled a total of 198 economic items during his presidency. He also ordered that a progress report be made and submitted by each ministry before the start of the fiscal year, thereby ensuring that over 60% of the fiscal budget would be executed within the first half of the year. The country also prepared and implemented the largest economic-stimulus package among the OECD member states while implementing a series of nimble and preemptive measures, including the signing of an agreement to swap currencies with the U.S., Japan, and China

Korean society joined the president in his swift response to the changing global situation.

The nimble and closely coordinated responses to the global financial crisis by the government and the private sector eventually helped the country succeed in becoming a member of the club of advanced economies faster than it had anticipated. While most of the advanced economies were still struggling with a minus economic-growth rate in 2008, three OECD member states (among them, South Korea) recorded a plus economic-growth rate. According to the sovereign credit ratings announced in 2012, the ratings of majority of the advanced economies, including the U.S., were downgraded, while South Korea was the only country in the world that saw its ratings upgraded by all three major credit rating agencies. Among them, Fitch Ratings even rated South Korea one level higher than Japan.

As a result, South Korea's prestige in the global stage was pushed up, and the country's influence also markedly grew. The G-20 Summit was organized as a global control tower for overcoming the financial crisis, and the 2010 Summit was held in South Korea, with the country being appointed as the chair state. Two years later, the 2nd Nuclear Security Summit was also held in, and South Korea became the first country in the world to change its status as an aid giver from a beneficiary of international aid by joining the OECD Development Assistance Committee as the 24th member state. In addition, in 2012, the country became the 7th state to be included in the group of 20 - 50 countries (countries with an over 50 million population and with a per-capita GNI surpassing $ 20,000; in other words, large-scale advanced economies).

A country's advancement, however, cannot be assessed in terms of economic indicators alone; it should be realized in terms of the daily living environment of the people as much as in terms of economic indicators. The Lee Myung Bak administration concentrated its resources on climate change which was apparent long before it came into power. The administration took note of the fact that uncontrolled development projects that utilized coal and petrol, the energy sources well known for their disproportionate contribution to global warming, were destroying the environment and worsening humanity's living conditions by environmental contamination. Furthermore, the administration realized that the country was also not free from the global water shortage caused by such environmental destruction. Likewise, the administration presented its answers to such concerns by preparing and implementing the Four Major Rivers Project and the Low Carbon, Green Growth initiative at the beginning of the administration.

With the Four Major Rivers Project completed after two years of construction,[24)] the administration laid the policy platform for green growth by enacting a related law (Basic Act on Low Carbon, Green Growth, enacted in 2009). The effectiveness of the two policy initiatives over an extended period shall be evaluated in the future, but it is significant that the country pushed forward the green-growth policy well ahead of the majority of advanced countries in the world.

Economic advancement should be realized simultaneously with the advancement of the living

---

as well as the signing of FTA agreements with key advanced economies.

24) The Four Major Rivers Project was a massive construction project involving the building of a series of dammed pools for irrigation in the four major rivers in South Korea, and the streamlining of its surrounding areas in preparation for some climate irregularities such as famines and floods, while securing spaces for leisure and cultural activities at the same time. The Lee Myung Bak administration pushed forward with the project and eventually completed it, investing over KRW 22 trillion therein. Opinions are divided over the merits of the project, but it cannot be disputed that the country became capable of managing its water system effectively with the completion of the project.

and welfare conditions of the people, including the overall culture as well as the advancement of the business practices and state administration. However, the country has yet to realize sufficient maturity in these areas; after all, such goals require an extended period of time and continuous efforts for meaningful results to be seen. The national effort to realize such goals remains as the country's ongoing duty, to be continued well into the future.

6. Conclusions

The policies of the governments of the Republic of Korea that this report will cover in the main text are the key policy initiatives that were indispensible for the development of the country. These policies should be reviewed in detail and should be classified organically so that they would remain as important reference materials for the future generations in their advancement of the Republic of Korea into a unified country with immense significance in the global stage.

Chapter 1

The Syngman Rhee/ Jang Myeon Administration

Section 1

Inauguration of the Syngman Rhee Administration and Foundation of Key Policy Administration

1. Inauguration of the administration and introduction of its organization

The development of modern South Korea began with the conclusion of World War II and the subsequent liberation of the Korean Peninsula from the iron grip of colonial Japan. With the legitimacy of the various liberation efforts fought in the peninsula and in other parts of the world not recognized by the Allied Powers that won the war, Korea greeted its liberation as if it were the war booty given to it by the Allied Powers. When the U.S. and Soviet armed forces, respectively, advanced to the Korean Peninsula after the conclusion of World War II, President Roosevelt had the intention of applying trusteeship to the newly liberated countries, including Korea. The most urgent agenda for Moscow, however, was the expansion of its influence over the newly independent nations as part of its strategy to communize the world. As a convenient compromise between Washington and Moscow with regard to their strategy of implementing their respective foreign policy agenda, a line was drawn along the 38th parallel of the peninsula followed by the establishment of the U.S. and Soviet Military Government in the southern and northern parts of the peninsula, respectively.

For the three years (September 1945~August 1948) that South Korea was under the U.S. Military Governance, any remaining vestige of the Japanese imperial rule was purged and preparatory work for the establishment of a new government was implemented. While assisting the South Koreans in the establishment of their own democratic government during the period of the Military Governance, Washington successfully overcame the political, economic, and social upheavals as well as the infiltration attempt by the communists.

The U.S. Military Government started to rule the country by establishing the "United States Army Military Government in Korea," and assigned U.S. Army officers to head each bureau. In an attempt to ensure the efficient administration of the trusteeship, the U.S. Military Government appointed the Japanese officials from the Japanese Government-General of Korea as advisors, who would offer advice on the administration of the peninsula, thereby utilizing the ruling apparatus of the Japanese.

It was not that no Korean participated in the bureaucratic system; a group of 11 Koreans chaired by Kim Seong Su were appointed as advisors of the Minister of Military Administration, and dual directorship by a Korean and an American was announced in December. The U.S.

Military Government strove to establish the foundation of the new government organization with a series of measures, including the launch of the Korean Democratic Representatives in South Korea as an advisory body to General Hodge of the USFK on February 14, 1946, the opening of the Korean Interim Legislative Assembly (chaired by Kim Kyu Shik), the expansion and restructuring of the central government in 1947, and the renaming of the Korean organization in the U.S. Military Government to "Korean Interim Government."

The countless political parties and social organizations that were formed during the period of the U.S. Military Government scrambled along the lines of their respective political ideologies. The leading political powers among them were the left-wing group represented by the Communist Party of Chosun and the Workers Party of South Korea, the moderate left-wing group represented the People Party led by Yeo Woon Hyeong, the moderate right-wing group that formed the Federation of Korean National Independence, and the right-wing group represented by the Korea Democratic Party, the Korean Independence Party headed by Kim Koo, and the group led by Syngman Rhee, including the Central Council for the Rapid Realization of Korean Independence and the National Association for the Rapid Realization of Korean Independence. The groups pushed forward their respective political agenda according to the base and interest of their class and their political ideology.

Figure 1-1. The Political Powers during the Rule of the U.S. Military Government

Left-Wing Group	Moderate Left	Moderate Right	Right-Wing Group
The Workers Party of South Korea	The Labor People's Party	The Federation of National Independence	The Korea Democratic Party, The Korean Resistance Party, The National Association for the Rapid Realization of Korean Independence

Source: Jeong Yeong Hun (1995).

Even though the right-wing group, at first, disagreed with the U.S. Military Government on many political ideologies such as the trusteeship, it, after the botched 1st Joint U.S. - USSR Commission, rescinded its opposition to the trusteeship and started to support the establishment of a single government in the southern part of the peninsula. The right-wing group finally emerged victorious in the realpolitik with the inauguration of the Syngman Rhee administration (the 1st Republic) in 1948.

A more detailed look at the process of the foundation of the 1st Republic is the following; in accordance with the resolution of the United Nations Little Assembly, which allowed feasible areas to hold elections, the first elections in Korea, which signaled the beginning of democracy in the country, had become a reality with the announcement of the general elections in the southern part of the peninsula from May 1 to 10. Such announcement of the general elections laid the foundation for the elections of legislators that would make up the Constituent National Assembly. Likewise, the United Nations Commission on Korea confirmed May 10 as the elections day, and proposed the abolition of unfair laws and orders and the release of political prisoners to the authority of the occupation forces to ensure a free elections campaign. Amidst the destructive sabotage operations by the left-wing groups, and the official boycott of the elections by the proponents of inter-Korean negotiations and moderate politicians, the elections were eventually held in all areas except in Jeju Island.

A total of 948 aspiring politicians[1)] registered as candidates for 200 legislator seats in the Constituent National Assembly, recording a competition ratio of 4.7 : 1. The Constituent National Assembly, which was established amidst the confusion and unstable social environment, elected Syngman Rhee as the Speaker of the National Assembly, followed by a series of legislations, including the Constitution of the Republic of Korea on July 12, the National Assembly Act on October 2, and the Elections Law, which became the early form of what is now the Elections of National Assembly Members Act. The Constituent National Assembly was named such because it formed the country's first national assembly and constitution as a result of the general elections held on May 10. A total of 198 candidates among the 902 aspirants emerged victorious in the first elections that were held only in the South Korean territory, and the Constituent National Assembly was subsequently inaugurated on May 31. The National Assembly elected Syngman Rhee as the Speaker of the National Assembly, and Shin Ik Hee and Kim Dong Won as the vice speakers. And Syngman Rhee was later elected as the first president of the Republic of Korea on July 20.

In the process of founding the 1st Republic, however, the country failed to purge the government of those who collaborated with the Japanese during the colonial rule. This exacerbated the rivalry between the right and the left, and thereby divided the Korean people and weakened the national spirit. The Syngman Rhee administration selected anti-communism as the overriding dogma of the country under the new national goals — freedom and democracy — in an attempt to overcome its limitations upon its birth. However, the outbreak of the Korean War triggered by the invasion of North Korea pushed the country further down, making it one of the poorest countries in the world that had to rely on the global community for its sustenance and security. At the time of 2nd presidential elections, which was held after the outbreak of the Korean War when the administration had evacuated to Busan from Seoul, Syngman Rhee, who was not confident that he would win in the indirect elections, pushed forward the constitutional amendment to the presidential elections (promulgation of the amended constitution on July 7, 1952; the presidential elections on August 5) at full speed on the premise of the so-called "Selected Constitutional Amendment." In the 2nd presidential elections held on August 5, 1952, where there were four candidates (Syngman Rhee of the Liberal Party; Cho Bong Am, an independent candidate; Yi Shi Yeong of the Democratic National Party; and Shin Heung Woo, an independent candidate), Syngman Rhee emerged victorious, obtaining 74.5% (5,238,769 votes) of all the votes cast.

Syngman Rhee also won in the 3rd presidential elections held in 1956, obtaining 70.0% (5,046,437 votes) of all the votes cast, and was thereby sworn in as the 3rd president of the Republic. The presidential candidate of the Democratic Party then was Cho Byeong Ok, who died

---

1) A total of 48 political parties and social organizations participated in the general elections, including the National Association for the Rapid Realization of Korean Independence, which fielded 235 candidates, the Korea Democratic Party with 91 candidates, the United Young Men's Party with 87 candidates, the Korean Federation of Labor with 12 candidates, and the Farmers Federation for the Rapid Realization of Korean Independence with 10 candidates.

of a disease during the elections campaign. Therefore, Syngman Rhee, who was the only remaining candidate in such elections, was elected as the 3rd president of the Republic. In the vice presidential elections, Lee Ki Poong won, obtaining 70.2% of all the votes. Both the presidential and vice presidential elections were direct elections. The infamous elections fraud perpetrated by the Liberal Party in the March 15 elections, however, triggered a cascading outbreak of nationwide popular protests by the democratic citizens. In the end, the presidential and vice presidential elections were both pronounced invalid, which again resulted in the collapse of the government of the Liberal Party.

The governing structure of the 1st Republic was a presidential system premised on separation of powers. Syngman Rhee opposed the draft bill of the constitution that contained a proposition for the establishment of a parliamentary government and changed the constitution to a compromised form featuring the presidential system. Such compromised structure left a seed for another round of constitutional amendments, thereby resulting in countless political upheavals and confusion in the government administration. The so-called "Selective Constitutional Amendment" in 1952 introduced some elements of a parliamentary government to the constitution. The unprecedented "Rounding-off Constitutional Amendment" in 1954, however, strengthened the power of the president even more, laying the foundation for the extended preservation of the presidential power and thereby reducing the constitutional amendment to simply a "new presidential system."

The first Government Organization Act, which was legislated and enforced on July 17, 1948, became Act No. 1 of the Republic of Korea with the promulgation of the constitution. The draft bill of the country's first Government Organization Act was prepared by the Commission on the Establishment of a Constitution and a Government Organization Act, which was composed of the lawmakers elected for the Constituent National Assembly and civilian experts. Formally, the Government of the Republic of Korea was inaugurated on August 15, 1948, followed by the actual transfer of the administrative power from the U.S. Military Government on September 3 of the same year.

The Central Government, at its inauguration, was composed of the following: president, the cabinet members, the prime minister, 11 ministries (Ministry of Internal Affairs, Ministry of Foreign Affairs, Ministry of Defense, Ministry of Treasury, Ministry of Justice, Ministry of Culture and Education, Ministry of Agriculture and Forestry, Ministry of Commerce and Industry, Ministry of Social Affairs, Ministry of Transportation, Ministry of Communication), 4 agencies (Government Administration Agency, Government Legislation Agency, Planning Agency, Public Information Agency), 2 commissions (Commission of Government Notifications, Inspection Commission), and 3 offices. All of the compositions were preserved in their original forms without significant changes from the early years of the administration to 1955 after the Korean War.

The Syngman Rhee administration had since expanded the number of new administrative bodies through either the amendment of the Government Organization Act or the legislation of a special act. It added the Ministry of Health, the Office of the Treasury, and the Foreign Procurement Agency in 1949. When the prime ministry was abolished with the 2nd amendment of the constitution in 1954, the administration modified the Government Organization Act to such an administrative system that was true to the spirit of the presidential system. Likewise, all the administrative rights that were either delegated or vested to the prime minister were given back to the president. In the wake of the reshuffling of the government organization, the central administrative body was also revamped to assume 12 ministries, 3 offices, 2 services, and 2 bureaus as well as the Secretariat of the State Council, the Secretariat General of the Former Imperial Estate, and the Reconstruction Committee, which was governed by the Ministry of Reconstruction. The former Ministry of Health and Ministry of Social Affairs were consolidated to form the Ministry of Health and Social Affairs. Finally, the Ministry of Reconstruction was newly installed.

2. Objectives and directions of the government administration

Among the visions and objectives of the Syngman Rhee administration, the one with an overriding importance was to establish a country that strives to realize the happiness of the people. Such vision had been appearing repeatedly throughout various remarks made by the president, including the "Independent Spirit" that he wrote in 1904, the resolution of the "First Korean Congress," which was held in Philadelphia and was led by Syngman Rhee, the "Summary of One People Principle" published in October 1948, and the "presidential inaugural speech" that he offered in the inaugural ceremony of the Government of the Republic of Korea held on August 15, 1948. He clarified that the sovereignty of the country originates from the people and laid out the vision of guaranteeing the people's right to pursue happiness based on economic reconstruction and egalitarianism.

Secondly, Syngman Rhee stressed the importance of the nation state. Specifically, he argued that the people need to overcome their partiality so that South Korea would become a powerful independent country. He went further to demand the sacrifice of the people in the short term. By partiality, while he claimed on one hand that the power needed to be concentrated on the president himself, he argued on the other hand for the unified voice of the people to establish a country that was independent of the U.S. and the Soviet Union and that was free of groups that were still associated with Japan. He also made it clear that freedom involves responsibility to the country; he argued that the people need to offer even their lives, if necessary, to promote the interests of the country and to ensure individual freedom and affluence in a unified country.

Third, Syngman Rhee intended to establish a liberal democratic system, which guaranteed a government based on separation of powers as well as freedom of speech, the press, association, and religion. Specifically, the ultimate goal that Syngman Rhee aspired to attain was to form an autonomous and independent country where the people enjoy freedom and democracy modeled after the American democracy. Such philosophy of his was the result of the education that he received at a young age, which was clearly reflected in the "Spirit of Independence" that he wrote: "The United States is a young country with a short history since its foundation, but no country would compare with America in the future as it becomes renewed with the advancement of enlightenment and civilization."

Syngman Rhee aspired to adopt American democracy partly due to the fact that America was then rising and was poised to become the most powerful superpower at the time, and that America was the only superpower then without explicit imperialistic ambitions. On the contrary, Rhee drew a clear line against Russia or communism early on. His antagonism and suspicious attitude towards

Imperial Russia after the Russo-Japanese War only deepened after the Communist Revolution.

The key governing spirit and tasks required to realize Syngman Rhee's vision of government operation were: (1) establishment of an independent government; (2) purging the country of the ancient regime and the vestiges of the Japanese colonial era; (3) establishment of liberal democratic constitutionalism; and (4) pursuit of anti-communism. Specifically, the establishment of an independent government was the most pressing issue for the country then. Towards this end, Syngman Rhee united those who shared his political vision and principles while trying to neutralize the opposition forces. At first, he collaborated with some of the leading figures affiliated with the communist bloc, such as Park Heon Yeong, Yeo Woon Hyeong, and Cho Bong Am, on a tentative basis if it was necessary for the establishment of an independent government. However, beginning in early 1946, he started to assume a thoroughly anti-communist stance while arguing for the establishment of an anti-communist government only in South Korea, thereby laying the groundwork for unification in the future. Syngman Rhee had since pushed forward with some practical efforts to establish an independent government, including the potential establishment of an independent government through international diplomacy and the possible recognition of South Korea as the only independent country in the Korean Peninsula by the international community.

The total abolition of the old social status system, which could be found in the four key platforms of the One People Principle proposed by Syngman Rhee,[2] was realized through the implementation of the following key policies intended to realize an egalitarian society: the abolition of the division between the yangban (the aristocrats) and the sangin (the lower class), the abolition of regionalism, and the abolition of the segregation between men and women. As part of the detailed policies designed to realize such goals, arable lands reform, economic democratization, education system reform, and eradication of social indecency were implemented. Also, in a series of efforts to remove the vestiges of the Japanese colonial rule, all the remaining vestiges that infiltrated diverse institutions, including the society, legal, and educational establishments, were purged. Also, the properties owned by the Japanese and Korean traitors were either confiscated or nationalized, and his administration maintained its vigilance against the ambitions of Japan after being freed from the control of the U.S. Military Government.

As part of its efforts to establish a liberal democratic system, the Syngman Rhee Government introduced the liberal democratic system of the West to the country. As for the political area, the Government established constitutionalism based on the liberal democratic principles that guaranteed each individual full constitutional rights and freedom by granting suffrage and eligibility to run for public office to any citizen over 18, protecting the citizens' freedom of speech, association, religion, the press, political movement. It also strengthened personal protection by banning detention without the issuance of an arrest warrant by the court, and banning the infiltration of a private territory without the issuance of a warrant by the court. Socially, the administration accepted the realization of an egalitarian society based on laws, and it accepted the American economic democracy.

Another key governing principle of the Syngman Rhee administration was anticommunism. He stressed the threat posed by the Soviet Union in his 1941 book Inside Story of Japan, and opposed

2) It means a chunk of government policies that a government, a political party, or another group plans to promise to the people and to realize according to the plan.

the attempt by the Chongqing Interim Government to strengthen the Interim Government through the establishment of a coalition between the left and the right. Likewise, in the statements that he issued through communications with the Diplomatic Council in the United States, he continuously stated his opposition to the establishment of a communist government in South Korea. However, because the left-wing group had enjoyed popular support right after the country's liberation, Rhee did not clarify his attitude towards anti-communism until December 17, 1945, when he made a speech titled "My Position on the Communist Party" on the radio. He claimed on the radio that "South Korea should proclaim to the world that it does not want communism given the current situation it is in."

Table 1-1. Vision and Directions of the Syngman Rhee Administration

Vision and Objectives	Governing Tasks
A powerful independent country	- Establishment of an independent country through international diplomacy
A democratic country that pursues the happiness of the people	- Liberal democracy based on constitutionalism - Adoption of American-style economic democracy
Establishment of a liberal democratic country based on egalitarianism	- Abolition of the feudal social status system (elimination of the vestiges of the old social status system as well as of regionalism and sexual discrimination) - Elimination of the Japanese colonial rule and recovery of economic sovereignty - Pursuit of anti-communism

Section 2

Key Policy Initiatives

1. Establishment of a legal system that would support the realization of a democratic constitutional state

Background

The process employed by the Syngman Rhee administration in establishing the country's legal system, which lasted for 12 years, beginning in 1948, was based on some historical peculiarities unlike any in the other administrations throughout the history of the Republic. Given that it was the first government of the fledgling new democracy then, the Syngman Rhee administration had to shoulder the extraordinary burden of state building after graduating from the stewardship of the U.S. Military Government.

As the legal system provides the basic framework required for the organizational structure and operation of a country, the Syngman Rhee administration, as the country's first government, was required to implement the constitutionalization process in accordance with constitutionalism and the ideology of a law-governed country, which had been inherited from the earlier human history. The key task related to the establishment of the legal system in this period was the formation of subcomponent of the legislation system aimed at establishing a new constitution and realizing the ideology and institutions provided for in such constitution.

As it is inevitable even for a fledgling new country to assume the existing political and social order rather than to build an entirely new system, it is natural and efficient to adopt the conventional legal system as the everyday legal system, for which it is not critically related with the fundamental nature of the national system. The Syngman Rhee administration, however, had no option but to push ahead with the establishment of a legal system by combining the two significantly different legal systems: the legal system that had existed for the over 36 years since the establishment of the Japanese colonial rule in the country and the new set of legal systems established during the short rule of the U.S. Military Government.

Meanwhile, another pressing issue that the first government of the Republic had to address was the legalization of the tasks that needed to be carried out to purge the country of its past history and to build a future-oriented order, an indispensable step for the construction of the new nation state. In particular, it was urgent to recover the legal status of the people who had been criminally persecuted in the ancient regime in accordance with the brand new legal system while at the same time to prosecute the traitors who had inflicted insurmountable suffering on the people by undermining the national spirit. In an effort to ensure legal support for such urgent tasks, the Amnesty Act and the Act on the Punishment of Antinational Activity were legislated, followed by a series of legislations of various other laws, such as those on the naming of an era and on the establishment of an official language. Finally, the laws governing the everyday life of the people were legislated carefully to ensure the stability and continuity of everyday life through the smooth transition of the existing legal systems.

Moreover, after having faced the Korean War, imposed by its fate as a divided country, the country could not ignore the fact that it faced extraordinary ideological constraints in streamlining the legal system. Furthermore, the extended war posed some practical challenges to the process of building the state governing system as an independent country, thereby delaying the due establishment of the full-fledged legal system. On the other hand, such urgency prompted the establishment of laws that dealt with the state of emergency as well as those on the war.

Implementation System

The key to realizing the principles of popular sovereignty and a representative system is to have the national assembly. The national assembly represents the people, establishes the key issues in governing the country in the form of laws and regulations, and takes the administrative and judicial power to enforce such laws. Such form of governing is generally called "parliamentary democracy." It can be inferred from the fact that the Syngman Rhee administration specified in Article 31 of the First Constitution of the Republic of Korea that the legislative right belongs to the National Assembly that the said administration chose parliamentary democracy to realize the principles of popular sovereignty and a representative system.

The key characteristic of the implementation system employed by the Syngman Rhee administration with regard to the constitution was that the first constitution did not stipulate the establishment of a constitutional assembly or the holding of a referendum but that an implementation system led by the National Assembly, which was to establish the constitution, was chosen.[3] The first constitution also stipulated that the right to amend the constitution belonged to the National Assembly. For sure, however, the role of the administrative body should not be ignored because the president retained the initiative for constitutional amendment in practice, and exercised such right whenever the situation called for it.

The legislation process of the Syngman Rhee administration was marked by the fact that once any bill was proposed by a lawmaker or the government, the bill was reported to the National Assembly by the Speaker before being passed and enacted after three rounds of reading and deliberations in the plenary session, without necessarily going through a review process by the

3) The Constitutional Assembly, which opened on May 31 after being established as a result of the general elections on May 10, 1948, was put together through a selections process in which 10 screening members elected to represent each province would appoint 30 people to make up a committee that was to draft the constitution on June 1. The draft constitution was prepared after 16 rounds of review from June 3 to 22, after which the finalized bill was submitted to the plenary session on June 23. The plenary session then confirmed the draft constitution on July 12, after three rounds of reading and deliberations.

Legislation and Judiciary Committee (Article 38 of the First National Assembly Law). A bill that had gone through three rounds of reading and deliberations was then delegated either to the Legislation and Judiciary Committee or to the Speaker for the clearance of the stipulation and text of the amended resolution, before being finalized (Article 41 of the First National Assembly Law).

Unlike the bills proposed by assemblymen, which were not subject to any special preliminary review process, the bills proposed by the government could be submitted as government-submitted bills to the National Assembly only after being submitted to and voted on by the State Council or the Cabinet, both legislative or deliberative bodies, after going through a consultation process with the related ministries. Moreover, the bills submitted by the government were drafted after going through a preliminary review by the Office of Legislation, which was belonged to the Prime Minister and which oversaw the legislative businesses in the government.

In the case of an administrative legislation process initiated by administrative right, a draft bill of the presidential decree was prepared by each concerned ministry before taking a certain form after going through a screening or voting process in a meeting of the State Council or Cabinet, which were both deliberative or review organizations in the administrative body. On the contrary, the decrees of the Prime Minister or of various ministries were not subject to the screening or voting requirement by the State Council or the Cabinet but were reviewed by the Office of Legislation before being promulgated by the Prime Minister or the concerned minister.

Implementation Process and Contents

The National Assembly during the time of the Syngman Rhee administration established a constitution. Such establishment again provided the foundation on which the key laws on the organization and operation of the three main powers, the National Government Organization Act, the National Assembly Law, and the Court Organization Act, were established. Other laws governing the organization and operation of other general national organizations that supported the basic administrative order were also established, including laws that dealt with the issues concerning the basic operation of the state, such as the Act on the Organization of a National Armed Forces, the Military Service Law, various tax laws, the Bank of Korea Act, the National Property Act, the Administrative Appeals Law, the Administration Litigation Act, and the State Tort Liability Act.

As the administration billed itself as the proponent of parliamentary democracy, the National Assembly, which retained the constitutional and legislative rights led the legislation of the Constitution (the foundation of the state laws), the Government Organization Act that formed the basis of the government organization, and of the National Assembly Law and National Assembly Rules that governed the operational details. The Constitutional Assembly made it clear, however, that it would concentrate on the extraordinary situation then characterized by the need for nation building by temporarily limiting its term to two years.

The governmental structure in accordance with the First Constitution was that of a parliamentary government, as suggested in the draft bill. Contrary to what was specified in the Constitution, however, the government was in practice run based on the presidential system, in which a country is led by a powerful president. With events like the abolition of prime ministerial office by the constitutional amendment instituted by President Syngman Rhee, the characteristics of the presidential system became even more pronounced in the 2nd constitutional amendment (the Constitution of 1954).

Various power struggles for political supremacy with regard to the power structure during the legislation process of the First Constitution soon escalated into a governmental conflict with the Korea Democratic Party over the constitution, and eventually triggered a political upheaval over the constitutional amendment.[4] The party at the time accounted for the majority seats in the National Assembly, along with President Syngman Rhee. After the series of political upheavals, a modified bill for constitutional amendments, which extracted elements of the direct presidential elections system and the state council system, respectively, was passed on July 7, 1952.

The proposed bill for constitutional amendments included a possible conversion of the unicameral system to a bicameral system composed of the House of Representatives and the House of Councilors. The 1st constitutional amendment, which would have come to be known as the "Selective Constitutional Amendment" in 1952, was revised again through the so-called "Rounding-off Constitutional Amendment" (2nd amendment) on November 17, 1954 to adopt a pure form of presidential system and to abolish the prime ministerial office.

The Constitutional Assembly established a legal system for the organization and operation of the constitutional institutions that would provide the foundation for the establishment of the government, as shown below.

Table 1-2. Legal System for the Organization and Operation of the Constitutional Institutions

Constitutional Institution	Applicable Laws and Regulations
National Assembly	- National Assembly Law, Elections of National Assembly Members Act
Administration	- National Government Organization Act,[5] General Accounting Office Act, Public Prosecutors' Office Act, Elections of President/Vice President Act
Court	- Court Organization Act, Act on the Temporary Organization of a Trial Agency on National Traitor, Public Prosecutors' Office Act, Attorney-at-Law Act
Local Government	- Local Government Act, Temporary Measure on the Local Administration Act

4) On January 28, 1950, just one year after the promulgation of the constitution, the Korea Democratic Party proposed a bill to revise the constitution that featured the parliamentary government system. Faced with intense opposition by the supporters of Syngman Rhee, the bill was voted down on March 13. President Syngman Rhee, however, who had been on the defensive since the landslide victory of the opposition party in the 2nd elections of the members of the National Assembly held on May 30, 1950, proposed a bill on January 18, 1951 to revise the constitution and to change the indirect elections of the president by the National Assembly to direct elections by the people. As the bill was again voted down in the National Assembly on January 18, 1952, the opposition proposed another bill to revise the constitution that featured the parliamentary government system. In response, on May 14, President Rhee proposed the same bill for a constitutional amendment that had been voted down earlier that year, fanning the flames of the political rivalry.

5) The General Accounting Office is a central administrative body that examines accounts on the balance of the receipts as well as the disbursement of the national coffers every year, and that governs the businesses related with the regular inspection and supervision of the accounts specified by the laws. The office was launched with the inauguration of the government of the Republic on December 4, 1948, and lasted until March 5, 1963, when it was consolidated with the Inspection Board, to be reborn as the Board of Audit and Inspection. The organization and authority of the General Accounting Office were stipulated by a separate law (General Accounting Office Act).

The administration prepared the foundation of the government organization that would provide the basis for the establishment of the government through the legislation of the Government Organization Act in 1948. The initial Government Organization Act specified an administrative body composed of 11 ministries as well as the installation of the Commission of Government Notifications and the Inspection Commission in the presidential office. The act had since been revised four times by the Constitutional Assembly and the 3rd National Assembly during the time of the Syngman Rhee administration.

Meanwhile, with regard to the execution of the duties of the president, who held the authority to promulgate the constitution and various laws in accordance with the constitution, and other issues associated with the form and requirements of the administrative legislation that would support the laws, Presidential Decree No. 1 on the promulgation ceremony — the first administrative legislation since the inauguration of the government — was enacted. Afterwards, the following various other laws were legislated: the National Assembly Act, which specified the organization and operation of the National Assembly based on the spirit of legalism; the Elections of National Assembly Members Act, which dealt with the elections of the members of the National Assembly; the Elections of President/Vice President Act, which specified the elections method of the administrative head, such as an indirect or direct elections system; the General Accounting Office Act, which granted the authority to examine accounts on the balance of the receipts and the disbursement of the national coffers; the Court Organization Act, which dealt with the legal organization; the Public Prosecutors' Office Act and the Attorney-at-law Act, which dealt with the establishment of prosecutors who would monopolize the right of arraignment, and of attorneys who would engage in legal practice, respectively; and the Local Government Act, which stipulated the regulations on local administration as well as the elections, organization, and operation of the local congress.

Beside the constitutional institution, a series of legislations of other laws governing the organization and operation of various national institutions that formed the basis of state operation were also implemented. The foundation of a military system was the most basic requirement, for the establishment of a nation state is feasible only on the premise of the preservation of the country and the successful defense of its sovereign territory. The Act on the Organization of a National Armed Forces was legislated on November 30, 1948 as Law No. 9, which governed the organization and make-up of the national armed forces based on the first constitution, followed by the legislation of the Military Service Law, which dealt with the recruitment of servicemen, who are indispensable for the formation of armed forces.

The first constitution was intended to establish fiscal democracy by adopting the "Principle of No Taxation without a Law." Specifically, the administration abolished the Korea Income Tax Decree, which was inherited from the Japanese colonial rule and was applied on a transitional basis, and legislated, instead, the Income Tax Act (July 15, 1949, Law No. 39) and the Corporate Tax Act (November 7, 1949, Law No. 62). In addition, the Bank of Korea Act, which effectuated the installation of the Bank of Korea as the legitimate successor of the Bank of Joseon as the national coffers, was legislated on May 26, 1950 as Law No. 138. Following the legislation, the National Assembly enacted the National Property Law on April 8, 1950 as Law No. 122, which governed the scope, classification, and type of properties and served as the related governing and disposal authority, thereby laying the foundation of the management of the state.

Meanwhile, the general administrative operation acts, such as the Administrative Vicarious Execution Act, were established separately from the earlier individual administrative operation acts in an effort to ensure the effectiveness of the administration. It was followed by the legislation of the Administrative Appeals Law, the Administrative Litigation Act, and the State Tort Liability Act to ensure the subsequent remedial of the damages inflicted by illegal administrative operation.

Following the simultaneous promulgation of the Government Act and the First Constitution, three laws, the Amnesty Act (Law No. 2), the National Traitor Law (Law No. 3), and the Act on the Era Name, were legislated as the foundation of the first government well before the National Assembly Act was enacted as Law No. 5. These laws were the administration's answer to the key issue of the time: the purge of all vestiges of the past colonial system.

Another legal issue that required urgent attention was the series of laws required to establish fundamental order and discipline in the new state, along with a purge of the vestiges of the past deeds. Towards this end, a series of acts, including those that follow, was legislated to establish the fledgling new country's identity as an independent autonomous state: the Act on the Era Name (September 25, 1948, Law No. 4) that aimed at reconfirming the country's status as an independent and autonomous state by promulgating the Dangun (the legendary founding father of Gojoseon, the first Korean nation) era name as the official era name of the Republic of Korea; the Act on the Exclusive Use of Hangul (Korean alphabet) (October 9, 1948, Law No. 6) that aimed at establishing the cultural foundation of the independent and autonomous country by promulgating Hangul as the official alphabet for all the official documents of the Republic of Korea; the Act on National Holidays (October 1, 1949, Law No. 53) that aimed at designating the joyous occasions of the country as national holidays; and the National Act that stipulated the qualifications of the people who constitute the Republic of Korea (December 20, 1948, Law No. 16).

The legal systems that had been established during the Japanese colonial rule or during the rule of the U.S. Military Government could not be deemed to have shared the fundamental values or ideology of the new country. Since they could not be regarded to have been established by the Korean people on an autonomous basis, the pressing issue at the time was the establishment of a legal system on everyday life that would accommodate the latest changes in the society and economy while at the same time remain committed to the new national ideology. Specifically, the civil and criminal law systems, which formed the basis of everyday legal life, needed to be revamped to establish the framework of a legal system on everyday life that coincided with the liberal and democratic national system both in form and content by overcoming the feudalistic heritages obtained from the Joseon dynasty as well as the oppressive and discriminatory elements of the Japanese colonial rule.

Such necessity was recognized relatively early on by the administration. On September 15, 1948, right after the inauguration of the new government, official positions for the Codification Commission were promulgated in accordance with Presidential Decree No. 4, followed by the installation of the Codification Commission. The Codification Commission "would collect and survey comprehensive materials with regard to the basic law books on civil law, commercial law, and criminal law as well as other materials on judiciary regulations, including litigations and criminal administration, and would draw up and screen the draft of each law." Given the severe lack of available legal experts, however, the codification process was limited in scale and depth. Furthermore, being a fledgling new country, the country did not put much importance on the codification of basic laws governing everyday life. For such reason, the Syngman Rhee administration did not see the completion of the codification process but instead continued with the tentative system that appropriated the legal systems inherited from the Japanese colonial rule.

It was only on February 22, 1958 when a civil code was legislated pursuant to Law No. 471, and it was enforced two years later, on January 1, 1960, when the country's old civil law system, which appropriated the civil laws of Japan, was perfunctorily abolished. The Civil Law was composed of five books: "General Rules," "Real Rights," "Creditors' Rights," "Relatives," and "Inheritance." Compared with the civil laws appropriated from the Japanese laws that were strongly influenced by the French civil laws, the new Civil Law is assessed to have been influenced more by the German laws.

The criminal laws, which, unlike the civil laws, may be abused by the regime to oppress the people depending on the nature of the administration, should have been reshuffled rather expediently given the undemocratic nature of the Japanese colonial rule. The proposed bill for the amendment of the laws, however, was submitted to the National Assembly on April 13, 1951 and was reviewed for two years before being legislated as Law No. 293 on September 18, 1953, followed by its enforcement on October 3 of the same year.

Meanwhile, the Act on the Government Purchase of Grains, which was legislated on October 9, 1948 as Law No. 7 in an effort to ensure socioeconomic stability in the extraordinary situation the country was in, was enacted to guarantee the egalitarian dietary ingestion of the people and foster their financial security by stipulating the basic rules governing the purchase of grains. In addition, a series of legislations ensued, including those related to living matters, such as the education system, which was aimed at guaranteeing the people's right to obtain education (Article 16 of the First Constitution); labor requirements, designed to guarantee the people's right to work (Article 17 of the First Constitution); three major rights for labor (Article 18 of the First Constitution); the protection of those with no means to procure their daily living needs due to aging, disease, or loss of other types of labor faculty (Article 19 of the First Constitution); the special protection of the chastity of marriage and family health (Article 20 of the First Constitution); and the redistribution of the country's arable lands (Article 86 of the First Constitution).

Performance and Assessment

The efforts made by the Syngman Rhee administration to establish a legal framework can be assessed as follows. First, as the first government of the fledgling new country, which had been inaugurated as a democratic republic, the Syngman Rhee administration not only had to consider the values that it aspired to achieve but also had to match organizational structure and operational methods with regard to the establishment of a legal system on the basic values and organization of the new state. Although it may not have been perfect, the administration is assessed to have completed the establishment of the legal system required for putting down to the basic constitutional order. It can be concluded that the legal systems of the succeeding administrations were able to develop to the next level based on the legal system built by the first administration.

Second, the abolition of the legacy legal system, which was established on the premise of the Japanese colonial rule, was another key mission of the new administration in establishing its own legal system. In that, it did not entail a regime change within a nation-state until the creation of a new nation-state after the liberation from the colonial rule of the foreign force. The purging of the country's past history, however, as intended by the legislation of the National Traitor Law, was not realized up to the promised level amidst the confusion of the extraordinary development that was brought upon by the Korean War. The legacy of the unfinished job of purging the country of the past wrong deeds has since become a source of endless social controversy from the authoritarian era up to the present democratic era.

Third, even the foundation of a new nation-state cannot be completely insulated from the influence of the existing system when it comes to the socioeconomic life of the people. As such attempt was not only difficult but also inefficient, it was inevitable that a regime that would stick to the existing legal system that formed the basis of the lower governing structure, which linked directly with the legal system governing the everyday life of the people, would be maintained for a while. Specifically, considering that the civil laws appropriated from the Japanese legal system lasted for ten years, even after the inauguration of the new nation-state, the administration was remorseful, believing that it should have accelerated its implementation of a new set of civil laws despite the fact that there were some practical limitations in doing so, such as the lack of legal experts. It should be considered, however, that the government's resources tended to be concentrated on resolving the urgent issues that required immediate attention rather than on establishing a legal system, which tends to assume a perfunctory nature during the period of nation building, where the tradition of the constitutional state tends to be weak and there are mountains of socioeconomic issues that need to be resolved.

Fourth, the division of the peninsula created a peculiar environment in which ideological deviation might happen with regard to the content of a legal system. With the prime example being the legislation of the National Security Law, it is also notable that the country's legal system had been active in legislating laws or regulations related with the contingency or wartime irregularities..

Fifth, for additional historical assessment, it remains to be seen whether or not the respect for law, which forms the basis of the establishment of a legal system, had firmly taken root because the creation of a formal rule of law alone cannot guarantee the realization of its objective. For instance, as it is obvious from the fact that the country ended up with a unicameral system despite the fact that the first constitutional amendment stipulated the implementation of a bicameral system, some key national institutions stipulated by the constitution were not installed at all, or the State Council was not operated to the fullest extent despite the fact that it was specified as a legislative body by the First Constitution. Therefore, it would be necessary to pay special attention to the development of some unconstitutional practices in the realpolitik in relation to all those aforementioned constitutional stipulations.

2. Establishment of a modern defense and security system

Background

For a country to maintain its status as an independent state in the international community, a level of defense capability that is sufficient to enable it to defend itself from external invasion is indispensable. Further, a police force is required to maintain law and order as well as security within the country's territorial boundaries. Without an appropriate level of defense capability and a functional police force, no country would be able to act as an independent nation-state. The Republic of Korea established its own constitution upon the inauguration of the first government on August 15, 1948, and legislated the Government Organization Act (Law No. 1, July 17, 1948), thereby providing a legal basis for the central administrative organization.

The main duty or role of the armed and police forces of the Republic of Korea (ROK) was to defend the country's territory and to maintain law and order. However, before the outbreak of the Korean War, the country's armed and police forces focused on carrying out their duty of ensuring security within the country by preventing armed clashes along the 38th Parallel Line or maintaining law and order by cracking down on domestic disturbances and riots, such as the Yeosu - Suncheon Rebellion on October 19. The country's armed and police forces had expanded their respective organizations and manpower since the Korean War to protect the country. The armed forces continued to grow and develop as the main force tasked to defend the national territory after the war, while the police went back to its original place as the keeper of law and order, with its organization and manpower scaled back to their states before the outbreak of the war.

Implementation System

The defense policy of the Syngman Rhee administration after the war was to solidify the South Korea - U.S. alliance based on the ROK - U.S. Mutual Defense Treaty signed on October 1, 1953 in Washington D.C. and to push ahead with the modernization of military equipment, the expansion and strengthening of military power, the realization of the principle of elite force,[6] the improvement of military discipline, and the strengthening of logistical support.

The defense organizations and institutions of the Republic of Korea have been constructed through a series of legislations since the inauguration of the government, including the Government Organization Act, which was enacted on November 30, 1948 as Law No. 1; the Act on the Organization of a National Armed Forces, which was enacted on November 30, 1948 as Law No. 9; the Department of Defense Organization Decree, which was enacted on December 7, 1948 as Presidential Decree No. 37; the Decree on a Temporary Measure on Military Service, which was enacted on January 20, 1949 as Presidential Decree No. 52; the Military Service Act, which was enacted on August 6, 1949 as Law No. 41; the Decree on the Marine Corps, which was enacted on May 5, 1949 as Presidential Decree No. 80; the Air Force Installation Decree, which was enacted on October 1, 1949 as Presidential Decree No. 254; and the Decree on Military Service, which was enacted on February 28 as Presidential Decree No. 282. The defense organization of the Syngman Rhee administration was composed of the Department of Defense, which governed the military administration; the Joint Chiefs of Staff, which governed the military command; and the tri-service system, which was composed of the Army, Navy (including the

6) A line of thinking in the military circle that a few members of the elite force should be trained with extraordinary care and attention and then armed with powerful weapons so that the country's army could compete with a foreign army many times larger than itself. It is the defense guideline adopted mostly by small powers to cope with the threats posed by larger powers.

Marines), and Air Force.

As a result of the series of legislations, the country's defense organization and set-up ended up being composed of the Headquarters of the ROK Department of Defense (Secretariat, First Bureau, Second Bureau, Third Bureau, Fourth Bureau, and Aviation Bureau), the Chief of Staff (presently the Chairman of the Joint Chiefs of Staff), the Combined Chiefs of Staff Council (presently the Joint Chiefs of Staff Council), and the Headquarters of the Army and of the Navy. Added to the aforementioned initial organization during the Korean War were the Central Prisoners of War Screening Committee and the Regional Prisoners of War Screening Committee, followed by the installation on March 4, 1952 of the Martial Law Command and the Regional Martial Law Enforcement Office in accordance with Department of Defense General Decree No. 57. The operation of the Military Police was commenced with the enactment of the Military Police Act on July 29, 1949 in accordance with Presidential Decree No. 153. As its management failed to live up to the lofty expectations of it, the Military Police General Headquarters was established in the Headquarters of the Department of Defense on March 20, 1953, thereby consolidating the military police forces run by the Army, Navy, and Air Force, respectively, under a single-command system. In addition, the Interim Joint Chiefs of Staff was installed in an attempt to provide valuable advice to the president during the Korean War with regard to the close consultation with the United Nations Forces; the mutual collaboration among the Army, Navy, and Air Force for key operations; and the key defense policies and plans. The Interim Joint Chiefs of Staff was later revamped and expanded into the Joint Chiefs of Staff, which performed diverse roles, including providing assistance to the president, recommending key strategic directions and plans to the president, and maintaining liaison among the Army, Navy, and Air Force.

The missions of the ROK Police after the inauguration of the Republic of Korea included ensuring the people's security, guarding the 38th Parallel Line, suppressing domestic riots and disturbances, mopping up the communist guerrillas, and providing security and escort services to the head of state and to the Capitol Building. It is, however, believed that the most important roles or functions of the ROK Police during the incumbency of the Syngman Rhee administration were ensuring the people's security and carrying out a series of activities, based on the National Security Law, aimed at preventing subversive actions by the communist force to topple down the government.

The ROK Police had belonged to the Ministry of Internal Affairs since the inauguration of the ROK government in accordance with the Government Organization Act. The supreme commanding/superintendent organization of the ROK Police was the Bureau of Public Security, which was under the Ministry of Internal Affairs. Along the line of command, the police organization was made up of the Bureau of Public Security, the provincial police bureaus and police stations. In addition, the Presidential Office Police Command Station was installed on February 23 to provide security and escort services to the head of state and to the Capitol Building, followed by the installation of the Railroad Constabulary Unit on April 22, 1949 in accordance with Presidential Decree No. 75 in an effort to guarantee the security of the country's rail services.

As the ROK Police was required to play the role of a combat police force rather than to ensure the people's security with the outbreak of the Korean War, the Bureau of Public Security newly installed the deputy chief of bureau position on July 27, 1950, followed by the installation of the Supply Division, in an attempt to ensure the efficiency of the organization during the war

(Presidential Decree No. 378 and 379, July 27, 1950). On August 10 of the same year, the Inspection Department and the Investigation Department were consolidated into the Intelligence and Investigation Department, which performed civilian inspection, foreign inspection, criminal investigation direction, crime inspection and inspection by special order of the Ministry of Internal Affairs. The police engaged in combat missions and directed the provincial police forces throughout the country under the command of the Emergency Guard General Headquarters. Moreover, ever since the communist guerillas began rising en masse in the home front, including Mt. Jirisan, in the wake of the intervention by the Chinese troops, the ROK Police embarked on various combat missions to ensure stability and security in the home front. The United Nations Forces Command also dispatched U.S. military advisors consisting of high-ranking officials to the combat police force and to each provincial police, thereby assisting them in mopping up the communist guerillas in an organized and decisive fashion.

Only in 1955, nearly two years after the signing of the armistice agreement, was the organization and set-up of the Bureau of Public Security released from the state of war. The deputy chief of bureau system was abolished on May 10, 1954, followed by the abolition of the Supply Division on February 17, 1955. Whereas, the Bureau of National Security was left intact along with the Police Administrative Division, the Security Division, the Investigation Direction Division, the Special Intelligence Division, and the Communication Division, in the wake of the amendment of the organization of the Ministry of Internal Affairs (Amendment of the Organization of the Ministry of Internal Affairs, February 17, 1955: Presidential Decree No. 996). Such organizational state of the Bureau of Public Security had been preserved throughout the incumbency of the Syngman Rhee administration.

Implementation Process and Contents

On May 3, 1954, the Joint Chiefs of Staff was installed in accordance with Law No. 367 and Presidential Decree No. 895 (Republic of Korea Department of Defense, 1955: A61, C106). The Joint Chiefs of Staff was installed under the immediate control of the president to act in a military advisory capacity for the president with regard to the execution of the military command and to provide recommendations on defense policies and plans, thereby promoting liaison among the Army, Navy, and Air Force. The Chairman of the Joint Chiefs of Staff was appointed to handle the administration of the headquarters.

The key missions of the Joint Chiefs of Staff were to govern the establishment of consolidated strategic plans and consolidated operation plans for the ROK Armed Forces; to organize troops for consolidated operation, training, and education; and to handle the operation control and military envoys. As such, the ROK Armed Forces was finally able to achieve the strategic preparedness of its three branches independently, and to unify the chain of command in the military operations.

In addition, regulations on the terms of the Army Chief of Staff, the Navy Chief of Staff, and the Air Force Chief of Staff as well as of the Marines Chief of Staff were established. Diverse companies were established in an attempt to ensure the systematic management of the Army. For instance, the Field Army Command, which aimed at governing the operation/training and the military administration within its territorial jurisdiction by establishing a field army, was created (henceforth, the First Army Command), followed by the creation of the Rear Echelon Command (henceforth, the Army Command), which aimed at governing the provision of logistic and military administration support to all the companies within the Army as well as the operations within and guarding of the territorial jurisdiction of the respective army units, and the Army Training & Doctrine Command (henceforth, the Training & Doctrine Command), which aimed at controlling the training and education of the Army.

The ROK Army had eight infantry divisions and two independent regiments when the Korean War broke out. The ROK Army had since built up its forces remarkably during the war, having had 18 divisions by the end of the war, with the total number of troops having ballooned from 94,000 to 550,000. By the end of October 1952, Washington and Seoul had agreed on the expansion of the number of troops from 250,000 to 463,000, which resulted in the addition of eight divisions (12th, 15th, 20th, 21st, 22nd, 25th, 26th, and 27th Division) from the end of November 1952 until the ceasefire. By the time of the signing of the armistice agreement, the total number of ROK troops had grown to 550,000 (excluding the KATUSA troops). With the addition of the 28th and 29th Division upon the ceasefire, the ROK Army had come to possess a total of 20 divisions, with its troops totaling at 600,000.

The ROK Navy had a total of 33 warships distributed over four small fleet forces when the war broke out, but they were not equipped with the most basic navy equipment, such as guns, torpedoes, and communication equipment. Thanks to the continuous build-up during the war, however, the ROK Navy had grown to own one fleet composed of six warfare groups by the end of the war, with its total troops having grown from 6,954 to some 12,000. The ROK Navy renamed its First Fleet as "Korea Fleet" in September 1953, upon the signing of the armistice agreement in July 1953, and continued with the expansion of its naval forces by establishing the Five-Year Plan to expand the Naval Force (1954~1958). Meanwhile, the ROK Marine Corps started to perform its own operations independently after it took over the operational command authority from the U.S. First Marine Division on March 14, 1955.

The ROK Air Force also had a fleet of 22 small aircrafts, including liaison aircrafts and trainers, but its fleet had since grown remarkably to one air wing, which was capable of performing independent operations, and one training wing by the end of the war. As the number of fighter jets in its fleet grew after the air wing became the First Air Wing on August 1, 1951, the 10th Air Wing Group under the control of the First Air Wing was separated on February 15, 1953 to become the 10th Air Wing. With the separation of the 10th Air Wing, the First Air Wing became the First Training Wing on February 15, 1953. As a result of such revamping work, the ROK Air Force, which was forced to fight the enemy with only 22 light aircrafts, had grown to fly two air wings (one air wing and one training wing) by the end of the war, with its total fleet amounting to 110 aircrafts, including 80 F-51 fighter jets, and with the number of its airmen having ballooned from 1,897 to 11,000.

The two-year period from the birth of the Government of the Republic of Korea until the outbreak of the Korean War was the period of childhood of the ROK Police. Faced with the urgent mission of blocking the threats posed by North Korea as well as the communist insurgents in the South, the ROK Police had to maintain the public order and security on one hand and defend the country on the other. However, despite its urgent mission of meeting such goals, the organizational characteristics of the ROK Police took a markedly different form compared to the period of the U.S. Military Government. Specifically, the supreme executive institution of the police during the rule of the U.S. Military Government was the Department of Police, but it was stripped down to one bureau after the inauguration of the ROK government. What was once the Department of Police during the Japanese colonial rule was elevated to the Department of Police of the Interim Government of South Korea during the rule of the U.S. Military Government. However, after the inauguration of the government, it was again stripped down into the Public Security Bureau, which was only one bureau under the Ministry of Internal Affairs. The overall prestige and status of the police institution in the central government was reduced under the premise of an independent state, and the organization of the police was revamped and reduced in accordance with such policy direction.

The Korean War broke out amidst such transitional period, and the ROK Police was forced to engage in combat activities right away. During the first year of the war, the police force fought at the frontline, and thereafter, it engaged in combat activities in the rear. They blocked the retreat path of the remnants of the defeated North Korean troops in Mt. Jiri and Mt. Taebaek, and suppressed the activities of what had then transformed into communist guerillas.

After the signing of the armistice agreement, the police concentrated on mopping up the remaining armed guerillas. The South-West Combat Constabulary Unit, which was installed three months before the signing of the armistice agreement, tightened up the siege of the communist guerillas who had already been chased down to Mt. Jiri before pushing ahead with the mop-up operation. With the installation of the Security Department in the Bureau of Public Security, the Railroad Constabulary Unit was dismantled. The ROK Coast Guard, which was established in December 1953 as the police took over the duty of guarding the so-called "Peace Line" in the wake of the declaration of sovereignty over the territorial waters by the government, was dismantled as well with the conclusion of the mop-op operation of the communist guerillas. As the extraordinary wartime duty of the ROK Police was no longer needed after the ceasefire, the Intelligence and Investigation Department, which was created through consolidation during the war, was again divided into the Investigation Department and the Special Intelligence Department, and the deputy chief of bureau system and the Supply Department were also dismantled. In addition, in an attempt to modernize the technique of criminal investigation in preparation for the expected increase in the sophistication of the crimes in the postwar era, the Department of Criminal Identification was abolished and was replaced by the National Forensic Service under the direct control of the Ministry of Internal Affairs.

The ROK Police also strove to improve the efficiency of the police administration through the consolidation and abolition of various laws and regulations related with the police. The Act on the Performance of Duties by Police Officers was enacted to stipulate the duties of the police officers while the enactment of the Administrative Vicarious Execution Act provided legal grounds for the execution of the enforcement authority of the police. The Minor Offenses Act was legislated to replace the Police Offense Regulation inherited from the Japanese colonial rule while the sustenance of the Special Disciplinary Decree on Police Officers in Contingency ensured the discipline of the police officers, which was followed by the enactment and enforcement of the Policemen Appointment Regulation and the Regulation on the Police Officer Promotion Test.

Performance and Assessment

The ROK Armed Forces achieved astonishing growth during the incumbency of the Syngman Rhee administration, until it came to have the present defense system and army structure. The performance of the Syngman Rhee administration in building up the defense system during its incumbency can be summed up as shown below.

First, the restructuring of the ROK Armed Forces, which established the dual system in which the Department of Defense governs the military administration while the Joint Chiefs of Staff governs the military command, created a modern defense system and structure that is capable of engaging in modern warfare that exists until the present. The Army advanced the structure of its armed force to one that is capable of ensuring fighting efficiency by establishing a system[7)] through which it can execute the three key army functions: operation, logistic support, and training.

Second, the administration strove to achieve self-reliant defense capability through a build-up of its armed forces during the postwar era. The prewar ROK Armed Forces, a 100,000-strong army composed of eight infantry divisions supported by a fleet of 33 small warships and 22 light planes, had grown to a 600,000-strong army[8)] after the war.

Third, the stationing of U.S. forces in South Korea based on the ROK - U.S. Mutual Defense Treaty was instrumental in forming the Joint Korea - U.S. defense system, which is not only playing the role of deterring war in the Korean Peninsula but also maintaining the balance of power in Northeast Asia.

In summary, after the inauguration of the Syngman Rhee administration, the ROK Armed Forces, having escaped from the tri-service system that is composed of the Army, Navy, and Air Force only in name, started to build up practical military strength that would make it capable of executing joint operations effectively during the war. Furthermore, it succeeded in strengthening its military power and army structure up to the capacity requirement for modern warfare, and thereby became a critical deterrent against the North Korean threat. This can be said to be the biggest accomplishment of the Syngman Rhee administration.

On the contrary, in terms of size and organization, the ROK Police was reduced compared to how it was during the rule of the U.S. Military Government. The Department of Police, which was one of the central departments during the rule of the U.S. Military Government, was demoted to one bureau of the Ministry of Internal Affairs after the inauguration of the government. This did not mean, however, that the duty and function of the supreme organization of the ROK Police were reduced as well. Given the conditions in South Korea at that time, the ROK Police had to maintain the public order and security on one hand and defend the country on the other, making

7) The Field Army Command, which would command the combat divisions at the frontline, was created, followed by the creation of the 2nd Operations Command as a rear echelon command, which would govern the provision of logistic and military administration support to all the combat forces at the frontline. The Army Training & Doctrine Command was also established, aimed at controlling all the military academic institutions, excluding the Korean Military Academy.

8) The Joint Chiefs of Staff, the supreme institution in the military command line, was established for the ROK Armed Forces, which had come to possess one field army command, one rear echelon command, an army training & doctrine command, and 5 armies, 5 military district headquarters, 20 combat divisions, 10 reserve army divisions, one navy fleet, and one fighter wing with 110 aircrafts.

it inevitable for its duty and role to become much bigger than before. Specifically, the police was given the additional duty of providing security and escort services to the head of state by taking over the duty of ensuring the security of the Presidential Office and the Capitol Building.

Another key duty of the ROK Police at the time was to protect the regime of the Republic of Korea, an advocate of liberal democracy, by engaging in a clean-up operation of the communist group that was operating clandestinely in South Korea, and by participating in the mop-up operation of the communist guerillas who had hidden themselves in Mt. Jiri in the wake of the Yeosu - Suncheon Rebellion on October 19. Towards this end, the riot police system was introduced to the country.[9] Under the riot police system, the police participated in the war as the guardians of public security as well as the defenders of the country and in diverse postwar activities, such as controlling the refugees, facilitating the evacuation of the refugees to their respective shelters and refugee camps, and installing security checkpoints in an effort to maintain the public order and to ensure public security, which had deteriorated during the war. In addition, the riot police strove to mop up the armed guerillas scattered around Mt. Jiri, and to stabilize the rear area. After the stabilization of the rear area and the conclusion of the operation to clean up the communist guerillas, the riot police turned their attention to everyday security assurance, cracking down on economic and public safety offenses and preventing the commission of various crimes.

Finally, the ROK Police advanced its structure markedly through the Korean War and the postwar rehabilitation. With the dismantlement of the riot police, which was installed to mop-up the communist guerillas, the police task force formed and operated to prevent the outbreak of emergency incidents and the disturbance of the public order in isolated areas. In addition, the ROK Coast Guard was established and operated to block the infiltration of its territorial waters by Japanese ships and seaborne infiltration by the 5th column and North Korean spy forces and to prevent seaborne crimes such as the import/export of gold products during the war. Furthermore, to enable the management of theater by the police alone from multiple dimensions, the police air wing was established in an effort to strengthen the airborne operation capability of the police.

As such, even though the ROK Police during the incumbency of the Syngman Rhee administration was just one bureau of the Ministry of Internal Affairs, it continued to push forward despite such limitations, and performed its role excellently as the keeper of public security and as riot police. The ROK Police did its best to fulfill its diverse roles, including ensuring the security of the president, mopping up the communist guerillas, controlling and facilitating the evacuation of refugees, and maintaining law and order in 1950s, and succeeded in achieving each of these goals.

---

9) The ROK Police established the "Riot Police Command," which was solely dedicated to carrying out combat duty and was organized in the fashion of armed forces. The Riot Police Command controlled the general police force within the tactical area of operational responsibility under its command. The Riot Police Command was composed of the Mt. Palgong District Combat Command, the Taebaek District Combat Command, the Mt. Jiri District Combat Command, and the Southwest District Combat Command.

3. Farmland Reform

Background

Land (farmland) reform, the policy initiative that at its core re-established the land ownership and cultivation rights of the South Korean farmers, was one of the key imperatives for the fledgling new government's task of building a new country in the Korean Peninsula after the demise of the Japanese colonial rule. Farming is the foundation of the people's economic life and of the national treasury for a fledgling new country with no sufficient build-up of secondary and tertiary industries. As majority of the Korean farmers at the time had no arable land in their exclusive possession, farmland reform was one of the most important imperatives with utmost urgency for the construction of the country. The Korean farmers at the time of the liberation in 1945 were either controlled by the Oriental Colonization Company or enslaved to the Japanese landlords. In the wake of the demise of the Japanese colonial rule, however, the disposal of the lands owned by the Japanese was inevitable and, therefore, the seed of land (farmland) reform was planted. The Syngman Rhee administration remained committed to the task of farmland reform throughout the 1950s, which saw the outbreak of the Korean War and the implementation of postwar rehabilitation, with the reform concluded close to the early days of the Park Jung Hee administration in the 1960s.

Farmland reform was one of the most important imperatives not only for South Korea but also for all the fledgling new countries that were born after World War II. Among them, those that adopted communist socialism realized impressive achievements in their respective pushes for farmland reform in the process of "abolishing the landlord class and nationalizing the land." As soon as Kim Il Sung advanced to the North Korean territory, he confiscated all the lands and redistributed them to the North Korean farmers (March 1946). In the process of the implementation of the reform, the landlords with over 50,000m^2 of land in their possession were purged by force, and the confiscated lands were redistributed to all the farmers according to their respective scores calculated by rating the labor condition of each family member. The farmers who used to be serfs were given their own land as per the decision of the Communist Party. Many communist states in Eastern Europe also went through a similar reform process. Things were quite different, however, in those states that adopted democratic capitalism, such as South Korea, Japan, Taiwan, the Philippines, and India. As their ideological intention was firmly focused on the liberal market economy, they could not push forward with the wholesale reform implemented by the communists.

Implementation System

Land reform was initiated by the U.S. Military Government upon the liberation of Korea. The new government inherited the task in 1948, and it made decisions on the details of the reform process, and executed them. Based on Article 86[10] of the Republic of Korea Constitution

10) Farmlands shall be distributed to the tillers, and the distribution method as well as the limit, content, and scope of farmland ownership shall be governed by law.

established and promulgated on July 17, 1948, President Syngman Rhee made it clear in his first speech on the administrative policy which he delivered in the first regular session of the National Assembly on September 30, 1948, that farmland reform should be implemented without any hesitation in accordance with the "Land to the Tillers" principle.[11] In the process of legislating the Farmland Reform Act pursuant to the first constitution, diverse related parties, including the government, politicians, landlords, farmers, and various interest groups clashed with each other in a prolonged confrontation. Various ministries, including the Ministry of Agriculture, the Ministry of Culture and Education, the Industry Committee, as well as the Farming and Forestry Subcommittee in the National Assembly, and the Farmers' Federation for the Independence of Korea, proposed their own reform bills before the final legislation of the Farmland Reform Act "for the purpose of improving the lives of the farmers and ensuring the balanced development of the national economy through the economic self-reliance of farming family and the expansion of the country's agricultural output by distributing the farmlands to the farmers based on the Constitution" (June 21, 1949, Law No. 31). The act included stipulations on the acquisition of farmlands (Article 5), the prohibition of purchasing (Article 6), compensation (Article 8), distribution method (Article 11), upper limit of ownership (Article 12), and reimbursement method (Article 13).

The government established the Ministry of Agriculture and Forestry on November 4, 1948 which would oversee the farmland reform process (Presidential Decree No. 23). The Bureau of Farmlands in the Ministry of Agriculture and Forestry, had the Designation Department, the Screening Department, the Adjustment Department, and the Farmland Improvement Department under its control, and the government created the Bureau of Reverted Farmland Management under the control of the Ministry of Agriculture and Forestry (January 6, 1949), which assumed the function of the Office of Central Land Administration. The bureau was then divided into the Designation Department, the Distribution Department, and the Farmland Improvement Department on March 31, 1950 in an attempt to push forward with full-scale farmland reform. On April 12, 1952, the Bureau of Farmlands and the Bureau of Reverted Farmland Management were merged to form the Farmland Management Bureau, and the Land Policy Department or the Farmland Department was installed in Seoul Special City as well as in other provinces, cities, and counties to carry out farmland reform. The Ministry of Agriculture and Forestry held the First Central Farmland Committee meeting on March 24, 1950. Although the Committee did not have any policy-making or policy enforcement function, by responding to the request for advice by the Minister of Agriculture and each provincial and municipal farmland committee, the Committee greatly expedited the farmland distribution, the adjustment of the distributed farmlands, and the filing of formal objections to the allocated farmlands.

Implementation Process and Contents

First, when the process of policy is analyzed in its entirety, it is marked by an extended

11) It signifies that farmlands can be owned only by the agricultural-sector workers and farming corporations, and it was stipulated in the ROK Constitution and the Farmland Act to prevent the speculative ownership of farmlands by non-farmers.

period of deliberation as well as policy formulation and execution. The discussion on farmland reform started in the early days of the U.S. Military Government as the lands and real estate confiscated from the Japanese had to be given back to and distributed among the Korean people. Actively supported by the Korean advisory councilors, the U.S. Military Government discussed how to dispose of the reverted property and initially decided to allocate the farmlands controlled by Shinhan Corporation to the tillers. The Syngman Rhee administration succeeding the U.S. Military Government, which considered farmland reform its key policy, continued the discussion on farmland reform until it completed the process throughout the nation in 1950. However, due to the outbreak of the Korean War, the agreed-upon reform policy was not implemented.

Even when the war went into prolonged doldrums, the government still pushed forward with the implementation of the farmland reform policy that it had laid out earlier. The problem was that the reform policy could not be executed according to the planned schedule as the additional burden of providing wartime logistic support fell on the shoulders of the farmers. Since the farmlands were not be reverted to the tillers according to the planned schedule, the farmland reform was completed only after the inauguration of the Park Jung Hee administration.

Second, the Syngman Rhee administration strove to reflect the conflicting interests of diverse groups in the process of farmland reform. The worst conflict among them was the one between the landlord class who were in possession of lands and the tenants who had no land or who had a very limited amount of land. The landlord class, in general, had a say in the land reform process by expressing their opinions through the members of the Legislative Committee under the U.S. Military Government and through the members of the National Assembly in the Syngman Rhee administration. The opinions of the tenant class, however, were barely heard and were expressed only through street protests or through the publication of the statements made by the farmers' association or the communist/socialist group. The conflicting opinions of the two main camps were substantially reflected in the reform plan in the process of its deliberation by the National Assembly before the finalization of the policy package.

Third, farmland reform was fundamentally implemented through the vehicle that had been created amidst the ongoing ideological clashes between the democratic and communist camps. Given that Kim Il Sung had already won the hearts of the North Korean residents by realizing the reform based on the principle of "free confiscation, free distribution," the tenants and communist/socialist groups in South Korea showed their wholehearted sympathy with the North Korean reform. Furthermore, the communist group strove to take over the political power in South Korea on the platform of farmland reform while the democratic group struggled to preserve the regime in the face of such offensive protest, a conflict that was explicitly chronicled throughout the process of farmland reform. A key instance of such ideological clashes can be seen in a move intended to assist the democratic camp in earning the votes in the general elections; with the May 10 general elections fast approaching, the U.S. Military Government swiftly distributed the lands controlled by Shinhan Corporation to the tenants.

A detailed examination of the formulation of the farmland reform policies will reveal that the government officials thought hard for the best way to expropriate the farmlands in the first place. Given that the prevailing sentiment in the peninsula after the demise of the Japanese colonial rule was to strongly support the purge of the colonial legacy, the people strongly advocated the elimination of the landlords during the colonial era, which was exactly the path that North Korea took. Plenty of political and social groups led by workers and farmers also preferred such drastic approach in South Korea. However, plenty of people among the U.S. Military Government, its Korean advisors and high-ranking officials, and the members of the National Assembly during the Syngman Rhee administration opposed the wholesale rejection of the landlord class, including those from the Korea Democratic Party. Therefore, while majority of the countries were pushing forward with the free confiscation policy, the administration ended up selecting the paid confiscation method, which had been preferred by other advanced countries, such as the U.S. and the U.K. Instead, due to the existence of various hurdles, such as the outbreak of war, the resulting inflation, the insufficient funds available for compensation, the delay of the compensation, and the subsequent currency reform, the administration ended up implementing "compensation close to confiscation."

Second, the administration studied ways of repaying the land price of distributed farmlands. The government opted for the "paid distribution" method, thereby rejecting the free distribution favored by many communist regimes at the time. The farmers, on the other hand, favored free distribution, but given that farmland confiscation should be done on a paid basis, the subsequent step was naturally paid distribution. The repayment of the price of distributed farmlands would be realized by paying 30% of the annual crop production for a period of five years. However, in the confusion of the war when massive mobilization of logistic support for the war was required, the repayment was not realized as originally intended. The farmland reform was finally concluded as late as in the 1960s, based on the policy consideration at the time.

Third, the administration decided to put an upper limit to farmland ownership. It was decided that the upper limit would be about 30,000m^2 (9,000 Pyeong) which indicates that the administration, first of all, intended to recognize the current ownership of the landlords to a certain extent but instead focused on deciding whether or not any plot of land exceeding this upper limit should be confiscated. Additionally, a decision had to be made on up to how much land the tillers with no farmland in their possession should be allowed to cultivate. In fact, the lands that were distributed to the farmland tenants were about on average 10,000m^2 in size.

Fourth, the key agenda in the discussion of farmland reform were the calculation of the tilling capability or farmland fertility per farming family, the confiscation of the farmlands owned by clans or academic foundations, and the confiscation of orchards or mulberry fields. In addition, the distribution of the farmlands north of the 38th Parallel Line, which was thought to be recovered after the war, was discussed.

A host of impediments hindered the implementation of farmland reform, including, first, the early inability to implement the reform due the outbreak of the war, and the late execution of the entire reform process after the recovery of the lost lands. Reform policies such as farmland reform are impossible to implement without a powerful enforcement capability. Despite being faced with such extreme situation, the government was still able, if not flawlessly, to control the people and enforce the policy. President Syngman Rhee promoted the formation of a powerful government-led policy environment during the war and in the postwar rehabilitation period. Such powerful leadership of the government may have played a substantial role in implementing the revolutionary policy of farmland reform.

Second, the repayment of the land price with the annual harvest could not be successfully implemented because the farmers were required to provide crops to the military during the war.

Given that majority of the adults then were conscripted for the war, with many of them either killed or injured, the very act of farming was a great challenge. Faced with the additional challenge of enforcing the agricultural policy, the harvest of rice and barley did not increase considerably. Naturally, the provision of crops to the military and the use of crops to repay the land price were delayed.

Third, the landlords whose farmlands were confiscated could not be compensated. With the grain production far lower than the annual average, the farmers were not able to provide additional grains to the military, to say nothing of the payment of 30% of their annual harvest for the land price. For this reason, the government had no choice but to postpone the compensation of the landlords. With the delay of the compensation schedule, the compensation amount, which was calculated based on the government purchase price of the grains, was being depreciated while the inflation owing to the war further pushed down the compensation amount. Thus, the actual amount of the compensation that the landlords were paid in the end was further pushed down.

Performance and Assessment

With regard to the eventual execution of the reform policy, the government was able to allocate 20,000m^2 of farmland on average to all the tillers throughout the county, which implies that all the people were able to own a piece of land upon the inauguration of the new state. By 1957, 96% of all the South Korean farmers had come to own land. The number rose to 98.2% in 1963, and 15.2% of all the farming families that were either newly formed or that had some special situation had to till additional lands owned by other people after finding that the farmland that they had come to own was not sufficient for their needs. As a result of the reform of farmland ownership, the Korean people, who had to shoulder massive taxes and endure forced labor throughout the Joseon era or the Japanese colonial rule while "alienated from the state," were given an opportunity to become the "true people" of the country in form and substance. Finally, all the Korean people were able to participate in the nation building process while carrying out the economic activities that matched their respective capabilities.

Second, the era of the "homogenized people" was opened with the abolition of the gentlemen (yangban) landlord class and the tenant class. After World War II, the world went through massive waves of changes, including farmland reform and the abolition of entrenched power. Specifically, the rise of communist regimes all over the world sparked a firestorm of land confiscation and distribution in many countries. Riding the wave of such global reform, the country was able to successfully complete farmland reform, thereby enabling "wealth accumulation according to individual capability" and "evolution into a society based on unlimited competition" as well as realizing "Korean-style democracy."

Third, the transition of the properties of the landlord class into industrial capital, which had been the focus of the farmland reform, did not materialize in a desirable fashion because an adequate level of compensation was not offered in the end. Due to the following impediments, the actual amount of compensation paid to the beneficiary was far lower than what would have been reasonable: the compensation amount was determined based on the grain prices in the 1950s; the compensation was delayed due to the Korean War; the compensation amount was depreciated due to the currency reform; and finally, the amount was further depreciated due to inflation.

4. Declaration of the Peace Line: Defending the country's sovereignty over territorial waters

Background

President Syngman Rhee declared the Peace Line to demarcate the country's territorial water, a body of water 50~100 nautical miles off the coast of Korean Peninsula that needs to be defended amidst the squabbles over fishing rights between South Korea and Japan. He issued the "Presidential Decree on the Sovereignty over the Adjacent Ocean" on January 18, 1952, thereby clarifying the steadfast resolution of the four-year-old country to the world to protect its resources and to ensure its security and defense. The official declaration of the country's sovereignty over its territorial waters by the ROK government was made on February 8, 1953 with the declaration of the Peace Line, in which the government clarified that the "prime intention of the Republic of Korea in declaring its sovereignty over the waters surrounding the country is to keep the peace between the Republic of Korea and Japan."

The opinions as to why the Syngman Rhee administration declared the Peace Line are divided. Some argue that the declaration was intended to protect the country's fishing resources and to secure exclusive fishing rights over the waters. Others argue that it was a bargaining chip that would be put on the negotiation table with Japan so that South Korea would have the upper hand in the negotiations. Another conjecture is that the administration declared the country's jurisdiction over the territorial waters for the purpose of strengthening the country's territorial rights over various islands. Finally, other observers believe that the declaration was intended to achieve double goals: protection of the country's fishing rights and provision of a bargaining chip for the negotiations with Japan. Everyone agrees on one thing, though: the territorial dispute was one of the key pending issues in the series of talks held between Korea and Japan, as well as a source of constant conflict and confrontation between the two countries. Below are the reasons behind the diplomatic decision of the Syngman Rhee administration to declare the Peace Line even though it braced for potential backfire from the international community.

First, the declaration of the Peace Line was prompted by the personal determination of President Syngman Rhee, who accepted the policy recommendation by the public officials at the Bureau of Fishery in the Ministry of Commerce and Industry. The public officials in the Ministry of Commerce and Industry argued that it would be better to focus on growing the country's fishing industry based on the country's rich oceanic resources than on advancing the agricultural industry considering that it would take a long time before the crops could be harvested. They reasoned that the country would be able to further proceed with agricultural and industrial development by accumulation of plenty of foreign currency reserves by expanding the export of fishery products, alongside acquiring a bigger potential for export. The breakdown of the country's gross national product (GNP) in 1954 by industry shows that the primary industry accounted for close to half of the country's GNP, with a 47.3% share, followed by the secondary industry, with a mere 10.2% share. This suggests a disproportionate share of the fishery industry in the GNP. At the backdrop of such consensus, the effort of the Syngman Rhee administration to protect the rich fishery resources in the waters of the Korean Peninsula, which is blessed with seashores on its three sides, prompted the demarcation of the Peace Line.

Second, as per the decision of the General Headquarters after the defeat of Japan in World War II, all the vessels in Japan were prohibited from sailing flat out. Japan, however, after concluding that it should foster its fishery industry rather than farming to tackle the food shortage that it faced after its defeat in the war, requested approval for the operation of fishing boats. Therefore, fishing in the territorial waters within 12 nautical miles off the coast of the Japanese archipelago as well as some deep-sea fishing were permitted. The line drawn as such was named "MacArthur Line," after General Douglas MacArthur.[12] The MacArthur Line had since been expanded in three phases, along with the expansion of the fishing area, thereby resulting in increased incidences of clashes between Japanese and Korean fishermen. Of particular concern was the reckless fishing carried out by the Japanese fishing boats, which engaged in fishing in the shores of South Korea or China without subjecting themselves to regulation by the Japanese authority or by the South Korean or Chinese authority. The illegal fishing by the Japanese fishing boats on account of their breach of the MacArthur Line culminated in the outbreak of the Korean War. Seoul opposed any further expansion of the MacArthur Line for the fear of the impediments that might be placed by the Japanese fishing boats on the South Korean fishing industry, of the potential depletion of some species, of the eventual justification of the rearmament of Japan, and of the resulting threat to the national defense. Washington, however, approved the further expansion of the MacArthur Line as proposed by Japan. To cope with such development, South Korea decided to take some special actions internally. One of such is the Syngman Lee administration's declaration of the Peace Line.

Implementation System

The declaration of the Peace Line was originally an idea of the public officials at the Bureau of Fishery in the Ministry of Commerce and Industry. Understanding that the advancement of the country's fishery industry would be indispensable for the country's economic development, they came up with a draft plan through close consultation with the experts in the Bureau of Waterways in the ROK Navy and through collecting related maritime materials with the help of the Korean embassies around the world. They then started to work in earnest on the basic framework of the Peace Line by seeking legal and diplomatic advice from the Ministry of Justice and the Ministry of Foreign Affairs, respectively. The idea began as an exclusive fishery zone in the Proposal for an Exclusive Fishery Jurisdiction Zone[13] drafted by the Ministry of Commerce and Industry, but

---

12) It covers the area located at 36°00'N and 130°30'E, 33°00'N and 127°40'E, and 32°30'N and 120°00'E. The distance to the MacArthur Line is 60 nautical miles from Geomundo Island, 30 nautical miles from Busan, and 25 nautical miles from Jeju Island.

13) In close collaboration with the Ministry of Foreign Affairs and the Ministry of Justice, the Minister of Commerce and Industry proposed on June 16, 1951 that it be made clear that the government has a legitimate right to issue an "appointment of protection" on "protected fish species, including the sea bream," and that exclusive protection rights be established on the "No-Trawl-Fishery Zone." The "Proposal for a Fishery Jurisdiction Zone" submitted by the Ministry of Commerce and Industry was based on the precedent made by the Japanese Government-General of Korea, in which it designated a no-fishing zone in some parts of the territorial waters of Korea to prevent the drastic drop of the available fishery resources as a result of the reckless fishing by Japanese fishing boats near the shores of Korea. The lines proposed by the Ministry of Commerce and Industry did not include Dokdo, however, as the east line was drawn between Uleungdo and Dokdo.

it soon evolved into an exclusive fishery protection zone as the Ministry of Foreign Affairs insisted on the inclusion of Dokdo in the territorial waters. It had since been renamed and made the sovereign power line of the sea after going through a deliberation process in the Presidential Office.[14)]

The demarcation of the Peace Line was strongly influenced by the final report submitted by the Korean Mission to Japan. In the report on the political circumstances in Japan and the Allied Forces with regard to the San Francisco Treaty, which was submitted by the Korean Mission to Japan, Seoul was advised to prepare its fishery policies independently as Washington was engaging in diplomatic bargaining with Japan based on the premise that the MacArthur Line would be abolished. The advice was based on the view that the abolition of the MacArthur Line would make it very difficult to regulate the Japanese fishing boats given the presence of the principle on free international waters. Based on the report submitted by the Korean Mission to Japan, the Ministry of Foreign Affairs started its review of South Korea's fishery policies against Japan beginning in February 1951, while the Ministry of Commerce and Industry, which was governing the fishery policies at the time, collaborated with the Ministry of Justice in considering the associated legal issues. Finally, the Preparatory Committee on the Fishery Agreement with Japan was inaugurated on April 3, 1951.

Implementation Process and Contents

Based on the "Fishery Protection Zone" whose establishment was decided by a majority vote in the cabinet meeting on September 7, 1951, the Bureau of Fishery in the Ministry of Commerce and Industry came up with a draft bill on the Peace Line in multiple meetings before the bill was verified and subjected to historical research in collaboration with the Bureau of Waterways in the ROK Navy, and sought additional counseling from the Ministry of Justice with regard to the international laws. On November 29, 1951, the Ministry of Foreign Affairs delivered the "Additional Opinions on the Legal and Regulatory Materials in Foreign Countries with regard to the Declaration of Territorial Waters" to President Syngman Rhee as a bill through which the country may exercise its sovereign right over its territorial waters. In other words, the Peace Line was modified and expanded while it was being formulated by the Ministry of Commerce and Industry, the Ministry of Justice, and the Ministry of Foreign Affairs, and finally by the Presidential Office before it was reborn. Nearly five months passed before the Peace Line was declared after being approved in the 4th Cabinet Meeting on January 15. After detecting the diplomatic bargaining between Tokyo and Washington, which implied that the MacArthur Line would be automatically terminated once the San Francisco Peace Treaty took effect (April 28,

14) The initial proposal was modified and expanded to include Dokdo, upon the request of the Ministry of Foreign Affairs, in an attempt to protect the country's territorial waters, and was further strengthened compared with the "Proposal for a Fishery Protection Zone" submitted in September, by reflecting the determination of President Syngman Rhee. The proposal did not only contain the protection of the country's fishery resources but dealt with more comprehensive issues, including the "protection and development of the underwater mineral resources in the continental shelf" and other "defense issues." The demarcation proposal prepared by Seoul included Dokdo in the east while also drawing a line from one area near Shinuiju in North Korea all the way down to another area southwest of Jeju Island in the west, instead of drawing an oblique line from the shore near Small Heuksando Island to the waters near Jeju Island. Moreover, another line, which had been much expanded compared with what was originally proposed, was drawn over East China Sea and Yellow Sea.

Table 1-3. Actions Taken by the ROK Government after the Declaration of the Peace Line (1952~1954)

Date	Key Development
Jan. 18, 1952	The ROK government issued the "Presidential Declaration of Sovereignty over the Adjacent Seas of the Republic of Korea."
Jan. 19, 1952	The ROK government notified Japan of the promulgation via SCAP (Supreme Commander for the Allied Powers).
Jan. 28, 1952	The Ministry of Foreign Affairs of Japan delivered a verbal note to the ROK government rejecting the legitimacy of the promulgation.
Feb. 4, 1952	A Japanese trawler fishing steamer was shot by an ROK Coast Guard ship while fishing in the purported territorial waters after crossing the Peace Line, resulting in the death of one Japanese seaman.
Feb. 11, 1952	The U.S. Ambassador to Korea delivered a letter and a memorandum to the Korean Minister of Foreign Affairs specifying the illegality of the declaration made by Korea.
Feb. 13, 1952	The Ministry of Foreign Affairs delivered an answer to the U.S. Ambassador to Korea.
Apr. 18, 1952	The ROK government delivered its opinion letter in response to the verbal note delivered on January 28 by the Ministry of Foreign Affairs of Japan.
June 11, 1952	The Republic of China (Taiwanese) Ambassador to Korea delivered its opinion to the ROK government stating that the declaration made by Korea infringes on the rights and interests of the Republic of China.
June 26, 1952	The Deputy Minister of Foreign Affairs in Korea delivered its opinion to the Republic of China government stating that the declaration made by Korea does not infringe on the rights and interests of the Republic of China.
Oct. 4, 1952	The Capture and Trial Decree was enacted and promulgated as Presidential Decree No. 12, followed by the establishment of the Capture and Trial Court and Higher Court of Capture and Trial.
Jan. 12, 1953	The British Minister to Korea delivered a letter to the ROK government stating that Britain could not acknowledge the declaration made by Korea.
Jan. 28, 1953	The ROK Government sent a letter to the U.K. government in which it tried to persuade the latter of the necessity of the "Declaration of Sovereignty Over the Seas," including the protection of Korea's fishery industry, the prevention of disputes between Korea and Japan, and the other objectives of the promulgation associated with peacekeeping.
Sep. 11, 1953	Officials of the ROK government started to officially name the Declaration of the Sovereignty over the Seas as the "Peace Line."
Dec. 12, 1953	The ROK government promulgated the "Fishery Resources Protection Act" (Law No. 298).
May 6, 1954	The ROK government notified the Japanese government of the promulgation of the "Fishery Resources Protection Act."

Source: The Diplomatic Archive, "The Dispute between Korea and Japan on the Promulgation by Korea of the Fishery Resource Protection Act" Book 743.41, 1953-1955, p. 460, 1528-598.

1952), Seoul proposed the bill rather urgently in an attempt to secure the country's sovereignty over its territorial waters and so that the country could exercise its right of autonomy.

Anticipating that the potential reckless and excessive fishing by Japanese fishing boats armed with advanced technology after the planned abolition of the MacArthur Line would wreak havoc on the country's fishing grounds, thereby sparking another round of diplomatic dispute between Korea and Japan over fishing rights, the Syngman Rhee administration decided to declare the Peace Line before the abolition of the MacArthur Line.

The bill for the fishery protection zone, which was passed with a majority vote in the 98th Extraordinary Cabinet Meeting, was modified and expanded by the Presidential Office before being passed again with a majority vote as the Presidential Declaration on Sovereignty over the Adjacent Seas with the promulgation of the bill completed with Notification of State Council No. 14 on January 18 of the same year. With the declaration, whose ratification was delayed by four months in the National Assembly, the ROK government demonstrated its strong will to protect the country's sovereignty over the seas, which encompassed the protection of the country's resources as well as the security and defense of its territorial waters. President Syngman Rhee made an important political choice with the declaration, which effectively set the body of exclusive waters that it was to defend in the event of a fishery dispute with Japan as the zone up to 50~100 nautical miles off the coast of the Korean Peninsula.

The Presidential Declaration of Sovereignty over the Seas was not a spontaneous decision triggered by the anti-Japan sentiment prevalent in the Syngman Rhee administration. Rather, it was modified, supplemented, and expanded by the Presidential Office, led by President Syngman Rhee based on elaborate researches on related materials and an analysis of international laws. It was then made known to the international community after its establishment under the leadership of the Ministry of Commerce and Industry, in close collaboration with the Ministry of Foreign Affairs and the Ministry of Justice. To conclude, the Presidential Declaration of Sovereignty over the Seas was the result of the political decision made by President Syngman Rhee. President Rhee, who witnessed the sovereignty of the country being raped by the neighboring powers near the end of the Korean Empire, was convinced that the U.S. was not the protector of Korea's security, and that Japan had yet to give up its imperialistic instinct for invasion even though it had been vanquished in the war. It would be fair to conclude that the promulgation of the Presidential Declaration of Sovereignty over the Seas was largely driven by the practical desperation to protect the sovereignty of the country from the attempted exploitation of its resources and infiltration of its territory by Japan.

When the Peace Line was promulgated, however, the international community did not understand the desperation of the small country with an insignificant maritime presence. Likewise, many international institutions related to the maritime issues in the U.S., U.K., and Canada expressed harsh criticisms of the declaration. The reactions of the international community towards the declaration of the Peace Line are summed up below.

First, Japan criticized Korea via the diplomatic channel for violating the principle of free international waters, undermining the friendship between Korea and Japan, and infringing on its territory by including Dokdo in the Peace Line. The opposition to the declaration was particularly strong among the members of the fishery industry in Japan, who had to bear the brunt of the shock triggered by the declaration. Some from the right-wing group held a rally in which they demanded the abolition of the Peace Line while mentioning the issue of Dokdo, and pushed ahead with a popular movement to expel all the Koreans living in Japan.

With the deterioration of the relationship between Korea and Japan during the squabbles over the declaration of the Peace Line, the position of the allied states in the Free World slowly emerged. On February 11, 20 days after the declaration of the Peace Line, Washington protested that "Korea's unilateral setting of exclusive waters on the international waters is unfair," which was soon followed by a series of protests by the Republic of China in June of the same year, and by the U.K. in January of the following year, making Korea the target of international attack for a while. Australia and Norway, however, showed a deep interest in Korea's Peace Line and went further by requesting a copy of the promulgation of the Peace Line via their respective missions in Japan. Specifically, Australia, which was negotiating with Japan over fishing rights, showed a deep interest in the declaration of the Peace Line. The ROK government announced that the declaration of the Peace Line would not restrict the passage of the ships of the friendly nations, and spent much time clarifying the background of the declaration. Such process, however, gave the government an opportunity to taste the sorry state of the country with a weak maritime presence, but when the advanced maritime states began to expand their respective exclusive fishery zones in the mid-1950s, the negative international opinion on the Peace Line began mitigating.

The Peace Line disappeared in principle in 1965 as the exclusive fishery zone, which covered the waters until 12 nautical miles off the coast of the peninsula, and the jointly controlled waters, were abolished with the announcement of the joint statement and the initial signing of the fishery agreement on April 3, after the 2nd bilateral talks of the ministers of agriculture in Korea and Japan, while the protection and preservation of the fishery resources were allowed only within the waters specified in the agreement. A total of 320 Japanese fishing boats, including 3,900 Japanese fishermen, who violated the Peace Line before the normalization of the diplomatic relations between Korea and Japan in 1965 and the subsequent signing of the new Korea - Japan Fishery Agreement, were seized or arrested by the ROK coast guards, and in the process, 40 people either died or got injured.

Performance and Assessment

The declaration of the Peace Line highlighted Korea's "resource nationalism in the territorial waters," with the intent of protecting the fishery resources in the territorial waters by preventing the reckless fishing by Japanese fishing boats. Such protection ensured the survival of the Korean fishermen who possessed considerably much laggardly fishing technology after the war compared to the Japanese fisherman who possessed advanced fishing technology. Korea kept pestering Japan to come to the negotiation table to formulate a fishery agreement, but Japan did not respond to Korea's request due to its lack of preparation for the negotiation, for Japan had no reason to embark on the negotiation hurriedly. Japan was convinced that the abolition of the MacArthur Line would eliminate the possibility of any future dispute over fishing rights with Korea. Because Korea was far behind Japan in terms of the technological sophistication of its fishing vessels and fishing equipment, coupled with the abolition of the MacArthur Line, the ROK government would find it increasingly difficult to protect the fishing activities of the impoverished Korean fishermen. Therefore, the administration pushed Japan to sign the fishery agreement by declaring the Peace

Line, while at the same time preventing any future dispute over fishing rights between Korea and Japan even before the signing of the agreement. The administration made it clear in Article 3 of the declaration of the Peace Line, however, that the line is not permanent but could be modified in the future, which suggests that the administration anticipated the signing of the fishery agreement between Korea and Japan. As such, the declaration of the Peace Line may be remembered as an excellent example of how the keen observation of the trend in the international laws was used in diplomacy and politics.

With regard to the negative aspects of the demarcation of the Peace Line, for one, the plan of the Korean government, which came to the negotiation table with the objective of closing the gap between the fishing industries of Korea and Japan and preventing any future dispute in the territorial waters, turned out to be a failure. This was partly because Japan consistently argued about the illegality of the Peace Line in view of the international laws, but more importantly, it was because both Korea and Japan were not free from the influence of the U.S. as they both sought support and aid from Washington.

Second, the administration anticipated the opposition of Japan but failed to control such opposition given its limited capacity as a fledgling new country. The dispute deepened the conflicts between the Korean residents in Japan and the Japanese people, forcing the Koreans to bear the brunt of the deteriorating relationship. In 1961, at the height of the issue, a Japanese movie depicting the conflict between the Korean residents in Japan and the Japanese fishermen was released in Japanese theaters and gained considerable interest by many viewers. When Tokyo raised the issue of sending the Korean residents in Japan to North Korea in 1959 in view of its frustration over the poor prospects of resolving the Peace Line issue, the administration demonstrated its limited diplomatic bargaining chip as it achieved no effective results despite the fierce opposition.

Third, as the maritime superpowers insisting on the 3-nautical-mile territorial waters advocated the principle of freedom in the international waters, the Korean government was criticized by such countries, even receiving protests from the friendly nations in the Free World, including the U.S., U.K., and the Republic of China, thereby putting the country in a diplomatic trap.

5. Overcoming the damages wrought by the Korean War and reconstruction of the country

Background

Freed from the Japanese colonial rule, the Korean people aspired to achieve complete independence from Japan both politically and economically. Priding themselves in being ahead of Japan in terms of history and civilization, the Korean people were deeply scarred by the experiences under the Japanese colonial rule. As such, the strongest consensus among the members of the Korean society was to realize a level of economic growth that was comparable to that of Japan. As Japan succeeded in rehabilitating its economy during the Korean War, such voice in the Korean society only grew louder with time.

The competition with North Korea was also one of the crucial issues at the time. As majority of the country's heavy industries were concentrated in North at the time of the liberation, North Korea's condition then was more conducive to economic growth compared to South Korea's. Most of the industrial facilities were pounded to dust during the war, but Pyongyang succeeded in recovering those facilities, thanks to the postwar aid it obtained from Eastern Europe. East European countries set up a sisterhood relationship with North Korean cities, thereby assisting them with the reconstruction.

The unique situation of Korea then, as described below, also played an important role in the reconstruction of the country.

First, the control of the national economy and the general mobilization of the people towards the end of the Japanese colonial rule required a highly sophisticated capability to implement comprehensive planning works. As a result, the General Staff Office for Economic Planning was installed in Tokyo while the Planning Office, the Department of General Mobilization of the People, and Planning Committee were installed in the Japanese Government - General of Korea in Seoul. Given such political environment during the colonial era, many public officials conversant with the administrative process employed by the Japanese colonial government were hired by the ROK government to play key roles in the early days of the administration. The aforementioned organizations controlled the overall plans on the higher ground in the process of establishing and implementing the state-level policies. The South Korean bureaucrats and intellectual class had already experienced the efficiency of such administrative system.

Second, regardless of the ideological differences between the right- and left-wing camps among the various political forces after the liberation, they all stressed the need for state-led economic planning activities. Specifically, the left-wing forces had not yet been completely purged during the establishment of the government in South Korea, while other groups, such as the one led by Cho Bong Am, had been absorbed by the political establishment. Furthermore, the Korea Democratic Party, which endorsed a free market economy rather than a state-planned economy, also included in its platform policy the need for state intervention in the economy to ensure the reconstruction and growth of the economy after the liberation. An Jae Hong, one of the leading political figures in the "moderate camp," also stressed the need for establishing an economic system that combines capitalism and socialism while proposing the New Nationalism and New Democracy.

Third, the U.S. Military Government adopted an institutional framework that put emphasis on the economic planning function despite the fact that it aimed to establish a liberal economic system in the fledgling new country. As well as 10 various committees that directly reported to National Economic Board, the Office of Planning, which had the functions of analysis, research, and statistical survey, the Office of Food Administration, and the Office of Consumer Prices Administration were installed in the National Economic Board. The U.S. Military Government intended to resolve the social confusion and economic challenges that existed during the military administration through such committees. Although the performances of such committees were not satisfactory, they at least promoted the conditions that the people had been familiar with since the Japanese colonial rule.

Fourth, as a government of a fledgling new country that had just liberated, the administration aspired to accelerate the speed of economic growth not only to meet its urgent political agenda but also to achieve economic independence.

Another key background truth behind the adoption of the aforementioned economic policy was that the aid that South Korea was receiving from the U.S. began to shrink rapidly beginning in 1958. The ROK government, which largely relied on U.S. aid for its fiscal needs and military spending, felt pressured by the looming onset of a potential economic crisis as the Eisenhower administration started to scale down its aid to South Korea by adopting the New Look policy. Adding salt to the wound, the Eisenhower administration introduced the Development Loan Fund (DLF). According to the new framework, loans would be provided to the beneficiary country provided that the economic development plan submitted by the beneficiary country was deemed realistic in terms of its feasibility.

The ROK government had no choice but to push forward with economic development to cope with post-war crisis; it also had to establish its own economic development plan so it could obtain loans from foreign aid institutions, like DLF. The plan for such administrative process had been established since the inauguration of the ROK government, but the confusion due to the war and the markedly changed environment gives us a clue to why the full-fledged economic development plan began to be formulated in earnest only in the late 1950s.

Implementation System

The Office of Planning

The Syngman Rhee administration installed the Office of Planning in September 1948 according to the constitution, followed by the installation of bureaus with sub functions under the Office of Planning, such as the Bureau of Budget, the Bureau of Price Statistics, and the Bureau of Price Planning. Also, the National Economic Board, which was chaired by the head of the Office of Planning and was staffed with representatives of the Ministry of Agriculture and Forestry, Ministry of Commerce and Industry, Ministry of Transportation, Ministry of Communication, Ministry of Social Affairs, and Ministry of Internal Affairs as well as four members representing the industrial and financial sector and two members from the academic circle, was installed. The Office of Planning drafted the Five-Year Plan for Material Mobilization and the Five-Year Plan for Economic Rehabilitation while at the same time resolving short-term economic issues and reviewing budgetary proposals. As the implementation of the economic rehabilitation plan became unrealistic, however, with the outbreak of the war, ensuring the country's economic stability rather than rehabilitation had become a more urgent issue. To address such urgency more effectively, the Minister of the Treasury was required to head the Office of Planning, and the Vice Minister of the Treasury was required to be its vice head.

The Economic Board

Installed in the Office of Planning in accordance with Article 35 of the Government Organization Act, the Economic Board was initially required to survey and review the overall fiscal budget and the economic plans that were to be submitted to the Cabinet upon the request of the State Council, and to provide advisory support. Its activities consisted of deliberations on key pending issues before submitting a report to the Cabinet. Given that the Office of Planning was unable to control all the other ministries, the vice ministers of diverse ministries that were related with the economic issues then played the role of reconciling the varied interests of multiple ministries by participating in the Economic Board.

As the necessity of an administrative body that would plan and fine-tune the economic policies aimed at supporting the recovery of the country's industrial facilities and social overhead capital and the economic rehabilitation emerged, the Ministry of National Rehabilitation was installed in February 1955 to replace the Office of Planning and to take the role of directly controlling the ministers of the four economic ministries. As the long-term plans prepared by diverse ministries began to emerge,[15)] the Minister of National Rehabilitation performed various functions, such as the establishment and implementation of comprehensive plans on the rehabilitation of the country's industry and economy as well as the management and adjustment of the potentially conflicting individual agenda of different ministries.

The Industrial Development Committee in the Ministry of National Rehabilitation

With the abolition of the plan established in 1956 facing negative domestic opinions and criticisms from Washington, the ROK government embarked on the full-fledged establishment of the economic development plan. Towards this end, the Industrial Development Committee was installed as a subsidiary organization of the Ministry of National Rehabilitation on March 13, 1958. The Committee played the role of giving advice with regard to the establishment of the economic rehabilitation plan by surveying and assessing the status of the human, material, and capital resources in the country as well as maximizing the availability of such resources.

The Office of Foreign Capital

The Office of Foreign Capital was the central administrative body that oversaw the works related with the purchase and management of foreign capital, and was installed on February 17, 1955 by consolidating the Office of Foreign Procurement and the Interim Foreign Capital Management.

As an external office of the Ministry of National Rehabilitation, the Office of Foreign Capital had been responsible for lining up the foreign capital required for the rehabilitation projects until the installation of the Public Procurement Service in October 1951. The Office of Foreign Capital played the role of lining up and distributing the capital for the industrial development plans of the ROK government while managing the foreign capital provided by the U.S. Specifically, the role of the Office of Foreign Capital had a disproportionate significance because much of the aid provided by the Eisenhower administration was intended for military spending. However, since the special account of the Bank of Korea, which managed the counterpart funds raised from the aid, was controlled by the economic advisor of the Commander of the United Nations Forces and the economic coordinator of the U.S., the role of the Office of Foreign Capital was restricted.

---

15) Five-Year Plan to Increase Agricultural Production (1955), Three-Year Plan to Rehabilitate the Livestock Industry (1953), Plan to Rehabilitate and Reconstruct the Industrial Sector (1954), and Five-Year Plan to Develop the Pastoral Areas (1954).

Implementation Process and Contents

The Five-Year Plan for Material Mobilization

The Five-Year Plan for Material Mobilization (1950~1954) formulated in 1949, which dealt with the supply of insufficient materials along with the industrial development and rehabilitation plan, was drafted by the Office of Planning during the period when the ECA (Economic Cooperation Administration) aid plan of the U.S. was being prepared. The Five-Year Plan for Material Mobilization was aimed at achieving the goal of a self-sufficient economy by ensuring a stable supply of agricultural produce and fishery products as well as the products of mining and manufactured goods.

Additionally, the Syngman Rhee administration pushed forward with the Five-Year Plan to Rehabilitate Industries (1949~1953) beginning in 1949. The goal of the plan was to markedly advance the level of heavy and chemical industries to raise the organic construction of the domestic industry and to promote the transition from an agricultural country to an industrial one. According to such design, the plan concentrated on focusing investment and boosting the production volume for five years in the 14 key sectors spanning the country's most vulnerable areas, such as the fuel, energy, and heavy and chemical industries.

The ECA aid allocated 28.3% and 25.1% of the total funds to the rehabilitation projects in the 1950 and 1951 fiscal years, respectively, an amount surpassed only by the funds spent for importing fertilizer and farming products. The rehabilitation plan was made up of coal and the construction of railroads and bridges, but it was not easy for the Office of Planning to establish the rehabilitation plan through collaboration with the U.S. alone. More than anything, Washington was not enthusiastic about the rehabilitation plan. This was partly due to the fact that the U.S. Parliament voted down the bill to aid Korea mainly because the economic situation of South Korea at that time was not yet stable. The biggest reason was inflation and the outbreak of the war. Unlike the Korea's situation at the time, the establishment of plans to promote industrial development and to build infrastructure required a stable political situation.

Amidst such challenging situation, the U.S. Ambassador to Korea requested the administration to implement a fiscal stabilization plan to ensure the country's economic stability, which was soon followed by the inauguration of the Korea - USA Economic Stabilization Committee in January 1950. The Committee aimed at controlling inflation and stabilizing the economy, including the establishment of a balanced fiscal budget, the restriction of expenditure on government subsidies, the control of the bank credit line, and the justification of the foreign currency management system, in close consultation with the Office of Planning. The inflation was further exacerbated, however, with the outbreak of the Korean War.

The Five-Year Plan for Economic Rehabilitation

The Korea Economic Rehabilitation Plan of 1954, which was prepared by the Office of Planning, was intended for a full-fledged postwar rehabilitation project. According to the plan, the agricultural and fishery funds shall be spent for soil improvement, restoration of the agricultural warehouse, and construction and repair of fishing boats; the funds for transportation, communication, and electric power, for the construction of railways, the restoration of vehicles, the dredging of ports, and the expansion of power plants; and the mining and industrial funds, for the construction of fertilizer, cement, and glass panel manufacturing plants as well as the restoration of textile manufacturing facilities, machinery assembly factories, and mining facilities. To sum up, the funds were spent mainly on expanding the social overhead capital required for industrial advancement and on developing the country's heavy and chemical industries as planned before the war.

The change in the plan, if any, compared to the one prepared before the war, was that the earlier intention to rectify the imbalance of wealth through the implementation of the plan morphed into the strong will to win the race that would determine the supremacy of either regime (the South Korean or North Korean regime) through the expansion of the country's manufacturing capability led by the capitalists. Also, the economic aid from the U.S., which had been shunned for fear that the country would become politically and economically dependent on Washington, started to be considered the only tool left for the country to use for reconstructing the South Korean economy and thereby achieving economic self-reliance. The Syngman Rhee administration embarked on a full-fledged economic rehabilitation project led by the capitalists, based on the dependence on foreign economic aid.

With the New Five-Year Rehabilitation Plan (1957～1961), the ROK government planned to invest a total of US$ 1,075 million in a span of five years. Of such amount, US$ 563.5 million was allocated for the restoration of the power, transportation, and communication infrastructure for industrialization as well as for housing, education, health, and public welfare facilities while US $ 93 million was allocated for agricultural production. An additional US$ 418.4 million was allocated for the reconstruction of the manufacturing, steel, mining, fishery, vessels, and shipbuilding industries, which included such projects like the construction of fertilizer plants to replace the imported fertilizers and cement manufacturing plants; the restoration of the Ulsan oil refinery; and the restoration of the textile industry to improve the living standards of the people. The ROK government requested Washington to guarantee the payment of the fund amounting to US$ 2.3749 billion over the period of five years so that it could implement such reconstruction plan.

As such, since its inauguration, the government had already prepared in the early days the long-term economic plan, but the outbreak of the Korean War invalidated all such plans. After a comprehensive review of the country's economic reality, the discussion of economic self-reliance and the development plan was triggered by the discovery that while the economic dependence on foreign aid had deepened, the country's manufacturing capability had been recovered to the level before the war but the imbalance of the industrial structure had not been rectified. The plan, which was intended to realize the international balance of payments, the first step towards economic self-reliance, was the result of such awakening of the Koreans to the need for economic self-reliance.

As the postwar reconstruction project began to stumble upon unexpected roadblocks, the government issued industrial rehabilitation bonds totaling KRW 6.167 billion over eight rounds of issuance, from March 31, 1954 to 1957. Also, the government pushed ahead with a series of ambitious fiscal investments and loan programs funded by the industrial rehabilitation bonds and the counterpart fund. The government revamped and repaired the irrigation, ports, roadways, transportation, and communication infrastructure through fiscal investments, while it relied on the fiscal loan program for streamlining and strengthening the industrial structure in the wake of the construction of the key industries.

The Three-Year Industrial Development Plan

The Industrial Development Committee announced the Three-Year Industrial Development Plan right after the presidential and vice presidential elections in 1960, after several rounds of subcommittee discussions and plenary reviews since the committee's preparation of the draft proposal in early 1959. The plan assumed that the annual growth rate would be 5.2% on average for the three years. While the plan assumed that the required capital would be financed by foreign funds, when the foreign aid to Korea by the U.S. was declining, it nevertheless considered the changing economic situation at the time. The disproportionate emphasis on the fertilizer, cement, pulp, and machinery industries seems to have been influenced by the balanced-growth theory.

Another characteristic of the Three-Year Industrial Development Plan was that it stressed the importance of agricultural development. Given the traditional influence of farming and the country's underdeveloped industrial structure back in the 1950s, the plan stressed the absolutely critical status of the country's agricultural industry then. Another reason that the plan stressed the importance of farming was that it would be able to foster the development of the manufacturing industry through the expansion of the consumer market by boosting the income level of the rural areas.

A third reason was that the export of rice was practically the only viable option left for the country then to earn back foreign currency. The Three-Year Industrial Development Plan put a disproportionate importance on the farming sector, especially on the increased yield of rice and barley. As discussed earlier in the chapter, however, the plan was not put into practice in the end, after its approval in the Cabinet Meeting on April 15, 1960, due to the demise of the Syngman Rhee administration after the April 19 Revolution.

Performance and Assessment

The Syngman Rhee administration's plan to utilize foreign aid and reconstruct the country in the 1950s succeeded in realizing the results cited below.

First, the administration successfully completed the postwar recovery project by 1956, and established the economic development plan despite the fact that it had to struggle through the war for three years. As with the many new countries that were liberated after World War II, South Korea did not have sufficient capital or technology, which were indispensable for economic growth and industrialization. Making matters worse, the Korean Peninsula was divided along the 38th Parallel Line in the process of enforcing the surrender of the Japanese imperial army. For this reason, the country was not able to mobilize its economic potential nationwide while the Korean War that lasted from 1950 to 1953 contracted the already-challenging economy even more. Given the challenging situation created by such ordeals, the herculean effort poured into the establishment of the economic development plan definitely cannot be underestimated.

Second, the administration built the platform for future growth despite the difficult economic challenges they had to grapple with. The U.S. Armed Forces advanced to the part of the Korean Peninsula south of the 38th Parallel Line, and governed the territory by establishing the U.S.

Military Government, but the promised aid from the U.S. did not come according to the agreed-upon schedule. Since the U.S. was involved in almost every pressing issue throughout the world at the time, the Korean Peninsula did not rank high on the chore list of Washington. The country was therefore plagued by the exploding amount of money in circulation and the resulting inflation due to the insufficient aid from the U.S. Making matters worse, the loans offered to the United Nations Forces during the Korean War further exacerbated the inflation. After the signing of the armistice agreement in 1953, the factories slowly recovered, and started to pump up their production volumes, thereby laying the groundwork for economic recovery. Still, the economy had not recovered enough to warrant an increase of tax receipts for the government in the postwar confusion. Therefore, the Syngman Rhee administration had no choice but to increase the amount of money in circulation to boost fiscal spending. All the stimulus policies aimed at economic growth ended up boosting the amount of money in circulation. Amidst such challenging situation, the inflation rate of the South Korean economy reached a precarious level during the period from 1948 to 1957. The U.S. struggled to cap the amount of money in circulation and to reduce the trade deficit by boosting exports. Despite such efforts, however, it failed to curb the rising inflation rate. The unbridled inflation started to lose steam, however, by 1958, with the implementation of the fiscal stabilization plan, but the stabilization policy in turn lowered the overall production volume. Despite such problems, however, the ROK government still pushed ahead with the establishment of a related ministry (Ministry of National Rehabilitation) and institution (Industrial Development Committee) to draft economic development plans, a move that became an important stepping stone for future economic growth after the 1960s.

Third, the administration formed many groups of professional bureaucrats who were capable of planning and implementing economic development policies. As many public officials who were groomed while studying or being trained abroad started to return and take their posts in the economic ministries, they grew as professional public officials specializing in the area of economic planning. Some public officials who studied in the U.S. returned to their homeland after the liberation while the others were trained by key institutions throughout the 1950s. A special curriculum on how to formulate and implement an economic development plan was installed in the World Bank located in the U.S., to which the government sent at least one public official every year. Officials were also sent to the ECAFE and Colombo Plan every year, where professional bureaucrats hailing from all parts of Asia gathered together to share the experiences they had accumulated while implementing their respective economic development plans. Such education and training activities formed an important backdrop for the establishment of the Economic Planning Board as well as the formation of professional bureaucrats capable of drafting and implementing economic development plans during the period after the 1960s. To sum up, the rapid economic growth since the 1960s would have been unlikely without the economic achievement realized in the 1950s.

Section 3

The Government Reform of the Syngman Rhee Administration

1. Background and direction of the government reform

Background of the Government Reform

Korea has gone through diverse types of government reforms since its liberation, including scores of reshuffling of its organizational structure. Such reforms were triggered by the changing expectation about the role of the government that resulted from the changing external geopolitical environment and internal socioeconomic environment as well as the interaction between the political power and the social power. The government reform of the 1st Republic was not just another reform. As the government was not just the one that saw the birth of the Republic of Korea but was also the one that created various institutions as an independent state. While leaving a procedural precedent on the formation of various government organizations, its history is still exerting influence not only on the present situation after 60 years but also on the future of the country.

All reforms, including government reform, would inevitably aim to break the status quo and to bring about changes in the present state. Therefore, any reform would eventually be accompanied by changes in the existing power structure. Furthermore, if reform can be defined as a process through which a certain political leader or group changes the existing power structure or institutions and creates a new power structure and order based on its explicit will and desire, then the very presence of the U.S. Military Government and its power structure as well as the process of reforming it into that of an independent state can only be considered one of the typical examples of government reform. Therefore, the government reform of the 1st Republic, which aimed to shorten the duration of the U.S. military rule as well as to construct a nation-state and to unite the people, started in earnest with the establishment of an autonomous independent state.

Goal and Direction of the Government Reform

The goal and direction of the government reform of the 1st Republic shall be analyzed by dividing the period pegged on the inflection point when the constitutional amendment was carried out. The period shall be divided into three phases. The first phase covers the era of the first president, from 1948 to August 1952, during which a nation-state was formed; the second phase covers the period from August 1952 to August 1956, when the presidential elections to elect the second president was held in the wake of the first constitutional amendment; and the third phase covers the period from August 1956 to April 19, 1960, when the constitutional government of the 1st Republic was suspended due to the student revolution that broke out.

The key national goals of the government during the first phase were the construction of a nation-state and the formation of citizenship as well as the realization of European/American-style democracy, the establishment of a capitalistic economic system, the proclamation of the anti-communist policy, and the formation of a national system. Towards these ends, various advisory apparatuses were scaled down through consolidation while the Ministry of Foreign Affairs, Ministry of Defense, and Ministry of Internal Affairs, the key governmental infrastructure that would take on the mantle of constitutional legitimacy, were put ahead of other economic and social institutions. Moreover, the key imperatives that were made public included meritocracy in personnel administration and the establishment of organizational operation plans and economic development plans, while the official goals included the simplification of the administrative process, the fostering of convenience for the people, and reform towards decentralization. The reform is assessed to have largely failed, however, due to the hiring of public officials who lacked the required professional specialization and will to implement the reform.

In the second phase, the unification of the Korean Peninsula, economic stabilization, and postwar recovery were proclaimed as the urgent goals of the republic. Comprehensive economic planning and stabilization of the economy were required to reconstruct the industrial facilities and social overhead capital that were reduced to rubble during the Korean War. The government needed to come up with its own plan for national rehabilitation and economic self-reliance as the U.S., which provided most of the foreign aid that Korea received at that time, scaled back its aid. Specifically, the past practice of allocating key government posts among different political camps was ditched in favor of appointment of public officials armed with specialization in the economy in an attempt to ensure economic stability and recovery. The Ministry of National Rehabilitation and the Office of Foreign Capital were newly installed in the context of expanding the government institutions addressing the economic issues then.

In the third phase, the practical goal of the Syngman Rhee administration was the preservation of the regime in the aftermath of the administration's attempt to extend its incumbency, while the goals of nation building and reform of the administrative system were pushed to the sidelines. An oligarchical system led by the Liberal Party was formed amidst the characteristic atmosphere befitting a police state.

Government Reform Implementation System

The government reform of the 1st Republic was marked by the emergence of a political power headed by the president without any organization that will push forward with the reform, such as the Administration Reform Committee or the Economic Growth and Development Committee in the 5th Republic, or the Administrative Renovation Committee of the Kim Young Sam administration. Meanwhile, Lee Han Bin defined the Syngman Rhee administration as a very special type of regime driven by the autocratic leadership of President Rhee, which was supported by the oligarchical elite bureaucrats. Majority of the members of the administration, from the ministers down to the street-level public officials, did not have previous experience in governing the country. While there was formally an administrative organization from the outset, they were generally incapable of playing their roles and/or performing their responsibilities. Therefore, considering that the administration failed to push forward with the government reform systematically but instead copied the administrative practices inherited from the Japanese colonial rule, the Syngman Rhee administration is deemed to be a pre-modern-era bureaucratic system with no accumulation of professional specialty. The practice of state control over ideology set the tone of the future administrations in their comprehensive intervention in the civil society. The policymaking structure of the Syngman Rhee administration can be defined as a paternalistic and authoritarian policymaking system based on the autocratic personality of President Syngman Rhee.

Such authoritarian decision making structure of the Syngman Rhee administration becomes obvious when one looks deeper into the policy proposal or screening process of the administration. First, according to the ratio of the number of people who came up with any policy initiative or proposal, the very proposal of the policy was made by none other than the president himself, followed by the prime minister, a political apparatus containing elements of the parliamentary cabinet system designed to check the president. The negligible number of bills proposed by the National Assembly or other political parties indicates that President Syngman Rhee saw the National Assembly and the political parties as groups of imbeciles. Seen from a different perspective, this was partly due to the fact that the National Assembly and the members of the political parties at that time had yet to build a sufficient pool of talents who were capable of coming up with policy proposals. The prime ministerial system, which was designed to check the power of the president, and the Parliament, and the political parties had been practically incapacitated. The president relegated his power only to the members of his cabinet.

2. Contents of the government reform

Organizational Reshuffling

The Syngman Rhee administration went through three rounds of organizational reshuffling. First, the administration steadily increased the number of administrative bodies either through the amendment of the Government Organization Act or the enactment of a special law. In 1949, it established the Ministry of Health, the Office of the Treasury, and the Foreign Procurement Agency. With the abolition of the prime ministerial system in the 2nd constitutional amendment in 1954, the Government Organization Act was amended as well to construct an administrative system that was more in keeping with the spirit of the presidential system.

Second, in managing the government organization, the Syngman Rhee administration merely copied the practices of the Japanese colonial rule. Given the political and social confusion that existed in the wake of the Korean War, the administration could not yet afford to introduce a new administrative system. Despite such challenging situation, however, the administration realized the need to establish an organizational operation plan and an economic development plan. Albeit negligible in scale, the administration took a series of measures for reform, including the simplification of the administrative proceedings, the improvement of the convenience of the people, and the fostering of decentralization. While it strove to carry out the administrative works in a transparent manner by publishing a series of white papers composed by different government organizations, the administration pushed forward with the accelerated and fluid processing of civil matters and complaints through the enactment of the Administrative Work Simplification Decree in October 1949 and the Administrative Work Simplification in Time of War Decree in February 1951. In addition, the administration transferred a total of 26 administrative works previously handled by the central government to the local administrative body.

Third, the Syngman Rhee administration also showed interest in drafting comprehensive national plans. The installation of the Office of Planning alongside the inauguration of the government can be understood as an institutional step to establish such plans. The Industrial Development Committee, which inaugurated in 1955, pushed forward with the formation of long-term economic development plans. However, due to the demise of the Syngman Rhee administration in the wake of the April 19 Student Revolution, the Three-Year Economic Development Plan, which was completed in 1959 and adopted in the Cabinet meeting held on April 15, 1960, could not be implemented in the end.

Therefore, a clear example of the legacy of the previous administrative organization can be found in the government organization of the Syngman Rhee administration. Being the government of an independent state, the administration strengthened the ministries governing foreign affairs and defense while also adopting an organization with the characteristic of an independent regulatory committee, or consolidating several organizations. The main administrative framework of the government was formed, however, by adopting that of the Japanese colonial government, with only minor modifications. Furthermore, the principles and practices of organizational management were almost identical to those of the Japanese colonial government.

Fiscal Reform

The Syngman Rhee administration pushed forward with fiscal reform through organizational reshuffling and the streamlining of the related laws or institutions. It also attempted to implement fiscal stabilization initiatives indirectly — in other words, fiscal reform — through the management of the foreign-aid-based economy and the establishment of policies aimed at substituting imported products with local ones. The administration also promulgated the Finance Act and its enforcement decree, followed by the completion of the budget classification system featuring functional classification as well as classification by economic property by early 1959. Functional classification, including the general expenditure account, social expenditure account, economic expenditure account, and other accounts, began to be applied in 1962.

Personnel Reform

The first step in the personnel reform pursued by the Syngman Rhee administration was to stipulate the basic regulations governing the handling of personnel affairs related with the employment of public officials. The Civil Service Act[16] was enacted to rule out the patronage system in the hiring of public servants while also clarifying the advocacy of meritocracy in the assessment of the performance of public officials. The legislation was followed by the establishment of other related regulations, including the Civil Servant Employment Decree, the Higher Civil Service Examination Decree, the Civil Servant Payment Rules, and the Employment Rules. However, there were too much leeway in such laws and regulations that allowed a stunningly easy and arbitrary interpretation of the related laws and regulations. In fact, they were implemented by the Liberal Party often based on the patronage or spoils system.[17)]

Anti-Corruption Reform

The Syngman Rhee administration had to struggle through one of the greatest fratricidal disasters in the history of Korea from the early years of the nation building: the Korean War. The key group that was prepared to overcome such extraordinary situation was the armed forces. The moral and ethical standards of the armed forces were yet to be formed, however, considering that it had been just five years after the liberation. Moreover, even though a massive amount of war supplies was provided to the military organization, no department that would ensure the transparency of the distribution process by monitoring or supervising the military organization was in place, a structure that invited corruption in the ROK Armed Forces. As corruption was rampant in the armed forces, which formed the foundation of the governing group in the Syngman Rhee administration, the administration's drive for anti-corruption reform was merely perfunctory in nature.

Although not sufficient in extent to be considered as an anti-corruption activity, Watchword for Public Servants was created to stress the key discipline required for public servants, including punctuality, obedience to authority, fulfillment of one's responsibility, and fairness.

Watchword for Public Servants was the set of maximum guidelines that the Syngman Rhee administration would be able to propose to the public officials then as an indirect anti-corruption initiative.

Reform of Local Administration

The Syngman Rhee administration pushed forward with the reform of the local administration with the promulgation and enforcement of the Act on the Local Self-governing System, which stipulated the application of a stratified structure to the design of the local self-governing system,

---

16) It was on August 12, 1949, when the Civil Servant Act was promulgated, that the foundation of the country's civil servant system was created. The act was intended to ensure fairness in personnel administration, and to help the public officials maximize their work efficiency as the servants of the people by stipulating the basic requirements for becoming a civil servant. In reality, however, the act was nothing but a downright translation of the imperial order promulgated during the Japanese colonial rule, and a certain amount of democratic elements was added. As such, the Civil Servant Act was proven to be problematic when applied to real-world situations because its provisions were miles apart from the realities of the country, and because the country's administrative technique had not yet fully matured at that time, even though the act formed the basis of the personnel administration, along with the law that stipulated the details of meritocracy.

17) The patronage or spoils system perpetrated by the Liberal Party administration is not identical to the massive replacement of civil servants that is done to democratize the government bureaucracy, which was common in the U.S. back in the early 19th century, but indicates some small-scale personal transfers designed to fill in vacancies, or transference or promotion under the connivance of the Liberal Party.

such as that of Seoul Special City and the provinces in one strata and city, town (eup), and county (myeon). Another aspect of the reform pursued by the local administration during the Syngman Rhee administration was the formation of the local assembly at the soonest possible time. The councilmen of the cities, towns and counties were elected on April 25, 1952, followed by the elections of the provincial councilmen on May 10, thereby forming the first civilian local council throughout the country. As President Syngman Rhee ensured the holding of the first local elections in an attempt to mobilize his political supporters, the elections were held and managed haphazardly, without the sufficient preparation for such of the local self-governing system. The negative side effects of the first elections reverberated in the history of the country's local self-governing system as the elections were imbued with the atrocious politics of Seoul.

3. Performance and assessment of the government reform

The assessment of the 1st Republic and of President Syngman Rhee is sharply divided depending on the ideological slant of the evaluator. On one hand, President Rhee is praised for having founded the Republic of Korea based on the liberal democratic ideology, and for succeeding in reflecting the presidential system in the first amendment of the Republic of Korea, thereby laying the foundation for national development. On the other hand, he is criticized for having nurtured a political ambition that, coupled with Washington's foreign policy, contributed to the division of the Korean Peninsula. A closer look at the international circumstances and political situation of the fledgling new country would reveal, however, that he could not be held responsible for the division of the Korean Peninsula.

President Rhee ruled out socialism on the premise of anti-communism, and established the 1st Republic. He also strove to ensure the basic survival of the country by recognizing the defense and maintenance of public order as one of the most pressing tasks facing the country for it to effectively respond to the threat of the communist force during the establishment of the government and during the Korean War.

The 1st Republic can be said to have accomplished government reform in that it built an autonomous independent state based on liberal democracy, which in the historical context dates back to the late Joseon period, the Japanese colonial rule, and the rule of the U.S. Military Government. Other than this, however, the republic largely failed to promote the creation of circumstances conducive to the effective implementation of social integration by overcoming the confusion and poverty that it encountered after struggling through the Japanese colonial rule. To sum up, the so-called "government reform" was implemented well before the necessary political base and administrational foundation was systematically prepared. Still, the Syngman Rhee administration was not without accomplishments, and these could be summed up as shown below.

First, the administration signified the inauguration of an autonomous democratic government. Like many other fledgling new countries that acquired political freedom upon liberation after World War II, which were required to establish their identity as a national state and to build a new policymaking system, the 1st Republic of Korea was also required by the era to embark on the task of nation building and the formation of the people ahead of anything else so as to establish an autonomous government and to exercise the right of self-determination. The shortening of the U.S. military rule and the establishment of a national state based on liberal democracy can be deemed as the most important achievements of the 1st Republic.

Second, the administration succeeded in migrating to the presidential system. President Rhee completely abolished the prime ministerial system, whose practical function and responsibility is currently being questioned, but established a fully functional president-centric government, a significant achievement when seen from the perspective of administrative consistency or policy direction.

Third, the administration signified the inauguration of a functional government system, which was formed on account of the need to carry out national tasks. The government of the 1st Republic failed to come up with its own goal or vision in forming the government organization but designed it by appropriating the form and function of the administrative bodies of the U.S. Military Government, the Japanese Government-General in Korea, and the Japanese government. The administration minimized the government organization by taking over the administrative bodies of the U.S. Military Government without any modification, with the exception of the foreign affairs and defense functions, based on the principle of conservation and simplification of the administrative process. Such choice leaves room for the potential interpretation that the administration had no sense of the new demands for administration service, or that their purported goal of promoting the people's convenience may have just been a bogus claim. Despite such limitations, however, the fact that the administration still launched some form of institution and organization, albeit limited to the minimal level, should be acknowledged. In addition, the administration listed the unification of the two Koreas, economic stabilization, and postwar recovery as its urgent goals, and expanded the postwar administrative organization by widening the scope of the national functions through the establishment of the Ministry of National Rehabilitation for economic stabilization and recovery, and the consolidation of the Ministry of Health and the Ministry of Social Issues for postwar recovery.

The 1st Republic lacked internal fidelity and continuity in its pursuit of government reform due to the absence of a standing body dedicated to the handling of government reform. It also understood the government function in a narrow sense, as being centered on the maintenance of law and order. This was largely due to the disproportionately high percentage of government officials from the legal circle, who did not have a sufficient understanding of government reform. Furthermore, the Government Organization Act was legislated without a clear forecast of the diverse needs of people spanning politics, the economy, the society, or culture, thereby making the government reform fizzle out in the end. In addition, the government reform was limited to institutional reshuffling rather than aiming to change the bureaucratic behavior or advancement of the management techniques. The reform covered wide-range of areas in an attempt to lay the foundation for an independent state. As the diverse attempts at reform were implemented in a sporadic, timid, and distributed manner, however, the reform failed to institutionalize the fresh practices that the administration hoped would take root throughout the government organization.

Therefore, due to the inefficiency of the administration, the Syngman Rhee administration failed to respond to the explosion of diverse demands spanning politics, the economy, the society, and culture, but rather focused on preserving the regime. The authoritarian minds of the governing class deepened the anti-democratic practices caused by the one-man autocracy as well as the fraud and corruption perpetrated by the civil servants. In conclusion, it is assessed that the government reform of the Syngman Rhee administration failed to achieve its stated goals because it focused on protecting the existing framework in a passive manner rather than proactively responding to the social changes that occurred then.

Section 4

Inauguration of the Jang Myeon Administration and Foundation of Key Policy Administration

1. Inauguration of the administration and introduction of its organization

With the passing by a majority vote of the constitutional amendment featuring the parliamentary cabinet system on June 15, 1960, after the demise of the Syngman Rhee administration in the wake of the April 19 Student Revolution, the interim government announced the July 29 general elections for the members of the Lower and Upper House who will make up the 5th National Assembly. In the elections, which were held in a freer and fairer environment compared to the elections held during the time of the Syngman Rhee administration, the Democratic Party[18] won with a landslide, as expected. The political turmoil worsened, however, as the competition among the different political clans in the Democratic Party kicked into high gear in the run-up to the July 29 general elections.

The competition among different clans within the Democratic Party, which first emerged during the nomination process for the July 29 general elections, grew progressively worse and eventually went beyond control, paralyzing the screening and voting process on the ordinary budget bills. In the end, the National Assembly degenerated into an arena of struggle for political supremacy in the party rather than of desirable political competition aimed at the development of the country.

Given the absence of a functioning national governance system and social infrastructure since the end of the Korean War, the armed forces was then the most systematic and organized group armed with administrative capability in the South Korean society. Therefore, military intervention in politics was highly likely in such a precarious social environment, an observation shared by President Syngman Rhee. For this reason, the president believed he should exercise effective control of the armed forces, and he eventually utilized them as his political base. The Heo Jeong Interim Government also singled out the stabilization and effective control of the military as the key goal in the government administration, and concentrated its resources on coming up with an

18) A detailed look at the results of the July 29 general elections will show that the Democratic Party swept the Lower House by winning 175 of the 233 seats (over 75%). Of the 301 candidates who ran in the elections, 175 won seats, thereby recording a 58.1% winning ratio. In the Upper House, the Democratic Party had 31 successful winners out of 60 candidates, thereby recording a 51.7% winning ratio.

effective method of controlling the military.

Contrary to such moves, Prime Minister Jang Myeon of the 2nd Republic focused on incapacitating the military based on his political beliefs regarding the foundations of liberal democracy, and while also anticipating military support from Washington. In his inaugural speech as the prime minister, he stressed the need for arms reduction and for reform of the armed forces. He laid out his plan to slash the defense spending, which accounted for nearly 40% of the total fiscal budget, down to a 20% level, with the saved amount to be spent on economic development, with the insufficient troops to be supplemented with the modernization and expansion of the military equipment. His reform initiative, however, was entirely his own, with no advanced consultation conducted between the ROK Armed Forces and the U.S. government. His announcement, therefore, faced considerable resistance and opposition from the ROK and U.S. military.

In the meantime, the ROK Police also grew with the support and sponsorship of the political establishment of the U.S. Military Government and the Syngman Rhee administration.

Convinced that the police would play a critical role in pushing forward with the reform of the South Korean society, however, Prime Minister Jang Myeon tightened the regulation and management of the police to establish discipline in the organization. First, the over 4,500 police officers who were involved in the rigging of the elections by the Liberal Party were punished, followed by massive personnel replacement, including the three-time replacement of the Minister of Internal Affairs. Despite the potential the armed forces and police had of forming the key political base for the administration, through which the administration could minimize the social unrest and gain public trust, Prime Minister Jang Myeon failed to effectively control them and resulted in the collapse of the regime.

The voices asking for a democratic society among the citizens grew louder in the wake of the April 19 Student Revolution. In response to such request, Prime Minister Jang Myeon minimized the restriction on political participation while proclaiming its advocacy of liberalism and democracy. This resulted in the explosive release of the people's pent-up desire for political participation, which was placed under tight control during the Syngman Rhee administration. In what was later called "The Spring of Seoul," endless streams of protesters and sit-in demonstrators lined the streets every day, across the country. Various interest groups representing the country's labor, education, press, and religious sectors took to the streets for rally after rally. Such atmosphere even spread to the public sector and grew to such an extent as to intoxicate the people into attempting to solve any problem with a protest rally. The reformist group, which remained largely hidden behind the curtain during the Syngman Rhee administration due to its political oppression by the administration, came up to the front stage of the political arena to raise their voices.

As such, the Jang Myeon administration took a more receptive and moderate attitude towards the diverse political desires of the people compared to the previous administration. Unfortunately, however, such moderate attitude was reflected even in the punishment of the high-ranking officials who were involved in the corruption and the rigging of the March 15 elections, who received a light punishment. Such lenient attitude towards public offenders backfired as the citizens eventually grew furious: in October 1960, some 50 activists who were injured during the April 19 Revolution stormed the National Assembly Building and occupied the main hall, demanding the legislation of a special law to punish the traitors of democracy.

During the time of the Jang Myeon administration, the discussion on unification by the reformist group and the student activists who supported the unification of the two Koreas and socialist ideas started to show a more colorful development. The only idea concerning the unification that was allowed to be discussed during the Syngman Rhee administration was unification by advancing northward, but scores of ideas on the unification and inter-Korean exchanges, such as peaceful unification, unification through the neutralization of the peninsula, and the proposal for the holding of inter-Korean negotiations, were actively discussed. Specifically, the student activists and the reformist group actually attempted to engage in inter-Korean talks on the unification by trying to establish direct contact with Pyeongyang. In November 1960, some 600 students of Seoul National University formed the National Unification League and published a statement, arguing Prime Minister Jang Myeon to visit Moscow and Washington to push for the two countries' support for Korean unification. Such radical move by the reformist group and student activists backfired in the end, triggering strong opposition by the conservative politicians and social organizations, and further complicating the North Korean policy of the Jang Myeon administration.

Prime Minister Jang Myeon promised that he would guarantee freedom of the press, assembly, and association when he was inaugurated as the prime minister of the 2nd Republic. In fact, freedom of the press was allowed with practically no limits. The power of the press exploded in the context of democracy during the 2nd Republic, to an extent that would warrant the nickname of "The Press Republic" for the 2nd Republic. On the other hand, the uncontrolled explosion of sudden freedom ended up creating social confusion and unrest.

Since newspapers and news agencies were not required to register with the authority and since the submission of a simple report by their foundation would be sufficient after the introduction of a new report-based system, countless numbers of small newspapers started to print news reports, filling their papers with materials criticizing the government. Despite such overwhelming exercise of freedom of the press, the Jang Myeon administration maintained an extremely generous attitude towards the attacks by the press while also exercising limited regulation of the press.

The Syngman Rhee administration concentrated on growing the economy based on the industrialization strategy so as to accelerate the postwar rehabilitation of the country, but the country's economic growth was less than satisfactory until the early 1960s due to the mounting political upheaval and the lack of the needed infrastructure. While the index of industrial production and the amount of currency in circulation did not rise at all for about one year since April 1960, the wholesale price index jumped by nearly 10%. Such prolonged economic slump and rising prices further worsened the chronic unemployment rate. To cope with such challenges, the Jang Myeon administration attempted to tackle the unemployment plaguing the economy by introducing the so-called "New-Deal style" public projects, through which millions of unemployed people, especially those with higher education, would be able to find a job.

Prime Minister Jang Myeon put industrial advancement and economic policy first in the government administration agenda, and the Economic Development Committee, which was founded in 1961, embarked on the formulation of the Five-Year Economic Development Plan, which was praised as it was said to have come up with the macroeconomic framework for the country's economic policies. The content of the economic development plan prepared by the Jang Myeon administration was very down-to-earth and practical in that it showed a keen awareness of the key issues then of the South Korean economy. Unfortunately, however, the plan prepared by the Jang Myeon administration did not enjoy wholehearted support from the politicians and people alike, and did not even have a chance to be implemented due to the untimely demise of the administration early in its incumbency.

As the South Korean economy largely relied on the economic aid from Washington, it was swayed by the scale and provision policy of the foreign aid provided by the U.S. While the aid methods were divided into the planned aid, in which materials required for industrial facilities were provided, and unplanned aid, in which consumables were provided to stabilize the people's livelihood in the short term, the U.S. aid policy was implemented through the provision of defense support and economic aid at the same time. The overall size of the U.S. aid decreased slowly, and the percentage of the unplanned aid rose slowly compared to the planned aid. Moreover, Washington pressed the ROK government to depreciate the Korean won on the pretext that this would pave the way for the more effective spending of the relief and development being supplied by the export economy. As the exchange rate between the U.S. dollar and the Korean won skyrocketed, the prices rose rapidly. To sum up, the ROK government pushed forward with the industrialization strategy in an effort to build a self-reliant economy by escaping the Japanese colonial system beginning in the Syngman Rhee administration, but the country's economic dependence on the world powers persisted in that the imbalance in the industrial structure was retained and only the country on which Korea depended on economically was changed: from Japan to the U.S.

The unbalanced industrialization, coupled with the economic structure that was disproportionately dependent on the U.S., further worsened the poverty level of the country's rural region. The biggest reason that the country's rural area had grown poorer was the influx of excessive amounts of imported surplus agricultural produce. In the short term, the influx of surplus agricultural produce increased the benefits to the end consumers, but the fixation of the low income and the high interest rate resulted in the deepening of the poverty rate in the rural areas. Moreover, with the import of fertilizers, the Korean rural homes had to struggle with worsening economic difficulties due to the expensive fertilizers. The gap between the urban and rural regions was further exacerbated as the farming population migrated to the urban areas, further contracting the foundation of the agricultural economy.

2. Goal and direction of the government reform

The vision of the Jang Myeon administration consisted of the "completion of the April 19 Revolution" and "order and advancement," ahead of any other. The completion of the April 19 Revolution would be realized with the guaranteeing of the freedom to engage in political activities and with the purging of the past deeds, making the spirit of the April 19 Revolution felt. "Order" here signified the political and economic order while "advancement" signified the economic development of all.

To realize the "Completion of the April 19 Revolution," which was the key vision of the Jang Myeon administration, "political freedom" had to be guaranteed to the maximum extent and "autocratic rule" had to be ruled out. The Jang Myeon administration strove to fulfill its campaign pledges amidst the explosion of the people's pent-up demands for social change, which had been suppressed under the Syngman Rhee administration. The administration strove to cling to the mandate of the government: gradual establishment of "order" while ensuring "freedom" to its maximum allowable limit. The Democratic Party was determined to offer the "perfect freedom" that the people had been aspiring to have.

Another vision and goal in the government administration of Jang Myeon was "order and advancement." Towards this end, the country needed to realize "democracy" and "economic development" at the same time. Therefore, the Jang Myeon administration strove to recover democratic politics through "the reestablishment of the democratic political system," while in the area of the economy, it strove to "realize a self-sufficient economy" through "the establishment of economic order" and the formulation and implementation of a long-term economic development plan.

Having struggled under the oppressive rule of the Syngman Rhee administration, the Jang Myeon administration clung onto one principle that was non-negotiable: never trace the footsteps of the Syngman Rhee administration in any situation. Based on this principle, the Jang Myeon administration strove to guarantee "freedom to its maximum allowable limit," recovery of democratic politics, purging of the autocratic legacy and corruption of the Syngman Rhee administration, implementation of the economy-first rule, realization of a self-reliant economy, and a "rational" unification and foreign defense policy. The key administrative tasks of the government to achieve these goals are discussed below.

First, the party platform and key policies of the Democratic Party were "unification and foreign policy," "completion of the April 19 Revolution," "promotion of the development of the rural and fishing towns," and "establishment of a fiscal, financial, and economic platform." Accordingly, the key tasks that were proposed to realize the party platform and policies were laid out in the 15 Pledges for the July 29 General Elections.

To review the party platform and policy and campaign pledges of the Democratic Party, the administrative policy speeches of Prime Minister Jang Myeon, the key principles and goals proposed by the related ministers, and the budgetary plans, the key mandates of the Jang Myeon administration are summed up as follows: completion of the April 19 Revolution through revolutionary legislation, laying the groundwork for civil rights and advancement of party politics, starting economic construction anew, realization of social justice, rehabilitation of the rural and fishing towns, fostering of the development of small businesses, reducing the burden of the people, popularization of financial services, healthy development of a labor movement, educational innovation and expansion of scholarships offered, proactive implementation of a unification foreign policy, normalization of the relationship between Korea and Japan, establishment of a foreign policy aimed at obtaining foreign aid from the U.S., renovation of the defense policy and arms reduction, strengthening of the country's national security preparedness, and improvement of the treatment of civil servants.

Chapter 2

The Park Jung Hee Administration

Section 1

Inauguration of the Park Jung Hee Administration and Foundation of Key Policy Administration

1. Inauguration of the administration and introduction of its organization

The inauguration of the Park Jung Hee administration (1963~1979) signaled the emergence of a new power elite group that would take the helm in the country's drive for modernization. On May 16, 1961, near the end of the 2nd Republic but still during the incumbency of the Jang Myeon administration, some 3,000 troops led by Major General Park Jung Hee advanced to the Capital Building in Seoul via the ROK Army Headquarters in Yongsan and took the helm of the state by taking over the key governmental organizations and broadcasting stations.

Led by the junior group in the South Korean military, a host of army officers started a move to purify the armed forces in response to the political confusion and anomic conditions during the Jang Myeon administration, particularly after the April 19 Student Revolution. They were thought to harbor the vision of steering the country towards a new direction. Some officers were known to have been criticizing the inability of the Liberal Party to address the ever-worsening poverty as well as the country's growing dependence on the military and economic aid of the United States. Moreover, their aim to modernize the country through economic development and through the eradication of the societal anomy and of the administrative and political lameness, owing to the political rivalry between the old and new factions in the Democratic Party, became the key motivations behind the May 16 revolution. The military made five "revolution pledges": (1) to prepare for infiltration by external forces based on the principle of anti-communism; (2) to forge an alliance with the friendly countries in the free world by adhering to the Charter of the United Nations; (3) to strengthen the people's moral armaments and to foster the development of a national and democratic spirit by ruling out social corruption and political misdeeds; (4) to address the people's hunger by concentrating on building a self-reliant national economy; and (5) to accomplish the reunification of the Korean Peninsula by rooting out the communists in North Korea.

General Park Jung Hee, who seized power through the May 16 revolution, was sworn in as the acting president in March 1962, and remained in office until December 1963. Having won in the presidential election that was held the following year, the acting president Park Jung Hee was sworn in as the 5th president of the republic for a term that lasted until June 1967. President Park won again in the succeeding presidential election and was sworn in as the 6th president of the republic for a term that lasted from July 1967 to June 1971. Again, elected as the 7th president of the republic based on the October 21, 1969 constitutional amendment allowing presidency for three consecutive terms, President Park was in the middle of his third term as president (July 1971 ~December 1972) when he established the Yushin Constitution on December 27, 1972, thereby installing himself as the 8th president of the republic for another six-year term as president that lasted until December 1978. President Park was again sworn in as the 9th president of the republic in December 1978, and remained in office until he was assassinated by his close aide on October 26, 1979.

The government of the 3rd Republic consisted of 2 boards, 13 ministries, 3 agencies, and 6 offices, with the president as the head of state, supported by the prime minister, the Board of Audit and Inspection, and the Central Intelligence Agency. As for the administrative bodies controlled by the president, the Presidential Office (Cheongwadae) had the Presidential Secretariat and the Office of Presidential Security. The Board of Audit and Inspection, a constitutional institution controlled by the president, performed audits and inspections of the duties of the various administrative bodies and local autonomous governments, while the Central Intelligence Agency gathered intelligence related with the national security and performed anti-communist investigative functions. The Presidential Committee on Economy and Science, a presidential advisory body, was installed to screen and review the key economic issues in the country and to advise the president with regard to such issues. The National Security Council, another presidential advisory body, was also installed to screen and review the key security-related and defense issues in the country and to advise the president with regard to those issues.

The prime minister was given the role of supervising the general administrative bodies, comprehensively supported by its internal administrative bodies, including the Office of Planning and Coordination and the Prime Ministerial Secretariat. The ministries that were directly controlled by the prime minister among the central administrative bodies were the Economic Planning Board, the Office of Government Administration, the Office of Legislation, and the Office of Veterans Administration as well as a nuclear safety body called the Board of Nuclear Power. There were also external bureaus, which were independent administrative bodies installed outside the ministries and were not auxiliary agencies within the central administrative bodies, such as the Office of Cultural Properties under the Ministry of Culture and Education, the Patent Bureau, the Central Metric Bureau, the Bureau of Standards under the Ministry of Commerce and Industry, the Railway Bureau and the Hydrographic Bureau under the Ministry of Transportation, and the Radio Management Bureau under the Ministry of Communication.

The government organization of the 4th Republic was remarkably expanded compared to that of the 3rd Republic. Specifically, the Board of National Unification was newly installed to push forward with the unification policies, and the Office of Science and Technology was installed to promote the development of science and technology. Office-level central administrative bodies were extensively installed to ensure the down-to-earth and effective implementation of the national policy initiatives or projects. All in all, the government of the 4th Republic consisted of 2 boards, 13 ministries, 4 agencies, and 13 offices, with the president as the head of state, supported by the prime minister, the Board of Audit and Inspection, and the Central Intelligence Agency.

As an internal administrative body of the Prime Ministerial Office, the Administrative

Coordination Office, which did not exist in the 3rd Republic, was installed. Such installation was a significant move in that the power of the prime minister was strengthened by empowering him with the coordination function of the implementation of key policies and government administration. The central administrative bodies additionally controlled by the prime minister were the Board of National Unification, which was established to push forward with the unification policy, and the Office of Science and Technology, which was established to assist in the development of science and technology.

In general, the legislative branch retained the right to review the proposed bills, budget proposals, and year-end settlements of account, but the administrative branch held the predominant power over the legislative branch in the presidential system. The parliamentary cabinet system that existed in the 2nd Republic was changed to the presidential system after the establishment of the 3rd Republic. The military group that assumed power listed the following reason for their introduction of the presidential system in the country: the parliamentary cabinet system failed to demonstrate its benefits and advantages and only caused unnecessary factional disputes, thereby resulting in increased political confusion and instability of the social order, with the administration less enthusiastic about executing the key national policies. As such, the military justified the adoption of the presidential system on the pretext that the system would ensure stability in the government administration, and would help the government push forward with its national development policy.

In fact, since the relationship between the National Assembly and the president was largely influenced by the power and authority of the president himself, it can be assumed that the National Assembly might have found it difficult to check the power of the president. Furthermore, the key posts were filled in by influential politicians; in particular, the main posts in the National Assembly were filled in by influential politicians belonging to the ruling party. Therefore, it would be fair to assume that the National Assembly maintained a friendly attitude towards the policies of the administration and towards the president himself. The opposition party politicians, however, might have maintained a confrontational attitude towards and fought against the administration as they were critical of the authoritarian attitude of the president and his administration. Their role of checking the executive's exercise of power might have been limited by their limited seats in the National Assembly, or by the constitutional restrictions that existed then. In particular, the fact that the opposition and resistance posed by the opposition party then was largely based on such party's political opposition against the overall government administration rather than on its rational criticism of the practical contents of various policy initiatives of the government may have weakened the legitimacy of the party's role of checking the exercise of power by the country's chief executive.

Meanwhile, it was stipulated in the 1962 Constitution of the 3rd Republic that the president appointed Chief Justice of the Supreme Court based on the recommendation of the Judiciary Recommendation Committee. Likewise, the judges of the Supreme Court were to be appointed by the president after approval by the Judiciary Recommendation Committee and based on the recommendations of the Chief Justice of the Supreme Court. The other judges were to be appointed by the Chief Justice of the Supreme Court based on the recommendations of the Judges' Council of the Supreme Court. The fact that the president retained the power to appoint the judges of the higher court indicates that the president was allowed to exert an influence on the judicial branch.

With the introduction of the so-called "Yushin Constitution" in 1972, the previously existing Judiciary Recommendation Committee was abolished. The Chief Justice of the Supreme Court was to be appointed by the president after approval by the National Assembly, and the other judges were to be appointed by the president based on the recommendations of the Chief Justice of the Supreme Court. Furthermore, a disciplinary system for the judges was introduced, and the system whereby the judges were appointed by a panel of judges was abolished. These moves may be interpreted as moves to eliminate the collective influence of the judges; at the same time, allocating the power to appoint all judges to the president may be understood as an expansion of the influence that the president and the administrative body could wield over the judiciary. While it was stipulated in the Yushin Constitution that the Constitutional Council would judge the unconstitutionality of any law, in reality, the Constitutional Council was never called on to review the unconstitutionality of any law under the Yushin Constitution.

2. Objectives and directions of the government administration

When prompted to single out one key objective of the Park Jung Hee administration, one may cite economic development. Given the situation at the time, President Park Jung Hee had no choice but to concentrate on economic and industrial development rather than on other issues related with culture, society, or social welfare. Hampered by the political and fiscal impediments that were still dogging the country then, it had yet to construct the economic platform required for the country to leap past the postwar reconstruction stage. On top of that, the persistent armed provocations by the North further slowed down the implementation of the economic development plans.

Meanwhile, President Park enlisted administrative officers and put them up as the country's vanguards in its march towards a singular goal. In the words of one observer, President Park embraced a philosophy that "puts efficiency and effectiveness ahead of anything else in running the bureaucratic apparatus." Anything that would hinder the realization of the national interest was to be ruled out and restricted by the law.

President Park aspired to achieve a society that values efficiency and effectiveness and that respects ethics and order. He also valued ethics in political behavior, in social life, and the ethics of workers, and envisioned an ethical, corruption-free administration. For instance, he considered the elimination of corruption and fraud as one of his top priorities, referring to it as one of the country's top three public enemies in his inaugural address. He laid out a roadmap for rooting out the causes of corruption and fraud through the modification or abolition of various corruption-laden institutions or regulations in the process of reforming the bureaucratic system.

As mentioned above, in his inaugural address after being sworn in as the 6th president of the republic, President Park singled out three key public enemies that he believed had to be eliminated for the rehabilitation of the nation: poverty, corruption and fraud, and communism. Poverty, here, seems to be the problem that had to be addressed for the country to attain economic self-supporting; communism, for the country to attain political self-reliance; and corruption and fraud, for the country to attain social harmony and stability. The speech is significant in that it attempted to stress the general direction of the government administration by suggesting the negative issues that had to be addressed before pushing forward with positive goals for the country.

However, President Park failed to come up with clear goals or a vision for his government administration in his inaugural address after becoming the 7th president of the republic by winning in the indirect election held in the form of the National Council for Unification. Instead, he put emphasis on justifying the legitimacy of the Yushin administration by demonstrating its economic achievement and flying the flag of "South-Koreanstyle democracy." In his succeeding inaugural addresses after being sworn in as the 8th and 9th president of the republic, respectively, he seemed to have sought to justify the Yushin administration and the legitimacy of the regime by demonstrating its economic achievements to the people.

President Park also defined the mid-1970s as the era for "growing the national power required to unify the peninsula," by stressing that "the goal of the 3rd Five-Year Economic Development Plan (if achieved) will provide the nutrients needed for democratic development, which will help secure the basis for unification." The national power required for the unification of the peninsula, however, would not be realized with security and diplomatic efforts alone, but by absorbing the northern half of the peninsula through the economic supremacy of the south, he suggested.

In the wake of the introduction of the Yushin Constitution, President Park proposed more detailed policy directions compared to those that existed during his 5th and 6th administrations. In his inaugural address after being sworn in as the 9th president of the republic, he said, "Our key policy directions in the coming years will be the realization of a completely self-reliant economy, the preparation of a self-reliant defense system, the expansion of the scope of social development, and the development of a moral culture. We will do everything that we can together to realize these goals." The president specifically laid out four key policy directions in his speech: (1) establishment of a completely self-reliant economy; (2) preparation of a self-reliant defense system; (3) expansion of the scope of social development; and (4) development of a moral culture. A "completely self-reliant economy" does not necessarily mean a self-sufficient economy in the contemporary context, but the localization of imported products, including the daily necessities, and "preparation of a self-reliant defense system" means escaping from the country's reliance on the U.S. Armed Forces for its security assurance. President Park's repeated use of the word "self-reliance" suggests that he might have wanted to gain the support of the people to a certain extent.

The goal of economic development materialized in the form of the policy direction "growth first, then democratization." The president had the urgent goal of addressing the hunger of the people due to the chronic shortage of grains in spring, or in common parlance, "barley hump." The fact that the economic issue took precedence over the political issue suggests that the president had already set some significant policy directions. The state-led economic development policy that started as such sometimes led to the suppression of dissent, which was triggered by the unbalanced development policy. The Park Jung Hee administration was clearly aware of the fact that "parliamentary or party politics is often inefficient, and administrative efficiency often plays a decisive role in driving economic growth in lieu of parliamentary politics" when a belatedly industrialized nation aims to accomplish national prosperity and military power by proactively intervening in the market, even it was built on the market economy and private property.

It is evident from the various policies the Park Jung Hee administration implemented that the administration, in an attempt to infuse life into the aforementioned stagnant economy, pushed ahead with a "foreign-centric economic development strategy" beginning in the 1960s. Even though market liberalization was realized to a certain extent through the administration's attempt to achieve foreign-centric economic growth, the key characteristic of the economic development strategy of the administration was the proactive intervention in the economy by the government, as the country's economic development was pushed forward under the regime of the development state by the Park Jung Hee administration.

In his inaugural address after being sworn in as the 7th president of the republic in the 1970s, President Park reflected on the South Korean situation in the 1960s, saying, "We may take pride in having focused on internal growth during that period." He went on to say, "We will have to jump on the international trend that stresses the value of peace based on such accomplishments, while at the same time strengthening our foreign participation, through which we will search for a way to realize our national goals." "Internal growth" may signify that the country had barely succeeded in eradicating hunger, thanks to the growth it achieved in the light industries. President Park laid out a clear policy goal for future economic growth, which was to be realized by turning to the international market and expanding the country's exports rather than remaining in the limited market in the Korean Peninsula.

That did not mean, however, that the rural residents were excluded or alienated from the policy goals of the government administration. The previous policy goal, which was to achieve agricultural and industrial development simultaneously, was steadfastly upheld. The administration clearly understood that the country's rural population would be the key to the industrialization of the urban areas, and pronounced this as its policy goal. President Park, however, recognized that the industrialization policy, which focused on the development of industrial cities, had widened the income gap between the rural and urban areas. In an attempt to resolve this dilemma, the government came up with the policy goal of "building the domestic market base by pushing up the income level of the farming families" while at the same time stressing the need to raise the country's grains harvest to address the country's chronic food shortages. The motivational drive that promoted the spirit of self-reliance among the rural population by introducing the Saemaul Movement was part of the Park Jung Hee administration's human resource development plan.

The government policies during the Cold War era, however, cannot be freed from the restraints imposed by the Cold War system and the resulting division of the Korean Peninsula. The armed provocation from the northern half of the peninsula grew more daring as Pyongyang kept sending its armed guerrillas to the south in the late 1960s. Since, in terms of military power, the country could not rival North Korea then, South Korea relied almost entirely on the U.S. for its security assurance. Washington, however, did not respond proactively to such predicament. Making matters worse, the U.S. came up with the Nixon Doctrine, in which Washington argued that the Asian countries should build up their own national defense system. Faced with such challenges, the Park Jung Hee administration was forced to come up with a policy goal designed to ensure the continuity of the state.

In the 1970s, when the importance of the policy goal of realizing economic development became even more important, the need to strengthen the structural base of the country's key industries emerged, which made the administration shift its policy direction from the previously labor-intensive industries to the technology-intensive industries. Sensing that the international competence of the country's light industries in the global market was weakening fast, the Park Jung Hee administration decided to foster the development of 6 key strategic industries, including the "steel, chemical, non-ferrous metal, machinery, shipbuilding, and electronic industries," by importing Japanese capital despite Washington's opposition. This manifested the Park Jung Hee administration's strong will to clarify its policy goals and to push forward with them. The development of the country's machinery, electronics, and shipbuilding industries, which were considered high-value-added at that time, as well as of the heavy chemical industries, such as the steel, chemical, and metal industries, which were based on materials, delivered a much-needed kick for the government to push forward with a systematic policy implementation that ultimately resulted in the sophistication of the country's industrial structure.

The Park Jung Hee administration was also interested in tapping various areas other than the economy to realize national prosperity and military power through sustainable economic development in the long run. Even though the actual planning and implementation of the national policy was centered on the economy, the country was still required to do it right in the area of social welfare and others so that the people would feel the impact of the economic development through the overall improvement of the quality of their lives.

Section 2

Key Policy Initiatives

1. Gyeongbu Expressway: Construction of a transportation network interconnecting the entire nation

Background

The year that was closely related with the birth of the plan to construct Gyeongbu Expressway was 1967, when the implementation of the 2nd Five-Year Economic Development Plan started after the successful completion of the 1st Five-Year Plan. It was when the country achieved a moderate level of economic improvement thanks to the 8.3% average annual growth rate during the period covered by the 1st Five-Year Economic Development Plan. In particular, due to successful completion of the 1st Five-Year Plan, the period was marked by the South Korean people's confidence that they are capable of realizing economic development and by the steady progression of urbanization and industrialization in the country.

Despite overall traffic increase that followed the economic expansion, the country's transportation infrastructure was far less developed than it should have been, causing severe shortage in the country's transportation capacity. The annual increase in the demand for transportation was recorded as 13.5% on average due to the rapid economic growth during the period covered by the 1st Five-Year Economic Development Plan. The country's road infrastructure at the time was poorly developed considering the rapid increase in road traffic and the remarkable improvement in vehicle performance. The South Korean people started to understand that road expansion may contribute to industrial development, and that the building of a more sophisticated transportation system and the lowering of transportation cost may improve the quality of life of the people.

Besides the impending explosion of the number of cars, the rising demand for transportation along with the economic growth, and the country's need to foster the heavy chemical industries as the foundation for national economic growth, another factor that made the people understand the need for an expressway was the global trend, particularly in advanced countries, in building expressways then. Japan started the trend, constructing an expressway linking Nagoya and Osaka, followed by the construction of two additional lines, all of which seemed to have had a significant influence on the related discussion in South Korea.

Implementation System

As a move to keep his campaign pledge, President Park announced on April 29 that the government would embark on the construction of an expressway within the period covered by the 2nd Five-Year Economic Development Plan (1967~1971). He also made it clear in the press conference held on May 2 of the same year that the government would "construct a trunk line expressway connecting Seoul to Incheon, Gangneung, Busan, and Mokpo." As such, the reform of the country's transportation infrastructure from one based on the railway to another based on roads began.

The Presidential Office formed an interim task force with a group of army officers recommended by the Directorate General of the Army Procurement Office of Chief of Engineers, and the public officials affiliated with the Territorial Preservation Bureau in the Ministry of Construction. The task force started the project near the Office of the Senior Secretary to the President for Economic Policy. Although small and lasting only for 10 weeks, until January 31, 1968, the task force signaled the genesis of the organization that would eventually take the helm in the total planning of the project, and provided the basis for the formation and operation of the Construction Plan Research Team. The task force had no official title at the time and was simply called the "Delegation to the Presidential Office."

The Delegation to the Presidential Office was supposed to report to the Chief Presidential Secretary, the Senior Secretary to the President for Economic Policy, and the Secretary to the President for Construction, but in practice, it reported directly to President Park while acting as an independent organization dedicated to collecting the materials required for the ideation work on the expressway. The key assignments that were given to the delegation were to draw maps based on which the budget estimates for the different planned lines were to be compared, to collect and edit the materials required to acquire right of way, and to draw standard cross-sectional diagrams of the planned lines and to perform a field survey thereof.

When President Park was involved in the planning of the expressway, including the installation of the Delegation to the Presidential Office, the Ministry of Construction was working on its own plan separately. As the office of primary concern, the Ministry of Construction formed the Expressway Construction Advisory Committee, which was to advise the Minister of Construction on the planning of the project. The ministry requested the service to perform a research on the basic plan for an expressway connecting Seoul and Busan and completed the project in December 1967. Given the massive scale and nature of the project, the Gyeongbu Expressway Construction Project was not something that could be pushed forward as a project of one ministry, but was a project that required comprehensive liaison and collaboration across the government organizations. Based on this understanding, a policy organization that would drive the project implementation through close liaison and collaboration with different ministries was installed.

On December 13, 1967, the Key National Expressway Construction Promotion Committee was formed. It was chaired by the Prime Minister and co-chaired by the Minister of the Economic Planning Board and the Minister of Construction. Its members consisted of the affiliated ministers as well as the municipal and provincial heads and experts from the private sector. The committee was given assignments covering wide-ranging areas, including establishing policies on expressway construction, drawing up basic and implementation plans, securing the necessary funds, providing technical and administrative support, facilitating collaboration and liaison among relevant ministries, and discussing the delivery of the services ordered directly by the president.

The Construction Planning and Research Team was intended to be an "organization dedicated to planning and researching on the materials needed by the Key National Expressway Construction Promotion Committee," but in practice, it was the centerpiece of the construction project. The Construction Planning and Research Team was chaired by a former minister, with its participating members consisting of working-level officials from each ministry, including the Ministry of Construction and the Office of Chief of Engineers, as well as other experts from the academe and the private sector. Backed by President Park, the committee was able to play some key roles in implementing the project. Specifically, the committee could expedite the implementation of the related businesses, thanks to its unique organizational structure marked by the disproportionate share of members from the military and the Ministry of Construction.

The Construction Planning and Research Team consisted of three sections: the planning section, which dealt with planning and research, selection of line, and compensation for the right of way; the technical section, which dealt with measurement, supervision, and design work; and the finance and economy section, which dealt with project funding. The team existed for about one month and a half and was closed thereafter, but while in existence, it performed diverse feasibility studies as well as planning and research activities. Its other responsibilities covered wide-ranging areas, including line selection, land compensation, measurement, supervision, design, and lining up of the necessary funds.

The Construction Office, the organization that implemented the construction of Seoul-Busan Expressway, was installed on January 29, 1968 in accordance with the Ministry of Construction Decree No. 48 (amended on January 29, 1968), which was the decree of the Ministry of Construction and the Regional Construction Bureau on the installation of the construction office. The office was installed before the construction started in the Seoul-Suwon section of the Seoul-Busan line, but its actual operation started on February 1 of the same year. The Construction Office opened with the signboard hanging ceremony on February 12, and took over the duties that were previously carried out by the Construction Planning and Research Team to take the helm of the construction management.

Implementation Process and Contents

As the construction of Gyeongbu Expressway became official with President Park Jung Hee's announcement of his campaign pledge, the government embarked on a research to establish the basic plan by commissioning Korea Engineering Consultants Corporation (KECC) to conduct a feasibility study on the proposed Seoul-Busan Expressway Construction Project. The report of KECC covered diverse areas associated with the Gyeongbu Expressway Construction Project, including the projected transport demand, the clustering of industries along the candidate lines, and comparisons of the competing proposals: construction of an expressway vs. expansion of the existing roads. The report, however, was biased towards the construction of an expressway as it stressed the need for an expressway rather than comparing the pros and cons of constructing competing transportation infrastructures such as a railroad and a standard road. As expected from such a biased analysis, the report proposed in its conclusions several candidate expressway lines as well as a matching project budget and a possible financing plan.

Meanwhile, President Park believed that the growing worries over the construction of an expressway were caused by the lack of governmental efforts to publicize the validity of constructing an expressway. In an effort to demonstrate the validity of the project and to persuade the people that an expressway needs to be constructed, the government made the feasibility study prepared by the Expressway Construction Project Research Team, titled "Executive Summary of the Key National Expressway Construction Plan," publicly accessible. The report covered the diverse implications of the project, including the relationship between economic growth and the construction of expressways, the need to construct an expressway connecting Seoul to Busan ahead of other potential lines, the direct and palpable benefits of the project to the everyday lives of the people, the development of rural and fishing towns, the narrowing of the gap between the regions, the direct benefits of the project itself, and the project's other benefits in relation with defense. The report, however, failed to overcome its inherent limitations as it stopped at improvising a counter-logic against the series of issues posed sporadically, without conducting a thorough study on the economic validity of the project.

The Expressway Construction Project Research Team finalized the line in January 1968, which would connect Seoul to Daejeon and Daejeon to Gimcheon. It was followed by the finalization of the remaining lines connecting Daegu to Busan in April 1968 and Gimcheon to Daegu in October, respectively, thereby concluding the design of the 428-km-long expressway that starts at the southern end of the 3rd Han River Bridge (presently Hannam Bridge) and then passes through Suwon, Osan, Cheonan, Daejeon, Yeongdong, Hwanggan, Gimcheon, Gumi, Waekwan, Daegu, Yeongcheon, Gyeongju, Eonyang, and Yangsan before terminating at Guseo-dong, Dongrae-gu in the city of Busan.

After the publication in 1966 of an IBRD report containing a recommendation to expand the road network in South Korea, the Ministry of Treasury requested the president of IBRD to provide the loans worth US$ 30.03 million that are required for the purchase of construction materials and equipment, but the request was rejected flat out. Thereafter, the government gave up its effort to import foreign capital; instead, it decided to finance the project internally by raising the petrol taxes, imposing toll fees, and issuing road bonds. The financing plan for the Gyeongbu Expressway Construction Project was finalized with a total budget of KRW 33.1 billion in the 8th Meeting of Economic Ministers on February 5, 1968; the budget was to be funded by the native capital raised from the imposition of gasoline taxes, toll fees, and the KRW 2.7 billion the country received as a claim from Japan for the damages the latter inflicted on the peninsula during its colonial rule (Korea's property claims against Japan).

With the financing plan by different revenue sources finalized, the government took a series of actions to funnel the road taxes to the road construction budget so it can finance the required construction costs. Towards this end, the government amended the Petroleum Products Taxes Act to raise the tax slapped on gasoline twofold, from 100 to 200%, and the Road Maintenance Promotion Act to raise the upper limit of the taxes from the petroleum products that could be spent on the road maintenance project from 50 to 75%.

Equally complicated and wide-ranging were the procedure and proceedings involved in the acquisition of the required land. To expedite the administrative handling of such arduous process, the government inserted a special administrative component in the existing structure. Specifically, the authority to exercise administrative proceedings with regard to the construction was delegated almost entirely to the governors presiding over each regional administrative jurisdiction, under the supervision of the Minister of Construction. In addition, the Commission for the Promotion of the Expressway Project was installed at each provincial, municipal, county-level, and town-level administrative body to push forward the related businesses, including consultation on the measures to be taken to acquire the required land, implementation of land transactions, and payment of the fair price of the land. The committee was given the supreme right to deliberate and vote on the fair price of the lands to be appropriated for the expressway project.

The required budgets and funds were allocated to the respective regions, and given the urgency of the project, the understanding and participation of the local residents who were going to be affected by the project were sought by tapping into the regional expertise of each administrative body. The acquisition of the required land was not pursued simply by following the proceedings specified in the laws; it was pursued by bargaining based on the voluntary will of the landowner to the extent allowed, with the compensation made pursuant to the market price. The Ministry of Construction and the Construction Office did not commence the construction of any section until the full compensation for the required land and the other installations in the section had been given.

The total land area required along all the planned sections of Seoul-Busan Expressway amounted to 20.5 million m^2. Of this, some 1.22 million m^2 was the state's property, which was subsequently acquired through collaboration with the pertinent governing authority, while the remaining lands (19.24 million m^2) were all acquired through bargaining with the landowners. The total amount spent for acquiring the required land along all the planned sections amounted to KRW 1.963 billion.

The 428-km-long expressway connecting Seoul to Busan was divided into nine construction sections before the detailed design of each section was made. With seven construction offices built along the line, the construction was performed by subsection, with the subsections being the subdivisions of each construction section. Since the groundbreaking ceremony on February 1, 1968, all the available resources from the civilian, government, and military sectors were mobilized until the completion of the construction on July 7, 1970, some 29 months after the commencement of the project.

Performance and Assessment

The significance of Gyeogbu Expressway in the 1970s, when economic development was being pushed forward at full speed, was that it was an industrial road that would support the nation's economic development plan. The expressway helped the people save on transportation costs, increased the interdependence among wide-ranging regions, and promoted the spatial role division in the country's economic activities, thereby ensuring the price competitiveness of the country's exported goods in the international market.

The construction of Gyeongbu Expressway is assessed to have been a rational and effective policy decision in that it helped expand the market for the country's goods and maximize the country's transportation capacity by connecting the Busan region, which accounted for some 40% of the country's total export/import volumes, to the Incheon region, accounting for some 20% of the country's total export/import volumes. In the 1970s, upon the completion of Gyeongbu Expressway, industrial clusters began to form along the expressway, reshuffled into two large industrial clusters (the greater Seoul area and the southeast area), and the accelerating regional interconnection along the Seoul - Daejeon - Daegu - Busan line laid the foundation for the country's future economic development.

The most pressing issue related to the establishment of the National Development Plan was the rational reshuffling of the country's industrial locations, which again required the distribution of the industrial clusters concentrated in the metropolitan area as well as the formation of large-scale industrial complexes. Gyeongbu Expressway enabled an organic interconnection among the expressway, national roads, and local roads, prompting a qualitative change of each location into an industrial site. Furthermore, it also made it easier to redistribute the industrial areas to other regions by allowing the geographic realigning of the manufacturing and consumption centers. As a result of such geographic realigning, some large-scale manufacturing plants that required massive lands gradually migrated to regional areas while the industrial complexes clustered in the metropolitan area were transformed into high-tech industry complexes.

Meanwhile, the construction of expressways made it possible to earn surplus margins both spatially and economically by shortening the turnover cycle of the invested capital. The construction of Gyeongbu Expressway delivered a decisive kick that led to the growth of the construction capital. The construction industry started to accelerate the compartmentalization and specialization of the construction management by honing its engineering skills and growing capability to implement large-scale construction projects. Additionally, the industry realized the need to further train and educate the professional construction engineers as well as to integrate the affiliates and to rationalize management. As a result, the prestige and reputation of the country's construction technology in the international market markedly improved, triggering the industry's expansion to the overseas construction market.

Gyeongbu Expressway, as a key social overhead capital of the country, prompted an organic flow of logistics, a change in the living area, and the rapid reshuffling of the population. Specifically, the development of the lands along Gyeongbu Expressway resulted in rural development, including increased land use and home improvement, while enabling the redistribution of social values through the improved access between the urban and rural areas, and the development of tourist attractions. Therefore, Gyeongbu Expressway can be said to be the key social road network that expanded the exchanges among different regions.

The key objective of the Park Jung Hee administration was to achieve economic growth, national prosperity and military power as to achieve supremacy over North Korea, with which it maintained a hostile relationship. In other words, economic advancement and political stability were sought because the administration aspired to build a strategic foundation on which it would enjoy supremacy over North Korea. President Park intended the Gyeongbu Expressway Construction Project as a monument to his administration's anti-communism drive.

Given the administrative culture of the Park Jung Hee administration, the president's campaign pledge could not be seriously scrutinized for its economic feasibility; the faithful implementation of the project, true to its spirit, was the only option left for the public officials. As it is obvious from the fact that the schedule of the feasibility study for the proposed expressway was confirmed only after the decision to undertake construction was made, the feasibility study was a measure designed to persuade the people of the necessity of constructing an expressway. As such, the policy, which was decided based on the authoritarian mobilization model, met much opposition, thereby hindering the smooth implementation of the project.

The construction of the expressway promoted the integration of social spaces, but it also prompted social disintegration. Such social disintegration led to political conflicts because the expressway compartmentalized the nation's territory as it provided a platform for an unbalanced development strategy between south-east and south-west areas. Such results were not intended when the expressway was being constructed, but it put substantial political pressure on the succeeding administrations. Furthermore, Gyeongbu Expressway deepened the environmental contamination in the areas accessible therefrom as it accelerated the use of resources in those regions and boosted the traffic therein. The construction of the expressway itself destroyed the natural environment in the affected areas by ruining the ecosystem therein, and divided the residents' living areas.

It would, however, be fair to evaluate Gyeongbu Expressway not on the basis of the situation at the point of evaluation but on the basis of the situation at the point of construction. To sum up, the Gyeongbu Expressway Construction Project shall be understood as the combined result of the economic situation at the time and the entrepreneurial leadership of President Park. Therefore, Gyeongbu Expressway should be seen as one of the most successful examples of entrepreneurship that changed the paradigm of South Korea's road network from its core, whereas the negative side effects of the construction should be overcome by expanding the human space required to improve the quality of life of the people, and by fostering the balanced development of the territory.

2. The Saemaul Movement: Rural modernization realized through collaboration between the government and the private sector

Background

It was in the 1970s, when South Korea was going through rapid urbanization in the wake of industrialization while its rural economy was decaying in the dust that the South Korean government started to push ahead with the Saemaul Movement (New Community Movement) as one of its key national initiatives. The Saemaul Movement at the time was a comprehensive policy package designed to consolidate the wide-ranging rural development initiatives that had been implemented without any organized cooperation, and to realize such ambition by building up the capabilities of the village residents. Despite a series of governmental efforts to boost the country's agricultural productivity by alleviating poverty in the rural areas through diverse means, the South Korean government largely failed to overcome the barriers to realize each policy unit's goal by interlocking the traditional and modern industries and adjusting the interaction between the rural and urban regions. Furthermore, the term "Saemaul Movement" had been used by the rural development project implemented throughout Gyeongsangnam-do Province beginning in March 1962.

Given the confrontation between the two Koreas in the Cold War era, it is understandable that North Korea's superior military power then may have put added pressure on Seoul, which was busy industrializing the country's fledgling economy. Specifically, the 1st and 2nd Five-Year Economic Development Plan, which had been implemented since 1962, was widening the gap between the country's urban and rural areas and between the traditional agrarian economy and the manufacturing sector in the wake of the rapid economic development. Should such gap between different living spaces and industrial sectors widen, those living in the rural areas, such as the farmers, fishermen, and the other constituents alienated from the rest of the country, may be left behind, segregated from the mainstream movement to build the country. Such concerns sparked discussions on the need to strengthen the bonds among the people at the level of the local communities, especially of villages, the peripheral nervous system when seen from the perspective of running the country. As such, the periodic backgrounds associated with the adoption of the Saemaul Movement as the key development package are closely related with the diverse initiatives aimed at developing the local communities. In other words, the enhanced bonding at the level of villages and the gearing of the development engine on the strength of the Saemaul Movement were interlocked with the continuous industrialization efforts of the South Korean government as well as its political intention to try to gain support from the rural voters while at the same time ensuring national security.

Implementation System

From the very beginning (in the 1970s), the implementation organization of the Saemaul Movement was assembled and worked on based on the division of roles between the government and the local residents. The government organization assumed the responsibility of promoting environments conducive to regional development by empowering the local residents with the initiatives on ownership of the movement. Meanwhile, the residents were able to start their long-overdue projects with the construction materials like cement and rebar rationed by the government, which again helped them improve the quality of their lives by reviving the community life in each village unit. As such, the Saemaul Movement made a substantial contribution to the formation of a virtuous cycle for an ever-expanding forum conducive to the overall national interest, through the interaction between the public and private sectors.

As mentioned earlier, the Saemaul Movement was implemented based on the harmonious division of roles between the public sector (in which the government held the leadership) and the private sector (led by the members of the local communities). In other words, the implementation organization of the Saemaul Movement was imbued with the characteristics of the 3rd sector, based on the collaboration between the government and civil groups, which was enabled by creatively combining the public and private sectors. The entirely new implementation structure enabled the central government, local administrative agencies, and local communities to establish a vertical governance structure; the open competitiveness among the local administrative agencies and villages, combined with the division of roles among the central governmental ministries, resulted in the formation of a horizontal governance structure. The South Korean society was then able to maximize the efficiency of the national administration system on the strength of the grid-type governance structure, which was formed by interlocking the vertical and horizontal governance structures, thereby creating a new growth engine.

The Saemaul Movement was interlinked with almost all the central ministries in one way or another, making it necessary to form a consultative body in which the various projects pushed forward by these ministries would be discussed and fine-tuned. With such circumstances as the backdrop, the Council for Comprehensive Planning of the Saemaul Movement was installed in Seoul and in each regional unit in an attempt to mediate the various administrations by the related agencies and organizations. Specifically, the Saemaul Movement Council was formed across all regional levels, including in the central government ministries as well as in the municipal, provincial, county, and village levels. First, the Saemaul Movement Central Council was established as a steering and mediation organization that encompassed all the governmental administrative bodies under its umbrella, including the Economic Planning Board, Ministry of Internal Affairs, Ministry of Treasury, Ministry of Culture and Education, Ministry of Agriculture, Fisheries, and Forestry, Ministry of Commerce and Industry, Ministry of Construction, Ministry of Health and Society, Ministry of Postal Service, Ministry of Culture and Communication, Ministry of Science and Technology, and Office of the 2nd Ministry without a Portfolio as well as the Forest Administration, Public Procurement Agency, Rural Development Administration, National Agricultural Cooperative Federation, National Fisheries Cooperative Federation, and Seoul municipal government.

The restructuring of the local administrative organizations that was implemented at the time met the requirements of the governmental innovation that was necessary to push forward with the Saemaul Movement. These regional administrative agencies introduced a new function (development of local communities) to their job portfolio, and utilized a new type of field-centered work implementation method, unlike any utilized in the past. In particular, made up of the heads of the local administrative agencies and the Saemaul leaders, the Implementation Council was formed in an attempt to give a helping hand to the movement. In addition, the General Meeting of Villages and the Village Development Council installed in each rural community held the leadership in pushing ahead with the Saemaul Movement. The support for the Saemaul Movement provided by the local administrative agencies can be summed up as having come in the form of the provision of public property and the delivery of resources rationed by the central government as well as the provision of various forms of administrative support, technology training, and identification and dissemination of model cases by the dedicated public official installed in each village.

As such, the Saemaul Movement was implemented by way of the unique "governance" structure that featured joint collaboration between the government and the private sector, focused on field work, and considered the feedback from the village residents in the future planning. Additionally, villages' performances made through the Saemaul Movement were compared and evaluated against those of other villages that weren't affected by the movement, and the movement's success was propagated nationwide. Another notable achievement was that the work manners of the public officials engaged in the local administrative agencies changed during the process of implementing the Saemaul Movement. The "one public officer to one village" charge system took root as a department dedicated to the implementation of the Saemaul Movement was installed in the municipal, county, and town levels. Although the "one public officer to one village" system acted as an apparatus through which the village members and the public institutions could collaborate, it also sometimes. became a source of conflict. Specifically, since a public officer's job promotion was interconnected with the performance in implementing the Saemaul Movement in the officer's corresponding village, many overzealous public officers often clashed with the village residents who were spontaneously implementing the Saemaul Movement.

The Saemaul Movement created a virtuous cycle for an ever-expanding forum conducive to the overall national interest through the interactions between the public and private sectors on the village and community levels. Such virtuous cycle of escalating development was largely indebted to the fostering of the implementation organization in the private sector as well as to the powerful implementation structure in the public sector. The Saemaul Movement expanded even more, thanks to the introduction of various reward systems, such as "more incentives for the better achievers." Specifically, by giving incentives to villages that make outstanding performance, the Saemaul Movement encouraged each and every member of the village to participate proactively in the movement while lining up the required resources internally.

Implementation Process and Contents

The key characteristic of the way the Saemaul Movement was implemented is that the government promoted the voluntary participation of the residents in the movement by rekindling Korea's traditional town-centric community spirit found in "Hyangyak (a tradtional community movement). Since the Saemaul Movement had a process-centric aspect designed to foster desirable changes in each town, some type of conversion vehicle that would link the input and output was required for it to work successfully. The government leadership that acted as driving agents of change and the voluntary participation of the residents were the aspects of the movement that ensured the effective functioning of such conversion vehicle. To conclude, the proactive early involvement of the government, specifically the successful work on an implementation structure that would organically link the motivational mechanism and the residents' voluntary participation, largely determined the success of the Saemaul Movement, for it is evident that the input of an identical resource would not always guarantee the equivalent output and that the government's effort to change promptly would not necessarily result in a matching level of resident participation.

The Ministry of Internal Affairs and Ministry of Agriculture and Fishery took the helm in the early stage of the implementation of the Saemaul Movement. As more government-led projects got integrated with the working mechanism of the Saemaul Movement, almost all the government ministries began to be associated with the Saemaul Movement in one way or another. Specifically, the project that was implemented in the form of the Saemaul Movement in 1973 was associated with the Ministry of Internal Affairs and Ministry of Agriculture and Fishery as well as with the Ministry of Commerce and Industry, Ministry of Construction, Ministry of Health and Society, Ministry of Postal Service, Ministry of Culture and Education, Ministry of Culture and Public Affairs, Ministry of Science and Technology, Office of Agricultural Promotion, and Office of Forestry. With the expansion of the Saemaul Movement, all the government ministries started to become involved in the planning and implementation of the projects related with the Saemaul Movement. Such complex implementation structure devised exclusively for the Saemaul Movement desperately needed a liaison and consultative body, a role that was eventually played by the Ministry of Internal Affairs in the central government and by the Saemaul Movement Central Council, which was organized separately to deal with such businesses. The responsibility, however, of making a decision on the budgetary priorities for the various projects that should be implemented with limited resources fell on the residents themselves. As a result, the residents themselves were given an opportunity to exercise their authority related with the formation and management of the shared assets by establishing their autonomous institutions, such as Saemaul Leaders Council and Saemaul Women's Association.

The explosive growth in the number of participants in the Saemaul Movement is believed to have been driven by the following factors: (1) the early Saemaul Movement was pushed forward by focusing on improving the living environment in an attempt to promote the formation of a community based on the regional network; (2) the achievements realized as such strengthened the people's confidence in obtaining the government's future rewards for the better performers; and (3) the residents themselves grew satisfied with the positive results of their concerted efforts. To sum up, the government support provided in the early days of the Saemaul Movement was perceived as the rewards for the concerted efforts of the community, which again fostered diligence in each township. The residents, who felt pride in their achievements in the process of implementing the movement, began to be motivated to cultivate a self-reliant spirit. Moreover, the residents slowly woke up to the effectiveness of community-level efforts, such as the Saemaul Movement, in achieving the public good, which could not be realized with individual efforts alone, thereby laying the foundation for collaboration in each township.

It is obvious from the decision-making process prevalent in the implementation of the Saemaul Movement that the movement was based on the upward community development model. No matter how much resources were poured into the movement, the desirable outcome would not have been gained without the voluntary participation of the residents. As with other innovations, the Saemaul Movement was required to select and present the change agent as a leader of the movement to create a following of like-minded people. The Saemaul leaders representing the residents were elected by the voters themselves in the town. As a result, all the aspects of the Saemaul Movement, from the project priority, the burdens on the residents, and the decision with regard to the beneficiaries, were imbued with an element of the upward procedure. As such, while the country was governed by the power structure marked by the powerful centralized government in Seoul, the decision-making process of the Saemaul Movement alone was thoroughly based on grassroots democracy. Such experience was the background of the birth of local governance in South Korea.

Since the Saemaul Movement was pushed forward with the anticipation of the development process of the movement, which progressed along the early-foundation-building phase, the self-reliance development phase, and the final phase, where the development of high-level of self-reliance was completed, the plan included the planning logic designed to foster the voluntary participation of the residents. The Saemaul Movement had been pushed forward from 1971 until 1973 with the early emphasis on building the everyday living environment and the production environment in the 34,665 villages. Then, beginning in 1974, the movement was pushed forward by relying on the self-reliant participation of the residents while ditching the past practices, where the government triggered and supported the movement. Such self-reliant version of the Saemaul Movement is assessed to have continued until 1976. The participation in the Saemaul Movement skyrocketed beginning in 1977, thereby helping the movement to enter the phase of a high-level of self-reliance structure. Likewise, the primary reason behind the success of the Saemaul Movement was the fact that the leadership anticipated the development process of the movement, which, as mentioned earlier, progressed along the early-foundation-building phase, the self-reliance development phase, and the final phase, where the development of self-reliance was completed, and applied the matching implementation structure to each phase.

The remarkable achievements of the Saemaul Movement became possible because the movement: (1) transformed the township unit based on the residents' blood links with one another to one based on the regional network; (2) installed the upward implementation logic by setting the development phases of the movement and by fostering the voluntary participation of the residents; and (3) thoroughly implemented meritocracy, which linked the benefits offered to the residents and the extent to which they carried out their responsibilities.

Performance and Assessment

It is entirely possible that the government did not intend to achieve what is now recognized as the stunning performance of the Saemaul Movement when it selected the movement as one of the key government projects. In such context, it can be assessed that the Saemaul Movement in South Korea was pushed forward in the form of a mutual learning process between the government and the resident organizations. Specifically, the movement had some inevitable negative side effects due to the push by the overzealous public officials as the movement was in the limelight as one of the key government projects. Still, the movement succeeded in alleviating the poverty in the rural areas to a certain extent, nurturing the governance structure of the state in the process by constructing a local administrative system. Also, the local public officials were able to drive the participation of the residents through the use of soft power such as persuasion and communication while building the mechanism for securing resources and the legitimacy required to carry out the project by linking diverse authorities and stakeholders outside the community.

South Korea's Saemaul Movement was effective in bridging the various spatial gaps (urban and rural areas) and industrial gaps (agriculture and modern industries) as well as the gaps between different classes, which had been the key objective of government administration beginning in the 1960s. Indeed, the movement succeeded in constructing a state operation system by effectively mobilizing the limited resources. The achievements of the Saemaul Movement make it one of the exemplary cases applicable to realizing the "accumulation of social capital," "governance building," and "sustainable development." The movement contributed to the formation of a social operation system capable of improving the efficiency of the South Korean society, accepting the environmental changes at the township level — the basic living zone of the country's residents — and realizing advancement based on this established platform.

3. The Five-Year Economic Development Plan, the driving force behind the rapid economic growth of South Korea

Background

The military government that was inaugurated after the May 16 revolution was enthusiastic about the country's economic development, through which it planned to resolve the everyday economic plight inherited from the earlier generations once and for all. Even though the resolution of the financial difficulties of the people was a key mandate of the era, it was also an urgent task for the new military regime in the political context, for its successful resolution would legitimize the "military revolution."

Furthermore, blessed with the pilot plan prepared by the 1st and 2nd Republic on a trial basis, the regime simply had to formulate the economic development plan based on this template. Still, a powerful institution that would drive the comprehensive implementation of the economic development plan was required. Armed with such understanding, the military government installed the Economic Planning Board on July 22, 1961, just two months after the May 16 revolution. This installation was immediately followed by the announcement of the Comprehensive Economic Reconstruction Plan, an illustrious evidence of the military government's strong will and commitment to realizing economic development.

Implementation System

The Economic Planning Board lasted from July 1961 to 1994, during which it played a decisive role in developing the South Korean economy through the establishment and implementation of the nation's Five-Year Economic Development Plan.

Figure 2–1. Structural Design of the Economic Planning Board

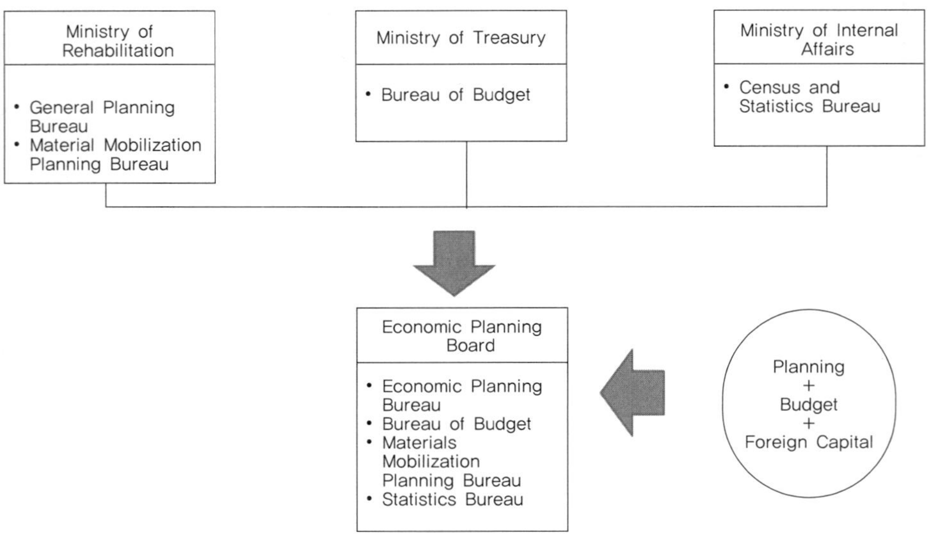

The Economic Planning Board started as an independent organization formed by consolidating various departments scattered across different ministries, including the General Planning Bureau and Material Mobilization Planning Bureau in the Ministry of Rehabilitation, the Bureau of Budget in the Ministry of Treasury, and the Census and Statistics Bureau in the Ministry of Internal Affairs, with an initial organizational structure composed of four bureaus and one section, including the General Planning Bureau, Bureau of Budget, Materials Mobilization Planning Bureau, Statistics Bureau, and General Affairs Section.

With such structure, the Economic Planning Board had come to be equipped with the function of lining up native and foreign funds as well as a planning function. The board was structured in such a way that it would maximize the returns by organically linking the three key means of economic development: planning, budget, and foreign capital induction. As the available funds required even for meeting the basic needs of the people were absolutely in short supply at the time and as the government's capability to establish and manage the economic policy remained at a very poor level, a powerful government institution capable of consolidating different functions on a whim was required to a certain degree.

Unlike other ministries, the Economic Planning Board was supposed to take the helm in shaping the national policy in the long-term perspective without being involved in the projects linked with interest groups. As a result, the board has since evolved into a ministry that deals only with the formulation of economic policies, without carrying out its own projects. The institutional neutrality of the board has since provided the basis for institutional autonomy, thereby ensuring the establishment of the future national policies only from the perspective of the national interest. Another benefit of having no responsibility in the project was that the Board was able to manage the policies on a long-term basis, an apparatus that helped the board strengthen its function of managing and planning the fiscal budget from the long-term perspective. Institutional autonomy was realized by having the same ministry handle the planning and budget functions. Such autonomy became the turning point for the ministry as it came to be equipped with powerful implementation capabilities thanks to the linking of such functions.

When the Economic Planning Board was established, it had a general budget section as well as administrative budget, investment budget, and enterprise budget sections under its immediate control. The Bureau of Budget in the Economic Planning Board had gone through several rounds of organizational reshuffling in the process of expanding its responsibility. In December 1968, the budgetary control officer was newly installed, tasked with maximizing the efficiency of budgetary spending through budget cuts. The Bureau of Budget has since steadily expanded in size and responsibility through several rounds of organizational reshuffling until it was promoted to the Office of Budget on June 26, 1979. The key roles of the Office of Budget were to establish budget policies and a mid-term fiscal plan and to prepare state budget proposals. The Economic Planning Board was able to play the critical role of linking the long-term plan and the short-term budget via the Office of Budget.

With the installation of the Office of the Vice Prime Minister, which was headed by the Minister of the Economic Planning Board, in December 1963, the status of the head of the board was promoted to the level immediately below that of the prime minister. As a result, the Vice Prime Minister-cum-Minister of the Economic Planning Board was able to exercise unprecedented power in the administration, including lining up and redistributing foreign and native capital and preparing and implementing the economic development plan. At the same time, the minister was able to preside over various meetings that dealt with economic issues in his capacity as vice prime minister, thereby demonstrating powerful leadership as a general mediator of comprehensive economic policies both in name and content.

Korea Development Institute was installed in March 1971, in the wake of the growing recognition of the need for a research institution that would conduct practical and systematic studies on the policy tasks spanning wide-ranging economic issues and that would help in the establishment of the Five-Year Economic Development Plan and in the preparation of policy proposals. In the 1970s, with the goal of "designing an economy for national prosperity," KDI actively participated in not only the development of the Five-Year Economic Development Plan but also the preparation of the Three-Year Interlocked Plan and Economic Operation Plan, which were controlled by the Economic Planning Board. KDI also conducted short-term studies aimed at supporting the establishment of policies dealing with the pending issues and held rounds of policy meetings, whenever deemed necessary, to promote discussion and consultation on the pending economic issues. Additionally, KDI contributed to the establishment of economic policies and to building the foundation of the South Korean study on the economy.

KDI also played the role of the government think-tank supporting the establishment of the Five-Year Economic Development Plan. Despite country's having many presidents with a military background, the installation of an independent professional research institute (KDI) to set the national agenda and to establish the country's economic development plan was a key reason behind the country's successful implementation of its economic policies.

Implementation Process and Contents

	Values and Key Policies	Key Policies and Objectives
1st Phase (1962~1966)	Establishment of a self-reliant economic base	- Raise the rural income levels by boosting agricultural production - Secure key energy sources, including electricity and coal - Establish key industries and obtain the needed social overhead capital - Improve the balance of international trade by concentrating on export - Obtain advanced technological competence
2nd Phase (1967~1971)	Acceleration of the establishment of a self-reliant economy	- Develop food self-support, afforest the mountains, and develop the fishery resources (concentrate on boosting the rural income level) - Lay the foundation for industrial sophistication by developing the chemical, steel, and machinery industries - Lay the foundation for the balance of international trade by boosting the country's exports - Foster the development of science and management techniques
3rd Phase (1972~1976)	Harmony between growth, stability, and balance	- Pursue the innovative development of rural and fishing towns - Realize a noticeable increase in exports - Develop the heavy and chemical industries

4th Phase (1977~1981)	Growth, fairness, and efficiency	- Realize a self-reliant growth structure (balance of international trade, industrial sophistication, etc.) - Promote social development (fair income distribution, improvement of living environment) - Pursue technology innovation and efficiency improvement (expand the country's technological capability, rationalize the economic management)

Source: The Economic Planning Board.

Through the implementation of the 1st Five-Year Economic Development plan, industries, including the coal, power generation, fertilizer, and oil refinery took form as the country's key industries. In an attempt to provide financial support to such efforts, several laws, including the Certificate of Payment for Loans Act and the Special Measure on the Introduction of Capital Goods via the Long-Term Payment Act were enacted in 1962, and the Commercial Bank of Korea, which was privatized in the 1950s, was nationalized again. Thanks to such efforts, the shares of the country's exports, which were 63% primary industry products and 27% manufactured products in 1962, changed to 27.5% primary industry products and 72.5% manufactured products in 1967. It is obvious from these figures that the economy was changing from an agricultural economy to an industrial one.

During the period covered by the 2nd Five-Year Economic Development Plan, the government strove to expand the scope of consensus through the increased participation of the private sector and the related professionals. Through such efforts, the government realized self-sufficiency in food supply and assured institutional support to corresponding industrial sectors in the area of seven industries (machinery, shipbuilding, textile, electronics, petrochemical, steel, and non-ferrous-metal industries) by enacting related Industrial Promotion Acts. The 2nd Five-Year Economic Development Plan was made up of three key axes: the general plan, the plan for the industrial sector, and the capital investment plan. In the general plan, respective targets were proposed for income, fiscal austerity, the banking industry, and balance of international trade. In the plan for the industrial sector, a future plan for different industries was established by segmenting different industries and performing input/output analysis. As for the capital investment plan, it was established by analyzing the investment ratio per income and the marginal effect of investment and international trade. It would be fair to conclude that the foundation of the South Korean economy was laid down throughout this period.

In 1973, during the period covered by the 3rd Five-Year Economic Development Plan, the 1st oil shock hit the country, but the South Korean economy was resilient enough to adapt to the changing situation, and still succeeded in accomplishing its proposed growth target. Moreover, efforts to narrow the gap between the rural and urban areas were made during the period by pushing forward with the Saemaul Movement. With the proclamation in 1973 of the vision to turn the country's economy into one based on the heavy and chemical industries, the government started to strategically push the steel, metal, petrochemical, and electronics industries. The successful realization in 1977 of the country's US$ 10 billion export target has since been perceived as the indicator of the success of the aforementioned strategy. Another characteristic of the period was that the government strove to stabilize the economy. The government exerted extraordinary efforts then to tackle the fundamental vulnerabilities of the country's economy, which had been exposed in the process of the rapid economic growth in the 1960s, such as the deteriorating financial structure of companies, the vicious cycle of rising prices, the depreciating value of the country's currency, the less-than-satisfactory progress of industrial rationalization, and the weakening of international competence. On January 14, 1974, the government announced the Emergency Presidential Measure to Stabilize the Lives of the People in the wake of the oil shock. The government attempted to turn the ship from the growth-centric policy in the past towards one focusing on economic stability by strengthening the government support to the low-income classes.

With the 4th Five-Year Economic Development Plan, the government aspired to achieve growth and stability in economy at the same time. The scope of the plan was further expanded to include social issues such as the balance among the different social classes or the labor-management relations. The economic development plan of South Korea was a strategy that assumed the five-year unit for each development period, but it provided the momentum for industrialization and modernization by accomplishing the goals for the previous period and laying out the succeeding strategy based on the earlier achievements.

In 1967, the government introduced the Overall Resources Budget (ORB) in an attempt to synchronize the economic development plan and the matching budget. The new scheme was intended to encompass private and government projects in the establishment of a material mobilization and financing plan before pushing forward with economic development. The ORB was intended to be prepared by considering the economic ups and downs from a macroeconomic perspective, with regard to the goals and policy direction of each Five-Year Economic Development Plan. The ORB provided a platform on which a short-term policy could be established in a consistent manner. Such budget provided key indicators for the year based on the analysis and projection of the economic trends in South Korea and the world, including the growth target for the year, the basic policy directions, the investment size per industry, the plan for the balance of international trade, and the key indicators in the finance and banking sectors. Therefore, the ORB provided key directions for each ministry's planning and for the activities in the private sector, which included budget planning and the establishment of a foreign currency supply plan.

Towards the end of 1961, as an attempt to strengthen the legal basis for the fiscal support activities for economic development, the military government enacted the Budget and Account Act to replace the Finance Act, which had been in place since the inauguration of the government of the Republic of Korea. The former Finance Act was copied from Japan's finance act and focused on sustaining healthy finances. Specifically, it was aimed at maintaining the balance between the receipts and disbursements. However, as a country in the process of pushing forward with an ambitious economic development plan, a more flexible and nimble fiscal management policy was required. In other words, the Budget and Account Act was enacted not from the perspective of responsibility or control but from the perspective of flexibility and discretion. The government supported the efficient fiscal management required for economic development by relying on this scheme.

By making the general accounting cover the current costs, the government's investment activities and the provision of financing were able to be managed separately. Towards this end, various special accounts or funds were established to support the ambitious investment policy. The special accounting and funds reflected the government's intention to respond more flexibly and nimbly to the changing situation, without being rigorously controlled by the National Assembly, compared to the general accounting.

In the 1960s, when the country was in the early stage of economic development, the country lacked capital, technology, talent, and other basic resources required for economic development. With the capital accumulation in the private sector still not on a satisfactory level, the private businesses were not prepared to implement the task of industrial development. The government responded to this challenge by establishing public enterprises, which would play the key role in economic development.

Performance and Assessment

Spurred by the potent drive fueled by the personal interest and care of the most powerful man in the country, the government achieved better performances than it initially targeted in the process of implementing the annual component of the Five-Year Economic Development. The double-digit growth rates it achieved throughout the 1960s and 1970s provided the basis for the future economic prosperity.

Even when the country had yet to realize self-sufficiency in food supply, the country's bold move to adopt an aggressive economic development strategy that included export-centric economic development and the fostering of the heavy and chemical industries allowed it to successfully join the club of advanced economies. The country was able to achieve a per-capita GNI of US$ 10,000 in 1994, and joined the OECD on the shoulder of the achievements realized by such efforts starting in 1962.

Their experience of implementing the country's economic development strategy and the success that they attained in the process imbued the South Korean people with a "can-do" spirit. Coupled with the Saemaul Movement in the 1970s, which was aimed at developing the country's rural areas, the experience also played the role of reviving the national spirit. The Five-Year Economic Development Plan is a typical example of a government-led economic development model pushed forward by an authoritarian regime.

Such excessive intervention of the government, however, would undermine the development of capitalism driven by the inherent energy of the market. The economic development strategy based on government intervention could deliver some successes in the take-off stage of economic development, but the strategy needed to be changed to another strategy once a certain degree of economic development was achieved. The imperative of the later administration is to secure the energy required for the further growth of the national economy so that it is supported solely by market logic and is free from government strategy.

The widening income gap, the flip-side of the rapid economic growth driven by the government, has risen as the political hot potato in the country. The economic policy emphasizing the dominant role of the chaebols or the conglomerates, derived from the "grow first and distribute later" attitude, left a thorny legacy that the succeeding administrations has to grapple with: political and economic democratization. The rural residents provided the much-needed labor in the process of the country's rapid industrialization by migrating to the urban areas, but they were gradually marginalized to the outskirts of the cities, thereby worsening the income gap between the different classes. In addition, the lopsided government support to the large conglomerates widened the economic gap between the small and large enterprises, which created another social dilemma that the present generation has to handle.

4. Export and heavy chemical industries for the leap forward to an advanced economy

Background

The Park Jung Hee administration had to go through various ups and downs during the period of the 1st Economic Development Plan, from 1962 to 1966, when it was still a revolutionary government. Based on the lessons it learned from such experiences, the administration successfully established and completed the 2nd Five-Year Economic Development Plan, which lasted from 1967 to 1971. The success of the 2nd Five-Year Economic Development plan helped not only realize self-sufficiency in food supply and afforestation of the country's mountains but also meet the target of US$ 700 million in exports through moderate industrial sophistication based on the development of the chemical, steel, and machinery industries. However, composed mostly of labor-intensive goods, such as wigs or agricultural products, the country's export goods at the time closely reveal how weak and vulnerable the country's economy was during the period.

Against the backdrop of such shifting situation, in the State of the Nation Address on January 12, 1973, the government, as an effort to stabilize the industrial structure, unveiled a plan to grow six key strategic industries (steel, electronics, petrochemical, shipbuilding, machinery, and non-ferrous-metal industries) during the period covered by the 3rd Economic Development Plan. The plan hinted at the government's ambition to overcome the limitations of economic growth centered on the light industries by choosing to foster the development of heavy chemical industries as an effort to realize stable growth in the future. The decision was also closely related with the changing defense environment marked by the announcement made by President Nixon in February 1970. In his announcement, President Nixon claimed that the U.S. would not provide military protection in Asia (the Nixon Doctrine) in view of the lessons the U.S. learned from the Vietnam War. The announcement was followed by a partial withdrawal of the U.S. forces in South Korea in July of the same year. To sum up, the government intended to hit two birds with one stone, specifically economic growth and a self-reliant defense system, by growing the heavy chemical industries, which could presumably be easily appropriated for the production of military equipment.

Implementation System

The key economic policies of the Park Jung Hee administration were personally determined by President Park himself. Faced with the choice between a self-reliant economy based on agriculture and an open economy supported by export, majority of the economists then supported the former. Likewise, President Park's announcement of the policy change to support the heavy chemical industries in the State of the Nation Address was met with opposition by not only the opposition party and the academe but also the Ministry of Treasury and the Economic Planning Board. The proposed plans to build POSCO and Gyeongbu Expressway were met with unanimous opposition both at home and abroad, but the president still pushed ahead with the plans. As a result, many economic policies were established by the task force team in the Presidential Office and announced by the president himself. As opposed to bottom-up decision-making, in which an idea proposed by the ministry is reported to the president for final confirmation, such decision-making was a typical case of top-down decision-making, in which the president comes up with an idea and the public officials in the related ministry mobilize the resources required to implement the idea with the full support of the president.

The export-driven policy was implemented with the concerted efforts of all the government organizations. Foreign capital was imported to promote export, followed by the provision of scores of tax breaks and financial support. KOTRA (Korea Trade-Investment Promotion Agency) and EXIM (Export-Import) Bank were established as public institutions that would support the export activities of private businesses. Such policies were established by the Presidential Office, the Economic Planning Board, the Ministry of Treasury, and Ministry of Commerce and Industry, but in practice, almost all the government institutions were enthusiastic about helping the export companies. Rather than striving to uphold the rights and improve the welfare of the workers, even the Ministry of Labor focused on suppressing the demand for wage increase by the workers for the fear of the potential deterioration of the competitiveness of the country's industries due to the wage level increase. Additionally, during the incumbency of the Park Jung Hee administration, what is now the Ministry of Environment was kept as only one bureau of the Ministry of Health and Welfare as to prevent the potential burden of tightening environmental policy that might be placed on the companies.

The best illustration, however, of the export-driven policy of the Park Jung Hee administration was the Monthly Extended Meeting for Export Promotion/Expansion that was presided over by the president. The meeting was held 152 times during the incumbency of the administration, and President Park invited scores of private businesses to the meeting from early on. Even though such invitation in an official meeting of the government was an extraordinary practice that is hard to find even in many underdeveloped countries, such practice eventually helped expand the country's export volumes. This was because the meeting was held in the following way: the business owners would appeal to the president with regard to the difficulties that their businesses were facing, and the president would resolve such issues on the spot. The practice thus worked as an extremely effective mechanism of promoting the country's exports.

Figure 2-2. Export Drive Promotion System

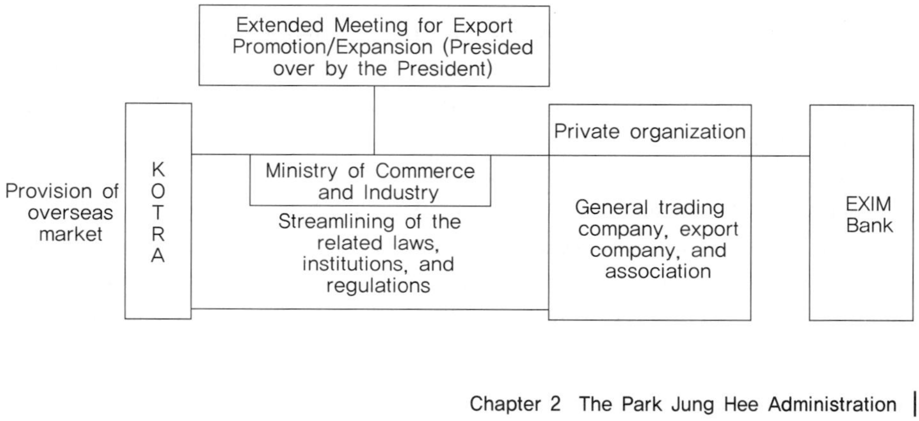

Figure 2-3. Administrative System for Driving the Growth of the Heavy and Chemical Industries

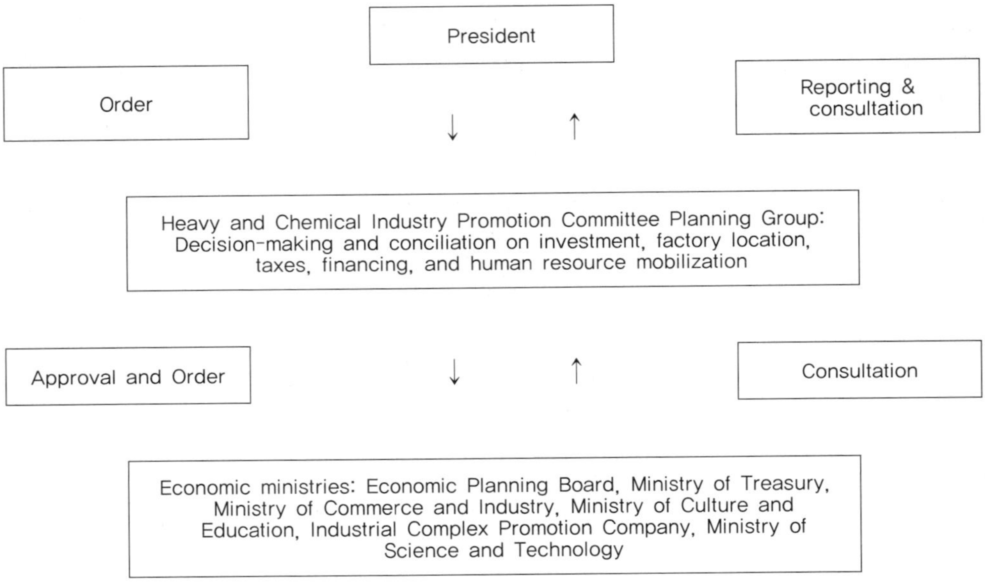

The conventional policy implementation system was not used in the formation and execution of the heavy chemical industry policy. Specifically, the Ministry of Commerce and Industry designed the details of the policy from the perspective of the national industrial policy, the Economic Planning Board mobilized the necessary financial support, and the Presidential Office installed the Office of the 2nd Senior Secretary to the President for Economic Policy and made this organization oversee the overall heavy and chemical industry policies. As the Office of the 2nd Senior Secretary to the President for Economic Policy reported directly to the president to obtain his approval, the effectiveness of the policy implementation was very high.

Implementation Process and Contents

The export support policies of the Park Jung Hee administration were extremely diverse and were executed effectively. In 1962, KOTRA was installed to help the export businesses explore and develop overseas markets. Established in an effort to improve the balance of international trade and to realize a self-sufficient economy, KOTRA carried out diverse functions, including conducting research on the overseas markets, developing the country's overseas markets and introducing trade opportunities, promoting the South Korean industries and products, participating in various expositions and hosting exhibitions, providing timely and accurate information on overseas products to the country's export companies, studying ways of increasing exports per product category, and identifying promising export products. In 1963, the government introduced the export-import link system, in which exporters were given the authority to spend the total proceeds from export for importing other products. Considering that importation was strictly controlled by the government at the time, such system was an extraordinary, and likewise, was later abolished with the introduction of a fundamental policy apparatus including the depreciation of the South Korean currency.

Revving up the country's already-hot export engine even more, the Park Jung Hee administration billed the policy goal for the fiscal year 1965 as the "Year of Export/Increased Production/Construction," and set the export target for the year at a level some 40% higher than what it had been in the previous year. The exporters were very skeptical about the proposed goal but exerted a variety of efforts to boost their export volume with the full support of the president. Specifically, the Extended Meeting for Export Promotion played a disproportionate role in the process as an official mechanism of promoting export. Created in 1965 by expanding and revamping the existing Export Promotion Meeting, the meeting was the key institution that "made decisions on the export plan and export promotion policy while also adjusting and implementing the decided plan policies." The institution illustrates the key characteristic of the Park Jung Hee administration's export promotion policies: collaboration between the government and the private sector. For instance, the meetings that were held during the 1967 fiscal year were attended by a total of 89 participants: the president, ministers and vice ministers, director-and department-level officials and various civilian participants, including participants from financial institutions, government investment institutions, and business and industry associations; professors of the related study areas; lawmakers; and representatives of private businesses. Out of the total of 152 meetings held during the incumbency of the Park Jung Hee administration, President Park presided over 147 meetings, indicating the strong will of the president to promote the country's exports.

Beginning in May 1972, the discussion of the possible sophistication of the country's industrial structure took center stage in the meetings held in the Presidential Office, signaling a policy shift towards the growth of the heavy chemical industries. Even though the need to develop the heavy chemical industries had been confirmed earlier during the fostering of the defense industry to produce weapons in preparation for potential outbreak of war, it was reconfirmed that the heavy chemical industries would be indispensible in meeting the US$ 10 billion export target proposed by President Park. Asked by the president how the country would be able to accomplish the US$ 10 billion export target, Won Cheol, the 2nd Senior Secretary to the President for Economic Policy, stressed the need to revamp the country's industrial structure from one based on the light industries to one based on the heavy chemical industries. The proposal was approved, and thereafter, the government embarked on the task to prepare the Heavy Chemical Industry Build-up Plan.

With the great interest of the president, the Heavy Chemical Industry Development Plan, targeted for the period from 1973 to 1981, was established. The plan proposed annual targets and suggested the year for the final completion of the project. It also contained the financing schedule required to turn the plan into a reality by obtaining the full support of the president. As a result, the plan did not stop at being just a plan but attained significant achievements in the end, thereby demonstrating its effectiveness during the period.

Lining up massive amounts of funds was critical to financing the development of the heavy chemical industries. Towards this end, the government provided various forms of administrative support, including financing through the fiscal investment and loan account and the provision of individual funds by industry and company in accordance with the various industrial promotion acts, of policy financing packages with low interest rates, and of industrial support funds. Specifically, the National Investment Fund, which was installed in accordance with the National Investment Fund Act, played an important role in financing the plan as the money raised by the fund was provided as low-interest loans to the heavy chemical industries. Beginning with the investment of 54.9% of the total funds in the heavy chemical industries in 1974, the investment amount has since ballooned to some 70% of the total funds in the period from 1977 to 1981. As a result, the funds invested in the heavy chemical industries accounted for 67.9% of the total funds held by the National Investment Fund on average from 1974 to 1981.

On top of such fiscal and financing support, other forms of policy support spanning the area of tax and human resource development were also provided in disproportionate amounts to the heavy chemical industries. Comparing the forms of policy support given to the heavy chemical industries with those offered to the light industries based on the related contents stipulated in the various industrial promotion acts, the share of the government support to the heavy chemical industries was disproportionately high. Specifically, the heavy chemical industries were provided with diverse forms of government support and preferable treatment across wide-ranging areas, including entrance barriers, regulation of facility investment and production, subsidies for R&D activities, fiscal support (tax breaks), public utility charge discounts, and financing and development of industrial complexes. The light industries were provided with equally diverse forms of government support with regard to entrance barriers, regulation of facility investment and production, and financing and development of industrial complexes, but no direct support was provided with regard to the subsidies for R&D activities, fiscal support (tax breaks), and public utility charge discounts. The tax breaks that were offered to the heavy chemical industries were a 100% tax break for inland duty for the first three years, a 50% tax break for the next two years, and 70-100% tax breaks for the applicable duty and tariffs.

Performance and Assessment

As a result of the export-driven growth policy of the Park Jung Hee administration, the country's export volume increased rapidly until US$ 119 million worth of exports was reached in 1964. "Export Day," which was established to commemorate the day that the country met its export target (November 30), was one of the most important anniversaries commemorated during the incumbency of the Park Jung Hee administration. The country never missed its annual export target throughout the period from 1964 to 1979. The lowest average accomplishment rate against the proposed annual target was recorded in 1972 (110%), and the highest was recorded in 1971 (245%). A review of the export growth rates for eight years, from 1964 to 1971, showed that it comfortably remained at around the 40% level. As government officials, government investment institutions, and private businesses employed every possible means at their disposal to meet the about 40% growth target year-on-year, largely spurred by the strong will of the president, the country is believed to have recorded a whopping 41.1% annual growth rate on average during the period.

As the president's personal attention as well as the country's administrative and fiscal resources was focused on the task of promoting export, other areas were rarely able to enjoy the benefits offered by the government, and sometimes even experienced significant damages to their businesses. Accordingly, the domestic industries did not enjoy any noticeable benefits; the farming and fishery industries, unlike the industrial sector, were excluded from the policy support by the government. Specifically, since any potential rise in the food cost would certainly push up the pressure for wage increase and thereby weaken the competitive edge of the exporters, the price of rice was artificially controlled, resulting in the government-orchestrated restriction of the income growth of the farmers. Likewise, the voice of workers demanding wage increase was suppressed thoroughly and no labor movement aimed at protecting and promoting the rights and benefits of the workers was allowed at all.

As the export companies started to cluster around the metropolitan areas, which were full of high-quality labor and had a well-developed transportation infrastructure, the government concentrated its investments on the urban areas in an effort to ensure an efficient supply of social overhead capital to the export companies, which is an understandable move as the government aimed to maximize the effectiveness of the fund distribution given the limited capital available for investment. Still, such policy eventually made the rural areas lag far behind the urban areas, and created a serious development gap between the rural and urban areas, which again escalated into a difficult political dilemma for the succeeding administrations to grapple with for years to come. Moreover, the reform of the administrative district, which differentiated the urban from the rural areas by promoting a town to a city and a general city to a wide-area city, also resulted in decreased investments in the rural areas for the sake of ensuring the competitive edge of the urban areas.

The artificially skewed distribution of resources that favored the export companies gave rise to substantial corruption as well. Given that the government had the authority to distribute resources, it was a common practice then for companies to lobby hard to politicians or officials, whom had such authority to distribute resources, for an opportunity to obtain rent privileges. The situation was made even worse by the extremely low wage levels of the public officials at the time and the country's less mature political culture. As such, a symbiotic relationship was formed between the export companies and the politicians and public officials, where the former kept expanding their businesses by obtaining privileges from the government while the latter received part of the profits that the businesses gained in the form of kickbacks or of the slush funds required to finance their political activities.

Meanwhile, the country's industrial structure and resulting portfolio of export products changed dramatically, thanks to the focused investment in the heavy chemical industries from the mid-1970s to the early 1980s. In the case of the industrial structure, the shares of the heavy chemical industries and the light industries were 37.8% and 62.2%, respectively, in the 1970s, with the latter having the dominant share. In the 1980s, however, the shares changed to 52.4% and 47.4%, respectively, with the former having nearly half of the total. The portfolio of export products changed as well: the shares of the heavy chemical industries and the light industries in the 1970s were 12.8% and 69.7%, respectively, but these changed to 41.5% and 49.4% in the 1980s, showing a marked increase in the share of the heavy chemical industries.

As the heavy chemical industry development policy was implemented by assuming massive investments, large conglomerates were the dominant participants of the projects, but the early reactions of these conglomerates were lukewarm at best. To encourage their participation in the heavy chemical industries, the government provided them with diverse tax breaks and financing support. As a result, the conglomerates grew in size due to the government support, a practice that soon backfired as it sparked a controversy over the extraordinary benefits enjoyed by the conglomerates, and the gap between the conglomerates and the small businesses widened. Furthermore, the decisive role that the government played in the process deepened the dependence of the private businesses on the government, thereby weakening their self-reliance and international competence.

5. The 10-Year National Land Development Policy: Key to comprehensive national land development

Background

The economic development of the Republic of Korea is characterized by the continuous expansion of the social overhead capital and the systematic implementation of a land development plan. The national land development policy is closely related with economic development when seen from the perspective of national development. In the wake of the start of the implementation of the 1st Five-Year Economic Development Plan, the country's national land development policy was pushed forward as part of the greater scheme to lay the groundwork for economic growth as it expanded the nation's social overhead capital.

It was after the establishment of the 1st Comprehensive National Land Development Plan that the country's full-fledged land development started in earnest. It was a comprehensive and long-term land development plan that covered the entire territory, and was intended to respond to the various dilemmas that started to appear amidst the rapid industrialization and urbanization of the country, by consolidating the various national land development plans that had been discussed since the 1960s.

The 1st Comprehensive National Land Development Plan had the following goals: (1) effective utilization of the national territory to support efficient economic growth; (2) laying the foundation for national land development that would support economic growth; (3) development of the country's abundant natural resources; (4) ensuring environmental protection in the wake of the development of large-scale industrial complexes; and (5) improvement of the country's living environment to resolve the urban problems and to guarantee the people's cultural-life enjoyment.

Towards these ends, the plan set following strategies: (1) develop large-scale industrial complexes that would lead the advancement of the national economy; (2) expand the communication, transportation, and energy supply networks that connect the metropolises, regional areas, and industrial centers; and (3) strengthen the functions of the rural and fishing towns and of the other laggard areas that started to appear due to the unbalanced development practices.

Implementation System

The national land development project in the 1960s can be considered part of the bigger economic development plan because it was implemented during the period covered by the 1st and 2nd Five-Year Economic Development Plan as a comprehensive policy package designed to break through the country's economic hardships, such as the low growth rate and the high unemployment rate. The government pushed forward with a series of civil works in the 1960s to support economic development, including the formation of an efficient territorial structure as well as the provision of basic infrastructure such as roads, railroads, industrial complexes, and dams. In Gyeonggi, Incheon and southeast regions, where excellent geographic locations and great growth potential made them strategic places for the building of economic infrastructure, the government pushed forward with an industrialization policy focused on the light industries and aimed to construct industrial complexes and Gyeongin and Gyeongbu Expressway.

Meanwhile, in the 1970's, a period marked by the laser-sharp concentration of resources to build a self-sufficient economic base to overcome absolute poverty, the key economic development policy was export-driven industrialization. Therefore, a national-level land development plan was required for an effective development of economic policies. Moreover, the construction of large-scale industrial complexes, which were aimed at ensuring efficient industrialization, required a systematic and comprehensive site and land supply strategy for the transportation facility, which was necessary to support the industrialization process. According to such logic, the 1st Comprehensive National Land Development Plan (1972~1981) was established. The key objective of the 1st Comprehensive National Land Development Plan was to expand the country's social overhead capital by using lands effectively to ensure efficient economic growth, and by laying the groundwork for national land development to support economic growth. The other objectives of the plan were the resolution of the environmental problems caused by the exploitation of natural resources and by the development of massive industrial complexes and the improvement of the living environment to cope with the urban problems and to ensure the cultural life of the city residents.

Implementation Process and Contents

The National Land Construction Project in the 1960s was implemented with the intention of living up to the following two policy imperatives: reform of the country's economic structure and formation of a social overhead capital. The short-term goals of the project were the completion of a national land construction basic plan, the preservation of the country's limited lands, the restoration of the lands damaged by floods, the surveying of the resources and technologies in a specific area, and the maximized utilization of the short-term unemployed people. The long-term goals of the project, on the other hand, were the completion of the national overall land development plan, the expansion of the land preservation projects, and the expansion of the employment of effective but jobless people.

In the latter part of May 1961, President Park Jung Hee announced the 1st Economic Development Plan (proposal), which was prepared based on the five-year development plan established under the previous democratic administration. The Comprehensive Economic Rehabilitation Plan was confirmed and was announced by the Economic Planning Board, which was founded on July 22 of the same year. The Economic Planning Board prepared and quantified the economic policies and supporting logic by consolidating diverse plans dealing with different segments before completing a proposal for the Five-Year Economic Development Plan on September 15 of the same year. The proposed plan was reviewed and screened by the Central

Economic Committee, which was formed for the sole purpose of performing this task, before it was completed in the latter part of December 1961, after the fine-tuning of its contents in a cabinet meeting and their review by the Supreme Council. The Park Jung Hee administration then unveiled its long-term development plan centered on the national economy as well as on the development of rural and fishing towns and key industries while specifying its intention to link the land construction project with the yearly economic development plan.

The land construction plan started to take form as each ministry was ordered in early November 1962 to establish its own "comprehensive national land construction plan." The preparation of the Comprehensive National Land Construction Plan was carried out by the Minister of Construction while the heads of other ministries established a detailed sub-plan and submitted it to the Minister of Construction on December 15, 1962. Finally, the Minister of Construction established the Comprehensive National Land Development Plan by modifying and fine-tuning the submitted sub-plans in anticipation of the scheduled promulgation of the plan on July 30, 1963. The Comprehensive National Land Construction Plan Advisory Committee was then installed on April 1, 1963 and was given the role of reviewing the details of the Comprehensive National Land Construction Plan by responding to the request of the Minister of Construction.

The legislation of the Comprehensive National Land Construction Plan Act on October 14, 1963 established the institutional basis for the basic long-term plan that would deal with the diverse issues related with the use, development, and preservation of land, water, and other natural resources; the rough locations, sizes, and structures of urban and rural areas; the selection and formation of industrial sites; the locations and sizes of key public facilities that would lay the groundwork for industrial development; and the locations and sizes of the facilities aimed at protecting culture and wellbeing, tourism, and other resources.

Based on the "Basic Design," the detailed planning work of the Comprehensive National Land Development Plan started in 1969. The plan was promulgated with Presidential Notification No. 26 on October 27, 1971, after deliberations on it by the Comprehensive National Land Construction Plan Deliberation Committee and its subcommittees as well as various seminars and public hearings on it and two years of screening and review by the United Nations Development Programme. Since the plan was published as a book authored by the government, it had the characteristic of a land development plan that was confirmed by the overall government organization, unlike the Greater National Land Construction Plan or "Basic Design" that was announced by the Ministry of Construction. Specifically, the 1st Comprehensive National Land Development Plan, which covered the 10-year period from 1972 to 1981, was aimed at realizing the balanced development of all the lands in the country, the simultaneous development of agriculture and industry, and the creation of an environment that would boost the overall efficiency of the national economy. It also aimed to revamp and expand the international transportation and communication network to catch up with the changing international community and the diversification of the international division of labor. The plan also adopted a development method by key regional area, by dividing the nation into four large (great) areas, eight medium-sized areas, and 17 small areas.

President Park unveiled his campaign pledge while running for president in the 6th presidential elections in 1967; it included the construction of the proposed expressway, railroads, and ports as well as the Comprehensive Four Major River Area Development Project during the period covered by the 2nd Five-Year Economic Development Plan (1967~1971). The announcement of the Greater National Land Construction Plan was the administration's move to keep this campaign pledge. The key contents of the Greater National Land Construction Plan were: (1) to obtain water and power, to control flooding, and to develop water transportation means through the comprehensive development of the four major rivers; (2) to build a key expressway network linking Seoul with Incheon, Gangneung, Busan, and Mokpo; (3) to build a railroad network linking the east, south, and west coast areas to one another; and (4) to build key ports (top 10 ports) in the east, west, and south coast areas.

The basic design of the national land development plan was proposed with the goal of "ensuring efficiency in the use of national lands and rationality in national land management," and of "creating methods of maximizing the highly compact utilization of lands," and more directly, of "establishing a basic design for the national land development plan." The basic design was a long-term plan, which was developed to provide guidelines on the provincial, county-level, and urban development plan with the goal of establishing the objectives and directions per given area that would be required to establish the Comprehensive National Land Construction Plan.

The 1st Comprehensive National Land Development Plan (1972~1981) was devised with the purpose of resolving the negative side effects of industrialization and urbanization caused by the successful implementation of the two consecutive economic development plans, and of laying the foundation for rapid growth in the future through the effective utilization and development of all the lands in the country. The plan consisted of an overview, which clarified the key ideology behind the establishment of the 10-year plan from 1972 to 1981, and of Part 1 (Basic Plan), Part 2 (Plan by Sector), Part 3 (Plan by Area), and Part 4 (Management and Implementation of the Plan).

Under the administrative motto of "economic development," the Park Jung Hee administration pushed forward with the national land development plan that corresponded with the economic and regional development plan for specific areas to resolve the country's economic difficulties, such as the low growth rate and the high unemployment rate. Specifically, the national land development plan was sometimes implemented as part of the bigger economic development plan. For instance, in the 1st and 2nd Five-Year Economic Development Plan, the land development project was implemented within the investment limits specified by the respective economic development plans.

Accordingly, the land development plan in this period was implemented centered on the regional land development plan for specific areas. Flanked by the Samcheok area to the north and Busan to the south, the Ulsan area, for instance, was assessed to be an ideal location for the development of a logistic center as well as an energy base. Further encouraged by other benefits, such as its neighboring satellite cities, the city was selected by the government as a target location for the construction of key industrial infrastructure, such as an oil refinery and a nitrogen fertilizer manufacturing plant, a thermoelectric power plant, small and medium-sized factory cities linked with Ulsan, a water supply facility, ports, a water management project, and factory lots. In addition, the Taebaek area was assessed to have a rich reserve of underground resources, such as coal, iron ore, limestone, and tungsten, as well as a potential to support the development of 12 key hydropower plants along the upper stream of Han and Nakdong River. Based on this assessment, the government pushed forward with projects to develop the part of Gangwon Province south of Ganneung, part of Chungcheong Province, and the part of Gyeongbuk Province north of Andong. The detailed projects included: the construction of key industrial roads and key port infrastructure to organize a coal export network; hydropower development; formation of coal, cement, and pulp-centric industrial complexes in Chungju, Jecheon, Danyang, and Yeongwol based on their rich reserves of underground and energy resources; and the construction of fishery and industrial bases in the Gangneung, Mukho, and Samcheok areas.

The land development plan in the late 1960s was aimed mainly at identifying various economic variables by setting the "zone (area)" concept, including the aspect of the distribution flow between the manufacturing and consumption centers as well as the link between the city center and the outskirts, to develop a basic unit area. The hierarchy and list of zones included the central economic zone centered around Seoul City and the southern economic zone centered around Busan City, which were followed by the stratified layers of other smaller zones, including four major zones (Han River Basin, Nakdong River Basin, Geum River Basin, and Yeongsan River Basin) selected along the river basins based on the available resources; eight medium-sized zones selected along the provincial administrative unit (the Greater Seoul zone; the Daejeon zone, Taebaek zone, Jeonju zone, Daegu zone, Gwangju zone, Busan zone, and Jeju zone); and finally, 17 small zones (eight medium-sized zones; the Chuncheon zone, Wonju zone, and Cheonan zone; the Cheongju zone; the Andong zone; the Pohang zone; the Jinju zone; the Suncheon zone; and the Mokpo zone), which were selected by considering the respective city center and outskirts that were deemed to have a potential to form a single economic zone by clustering four to five counties.

In the 1970s, the Park Jung Hee administration formed a structure of sectoral plans in accordance with the Comprehensive National Land Development Plan, which touched on the establishment of an industrial foundation, the expansion of the country's transportation and communication network, urban development, improvement of the country's living environment, hydro resource development, and preservation of lands. It also supplemented the structure of the sectoral plans with the zoning (area) plan. Specifically, the area plan aimed to promote an environment conducive to maximizing the efficiency of the national economy through the balanced development of the country's lands and the simultaneous development of farming and industry by designing Han River Basin to integrate the Greater Seoul and Taebaek zones, Geum River Basin to integrate the Chungcheong and Jeonju zones, Nakdong River Basin to integrate the Daegu and Busan zones, and Yeongsan River Basin to integrate the Gwangju zone.

Performance and Assessment

The Greater National Land Construction Plan can be said to have been prepared to modernize the country by reforming various structural bases in the country, and thereby forming a rational and balanced industrial structure, national land structure, and income structure. The Ministry of Construction then highlighted the significance of the Greater National Land Construction Plan by defining it as the development and construction plan of the national lands. The ministry claimed that such plan would be required for the great people of any advanced country on the premise that the South Korean people would evolve to become first-rate citizens of Asia in terms of politics, economy, culture, and society. In this respect, the plan has a historical significance in that it was the "first nationwide development plan," although its scope was limited to road, port, railroad, hydro resource, and river maintenance.

Second, the "Basic Design of National Land Development" played the role of the charter for national land development as it was the blueprint aimed at ensuring the consistency of the national land development plan through the adjustment of the various construction functions within the government organization as well as through the provision of directions and guidelines for the formulation of physical plans, including the specific regional, provincial, and city plans.

In addition, the plan is regarded highly for being the first plan in the country to stratify the national zones along the top-down layers: 4 great zones-8 mid-sized zones-17 small zones. It is also regarded highly for its significant role in the establishment of the 1st Comprehensive National Land Development Plan by setting the basic directions for the desirable future of the national land use. In the process, the national land development plan of the Park Jung Hee administration failed to live up to the level desired in terms of the methodological framework and the level of institutionalization back in the 1960s. The administration, however, succeeded in establishing a more systematic planning system that could respond to the economic growth in the 1970s when it came to understand that the national land development plan was a development mechanism that was closely interlocked with the national economic policy.

The 1st Comprehensive National Land Development Plan can be assessed to have accomplished the established performance goals, including the efficient utilization and management of the national lands and the expansion of the development foundation. Specifically, the plan succeeded in constructing the coastal industrial base, the heavy chemical industrial complex in the southeast coast industrial base, and the regional industries by introducing the growth pole development strategy. It also realized the one-day life territory by adding more expressways, including Honam Expressway, Yeongdong Expressway, and Namhae Expressway. An equally significant achievement was the comprehensive development of the four rivers aimed at managing and providing water.

Overall, the Park Jung Hee administration designed a systematic land development plan across the country during its incumbency, which started from a period of chaos, went through a germination period, and culminated in a renaissance period. In the process, the administration succeeded in realizing rapid economic growth, modernizing the country's industrial structure, and expanding the country's social overhead capital while at the same time attaining some basic accomplishments, such as the efficient utilization of the national lands, environmental protection, and deterring excessive population concentration in the urban areas.

6. Participation in the Vietnam War: First dispatch of the country's armed forces and a higher-level diplomatic/economic strategy

Background

It was during the Syngman Rhee administration that the ROK government started to mull over the potential dispatch of its troops to Vietnam. The Syngman Rhee administration proposed to John Hull, Commander-in-Chief of the United States Far East Command, that the ROK government would dispatch one division of troops to Vietnam, but Hull declined the offer because the situation in Vietnam at that time was not yet that serious, and because Washington and Paris were worried about the potential expansion of the war front. Additionally, Washington may have not found compelling benefits from receiving only one division of troops in terms of tipping the scale of the war, and it may have concluded that sending ROK troops to another country was not desirable when the U.S. forces were stationed in South Korea.

Before his summit meeting with President Kennedy, Park Jung Hee, the Chairman of the Supreme Council for National Reconstruction then, stressed in his meeting with the Secretary of State that U.S. assistance was essential to the economic development of and the maintenance 600,000-strong army in South Korea in order to defend the country against possible communist aggressions. He suggested that Washington offload part of the burden it was shouldering to defend the free world onto the Republic of Korea, and in return, Washington could provide economic aid to South Korea. The offer was not accepted by Washington, however, as the Kennedy administration had a negative opinion about sending ROK troops to other regions outside the Korean Peninsula.

Implementation System

President Park Jung Hee was enthusiastic about sending troops to Vietnam for military and economic reasons; he made his intention official by sending Kim Jong Phil, his close aide, to Vietnam in February 1962 on a fact-finding mission to assess the situation. Kim Jong Phil reported to the president that the situation had deteriorated and was actually much worse than what was described in the intelligence report provided to the ROK government by the U.S. Based on this observation, Song Yo Chan, then the Prime Minister of the administration, kept sending a message to Washington restating Seoul's intention to send troops to Vietnam.

Convinced that sending troops to Vietnam would be the best option left for the country to solve its impending economic challenges at the time, the top decision-makers in the administration, including President Park, made the maximization of economic returns the no. 1 goal in sending the troops. According to Lee Dong Won, who worked as the Chief of Staff in the Presidential Office from 1963 to 1964, and who was the Minister of Foreign Affairs until 1967, the president pushed forward with the dispatch of troops to Vietnam because he was convinced that (1) South Korea's participation in the Vietnam War would provide the country with access to the only export market left for it; (2) the country could also export its labor to Vietnam, thereby lowering its unemployment rate; and (3) it would be the only direct way for the country to raise U.S. dollars.

After receiving official request by the U.S. Ambassador to the Republic of Korea to provide support to South Vietnam, the Ministry of Foreign Affairs discussed with its U.S. counterpart the status of the ROK Armed Forces in South Vietnam and the command jurisdiction of the ROK Armed Force, and the Ministry of Defense took the helm in the preparatory work in South Korea. The official documents had no specific content with regard to the role of the Korea Central Intelligence Agency (KCIA). Still, KCIA is believed to have played a key role within the government in the process of sending ROK troops to South Vietnam in view of the fact that Kim Jong Phil, the KCIA Chief at that time, notified Washington of Seoul's intention to dispatch troops after sending a fact-finding mission to Vietnam and possessed high-quality professional intelligence on the local developments through his active engagement in various overseas activities to collect diverse intelligence.

The dispatch of troops was led by President Park Jung Hee and his administration, but the administrative decision had to be ratified by the National Assembly. Paragraph 2 of Article 56 of the Constitution states: "The National Assembly retains the right to consent to the declaration of war, the dispatch of troops to a foreign country, or the stay of foreign troops in the territory of the Republic of Korea."

The first dispatch of troops, which was scheduled in September 1964, was passed in the July 31 National Assembly plenary session according to the government proposal per se, but the opinions in the National Assembly over the second dispatch of troops were sharply divided. The motion was passed by the National Assembly with a majority vote in the end, as the ruling Republican Party enjoyed majority seats in the National Assembly and some members of the opposition party also voted for the motion. The opposition party, however, expressed its harsh opposition to the bill beginning with the third dispatch of troops, a move echoed by some members of the ruling party, including Representative Cha Ji Cheol.

Implementation Process and Contents

President Lyndon B. Johnson began to consider an all-out engagement as opposed to the "flexible response" strategy of President Kennedy. After failing to persuade the U.S.'s European allies in his attempt to mobilize the Southeast Asia Treaty Organization (SEATO), he instead proposed the so-called "More Flags" strategy, in which Washington welcomed the participation in the war of other allied countries. The U.S. Department of State confirmed on May 8 that "a total of 25 countries, including South Korea, pledged their support to South Vietnam, which was waging a war against the communists, by making a material contribution to the South Vietnamese government." This was echoed by the statement of the ROK government, in which it expressed its explicit intention to dispatch combat troops to the war should the South Vietnamese government make an official request for military support.

As Washington, however, maintained a negative attitude towards the dispatch of ROK combat troops, Seoul and Washington instead agreed on dispatching one mobile army surgical hospital (MASH) and 10 Taekwondo trainers to Vietnam. The government specified in the motion that it submitted to and was unanimously passed by the National Assembly on July 31 that "the Republic of Korea is required to support the Republic of South Vietnam to maintain the international peace and to deny the war based on the spirit specified in Article 4 of the Constitution."

On January 11, 1965, the government submitted a motion requesting for an "additional dispatch of troops" to the National Assembly, which the Republican Party expressed approval of, the Democratic Justice Party led by Yoon Bo Sun expressed opposition to, and the Democratic Party expressed passive opposition to. The motion was passed with 106 votes in favor, 11 votes in opposition, and 8 blank ballots out of the total of 125 representatives present in the National Assembly plenary meeting. As one of the reasons for its request for the dispatch of additional troops, the government specified in the motion that because the country was able to escape from the communist invasion thanks to the help of 16 allied countries, including the U.S., in the Korean War, it was required to protect Southeast Asia from communist invasion and to strive to make peace and freedom in Asia permanent. This was to clarify that the country was not participating in the Vietnam War involuntarily upon the request of Washington, but it intended to return the favor it received during the Korean War as a member of the international community, and to demonstrate that it was a sovereign state that recognized the value of the international community.

On June 14, 1965, the South Vietnamese government made an official request to South Korea to send one division of combat troops to the country. In response, the Ministry of Defense informed the USFK Command that it decided to dispatch one division of combat troops to the war (including one marine combat unit).

The motion requesting for the dispatch of combat troops to Vietnam was submitted to the National Assembly on July 12. Kim Hyeong Wook, the KCIA Chief then, stressed in a Foreign Affairs Committee meeting of the National Assembly that the dispatch would provide opportunities for South Korea to strengthen the combat readiness and mental strength of the ROK Army, which had had no combat experience since the end of the Korean War, and to modernize the military equipment of the ROK Armed Forces. Economically, Kim said that the country's participation in the Vietnam War would give it an opportunity to earn foreign currency. As the opposition party lawmakers declined to attend the plenary meeting after submitting their resignation letters in the wake of the ratification of the ROK-Japan Basic Relations Treaty, the motion was passed in the plenary meeting participated in only by the ruling party and independent lawmakers, with 101 yes votes, 1 no vote, and 2 blank ballots.

President Lyndon B. Johnson sent Vice President Hubert Humphrey as a special envoy to Seoul in two visits, on January 1 and February 22, 1966, and requested for a dispatch of combat troops to the war. After continuous negotiations, the negotiating partners drafted the U.S. Browne Memorandum, which dealt with diverse agreements, including military support such as modernization of the ROK Armed Forces, provision of all military equipment and other costs associated with the dispatch of the troops, and a pay raise for all the ROK troops stationed in Vietnam, as well as other forms of economic support, including the provision of additional loans on top of the previously promised loans, the provision of support to boost South Korea's exports to Vietnam, and the purchase of military supplies for the ROK troops.

Whereas the first-, second-, and third-round troop dispatches to Vietnam helped the South Korean government justify the country's engagement in the war, the fourth-round dispatch resulted in the implementation of the promised offers and the provision of additional support to the country. It can be concluded from these that the intricate and carefully vetted implementation system of the policy was effective in realizing the intended goals. The South Vietnamese government sent an official letter to Seoul on February 22 requesting for an additional dispatch of ROK combat troops. The motion requesting for the additional dispatch of troops to Vietnam was passed with 95 yes votes, 27 no votes, and 3 blank ballots on March 20, in the plenary meeting that was boycotted by the opposition party lawmakers.

When the fourth-round dispatch of ROK troops were agreed upon between Seoul and Washington, William Westmoreland, the commander of the U.S. forces in Vietnam then, proposed an additional dispatch of ROK troops to Vietnam. President Lyndon B. Johnson visited Seoul on October 31, 1966 and requested for an additional dispatch of ROK troops, but President Park said in the press conference held on November 11 that there would be no more additional dispatch of troops but that he was considering the potential dispatch of rear agents consisting of retired soldiers; in other words, the overseas employment of civilian technicians who were not at all related with the combat troops. On another note, a total of 2,936 troops were additionally dispatched to Vietnam to resolve the restrictions faced by the 2nd marine brigade, which had been dispatched earlier. The dispatch was decided without the approval of the National Assembly as the government argued that it did not require the approval of the National Assembly because it was a simple rotation of troops.

Richard M. Nixon, who was sworn in as the 37th president of the U.S. in 1969, announced the phased withdrawal of the U.S. troops from Vietnam, and started to pull back the troops beginning in July of the same year. The ROK government, however, postponed its announcement of its position on such withdrawal as the withdrawal of the U.S. forces in South Korea was interlocked with the withdrawal of the ROK troops in Vietnam. However, in July 1970, with a unilateral notification by Washington to withdraw one division of U.S. troops in South Korea, the agreement that "Washington would not scale back or withdraw the U.S forces in South Korea without advanced consultation with Seoul" was no more effective. As a result, the ROK government announced its plan for the first-round withdrawal of its troops on November 6, 1971, with the actual pull-out of some 10,000 troops completed in the period from December 1, 1971 to April 13, 1972.

The second-round withdrawal plan was originally intended to pull out all the remaining ROK troops by 1972, but it was postponed upon the request of the U.S. and Vietnamese governments. With the signing of the Vietnam Peace Agreement on January 23, 1973, the ROK troops started to pull out from Vietnam on January 30, 1973. The withdrawal was completed on March 23 of the same year.

Performance and Assessment

It has been confirmed by many studies that South Korea was able to strengthen its military power with the support of the U.S. by dispatching its troops to Vietnam. The ROK government requested Washington not only to support the arms build-up of the remaining forces in South Korea as a way to fill in the vacuum created by the dispatch of its troops to Vietnam but also to modernize the dispatched troops. With a substantial part of such demands having been realized, the dispatch of ROK troops to Vietnam played a decisive role in transforming the military alliance between the two countries from one characterized by unilateral military aid from the U.S., with South Korea being on the receiving end, to one characterized as an interdependent relationship.

The dispatch of ROK troops to Vietnam was not an option but a requirement if the economic aspect alone is to be considered. Given that the aid from the U.S. continued to slide down while the unemployment rate kept going up, the Park Jung Hee administration desperately needed to dispatch the country's troops to obtain expanded support from the U.S. and to secure the funds needed for the country's economic development.

In terms of its political implications and of security assurance, the country's participation in the Vietnam War helped strengthen the U.S. - ROK relationship. Of course it should be noted that the deteriorating state of the Vietnam War and the successful nuclear experiment of China significantly raised the strategic importance of the Korean Peninsula, thereby making it imperative for the U.S. and South Korea to maintain close ties. Despite such strategic importance of the Korean Peninsula, however, Washington still converted the military aid it had been providing to South Korea to economic aid, and pushed ahead with the reduction of the U.S. forces in South

Korea in an attempt to slash its budget. Amidst such looming changes, the dispatch of ROK troops to Vietnam pushed the discussion on the potential reduction of the U.S. forces in South Korea back to the drawing board. Specifically, Washington agreed that it would not pull out the U.S. forces in South Korea without advanced consultation with Seoul by linking the issue with the dispatch of the first ROK infantry division to Vietnam; additionally, the joint statement issued when President Johnson visited Seoul in 1966 made it clear that the U.S. had no plan to reduce the U.S. forces in South Korea.

One of the most important tasks of the Park Jung Hee administration was economic development, but the country's economic structure then, which was characterized by dependence on U.S. aid, ended up making the country's industrial structure more vulnerable while pushing up the unemployment rate. A special procurement of war is that a certain country provides the required materials upon the request of the country engaged in a war. Japan, for instance, was able to realize economic rebound thanks to the Korean War. Although the economic benefits that South Korea gained from its participation in the Vietnam War were certainly not comparable to those gained by Japan, it cannot be denied that South Korea was also able to lay the groundwork for its economic development through its participation in the Vietnam War. Furthermore, the loans provided by the U.S. to South Korea were invested in expanding and maintaining the social overhead capital and developing the key industries, thereby laying the groundwork for future economic growth.

Section 3

The Government Reform of the Park Jung Hee Administration

1. Background and direction of government reform

The administrative reform that the Park Jung Hee administration pushed forward was the typical macroscopic government reform. The Park Jung Hee administration consistently adhered to the principle of economic growth throughout its incumbency. The government reform of the Park Jung Hee administration, therefore, focused on supporting economic growth more than on anything else. The evidence supporting such observation is the total of 25 reshufflings of the central administrative institutions implemented during the incumbency of the Park Jung Hee administration, 12 of which were conducted on the premise of economic policy, such as economic development. In the same period, 7 reshufflings were carried out as a result of the readjustment of administrative functions, 3 reshufflings by constitutional amendment, and an additional 3 by political demand.

The key objectives of the government reform were: (1) to achieve human and institutional disconnection from the 1st and 2nd Republic, and to lay the foundation for nation building; (2) to build an institutional basis for economic development; and (3) to establish an authoritarian governing structure to maximize the efficiency of government administration.

More than anything else, the Park Jung Hee administration strove to disconnect itself from the past through the massive replacement of personnel during the rule of the military government. The military government pushed forward with an extensive replacement of the national leadership. Specifically, the military government punished the corrupt and fraudulent public officials who served during the 1st and 2nd Republic, as well as those who conducted anti-national and anti-revolutionary deeds. The punishment of corrupt politicians and entrepreneurs was part of the series of measures that were taken to justify the legitimacy of the military revolution.

The motivations and goals of the comprehensive organizational reshuffling implemented during the rule of the military government could be found in the revolutionary pledges and the "October 2 Administrative Reform," which included the following: (1) democratization of and fostering of efficiency in the administration; (2) separation of planning from implementation; (3) institutionalization of the control function; (4) consolidation of duplicate departments; (5) unification and concentration of the administrative system; (6) strengthening of the country's regional administrative apparatus; (7) tightening of the management of the project-implementing authority; (8) promotion of the national land development project; and (9) strengthening of the intermediary management organization.

The Park Jung Hee administration set the reform goals that put utmost importance on the economic build-up during the period of the 3rd Republic, and continuously pushed forward with wide-ranging reforms, including (1) government reform aimed at supporting economic growth and (2) comprehensive administrative reform aimed at ensuring efficiency in the internal management of the administrative system.

In accordance with the aforementioned reform goals, the 3rd Republic embarked on government reform that touched on wide-ranging aspects of the national system and various administrative organizations. The government streamlined and enacted scores of laws and regulations that had yet to be established amidst the confusion during the period of the 1st and 2nd Republic, while also pushing forward with the reform of the government organization by installing new offices, including the National Tax Service, Fisheries Agency, Korea Forest Service, Ministry of Science & Technology, Board of National Unification, Korea Customs Service, Military Manpower Administration, and Ministers without a Portfolio. The 3rd Republic's government focused on introducing American institutions and management techniques to South Korea, including organizational revamp modalities such as the introduction of the staff system, the improvement of the administrative process, and the provision of a systematic education and training system. With the comprehensive participation of countless civilians and scholars armed with American education, the government reform was implemented with the basic goal of realizing the principles and techniques of developmental administration.

The primary goals of the 4th Republic's government reform were (1) to support the developmental administration; (2) to enforce "official discipline" aimed at justifying the legitimacy of the Yushin regime; and (3) to establish a system aimed at solidifying the Yushin regime.

Beginning in 1975, the 4th Republic pushed forward with the enforcement of official discipline on an unprecedented scale and depth, as part of its political efforts to justify the legitimacy of the Yushin regime. Faced with the growing political and social protest against the Yushin regime, President Park Jung Hee embarked on a powerful "enforcement of official discipline (purification of officialdom)" in an attempt to justify the legitimacy of the Yushin regime by turning the people's attention to the purge of fraudulent and corrupt acts. The government of the 4th Republic defined "enforcement of official discipline" as an "endeavor to spark national revival and to build a prosperous country by maximizing the efficiency of government administration through the recovery of the people's trust in the government. It claimed that such trust would be realized by eliminating all the corrupt practices of the government officials and by implementing efficient and bright administration based on a servant spirit, while at the same time lifting such efforts to a new level of a spiritual-reform campaign aimed at fostering a healthy national spirit based on the social purification movement, which would eliminate the comprehensive fraud and inefficiency throughout the society, and on a new set of values." The enforcement of official discipline was ultimately aimed at realizing national revival through the strengthening of the national power. In addition, the movement aimed to push forward with three key action goals: purification of the government officials, purification of the general society, and a spiritual revolution.

The government of the 4th Republic also pushed forward with a hidden agendum: the establishment of a system aimed at solidifying the Yushin regime. The said government established five new departments in the Public Prosecutors' Office by amending the Public Prosecutors' Office Act in January 1973 upon the inauguration of the Yushin regime. It also implemented successive government reforms aimed at expanding the public security apparatus, such as the installation of the Police Squad in October 1974 and the expansion of the Public Order Bureau into the National Police Headquarters in December 1974. Likewise, during the time of the 4th Republic, which was known as the "Yushin Era," various apparatuses designed to maintain the power of the regime were significantly expanded.

The government reform system of the Park Jung Hee administration shall be reviewed by dividing the era into the aforementioned three key periods: the military government, the 3rd Republic, and the 4th Republic. The government reform of the Park Jung Hee administration during the rule of the military government was led by the Supreme Council for National Reconstruction and the Administrative Management Bureau in the Ministry of Government Administration.

The reshuffling of the government organization during the rule of the military government was implemented by the Supreme Council for National Reconstruction. The council had several subcommittees, including the Standing Committee and the Special Committee, which were directly under its control. Among them, the Government Organization Restructuring Special Committee was composed of 9 members of the Supreme Council.

The military government installed the Administrative Management Bureau in the Ministry of Government Administration in July 1961 as a working organization to implement the government reform. The Administrative Management Bureau had since been revamped into the Secretariat of the Cabinet, which was given the role of carrying out the government-wide administrative reform. The Secretariat of the Cabinet installed the Administrative Management Research Committee and put it directly under its control, with the task of conducting studies on the improvement of administrative management. The military government implemented a total of 11 organizational restructurings during its rule, which lasted for two years and seven months.

The government reform of the 3rd Republic was implemented by the Administrative Reform Investigation Committee, which was installed in June 1964 and was placed under the direct control of the president. The committee, which was originally intended to operate for a limited period of three years, was extended until 1966. With the amendment in January 1973 of the Government Organization Act, the committee was renamed as Administrative Reform Committee and became the staff organization of the Prime Ministerial Office.

The government reform of the 4th Republic was implemented by the Administrative Reform Committee. The committee had changed from the Administrative Reform Investigation Committee of the 3rd Republic, as mentioned earlier. Also mentioned earlier, the committee, which was installed in 1964 as a temporary institution directly controlled by the president of the 3rd Republic, became the staff organization of the Prime Ministerial Office and was renamed as Administrative Reform Committee in accordance with the amendment in January 1973 of the Government Organization Act. Even though the committee continued to exist until 1981 and took research and provided administrative proposals, due to the Yushin administration's markedly low interest in government reform, it failed to play the central role in the reform process that it used to play in the military government and the 3rd Republic.

2. Contents of the government reform

Organizational Reshuffling

The key characteristic of the reshuffling of the government organization of the Park Jung Hee administration is that numerous organizations and institutions associated with economic development were either newly created or installed. The 3rd Republic (1963～1972) coincided with the country's 1st growth phase when the country focused on exporting light industrial goods. Among the government institutions that existed during the period, the biggest change was observed in the government institutions associated mainly with industrial development. Specifically, the Rural Development Association went through organizational reshuffling 44 times; the Ministry of Commerce and Industry, 40 times; the Ministry of Agriculture and Fisheries, 26 times; and the Ministry of Construction and Ministry of Transportation, 22 times. What is notable is that the government paid as much attention to the agricultural policies as it did to the industrial policies, which was reflected in the changes that were made in the government institutions associated with agriculture. The 4th Republic coincided with the period of economic growth, where the emphasis was placed on developing the heavy chemical industries, which saw numerous changes in the government organizations associated with production, with the largest number of changes observed in the Ministry of Internal Affairs. This signifies that the regulatory function of the government that mobilized the government's enforcement capacity was markedly strengthened, along with the organizations associated with industrial production.

Figure 2-4. Government Organization of the Park Jung Hee Administration (As of 1979)

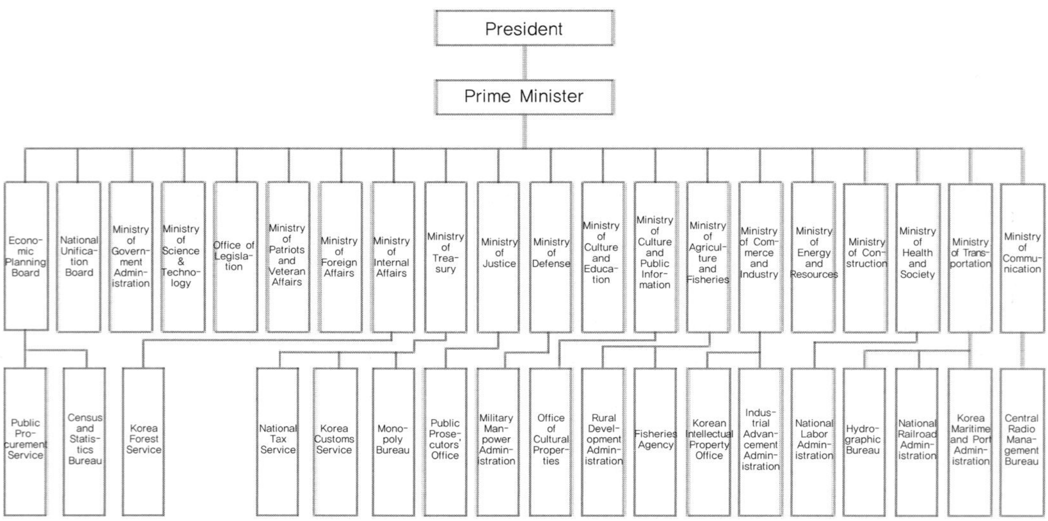

Fiscal Reform

The primary issues that had been dealt with by the budgetary guidelines, the presidential address on the annual budget proposal, and the supporting explanations from 1961 until the late 1980s were economic development, strengthening of the country's diplomacy and defense capability, fostering of exports, stabilization of the daily lives of the people, and advancement of science and education. As such, the key areas of the government budget proposal from the late 1960s until the 1980s were expansion of the country's social overhead capital, fostering of export, activation of a rural economy, and development of the heavy and chemical industries. The military government that emerged in 1961 established and implemented the Five-Year Economic Development Plan with economic development as the administration's top objective. The biggest hurdle that the government met in the process of implementing the economic development policies was the lack of sufficient domestic capital. To ensure rapid economic growth, the country needed more capital and investment. In an effort to maximize the mobilization of the available resources, the Park Jung Hee administration pushed forward with the policy marked for the fostering of export and the expansion of the country's social overhead capital, and focused the investment in the key industries until the early 1980s, through favorable interest rates and tax reform. Faced with the looming obsolescence of the past economic policy focused on the light industries due to the wage increases and the increasing competitive threats posed by the second-mover developing countries, the Park Jung Hee administration started to promote the development of the heavy chemical industries in an attempt to realize the sophistication of the industrial structure. The government also had to grapple with the widening gap between the urban and rural economies as an unwanted byproduct of rapid industrialization. In an effort to mitigate the worsening situation by activating the rural economy, the government pushed forward with the Saemaul Movement project beginning in the late 1960s.

Next, the changes in the size of tax spending by function in the central government (1962~1980) are as shown below. First, the most prominent characteristic of the tax spending during the incumbency of the Park Jung Hee administration was the fact that the share of defense spending was the highest (30%). The defense spending during the Park Jung Hee administration (1962~1979) accounted for some 30% of the total tax spending. The disproportionately high share of defense spending implies a substantial investment in the defense sector, but this was partly due to the practice of allocating a specific percentage of the GNP (6%) for defense spending when establishing the annual budget proposal. In other words, the share of defense spending automatically increased as it was interlocked with the increase of the GNP.

The next biggest item in the budget was the spending for economic development, which accounted for some 27% of the total budget. The budget allocated for economic development was invested in the agricultural and fishery industries, the mining and manufacturing industries, and the social overhead capital, such as electric power and the communication and transportation infrastructure. Specifically, the share of the spending on economic development was stressed as significant during the 1970s, as the administration's economic policy shifted from the development of the light industries to that of the heavy chemical industries. With the importance of the social development budget being increasingly stressed, however, beginning in the 1980s, the share of the economic development budget in the total budget started to decrease. Such change indicates that the private sector started to play a more dominant role in the economic development strategy. The third biggest item in the tax spending was the social development budget, which accounted for some 23% of the total budget. Education spending accounted for majority of the social development budget (over 20% of the social development budget in 1982, for instance), followed by home, health, culture, human resource development, and social welfare expenditures.

Personnel Administration Reform

The key characteristics and contents of the reform of the Park Jung Hee administration's personnel administration are as shown below. First, the National Public Service Law, which was newly enacted in 1963, specified meritocracy as the guiding principle in the employment/ assignment of public officials. The law states that public servants shall be assigned to a post based on the results of the evaluation of their respective test scores, job performances, and other capabilities (Article 26); that new public servants shall be recruited through an open competitive test (Article 28); that the recruitment test through an open competitive examination shall be open to all eligible people with identical qualifications, with the date and place of the test to be decided considering the convenience of the test takers (Article 35); and that information about the job description, compensation, qualifications, and number of people to be hired shall be provided for a substantial period during the administration of the recruitment test (Article 37).

Notable in the National Public Service Law enacted in 1973 are the establishment of the special employment system and contract-based public officials as well as the abolition of the job ranking classification system established in 1963. Specifically, the law allowed the employment of the top scientists and engineers in South Korea and other countries to conduct national research or engineering works through the newly installed special recruitment system, and the establishment of the contract-based public official system was allowed to complement and streamline the existing institutions across wide-ranging areas, including the employment and testing of public servants as well as compensation. Also, additional provisions on the special employment of those who would be made to work in islands or remote areas, or of those fluent in a rarely used foreign language, as well as the special employment of those who graduated from vocational high schools and of those with experience in conducting scientific and engineering researches, were also established. Such special employments were actively implemented beginning in 1977, but were significantly dropped in 1982, one year after the inauguration of the Chun Doo Hwan administration (1981).

Reform of Public Enterprises

The management system of the public enterprises during the incumbency of the Park Jung Hee administration fell within phase 2 of the transformation process of the public enterprise management system in Korea. Phase 2 is marked by the active utilization of public enterprises as primary means of realizing economic development in the wake of the implementation of the economic development plan. The period spans the years before the enactment of the Basic Act on the Management of Government Investment Institutions (enacted in December 1983). The applicable laws during the period included the Act on the Budgetary Accounting of Government Investment Institutions (enacted in August 1962) and the Government Investment Institution Act. In addition, the public enterprises were controlled by various ministries in accordance with the individual act on the establishment of government investment institutions and the Board of Audit and Inspection Act, the Government Procurement Fund Act, and the regulatory measures applicable to each concerned industry. The government investment institutions (public enterprises) were managed and controlled comprehensively by many central ministries across each applicable sector. For instance, the project planning and budgetary spending of the government investment institutions were controlled by the Economic Planning Board and other governing ministries whereas their personnel administration was controlled mainly by the governing ministry. With regard to other corporate functions, such as materials purchase, performance supervision, and audit and inspection, they were controlled by the governing ministry, the Ministry of Treasury, the Board of Audit and Inspection, the Government Procurement Service, and various other government organizations.

Anti-Corruption Reform

Depending on the applicable laws, the activities of the Park Jung Hee administration aimed at realizing anti-corruption reform can be divided into the following periods: (1) period of enactment of emergency measures for the National Reconstruction Act (1961); (2) period of establishment of the Board of Audit and Inspection (1963); (3) period of enactment of the National Public Service Law (1963); (4) period of installation of the Administrative Reform Inspection Committee (1964); and (5) period of installation of the Office of the Special Presidential Aide for Inspection.

The characteristics of the anti-corruption activities during the 3rd Republic are as follows: (1) the administration pushed forward with the harsh punishment of those who colluded with others in committing corruption by ignoring the existing laws and proceedings, beginning with the so-called "revolutionary pledges" and the "revolutionary tribunal", and (2) the scope of anti-corruption was expanded with the legislation of the Act on Handling the Fraudulent Accumulation of Wealth. In an attempt to gain social support and secure legitimacy for the revolution the Park Jung Hee administration focused on uncovering the identities of and punishing those who colluded with others mainly in the establishment in committing corruption, regardless of their social status or the level of seriousness of their act of corruption. On top of uncovering and punishing those who colluded with others in committing corruption, the key contributions of the 3rd Republic to the elimination of corruption in the government were the administration's establishment of the Board of Audit and Inspection as a central institution that was to perform audits and inspections and the administration's enactment and enforcement of the National Public Service Law, which laid the foundation for the management of public officials.

Key to the anti-corruption activities of the 4th Republic was the administration's introduction of a series of powerful and diverse institutions in an attempt to raise the level of punishment of those who colluded with others in committing corruption in the process of purging public officials, such as the system of enforcing the "joint responsibility of the affiliated persons," the "mutual punishment system," the "prohibition of employment characterized by a potential conflict of interest," and a "ledger of rewards/punishments with regard to the enforcement of official discipline." "Joint responsibility of the affiliated persons" signifies that the perpetrator as well as the supervisor who oversees him/her shall be held responsible for any misconduct. "Prohibition of employment characterized by a potential conflict of interest" signifies the banning of employment in an institution with which one has a potential conflict of interest with regard to the performance of official businesses to prevent corruption as a result of collusion with the interested party.

"Ledger of rewards/punishments with regard to the enforcement of official discipline" signifies that the names of the public servants who received prizes/donations or punishment in relation to their performance of their official businesses shall be recorded in the ledger, and that the ledger would be preserved permanently.

3. Performance and assessment of the government reform

The organization of the Military Revolution Committee as a supreme national authority right after the success of the May 16 revolution (renamed "Supreme Council for National Reconstruction" after the resignation of the Jang Myeon Cabinet on May 19), the establishment of KCIA, and the adoption of other measures to restrict political activities may be assessed to have contributed to the establishment of a powerful and efficient governing structure.

Not a few scholars, however, are maintaining a critical perspective on the administrative reform implemented by the military government from diverse angles. The most frequent criticism of the government reform by the military government is that the reform overwhelmingly leaned towards the pursuit of efficiency and away from the sustenance of democratic values. The military government is also being criticized for its pursuit of centralized authoritarian rule. Another criticism of the military government is that it aspired to realize a mega government and an administrative state while pursuing the building of a developmental administrative system.

The government reform of the 3rd Republic can be assessed to have been a success if one will focus on the objectives of the government reform. Specifically, such assessment would be justified in view of the realization of the reform goals. The reform goals that were proposed with the inauguration of the Administrative Reform Inspection Committee were as follows: (1) establishment of an administrative system capable of implementing government administration efficiently; (2) ensuring the comprehensive and balanced development of the national administration; and (3) getting rid of the inefficient and uneconomical elements of the management of administrative affairs. All these can be assessed to have been fully realized.

However, the administrative reform implemented by the 3rd Republic is criticized for its pursuit of the ideology of purposefulness rather than of the democratic property, and the reshuffling of the administrative institutions is being criticized for its failure to simplify the administrative process as its key principle. Indeed, many scholars claim that the goal of "simplification of the administrative process" was rarely realized in view of the fact that the government organization actually expanded during the incumbency of the 3rd Republic's government. Some claim that this criticism is based on the fact that the expansion of institutions, such as KCIA, is a violation of the democratic principles. Other scholars who are critical of the government reform implemented by the 3rd Republic point out that the administrative reform failed to live up to its promised goal in terms of qualitative improvement.

The assessments of the government reform by the 4th Republic can be divided into (1) the negative assessment of the expansion of the undemocratic institutions in an attempt to preserve the Yushin regime and of the expansion of the administrative organization and (2) the positive assessment of the performance of the reform on a microscopic level, including the enforcement of official discipline aimed at rooting out corruption and at instituting administrative management.

Many scholars put weight on the criticism of the Yushin regime itself, with regard to the government reform of the 4th Republic. Specifically, along with many criticisms of the expansion of institutions, such as KCIA and the National Police Agency, many criticize the government reform by the 3rd Republic, also in view of the principle of democratic values. Furthermore, the expansion of the government organization during the period of South Korea's rapid economic growth is sometimes criticized from the perspective of the "small government."

Chapter 3

The Chun Doo Hwan Administration

Section 1

Inauguration of the Chun Doo Hwan Administration and Foundation of Key Policy Administration

1. Inauguration of the administration and introduction of its organization

On December 12, 1979, General Chun Doo Hwan, the commander of the Army Security Command who was leading the investigation on the October 26 assassination of President Park Jung Hee, seized the power in the South Korean military by eliminating the martial law commander Jeong Seung Hwa, the top person in the country's power structure. With the elimination of Jeong Seung Hwa, the neo-military group led by Chun Doo Hwan emerged as the key power group in the country.

With various groups, including the Chun Doo Hwan group, which seized the power in the wake of the December 12 military coup d'état; the civil group, which hoped to realize the popular aspiration for the country's democratization in the political institution; and the political establishment co-existing in an awkward but precarious state, the period was marked by murky ambiguity[1] There are many factors that explain why they were able to co-exist, but chief among these are the facts that the neo-military group (1) did not have a clear will to seize the political power, or any comprehensive plan to turn this into a reality; and (2) had no compelling mandate sufficient to justify their advance to the front stage of the political arena then.

Therefore, the emerging military group was secretly establishing a power group by forming an alliance with large conglomerates (capital) and public officials who had escaped from the ancient regime. Meanwhile, the voice of the moderate minority group in the neo-military group, which practically controlled the power, grew weaker with time. The street protests of the allied forces for the democratization that unfolded in mid-May 1980 gave the neo-military group a convenient excuse to launch a brutal crackdown on the protesters. At 12 midnight on May 17, the neo-military group expanded the emergency martial law to cover the entire country and started a full-scale crackdown on the democratization movement. The military closed the National Assembly with armed troops and placed the opposition leaders under a restricted-movement order.

On May 18, the Martial Law Army, which was stationed nationwide after the expansion of the

1) The simultaneous existence of the military coup d'état and the liberalization and democratization movement was often called the "Spring of Seoul" with the phrase "simultaneity of the non-simultaneous," a concept quoted from an essay by Ernst Bloch and M. Ritter, the historical philosopher of Weimar.

emergency martial law, blocked the students of Chonnam National University in Gwangju from entering the school. In protest, the students threw stones at the army, and the street scuffle soon developed into a clash when the Martial Law Army tried to dispel the students with brute force. Later on that day at 4 p.m., the neo-military group sent the paratroopers of the 7th Airborne Brigade to Gwangju, and the random violence of the paratroopers targeted at the Gwangju citizens further enflamed the protest, resulting in bloody clashes. In the evening of May 21, when the citizens armed themselves in response to the bloody crackdown, the citizen militia occupied the Chonnam provincial government building after the Martial Law Army withdrew therefrom. Thereafter, the neo-military group started an armed crackdown on the stronghold of the citizen militia. The Martial Law Army entered the city in the morning of May 27 and killed the last remaining members of the citizen militia who were fighting to death before concluding their operation.

With such event in the city of Gwangju, over 200 people were killed and some 4,300 people were injured. Such tragedy is remembered as an unfortunate event in the history of the Republic of Korea, in which the ROK troops killed its own people en masse in an organized fashion.[2)]

After the brutal armed crackdown in Gwangju, the neo-military group started to eliminate its other competitors from within, and took a series of actions to bolster the regime: either arresting or placing its political competitors under a restricted-movement order in their respective homes, closing numerous periodicals and purging the media industry under the pretext of launching a "social clean-up," and arresting and putting some 30,000 civilians in the military training camp called "Samcheong Training Camp," where they had to go through "special training." The group also sent university students with a hint of student activism to the military camp and tried to brainwash them to embrace the group's entrenched ideology under the pretext of carrying out an "afforestation project." In conclusion, the armed crackdown on the Gwangju Democratic Movement was just a prelude to the inauguration of the Chun Doo Hwan administration, all of which casted some fundamental doubt on the legitimacy of the 5th Republic for years to come.

Many scholars defined the Chun Doo Hwan administration, which was born through the aforementioned process, as a neowarlordistic dictatorial regime. The old-fashioned warlordism has the following key characteristics: (1) it establishes and maintains the regime by spreading fear among the people; (2) its adherents exercise their power autocratically and rely on one-man governance; (3) governing elites are recruited based on their loyalty to the dictator; (4) structural corruption is perpetrated systematically; and (5) violence is usually employed in the competition to become the successor, and the present ruler usually cannot resign from his/her post safely. The Chun Doo Hwan administration can be said to have developed neowarlordism in that it not only attained all the aforementioned characteristics of warlordism but also preserved characteristics of democracy by maintaining the election system and of modern technocratic dictatorship established by the Yushin regime in a path-dependent manner. President Chun Doo Hwan can be assessed to

2) The tragedy in Gwangju may be said to have been triggered by the deliberate provocation of the Gwangju citizens by the neo-military group. Park Hyeon Chae argues that the neo-military group selected Gwangju as the perfect site for demonstrating its power and for reconfirming the appropriateness of the oppressive regime's rule, which resulted in the outbreak of the atrocities perpetrated in Gwangju. It would be difficult to accept such hypothesis, however, because the neo-military group had already seized power in Seoul even without the bloody clash in Gwangju.

have maintained the election system and by attempting to guarantee his safe resignation by anointing his own successor, to have brought about the collapse of neowarlordism by triggering nationwide popular protests.

2. Objectives and directions of the government administration

Chun Doo hwan, who was sworn in as the 11th president of the republic on September 2, 1980, was elected again as the 12th president on February 25, 1981 by the presidential electoral college that was formed in accordance with the new constitution, thereby leaving a rare record of having been sworn in as the president of the republic two successive times, within just six months. In the inaugural speech that he delivered when he was sworn in as the 11th president of the republic, President Chun Doo Hwan summed up the objectives and directions of the government administration of the 5th Republic into the four subjects cited below.

Naturalization of democracy

The president stressed that this objective would be realized through the promulgation of a constitution built on individual freedom, state preservation, and security assurance through the improvement of the political climate to overcome fraud, conspiracy, factionalism, and violence and through the realization of peaceful regime change. He also stressed the importance of the public morality of all the citizens as the foundation of a democratic society. Such objectives and directions of the government administration are believed to have actually been meant to persuade and control the people with the logic of the naturalization of democracy, thereby overcoming the inherent limitations of the regime in terms of legitimacy and morality. The objective is assessed to be particularly undemocratic in nature in that it put more emphasis on national security and stability than on individual freedom and rights.

Construction of a welfare society

This demonstrates one aspect of the regime that differentiates it from the Park Jung Hee administration, which focused on a growth-driven national development policy. Whereas the Park Jung Hee administration ran the country squarely focused on the development strategy pegged on the principle of rapid economic growth, the Chun Doo Hwan administration pushed forward with two separate goals simultaneously: economic growth based on stable prices, and policy-level effort on welfare and culture. This is the first example of the application of the concept of "cultural welfare" in South Korea.

Establishment of a just society

This was focused on forming mutual trust among the people and eradicating fraud and corruption in the ranks of the public servants. This goal shows the will of the administration to close the gaps in politics, the society, and the economy among the South Korean people that were formed in the process of the rapid economic growth and under the prolonged autocratic regime in the 1970s. On the other hand, the regime's illegitimacy and immorality, which were demonstrated in the process of the establishment of the 5th Republic, led to dispersion of people's distrust in the legitimacy of the regime and of people's will to fully embrace democracy. This administrative goal can be understood to have reflected the determination of the regime to form a sense of unity among the people and to promote government leadership by adopting a control mechanism aimed at ensuring public order.

Educational reform and fostering of culture

This focused on the promotion of a free cultural life among the people and the raising of future talents. Accordingly, there was particular interest in educational reform as well as in new areas in the cultural policy. The educational reform focused on transitioning to a more relaxed and liberal educational activities from the uniform educational methods of the past that put emphasis on control. The administration's cultural policy pushed for the development of diverse cultural media given the expanded freedom to engage in nighttime activities in the wake of the lifting of the curfew. In addition, the successful hosting of the 1986 Asian Games and the 1988 Seoul Olympic Games, coupled with the opening of the pro-baseball era, triggered the full-fledged development of the country's sports sector.

In general, as opposed to the practices under the Yushin regime, which were marked by oppression and heteronomy, the Chun Doo Hwan administration targeted the expansion of the market domain to ensure continued economic growth in the increasingly liberalized society, ensuring openness, which would enable creative blossoming and reform across the society. Such objectives can be assessed to have been ultimately aimed at attaining multiple goals, including the overcoming of the legitimacy crisis that was experienced when the regime was established as well as continued economic development, recovery of social trust in the government, and creative blossoming of culture during the incumbency of the administration.

Section 2

Key Policy Initiatives

1. Liberalization policy: liberalization of the hair and school uniform codes, lifting of the curfew

Background

The liberalization of the hair and school uniform codes and the lifting of the curfew were soft-line policies aimed at easing the popular pressure on the Chun Doo Hwan administration due to the lack of political legitimacy that had plagued it since its birth. Although it could not but push ahead with an undemocratic administration style due to its lack of political legitimacy, the Chun Doo Hwan administration was fully aware that it could not implement a hardline policy for an extended time. As part of its bigger plan to maintain the political status quo, the administration sought to introduce a variety of soft-line social policies aimed at eliminating the popular dissatisfaction with and widespread criticism of the administration. Chief among these were the liberalization of the hair and school uniform codes and the lifting of the curfew. These were not all that was done; more importantly, the policy included a policy known as the "3S policy," which promoted, or at least tacitly tolerated, the development of sports, including pro baseball, pro soccer, and pro Korean wrestling, and of the movie (screen) and sex industry. The hidden intention and background of the lifting of the curfew as well as the liberalization of the hair and school uniform codes, which was announced right after the cabinet reshuffling on January 4, 1982, can be said to be relatively clear. In other words, such changes were not designed to promote the freedom and happiness of the people and to expand the protection of the people's privacy but were nothing but a pack of political tools mobilized based solely on the political needs of the core power group. Therefore, such measures had some inherent structural limitations that made them inevitable to be planned and implemented by the core power group in the administration.

The liberalization of the hair and school uniform codes and the lifting of the curfew were huge political moves that had significant shares in the government administration of the 5th Republic, which was in its 2nd year from its inauguration when such policies were adopted. The key policy directions proposed by the 5th Republic included an expanded economic base for economic stability, liberalization, and the implementation of an open-door policy throughout the society, and the strengthening of the summit diplomacy. Just like the expansion of unlimited overseas travel and other comprehensive forward-looking liberalization and open-door policy that were in line with the administration's other liberalization policies, the liberalization of the hair and school uniform codes and the lifting of the curfew were also part of the bigger social policy of the administration that stressed self-regulation and openness.

Implementation System

Liberalization of the hair and school uniform codes

The Ministry of Culture and Education announced on January 4, 1982 that the hair and school uniform codes for the male and female middle and high school students across the country would be liberalized beginning in the first semester of school year 1982 in accordance with the order of President Chun Doo Hwan. Established in accordance with the order of the Ministry of Culture and Education in early December 1981, the measure allowed the schools in the country to soften their student hair length and school uniform codes to the allowed guidelines beginning in the first semester of school year 1982. The implementation system for the liberalization of the hair and school uniform codes can be summed up as follows: "preparation and report by the Presidential Secretariat → approval and order by the president → announcement by the Minister of Culture and Education, followed by the issuance of the related guidelines → notification of each school under the municipal and provincial board of education → implementation by the respective school principals."

The key point in the overall implementation process was the determination by the president, for which the Presidential Secretariat, in particular, Heo Hwa Pywong, played the decisive role. The fact that the announcement was made by the speaker of the presidential office, as opposed to the usual procedure (announcement by the public information officer of the Ministry of Culture and Education), shows the political significance of the measure. While delivering his order to the Ministry of Culture and Education in December 1981, President Chun Doo Hwan said, "The early enforcement of the liberalization of the hair and school uniform codes is desirable. Nobody should be allowed to restrict the color and aesthetic senses of the teenagers, who are rapidly growing."

Since the liberalization of the hair and school uniform codes was an administration-level political event that was pushed forward by Heo Hwa Pyeong, the first senior secretary to the president for political affairs then, with the full trust and support of the president, it did not require any complex implementation system. Neither the ruling party nor the opposition party, or anyone in the political circle or in the incumbent governing group, expressed opposition to such measure in the face of the heightened public interest in it.

Lifting of the curfew

President Chun Doo Hwan issued an order to the related ministries on January 1, 1982 by asking the related senior secretariats to the president to "make all the necessary preparations to introduce a bill on the lifting of the curfew in the cabinet meeting on January 5 so that curfew can be lifted on that same night." Lee Woong Hee, the speaker of the presidential office, announced that the president said, "Since the bill was passed with unanimous approval in the

National Assembly and no particular incident was reported from anywhere during the holiday seasons, such as the Christmas holidays and the New Year holidays, when the curfew was lifted, it would be possible to lift the curfew on the successive days beginning in the night of January 3. However, because the bill needs to satisfy the administrative proceedings requirements, it would be better to lift the curfew when the bill is passed with a majority vote in the cabinet meeting on January 5."

Following the due proceedings after the issuance of the presidential order, the curfew, after 37 years of enforcement, was lifted across the country on the night of January 5, 1982 (midnight of January 6), with the exceptions in those areas neighboring the front border and other vulnerable costal regions. The measure was implemented as a result of the issuance of the presidential order to all the related ministries, including the Ministry of Internal Affairs, in which President Chun Doo Hwan ordered on January 1 that the pertinent bill be introduced in the cabinet meeting scheduled for January 5 of the same year, and that the measure be enforced on the night of the very day of its approval.

The 5th Republic government needed to implement its plan to lift the curfew without revealing its ulterior motive: to soften the popular criticism of the abnormal usurpation of the government by the military elite. The bill received the support of the opposition parties, including the Democratic Korea Party and the Nationalist Party, which were merely rubber stamps of the ruling party. Accordingly, the leaders holding the three key posts in the ruling and opposition parties convened on October 19, 1981 and agreed to cast votes on the bill in the 108th regular session of the National Assembly. The National Assembly passed with unanimous approval the Bill on the Lifting of the Curfew earlier proposed by the Nationalist Party in the Assembly plenary session on December 15, before sending it to the administration.

Implementation Process and Contents

Liberalization of the hair and school uniform codes

The detailed guidelines on the liberalization of the hair code delivered to each municipal and provincial board of education across the country on January 4 are as shown below.

(1) The hairstyles of the middle and high school students shall be liberalized, with the detailed implementation to be left at the discretion of the school principals.

(2) The students shall no longer wear school caps.

(3) The female students will not be allowed to perm or dye their hair while the male students will not be allowed to grow their hair long as to cover their ears or touch their back collar.

(4) The hairstyles of the male and female students shall be liberalized under the condition that hair shaving shall be prohibited.

The hairstyle was indeed liberalized beginning in the first semester of school year 1982, but the restrictions on the style or length of the hair were still enforced, although softened to a certain extent compared to the previous practices. Therefore, the liberalization at the time was not a full-scale liberalization but was limited and relative in nature.

Below are the principles that were applied to the liberalization of the school uniform code.

(1) The school uniforms of the middle and high school students shall be liberalized, with the detailed implementation left at the discretion of the school principals.
(2) The students shall no longer wear school caps.
(3) The male students shall wear school caps during their military drill classes while the students of special-purpose schools such as railroad high schools and maritime and ocean high schools shall still be allowed to wear their respective school uniforms.
(4) The uniforms for PE or training classes shall be decided by the school principals depending on their respective conditions.
(5) Stiletto heels, boots, or other luxury shoes (e.g., enamel-coated shoes, lacquered shoes) shall be strictly regulated.
(6) School badges, name tags, and school bags shall be liberalized along with the school uniforms.
(7) The students shall be allowed to wear private casuals once a week in school year 1982, on a trial basis.

The Ministry of Culture and Education elaborated on the detailed guidelines on the liberalization of the school uniform code as follows: "The liberalization of the school uniform code was allowed on the assumption that the students wear school uniforms up to today, but the new liberalization policy shall be implemented based on the principle that the single uniform worn by the students of all schools shall be abolished. Henceforth, the school principals shall determine the rules befitting their respective schools, taking into consideration the opinions of the parents, based on the principle of liberalization of the attire to be donned by the individual students. The hairstyle shall also be liberalized, but on the condition that the past shaving practices shall be abolished."

Lifting of the curfew

As mentioned earlier, following the issuance of the pertinent presidential order, the curfew was lifted across the country on the night of January 5, 1982 (midnight of January 6), with the exception of those areas neighboring the front border and other vulnerable areas along the coastal region. A total of 292 towns (eup, myeon) scattered across 52 counties neighboring the front border and other vulnerable areas along the coastal region were excluded from the lifting of the curfew on the grounds of national security and maintaining the public order. Those areas where the curfew was continued to be enforced were 71 towns scattered across 10 counties in Gangwon Province, and 221 towns (eup, myeon) scattered across 42 counties along the coastal region, in the rear. The curfew was lifted, however, in all the cities, even those located in the coastal region, including the waters 3 nautical miles off the shore. While curfew was not lifted in the two islands in Incheon City and in 252 islands (including 58 inhabited islands) in Gyeonggi Province, it was lifted in those islands located in other cities and provinces, including Chungcheognamdo Province.[3)]

3) The curfew was lifted in those areas that had been excluded from the initial lifting of the curfew on January 1, 1988 (*The Dong-A Ilbo*, February 9, 1988).

Performance and Assessment

The liberalization of the school hair code actually helped foster an identity and autonomous spirit among the students and helped the students become responsible and creative persons. As it was the prevalent perception at the time that the shaved hairstyle of the middle and high school students was a legacy of the Japanese colonial rule or was an influence derived from the past military culture, the liberalization of the school hair code was seen as having effectively cleaned up the accumulated evils in the society and as having barred any further possibility of infringing on the students' right of self-determination. To conclude, the liberalization policy can be seen as an important turning point in the history of the promotion of the people's rights.

The liberalization of the school uniform code succeeded in resolving the psychological contraction and sense of alienation of the students in the middle development stage while instilling in them a sense of responsibility by strengthening their individual characteristics and developing their political awareness as members of a democratic society. Specifically, the growing emphasis on the individual spirit and autonomy of the students during the three-year liberalization of the school uniform code since 1983 may have been the biggest achievement of the policy. The liberalization of the school uniform freed the middle and high school students from the school uniform, which had been perceived as a symbol of uniformity and impersonality and as a Japanese colonial legacy.

Meanwhile, the lifting of the curfew reduced the number of means available for the government to constrain the people's personal freedom, thereby laying the precious foundation for the transition from the uniform and oppressive society under the military regime to one where diverse voices could be heard. The lifting of the curfew effectively demonstrated the country's commitment to protecting the basic human rights as well as its confidence in ensuring the national security and public order. In practical terms, the abolition of the curfew created an economic environment where 24 hour operations were feasible, including the early-morning auction of agricultural and fishery products.

However, given the significance of the issue, the liberalization of the hair and school uniform codes was criticized for having been pushed forward surprisingly fast and unilaterally, without going through a prior process of collecting the opinions of various social groups on such measures. For such reasons, the measures implemented in 1982 were criticized for having failed to help foster the basic rights of the students. Some argue that the measures were nothing but an abandonment of the responsibility of the schools and the government to guide the middle and high school students, who were in the middle of *Sturm und Drang*.

Some negative side effects of the lifting of the curfew soon surfaced as well. The energy consumption increased, and the extended operation hours of the entertainment businesses promoted a social atmosphere where people were overly indulgent in pleasure, while the pleasure-seeking teenagers bent on earning entertainment money triggered an outbreak of juvenile crimes. Amidst such unexpected developments, some suggested the revival of the curfew to control the wayward social atmosphere. In the early days after the lifting of the curfew, the police custody facilities were filled with people who had been caught for having gone wild after indulging in binge drinking, replacing those who had been arrested in the past for having violated the curfew, and the number of crimes perpetrated by those who took advantage of the night hours surged as well. The police revealed that the "number of additional police troops required to fill the urgent gap to be at least 16,000."

2. Policy initiatives to clean up the social evils

Background

The policies aimed at eradicating the social evils can be deemed to be part of the bigger policy packages that were established with the intention of granting legitimacy to the administration. Specifically, the 5th Republic attempted to justify the patriarchal and extremely authoritarian state system that it embraced on the pretext of fostering national discipline.

The pretext behind such policy drive was to lay the groundwork on which to reform the national spirit in the short term through the stern control and comprehensive enlightenment of the people by pushing forward with a reform policy touching on wide-ranging issues across the state and society, and to advance the realization of a just and democratic welfare society in the long term through the people's spiritual revolution. As a result of such line of thought, the Chun Doo Hwan administration thoroughly denied the legitimacy of the Park Jung Hee administration. Specifically, "In an attempt to differentiate himself from Park Jung Hee, Chun Doo Hwan deleted the provisions in the Constitution that mentioned the 'Spirit of the May 16 Revolution' in the process of the constitutional amendment. In addition, he eliminated the core power group in the Republican Party, which maintained a negative attitude towards the Hana Society in the military, by accusing them of accumulating illicit wealth by exercising their influence, and, at the same time, redefined the Park Jung Hee age as an age festooned with fraud, corruption, and irregularities. As such, he proclaimed that the 5th Republic 'strives to realize a just society.'"

The true motivation, however, behind such policy drive, which purportedly aimed to eliminate the social evils, was to suppress the people's aspiration for a democratic society by purging the social constituents who were unwilling to recognize the legitimacy of the new administration. To sum up, the neo-military group pushed forward with special measures to clean up the social evils in an attempt to justify the legitimacy of the new administration, because they knew fully well that they would not be able to establish their own regime through a democratic process given the people's intense desire then for the democratization of the country.

Implementation System

The system through which to implement the policies that were aimed at eradicating the social evils was realized by establishing the Emergency Committee for National Security Protection. The constituent members of the committee are shown below. The committee was composed of 26 members (10 assigned members and 16 ex officio members), with the president as the chairperson. Among the members, 8 were from the cabinet and 14 were army generals. With Chun Doo Hwan (also, ex officio member) as the chairperson, a Standing Committee endowed with the practical authority was installed in the committee with total of 30 members, 14 ex officio members and 16 assigned members (18 of whom were active military generals). An additional 13 subcommittees[4)] were installed in the Standing Committee.

The Emergency Committee for National Security Protection was established with the aims of "carrying out the duty of protecting the national security faithfully in response to a national crisis and ensuring close collaboration between the martial law authority and the administration." With such purported goals, the practical role of the committee was either to eradicate the antagonist groups in politics and the society, which were classified into the corrupt, the seditious, and the thugs, or to purge them on the pretext of eradicating the social evils. The acts of eradicating the social evils were again classified into five different types depending on the elimination target, with the plan to purge the government of them materialized in the form of Samcheong Plan No. 1 to 5.[5)]

Among such plans, the legal ground for eradicating the thugs and other social evils, the primary targets of the clean-up policy aimed at eradicating the social evils, was Samcheong Plan No. 5, which was implemented in the early days after the emergence of the neo-military group on the pretext of satisfying the national anticipation and of earning the people's trust through social clean-up, particularly by eliminating illegal acts and injustice. Samcheong Plan No. 5 was drafted by reviewing the National Land Construction Team installed right after the May 16 revolution. The planning work was led by Kim Man Ki, the head of the Subcommittee on Social Clean-up of the Emergency Committee for National Security Protection, beginning on July 10, 1980, while the actual plan was drafted by Seo Wan Soo, the assistant manager of the project, before it was implemented through Samcheong Training Camp or through an employment promotion project.

Implementation Process and Contents

The discussion herein of the implementation process and contents of the said policy will not deal with all the targets of the clean-up campaign but will be limited to Samcheong Training Camp, which focused on eradicating the social evils through the social clean-up by eliminating the thugs, who were explicitly singled out by Samcheong Plan No. 5 ("Eradication of Social Evils").

In accordance with the Special Measure for Eradicating the Social Evils announced on August 4, 1980, and Samcheong Plan No. 5 specified in Martial Law Decree No. 19, Samcheong Training Camp was established with the purpose of retraining and rehabilitating thugs and others. The groups that were singled out towards this end according to the martial law decree included (1) the perpetrators of violent crimes (including burglars, thieves, and pickpockets); (2) the perpetrators of threats, and imposters (including those who exploited ordinary citizens); and (3) those who

---

4) The ex-officio members of the Standing Committee assumed the positions of the 13 subcommittee heads. The 13 subcommittees were tasked to take charge of defense, legal affairs, foreign affairs, internal affairs, economy and science, treasury, culture and information, agriculture and fisheries, health and society, transportation, construction, commerce, industry and resources, and social clean-up, respectively.

5) Samcheong Plan No. 1 targeted those who amassed wealth illicitly. The key members of the previous administration, including Kim Jong Phil and Lee Hu Rak, were actually punished after being denounced as having amassed wealth through illicit means. Samcheong Plan No. 2 was aimed at eradicating the politicians during the Park Jung Hee administration, including those in the Republican Party. Samcheong Plan No. 3 was actually implemented to purge a total of 8,601 high-ranking officials in the legislative, judicial, and administrative branches of the government. Samcheong Plan No. 4 was aimed at identifying and purging the government of the public officials who did not reach 3rd grade, with the exception of the high-ranking officials who were the targets of Samcheong Plan No. 3.

muddled the healthy social climate (including smugglers, narcotics peddlers/pushers, and compulsive gamblers). According to the plan to eradicate the thugs announced on July 29, 1980 by the Emergency Committee for National Security Protection, the targets of the plan included people caught in the act of committing a crime, criminals who are feared to repeat their crimes, criminals condemned by residents as they are seen as having no hope of improving, and people living an unhealthy life. Based on such guidelines, the military and police jointly came up with a list of ex-convicts and thugs, totaling 20,022, who were to be rounded up in the first wave of the arrest campaign. Some 800,000 army and police troops were mobilized to arrest them. However, seeing that approximately 36% of all the arrested people were innocent citizens with no record of convicted crimes or with no clear association with habitual perpetrators of violent crimes (organized or habitual) mentioned earlier, it was obvious that not all those who were arrested were involved in organized crime or were habitual perpetrators of violent crimes.

Those who had been rounded up under such arrest campaign were reassigned to the clean-up camp called "Samcheong Training Camp" installed in 25 military bases in the front and rear parts of the country, with the exception of those who committed light crimes, or the patients. The training in such camps was implemented based on the militaristic organization, and the daily schedule of the inmates was no different from that in the regular military training or drills. At the end of the four-week clean-up training, the candidates were reclassified with A~D ratings respective to their performances, and those who received a B rating were made to engage in forced labor. Realistically, a total of 10,016 people were given ratings through such classification process, and they were mobilized to engage in diverse forms of forced labor in the military bases, including the construction of tank operation strongholds, the fortification of battle positions, and the construction of tactical roads, plazas, and communication cable facilities.

Performance and Assessment

Unlike the 5th Republic government's self-serving assessment of the Samcheong Training Camp policy, the policy's assessment by other groups was something else. First, as mentioned earlier, many of the citizens who had been arrested for having committed "social evils" or for being "thugs" did not really commit social evils and were not really thugs, as was later confirmed by countless testimonies (e.g., the Presidential Truth Commission on Suspicious Deaths, 2003). Furthermore, evidences suggesting that countless illegal elements were involved in the process of implementing the policy started to surface. The official report submitted by the National Assembly after the demise of the 5th Republic also confirmed that the campaign to eradicate the social evils through Samcheong Plan No. 5 violated the human rights of the people targeted by such campaign.

Given that input-oriented legitimacy signifies that the opinions and preferences of the people are reflected in the policy-making process in a democratic way, it can be concluded that the policy lacked input-oriented legitimacy in that, unlike the neo-military group's suggestion that the people recognized the urgency of eradication the social evils, it was unilaterally created by the neo-military group without ever considering the people's opinions.

Output-oriented legitimacy signifies that a specific policy is being implemented by following a democratic process, and that such policy implementation effectively produces the intended results.

In other words, it signifies the satisfaction level of the people who are the targets of the policy implementation. Based on this, it is well demonstrated by the selection and training process of the targets to be encamped in Samcheong Training Camp and by the fabrication of the protective custody provision, which was not in the original plan, that numerous human rights violations were committed and that the people's opinions were totally disregarded in the process of implementing the aforementioned policy. Likewise, it can be concluded that the policy also lacked output-oriented legitimacy.

3. Policy banning private education

Background

The 5th Republic banned private education practices because the country's private education or private lessons had been worsening for the past 20 years. The Emergency Committee for National Security Protection unveiled the "Policy Initiative to Normalize Education and to Resolve the Overheated Private Lessons," or the "July 30 Education Reform." The policy was aimed at resolving the diverse issues in the country's education sector, including the overheated private lessons fever.[6] According to one study at the time, approximately 15% of the students in the country were receiving some form of private lessons. However, private lessons were so widespread at that time that many evaluated such survey result to be an underestimation.

Likewise, amidst the growing popular worry that the "the overheated private lesson boom would lead to collapse the country," Chun Doo Hwan pledged to "eradicate the private lessons" when he was sworn in as president. The pledge was certainly driven by political motivation because the government needed to come up with some countermeasure to soften the mounting frustration of the people with the iron-fisted rule and the economic crisis. For this reason, the government stressed that the private lessons were undermining the desirable development of the national education system, and that socially, they were putting a heavy financial burden on households, thereby worsening the chronic disharmony among the social classes. Also, the government claimed that economically, the private lessons were a waste of valuable resources.

In an attempt to reduce the overall need for taking private lessons, the government embarked on a series of measures to ban private lessons, along with the dramatic expansion of the university entrance quota, which were summed up in the July 30 Education Reform[7] in 1980. The key issues covered by the July 30 Education Reform announced by the government included the downright banning of private lessons as well as the reform of university education aimed at

---

6) Some argue that the reform initiative was implemented in close relation with the political and social environment at the time. According to such observation, the 5th Republic government urgently needed to justify the legitimacy of the governing power group as they retained the characteristics of an authoritarian regime, which lacked political legitimacy. Therefore, the 5th Republic government came up with a proposal to ban private lessons as part of its initiatives to resolve the disharmony among the different social classes, thereby justifying the political legitimacy of the regime. Viewed from such perspective, some suggest that the banning of private lessons played the role of a political control mechanism.

7) The official title of the July 30 Education Reform was "Policy Initiative to Normalize School Education and to Resolve the Overheated Private Lesson Boom." The initiative banned private lessons, expanded the university entrance quota, and introduced the university graduate quota.

lowering the demand for private lessons. It can be said that the government intended to resolve the educational issues and to lower the education costs through such drastic measures.

Implementation System

The government commissioned the Emergency Committee for National Security Protection with the task of banning private lessons. Since the commission had no in-house research staff, however, it requested the Korean Educational Development Institute, which was controlled by the Ministry of Culture and Education, to come up with the measures that would eradicate the overheated private lesson boom. In accordance with the request, the institute prepared a policy study report aimed at eradicating the private lessons, which resulted in the July 30 Education Reform initiatives. Based on the initiative, a sweeping ban of private lessons was propagated, with the actual enforcement of the order upheld until April 12, 1981 with no legislative ground.

Faced with the criticism that the policy contained no clear guidelines, the government prepared the legal ground for regulating private lessons and punishing those who violate their prohibitions by enacting the Law on the Regulation of Private Lessons on April 13, 1981 in an attempt to fix the systemic issues experienced in the process of implementing the policy. Then, to ensure a more systematic policy implementation, the law was amended in April 1984 to supplement the banning of private lessons. The amendment included provisions redefining the private training school as a social educational institution, a greater emphasis on the social educational function of private training schools, the development of the existing private training schools through improvements in their guidance and supervision, and the assurance of the advancement of social education. The act on private training schools, namely the Act on the Establishment and Operation of Private Educational Institutes, went through two rounds of amendments during the incumbency of the Chun Doo Hwan administration.

Implementation Process and Contents

Since the report titled “A Study on the Possible Measures For Resolving the Overheated Private Lesson Boom and for Normalizing School Education,” which was prepared by the Korean Educational Development Institute and submitted to the Emergency Committee for National Security Protection, did not paint a good picture of the policy as a compelling policy alternative, the committee held a seminar titled “Measures for Resolving the Overheated Private Lesson Boom” that was participated by representatives of the Korean Educational Development Institute and the Ministry of Culture and Education as well as by university professors, high school principals, and parent representatives. After going through the aforementioned deliberation process, the July 30 Education Reform, officially titled “Initiative to Normalize Education and to Resolve the Overheated Private Lesson Boom,” was announced on July 30, 1980.

The policy banning private lessons was originally intended to first be applied to the social leaders, but it ended up being applied to all parents and students from the start, regardless of the social class to which they belonged. In addition, private tutorials by university students were also banned. In other words, the no-exception-allowed principle was established in relation to private lessons. The ban was also applied to the schoolteachers to enable them to earn the trust of their students and the latter's parents. Specifically, the schoolteachers were not allowed to offer any type of private lesson regardless of whether it was offered to help their students score better at the entrance exams or primarily for the payment or fee, except for the regular or supplemental classes offered by schools. Also, the offering of private lessons to the enrolled students was completely banned beginning on August 1 of the same year. The government added more details to the regulatory policy governing private lessons by defining private lessons as "all acts of instruction that offer lessons outside the realm of the school classes." In accordance with such directions, the official guidelines on the regulation of private lessons that were equipped with enforcement capacity were established as the first step in the implementation of the policy banning private lessons, with the aim of resolving the overheated private lesson boom. The government legalized the banning of private lessons in the next year (1981) and revised the policy again in 1984. As a result of such legislation, the regulation and punishment of the act of giving private lessons was finally legitimized. Additionally, the government pushed forward with a national campaign to root out private lessons. In an effort to ensure the strict enforcement of the policy banning private lessons, the Chun Doo Hwan administration cracked down on illegal private lessons by forming the "Private Lesson Control Squad."

What follows is a summary of the issues related with the banning of private lessons by the 5th Republic. The government intended to cool down the overheated private lesson boom with the July 30 Education Reform, and then tightened the banning of private lessons by enacting a series of laws governing private lessons. Such laws are summed up as follows: (1) the executives and employees of all state-owned corporations as well as public officials and leading social figures shall demonstrate leadership in prohibiting their children from taking private lessons; (2) all the teachers in the public and private schools are not permitted to give private lessons and should leave their school post if they violate such order; (3) private tutors and teachers should register in the governing authority without exception, and should pay the applicable taxes associated with their earnings from giving private lessons; and (4) private educational institutions are not permitted to offer classes to the enrolled students, and should they violate this regulation, their permission to operate shall be rescinded. To sum up, all acts of private education shall be regulated and performed under the watchful eyes of the government, and any violation of this order was considered a breach of law and was punished as such. As discussed above, the 5th Republic government ensured the enforcement of the said laws by establishing the Private Lesson Control Squad and by tightening the supervision of private educational institutions.

Performance and Assessment

The following are the positive accomplishments of the banning of private lessons: (1) the students participated in the school classes more proactively, and started to develop a self-learning attitude, or learning without the help of private lessons; (2) the parents and students began to pay more attention to and concentrate more on school education, and the changing climate in the public education institutions helped restore the deteriorating prestige of the teachers as they began to recognize their responsibilities and rewards as teachers; and (3) the households were able to reduce their deficits and lower their financial burden associated with education as they no longer spent for private lessons for their children.

The overall assessment of the banning of private lessons, however, was that the policy was swayed by public opinion and was a failure in that it was nothing but a shock therapy that reduced the private lesson fever ostensibly. It only restricted private lessons and did not show any interest in the resolution of the fundamental educational issue: the stabilization of public education. Despite all the efforts to crack down on and punish the persons responsible for illegal private lessons, the banning of private lessons only intensified the practice of secret and illegal private lessons[8] because no notable changes was observed in the national aspiration for enrolling in the top schools, the overall social environment, and the psychology of the parents and students.

The illegal and secret private lessons only grew in diversity, and as the government intensified its crackdown on them, the private lessons fees skyrocketed. As a result, only the children from the few privileged families could afford the exorbitant tuition, and word of such secret private lessons prevalent among the privileged families spread to the other classes alienated from such perks, thereby worsening the relative sense of deprivation of such students and parents. To conclude, contrary to the intention of the 5th Republic leadership to bridge the gap between the social classes, the initiative of banning private lessons ended up promoting the conflict even more.

In other words, the banning of private lessons by the Chun Doo Hwan administration lacked the democratic element and ended up spawning more negative outcomes educationally, economically, and socially. The variety of negative side effects of the all-out banning of private lessons made the Supreme Court reconsider the effectiveness of the ban. Eventually, the implementation of the policy started to become lax beginning in 1981, barely one year after its enforcement. Accordingly, the July 30 Education Reform was eventually either discarded or modified extensively.

4. Economic stabilization policy

The economic policy of the Chun Doo Hwan administration can be divided into the following three phases in view of the background of the implementation and the implementation system:

Phase 1: September 1980 to December 1981, the final 16 months of the period covered by the 4th Five-Year Economic Development Plan

Phase 2: 1982~1986, the five-year period covered by the 5th Five-Year Economic Development Plan

Phase 3: January 1987~February 1988, the first 14 months of the period covered by the 6th Five-Year Economic Development Plan

8) The various colloquial terms for illegal private lessons, such as "midnight private lessons," "second-house private lessons," "boarding house private lessons," "mobile private lessons," and "secret private lessons," were all used in the private circles during the time of the 5th Republic.

Background

Phase 1: Measures for economic stabilization implemented from September 1980 to December 1981

This period is marked by the political confusion in the early years of the 5th Republic, and the resulting loss of opportunity in terms of economic policy and economic trends. The 2nd international oil shock that hit the global economy from late 1979 until the end of 1980, and the resulting double whammy of high interest-high dollar value pushed the South Korean economy, which had traditionally been highly dependent on the global economic climate, further down the abyss, thereby subjecting it to triple distress: "low growth-high prices" and worsening of the international balance of trade.

Among the items making up the "triple distress," the high inflation rate (23% on average from 1980 to 1981) that plagued the South Korean economy then was second to the worst since the 1960s, almost as high as the 25% annual inflation rate recorded during the period of the 1st international oil shock (1974~1975).

Coupled with such internal factors, the "neo-protectionism in the international trade" that swept the world also dogged the South Korean economy. One of the most serious global developments that emerged during Phase 1 of the Chun Doo Hwan administration's economic policy was the advanced economies' "growing wariness of the semi-developed countries," with such advanced countries on high alert since the group of the "newly industrialized countries (NICs)" first appeared in the 1978 OECD Annual Report. Further, the value of the U.S. dollar began to appreciate after an extended period of weakness in the late 1970s due to the widening current account deficits, thereby posing a new threat to the international currency market. Amidst such developing situation, the international community began to pay attention to the foreign currency crisis of the developing countries, mainly that of the Latin American debtors, which again practically pushed South Korea, then laden with a nearly US$ 20 billion foreign debt burden, into its first foreign exchange crisis.

Phase 2: Stabilization policy during the period covered by the 5th Five-Year Economic and Social Development Plan (1982~1986)

The period covered by the 5th Five-Year Economic and Social Development Plan (1982~1986) was the phase when the problems that the country ran into during the period of its rapid growth were rectified, and when the country's economic policy started to put more weight on stability. In other words, the overall policy directions were refraining from pursuing excessively high growth and laying the foundation for the next economic leap forward based on a more stable and balanced economic and social foundation. Additionally, the issue of consumer protection emerged as the key economic agendum during the period covered by the 5th Five-Year Plan, and diverse changes in the economic environment, including the maintenance and streamlining of the greater Seoul area, rural development, establishment of a draft plan for the minimum wage system, introduction of the land transaction report system, and balanced growth across sectors and social classes, all of which aimed at stabilizing the overall economy, began to materialize.

Globally, although riddled with occasional risk factors, an increasingly positive environment started to form: the falling oil prices since 1982, the improved stabilization of the interest rates in the advanced economies in the wake of the falling U.S. interest rates beginning in 1982, and the downward trend in the value of the U.S. dollar beginning in late February 1982, all of which were extremely positive developments conducive to stabilizing the South Korean economy.

Phase 3: Stabilization policy from January 1987 to February 1988

Substantial changes transpired in the economic environment throughout 1987, which was the first year of the period covered by the 6th Five-Year Economic and Social Development Plan as well as the last year of the Chun Doo Hwan administration. The series of political events throughout the year, including the June 29 Declaration, the referendum in October of the same year to decide the adoption of the direct presidential election system, and the presidential election in December of the same year, triggered an outpouring of exercises of political freedom, which had been put under the lid for an extended time. Such development was more pronounced in the labor - management relationship, which had been heavily regulated and suppressed for various reasons. The nationwide spread of the labor - management dispute that began in late July 1987 soon developed into a social and political issue that was enough to deal a severe blow to the economy, far more serious than the initial conflict over the distribution of corporate income between management and labor. In response to such development, which was beyond its control, the Chun Doo Hwan administration focused on minimizing the impact of the political and social development on the economy in an effort to maintain economic stability as part of its economic policy.

Meanwhile, substantial financial development, enough to turn the trend in the international economy, was observed in the global economy: the joint February 1987 statement of six advanced economies that they would endeavor to stabilize their exchange rates; the coordinated interest rate cuts of key European countries in March; the emergency economic package from Japan in May; the Black Monday Wall Street stock market crash in October; and the adoption by 11 Latin American states of the Acapulco Declaration in November.

Implementation System

Phase 1: Stabilization policy from September 1980 to December 1981

The economic policy during this period was mainly focused on completing the 4th Five-Year Economic Development Plan and overcoming the unanticipated 2nd international oil shock and the aftershock left by the massive U.S. fiscal deficits. Specifically, the monetary policy was centered on the low interest rate policy aimed to respond to the high global interest rates caused by the deliberate fiscal deficit policy that Washington initiated in an attempt to overcome the 2nd international oil shock, as well as on the long-term plan to supply homes and the accelerated disposal of real estate in an effort to cool down the overheated speculative investments on homes and lands. The policy of developing the heavy chemical industries, which was pushed forward by the Park Jung Hee administration during the period covered by the 4th Five-Year Economic Development Plan, can be said to have met the critical point in terms of its effectiveness due to the rising interest burden from foreign loans and the rapid drop in the operation rate of related facilities. The successful handling of such challenges emerged as another key issue in the laundry list of the Chun Doo Hwan administration.

Responding to such macroeconomic development challenges, the Chun Doo Hwan administration pushed forward with a bold restructuring policy aimed at boosting the efficiency of the heavy chemical industries, which was the key policy focus of the previous government. Along with this policy, the administration also pushed forward with other policies designed to open the national economy and to improve the country's efficiency on the foundation of economic stabilization as part of the bigger policy package aimed at overcoming the foreign exchange crisis for the first time since the period covered by the 1st Five-Year Economic Development Plan.

Phase 2: Stabilization policy from 1982 to 1986 (the period covered by the 5th Five-Year Plan)

During Phase 2 of the Chun Doo Hwan administration's economic policy, the administration focused on the faithful implementation of the 5th Five-Year Economic and Social Development Plan, which it had established. The primary characteristic of the plan was that it was an "economic and social development plan," a shift intended to give greater policy consideration to the social sector that received less attention from the previous administrations. To conclude, the objectives of the economic policy of the Chun Doo Hwan administration were economic stabilization, balanced development of the economy and society, activation of the market economy, fostering of the autonomy of the private sector, and improvement of the labor - management relations. The administration achieved intensive growth through the realization of these objectives.

Phase 3: Stabilization policy from January 1987 to February 1988

The key characteristic of the economic policy of the Chun Doo Hwan administration can be summed up as a policy that inherits the economic development pattern of the Park Jung Hee administration on the condition that it would evolve into a sustainable form. Such characteristic was applied to the economic policy that was implemented during the so-called "Phase 3" of the incumbency of the Chun Doo Hwan administration.

Table 3-1. Key characteristics of the 6th Five-Year Economic and Social Development Plan

Directions and Objectives of the Plan	Development Strategy	Average Annual Growth Rate	Key Tasks
• Efficiency, equality, and welfare • Development of economic and social institutions and advancement of the socioeconomic order • Improvement of the industrial structure • Technology-based national development • Regional equality	• Industrial restructuring and advancement • Fostering of autonomy and competition • Open and internationalized economy • Balanced growth	7.8%	• Appropriate level of growth and stabilization of prices • Improvement of the international balance of trade and lowering of the burden of foreign loans • Industrial restructuring and technological advancement • Regional balance and rural development • Improved welfare level • Establishment of economic order in the market • Re-establishment of government functions

Therefore, the 6th Five-Year Economic and Social Development Plan put emphasis on the following issues more systematically and in more diverse forms: stability, appropriate level of growth, balance, efficiency, expansion of welfare benefits, improvement of the international balance of payments, establishment of an order based on the market economy, technology advancement, and re-establishment of government functions. Such policy directions are summed up in the following table.

Implementation Process and Contents

Phase 1: Stabilization policy from September 1980 to December 1981

The speculative investment in real estate rose to an unprecedented level during the first half of the period covered by 4th Five-Year Economic and Social Development Plan, due to the growing liquidity and unstable price trend in the domestic market, which was triggered by the exploding demands associated with the development of the heavy and chemical industries. Such economic instability eventually led to social instability by hindering the mass supply of homes to the low-income classes and by worsening the redistribution of the gross income, thereby prompting the government to make two rounds of announcements on the "pending tasks and counter-measures" in June and September 1980, respectively, when the 2nd international oil shock was unfolding at full speed. Specifically, the "June 5 Measure" announced on June 5, 1980, which focused on preventing the further worsening of the "economic and social instability" that may have been arising due to the widespread social instability observed in April and May 1980, dealt with the following issues: employment and stabilization of the everyday life of the people, measures to prevent the further worsening of the international balance of trade, provision of support to businesses and development of their growth potential, and rationalization of corporate management practices.

The difficulties faced by the South Korean economy were obvious across the key domains: money supply, finance, interest rate, and foreign exchange. In such a difficult circumstance, the size and interest rate determined for the currency stabilization bonds issued by the Bank of Korea to control the money supply played the key role in maintaining the country's fiscal stability. In terms of the financial policy, the principal banking institution system introduced in June 1976 under the formal leadership of the Korea Fiscal Syndicate was taking root after a series of modifications and complementary measures. In terms of the changes in the interest rate policy, the period was marked by a drastic rise in interest rates in January 1980 and by overall interest cuts during the period from June 1989 to February 1981. Meanwhile, the core of the foreign exchange policy during the period can be summed up as the relaxation of the foreign currency control, the expansion of the forward exchange market system, and the revamp of the foreign exchange system. A more relaxed control of the foreign currency was applied during the second half of the 1981 fiscal year, with the initial impact of the 2nd international oil shock dissipating slowly; the measure to improve the foreign currency management system enforced in July 1981 included the simplification of the certification of payment process for international trade, the relaxation of the requirements for overseas investments, the expansion of the candidate industries for investment, the expansion of the local foreign currency reserves of the construction companies engaging in overseas projects, and the allowing of the overseas branch offices to acquire business-use real estate.

Another notable feature of the 4th Five-Year Economic and Social Development Plan was that the heavy chemical industry policy began to be implemented in earnest. Specifically, the heavy chemical industry investment adjustment policy was implemented more intensively while many key investment projects in the area of heavy chemical industries started to come to fruition, with the key background of such policy initiatives being the stabilization of prices. The investment adjustment was aimed at overcoming the limitations of the policy funds that were allocated for the investment in the heavy chemical industries in early 1979, during the 2nd international oil shock, and for the vicious cycle of the fiscal support pegged on the inflation-adjusted method. The measure was introduced in accordance with the objective of the policy initiative to allocate the remaining surplus funds to the area of daily necessities after the adjustment.

Also notable was that the policies governing the home and real estate issue were implemented in relatively more diverse forms. Specifically, faced with the serious contraction of the economy, the government pushed forward with the policy of promoting the simultaneous boom of the real estate and construction businesses as part of the overall stimulus package. On November 8, 1980, the government announced the comprehensive stimulus package that included the following key measures: interest rate cuts and expansion of business operation loans, special consumption tax rate cut and expansion of the financing for the banking consumers, and the purchase of corporate lands by Korea Land Development Corporation, which coincided with the announcement of the Long-Term Home Building Plan (November 1980) by the Ministry of Construction, and the Policy to Boost the Real Estate Businesses (December 1980) by the Ministry of Treasury, with its key component being the transfer income tax cuts and the depreciation of the special value-added tax rate cuts.

Phase 2: Stabilization policy during the period covered by the 5th Five-Year Plan (1982~1986)

The economic policy during the period covered by the 5th Five-Year Plan was initially implemented with the economic stimulus package through the firm establishment of stabilized price trends and the fostering of exports and investment. A variety of measures were taken in the first half of 1982, the first year of the plan, including the Directions for the Impending Economic Measures (January 14 measure), the Impending Economic Measures (May 18 measure), and the Measure to Boost the Economy through Accelerated Investment. The three impending economic measures can be summed up as the activation and advancement of the overall economy, with the details being categorized into the sectors shown below.

The key issues in the money supply policy included the policies governing the money supply management; the policies governing the currency stabilization bonds; the policies governing the financing for small businesses; the policies related with export financing, credit cards, and certificates of deposit; and the policies governing the target organizations of the open market. In addition, the government opened the "era of credit cards" by granting credit card business permission to the top five commercial banks, with the actual business operation commenced in the June of the next year, coinciding with the start of the 5th Five-Year Plan.

As for the credit line control policy, in the wake of the severe damages inflicted on the public reputation of the banks by the illegal transactions of bogus private loans (known as the "Myung

Sung Group scandal" in private circles) for over four years, from April 1979 to August 1983, the government enforced the Credit Management Improvement Measure in March 1985. In addition, the government revised the Regulations on the Credit Management of Financial Institutions (February 1985), through which it reduced the scope of regulated businesses with regard to the credit line from "affiliated companies with combined credit loans of over KRW 20 billion and from non-affiliated companies with combined credit loans of over KRW 10 billion or a total invested capital of over KRW 5 billion" down to affiliated companies with a combined total credit of over KRW 100 billion, while at the same time allowing the selection of the principal banking institution by individual company, and consolidating the multiple credit line management indices into the ratio of owner's equity.

The changes in the foreign currency management included the relaxation of the concentrated foreign currency management rule from the selling-based concentration system to the selling- or deposit-based concentration system. What is notable with regard to the extending/receiving of foreign currency credit is that the base rate previously specified by the Minister of Treasury was abolished and was replaced with the new system, in which the foreign exchange bank could determine the interest rate independently within the limits of the maximum allowable interest rate specified by the Bank of Korea. The series of measures aimed at relaxing the foreign currency control were interpreted to be part of the money supply and credit line management policy aimed at suppressing the increased issue of currency in the foreign sector, which was caused by the growing surplus in the international balance of trade. Meanwhile, the foreign exchange rate policy adopted in 1981 shows that the administration strove to utilize the aforementioned foreign exchange rate institutions "strategically" by considering the impact of the foreign exchange rate on the international balance of trade, on the current account, and on the domestic prices.

The policy of import liberalization continued to be implemented during the period covered by 5th Five-Year Plan, an inevitable measure given that the international trade environment put growing pressure on Seoul to adopt a more flexible import policy. The phased liberalization of imports was pursued in accordance with the Proposal for the Phased Liberalization of Imports (February 1983), with its key contents shown in the table below. Additionally, the government switched the custom tariff system from the accumulative tariff rates in the past to uniform tariff rates, followed by the phased lowering of the custom tariff rates by way of the custom tariff forecast system, all of which were aimed at stabilizing the domestic prices.

What is notable about the various taxation policies that were implemented during the period covered by the 5th Five-Year Plan is the extension of the applicable period and the expansion of the scope of the laws regulating tax breaks. The special act on the tax exemption, which was

Table 3-2. Proposal for the Phased Liberalization of Imports

Phase	Period	Target of Liberalization
Phase 1	1983~1985	Products with a competitive advantage and those with a competitive disadvantage
Phase 2	1986~1987	Products with a relative comparative advantage and other items required to stabilize the everyday lives of the people
Phase 3	1988~	All products, with the exception of those produced by the strategic industry

Source: Korea Development Institute (1995), The Half Century of the Korean Economy: Policy Source Book.

temporarily enforced until the end of 1986, was extended by five more years to ensure continued support during the period covered by the 6th Five-Year Plan. Such extension was an attempt to provide tax-related support to the administration's key policy initiatives, including the establishment of the foundation for small startups, the training of engineers and technicians, the construction of rental houses, the balanced development of urban and rural areas, the fostering of overseas industries, and the execution of Olympic projects.

Diverse policies to support the agricultural, dairy, and fisheries industries (henceforth, "agricultural policies") were also established. The agricultural policy mainly consisted of measures to support the development of vocational jobs; the improvement of the distribution of agricultural, dairy, and fisheries products; and the regional development. Specifically, those measures were again consolidated into the Comprehensive Measure for Rural Development (March 1986) in the last year of the period covered by the 5th Five-Year Plan. In the distribution sector, the Measure to Strengthen the Information Network on the Distribution of Agricultural and Dairy Products (March 1983) was established to push forward with the computerization of distribution-related data. Afterwards, in accordance with the Detailed Implementation Plan to Improve the Distribution Structure of Agricultural and Fisheries Products (February 1984), a wholesale market was built in Seoul, Daejeon, Daegu, Busan, Gwangju, and Incheon.

Phase 3: Stabilization policy from January 1987 to February 1988

Due to the rapid increase of currency in the overseas sector, caused by the turning of overall balance of payments to surplus from deficit, the annual growth rate of the total currency amount (M2) hovered at around 19% on average from 1986 to 1987. This was mainly due to the surplus recorded in the current account balance, which again resulted in an explosive increase of the money supply. Such high growth rate in the money supply during the period when both the current account balance and the overall balance of payments were showing a surplus meant that the money supply via the overseas segment could not be sufficiently clawed back or neutralized within a short time. This implied that the authority governing the money supply had to grapple with the emergency situation because the surplus recorded in the current account balance and overall balance of payments was never anticipated, and the size of the surplus was far greater than the country's economic size at the time could handle. Therefore, the authority governing the monetary policy continued to take diverse measures to suppress the increased issue of currency in the overseas sector, including suppressing the lining up of commercial loans and annually paid incomes, reducing the SWAP in the local branches of foreign banks, and suppressing the trade financing and reducing the facility financing for the export industries.

The key contents of the policy established to support the rural economy included the "Measure to Lighten the Debt Burdens of Farming and Fishing Towns" (March 1987) and the "Comprehensive Plan to Activate the Rural Economy" (December 1987). Towards these ends, the policy of easing the actual debt burdens of the rural and fishing towns was prepared to cope with the situation in which the debt repayment capability of the farming and fishing towns was deteriorating every year. The detailed measures included the provision of loans to refinance the private loans, the refinancing of the long-term loans offered to the low-income rural families with low-interest loans, and the interest rate cuts of the farming and fishery loans.

The rationalization of the industrial structure was also one of the key policy objectives at the time. In 1986, a total of 56 companies was restructured or liquidated in an attempt to eliminate the marginal businesses (48 companies were designated as targets for management rationalization, 6 companies were acquired by a third party, and 2 companies were liquidated). Moreover, the industrial rationalization measure announced in 1987, following the resolution by the Industrial Policy Deliberation Committee, laid out the guideline that industry-wide rationalization shall be applied to the unpromising industries struggling with slumping sales and that those companies with no hope of a management turnaround despite such rationalization measure shall be liquidated in accordance with the procedure applied to insolvent enterprises.

The Measure to Realize the Early Establishment of Universal Healthcare and Medical Insurance Benefits (December 1987) contains the ambitious healthcare initiatives that the administration adopted near the end of its incumbency to improve the medical welfare benefits of the people. The policy was aimed at boosting the percentage of people covered by medical insurance from 58.9% of the total population as of June 1987 to 100% by 1989. The proposal included the establishment of a healthcare service foundation in the rural and fishing towns, the improvement of the medical charge system, and the establishment of the medical service delivery system.

As the international balance of trade and the current account reached the highest levels in the history of South Korea in 1987, the government's trade and foreign loan inducement policy focused on lowering the tariffs slapped on imported goods, expanding the self-regulation of exports and the scope of the target industries open to unrestricted foreign investment. The country saw marked improvements in the liberalization of imports in 1987, with five rounds of custom tariff cuts implemented. The increased supply of imported goods through the expanded liberalization of imports, and the falling prices of imported goods as a result of the tariff cuts, can be understood as being part of the policy initiatives aimed at stabilizing the prices and the overall economy.

Performance and Assessment

Phase 1: Stabilization policy from September 1980 to December 1981

The Phase 1 economic policy of the Chun Doo Hwan administration mainly aimed at completing the 4th Five-Year Economic Development Plan, which was started by the previous administration, and at overcoming the aftereffects of the 2nd international oil shock. The Phase 1 financial policy was centered on the low-interest policy to cope with the unusually high global interest rates, while high priority was given to calming down the speculative investments on houses and lands. Another notable characteristic of the Phase 1 economic policy implemented by the administration is that policies aimed at opening the national economy and improving the operational efficiency to overcome the practical foreign currency crisis caused by the worsening international balance of trade and the ballooning foreign debts were pushed forward with unprecedented administrative determination.

In an attempt to improve the operational efficiency, the Chun Doo Hwan administration pushed forward with the bold restructuring of the heavy chemical industries that were built during the incumbency of the Park Jung Hee administration. Recorded as the third massive-scale industrial structuring since the restructuring of insolvent companies from the late 1960s to the early 1970s and the restructuring of the construction industry in the mid-1970s, it was the largest in terms of scale and the related industrial sectors. Although the policies that the Chun Doo Hwan administration adopted in an effort to stabilize the economy largely failed to push down the prices significantly due to the massive aftereffect, beyond the expectations, of the 2nd international oil shock, they can still be evaluated highly for their strategic significance in view of the fact that the administration exerted diverse policy-level efforts to prevent extreme development and to take advantage of the economic crisis to strengthen the structural make-up of the economy.

Phase 2: Stabilization policy from 1982 to 1986 (the period covered by the 5th Five-Year Plan)

The Chun Doo Hwan administration concentrated on the faithful implementation of the 5th Five-Year Economic and Social Development Plan that it directly drafted during Phase 2 of its incumbency. The key characteristic of the administration's economic development plan is that it evolved from the previous "economic development plan" into an "Economic and Social development plan" as a result of the administration's attempt to pay more policy-level attention to the social sectors that were relegated to the sidelines by the earlier administrations. The move is significant in that it was an inevitable change of the overall direction aimed at a mutually beneficial effect between the two sectors considering the interlocking mechanism between the economic and social phenomena.

The second characteristic of the administration's economic development plan is that it aimed to eliminate the various negative side effects accumulated during the incumbency of the Park Jung Hee administration, to construct a more rational and efficient economic system and ensure balance and equity between the different regions and industrial sectors, and to foster the autonomy of the private sector and expand the market function. To sum up, the key direction of the economic policy of the Chun Doo Hwan administration was to inherit and improve the economic development pattern of the Park Jung Hee administration, and to turn it into a more sustainable form.

The economic policy during this period can be given positive ratings in that the "high prices-low growth" pattern in the past was changed to a "low prices-high growth" pattern while achieving a "3% inflation rate" in the process. The key drivers behind such positive achievements remained active until 1987, the first year of the period covered by the 6th Economic and Social Development Plan, thereby helping the country crawl out of the chronic inflation that dogged its economy. It is believed that the government's comprehensive money supply and credit line management policy, coupled with the restructuring of the heavy chemical industries, measures to promote the growth of the rural economy and small enterprises, and the stabilization of the management-labor relations and liberalization of imports, played the decisive role in achieving such accomplishments.

What should not be overlooked when evaluating the successful policy implementation of the Chun Doo Hwan administration during Phase 2 of its incumbency, however, is the impact that the so-called "three lows" had on the South Korean economy. While the full-fledged falling of the interest rates in the global financial market practically solved the foreign currency issue of the country, which was practically on the verge of a foreign currency crisis, the falling oil prices helped the country improve the international balance of trade and stabilize the prices in the domestic market. Specifically, the appreciation of the value of the South Korean Won further solidified the downward trend of the domestic prices. To conclude, the successful policy implementation during this period can be largely attributed to external variables; therefore, had any of these factors changed direction, the stability of the domestic price level could have been shattered at any moment. For this reason, the stabilization of prices and the so-called "three lows" that characterize the booming conditions of the country's internal foundation that were achieved in the 1984 fiscal year by the administration cannot be concluded to be robust enough to be compared with the improvement recorded in the key economy indicators.

Phase 3: Stabilization policy from January 1987 to February 1988

The 6th Five-Year Economic and Social Development Plan took into account some long-term goals that could not possibly be expected to be accomplished by the Chun Doo Hwan administration. Various additional goals were included in the plan, which assumed more systematic and diverse forms compared to the 5th Five-Year Plan, including economic stability, an appropriate level of growth, balance, efficiency, improved welfare provision, improvement of the international balance of trade, establishment of an order based on the market economy, technology improvement, and re-establishment of government functions. It can be concluded that the economic policy of the administration during the first year of the period covered by the 6th Five-Year Economic and Social Development Plan contained extremely proactive economic aspects and exerted a substantial influence on the economic policy of the succeeding Roh Tae Woo administration. The "single-digit inflation rate" of the Chun Doo Hwan administration was carried on in the 1987 fiscal year, thereby emphasizing the South Korean economy's complete escape from chronic inflation.

The stable prices that were maintained throughout 1987 can be largely attributed to the Chun Doo Hwan administration's continuous and stable implementation of price stabilization policies throughout the seven years since 1980. Also, other factors such as falling international oil prices and interest rates since 1980 and the sharp appreciation of the South Korean Won due to the mounting international pressure in the wake of the depreciation of the value of the U.S. dollar contributed to the stable prices. In addition, the country was able to endure the dramatic appreciation of the value of the South Korean Won because the import prices, one of the top three deciding factors of the domestic prices, was kept at 10.9% along with the capacity utilization rate of the manufacturing sector and the unit labor cost, a sharp contrast to the situation that was observed during the period after 1988.

5. Successful bid for the 1986 Seoul Asian Games and 1988 Seoul Olympic Games

Background

As the race to host the Seoul Olympic Games started during the incumbency of the Park Jung Hee administration, with many related achievements accomplished in the same period, it would be a stretch to claim that the successful bid for the Games is solely attributable to the Chun Doo Hwan administration. Still, it can be regarded as the policy of the Chun Doo Hwan administration as such administration dealt with the core part of the bidding process.

The Park Jung Hee administration's efforts to bid for the Olympic Games was met with vehement opposition from the officials of Seoul City, which was to host the Games, and from the economic ministers, after the October 26, 1979 incident. President Chun Doo Hwan's confirmation of his desire to bid for the Games, however, triggered a powerful drive to push forward with the bid efforts. On September 4, 1981, the government convened an emergency meeting to decide whether to bid for the Games, and an affirmative decision was arrived at. The administration successfully bid for the Games, beating Nagoya with 52 : 27 votes in the IOC General Assembly held on September 30, 1981. The successful bid for the Games can be attributed to the following factors, among others: the emergence of Juan A. Samaranch, the reformist chairman of IOC; the state-centric bid for the Games, which mobilized the full capabilities of the country; and the passionate bidding activities of the chairmen of large South Korean conglomerates, who usually chaired various international sports federations unlike those chaired by their Japanese counterparts, the most powerful bid participants.

At the time when the country's bid for the Games was successfully concluded, the South Korean society was mired in a political quagmire due to the dubious legitimacy of the Chun Doo Hwan administration. The political squabble that started with the attacks on the hosting of the Games by the opposition leaders had grown into a full-force gale by the time the June 10 democratic uprising swept across the country, just one year before the opening of the Games. Unable to launch an armed crackdown on the protest in the city that was to host the Olympics within just one year, the government came up with a solution in the form of the June 29 Declaration for Democratization in view of the high stakes involved in the stabilization of the political situation, the recovery of its legitimacy, and the successful hosting of the Olympics. Such solution enabled the government to push forward with a full-scale campaign for the successful hosting of the Olympics. The declaration allowed the South Korean voters to elect the president in the direct presidential election. Roh Tae Woo, the supreme representative of the ruling Democratic Justice Party, who orchestrated the June 29 Declaration, and the ruling party candidate emerged victorious in the election held in the same year. Likewise, the South Korean people began to feel the impact of the democratization deep in their skin while their enthusiasm for the Olympic Games started to heat up, riding the crest of the democratization fever.

Internationally, the Seoul Olympic Games deserves to be highlighted from the perspective of the new détente. During the years leading up to the Seoul Olympic Games, the rivalry between the free world and the Socialist bloc was intensifying, thereby politicizing the Olympics to new heights ever since the invasion of Afghanistan by the Soviet Union. The leaders of the two blocs, who were seeking an opportunity to break the political gridlock, hoped to make some sweeping turnaround in the wake of the Seoul Olympic Games. In 1985, Mikhail Gorbachev, the new secretary-general of the Communist Party of the Soviet Union, who emerged as the leading figure in international politics by pushing forward with the Perestroika and the glasnost policy, started to promote a conciliatory mood with U.S. President Ronald Reagan. As one news commentary pointed out, "the revolution led by Mikhail Gorbachev triggered a political revolution in the Western corner of the Eurasian continent while its butterfly effect rippled through the continent until the Seoul Olympics, thereby turning the Games to a venue for global harmony and reconciliation between the East and West." To sum up, the world opened the floodgate for the new détente to flourish with the Seoul Olympic Games.

Implementation System

The government formed a full-scale national support system unprecedented in scale. The government organized a state-level implementation system and provided policy-level support. It established not only an organization that would orchestrate such support activities but also the Ministry of Sports that was separate from the Seoul Olympic Organizing Committee, which was to be responsible for the official operation and organization of the Games. It, also, installed a supporting committee composed of the cabinet members, including the Prime Minister.

The 1988 Seoul Olympic Organizing Committee, which was inaugurated on November 2, 1981 with a secretary general, two vice secretary generals, one planning office, and a 36-strong staff, was soon consolidated with the Seoul Asian Games Organizing Committee in February 1983, thereby enabling the unified handling of the two games by a single organization. After the successful completion of the 1986 Seoul Asian games, the organizing committee was expanded over several rounds of reshufflings, with the addition of functions, as necessary, before it was changed to a system that was fully ready to implement the operation of the July 1988 Olympic Games. Meanwhile, while maintaining a collaborative relationship with the IOC, various international sports federations, and the NOC, the Seoul Olympic Organizing Committee

Figure 3–1. Organization of the Seoul Olympic Organizing Committee

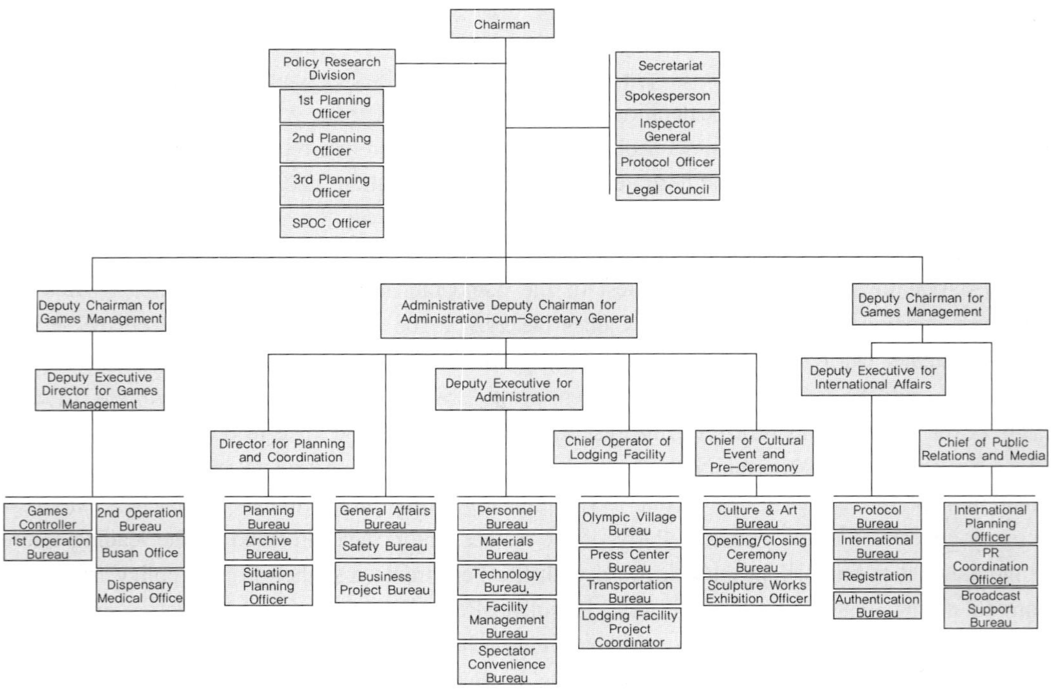

Source: Seoul Olympic Organizing Committee (1990a: 1988).

established an organic collaborative system with diverse administrative ministries, including the Ministry of Sports, the Government Support Committee, the Korea Olympic Committee, the Seoul Municipal Government, and the Pan-National Central Olympic Promotion Council to develop an implementation plan that would help the committee to execute the entire array of projects in a phased manner.

The Ministry of Sports was newly established and designated as the primary government authority that was to support the two games after the successful bidding for the Seoul Olympic Games and the 10th Asian Games in 1986. The Ministry of Sports, which was inaugurated with 1 office, 3 bureaus, 10 departments, and 3 officers, soon went through several rounds of partial organizational reshuffling. The ministry's responsibilities touched on diverse areas, including the mobilization of nationwide capabilities, the overall coordination of the related projects, the efficient preparation of the two games, the establishment of short-and long-term plans for national sports, the identification and training of top athletes, and the implementation of sports promotion projects. Furthermore, the Ministry of Sports supported the construction of various athletic facilities designed with the exact specifications of the matching sport, including the Jamshil Olympic Stadium, as well as other facilities for varying sports, including gymnastics, fencing, swimming, tennis, and cycling. The ministry also push forward with overall sports promotion activities, including the doubling of the pension paid to the athletes. With regard to the government-wide support initiative, the government installed the Government Support Committee on December 8, which was given the role of establishing a wide-ranging support apparatus, including the review and adjustment of the key policies related to the games as well as administrative and fiscal support to the organizing committee. The Government Support Committee was chaired by the Prime Minister, with its membership held by the key government officials, including the Minister of the Economic Planning Board and the Minister of Sports (each in the capacity of vice chairman), all the members of the cabinet, the mayor of Seoul City, the Chief Presidential Secretary, the head of the Agency for National Security Planning, the head of the Office of Legislation, and the head of the Ministry of Patriots and Veterans Affairs.

Meanwhile, the National Assembly formed a special committee aimed at supporting the preparation of the Olympic Games, with its members elected from the standing committees in the National Assembly related with the Olympics. The special committee provided legislative support for the games by enacting and amending the related laws. The Seoul Olympic Games Organizing Committee Support Act promulgated on December 31, 1981 by the special committee was not just aimed at supporting the Organizing Committee at the level of the National Assembly but had a characteristic of a nationwide support mechanism: the Organizing Committee retained the authority to request the municipal governments to provide administrative and fiscal support as well as to dispatch public servants and top talents from corporations, and other social organizations.

Implementation Process and Contents

For the purpose of this discussion, the projects related to the hosting of the Seoul Olympic Games were classified based on the preparation stages, with the key projects implemented in each phase classified based on the matching area. The preparation process was divided into the following four phases: the phase from the confirmation of the successful bid for the Olympic

Games until the foundation building for the preparation of the basic plan, the full-fledged preparation phase from the preparation for the participation in the Los Angeles Summer Olympics until the opening of the Seoul Asian Games, the final preparation phase from the hosting of the Seoul Asian Games until the time before the opening of the Seoul Olympic Games, and the final phase covering the hosting of the Seoul Olympic Games and the post-Olympics management.

Phase 1. Foundation Building (November 1981 ~ December 1983): Confirmation of the successful bid for the Seoul Olympics to preparation of the basic plan

In the basic preparatory stage for the Seoul Olympic Games, projects focused on establishing the preparatory infrastructure for the games, such as the inauguration of the Organizing Committee, the establishment of the project implementation system, the legislation of the Seoul Olympics Support Act, the establishment of the consolidated plan for the games preparation, the operation of the games organization, and the construction of the games facility, were implemented. The projects that were implemented during the preparatory phase were very important because the country had no previous experience of hosting a mega sports event.

The games organizations were adjusted and expanded in pace with the progress of the project implementation. The Seoul Olympic Organizing Committee, the key organization that was to prepare for the games, elected Kim Yong Shik, then the president of Korea Red Cross, as the first chairperson, with its board members consisting of 4 deputy chairmen, 5 executive committee members, and 19 members, and Lee Won Kyung, the standing advisor to the Korean Olympic Committee, as the Secretary General of the Committee. Meanwhile, the National Assembly formed a special committee aimed at providing parliamentary support for the Seoul Olympic Games in its 108th regular session, followed by its legislation in December of the same year of the Seoul Olympic Games Support Committee Regulation as Presidential Decree No. 10640, and the formation of the Government Support Committee chaired by the Prime Minister. The IOC was notified of the official establishment of the Seoul Olympic Games Organizing Committee, which was to perform the tasks associated with the Seoul Olympic Games, as an implementing institution.

Phase 2. Full-Fledged Implementation (January 1984 ~ August 1986): Preparation for participation in the Los Angeles Summer Olympic Games to the period before the opening of the Seoul Asian Games

As part of the full-fledged project implementation by area, the projects associated with the games preparation were carried out in earnest, including the focused implementation of the investment projects, such as the venue facilities, proactive overseas and domestic publicity, interim check in view of the experiences with the 1984 Los Angeles Summer Olympic Games, preparatory work for the hosting of the 1986 Seoul Asian Games, and active development of profit-making businesses.

The Organizing Committee was reshuffled through expansion as it entered the full-fledged implementation phase. The secretariat organization of the Organizing Committee was revamped to a new structure, staffed with a total of 456 members and composed of 3 deputy heads of department, 1 office, 1 spokesperson, 10 bureaus, 33 departments, and 7 officers. Moreover, the corporate leaders who headed the various sports associations sent their senior executives and junior staff members to the Organizing Committee, and they continued to provide their services to the committee until the closing of the Olympic Games. The committee accelerated the speed of the games preparation even more with Park Se Jik, the Minister of Sports, taking office (May 1985) in the Seoul Asian Games and the Seoul Olympic Games Organizing Committee. The executive and general committees of the Seoul Olympic Games Organizing Committee decided to hold the Seoul Olympic Games from September 17 to October 2, 1988 and submitted their decision to the 88th IOC General Assembly (July 1984) held in Los Angeles, where it was later confirmed through its ratification by the General Assembly.

The construction of most of the venue facilities was completed during the full-fledged preparatory stage, and the facilities were fully ready for use way before the Seoul Asian Games and the Pre-Olympics, thereby allowing the committee to check the facility operation status and to supplement any missing elements (if any) for the perfect construction of the facilities. A groundbreaking ceremony was held for the construction of the Olympic Park (April 1984) on the piece of land that was once occupied by the National Stadium, located in Songpa-gu, Seoul, followed by the commencement of the Seoul Equestrian Park construction project at the lot located in Gwacheon-si, Gyeonggi Province by Korea Racing Authority, as a private capital inducement project. The construction of the Olympic Park, which housed six stadiums, one each for cycling, fencing, gymnastics, weightlifting, swimming, and tennis, and of the 17-story (2 basement floors, 15 ground floors) Olympic Hall and other park facilities, including an artificial lake, a green area, and an open-air arena, was completed on May 28, 1986. In June of the same year, the construction of the Han River Rowing and Canoe Race Track, which can accommodate up to 25,000 spectators, was completed in Misa-ri, Gyeonggi Province, followed by the completion of Seoul National University Gymnasium, which was to be used as the venue of the Olympic table tennis games, and Hanyang University Gymnasium, which was to be used as the venue of the Olympic volleyball games.

Phase 3. Final Preparation (September 1986 ~ July 1988): Hosting of the Seoul Asian Games to the period before the opening of the Seoul Olympic Games

The comprehensive inspection phase was aimed at checking the final preparedness for the games by maintaining and strengthening the games operation organization through an analysis of the preparation status and the resolution of any problem found in the process and by concentrating all the government resources on the preparations for the games. During the inspection phase, the Olympic Village and the main press center were constructed, along with the final check-up of numerous facilities, equipment, and operating staffs. Moreover, after the successful completion of the Seoul Asian Games, the secretariat of the Organizing Committee was reshuffled to a new structure that was headed by the secretary general and that was made up of 3 deputy heads of department, 2 heads of offices, 1 spokesperson, 1 inspector-general, 1 mediator, 1 branch office, 23 bureaus, 74 departments, and 24 officers. In the final preparation phase, numerous activities were implemented for the successful operation of the Seoul Olympic Games, based on the operational experiences gained from running the 10th Seoul Asian Games.

About one year before the opening of the Olympic Games, the Pre-Olympic was held for each sport in an attempt to perform a pilot test on the venue facilities and operation. First, the hosting of the World Junior Modern Pentathlon Competition in September 1987 was held in the Seoul

Equestrian Park and was participated in by over 110 athletes. Then, the International Yacht Racing was held in the Busan Yacht Racing Venue and was participated in by 498 athletes hailing from 29 countries. The International Cycling Race was held in the cycle racing track located in the Olympic Park, and was participated in by 136 athletes hailing from 16 countries, followed by the Seoul International Canoe Race held in the Han River Rowing and Canoe Track, participated in by 297 athletes hailing from 27 countries.

Phase 4. The Games and After (August 1988 ~ June 1989): Hosting of the Seoul Olympic Games and post-Olympic management

Numerous activities were implemented by the Organizing Committee during the final phase in an effort to ensure the successful hosting of the Seoul Olympic Games by boosting the enthusiasm and excitement of all the concerned organizations and all the South Koreans. First, an inauguration ceremony for the volunteer translators consisting of overseas South Korean residents was held at the Olympic Park, participated by over 400 people, including the volunteer translators, the executives of the Organizing Committee, and other related officials. Also, the Seoul Olympic Torch, which was lit up at Hera's Temple in Greece, embarked on a 22-day journey across the country after its arrival at the Jeju International Airport on August 27 of the same year. The Olympic Torch had been carried along the 1,595 sections crisscrossing the country until it arrived at the Seoul City Hall Plaza, its final destination, on September 16, after the 4,167-km-long race. Each of the 21 cities where the Olympic Torch stayed for one night greeted the torch by holding performances by foreign folk dance teams, or local cultural festivals, to boost the people's enthusiasm for the Olympics. The opening ceremony was held at Flags Plaza in the Olympic Village (September 3, 1988), where a total of 9,627 athletes and 3,999 officials hailing from 160 NOCs checked in. The final number of participants who actually entered the country and got accredited amounted to 9,417 athletes and 3,887 officials (total of 13,304 people were accredited into the Olympic Village) from 160 NOCs.

Performance and Assessment

The South Korean people remained worried about the Seoul Olympic Games until its opening. Although partly attributable to the slanderous campaign by the opposition groups, even the cabinet members were convinced that the hosting of the Games was a bit too early for the country to handle. They were also worried about the economic resources required to host the games as well as about the possibility of the country being alienated in its very territory due to the stellar performances of other sports powerhouses. Some were convinced that the hosting of the Games was a convenient scheme of the administration to neutralize the popular angst with regard to its armed assumption of political power through the military coup d'état, its armed crackdown on the Gwangju Democratic Movement, and its various other oppressive policies. For such reason, many belittled the policy of promoting the sports and cultural industries, claiming that it was actually aimed at dumbing down the people (3S: sports, sex, and screen).

The Seoul Olympics, however, has been to this date praised as the most perfect Games ever held in the history of the modern and contemporary Olympics. Such glowing assessment can be attributed to a couple of developments triggered by the Seoul Olympics: the Games not only provided the global community with a precious momentum to pull the world out of the suffocating grip of the Cold War and to build a new world order commonly known as the "new détente," but also helped South Korea to gain the trust of the superpowers in the East and the West, as well as of the Third World countries by strengthening South Korea's capability to suppress the potential outbreak of war in the Korean peninsula. In addition, South Korea has since succeeded in establishing diplomatic ties with the Soviet Union, China, the socialist countries in Eastern Europe, and the Third World countries, thereby successfully laying the groundwork for the "Northern Diplomacy," which again helped the country to open a new economic horizon through the development of new trade partners. Furthermore, the country was able to solidify its supremacy over North Korea, which at the time enjoyed a higher status across many areas, including the economy, defense capability, sports, and the supremacy of its governing ideology. Finally, the Games helped the country boost its national brand power to an unprecedented level.

Internally, the June 29 Declaration for Democratization, which was concocted partly aimed at assuring the successful hosting of the 1988 Seoul Olympics, helped the country realize what can be considered democratization for all practical purposes, thereby promoting the stabilization of the political situation and the improvement of the human rights condition. The realization of genuine democratization, which the South Korean society had so fervently yearned to achieve, resulted in marked advancement across all areas, including politics, the economy, the society, diplomacy, culture, and sports. After the closing of the Seoul Olympics, the two Koreas simultaneously joined the United Nations, and President Roh Tae Woo was given an opportunity to deliver a keynote speech at the United Nations General Assembly (1991). Would such achievement have been possible even without the country's contribution to the international community and the marked improvement in its human rights condition as a result of its democratization? The utility of South Korea's successful hosting of the Seoul Olympic Games did not stop at the aforementioned achievements. About a year after the successful hosting of the Seoul Olympics, an assessment of the Games by the South Korean people was conducted. The survey performed jointly by Korea Development Institute and Gallup Korea (1989) revealed that the respondents believed that the Olympics had a very desirable impact across the society, including politics, the society, diplomacy, culture, and sports. It was also discovered in another survey conducted four years after the closing of the Seoul Olympics that "the Seoul Olympic Games triggered wide-ranging social changes, from the people's value system to the social norms, and that the social transformation is clearly pointing to the direction of advancement."

What, then, might be the key factor behind the successful bid for and hosting of the Seoul Olympic Games by the Chun Doo Hwan administration? It is perhaps the firm will and determination of the president, which is evident from the fact that the president allowed Roh Tae Woo, the supreme representative of the ruling Democratic Justice Party as well as the most promising presidential hopeful then, to head the Seoul Olympic Games Organizing Committee as the chairperson, as well as the Ministry of Sports and the 2nd Ministry of State for Political Affairs. Additionally, the successful hosting of the Seoul Olympic Games became possible because the president put his full support behind the key figures in the power group, including Park Se Jik, the chairperson of the Seoul Olympic Games Organizing Committee.

Finally, the 24th Seoul Summer Olympic Games has been highly regarded for its historical significance: it helped the world escape from the entrenched division of the East and West, and realized the harmony that the Olympics represented or aspired for, thereby satisfying the mandate given to the South Korean people at that time. It is also noteworthy that South Korea was able to defy the threats of war and terror attacks that came with its being part of a divided country in the wake of its successful hosting of the Seoul Olympics. Also, the pride and newfound confidence that the South Korean people had come to possess as the citizens of the host country of the Olympics created new energy in the South Korean society, along with the economic growth and globalization trend. Also, the unquestionable support given to the 1988 Seoul Olympics by the Western and Eastern blocs forever changed the directions of the Olympic movement, which was formerly centered on the advanced and powerful countries, thereby demonstrating the spirit of equality that the Olympic movement aspired to showcase.

Section 3

The Government Reform of the Chun Doo Hwan Administration

1. Background and direction of the government reform

Inaugurated without gaining the necessary democratic legitimacy, the government of the 5th Republic can be deemed as the regime that was formed as a result of the joining of forces of the military elite that led the coup d'état and the civilian bureaucratic elite. In such situation when their opportunity to participate in the policymaking process was completely blocked due to the significantly weakened the role and function of the National Assembly as the body representing the people, the civil society had no choice but to concentrate on the resistance and on the move for democratization. The Chun Doo Hwan administration, however, was able to sustain the undemocratic and autocratic regime of the ruling elite despite the constitutional amendment. The administration thoroughly suppressed the resistance of the pro-democracy group, who rose against the military government, while at the same time pushing forward with measures to realize economic stability and growth in an effort to overcome such resistance. As part of the extraordinary measure to support such policy initiative, the administration took a decisive action in the form of the so-called "October 15 Administrative Reform" on October 15, 1981.

The reform that was implemented by the regime was driven largely by political necessity, but the country also desperately needed to respond to the changes in the socio-economic environment. Having graduated from the early stage of economic development, the South Korean society was evolving into an industrial society. Likewise, there was an increasing demand for a corresponding level of improved popular consciousness and for quality administration services befitting the advanced society. However, since the government organization and function optimized for the compressed economic growth in the past had been modified only partially without major changes, a wholesale review of the roles and working methods of the government was required at the time. Therefore, efforts aimed at overcoming the challenges posed by the administration's external environment and the irrationality of the existing administrative system, at recognizing the reform tasks that needed to be carried out to establish a future-oriented administration goal, and at re-establishing government roles were absolutely necessary regardless of the motivation or direction of the administrative reform at the time.

Another key component of the government reform that the administration pushed forward with, along with the administrative reform focused on the revamp of the government organization and functions, was the institutional improvement. The Chun Doo Hwan administration embarked on the "Project of Revamping Government Institutions for Growth and Advancement" upon the inauguration of the 5th Republic in 1981. Therefore, it pushed ahead with the abolition or improvement of the irrational laws and institutions across all areas of the government administration because the existing government institutions were not able to catch up with the changing environment given that no qualitative transformation in the government organization or functions had been made for a considerable time.

Established simply by inheriting the institutions that existed during the Japanese colonial rule, the country's institutions had substantial irrationalities, and the subsequent works aimed at improving the legacy institutions largely failed to reflect the growing demand for new administrative services as they remained at the level in the 1960s. As a result, many institutions were "designed to serve the administrators instead of the service consumers," and the evils of the outdated bureaucracy were undermining the administrative efficiency, thereby hindering the evolutionary development of the administrative system into one that would be capable of responding to the growing demand for new administrative services and to the changing internal and external environment. Moreover, the various regulatory measures devised to support the government-led development drive in the past were intensifying the dependence of the private sector on the government rather than promoting the autonomy of the economic activities, which again undermined the country's economic growth and the advancement of the society. In addition, the growing interest in environment protection, the increasing demand for a welfare and labor policy, and the rising expectations of the people with regard to their cultural enjoyment, which is directly linked with the improvement of their quality of life, also made it an urgent matter for the government to expand its role in the policies governing such areas.

Therefore, the October 15 Administrative Reform was aimed at changing the method and character of the government operation by implementing two separate tasks: the revamp of the government organization and the "institutional improvement for growth and development." The two pillars of the government reforms, which began in the early days of the Chun Doo Hwan administration, showed the basic directions of the government administration during its seven-year incumbency and formed the basis of the infrastructure required to implement the reform of detailed policies and functional areas.

Therefore, the author intends to explore in a detailed way the political context that defined the limitations and achievements of the government reform in analyzing the overall directions of the government reform that was pushed forward by the administration, all of which will be realized by analyzing the objectives and implementation directions of the government reform as well as the implementation system, performance, and assessment from two key perspectives: the organizational reshuffling and institutional improvements.

The objective of the reform that the administration intended to realize with the October 15 Administrative Reform was to affect a higher-level change through the redefinition of the government roles rather than through some small-scale reshuffling, such as the reduction of the overall workforce or the lessening of the high-ranking officials. Towards this end, the administration defined the re-establishment of the government roles as a task that it needed to carry out to re-establish the government functions and the scope of administrative engagement well past the limit of the conventional reform practices, such as the simplification of the administrative processes or the revamp of the government constitution from public officials to a few elite officials. To sum up, the official goal of the administrative reform pushed forward by the Chun Doo Hwan administration was to pose fundamental questions regarding the roles of the government. The administration suggested the detailed goals required to redefine the government roles, which touched on a comprehensive range of issues, from the redefining of the scope and contents of the government responsibilities, including the rationalization of the administrative processes, to the instrumental objective aimed at boosting the administrative efficiency. Noteworthy among these reform goals is the fact that the "small government" theory had already emerged as one of the key goals instrumental to the administrative reform during this period. The fact that the plan not only aimed to reduce the number of government organizations and scale back the manpower size but also to expand the scope of the reform as to redefine the coverage of the administrative responsibilities shows that the reform implementation group not just mulled over the management reform that would yield palpable outcomes instantly but was also interested in fundamental administrative reform from its core. The detailed guidelines suggested for the realization of such objectives included "reduction of administrative organizations through the consolidation of duplicate or similar functions," "establishment of an accountable and service-oriented administrative system through the alignment of the government authority and responsibility," "optimized appointment and improved capabilities of public officials through the selection of a few elites, and appropriate distribution of the workforce," and "democratization and improved efficiency of the administration by minimizing the range of administrative interference."

The key objectives of the institutional reform that was implemented along with the administrative reform are clearly shown in the "Guidelines to Improve the Factors Undermining Growth," which was enclosed in the presidential order issued by President Chun Doo Hwan in April 1981. According to the guidelines, the key characteristics of the government's institutional reform were that it would "turn a new page in the government administration for the new era" and "toughen the resolve for an efficient implementation of the key directives in the government administration." Towards these ends, the administration put out the basic goals of "identifying the laws, institutions, and practices undermining growth and advancement" by "eliminating as many elements worth abolishing as possible" and by "creating only essential elements, as few as realistically possible." Therefore, the administration aimed to "boldly improve the inefficient and irrational elements in the laws, institutions, practices, and administrative precedents that were undermining the growth and development in each area of the government administration" and "facilitate the realization of a fully advanced South Korea, as desired by the people, by improving the quality of administration." Compared with the goals of the administrative reform as discussed earlier, it can be said that the objectives of the government's institutional reform stopped at declaring the basic principles of the institutional improvement rather than suggesting the detailed reform targets and implementation goals. Since the guidelines covered a comprehensive range of reform targets, compared to the October 15 Administrative Reform, it is believed that the detailed goals would be custom-designed for each institution that was the target of improvement. This was inevitable as far as the government reform group was concerned because the processes of fine-tuning and consensus building would be required to ensure the smooth improvement of the institutions.

To sum up the two major streams of the government reform, the October 15 Administrative Reform centered on the reform of the administrative organization focused on the institutions that would implement the government policies, whereas the "institutional improvement for growth and development" centered on the institutional reform focused on the reform of the contents and implementation method of the required tasks, respectively. Although driven largely by political necessity, the two reforms boldly diagnosed the key pending government tasks regardless of the actual performance of the reform, thereby clearly showing the reform targets and reform direction. It can be assessed, therefore, that the implementation directions and objectives of the two different reforms established the key issues of the administrative reform that should be implemented by the government rather appropriately.

2. Contents of the government reform

Organizational Reshuffling

The Chun Doo Hwan administration attempted to reduce the function of economic policy management by consolidating the three Senior Secretaries to the President for Economic Policy bequeathed from the 4th Republic into one office in the early days of its incumbency. Also, while retaining its existing function of economic growth management, the Economic Planning Board strengthened its fair trade supervision function as to stabilize the prices and to ensure balanced growth. Its earlier initiative for a small and efficient government lost its momentum, however, as the central government organization, which had earlier been reduced to 2 boards, 15 ministries, 4 offices, 4 services, and 4 external bureaus in the wake of the October 15 administrative reform, was expanded by 1 ministry and 9 services, thereby returning to the administrative system composed of 2 boards, 16 ministries, 4 offices, 13 services, and 3 external bureaus at the end of the administration in 1987.

The reshuffling of the government organization during the incumbency of the administration was closely related with the political-economic situation at the time. Unique to the administration, among others, was the fact that it did not have to grapple with various resistances, such as those that occurred after the democratization or the opposition by the opposition party during the organizational reshuffling because it was an extremely authoritarian government capable of pushing ahead with its iron-fisted rule. The rise of those who adhered to the principle of market economy, led by Kim Jae Ik, the Senior Secretary to the President for Economic Policy, coupled with the full support of President Chun Doo Hwan, allowed the administration to transform the past economic policy centered on a planned economy to one centered on stability, autonomy, and a market-driven mechanism. Moreover, the reshuffling of the government organization aimed at minimizing the government function of mostly the economic ministries in the process was an inevitable task. The stabilization of prices was set as the predominant goal of the administration's economic policy given the extremely challenging economic situation at the time, which was represented by the "triple devils": inflation, which shot up to a whopping 44% in 1980; the worsening international balance of trade, which accounted for some 50% of the GDP then; and the numerous insolvent companies and high interest rate. The administration tolerated no attempt at political justification or contrarian logic to achieve this goal. Paradoxical as it may sound to some, such drastic measures would have been virtually impossible to enforce had it not been for the authoritarian regime of President Chun Doo Hwan. The reshuffling of the government organization that was implemented in the early years of the administration can be assessed to have been the administration's effort to implement such tasks while justifying its political legitimacy in the process.

Fiscal Reform

In the area of budgetary policy, accounting institution, or fiscal policy, no significant change in the basic direction was implemented by the Chun Doo Hwan administration on top of those that it had inherited from the Park Jung Hee administration. The administration minimized its operating expenses and minimized, reduced, or delayed public investments when the stabilization of the prices emerged as the most urgent policy goal and was made as the top priority. The massive export support policy during the development of the heavy chemical industries was scaled back greatly according to the policy initiative targeted at realizing a market-driven economy and economic stabilization. Likewise, as part of this effort, draconian fiscal belt-tightening was enforced, including suppression of wage hikes.

President Chun Doo Hwan fully supported the position of the economic ministers that the only way that the economy could rebound from the weakened state caused by the excessive duplicate investments and the 2nd international oil shock in the process of developing the heavy chemical industries was for the government to stabilize the prices, while rejecting any policy proposal that would potentially raise the prices for any reason imaginable. As a result, the administration attained the marvelous feat of deflating the wholesale price inflation rate from 44% in 1980 to 4% in the next year. The stabilization policy continued on a steady basis for long, thereby steadily pushing down the ratio of the GNP per the general account budget of the central government from 17.6% in 1982 to 14.6% in 1988. The zero-base budget was adopted in 1982, but the zero-base review of the ever-growing budget in the period of economic growth was practically impossible, with no great results achieved either without a fundamental reform of the budgetary policy.

In the end, the Chun Doo Hwan administration decided to maintain the government accounting system based on the Budgetary Accounting Act, which it had inherited from the Park Jung Hee administration, with no fundamental institutional reform or change. Instead, the administration changed the institution only incrementally, by reflecting the new economic policy, such as stabilization, open market, and market-driven economy, as well as new policy initiatives in labor, environment protection, and balanced development, which resulted in the reprioritization of fiscal spending.

Personnel Administration Reform

As with the organizational reshuffling, the administration embarked on the reform of personnel administration based on the reshuffling of the government organization and the October 15 Administrative Reform. Beginning with the selection of the innovation of the government administration as the central message of his inaugural speech, the president embarked on a sweeping personnel administrative reform and renovation of the working environment. The reform included a full-scale revamp of the training contents for the public officials, centered on anti-communism and integrity, along with the comprehensive organizational reshuffling in the early phase of the incumbency, the declaration of the ethics code for public officials, and the implementation of ideological education for the high-ranking officials over grade 3. The moral rearmament and ideological education of the high-ranking officials were largely driven by the ulterior political motive of the newly inaugurated Chun Doo Hwan administration, which hoped to overcome the controversy on its political legitimacy in the early phase of its incumbency while at the same time tightening its control over the bureaucratic community. There was a clear need, however, to establish a new institution to govern the national public servants that would reflect the changes in the administrative environment, now that 18 years had passed since the full-fledged amendment of the Civil Service Act in 1963, without any sweeping reform in personnel administration.

In view of such shifting circumstances, various changes were introduced in an attempt to establish an institution for qualified professional public servants with the necessary expertise and efficiency. The biggest among them was the revamp of the public servant ranking system from five grades (A, B) to one consisting of grades 1 to 9. In addition, the administration attempted to foster the development of professional expertise in the civil servants through the segmentation of the job positions and ranks by newly installing five more job rows in the job position classification system, and by introducing the job type concept, thereby assigning 120 new job types under the job rows. Also, with the professionalization of the civil service being firmly rooted in the ground, the system of promotion and demotion based on the principle of individual work history and meritocracy started to be adopted universally while the concept of a "lifetime job" grew stronger in the minds of the civil servants as the government nudged them to continue to serve until their retirement age.

Electronic Government

Given that the very concept of "informatization" had not been introduced in the country at that time, the term "electronic government" was not used at all during the incumbency of the Chun Doo Hwan administration. Still, the seed of the country's info-communication revolution was sown during the period: a series of major policy decisions on the info-communication industry were made, including the establishment of the Korea Electric and Telecommunication Corporation (presently KT), which was formed by turning the telecommunication services provided by the Ministry of Postal Service into a public corporation, as well as the establishment of DACOM, which introduced an element of competition to the country's telecommunication market, formerly governed by the state monopoly. The administration also laid the foundation for the country's info-communication industry, which has since evolved to become one of the leading IT powerhouses today, by embarking on the Big 5 National Basic Computer Network Projects beginning in 1987, after the inauguration in 1986 of the Computer Network Coordinating Committee.

The key contributing factors to the successful construction of the info-communication infrastructure by the administration were its excellent policy leadership and its mobilization of appropriate financial resources. The stellar leadership formed by the encounter between Oh Myung, a technocrat who studied in the Korea Military Academy, and Kim Jae Ik, a neoclassical economist, in the early phase of the administration gave the two an opportunity to experiment with the maximization of the synergy between telecommunications and the economy. In the area of the financial resources required for the IT projects, the government made it mandatory for the new telephone services subscribers to purchase a specified amount of government bonds (KRW 200,000 for the subscribers in Seoul) with the amendment in 1981 of the Temporary Act on the Expansion of the Public Electric Telecommunication Facility, which was enacted in 1979, and raised the message rate from KRW 12 to KRW 20. As a result of such combined efforts, the funds available for investments in the telecom sector jumped from KRW 231.7 billion in 1979 (2.27% of the total investments then) to KRW 817.1 billion in 1981 (6.32%), KRW 1.0875 trillion in 1982 (7.02%), and KRW 1.0591 trillion in 1983 (5.37%), until it expanded up to KRW 1.5392 trillion in 1987 (5.30%).

To conclude, the Chun Doo Hwan administration laid the qualitative and quantitative foundation for the telecommunication industry by advancing the telecommunication services industry through the resolution of the pent-up demand for telephone subscriptions and through the opening of the market. The full-scale implementation of the five key national computer networks, which began in 1986 based on these achievements, can be assessed to have provided the basis for the info-communication infrastructure construction project that began in the mid-1990s, and to have laid the foundation for the development of an electronic government.

Regulatory Reform

The Chun Doo Hwan administration was the first government that implemented regulatory reform among all the administrations in the history of the Republic of Korea. The administration was forced to embark on a paradigm shift from state-led development in the 1960s to market-driven development while, it was required to resolve the maladies caused by the excessively heavy-chemical-industries-concentrated investment in the 1970s. Externally, the administration was inaugurated with a burden imposed by the era for it to respond to the growing influences of free trade and neoliberalism. To overcome such challenges, the administration recruited young economists in their 40s, including Kim Jae Ik, Seo Sang Cheol, Kim Ki Hwan, and Sa Gong Il, and gave them key posts in the government. They collaborated with one another to shift the paradigm across the country's economy and industrial policies based on the principle of the transition to a market-driven economy, the opening of the market, and autonomy.

During such process, regulatory reform emerged as the inevitable task required for boosting the creativity, vitality, and autonomy of the private sector. With the formation of the Screening Committee to Improve the Factors Undermining Growth and Development as ordered by President Chun Doo Hwan in the cabinet meeting in April 1981, the administration continued with the drive for institutional improvement commensurate with the strong will and commitment of the president. The task of institutional improvement was implemented based on the following seven principles: the people's convenience, autonomy/productivity, fitness to the economic reality, healthiness of the people's mentality, trust of and harmony among the people, democracy, and administration efficiency. However, those who were critical of the drive for institutional improvement argue that these standards were too abstract and philosophical in nature, with no clarity, and therefore could not be applied to the real economy. Furthermore, as it is obvious from the committee's title, purporting to "promote growth and development," the regulatory reform did not pay sufficient attention to social equality or safety as it focused disproportionately on administrative efficiency and effectiveness.

To sum up, the regulatory reform can be assessed to have been aimed at boosting the efficiency and effectiveness of the government intervention by realizing administrative efficiency, by forming a market-centric economy, and by opening the economy while at the same time maintaining the overall direction targeted at economic growth. Notable, among others, is the fact that as the regulatory enforcement on the labor movement was strengthened, the protection of the workers' rights was further weakened compared to the practices that were enforced during the Park Jung Hee administration. Moreover, since the policy caused the conglomerates to focus only on importing goods, the liberalization of imports had a negative impact on the small enterprises and the agricultural sector, which were yet to fully mature to attain a sufficient competitive edge. Some studies suggest that the policies of the Chun Doo Hwan administration aimed at stabilizing the prices and liberalizing the economy further worsened the income distribution. In conclusion, the regulatory reform of the administration succeeded in preventing the free fall of the South Korean economy in the early 1980s, but had a detrimental impact on social integration as the benefits of the economic reform were mostly given back to the large conglomerates and economic powerhouses rather than to the small businesses and the economically vulnerable group.

Reform of Public Corporations

Some fundamental changes started to appear in the policy of managing public corporations in the wake of the inauguration of the administration. A study conducted by Korea Development Institute in August 1982 revealed the key problems in the management system of the public corporations and in the improvement measures, which again prompted the proposition of various measures for improvement, including the weakening of the governmental oversight, the strengthening of the internal management system, the installation of the Government Investment Institutions Assessment and Coordination Committee, the revamp of the assessment and incentive system, and the reshuffling of the top management of the government investment institutions. As a result of such varied efforts, the public corporations that were formerly governed by the Government Investment Management Act began to be governed by the newly enacted Basic Act on Government Investment Management. The new basic act differed significantly from the then-existing laws governing the management of public corporations in that it stressed the importance of the autonomy and responsible management of the government investment institutions and came up with measures aimed at minimizing the intervention of the governing ministry or of the authority performing oversight roles over them.

First, in terms of the organizational management, the internal monitoring and supervision function were separated with the installation of the non-executive director and chairman of the board on top of the existing chief executive and standing auditor seat, while the terms of the executive directors, which varied substantially depending on the government investment institution, were unified in accordance with the provisions specified in the basic act. Moreover, the role of the board of directors as the supreme voting body was clarified, dividing the executive body and the voting body in the public corporations in an attempt to guarantee autonomy in management. Whereas the top management, including the president, vice president, and executives, were usually recruited from outside in the past, the amended basic act specified that the executive members, including the vice president, shall be recruited only from among the internal staff, thereby assuring the independence of the institutions and boosting the morale of the employees. The act specified that the budgetary review and confirmation shall be decided by the board of directors, while the material purchases and construction contracts, which used to be handled by the Government's Public Procurement Service, were now to be decided by each government investment institution.

The new basic act also contained substantial changes in the oversight of business management. In the past, each government ministry retained the direct oversight and management authority over the government investment institutions under their supervision. The new basic act, however, substantially scaled down the scope of the government ministries' preemptive management oversight capacity. Instead, it installed the Management Assessment and Screening Committee, thereby changing the assessment of the management performance to one based on posterior control. In addition, the efforts to link the performance assessment results with the incentive payment started to materialize; beginning in 1983, the amount of incentive bonuses was determined in accordance with the corresponding management performance assessment result.

Anti-corruption Reform

The anti-corruption reform of the Chun Doo Hwan administration, which was implemented as part of the social clean-up campaign, was aimed at strengthening the ethical armament of the civil servants community, thereby rooting out the rampant complacency and corruption among them. Moreover, the administration pushed forward with a wide-ranging and radical social clean-up campaign on the pretext that it would root out the bad practices and the harmful consequences accumulated from the past in the wake of the inauguration of the new administration. In reality, however, the anti-corruption drive was spurred by the regime-level attempt to address the growing criticism of its political legitimacy as much as it was driven by the political motivation to intensify the enforcement of official discipline.

The government institutions associated with the anti-corruption drive, which were installed in the early phase of the administration, include the Standing Committee for Emergency Measures for National Security Protection, the Social Clean-up Committee, and the Contemporary Society Research Institute. The Legislative Council for National Security Protection, the key power structure before the inauguration of the administration, led the anti-corruption drive, including the political purge, but it was soon replaced by the Social Clean-up Committee as the key institution governing the anti-corruption policy after the inauguration of the administration. The Legislative Council for National Security Protection pushed forward with the handling of the cases involving the fraudulent amassing of wealth by exercising its power in an attempt to renovate the political climate, as well as with various other measures, including the dismissal and prosecution of corrupt public officials, the rooting out of the perpetrators of social evils, the normalization of public education (including the flat-out ban of private lessons), and the simplification of the public administrative service procedure associated with permissions and licensing. Also, countless illegal and anti-humanistic atrocities were perpetrated in the Samcheong Training Camp, which was introduced in an attempt to suspend the activities of many politicians that had the potential of becoming stumbling blocks for the regime, or to eradicate the social evils. In particular, numerous innocent people were arrested and put into the camp with no legitimate ground, simply because the government authority wished to meet the quota imposed on it.

It is an accepted fact that the policy of the Chun Doo Hwan administration aimed at assuring the ethical behavior of the civil servants and supporting the anti-corruption drive was appropriated for the purpose of suppressing the corrupt activities of the old politicians and of creating a new political order centered on the new military elite group. However, because the policy was pushed forward comprehensively along with the social clean-up campaign, on the premise of rooting out the corruption entrenched in the government and society, it also succeeded in rooting out crime and fraud that threatened the people's lives. Furthermore, the corruption control was not limited to the corrupt and fraudulent activities but was pushed forward as part of the nationwide enlightenment campaign encompassing the ethical/moral aspect of social purification, in an attempt to earn the public recognition of the legitimacy of the regime. It is deplorable, however, that the anti-corruption control activities were not pushed forward in an objective and fair manner by a legitimate inspection authority based on the related laws or institutional ground, but was enforced driven by a personal determination of a ruler and a ulterior political motivation.

Reform of Regional Administration

The country's regional administration, which had developed based on the government-controlled regional administrative system, evolved into the local autonomy system in accordance with the Temporary Act on Regional Administration (November 17, 1948; Law No. 8) and the Local Autonomy Act (July 4, 1948; Law No. 32), which replaced the earlier act. Afterwards, the local autonomy system was abolished during the incumbency of the Park Jung Hee administration and was followed by the establishment of a local administrative system that was dependent on the central government. The reform of the Chun Doo Hwan administration in the area of local and regional administration is represented by the 1980 constitutional amendment, which specified that the local government that had been postponed until the unification of the two Koreas during the incumbency of the Park Jung Hee administration shall be introduced again after considering the fiscal self-reliance of the local government. The provision was deleted in the 1987 constitutional amendment, thereby eliminating the last stumbling block in the path towards the realization of the local self-government system.

The biggest changes that were made through the 1980 constitutional amendment were that the local government was guaranteed as a local self-governing body, whose actual method of implementation was to be specified by law, and that the legal ground for the installation of the local assembly was established. In reality, however, just like the case during the Park Jung Hee administration, the implementation of the local government system was postponed through the legislation of the Temporary Measure on the Local Government until the heads of the local governments were to be appointed by the central government. With regard to the local assembly, the higher local administrative body would assume the duties of the local assembly in the case of the primary local governments, while in the case of the higher local administrative bodies, the prime minister would assume the duties of Seoul Special City and the Ministry of Internal Affairs then would assume the duties of a wide-area administrative body. Although it was specified in the supplementary provision, as mentioned earlier, that the local government system was to be implemented after considering the fiscal self-reliance of the local administrative body, it was also stated that the time of early implementation was to be specified by the applicable law, thereby raising the possibility of its early implementation compared to the provision during the Park Jung Hee administration, which specified that the postponement would extend "until the unification." Still, however, the local self-government system was never implemented in practice during the incumbency of the Chun Doo Hwan administration. The Local Government Act was amended in 1988, during the incumbency of the Roh Tae Woo administration, in which the structure of the local administration was to be a two-tier system (wide area and primary area), with Seoul Special City and the city under the direct control of the central government being designated as the wide-area self-governing bodies, and the city, county, and district being designated as the primary self-governing bodies.

Privatization

The Chun Doo Hwan administration was inaugurated with a significantly weakened economy due to the excessive investment in the heavy chemical industries, the disproportionate government intervention in the market economy, two rounds of international oil shocks, and the growing spread of protectionism. In an attempt to overcome such challenges, the administration turned the direction of the economic policy to economic development led by the private sector on the premise of the transition to the market economy and the opening and stabilization of the economy. The most notable change that was observed during the transition to economic development led by the private sector was the privatization of the public corporations. The privatization of the public corporations during the administration was aimed at minimizing the government intervention in the market based on the principle of the improvement of efficiency and expansion of autonomy in accordance with the application of the market principles. However, among the corporations that invested in the industrial sector and that still engaged in manufacturing activities, there were not many public corporations that were privatized during the administration. This is because many of them were created by converting the goods and services provided by the government organization into public corporations. Therefore, this period can be understood as the preparatory stage for the full-fledged privatization that started during the Roh Tae Woo administration.

The targets of the privatization that began in the Roh Tae Woo administration were a total of 11 blue chip public corporations, including Korea Power, Korea Telecom (KT), and Pohang Steel (presently POSCO). The public offering of government-issued stocks targeted at general people, which was adopted as a means of privatization of the aforementioned public corporations and aimed at preventing the type of privatization that is unilaterally advantageous to large conglomerates and chaebols, was quite successful. Via the government-issued stock system, the 34.1% share of Pohang Steel and the 21% share of Korea Electric Power were sold to the people in small units. The method had benefits in that it was welcomed by the people and could limit the dominance that the chaebols could exercise over many blue chip public corporations. Due to the excessive interest in raising the fiscal revenues and in the creation of wealth for ordinary people, it is assessed, however, that the administration did not show the corresponding interest in improving the management efficiency of the public corporations, in introducing a competitive system, and in deregulation, which were important goals of the privatization policy. To conclude, the privatization policy of the Chun Doo Hwan administration, including the privatization of the financial institutions, is assessed to have enabled the management of the market-driven economy while at the same time have changed the policy methods across the overall industrial policies.

3. Performance and assessment of the government reform

The performance of the government reform can be assessed from many different angles. First, it can be assessed from the perspective of effectiveness, which evaluates if the goal of the reform was realized; or from the perspective of efficiency, which measures the amount of resources that were mobilized to accomplish the desired effect of the reform. Other important criteria that can be used in assessing the performance of the reform include the following: if the implementation method and process of the reform was faithful to the principle of the democratic administration; if the entire process of the implementation of the administrative reform was transparent; if the selected reform tool succeeded in gaining comprehensive public sympathy; and if the individual safety or rights were infringed upon during the process of the implementation of the administrative reform, and as a result of it. On top of the assessments according to the aforementioned standard criteria, another important criterion that could be used in assessing the pros and cons of the government reform implemented during the incumbency of the Chun Doo Hwan administration is how much influence the inherent limitation of the administration as a result of the undemocratic nature of the regime had on the implementation process of the reform.

The positive aspects of the government reform implemented by the administration would include the fact that the administration demonstrated some short-term effect in eliminating some technical-level maladies among the administrative maladies accumulated from the preceding administrations, and in pushing forward with the government administration efficiently. The political pressure exerted on the overall civil servants community was quite strong as the administrative reform and institutional improvement were pushed forward simultaneously. The government reform succeeded in attaining some visible achievements from the quantitative perspective, thanks to the direct intervention of the power group and the personal interest of the supreme decision maker in the early phase of the reform. Although limited under the rule of the authoritative government, the improvement of the government institution can be assessed in a positive light in that the desire for rational reform of the bureaucratic elites was reflected in the reform process. Moreover, a future-oriented reform ideology ended up being reflected to some extent on the plan level at most because the authority was given not only to the neo-military elites but also to the professional bureaucrats. As a result, the organizational reshuffling laid out by the October 15 Administrative Reform and the efforts to improve the institutions that had been pushed forward during the seven-year incumbency of the administration made some significant contribution to the overall improvement of the operational efficiency of the government. Also, considering that many potential tasks then covered by the administrative reform and institutional improvement of the Chun Doo Hwan administration had since reappeared as key tasks of the government reform in the succeeding administrations, the reform can be assessed to have been firmly adopted as an important precedent in designing and implementing administrative reform in the coming years.

Attempts at comprehensive reform were also observed in the individual policy area and functional segments. The five key national computer networks construction project implemented during the incumbency of the Chun Doo Hwan administration laid the groundwork for the country to soar as the leading country in the area of electronic government in the coming years. It is also true that the efforts to realize a market-driven economy, autonomy, and the opening of the economy as well as other efforts for deregulation contributed to the enhancement of the competitiveness of the country's economy. Also notable is that the administration strove to maintain quantitative growth throughout its incumbency while at the same time pushing forward with incremental changes of the fiscal input, although limited in extent.

The government reform implemented by the administration succeeded in attaining positive outcomes, as discussed earlier, but it would be difficult to conclude that it led to the practical strengthening of the government capability and the future-oriented progression of social development. Being the government reform that had been pushed forward throughout the administration's incumbency by suppressing the popular aspiration for democracy and liberalization, it ended up undermining the potential of the ROK government in the end. When the desire to preserve the regime and the effort for government reform and advancement clashed with each other, as was inevitable, the political objective took precedence over the reform, thereby obliterating the significance government reform attempted in the early phase of the administration's incumbency as the administration neared its end. As a result, the reform promoted distrust and created an authoritarian climate throughout the society, contrary to the purported goals of government administration, such as "realization of a just society," which had been proposed officially by the reform leadership. Considering that the aftereffect of such failed reform still lingers in the present South Korean society and has sown the seed of a deep-rooted distrust of the government, the government reform of the Chun Doo Hwan administration can be assessed to have tarnished the positive effect of the reform.

Chapter 4

The Roh Tae Woo Administration

Section 1

Inauguration of the Roh Tae Woo Administration and Foundation of Key Policy Administration

1. Inauguration of the administration and introduction of its organization

"The June democratic uprising" in 1987 provided the key momentum for the inauguration of the 6th Republic as it played a decisive role in improving the country's political environment, including the constitutional amendment for the adoption of the direct presidential election. The political squabbles over the possible transition to the direct presidential election system began in early 1985, in the wake of the 12th General Election, some 3 years before the scheduled date of the 13th presidential election. Faced with the ever-expanding June democratic uprising, Roh Tae Woo, then the head of the Democratic Justice Party, announced the June 29 Declaration, in which he laid out eight key measures to quell the political unrest by succumbing to the popular demand for democratization, including the constitutional amendment to adopt the direct presidential election.

Table 4-1. Special Declaration for National Harmony and March Towards a Great Country (June 29 Declaration)

A. The ruling and opposition parties shall initiate the process of constitutional amendment for the immediate adoption of the direct presidential election system, and for the realization of a peaceful handover of power in February 1988 by conducting the presidential election in accordance with the new constitution.
B. The presidential election law shall be amended so that it would not only adopt the direct presidential election system but would also guarantee free candidacy that is open to all eligible people, as well as fair race, thereby subjecting them to fair assessment by the voters.
C. Kim Dae Jung and other politicians shall be given pardon and reinstated while all political prisoners shall be released.
D. Human dignity shall be respected all the more, and institutional improvements shall be expedited to guarantee the basic rights of each individual to the maximum allowable limits while aiming to achieve practical improvements in the human rights conditions through the immediate rectification of any infringement.
E. All institutions and practices associated with the press shall be improved to an unprecedented level to advance press freedom, while guaranteeing press freedom to the maximum allowable limits.

F. The self-governance and autonomy of each social segment shall be guaranteed to the maximum allowable limits. The local self-governing system as well as the liberalization of universities and the self-governing education system shall be realized at the earliest time.
G. The activities of political parties shall be guaranteed, and the political environment based on dialogue and compromise shall be promoted.
H. Seek bold social clean-up measures to build a bright and transparent society. Root out criminals inflicting damage on the everyday lives of the people, and boldly rectify the entrenched corruption and irrationalities.

The underlying spirit of the June 29 Declaration was "declaration for democratization." It aimed to terminate the decades-long authoritarian regime and boldly accept the desire for democracy prevalent among the South Korean people, thereby providing an important turning point for democracy across the diverse aspects of the country, including politics, economy, society, and culture. The period from the June 29 Declaration until the presidential election on December 16 was marked by the political haggling between the ruling and opposition parties over the constitutional amendment.

The June Democratic Uprising and June 29 Declaration signify the falling of the curtain for the 5th Republic, thereby providing a key turning point for the inauguration of the 6th Republic. The proposal for the constitutional amendment was drafted through negotiations between the Democratic Justice Party and the Unification Democratic Party, the opposition party with the largest number of seats, after which the motion for constitutional amendment was jointly submitted to the National Assembly by representatives from the ruling and opposition parties. The proposed bill for the constitutional amendment, which was submitted by the National Assembly and transferred to the government on September 18, 1987, was put to a vote and was passed with 254 "yes" votes and 4 "no" votes, with 258 representatives out of the 272 registered members present during the voting. In accordance with the regulation (Article 131 of the Constitution) specifying that "the proposed bill for the constitutional amendment should be put to a vote through a referendum within 30 days after its legislation by the National Assembly," the 6th referendum was carried out. In the referendum held on October 27, the bill was passed with 93.1% "yes" votes and with 78.2% of the total registered voters participating in the referendum. Upon the final confirmation of the constitutional amendment, the new constitution was promulgated on October 29, 1987 with the actual enforcement of the constitution taking effect beginning February 25, 1988, some 4 months after the promulgation. The proposal for the 9th constitutional amendment (the constitution for the 6th Republic) was composed of the preamble of the constitution, the main provisions consisting of 130 articles, and the supplementary provisions consisting of 6 articles. Some 37% of the provisions contained in the 5th Republic constitution were amended in the new constitution, with a significantly higher share of democratic elements in the said constitution compared to the constitution of the 5th Republic.

The key contents of the proposal for the 9th constitutional amendment were that the presidential election system was to be changed from the indirect elections to the direct elections, and that the term of the president was to be reduced from the current 7-year single term to a 5-year single term. Moreover, the parliamentary inspection of the administration was revived with the constitutional amendment. Other changes include: (1) the Supreme Court judge was changed to "chief justice," and the president was required to obtain the consent of the National Assembly when appointing the new chief justice, (2) the Constitutional Council was abolished and was replaced by the Constitutional Court, which was to perform the following functions: (i) ruling on the constitutionality of laws; (ii) issuing judgments on the impeachment and dissolution of political parties; and (iii) making a ruling with regard to disputes between state institutions and with regard to constitutional complaints.

On December 16, 1987, Roh Tae Woo, the presidential candidate for the Democratic Justice Party, emerged victorious in the 13th presidential elections, becoming the 13th president of the Republic, winning 36.5% of the valid votes. On February 25, 1988, two months after the presidential elections, president-elect Roh Tae Woo was sworn in as president in the front garden of the National Assembly building, starting his five-year presidency.

The Roh Tae Woo administration installed the Administrative Reform Committee upon its inauguration, in an attempt to come up with an improved proposal for the reshuffling of the government organization. The committee lasted until July 1989 on a temporary basis, and set up the following guidelines for the administrative reform: (1) pursue democratization and guarantee human rights protection; (2) boost the autonomy and creativity in the private sector; (3) realize the reunification; (4) respond to the internationalization era; (5) prepare for the era of localization; (6) ensure sustainable economic growth; (7) realize equality in the welfare services; and (8) improve the efficiency of the administrative system.

In what was recorded as the first reshuffling of the government organization by the Roh Tae Woo administration, the National Government Organization Act was amended by the end of 1989, splitting the Ministry of Culture and Information into the Ministry of Culture and the Ministry of Information, while the Environmental Office was promoted to the Ministry of Environment, which came to be directly controlled by the Prime Ministerial Office with the amendment (the amended National Government Organization Act, Law No. 4183, December 30, 1989). Also, in a move to prepare the country for the deepening globalization, industrialization, and urbanization trends, the administration strengthened some functions of the Ministry of Foreign Affairs, Ministry of Health and Society, Ministry of Labor, and Ministry of Transportation, and transferred and adjusted the partial functions of the Ministry of Sports and Ministry of Culture and Education. In the 2nd reshuffling that was done in 1990, the Board of National Unification was renamed "Board of Unification" while the Minister of the Board of Unification was promoted to vice prime minister, followed by the renaming of the Ministry of Culture and Education to the Ministry of Education, and the Ministry of Sports to the Ministry of Youth and Sports. The Census and Statistics Bureau in the Economic Planning Board was also revamped and promoted to the National Statistics Office; the Central Meteorological Observatory was promoted to the Korea Meteorological Administration; and the Headquarters of the National Police under the Ministry of Internal Affairs was revamped and promoted to the National Police Agency, along with the installation of the National Police Commission (amended Government Organization Act, Law No. 4268, December 27, 1990). The Roh Tae Woo administration pushed forward with the reshuffling of the government organization on the pretext of instituting a "small government" by installing the Administrative Reform Committee, but ended up expanding the size of the government organization by the end of the administration compared to the one at the administration's inauguration.

2. Objectives and directions of the government administration

The Roh Tae Woo administration was inaugurated amidst the shifting trend of the times marked by a significantly expanded political and social room for democracy and autonomy in the wake of the June 29 Declaration. The need to change the style of government administration emerged to ensure that the government could respond effectively to the shifting social and economic environment, including the expansion of human rights and popular participation, the growth of creativity and spontaneity in the private sector, the opening and globalization of the country's economy, and the popular demand for the democratization of the country's political system.

In his inaugural address on February 25, 1988, President Roh Tae Woo declared the new age of national independence and proposed democratic reform and national harmony as the key directions of the government administration. Just as President Roh had advocated ever since the June 29 Declaration, the vision of the government administration of the 6th Republic was to realize the "great age of the ordinary people."

With regard to the objectives of the government administration, its political objective was to root out the legacy of political oppression and abusive exercise of power while at the same time establishing the foundation for the peaceful transition of power. Its economic objective was to realize liberation from poverty. As for its goals in the social welfare area, it stressed the need for popular participation for national growth while at the same time proposing the goals of government administration, including the creation of a social consensus based on reconciliation and discussion, marching forward towards an open society on the foundation of a liberal democratic society, and leaping forward into an industrialized welfare state capable of delivering welfare benefits to the people. Furthermore, the administration stressed the need to realize peaceful reunification through the establishment of peace in the Korean Peninsula while also aiming to promote an environment of mutual trust between the two Koreas. Towards this end, the administration drew attention to the closed nature of the North Korean regime and urged the immediate opening of the country. Among all the pending objectives, however, the Roh Tae Woo administration put forward national security as its overriding goal.

Upon the inauguration, the Roh Tae Woo administration laid out the directions for its government administration, including national independence, democratic reconciliation, balanced development, and prosperity through reunification. The key directive of the government administration of the 6th Republic was to realize the great age of the ordinary people, as had been advocated since the June 29 Declaration, which was aimed at making the Republic of Korea a country where the good citizens would rise as the masters of the country, without receiving privileged or discriminatory treatment, and at creating the great age of popular participation.

First, the administration proposed the objective of national independence in an attempt to foster an independent spirit so that each individual Korean would demonstrate the national capabilities in the global competition, armed with pride and self-esteem. The objective was intended to confirm the people's capabilities, pride, and independent spirit, thereby growing them as the principal agents recognized on the global stage. Specifically, the administration anticipated that the cultural creative power of the people would play the central role in realizing the creative fusion of the Western and Eastern cultures and in advancing in the race for an information society, which had been dominated by the advanced economies of the world. With this serving as a momentum, the administration intended to recover the mutual trust between the government and the people, and to derive public support for the democratic government.

Second, the administration proposed to abolish the legacy of the past authoritarian rule and to promote democratic harmony for the development of democracy. The administration believed that genuine democracy would be achieved in the 6th Republic if harmony among the different regions, social classes, and generations as well as understanding and reconciliation between individuals and groups would be realized. The administration also stressed that the growing social diversity resulting from the rapid industrialization should be accepted as a given fact, but that the government would do away with the past governing practices centered on administrative oversight. Therefore, the administration intended to implement the measures of democratic reform aimed at the democratic reconciliation of the country.

Third, the 6th Republic was clearly aware of the negative side effects of the country's rapid industrialization in the process of the country's economic and social development during the period of rapid growth. In other words, the administration started to put more weight on the value of balanced development across politics, society, and culture in its government administration in the wake of the country's graduation from a developing country. The administration understood the series of such measures as the efforts aimed at pursuing and harmonizing the people's mental values and quality of life simultaneously in a paradigm shift from the past national development strategy marked by the "economy first" principle.

Fourth, the administration aimed to link its diplomatic efforts with the growth of the national power in designing the initiatives for the country's prosperity through reunification, which again signified that the administration would push for the expansion of the country's exchanges with the Communist bloc, thereby making the country's relationship with it official in the implementation of its diplomacy. As such, the administration strove to improve the country's relationship with Pyongyang and with the countries surrounding the Korean Peninsula at the same time by concentrating its diplomatic and unification capabilities. Such directions of the government administration were implemented as the key tasks of the government administration spanning all areas, including the economy and culture.

Section 2

Key Policy Initiatives

1. The Northern Policy

Background

The Northern Policy signifies the new foreign policy initiative that was established by the Roh Tae Woo administration upon its assumption of power in 1988. The policy was established based on the groundbreaking idea that shifted the traditional anti-Communist-bloc direction of the Republic of Korea's foreign policy, and that contains the bold idea of reunifying the Korean Peninsula by advancing the inter-Korean relations through growing exchanges with Pyongyang. In the larger context, the Northern Policy defines the country's foreign policy aimed at the Asian socialist states, including Communist China, the former Soviet Union, and the socialist states in Eastern Europe, as well as those policies aimed at Pyongyang. The Northern Policy was part of the proactive unification foreign policy that capitalized on the changing political environment in the Korean Peninsula and the surrounding regions, which was propelled by the shifting international politics and the resulting positive developments, including the spread of a conciliatory climate between the East and the West, the reform and open-door policy of the former Soviet Union and Eastern Europe, and the rising status of the Republic of Korea on the international stage.

Implementation System

The measure in the series of actions implemented as part of the Northern Policy was the Special Presidential Declaration for National Self-Respect, Reunification, and Prosperity (henceforth, "July 7 Declaration") unveiled before the opening of the 1988 Seoul Olympic Games. President Roh Tae Woo clarified his aspiration to usher in a new age of national self-respect, reunification, and prosperity with the six key initiatives outlined below, which would be realized by building a social, cultural, economic, and political community participated in by all the citizens of the country based on the principles of self-reliance, peace, democracy, and welfare:

1. The administration will push forward with mutual exchanges between the North and South Korean people, including politicians, businessmen, journalists, priests, cultural representatives, artists, athletes, scholars, and students, while also opening the doors for the overseas Koreans to visit the two Koreas freely.
2. Even before the final resolution of the North-South Korea Red Cross Talks, all available means shall be exhausted to help the separated families determine their mutual survival statuses and addresses, and to enable exchanges of letters and visits to their mutual homes.
3. Open the doors for all kinds of exchanges between the two Koreas, and consider the inter-Korean trade as internal trade within the Korean people.
4. The administration hopes to see the balanced development of the economy of the Korean people, which would lead to the improvement of the quality of life of both the North and South Koreans, and would not oppose the trade of non-military materials with North Korea by South Korea's allies.
5. End the unnecessary competition and confrontational diplomacy between the two Koreas, and instead help Pyongyang contribute to the good of the international community. The administration also hopes that the representatives of the two Koreas would freely meet with each other on the international stage, and would cooperate with each other to promote the shared interests of the Korean people.
6. The administration is willing to cooperate with Pyongyang in its efforts to improve its relations with South Korea's allies, including the United States and Japan. It will also strive

Figure 4–1. Implementation System of the Northern Policy

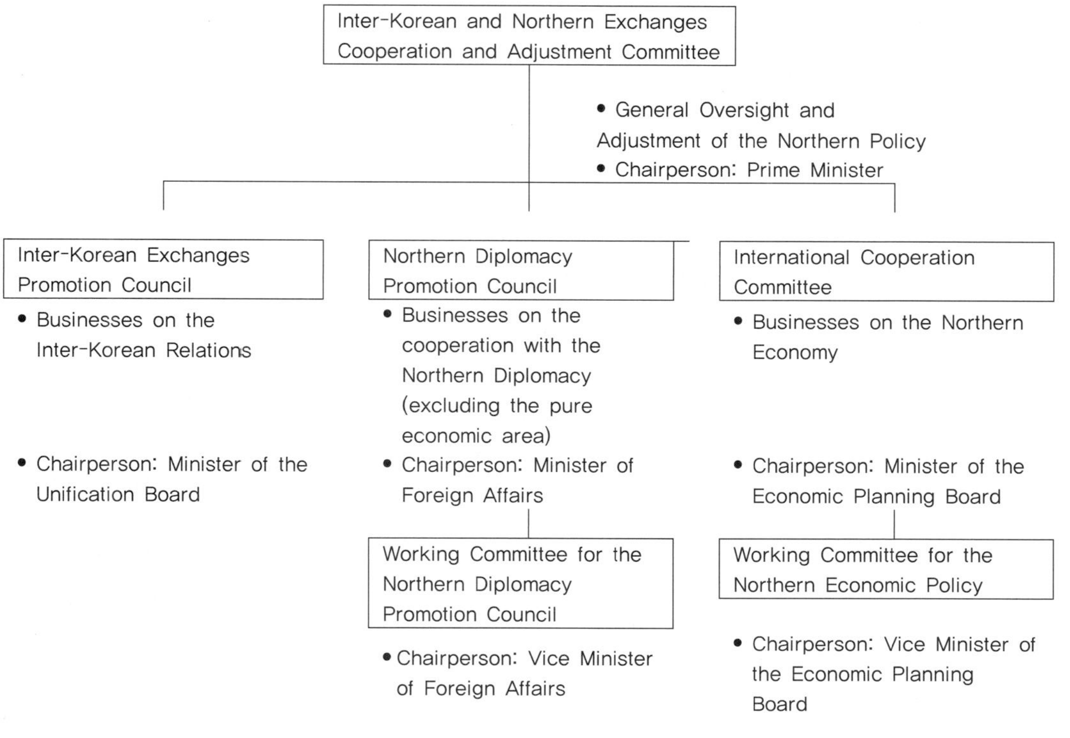

to improve South Korea's relations with the socialist states, including the Soviet Union and China.

What follows is a summary of the established measures as a result of the implementation of the Northern Policy. First, the ROK government installed and operated the Inter-Korean Exchanges and Cooperation Promotion Committee on March 31, 1989. The committee was composed of fewer than 14 vice-ministerial officers from the related ministries and was chaired by the Minister of the Unification Board. The committee was given the role of screening and adjusting the key policies on the inter-Korean exchanges and cooperation. The committee then prepared the "Basic Guidelines on the Inter-Korean Exchanges and Cooperation" to specify all the issues related with the promotion of the inter-Korean exchanges and cooperation, which was enforced on June 12, 1989. In a move to specify the provisions required for the enforcement of such guidelines, the "Detailed Implementation Guidelines for Inter-Korean Exchanges and Cooperation" was enacted and enforced on July 21, 1989. Then the government promulgated the Inter-Korean Exchanges and Cooperation Act on August 1, 1990, which was followed by the promulgation of the Inter-Korean Exchanges and Cooperation Enforcement Act on August 9, 1990. The key provisions in the laws governing the inter-Korean exchanges and cooperation specified weekly and daily contacts between the two Koreas, inter-Korean visit, inter-Korean trade, and inter-Korean cooperative projects.

Second, as the human and material exchanges between the two Koreas began to pick up after the tentative enactment and enforcement of the "Basic Guidelines on the Inter-Korean Exchanges and Cooperation," which was aimed at providing an institutional guarantee for the inter-Korean exchanges and cooperation, the government enacted the Inter-Korean Cooperation Fund to support the booming traffic. The key provisions of the said act specified that the inter-Korean cooperation funds shall be used only to cover the expenses or provide the loans required for the various exchanges and cooperative projects between the two Koreas, and that the oversight of the management of the funds shall be assumed by the Minister of the Unification Board, with its actual businesses delegated to financial institutions.

Implementation Process and Contents

The Northern Policy was implemented roughly in five phases, as discussed below. In the first phase, the administration embarked on clarifying its overall policy directions before its full-fledged implementation of the Northern Policy. In his special presidential declaration made on July 7, 1988, President Roh Tae Woo declared to the world the directions of his administration's reunification and foreign policy as part of the administration's move to promote an environment conducive to the successful hosting of the Seoul Olympic Games. Additionally, in the address he delivered in the 44th United Nations General Assembly on October 18 of the same year, President Roh Tae Woo made it clear to the world that the administration would advance a cooperative partnership between the two Koreas, in which Seoul and Pyongyang would cooperate with each other for the commonwealth of the Korean people. President Roh Tae Woo announced the "Plan to Reunify the Korean Ethnic Community" in his special address in the National Assembly on September 11, 1989, which was prepared by responding proactively to the changing local and global environment and by reflecting the diverse opinions of the people.

In the second phase, the establishment of diplomatic ties with the Communist bloc states emerged as the biggest task for the administration. The ROK government eyed the establishment of diplomatic relations with Hungary, one of the first states in Eastern Europe that pushed forward with the transition of its economic system to one based on the market economy, which became a reality in February 1989. Shortly after, in November and December 1989, respectively, the administration successfully established diplomatic relations with Poland and Yugoslavia, and in March 1990, with the Czech Republic, Bulgaria, Romania, and Mongolia in Asia.

In the third phase, the administration concentrated on establishing diplomatic relations with the Soviet Union, the leader of the Communist bloc, on the strength of the performances and experiences it had accumulated in the previous phases. Moscow was in the midst of extreme confusion during the transition period; it was struggling to dispose of the socialist regime it had been running since the success of the Bolshevik Revolution in 1917 while at the same time pushing forward with the simultaneous introduction of the market economy and democracy. Likewise, the administration had to go through a markedly more complex and challenging process of establishing diplomatic relations with the Soviet Union compared to the other Communist bloc states in Eastern Europe, but it eventually succeeded in normalizing its diplomatic relations with Moscow on September 30, 1990.

In the fourth phase, the administration succeeded in normalizing its diplomatic relations with China and with the rest of the Communist bloc states. However, due to various complicated factors that were involved, establishing diplomatic relations with China was not an easy task. Seoul and Beijing finally succeeded in establishing full diplomatic ties by signing a joint statement on August 24, 1992.

In the fifth phase, the administration pushed forward with the normalization of the inter-Korean relations on the strength of the performances it had achieved with the normalization of its diplomatic relations with the Communist bloc states. However, despite efforts by the communist states in Eastern Europe and Asia to transform their respective regimes through the adoption of the market economy and democracy, Pyongyang insisted on sticking to the socialist regime. With the normalization of the inter-Korean relations being the key task, with overriding significance, for the Roh Tae Woo administration, it finally succeeded in concluding the Inter-Korean Basic Agreement on December 13, 1991 after a series of talks with Pyongyang, starting with the preliminary talk for the High-Level Inter-Korean Talks scheduled for February 1989. The adoption and enforcement of the Inter-Korean Basic Agreement was realized nearly half a century after the division of the Korean Peninsula. South Korea had since maintained the policy for its exchanges and cooperation with North Korea; by the early 1990s, many conglomerates and small enterprises in South Korea wished to implement North Korean projects, emboldened by the prospect of improvement in the inter-Korean exchanges and cooperation. As part of such moves, leaders of top South Korean conglomerates visited Pyongyang and had discussions on the potential economic cooperation with North Korea; some even succeeded in importing materials from North Korea.

Performance and Assessment

For an overview of the achievements of the Northern Policy, the key achievement of the policy was that the country was able to demonstrate the superiority of the market economy and democracy through the policy by riding the crest of the global tectonic shift marked by the victory of the Western world led by the United States over the Communist bloc led by the Soviet Union. In addition, the successful establishment of diplomatic ties with the states in the former socialist bloc, which were formerly inaccessible to South Korea, provided immense economic opportunities to the country and at the same time expanded the country's diplomatic horizon. Meanwhile, the administration was able to accumulate valuable experiences in terms of the inter-Korean relations as it pushed forward with the direct inter-Korean negotiations. In other words, unlike the inter-Korean relations before the implementation of the Northern Policy, during which Seoul and Pyongyang ran their respective regimes as if their northern/southern counterpart never existed, the two Koreas were finally able to make practical contact and have exchanges with each other after the introduction of the Northern Policy.

In conclusion, the Northern Policy would be considered a success if its assessment would be limited to the achievements realized during the presidency of Roh Tae Woo, but its success would be considered less than satisfactory if the development of the inter-Korean relations after the 6th Republic would be evaluated as well. Therefore, it would be critical to examine the potential insufficiencies found in the planning, establishment, and implementation of the unification policies in the Northern Policy package to meet the future policy demands triggered by the urgent need for reunification of the Korean Peninsula led by South Korea.

2. High-speed rail construction project (KTX)

Background

As the existing transportation infrastructure grew increasingly inadequate to handle the ever-expanding transportation demand in the wake of the country's rapid economic growth, the share of the transportation costs in the total logistic budget ballooned to unprecedented levels, thereby triggering a series of discussions on the potential need to renovate the conventional transportation system. Particular concerns were the chronic traffic congestion and the excessive transportation demand along the Seoul - Busan axis, which accounted for near 70% of the country's GDP. Such problem had to be resolved as soon as possible to ensure the continued improvement of the country's international competence. According to the official estimates, the Seoul - Busan axis would be filled up to capacity by 1985 if the conventional transportation system would be maintained, and would begin to experience transportation difficulties in the period from 1985 to 1990. Moreover, the economic loss due to the excessive logistic costs was projected to add up to KRW 2.4 trillion by 2001 as the national logistic cost per GDP was about two times higher than that of the United States or Japan. To resolve this growing dilemma, Korea Advanced Institute for Science and Technology (KAIST) came up with a proposal to build a new rail network as an optimal solution to the country's transportation woes as the limited transportation capacity of the Seoul-Busan axis would seriously undermine the national competence if the then-existing transportation system were to be maintained.

Implementation System

KAIST submitted two proposals (an additional double-track railroad between Seoul and Busan and a passenger-only Seoul - Busan high-speed rail) to the government. In February 1979, when KAIST was still weighing various options, President Park Jung Hee ordered the establishment of a long-term transportation alternative in the State of the Nation Address that he delivered, in his meeting with the Ministry of Transportation. The plan he delivered was then reflected in the 5th Economic and Social Development Plan (1982～1986) in the form of a 160-km-long Seoul - Daejeon high-speed rail plan (1986～1989). While revising the 5th Economic and Social Development Plan in 1983, a decision was made to construct a high-speed rail depending on the results of a feasibility test on the Seoul - Busan high-speed rail. The "Feasibility Study on the Long-Term Transportation Investment in the Seoul - Busan Axis and on the Construction of a High-Speed Rail" was jointly performed by Louis Begen in the United States, Compsax in Denmark, Korea Research Institute for Human Settlements, and Hyundai Engineering for a period of 21 months, from March 1983 to November 1984. The need to build a high-speed rail started to be accepted widely after the completion of the feasibility study. The construction of a high-speed rail was supposed to be reflected in the 5th Five-Year Economic and Social Development Plan, but it was postponed as it was concluded that investing in a massive social overhead capital project would be unrealistic given that the country was concentrating all its available resources on the preparations for the 1988 Seoul Olympic Games, after the country's successful bid for the Games. After the successful hosting of the 1988 Seoul Olympic Games, the government decided to perform a technological survey for the construction of the high-speed rail during the period covered by the 6th Five-Year Economic and Social Development Plan. Finally, the decision to construct the Seoul - Busan high-speed rail was announced in May 1989.

As part of the measures taken after the announcement, on July 24, 1989, the government inaugurated the Committee for the Promotion of the Construction of the High-Speed Rail and the New International Airport, which was chaired by the Vice Prime Minister and Minister of the Economic Planning Board and was vice-chaired by the Minister of Transportation. Afterwards, the government installed the High-Speed Rail Planning Office in the National Railroad Administration, which was revamped and expanded to the High-Speed Rail Project Planning Group in February 1991. On June 15, 1990, the Basic Plan for the Seoul - Busan High-Speed Rail Construction Project was finalized and was announced after the resolution by the 3rd Committee for the Promotion of the Construction of the High-Speed Rail and the New International Airport. According to the resolution, the total extension of the high-speed rail would be 409 km between Seoul and Busan, the maximum design speed would be 350 km/h, the scheduled operating time would be 90 minutes for a non-stop run, the project duration would be from 1992 to 1998, the construction budget would be KRW 5.8462 trillion (rolling stocks: KRW 1.2144 trillion as of 1989), the projected number of passengers would be 218,000/day, and the service route would be Seoul - Cheonan - Daejeon - Daegu - Gyeongju - Busan.

Upon receiving the initial RFPs on the import of rolling stocks from France, Germany, and Japan, six rounds of submission and assessment of the modified RFPs were implemented. The Alstom consortium of France was selected as the preferred bidder in 1993, with the final signing of the contract for the import of the rolling stocks done in 1994, after eight months of negotiations.

However, the Seoul - Busan High-Speed Rail Construction Project needed to be readjusted to reflect the various incremental changes that had occurred across several areas, including the construction volume, the complementary design for the rail bed after the selection of rolling stocks, and the inflation and ballooning budget due to the continuous demands posed by the local governing bodies and other associated organizations. The government came up with a revised decision to construct the high-speed rail according to the original basic plan but in a phased manner, by taking into account the difficult economic situation and other aspects of the social environment.

Implementation Process and Contents

As part of the preparation for the opening of the first-phase section, the Comprehensive Plan for Operation Preparation and the Consolidated Operation Plan were established, followed by comprehensive high-speed train trial runs, commercial trial runs, and facility inspection and system construction, in an attempt to fix any potential issue that may arise during the commercial operation of the high-speed trains. The opening ceremony of the high-speed rail was held on March 30, 2004 at the new consolidated Seoul Station, amidst the great interest of all the people. The second-phase project covered the construction of new high-speed rail tracks in the Daegu-Busan section from 2004 to 2010, and in the Daejeon and Daegu city sections, respectively. The overall construction schedule was shortened by two years through the efficient use of construction equipment and labor, thanks to the economic rebound from the severe recession triggered by the global financial crisis.

The construction of the high-speed rail gave rise to conflicts over the environmental issue. Wonhyo Tunnel, which crosses Mt. Cheonseong, was designed to pass an underground section 300 to 400 meters deep from the surface and was composed of hard rocks, so that it would not interfere with the wetlands. The Buddhist groups and environmental activists in the Busan, Ulsan, and Gyeongnam region, however, demanded a flat-out cancellation of the Mt. Cheonseong section due to the potential damage that it might inflict on the natural environment and ecosystem. The conflict over the high-speed rail project further deepened as the activist groups in Busan released a statement in which they argued that "although the environmental issues should be resolved, the construction should not be delayed for the sake of the Busan economy." When the presidential candidate who pledged during the campaign that he would "cancel the Seoul - Busan High-Speed Rail passing the Mt. Cheonseong and Mt. Keumjeong sections after a comprehensive review" emerged victorious in the December 2002 election, the construction was suspended, followed by the formation of the Line Reappraisal Committee to reassess the economic and environmental aspects of the concerned sections. The construction resumed, however, after it was decided in the Policy Readjustment Meeting on Pending Administrative Issues that it would be best to stick to the original plan. The activist group countered this decision by "filing an injunction to stop the construction." A total of 12 field surveys were conducted to determine the potential impact of the project on the environment and ecosystem, and based on the results of such surveys and after comparing the states before and after the drilling of Wonhyo Tunnel, it was concluded that no environmental impact could be reasonably expected from the tunnel. The five-year conflict over the Mt. Cheonseong section ended in June 2006, when the Supreme Court rejected the appellate injunction to stop the construction. In view of the lessons it learned from the conflict over Wonhyo Tunnel, the Korea Rail Network installed the Conflict Management Review Committee, an institution designed to manage conflicts preemptively, thereby ensuring the smooth implementation of any future construction project.

The opening ceremony of the second-phase section was held on October 28, 2010, along with the building dedication ceremony for Osong Station, Gimcheon (Kumi) Station, New Gyeongju Station, and Ulsan Station constructed along the Phase 2 section. With the second-phase construction, the Seoul - Busan Trunk Line High-Speed Rail was finally completed.

Meanwhile, the Honam High-Speed Rail Basic Plan was established during the period from 1991 to 1997, beginning with the feasibility study in 1990 on the Honam High-Speed Rail Project. The commercial feasibility of the Honam High-Speed Rail was assessed in 1999, which was followed by the survey and research service performed jointly by the Ministry of Construction and Transportation, Korea Transport Institute, and Korea Research Institute for Human Settlements.

The plan to transform the Honam Line into a high-speed electric rail by 2004 was incorporated in the Plan for a Key National Traffic Network established towards the end of 1999. As the economic feasibility of the Honam High-Speed Rail Project was confirmed in the preliminary feasibility study in 2000 by Korea Development Institute, the budget for design and construction works amounting to KRW 55.5 billion was secured in the FY 2001 budgetary proposal. The plan laid out the construction schedule, in which the electrification of the existing Daejeon - Mokpo Line was to be implemented first so that the high-speed trains would already be running along the tracks by the opening of the first-phase section of the Seoul - Busan High-Speed Rail, with the annual investment plan for the necessary project costs finalized as well. The construction of the Honam High-Speed Rail started in October 2001 and was completed in 2004.

Performance and Assessment

In the second-phase construction, after struggling through numerous challenges in the first-phase construction of the high-speed rail project, the project team performed the detailed design verification and P.C. Box standardization drawings it had skipped during the first-phase construction. Also, the engineers specializing in SYSTRA, with rich experiences in the related projects, were stationed as residents so that they would collaborate with the field engineers and transfer the necessary technologies. Such design verification service enabled the transfer of the advanced technologies to the local engineering staff, thereby helping them enlarge the technological capability to implement high-speed rail construction projects not only in South Korea but also in other overseas sites.

The speed revolution triggered by the opening of the high-speed rail led to a paradigm shift in the people's everyday lives. As the people, capital, and technologies started to cluster around the KTX stations, the stations emerged as the traffic and commercial center of each region while the entire country turned into a half-day life zone. Moreover, the Act on Railway Station Sphere Development and Utilization was revised with the intention of strengthening the KTX station in each region into the hub of regional economic development as well as the local traffic center, thereby promoting the active development of the respective railway station spheres.

In addition, the localization of the high-speed train rolling stocks and electrical and signaling technologies, and the related facilities that were developed locally in relation to the high-speed rail project, helped the country shave off the related costs. The country had to struggle through numerous difficulties from the commencement to the completion of the Seoul - Busan High-Speed Rail Construction Project, but the efforts of the engineers to realize the thorough transfer of the related technologies bore fruit and yielded several achievements. Furthermore, the country's self-reliance in high-speed rail technology achieved in the process of project implementation allowed it to attain the necessary competence in the overseas markets. The country became the fifth country in the world to own a high-speed rail through the establishment of a self-sufficient rolling stock manufacturing technology and by signing a technology transfer contract with Alstom of France. In the area of railway construction project management, construction supervision, and consulting, the Korea Rail Network was so highly regarded for its technological excellence that it was able to open an office in China, thereby laying the groundwork for exporting related technologies. The country failed to win the bid for the railway construction projects in Nigeria and Brazil, respectively, but the South Korean engineers are currently involved in many railway projects in Algeria, Iraq, Vietnam, and Uzbekistan, and they are working hard to enter other markets, including Malaysia, the United States, Nigeria, Italia, and Brazil.

3. Incheon International Airport construction project

Background

The Incheon International Airport construction project was driven by the prospective demand for international airport services in the greater Seoul area and by the changing social and economic environment in South Korea and in other parts of the world. The international politics began to change dramatically beginning in the mid-1980s, with the rough direction of such changes pointing to the end of the Cold War, the spread of the open - door policy, and the renewed battle over economic supremacy. Such shifting global mega trends sparked a series of changes in the logistics and human exchanges between countries, regions, and cities, as well as fresh changes in the flow of capital, information, and technology and in the international network.

The rapid structural changes in the South Korean economy, society, and culture boosted the demand for air travel in the country. The country became the 10th largest economy in the world, thanks to its rapid economic growth in the 1960s and 1970s, which again triggered a dramatic increase in the logistic volumes and international human flow, along with the remarkable improvement in the people's living standard. Specifically, South Korea's successful hosting of the 1986 Seoul Asian Games and the 1988 Seoul Olympic Games boosted the country's prestige and reputation, thereby making the world rediscover the country's hidden potential and prospect for development. The liberalization of overseas travel enforced in 1989 further accelerated the country's adoption of an open-door policy while dramatically increasing the number of South Koreans traveling to overseas destinations. The number of international passengers jumped by 13% annually since the liberalization of overseas travel, with a corresponding 30% yearly increase in domestic travel recorded as well. It was by far the highest growth in air travel demand throughout the world.

Such dramatic rise in the demand for international air travel revived the old question about the handling capacity of Gimpo International Airport, which had been handling the country's airfreight and air passengers for some time. The government began to review the potential of Gimpo International Airport in earnest beginning in the early 1980s. Having concluded that the handling capacity of Gimpo International Airport would be breached by the mid-1990s, the government started actively deliberating on the possible construction of a new international airport in the greater Seoul area.

In its beginning-of-the-year report to President Roh Tae Woo in January 1989, the Ministry of Transportation mentioned the urgent need to construct a new international airport in the greater Seoul area, which eventually led to the official confirmation of the construction of a new international airport in such area. In March of the same year, the proposal to construct a new international airport was established based on the research materials that had been collected thus far. Based on such proposal, a feasibility study for the selection of candidate sites for the new international airport in the greater Seoul area was conducted in June of the same year, followed by the promulgation of the regulations governing the New International Airport Construction Promotion Committee by Presidential Decree No. 12762 on July 24 of the same year. Based on the results of the feasibility study, the candidate sites for the new international airport were selected, and among them were Yeongjong Island and Sihwa District. In June 1990, after assessing the climatic conditions, noise levels, accessibility, and prospects for future expansion of the candidate sites, the government confirmed and announced that Yeongjong Island was the ideal site for the construction of the new international airport.

Implementation System

For the construction of Incheon International Airport, the government formed an organizational structure within the administration, including a dedicated department. The Ministry of Transportation took charge of the project, which was again followed by the formation of an advisory committee composed of aviation specialists who were to provide advice on the construction of the new international airport in March 1989, right after the inauguration of the Roh Tae Woo administration. In July 1989, the New Airport Construction Promotion Committee, which was composed of the heads of 17 government agencies, was formed in accordance with the aforementioned presidential decree. The New Airport Construction Planning Group was installed in the Ministry of Transportation, along with the formation of the working-level committee for the construction of the new airport. The New Airport Construction Planning Group took charge of the project, including the establishment of the basic plan for the construction of Incheon International Airport. In January 1992, the New Airport Construction Headquarters was inaugurated in Korea Airport Corporation as the dedicated institution for the construction of the new airport. Korea Airport Corporation thus took charge of the construction of the new international airport.

On May 31, 1991, the Greater Seoul Area New Airport Construction Promotion Act was promulgated as Law No. 4384. The act was aimed at preparing for the ballooning demand for air travel in the greater Seoul area and, thereby, contributing to the advancement of the national economy through the efficient execution of the new-international-airport construction project in the greater Seoul area by specifying the provisions required for the speedy construction of the airport.

Since any massive project would entail corresponding costs, the timely acquisition of the necessary funds largely determines the success or failure of any project. The financing of the Incheon International Airport construction project was realized by tapping the various means available at the time. A total of KRW 6.7712 trillion was forecasted to be required for the Phase 1 project of Incheon International Airport. Of such amount, the total amount available for the actual construction of the airport, excluding the construction administration costs, was about KRW 5.6 trillion. The financing of the project was to be realized through the following means: (1) through the fiscal support from the government; (2) through internal financing by the project implementer (Korea Airport Corporation in the initial stage of the project, Incheon International Airport Corporation beginning in 1999); and (3) by attracting private investment in the airport facility, to be participated in by the private sector. The fiscal support from the national coffers accounted for 39.9% of the total project budget. The other 43.3% of the budget was financed internally by Incheon Airport Corporation and the remaining 16.8% was financed by private investors. The funds from the national coffers were invested in constructing the basic facility of the airport, including securing the right of way, site renovation, and constructing an airfield facility.

On March 29, 2001, some 8 years after the groundbreaking ceremony in November 1992, the historic opening ceremony of Incheon International Airport was held. The airport was modeled after Singapore's Changi International Airport during the construction stage, but it soon went past the level of Changi International Airport in terms of overall operational quality. Beginning in 2005, the airport was consistently touted to be the No. 1 airport in the world.

Implementation Process and Contents

Conflict management emerged as one of the key imperatives for the Incheon International Airport construction project as it faced substantial opposition from many activist groups and experts during the construction process and even before, since the announcement of the plan. The controversy centered mainly on the issue of soft ground, environmental/ecological impact, and airport noise. The government managed to control diverse forms of conflict associated with the construction of the airport using multiples approaches. First, the issue of the potential problems in the finished runways due to the soft ground was raised. Since the lot for the new airport was to be formed by reclaiming the mudflats, the 24-meter-deep sediment on average underneath the reclaimed mudflat may show differential settlement along the paved runways during airplane takeoff and landing. Specifically, some argued that the prospective reclamation sites that were to be the runway might not be able to perform at the desired level because the paved surfaces would become uneven overtime due to the differential settlement along the runway. The expected subsidence rate of the reclaimed lot in Yeongjong Island, however, would be lower than expected because the runways were to be built on the underlying rock formation by reclaiming some 5-meter-deep mudflats on average, whereas Kansai International Airport in Japan was built on the lot where it now stands by reclaiming some 20-meter-deep mudflats on average. The government also argued that it would be able to minimize the subsidence rate by employing cutting-edge reclamation techniques such as sand piling work, paper drain, pack drain, and preloading.

On the environmental front, opposition was posed due to the concerns over the bird habitats near the proposed site. The incidences of the spotting of migratory birds near the proposed airfield changed annually depending on the survey conditions, but the number of avian species and the total number of individual birds did not change significantly, according to the survey.

The demand for international air travel and airfreight exploded in the wake of the Asian financial crisis that hit the country towards the end of the 1990s. The design capacity of Incheon International Airport was forecasted to be saturated as the demand for international air travel was projected to grow by 8.8% per year for the next 10 years. The passenger terminal ramps were forecasted to be filled up to the design capacity by 2001, the airfreight terminal by 2004, the passenger terminal by 2005, and the runways by 2008, thereby potentially deteriorating the overall service quality of the airport. Moreover, the rising number of prospective new airlines flying international routes from Incheon International Airport raised the issue of facility expansion. The Ministry of Transportation finalized the Phase 2 Project and announced that it would be implemented from 2002 to 2008, after conducting comprehensive reviews across diverse issues, including the absolute construction period required for the expansion of the airport facility and the early realization of the Northeast Asian hub airport. Since the timely introduction of a new facility was critical in ensuring the competitive edge of the airport in its race to rise as the international hub airport by beating Japan and China, the expansion of the airport facility, including the passenger terminal and airport ramps, had to be expedited. Also, an airport complex city had to be constructed, which would include leisure and sports facilities and an international business center. In view of such shifting environment, the government is currently pushing forward with the Phase 3 Project of Incheon International Airport, which had begun in 2013 and is expected to be completed in 2017.

Performance and Assessment

Since its opening, Incheon International Airport has continued to grow at an unprecedented pace. It is now considered the best of the best airports in the world and is being emulated by over 1,000 airports operating in the four corners of the world. The airport has never been unseated from the top position in the global ranking of airports for 10 straight years, from 2005 to 2014.

The world-renowned speed and convenience of the airport's immigration/emigration and passport control service is perceived to have reached the world-class level, differentiating the airport from the rest of the pack. The ICAO agreement recommends airports to complete the emigration/immigration processing within 60 and 45 minutes, respectively, through the simplification of the passport control and customs clearance. However, Incheon International Airport managed to shorten the average processing time to 19 and 12 minutes, respectively, about three times faster than the international standard, thanks to the adoption of cutting-edge information technologies such as the installation of automatic immigration kiosks.

The key success factors of Incheon International Airport are as shown below.

First, the time-to-market and geographic conditions of the airport during the project implementation were exceptionally fitting. Its stellar success as a key national project was largely attributable to the unmatched level of fusion of the following two factors: (1) the excellent and fitting geographic location of the airport both internally and externally; and (2) the superb time-to-market that responded to the changing situation of the time, and the preemptive response to the prospective changes.

When viewed from the economic-geographic perspective, being located in the center of the Yellow Sea Belt of the Korean Peninsula and being close to the capital city of the country, the airport can be accessed primarily from the greater Seoul area, with a population of 25 million, and secondarily, from the entire South Korea, with a population of 50 million. Upon the reunification of the two Koreas, the airport shall have been located in the center of the Korean Peninsula, with the potential to emerge as the key hub airport of the unified Korea. Furthermore, the airport's characteristics make it an ideal candidate for a hub airport as well as a strategic gate to Northeast Asia. With 43 megacities with a population of over one million located within a 3-hour 30-minute flight from the airport, it has the potential to rise as the center of the super international economic bloc. Located in the geographic hub well-connected to China, Japan, Southeast Asia, and the United States, the airport enjoys the benefit of an unmatched international geographic location.

In terms of the time-to-market, the airport was constructed at the peak of a dynamic period strewn with major changes in the international economy, including the end of the Cold War, the spread of the open-door policy, the deepening economic war, the human and logistic exchanges between countries, the liberalization of overseas travel, the 1986 Seoul Asian Games, and the 1988 Seoul Olympic Games. In short, it was the period during which South Korea was urgently required to respond to the challenges of the time as well as to the given opportunities. Specifically, Incheon International Airport was pushed forward as the key national project during the period when a hub airport was urgently needed in Northeast Asia, thereby making it one of the timeliest national projects ever at the time.

Another success factors of the project were that the airport construction project was selected at the right time as the national project and that the government played an important role in implementing the project efficiently. With a clear focus on the public interest that permeated the entire project mechanism from the planning to the implementation phase, the excellent leadership is largely attributable for the frictionless application of the government roles throughout the process of constructing Incheon International Airport. The leadership shone brighter, in particular, in the oversight of the construction sites. The stellar public leadership demonstrated throughout the project proves that hiring the right people, which in the Incheon International Airport construction project was realized by delegating the responsibility to the selected leaders, is effective in accomplishing spectacular results. On top of the individual leadership observed during the implementation of the project, the project's success was also attributable to the "fusion leadership" or "group leadership," in which the leaders and countless project participants bonded with one another, driven by their collective determination during the construction process. The frictionless implementation of the related businesses through the collaboration between the government and the local governing bodies also contributed to the success of the project. On another note, the collaborative partnership between the government and the private sector and that among private businesses can be considered another key success factor of the project. Given that the attraction of private investment from many different enterprises was critical for the new-airport construction project, the establishment of the public-private partnership (PPP), in which the government and the South Korean/foreign companies managed to collaborate flawlessly under the shared vision and goal of the construction of Incheon International Airport, was also critical for the project's success.

The triple coordination of the administrative, fiscal, and legal mechanisms in the process of implementing the project is also believed to have contributed to the success of the project. In other words, the triple unity of the administrative, legal, and fiscal factors supported the fluid implementation of the project. Furthermore, the prompt response to the changing international aviation environment and the improvement in the service satisfaction level can be attributed to the unmatched application of information technology (IT) to the airport operation. From the very beginning of the construction, the latest info-communication technologies were fused with the overall airport system. It can be said that the development and installation of IT software through various consortia of IT companies, including Samsung Electronics, played a key role in the success of the project. The application of IT to the key facility and integrated system of Incheon International Airport, the unprecedented mega project in the history of South Korea, can be thought to have contributed to the consistent development of many South Korean and other global IT companies.

Finally, the appropriate management of the diverse conflicts that arose in the process of the airport construction can be considered another success factor of the project. Many stakeholders harbored doubts regarding the project at the time of the construction, but the project leaders prevailed in the end by sticking to the principle of candid communication and objectivity by attacking the problem head-on. It can be seen as the successful application of the thesis-antithesis-synthesis-thesis+ structure, the dialectic paradigm of a conflict, to the resolution of the conflicts. Specifically, conflict management was done based on the dialectic paradigm in accordance with the following process: project announcement by the government → emergence of an opposite logic → communication between the proponents and the opponents → scientific response and complementary measure on the insufficient aspect → resolution of conflicts and successful implementation of the project.

Incheon International Airport has some issues that need to be addressed before the eventual success of the airport operation. First, the base of the passenger demand has to be expanded, and the percentage of transit passengers has to be pushed up. Today, some 40 million passengers travel via Incheon International Airport annually. The airport will need to meet the long-term goal of 100 million annual passengers if it is to rise as the best hub airport in Northeast Asia. Furthermore, the percentage of transit passengers, currently hovering at 18%, has to be raised to north of 25% in the long term. In response to the growing number of Japanese passengers flocking to the Incheon International Airport, Japan's Haneda International Airport recently took some bold measures in an attempt to compete more aggressively with Incheon International Airport, including the expansion of the international routes by lifting the 30-year-old restrictions on such and the operation of the duty-free shops and restaurants 24 hours a day. Some extraordinary efforts would be required to improve the international transfer function of Incheon International Airport. To continue to hold the high ground over Japan's Narita International Airport and Haneda International Airport and China's Pudong International Airport and Beijing Capital Airport, Incheon International Airport has to push ahead with some bold marketing and with the creation of a new service strategy, including the continuous expansion of new international routes and the attraction of new airlines.

In addition, the airport needs to push ahead with the facility-space fusion strategy by linking itself to its neighboring area. The airport will have to strive to transform its vicinity to a global super business center from the wide-area level by capitalizing on the surrounding geographic environment, including the newly developed free economic zone, the greater Seoul area, the geographic location of Incheon International Port, the neighboring global market connecting Japan and China, and the global hub from which passengers can fly to the Americas and Eurasia. It is recommended that global marketing be pushed forward with in an attempt to attract blue chip multinational corporations to the greater metropolitan area surrounding Incheon International Airport.

4. Introduction of the concept of public land ownership

Background

The real estate prices started to soar along with the speculative investment boom on real estate beginning in the second half of 1987. During the period commonly known as the third real estate boom (1988~1990), the land prices skyrocketed at an annual rate of 26.6% on average. The land and home prices skyrocketed to unprecedented levels as to threaten the everyday life of ordinary people with no home ownership, thereby undermining the social stability. Therefore, the government was forced to announce the August 10 Real Estate Stabilization Measure (the so-called "August 10 Measure"), in which the government laid out its plan to reform the land-related institution fundamentally based on the concept of public land ownership. The announcement included diverse measures aimed at stabilizing the land prices, including the enforcement of a more stringent transfer income tax system, the enforcement of the obligatory use of the certified contract forms, the planned introduction of the obligatory real estate registration system, the introduction of the composite land tax system, and the unification of the land pricing system in the short term, and the fundamental reform of the land system based on the concept of public land ownership in the long term.

Implementation System

The government decided to install and operate the Research Committee on the Concept of Public Land Ownership in the 1st Real Estate Policy Deliberation Committee (chairperson: the Vice Prime Minister) meeting held on August 11, 1988. Such decision was followed by the confirmation of the composition of the committee as well as the research topics for the working-level committee meeting on real estate stabilization measures held on August 25 of the same year. Upon the beginning of the operation of the research institute, the government installed the Concept of Public Land Ownership Preparation Group (chairperson: Vice Minister of Construction), which discussed detailed methods of introducing the concept of public land ownership based on the study results of the research committee, and worked on the draft of related laws and regulations.

The government's efforts received overwhelming public support. The South Korean people wanted the government to radically resolve the real estate crisis after suffering from a repeated rise of real estate prices, a chronic shortage of housing supplies, and the conspicuous consumption of some social group that owned a disproportionate amount of real estate. Amidst such rapid development, Korea Research Institute for Human Settlements revealed the state of unequal land ownership in the country by analyzing the computer data on the lands managed by the Ministry of Internal Affairs with a super computer. The computer analysis proved the monopolistic land ownership structure of the country: the top 5% of the landowners owned 62.5% of all the privately owned lands in the country. Stunned by such astonishing computer analysis results, the social consensus that the land issue can no longer be ignored began to form among the South Korean people, playing a decisive role in making the South Korean society adopt the expanded concept of public land ownership.

Implementation Process and Contents

According to the definition by the Research Committee on Concept of Public Land Ownership, the concept of public land ownership "recognizes the individual ownership of lands, but their utilization should be regulated so that it would promote the welfare of the public." Specifically, the concept covers such matters as the land ownership ceiling system in accordance with the Act on Land Ownership Ceiling, the development surcharge system in accordance with the Act on Restitution of Development Gains, and the land excess-profits tax in accordance with the Land Excess-Profits Tax Act, all of which were legislated in the regular session of the National Assembly in December 1989. Separate from the legislations aimed at supporting the concept of public land ownership, a series of reforms associated with real estate were implemented continuously from 1988 to 1990, including the introduction of the composite land tax, the officially assessed land value index, as well as the obligatory registration of real estate and the measure to curb the excessive land ownership of businesses (the May 8 Measure).

Table 4–2. Implementation Schedule and Key Activity

Date	Key Activity
August 10, 1988	Installation of the Real Estate Policy Deliberation Committee (the working-level committee for the real estate stabilization policy) in accordance with the August 10 Measure
August 11, 1988	Formation of the Research Committee on the Concept of Public Land Ownership
September 9, 1988	1st meeting of the Research Committee on the Concept of Public Land Ownership
September 15, 1988	Subcommittee meeting by department of the Research Committee on the Concept of Public Land Ownership
September 30, 1988	2nd meeting of the Research Committee on the Concept of Public Land Ownership
November 11, 1988	1st draft proposal by the Research Committee on the Concept of Public Land Ownership
December 23~24, 1988	Panel discussion on ways to expand the concept of public land ownership
December 29~30, 1988	Policy meeting on the expansion of the concept of public land ownership
April 20, 1989	National debate on the expansion of the concept of public land ownership

The housing lot ownership ceiling system was aimed at stabilizing the residential quality of the people by encouraging the equally distributed ownership of lands and by increasing the supply of housing sites. Towards these ends, the government regulated the ownership of housing sites by not allowing individuals to own housing sites larger than the specified limits, and by not allowing corporations to own any housing site in principle, thereby suppressing the ownership of housing sites larger than what was reasonably acceptable. Any person who violated the aforementioned regulation had to pay an excessive ownership surcharge. However, the land ownership ceiling system backfired; it faced considerable opposition upon its enforcement, including resistance to the high taxation rates and various complaints associated with the tax imposition and collection. In the period from 1992 to 1993 alone, a total of 2,083 complaints were lodged.

The July 1994 ruling of the Constitutional Court, in which it ruled that the Land Excess-Profits Tax Act was unconstitutional, dealt another blow to the house lot ownership ceiling system, which had already been under review for its potential unconstitutionality from a separate constitutional petition filed earlier. In response to such developing situation, the government revamped the land ownership ceiling system by relaxing its key regulatory provisions in the related laws on August 30, 1997: the housing sites that had been under possession before the enforcement of the renewed system were exempted from the new regulatory system limiting the land ownership to one housing site per home, and any earlier issuance of land acquisition permission was assumed to have gone through the land transaction approval-declaration process. Despite such numerous efforts, the house lot ownership ceiling system was abolished in September 1998, in the wake of the Asian financial crisis that hit the country towards the end of 1997. Behind the unfortunate demise of the system lay the practical demand for activating the slumping land market and the less-than-satisfactory effectiveness of the earlier system that the government introduced.

The land excess-profits tax system is aimed at restituting the excess profits gained from idle lands. The system is aimed at stabilizing the land prices and at promoting the efficient use of lands by ensuring economic and social equality through the taxation of capital gains that have the characteristic of unearned income, thereby promoting the supply of idle lands. The transfer income tax makes it impossible to restitute the income from land price increases until the actual time of land transfer as it targets only the realized development gains; with the land excess-profits tax, however, the tax authority can restitute the unrealized capital gains by slapping a tax on the income from land price increases while the land is still under the possession of landlords. However, the land excess-profits tax system bumped into unexpected stumbling blocks in the early stage of its enforcement. Having faced substantial opposition and resistance to taxation owing to its intention of slapping taxes on unrealized capital gains, the system became the object of a constitutional petition, and the Constitutional Court eventually ruled that it was unconstitutional. On July 29, 1994, the Constitutional Court declared the Land Excess-Profit Tax Act unconstitutional while at the same time ordering the suspension of the application and enforcement of the act until the provisions that had been ruled unconstitutional were amended or abolished.

In compliance with the court ruling, the Land Excess-Profit Tax Act was amended on December 22, 1994 by reflecting what had been specified in the Constitutional Court's ruling. The amended act introduced the progressive marginal tax rates based on the taxation amount in an attempt to ensure the enhanced protection of the people's property rights and the application of appropriate tax burdens, along with the introduction of supplementary provisions in the event of land price decline. The revised act also specified that the land excess-profits tax shall be deducted in its entirety from the transfer income tax within the specified period and that the regular taxation shall not be applied at the national level during the time of stabilized land prices, but only in those areas that saw a dramatic rise of land prices, while also striving to supplement any insufficiency discovered during its enforcement.

As the pretext supporting the concept of public land ownership became tarnished in the wake of the Asian financial crisis that hit the country by the end of 1997, the land excess-profits tax became the first target of the deliberation for potential abolition. This is because the resistance to the taxation arising from the taxation of the unrealized capital gains grew worse despite the substantial revamp and supplementation of the system ever since the ruling on the unconstitutionality of the act while the grievances of the landlords grew louder due to the slumping land market. In December 1998, the government finally abolished the land excess-profits tax on the pretext of the difficulty of running the system due to the public resistance to taxation, and on the pretext of the elimination of the wastage of administrative resources.

The development surcharge system was aimed at preventing speculative land investment and at promoting the efficient use of lands by restituting the development gains arising from the development projects, including the housing site development by the project licensees. In other words, the system was designed to restitute the increased land prices due to the act of licensing and approval related with the development projects, which were initiated by the administrative authority. As the government specified in the regulations to restitute the increased land prices arising from idle lands in the form of taxation in the process of introducing the increased land price restitution system, the system became a dual structure composed of the development surcharge system and the land excess-profits tax system.

The development surcharge was slapped on those home lots development projects that were greater than the specified size and those projects specified in the laws. Those subject to the payment of the surcharge were the development project implementers that had been licensed or approved by the head of the central government or local self-governing body, or by those entrusted with such authority, to engage in development projects. The amount of the development surcharge (in other words, the development gains) was calculated by deducting the land price at the time of project initiation and the normal increase in the land price and development costs from the land price at the time of project completion, with the taxation rate being 50% of the total development gains. The development surcharge was initially slapped on those cases involving a physical form of development activity, but the taxation target was expanded in the end to include the land price increases arising from a simple change in land use, such as school lots being changed into home lots for home construction. The development surcharge was not to be slapped on those development projects initiated by the central government or the local self-governing body, and the surcharge was reduced by 50% for the development projects initiated by the state-owned corporations, such as Korea Land Corporation. Fifty percent of the restituted land development surcharge was to be paid back to the local governing body to which the land that had incurred development gains belonged, with the balance being used for the land purchase or development of underdeveloped areas via the special accounting for land development or for balanced regional development.

The development surcharge system started to be applied more flexibly in recent years in an attempt to stabilize the people's living conditions and to enhance the competitiveness of corporations. In 1996, the development surcharge was exempted for industrial-complex development projects as part of the policy initiative to improve the corporate competitiveness by more than 10%. Also, the rate was reduced by up to 50% in the case of industrial-complex development projects for small businesses, home lot developments for national housing projects, and other development projects where the mountainous areas account for over 70% of the given area. Specifically, the development surcharge system has gone through a series of changes since the Asian financial crisis: resumption of the taxation and reduction of the taxation rate (50%→25%) in January 2000; suspension of the taxation in all areas, excluding the greater Seoul area (January 2002); suspension of the taxation in the greater Seoul area (January 2004); and resumption of the nationwide taxation (January 2006).

The development surcharge system is assessed to have contributed to the suppression of speculative land investment and the fostering of the efficient use of lands by restituting the development gains, which were previously appropriated mostly by the development implementers in the process of the development and provision of lands. To sum up, the development surcharge system played the role of supplementing the function of the transfer income tax system, which was designed to restitute the realized development gains. Furthermore, the imposition of the development surcharge prompted the development project businesses to maximize the efficiency of their land use if they wanted to compensate for as much development gains as were restituted by the government. The system was also useful in raising the funds required for the balanced-regional-development projects initiated by the central government and regional self-governing bodies. The system, however, was not without inherent shortcomings. First, many argued that the system did not live up to its purported goal of restituting the development gains as the development surcharge system was aimed at restituting the development gains from those development projects that were implemented with one's own efforts and at one's own cost. Second, others argue that the system was not consistent in restituting the development gains as the development gains from the project sites developed by project implementers were restituted but the development gains from the areas surrounding the public projects were not.

Performance and Assessment

Overall, the development surcharge system is the only surviving apparatus to this date among the various concepts of public land ownership devised by the government. Specifically, the abolition of the land excess-profits tax system made it difficult to prevent the excessive privatization of the land capital gains generated in the areas surrounding the development project sites. The structural irony of the current restitution system is that the gains generated in the development site can be restituted with the application of the development surcharge system, but the area surrounding it cannot be subjected to such taxation scheme. Since the current system is fundamentally unfair in nature, some form of institutional apparatus should be established to keep the balance between the development gains and the regulatory losses. No more rapid urbanization is expected in the future with the projected low growth in the population and economy. If that is the case, some form of paradigm shift from the present land policy, which was established while the country was struggling to respond to the rapid growth age and urbanization in the past, needs to be effected.

5. Construction of new towns

Background

In the late 1980s, along with the geographical shift in the country's demand for homes from the Gangbuk to the Gangnam area in Seoul, the standalone homes shifted to small residential-type apartment homes, and mid-sized apartment homes shifted to large apartment homes in terms of size. The home prices soared due to the limited supply of new homes, and the resulting speculative home investment boom emerged as one of the serious problems plaguing the country. The demand for apartment homes, in particular, recorded explosive growth along with the rising income level, a phenomenon much more pronounced in the Gangnam area in Seoul, where middle-class people were concentrated. The large apartment homes in Gangnam rose by a whopping 30~50% within 6 to 7 months, which again triggered a ripple effect in the home prices not only in the greater Seoul area but throughout the country, leading to a speculative investment boom in apartment homes. The ordinary South Koreans could not afford their homes due to the abnormal rise of home prices. Moreover, the unearned incomes from such speculative home investment boom fanned the flames of social unrest and gave rise to uneasiness among different social classes.

Implementation System

Various related parties, including the central government, local governing bodies, project implementers, national research institutes, and public corporations were actively involved in new-town construction projects. Specifically, by newly establishing a special institution and a supporting organization dedicated to handling the new-town development businesses, the government made key policy decisions throughout the development process, including the arbitration of the conflicting interests among the project participants and of the conflicting opinions among the related ministries, while the local governing bodies coordinated with and supported the project implementers. In particular, Korea Land Corporation cracked down on various illegal activities jointly with the Prosecutor's Office in an effort to prevent the construction of unapproved buildings and false resident registration. As a national research institution, Korea Research Institute for Human Settlements (KRIHS) performed studies on key related policies, including development strategies and home policies covering the following areas: basic designs of new towns, basic planning, studies on the basic plan for a wide-area traffic network, and assessment of the influence of the construction of new towns on the affected population and traffic.

Implementation Process and Contents

Having arrived at the conclusion that the supply of a massive number of new homes is inevitable, the government embarked on the project of building 2 million new homes, which was one of the campaign pledges made upon the inauguration of the 6th Republic in September 1988.

Among the 2 million new homes planned for the project, 900,000 homes were to be built in the greater Seoul area. Of the 900,000 homes, 400,000 homes were to be built on the available lands, including the idle lands within the residential districts in Seoul, and the remaining 500,000 homes were to be built on the home lots that were to be secured along the outskirts of Seoul. The construction of new towns outside the commutable radius from the Seoul city center would pose substantial difficulties in moving the population and city function out of Seoul and would take an extended time to finish. In view of such prospects, five candidate sites (Bundang, Ilsan, Pyeongchon, Sanbon, and Jungdong) were selected based on their geographic location (within a one-hour commutable distance from Seoul) and their potential to attract middle- or higher-class Seoul residents into the new towns.

The selection criteria of the candidate sites were as follows: (1) it should be located within a 20km distance from Seoul, where the residents would be able to commute to Seoul within one hour; (2) it should be sufficiently large (over 10 million m^2) for building over 100,000 new

Table 4-3. Summary of the Phase 1 New-Town Construction Plan

Criteria	Total	Bundang	Ilsan	Pyeongchon	Jungdong	Sanbon
Location		Seongnam	Goyang	Anyang	Bucheon	Gunpo
Area (× 1000m^2) (× 1000 pyeong)	50,136 (15,167)	19,639 (5,941)	15,736 (4,760)	5,106 (1,544)	5,452 (1,650)	4,203 (1,274)
Population (× 10,000 people) (no. of homes)	116.8 (292,524)	39.0 (97,580)	27.6 (69.000)	16.8 (42,047)	16.6 (42,500)	16.8 (42,047)
Population density (person/ha)	231	197	174	327	301	396
Home building (× 1,000 homes)	292	97.6	69	42	41.4	42
Project duration		89. 8 ~96. 12	90. 3 ~96. 12	89. 8 ~95. 12	90. 2 ~96. 1	89. 8 ~95. 1
Total budget (× KRW 100 billion)	106.6	41.6	27.3	12.3	16.4	9.0
Project implementer		Korea Land Corporation	Korea Land Corporation	Korea Land Corporation	Bucheon City Korean Housing Corporation Korea Land Corporation	Korea Housing Corporation

Source: Ministry of Construction and Transport homepage (www.molit.go.kr).

homes, thereby absorbing the home demands of and assuming the city function of Seoul; (3) it should be close to the Gangnam area and well connected with the surrounding areas so that the new town would be able to absorb the potential demand for new homes in the Gangnam area; and (4) it should be able to sustain a pleasant environment and guarantee low land prices.

The Presidential Office formed the Working-Level Planning Group for the Construction of Homes for Ordinary People on April 4, 1989 and reviewed the home lots development strategy that would normalize the apartment home prices in Seoul. Korea Land Corporation drafted the development proposal and submitted it to the Presidential Office and the Ministry of Construction. Related officials from the Presidential Office (the Working-Level Planning Group for the Construction of Homes for Ordinary People), the Ministry of Construction (the Department of Home Lots Development in the Land Bureau), and Korea Land Corporation formed the working group, which again pushed forward with the detailed development ideation and the preparation of the review report. The government decided to implement the new-town development project as a housing site development project in accordance with the Housing Site Development Promotion Act.

The new-town construction projects in Bundang, Ilsan, Pyeongchon, Sanbon, and Jungdong helped resolve the chronic shortage of home supply in the 1980s, and helped stabilize the residential conditions of the people. Given severe shortage of homes, there were possibilities of serious social conflicts due to the soaring prices of apartment homes in the urban districts in the greater Seoul area, including Seoul City. Since there were insufficient lands available for home building in the greater Seoul area, including Seoul City, the early construction of new towns helped stabilize the housing market. The decision to build new towns within a 20km radius from the Seoul City center was particularly effective in calming down the housing market.

Performance and Assessment

The Phase 1 new towns in the greater Seoul area were superior to the ordinary homes built mostly in the smaller housing site development districts or on the pockets of lands scattered in the urban areas in terms of the residential amenities, including education and other convenience facilities. Likewise, many middle-income families moved to the newly built homes in the new towns, helping the ordinary homebuyers to purchase their homes. Such purchases were possible due to the stratified chain reaction of home selling and buying as families in certain income class sold their homes to the next lower-income class. As such, it is an undeniable fact that the massive home supply enabled by the new-town projects improved the overall residential environment in the greater Seoul area, thereby making a decisive contribution to the success of the housing policy that aimed to stabilize the residential environment.

One negative side effect of the new-town projects was the massive demand for labor and construction materials as multiple new-town construction projects were implemented simultaneously within a short period of time. Specifically, the smaller number of available jobs in the new towns compared to the massive number of new homes therein made those towns unable to gain self-sufficiency, thereby worsening the traffic congestion along the transportation link with Seoul. As the commuting distance became longer, numerous potential problems, such as traffic congestion, energy waste, and the lack of cultural and welfare facilities, were inevitable. Therefore, the urgent issues for the new towns are to attain a self-sufficient economy and to resolve the chronic traffic jam and the shortage of cultural and welfare facilities therein. Especially, the future new-town construction projects are required to build new towns systematically and completely over an extended period of time, and to build new towns infused with the green-city concept.

Section 3

The Government Reform of the Roh Tae Woo Administration

1. Background and direction of the government reform

It is necessary to review the local and international contexts, which would include the political background such as the democratization movement and the economic background to understand the government reform that was pushed during the incumbency of President Roh Tae Woo (1988~1992). The country's international balance of trade, which until 1985 had recorded deficits, turned black for the first time in 1986. The global economy was characterized by the so-called "three lows": low oil prices, low interest rates, and low dollar value. The country's international balance of trade turned black on the strength of increasing exports, which were largely attributable to the favorable global financial environment. Beginning in 1989, when the "three lows" finally vanished, the country's international balance of trade dropped significantly, and by 1990, it started to record trade deficits. Beginning in 1990, the country started to struggle with the re-emergence of inflation, while the real growth rate fell to one-digit levels.

The housing issue of the ordinary people resurfaced as well. The residents living in chartered homes in Seoul were priced out of the city due to the soaring home charter prices, and were eventually relocated to the city outskirts, while those living in the chartered homes in the city outskirts were priced out of their homes again and were forced to live in monthly rented housings. Amidst the worsening housing crisis, with some marginalized residents committing suicide out of financial frustration, thereby pushing the issue as one of the hottest social problems, the Roh Tae Woo administration unveiled the plan to build five new towns in Bundang, Ilsan, Jungdong, Pyeongchon, and Sanbon, all of which were located along the outskirts of the capital city. According to the plan, a total of 2.14 million new homes were built in the five new towns until 1991, thereby boosting the home ownership rate from 69.2% in 1987 to 74.2% in 1991.

The percentage of the age group over 65 rose rapidly during the period due to the rising income levels of the people, the advances in the medical science field, and the markedly dropped birth rate in the 1980s. The per-capita GNI rose from mid-3,000 dollars in 1987 to upper-7,000 dollars. The birth rate was close to 3 births per woman in the early 1980s but dropped to 1.5 births per woman after 1985. Due to the combined results of such various socio-economic developments, the percentage of the people over 65 rose from 4.3% in 1985 to 5.9% after 10 years, in 1995.

The incidences of labor-management disputes increased dramatically due to the great labor movement that swept the second half of 1987. The number of labor-management disputes jumped from 220 in 1986 to 2,400 per year on average after the June 29 Declaration until 1990. The real wage growth rate rose substantially in the early years of the Roh Tae Woo administration.

Against the backdrop of the commencement of the Uruguay Round Talks in September 1986, the country's trade surplus, and hosting of the 1988 Seoul Olympic Games, the advanced Western economies, including the United States, started to push for the potential opening of the South Korean market. Faced with the structural transformation of the industry, which was marked by the decline of the manufacturing industry and the rise of the farming and service industries, the advanced economies began to push other countries to open their markets for agricultural products and services. The country had to succumb to the growing pressure to open its markets for rice, beef, and financial services.

The 1988 Seoul Olympic Games, which was held for 16 days, from September 17 to October 2, 1988, played a critical role in raising the global profile of South Korea in the international community. Mikhail Gorbachev opted to push for the glasnost and perestroika policy upon assuming power in the Soviet Union as the General Secretary in March 1985, and took the initiative in realizing arms reduction talks by proposing that Washington open the talks. With the Soviet Union-United States summit held in November of the same year, the two superpowers embarked on the long journey for the eventual realization of arms reduction. Prodded by such moves of the Soviet Union, the communist states in Eastern Europe started to seek changes in their respective state systems.

In the context of aforementioned changes, the Roh Tae Woo administration pushed for a total of eight administrative reforms, as discussed below. First, the administration strove to ensure the democratization of the country and to protect the people's human rights. It exerted efforts to improve the people's understanding of and trust in the administrative process in an attempt to realize the democratic principles in the practice of administration by opening the policy-making and policy handling process as well as the various data held by the administrative bodies to the people.

Second, the administration focused on enhancing the spontaneity and creativity of the private sector. It strove to activate the private sector and to help them maximize their performance by redrawing the domains of the government and the private sector, respectively. Also, to improve the convenience of the people's everyday life, it strove to abolish, relax, or simplify any administrative regulation deemed unnecessary or inappropriate. The government revamped and streamlined the regulatory intervention process, including the granting of licenses or approval, as to limit the free and competitive system; boosted the efficiency of corporate management through the privatization of the government-owned corporations, such as Korea Telecom Corporation, Korea Electric Power Corporation, and other state-reinvested corporations; and expanded and revamped the administrative functions governing fair trade to establish a healthy market economy.

Third, the administration strove to realize the ideology supporting the reunification of the Korean Peninsula. It sought to implement some practical measures that would turn the hostile and strenuous relationship of the two Koreas into one based on coexistence and peace. At the same time, it streamlined the administrative system governing the reunification to maintain consistency in the unification policy, to promote interconnectivity between the administrative bodies governing the unification policy, and to ensure a systematic and efficient implementation of the unification policy.

Fourth, the administration attempted to bolster its preparedness for the era of internationalization. It strove to ensure a consistent surplus in the country's international balance of trade, and promoted the development of advanced science and technology to improve the international competitiveness of the economy. Furthermore, it exerted efforts to streamline the foreign trade cooperation system to push for more proactive economic diplomacy, to overcome the growing pressure to open the market, to resolve trade disputes, to establish an open economic system, and to respond better to the informatization and sophistication of the country's industrial structure. Additionally, the administration exerted efforts to gain a new diplomatic status in the international community while also pushing ahead with various diplomatic exchanges with the Communist bloc, including China and the former Soviet Union.

Fifth, the administration strove to prepare for the era of localization. It revamped the government's various businesses so that the central government would take charge of the key national and wide-area businesses that require unity and consistency at the national level, and transferred the other functions that could be better handled by the local self-governing bodies to the local governments. It also redefined the relationship between the central and local government levels in preparation for the full-fledged introduction of the local self-governing system. In addition, the government strove to come up with measures to improve the people's convenience and the efficiency of the local administration by ensuring the precise alignment of the people's living domain, the administrative domain, and the economic domain through the reassessment of the stratified local administrative structure, the skeletal structure of the local administration. Also, it came up with an institutional apparatus that would be used in revamping the administration in the wide-area governing bodies and in the greater Seoul area.

Sixth, the administration strove to ensure continuous economic growth. As an attempt to lay the foundation from which it may leap forward into an advance economy, it sophisticated the industrial and economic structure of the country, increased employment and promoted industrial development by strengthening the government support for small businesses, and narrowed the economic gap among the regions by coming up with measures to activate the economy in the less-developed regions.

Seventh, the administration pursued the realization of equal opportunities for welfare benefits. In an effort to improve the welfare support for the people and realize social stability, it strove to improve the equality in the distribution of income and wealth, expanded the public investment in the underdeveloped regions, and bolstered the government support for basic living facilities, such as providing housing for the low-income family, including the farmers and the poor urban residents. Specifically, the administration strove to ensure the balanced development of the underdeveloped areas and the advancement of the farming industry by strengthening the housing policy function in the Ministry of Construction, which was formerly concentrated on social-overhead-capital construction, and by turning the focus of the agricultural and fishery administration from the boosting of crop production to the development of farming and fishing towns. It also strove to ensure sustainable economic growth in the future through the improvement of the welfare services for the workers as well as through the productivity improvement of the economy, which could be realized by responding wisely to the environmental contamination and the labor-management disputes as well as by promoting a pleasant and healthy work environment and establishing industrial peace.

Eighth, the administration pursued efficiency improvement in the administrative system. It exerted efforts to lower the administrative costs by maintaining appropriate organization sizes and realizing a small but efficient government to ensure the effective implementation of the government tasks. The administration also strove to establish an efficient administrative business implementation system by rationalizing the standards for the installation of central administrative bodies and its umbrella organizations and by addressing the insufficiencies in the administrative system that were related to the revamp of the government organization. Furthermore, the administration reshuffled the work structure, improved the promotion and compensation system, and renovated the retirement age of the public servants in an attempt to promote an environment where public officials can work passionately and take pride in their work.

The Roh Tae Woo administration installed the Democratic Reconciliation Promotion Committee in the early years of its incumbency to rid the country of authoritarianism and to realize democratization. The committee proposed the installation of the Administrative Reform Committee jointly with the private sector to boldly implement administrative reform. As a result, the Administrative Reform Committee was inaugurated on May 13, 1988. The committee was composed of 21 members representing the academe, media, judicial community, economy, labor, and women, as well as four subcommittees handling general issues, general administration, economy and science, and society and culture, respectively, with each subcommittee having one working-level staff, another member from the academe, and two expert members. A total of 40 research professionals and investigators supported the activities of the subcommittee members. Among them, the Ministry of Government Administration dispatched two of its four expert members as well as 35 research professionals and investigators. Until it wrapped up its activities in July 1989, the committee was intended to be active for a few months upon its inception, but its active period was extended to one year upon the official launch of the committee and by two more months during its operation. The committee was dismantled in the same month, after submitting its policy recommendation.

The Administrative Reform Committee was unique in that it was almost entirely composed of civilians, not public officials. Such unique nature of the committee would enable its members to make independent judgments but could also encourage them to act irresponsibly as they were not involved in the implementation process. For instance, the Administrative Reform Investigation Committee, which was active during the periods of the 3rd and 4th Republic, suffered from low morale as all its members were public officials who felt that they were given insignificant posts. However, the Institutional Improvement Committee, which was active during the period of the 5th Republic, was a joint committee composed of both government officials and civilians whose resolution had a practical binding power. As such, the fact that the Administrative Reform Committee was a civilian committee drove its members to recognize the need for them to collect public opinions far and wide, which was exactly what they attempted to do in the end. Specifically, they embarked on such when they were selecting their future tasks or evaluating the given alternatives.

Second, the committee's relationship with the Presidential Secretariat was limited to the regular check-up of the prospective schedule in the Office of the Senior Secretary to the President for Political Affairs as well as to the submission of occasional reports to the president. Since the Administrative Reform Committee was a civilian advisory committee, the Presidential Office was not able to participate in its regular activities. The Administrative Reform Investigation Committee, which was active during the periods of the 3rd and 4th Republic, received much less attention from the Presidential Secretariat than the Administrative Reform Committee did. However, in the case of the Institutional Improvement Committee in the 5th Republic, the Office of the 2nd Senior Secretary to the President for Political Affairs expressed positive attitude towards the committee by assuming the leading role in running the committee.

Third, the Administrative Reform Committee invited related officials from the concerned ministries as well as other experts to obtain their advice, but made its decisions independently. According to the regulations, even though the committee had the authority to have expert and investigation members dispatched only from the related ministries, in practice, it had public officials dispatched only from the Ministry of Government Administration, the Prime Ministerial Office, and the Office of Legislation. In the case of the Administrative Reform Investigation Committee, which was active during the period of the 3rd and 4th Republic, its members visited related ministries for investigation, while in the case of the Institutional Improvement Committee in the 5th Republic, its members representing each ministry participated in the committee and expressed their opinions naturally.

Fourth, the Ministry of Government Administration assumed leadership in running the Administrative Reform Committee from its inception. The ministry was responsible for establishing its regulations and selecting its members, and two of the committee's four public official expert members and all its 35 research professionals and investigators were dispatched from the ministry. The Administrative Reform Investigation Committee in the 3rd and 4th Republic maintained an uneasy relationship with the Ministry of Government Administration due to the unclear division of roles with the ministry, while in the case of the Institutional Improvement Committee in the 5th Republic, the Presidential Secretariat assumed the leadership in the committee operation. The Ministry of Government Administration, however, started to play a stronger role beginning in 1983.

Fifth, when its will to reform the government organization was still relatively strong, the Administrative Reform Committee was launched amidst a favorable environment as it was installed upon the inauguration of the new administration. On the contrary, since considerable amount of time had passed since the May 16 coup d'état, the Administrative Reform Investigation Committee in the 3rd and 4th Republic was not able to demonstrate the strong level of will to reform the government. Meanwhile, the Institutional Improvement Committee in the 5th Republic can be said to have been inaugurated amidst a favorable environment as it was formed in the early stage of the administration, as was the case with the Administrative Reform Committee.

Sixth, the percentage of reform proposals finally selected by the Administrative Reform Committee was not that high. For purposes of comparison, whereas the selection rate of the Administrative Reform Investigation Committee in the 3rd and 4th Republic was not that high either, it was high in the case of the Institutional Improvement Committee in the 5th Republic.

Table 4-4. Proposal for the Revamp of Government Organization Submitted by the Administrative Reform Committee

Ministry	Proposition
Board of National Unification	- The minister was promoted to vice prime minister.
Economic Planning Board	- The Census and Statistics Bureau was expanded into the National Statistics Service; its implementation function, including trade negotiation, was transferred to the concerned ministries; the Review and Assessment Bureau was abolished; the oversight function on the government investment corporations was transferred to the concerned ministries; the Fair Trade Commission was to become an independent organization, with the Fair Trade Office changed to the Secretariat of the commission.
Ministry of Science and Technology	- The Central Meteorological Observatory was promoted to the Meteorological Administration. - The industrial and technology policy development and R&D support function was transferred to the other ministries governing the industrial policy.
Ministry of Internal Affairs	- The Headquarters of the National Police became an independent organization in the form of the National Police Agency. - The National Police Commission, which was to perform budgetary review and personnel management, was newly installed.
Ministry of Commerce and Industry	- The ministry was consolidated with the Ministry of Energy and Resources to form the Ministry of Industry, Trade, and Commerce.
Ministry of Energy and Resources	- The ministry was consolidated with the Ministry of Commerce and Industry to form the Ministry of Industry, Trade, and Commerce.
Ministry of Agriculture, Forestry, and Fisheries	- Korea Forest Service was merged with the Forestry Bureau in the ministry.
Ministry of Construction	- The ministry was renamed "Ministry of Construction and Housing." - The Housing Bureau was divided into the Housing Policy Bureau and the Housing Construction Promotion Bureau. - The industrial port management function in the Water Resource Bureau was transferred to the Port Management Authority.
Ministry of Transportation	- Korea Maritime and Port Administration was merged with the Ministry of Transportation.
Ministry of Culture and Information	- The ministry was divided into the Ministry of Culture and Sports and the Public Information Agency.
Ministry of Culture and Education	- The ministry was renamed "Ministry of Education."
Ministry of Health and Society	- The former vice-ministerial-level Environmental Office was promoted to the ministerial-level Environment Protection Agency.
Ministry of Labor	- A deputy vice minister to deal with the labor-management policy and the adjustment of the labor-management relations was newly installed.

Ministry of Sports	- The school sports and school meals management function was transferred to the Ministry of Education. - The ministry was consolidated with the culture administration function to form the Ministry of Culture and Sports.
Others	- The Advisory Council of Elderly Statesmen and the Social Clean-up Committee were abolished.

Overall, the policy recommendation proposal that the Administrative Reform Committee submitted upon its dissolution in July 1989 was significant in that it was the first report prepared through a democratic and objective research process that was ever attempted in the country. The proposal, however, had limitations in that it was prepared within a very short time and attempted to reform too many targets at the same time.[1] Also, instead of being seen as neutral or objective, its preparation process was led by the Ministry of Government Administration and did not offer sufficient opportunities for the related ministries, stakeholders, expert group, and news media to participate in the deliberation process and to express their opinions.

2. Contents of the government reform

Organizational Reshuffling and Reform of Personnel Administration

One of the key government reforms initiated by the Roh Tae Woo administration was the reform of the government organization. The reform was implemented roughly in two waves. In the first-wave reform, the government organizations under the Presidential Office were reshuffled, first through the readjustment of the function of the National Security Planning Agency, and second, through the abolition of the Social Clean-up Committee and the Advisory Council of Elderly Statesmen in February 1989. As part of the organizational revamp of the institutions under the Prime Ministerial Office, the Personnel Committee was installed in the Ministry of Government Administration as a collegiate institution, while the Office of the 4th Director-General for Coordination, which was to take charge of the inspection function, was newly installed in the Prime Ministerial Administrative Coordination Office. In December 1989, the Environmental Office was abolished and was replaced by the Environment Agency in the Prime Ministerial Office, and the Ministry of Culture and Information was divided into the Ministry of Culture and the Public Information Agency.

The readjustment of administrative functions was aimed mainly at responding to the internationalization, industrialization, and urbanization trends. Some functions of the Ministry of Sports and the Ministry of Culture and Education were transferred and adjusted: the Bureau of Youth was installed in the Ministry of Sports while the Ministry of Foreign Affairs, Ministry of

1) The committee submitted propositions not only on the central government organization but also on other government institutions with deep political connotations. The committee proposed to abolish the Advisory Council of Elderly Statesmen and the Social Clean-up Committee in the early phase of its operation, and eventually succeeded in abolishing such entities. In addition, the committee made numerous propositions regarding the regulatory and personnel administration, with a substantial number of them realized in the end.

Health and Society, and Ministry of Transportation were bolstered with additional functions.

The 21st-Century Committee was newly installed as a presidential advisory body during the period of the Roh Tae Woo administration. The committee was given the roles of establishing the long-term goals of the national development and advising the president on how such goals could be attained. In addition, the various committees installed across the government ministries were streamlined and revamped. Of the 398 installed committees, 101 were abolished and 17 were either downsized or adjusted.

The second-wave organizational reshuffling was implemented in response to the radical changes in Eastern Europe. As part of the organizational revamp, the National Unification Ministry was renamed Board of Unification, with the ministerial head promoted from the ministerial level to the vice prime ministerial level. The Ministry of Culture and Education was revamped into the Ministry of Education, and the Ministry of Sports into the Ministry of Sports and Youth. In the process, the two director-generals in the Ministry of Sports and Youth, including the director-general for policy coordination, were abolished. The Bureau of Census and Statistics was revamped and promoted to the National Statistical Office (1st grade), and the Central Meteorological Observatory to the Meteorological Administration (1st grade). Some functions of the Ministry of Construction, Ministry of Agriculture, Forest, and Fisheries, and Ministry of Internal Affairs were transferred to other ministries in the functional reshuffling, and the Headquarters of the National Police in the Ministry of Internal Affairs was revamped and promoted to the National Police Agency, along with the installation of the National Police Commission.

Fiscal Reform

The Roh Tae Woo administration laid out the following imperatives for the fiscal reform: (1) nurture the country's growth potential through industrial restructuring; (2) promote economic liberalization and the open-door policy; (3) foster balanced economic development; and (4) improve the national welfare level and equality. It is hard to believe that there was a special body that implemented the reform process in the case of fiscal reform, but the Concept of Public Land Ownership Research Committee chaired by the president of the Research Institute for Human Settlement was formed in September 1988 in relation to the reform of the land and taxation system. In addition, the Balanced Regional Development Planning Group was installed in the Presidential Secretariat to accelerate the balanced regional development, which was one of the four goals of the administration.

With regard to the reform to ensure the equal distribution of income, three key welfare systems — the universal medical insurance system, the national pension system, and the minimum wage system — were introduced based on the principle of welfare promotion on the foundation of fiscal stability, thereby maintaining fiscal health. Moreover, the fiscal system was steadily improved to expand the funds available for the local governing bodies. The improvement included the bold expansion of the fiscal grants for municipal finance and of the fiscal subsidies that had already been in place and the establishment of special fiscal accounts. As a result of such combined efforts, the fiscal grants to the local governing bodies that remained at KRW 2.2 trillion in 1987 had jumped to KRW 7.5 trillion by 1991 after counting in the funds from the tobacco consumption taxes, thereby enabling the central government to meet the growing demands for fiscal support for the municipal and provincial finances. In addition, the fiscal support for the local education finance was bolstered by changing the nature of the education tax scheduled for expiration at the end of 1991 to a permanent tax. In addition, the compulsory middle school education system, which was previously applied to special schools and to the schools in remote locations and islands, was expanded to the town areas (eup, myeon) beginning in 1992. Accordingly, the total fiscal support to the local education finance had grown from KRW 2.6 trillion in 1987 to KRW 7.0 trillion by 1992.

Land Reform

The rising land prices and the resulting real estate issue were the most serious social problems faced by the Roh Tae Woo administration upon its inauguration. The administration responded to such problems with the following measures: (1) tightening of the judiciary and tax measures aimed at restricting the traders and realtors engaging in speculative land transactions; (2) a series of long-term policies to increase the land supply, including the construction of new towns and the deregulation of land use and land development by local public corporations; and (3) measures aimed at suppressing speculative demands, such as the introduction of the appraised land value system and the enforcement of the composite land tax. With regard to the administrative aspects supporting such policy package, the government focused on expanding various real estate administrative systems, including the computerization of land management and the compulsory registration of lands. The appraised land value system was implemented beginning with the legislation in 1989 of the Act on Public Notice of Land Price and Land Appraisal, which was followed by the public notice of the land prices of 300,000 standard land lots beginning in 1990 as well as the land price survey on 24 million individual land lots. Also, with the additional supplementation of the system through the amendment of the Enforcement Ordinance of National Taxes beginning in 1991, the assessment standards for the transfer income tax, inheritance tax, gift tax, corporate tax, and special value added tax were calculated based on the appraised land value.

Improvement of Labor-Management Relations

Along with the advancement in the democratization process ever since the June 29 Declaration in 1987, a total of 3,749 incidences of labor - management disputes occurred in 1987 alone, a 14-fold increase from the previous year. Such dramatic increase made it inevitable to protect the rights of workers and to establish rational labor - management relations. Along with the strengthening of such unions' independence, the unrestricted establishment of labor unions was warranted through two rounds of bold amendments of the related labor laws, including the Labor Union Act in November 1987 and in April 1988. As a result, by the end of the administration, whereas the number of local unions had jumped 2.9-fold and that of registered union members jumped 1.8-fold, the number of labor - management disputes had dropped to 234 incidences by the end of 1991.

Liberalization of Interest Rates

On December 5, 1988, the interest rates were liberalized with the following key measures: (1) liberalization of the credit loan interest rates; (2) liberalization of the partial deposit interest rates; (3) readjustment of the regulated deposit interest rate system; and (4) revamp of the currency management system. However, as the real estate prices started to soar, the government tightened the regulation of interest rates, thereby destabilizing the market prices. Making matters worse, the international balance of trade turned from a surplus state to a deficit state, thereby worsening the overall business environment. The government attempted to liberalize the interest rates again on December 21, 1991.

Open-Door Policy

As the country's international balance of trade started to record a surplus beginning in 1986, the external pressure to liberalize the country's foreign currency trade rose. As the Roh Tae Woo administration was required to soften its regulation of the foreign currency to appropriately manage the rising surplus in the international balance of trade and the ballooning volume of external reserves, the administration joined Article 8 of the IMF Agreement as a member state in November 1988. Furthermore, as part of the policy of opening the country to the international market, the administration accelerated the opening of the domestic market through the Basic Tariff Rates Reshuffling Plan (1989~1993) in August 1988 and the Three-Year Import Liberalization Plan (1989~1991) in June 1989. The administration continued to liberalize the ordinary foreign currency exchange even after joining Article 8 of the IMF Agreement as a member state by softening the foreign currency concentration system, the payment method for trade transactions, and the restriction of payments, excluding those for international trade transactions. Also, beginning in March 1990, the multiple-currency basket system, which was introduced in February 1980, was abolished while the market average foreign exchange rate system was introduced as a transient measure before the implementation of the floating exchange rate system. Further, the allowable range of fluctuation for the exchange rate was expanded up to ±0.8% in July 1992 while the TT exchange rate for general customers was to be decided entirely by the banks. As a result, the import liberalization rate, which indicates the openness of the domestic market, rose from 95.4% in 1987 to 97.2% in 1991, near the end of the administration. Specifically, the rate was close to 99.99% in the case of the manufactured goods while the average tariff rate dropped from 19.3% in 1987 to 10.1% in 1991.

Policy to Lay the Foundation for an Electronic Government

The key objectives of the administrative computer network project, among the national basic computer network projects implemented by the administration, were to realize a small but efficient government by promoting the computerization of the administrative process and to improve the quality and quantity of the administrative services for the people so that the service users could comprehensively use the scattered administrative information. The key implementation system included the Computer Network Coordinating Committee. Before the committee was pushed forward as part of the basic plan confirmed in January 1989, the proposal of the Mid-and Long-Term Plan for Nation-Society Computerization was introduced in May 1988 after collecting the opinions of people from all walks of life and was modified and supplemented in November of the same year.

In accordance with the Administrative Computer Network Comprehensive Plan, the National Basic Computer Network was composed of five computer networks: the financial computer network, the education research computer network, the defense computer network, the public safety computer network, and the administrative network. Among these networks, the construction goals of the administrative computer network were to foster the realization of a small government bent on promoting the people's convenience and to support the realization of an advanced and conciliatory economy and society. In terms of the accomplished performance, the project largely succeeded in meeting its goals in many areas. First, comprehensive services were provided to the people in the six areas singled out as the top-priority areas. Second, the efficiency in the implementation of administrative works was markedly improved. The project succeeded in ensuring efficiency in the administrative process by establishing the pan-government shared utilization platform and by promoting an office automation environment through the expansion of the public officials' computer processing capacity. Finally, the project contributed to the growth of the country's information industry and to the early realization of the information society.

Regulatory Reform

The regulatory reform policy of the administration focused on lifting the excessive regulation of the private sector in the context of the improved autonomy, liberalization, and openness since the end of the 1980s. Towards this end, the administration pushed forward with the regulatory reform along two tracks: the regulation of the general administration and of the economic administration. Of the two, the regulatory policy in the economic administration was pushed forward as part of the measure to supplement the country's competitive system aimed at strengthening the country's macroscopic industrial competence, which started to reveal its limitations beginning in 1989. Accordingly, the administration focused on the microscopic approach, in which it would soften the regulation from the bottom through the institutional improvement of the individual industries. On the contrary, the general administrative regulatory policy began to be strengthened as the government pushed forward with the pan-governmental drive to implement the Administrative Innovation Measure to Root Out Inefficiency, which was aimed at boldly rectifying the society's inefficiency, waste, and irrational institutions and practices, marking the first anniversary on October 17, 1991 of the commencement of the "New Order, New Life" implementation drive. The key objective of the drive was to identify the potential target projects that would address the people's inconvenience practically through the comprehensive screening of the respective administrative institutions and business practices of each ministry.

The characteristic of the implementation system that drove the regulatory reform of the administration was that it started with an organization focused mainly on economic regulation in the early years since its inception but soon evolved into a comprehensive organization that covered all kinds of administrative regulation by expanding its regulatory coverage. First, the implementation system that had been responsible for the regulatory reform from the previous administration was the Fair Trade Commission. As the scope of activity of the Fair Trade Commission was limited to economic policy, however, another implementation system took the role of the commission beginning in 1989. Second, in an attempt to overcome the limitations of the role that the Fair Trade Commission played, and to resolve the pending economic issues then, the administration installed the Economic Crisis Overcoming Committee chaired by the vice prime minister in 1989. Furthermore, the Economic Liberalization and Competition Promotion Group, one of the 12 special task forces that were formed under the committee, took the lead in establishing the institutional improvement plan to soften the regulation.

Third, the administration installed the Administrative Deregulation Committee in April 1990, which was chaired by the prime minister and was composed of related ministers, as part of the Comprehensive Measures for Economic Stimulation. Also, installed under the committee were the Working-Level Committee for the Deregulation of Economic Administration (chairperson: Vice Minister of the Economic Planning Board) and the Working-Level Committee for the Deregulation of General Administration (chairperson: Vice Minister of Government Administration). Fourth, the administration operated the Non-governmental Advisory Committee for the Deregulation of Administration on a temporary basis as an institution to advise the prime minister in September 1991, in an attempt to comprehensively collect the opinions of the private sector.

The regulatory reform implemented by the Roh Tae Woo administration was clearly different from that implemented by the previous administrations. Whereas the previous administrations focused mainly on reforming the economic administration led by the Fair Trade Commission, the Roh Tae Woo administration was significant in that it prepared the comprehensive regulatory reform implementation system beginning in the middle of its incumbency, and approached the deregulation by dividing the regulatory targets into the general administration and the economic administration. Although it was part of the measures aimed at responding to the slumping exports then, the fact that the administration attempted to implement a systematic approach by establishing a regulatory reform system is significant in that it played the leading role in the regulatory reform in the succeeding years.

Reform of Public Enterprises

Unlike the case of the reform process in other areas during the time of the Roh Tae Woo administration, the administration did not establish an implementation system for the reform and privatization of public enterprises as a key means of reform. Instead, the implementation system for reforming and privatizing public enterprises, which was established in the Chun Doo Hwan administration, continued to be employed in the Roh Tae Woo administration. For instance, the Roh Tae Woo administration took advantage of the Government Investment Institution Management Basic Act that was enacted in 1983 by the Chun Doo Hwan administration for promoting an independent and responsible management environment for government investment institutions.

In an attempt to enhance the management autonomy of the government investment institutions and to appraise their management performance and ensure their institutional improvement, the management assessment system was introduced. Moreover, as independent institutions dedicated to performing actual management assessment, the Government Investment Institution Management Assessment Committee and the Management Assessment Group were installed. Therefore, no new

Table 4-5. Target Institutions for Privatization

Targets for Complete Sale	Targets for Partial Sale	Targets for Functional Readjustment
Korea Stock Exchange, Kookmin Bank, Small and Medium Industry Bank, Korea Exchange Bank, Korea Appraisal Board, National Textbook Publishing Corporation, Korea Engineering Development Co.	Korea Electric Power Korea Telecom Corporation Pohang Steel	Korea Overseas Development Corporation, Korea Trade Promotion Corporation, Korea Agro-Fisheries Trade Corporation, Korea Industrial Bank, Korea Housing and Commercial Bank, Korea Industrial Base Development Corporation

implementation system dedicated to the reform of public corporations existed during the Roh Tae Woo administration. It is significant that the administration simply reused the existing implementation system, which it had inherited from the previous administrations. The basic role of the Public Corporations Privatization Implementation Committee was to participate in the discussions on the basic directions of the privatization process, including the selection criteria for the target institutions and the implementation schedule.

Anti-Corruption Reform

Unlike other reforms, the anti-corruption reform of the Roh Tae Woo administration was implemented in close linkage with the political situation of the time. No clear policy or implementation direction was established for anti-corruption reform in the early phase of the incumbency of the administration. The anti-corruption reform was expanded in scope and began to be pushed for as part of the bigger social reform drive beginning in the middle of the presidency. As a result, the anti-corruption drive focused on coming up with institutional supplemental apparatuses, such as the modification or complementation of those regulations with a potential room for misuse of the discretion by public officials in the early phase of the presidency. Beginning in the middle of the presidency and until its end, however, the reform drive focused on strengthening the autonomous functions by pushing for the Public Official New-Spirit Movement and the New Order, New Life Movement, respectively. Therefore, in contrast to the drive in the early phase of the presidency, the anti-corruption drive, which was implemented beginning in the middle or second half of the administration, focused on conducting preventive inspection rather than posterior remediation. The drive also put weight on those inspections aimed at protecting the public officials by boosting their morale and improving their working conditions, including the improvement of the benefits for the junior public officials.

Given that the administration focused on democratization and liberalization and that the National Assembly was dominated by the members of the opposition parties, which enjoyed combined majority seats, during the early part of the administration's incumbency, the anti-corruption drive of the administration did not push for some bold measures for reform before 1990. The anti-corruption drive during this period stopped at establishing related institutions and ensuring official discipline. In response to the pressure on the administration to seize an opportunity for a political turnaround in the wake of the merger of three parties, the administration, which had been plagued by the past ills and by the political confusion arising from various issues for two years after its inauguration, pushed for the New Order, New Life Movement beginning in the 1990s by boldly reshuffling the cabinet amidst the huge shift in the political environment. The movement was a social reform drive initiated by the president, with its key contents including a project for suppressing corruption in the ranks of public officials.

Reform of Local Administration

The overall policy directions of the local administration reform by the administration focused on amending the related laws and regulations required for laying the groundwork for the local self-governing system as well as on the preparatory works for the implementation of the system. The plan to reinstitute the local self-governing system that started upon the inauguration of the administration can be assessed to have been the critical moment for the local administration reform project of the administration. The Local Government Act went through several ups and downs as the legal and political preparatory works required for the enforcement of the act got entangled with the complicated political situation then.

Finally, the deadlines for the election of local representatives and of the heads of local governments were pushed back to June 30, 1990 and June 30, 1991, respectively, as the proposed bill went through another round of modifications in December 1989 in the National Assembly, which was dominated then by the opposition party, enjoying the combined majority seats, but the renewed deadlines were not met in the end. The administration relinquished its hold on power only after succeeding in forming a local assembly, but it postponed the elections for the heads of local governments until 1995. The local administration reform that was implemented during the Roh Tae Woo administration, however, marked the start of the giant stride towards democratization. Despite its many limitations, the local administration reform of the Roh Tae Woo administration represented by the implementation of the local self-governing system was the result of the relentless march towards democratization based on decentralization.

3. Performance and assessment of the government reform

The government was composed of 2 boards, 16 ministries, 4 agencies, 13 offices, 3 external bureaus, and 1 committee upon the inauguration of the Roh Tae Woo administration, but its makeup had changed to 2 boards, 16 ministries, 15 offices, and 2 external bureaus by the end of the administration as the latter implemented several rounds of organizational reshuffling. The number of public officials was increased by 160,000 during the administration, with 60 more 1st-grade positions newly created in the higher ranks than in the lower ranks. As a result, the combined number of public officials added up to 553,103. The abolition or scaling back of the related institutions was not pushed ahead as initially planned due to the resistance of the stakeholders and professional bureaucrats amidst the climate of democratization.

The personnel administration reform implemented by the administration focused on guaranteeing the status of public officials and on improving their welfare benefits in accordance with the progress of democratization. Accordingly, the personnel administration reform was implemented by raising the wage level of the public officials incrementally or by introducing some measures aimed at boosting the morale of the public officials in the areas of their professional status and promotion system. The personnel administration reform by the administration made significant strides in the employment and welfare benefits but had no substantial achievement in the areas of training/education and capability improvement of the public officials.

Meanwhile, the fiscal reform of the administration focused on minimizing the governmental oversight but expanding the autonomy of the private sector. However, it ended up slowing down the overall economy as it heightened the sense of social crisis amid the deterioration of the international economy, the spread of labor-management disputes, the dropping enthusiasm of the workers, the drop in the overall productivity of the country's workforce, and the speculative real estate investment and conspicuous consumption by some classes. The administration's fiscal reform was received well in some areas, however, including the diversification of the country's export structure, the stability of the economic structure, and the expanded economic diversity. Even though the administration's attempt to liberalize the interest rates ended up as a failure, the attempt is still significant in that the liberalization alone made the market well prepared for the liberalization of the interest rates, as evidenced by the market's nimbler reaction to the fluctuation of the market interest rates.

In the area of the electronic government, the administration first revealed limitations in terms of efficient project management and control due to the lack of a standard project management technique, and its quality management system through internal inspection was also less than satisfactory. Second, the administration failed to ensure systemic safety and credibility to a sufficient level. The systemic failure arising from such limitations could disrupt the provision of administrative services to the people, but there was no adequate inspection system within the system to check such possibility. Third, the lack of fluid coordination between the work process development institution and the implementation institution often delayed the system development schedule. Fourth, the absence of a standardized work process development method prevented the systematic planning, implementation of efficient work process development, systematic schedule management, quality assurance, and unification of the interpretation of the related concepts, thereby creating confusion within the institution that requested the project or within the dedicated project implementer.

Meanwhile, the regulatory reform of the administration can be summed up as shown below. First, in the case of the regulatory policy on the economic administration, the validity of the objective and means of regulation implemented by industry should have been reviewed across the board in lock step with the changing national environment. The deregulation efforts to this date had succeeded in accomplishing some results, but, depending on the area, the efforts stopped at the level of a fragmented or localized approach, such as the simplification of the process under the existing regulation or the simple processing of administrative complaints. Therefore, a fundamental review of the regulation itself had to be continuously conducted. Second, the imposition or lifting of the regulation should have been reviewed in the overall context of technology innovation, but the administration did not meet the expectation in this regard. Therefore, the regulatory authority was required to adopt a more flexible attitude towards such areas, but in reality, it did not. Third, the related authority in the government should have done its best to come up with a consensus on deregulation through the open exchange of opinions with the stakeholders and interested outsiders before making a decision to implement deregulation. For this reason, efforts to make each individual feel the effect of deregulation deep in his or her heart was by far the most important imperative, but the related authority in the government did not exert any effort in this regard.

The reform or privatization of public corporations implemented during the administration in an attempt to upgrade such corporations' overall management level was aimed at maintaining the consistency of the policy in accordance with the laws or institutions established by the previous administrations. In this regard, the administration's effort is significant in that it was able to achieve popular assimilation into the policy and to ensure consistency in the policy's implementation. The administration's public-corporation reform policy, however, lacked creativity or freshness.

First, no significant difference can be found in the administration's policy on public corporations due to the administration's fundamental similarity with the Chun Doo Hwan administration. Accordingly, the administration's public-corporation policy can be assessed to have been faithful to the plan established by the previous administration. Second, no additional policy newly strengthened the management of public corporations, with the exception of the privatization policy, which was part of the administration's policy package. Therefore, no institutional reform was implemented by the administration in terms of the public-corporation policy.

Third, the privatization policy was frequently delayed or suspected of having hidden ill motives due to the lack of accurate predictions of the domestic and international economic environment. Therefore, it can be assessed that the administration's poor capability to manage the economy was the biggest stumbling block for the administration. Fourth, serious doubts can be raised about whether the privatization plan focused on expanding the fiscal coffers and boosting the national income level produced a desirable outcome. The deep-seated distrust of the populist political behavior with the spread of nationalism, and some privatization plans that failed to provide no significant fiscal build-up, expanded the distrust in politics and helped spread populist politics. Fifth, no fundamental factor causing inefficiency that the administration aimed to eliminate with the reform of the public corporations was actually eliminated in the end. In other words, no serious issue that was raised then — such as the lack of competition, the insufficient social oversight on public corporations, or the political influence or obscure ownership of public corporations — was resolved. Moreover, the promised improvement in management efficiency was not realized as a result of the reform of public corporations.

In addition, the characteristic of the anti-corruption reform that was implemented during the administration was that the overall policy direction shifted abruptly depending on the social climate in the early stage of the administration's incumbency or depending on the sudden change in the political situation, in which the ruling party assumed the majority seats in the National Assembly in the second half of the administration. The significance of the anti-corruption reform of the administration is that it demonstrated a somewhat autonomous or educational nature in its reform drive compared to the past administrations and that the administration strove to boost the morale of the public officials in an effort to minimize the negative side effects of the internal inspection. What is particularly significant is that the administration strove to elevate the anti-corruption drive to the level of a social-reform movement in the second half of its incumbency.

The failure of the administration's anti-corruption reform drive might have been on account of the factors presented below. First, the effectiveness of the anti-corruption reform drive was halved by the fact that no one held the clear leadership in the process of carrying out the reform drive. Second, the failure of the reform drive may have been due to the political situation then, but the anti-corruption drive should have been pushed forward in the early phase of the administration's incumbency. The anti-corruption drive, however, was not effective during this period. Third, the policy that was implemented to suppress corruption as part of the New Order, New Life Movement failed to rise up to the level of a social-reform movement but remained a government-led movement, thereby failing to obtain significant results. The anti-corruption drive was still significant, though, for its hint of a democratic nature in that the inspection put priority on boosting the morale and autonomy of the public officials.

Finally, the local administration reform implemented by the Roh Tae Woo administration marked the beginning of the country's long journey towards democratization. However, since the reform focused on streamlining the laws and regulations required for the implementation of the local self-governing system, no significant amount of practical improvement in the capability of the local governing bodies was realized. In other words, the seed of the perfunctory-local self-governing system was sown, but it was far from the real localization or from a truly balanced development.

Chapter 5

The Kim Young Sam Administration

Section 1

Inauguration of the Kim Young Sam Administration and Foundation of Key Policy Administration

1. Inauguration of the administration and introduction of its organization

The significance of the Kim Young Sam administration, which was inaugurated in 1993 amidst a complicated political situation and controversy, in the history of ROK politics cannot be stressed too much. The Roh Tae Woo administration (the 6th Republic) was elected by the people after the reintroduction of the direct presidential election system in the wake of the June 1987 Democratic Movement. Although established through a direct presidential election, the administration had some inherent limitations to be considered as a regime that is based on the democratic legitimacy.

The ruling Democratic Justice Party of the 6th Republic (inaugurated in 1981 and lasted until its dismantlement in 1990) failed to earn majority seats in the 13th General Elections, which was held in 1988 to elect the representatives of the National Assembly. On January 22, 1990, faced with a series of political burdens, including the instability in the government administration and the uncertain prospect of the successful recreation of the government, the Roh Tae Woo administration attempted to break through the political gridlock created by the opposition parties, which enjoyed combined majority seats in the National Assembly then, by establishing the Democratic Liberal Party (inaugurated in 1990 and lasted until its dismantlement in 1995) through the merger of the ruling Democratic Justice Party with the two opposition parties, the Unified Democratic Party and the New Democratic Republican Party.[1)]

The three-party merger can be understood as the behind-the-scenes merger driven by the three presidents of each party, President Roh Tae Woo, of the Democratic Justice Party; Kim Young Sam, of the Unified Democratic Party; and Kim Jong Phil, of the New Democratic Republic Party. However, the surprise merger of the ruling party with the Unified Democratic Party headed by Kim Young Sam, one of the two leading proponents of the democratic movement (along with Kim Dae Jung) in the country's political history, sparked a huge political controversy and had many ramifications.[2)]

1) In the 13th National Assembly Election in 1988, the ruling Democratic Justice Party won 125 seats (local constituency seats: 76; nationwide proportional seats: 38), followed by the Peace Democratic Party with 70 seats, the Unified Democratic Party with 59 seats (local constituency seats: 46; nationwide proportional seats: 13), and the New Democratic Republican Party with 35 seats (local constituency seats: 27; nationwide proportional seats: 8).

Despite such controversy, the Democratic Liberal Party created by the three-party merger came to dominate the National Assembly with a whopping 218 seats. In the aftermath of the power struggle among Roh Tae Woo, Kim Young Sam, and Park Cheol Eon, President Roh Tae Woo resigned as president of the Democratic Liberal Party on August 28, 1992, and Kim Young Sam emerged victorious and sworn in as the president of the Democratic Liberal Party.3)

As critical as the political dynamics in the presidential election was the economic situation at the time of the election. The collapse of socialism triggered by the break-up of the Soviet Union by the end of 1991, coupled with the full-scale integration of the world economy and the accelerating advancement of the transportation and telecommunication network, pushed economic growth through globalization towards the top spot in the agenda on the table of the world economy in the early 1990s. In 1992, when the presidential election was held, the South Korean economy was grappling with several key issues: the country's economic growth rate dropped from 8.4% in 1991 to 4.7% in 1992 while the high wage levels and the resulting cooling effect on the investment enthusiasm sparked fears with regard to the prospects of the country's economic vitality and growth potential. The world economy was going through accelerated regional economic integration starting in the mid-1980s, thereby highlighting the urgent need for the country to respond strategically to the globalization and market opening trends, given the export-driven nature of the South Korean economy.4)

Such economic environment was reflected in the presidential election in 1992. The ruling party presidential candidate, Kim Young Sam, ran his campaign on the premise of the "New Economy," and came up with detailed campaign pledges to support the said slogan, including minimizing the government intervention in the economy, strengthening the country's technological competence, and realizing a dynamic and autonomous economy through the establishment of proactive relationships with the country's foreign partners.

The 14th presidential election was characterized as a "two strong and one weak candidate (Kim Young Sam - Kim Dae Jung, Jeong Ju Yeong)" structure.5) The ruling Democratic Liberal

2) The three-party merger greatly shocked and enflamed the country's democratization and progressive groups. Kim Dae Jung, the president of the Peace Democratic Party who experienced the greatest political damage in realpolitik due to the three-party merger, attacked the behind-the-scenes deal with strong words: "The merger of the three parties is a coup d'état as well as an act of treason against the people. The act of artificially reversing the opposition's dominance of the National Assembly, which was created by the people's choice, without any consultation with the people amounts to a most despicable act unprecedented in the political history of the country. Therefore, the declaration of the three-party merger should be entirely invalidated. The members of the National Assembly who betrayed the campaign pledge they had made to the people practically lost their qualification as assemblymen."

3) President Roh Tae Woo tacitly hoped to anoint Park Cheol Eon as his successor, who was supposed to run for president as the ruling party candidate but faced the vehement opposition and resistance of Kim Young Sam. Meanwhile, President Roh Tae Woo was crowned honorary president of the party after his resignation as president of the Democratic Liberal Party, but he gave up all his party functions for political neutrality, and broke away from the Democratic Liberal Party on September 18, 1992.

4) A survey among university professors conducted after the conclusion of the 1992 presidential election showed that the respondents picked economic growth (32%), political stability (18%), and establishment of social order (12.6%) as the most urgent issues that the civilian government was required to handle.

5) There were eight presidential candidates: Kim Young Sam, Kim Dae Jung, Jeong Ju Yeong, Lee Jong Chan of the New Korea Party, Park Chan Jong of the New Justice Party, Lee Byeong Ho of the Korea Justice Party, Kim Ok Seon (independent), and Baek Ki Wan (independent). Lee Jong Chan withdrew his campaign after announcing his support for Jeong Ju Yeong, and the remaining seven continuing their run until election day.

Party candidate, Kim Young Sam, emerged victorious in the election, winning 41.96% (9,977,332 votes) of the total valid ballots, thereby beating Kim Dae Jung of the Democratic Party and Jeong Ju Yeong, who won 33.82 and 16.31% of the votes (8,041,284 and 3,880,067 votes), respectively. Both Kim Dae Jung and Jeong Ju Yeong promptly conceded their defeat, with no entailing controversy over the possibility of a rigged election as in the past. The 14th presidential election is significant in that it gave birth to the first purely civilian administration in the country as a result of an election; unlike the past, only two leading politicians and one leading entrepreneur ran for president, and no candidate from the military circle dominated the election.

The total number of cabinet members amounted to 111, with the exception of the president, during the presidency of Kim Young Sam. Among them, 6 were prime ministers and 105 were ministers. The average length of incumbency of the ministers was 11.45 months, slightly shorter than that during the Roh Tae Woo administration (12.88 months). Hwang In Seong was appointed as the first prime minister of the civilian government, but was sacked less than 10 months after assuming the post, amid the controversy over the Uruguay Round. He was succeeded by Lee Hoi Chang, Lee Yeong Deok, Lee Hong Ku, Lee Su Seong, and Ko Keon (in that order).

Overall, the status of the authentic bureaucrats seems to have been scaled back during the presidency of Kim Young Sam. The percentage of ministers with a bureaucratic background was reduced from 42.1% (48) in the Roh Tae Woo administration to 31.7% (13) in the Kim Young Sam administration. A similar reduction in the percentage of public officials with a pure bureaucratic background was also observed in the key posts in the Presidential Office. Among the senior secretaries to the president, the percentage of bureaucrats dropped from 44.4% (16) in the Roh Tae Woo administration to 20% (2) in the Kim Young Sam administration.

2. Objectives and directions of the government administration

The Kim Young Sam administration stressed the significance of the inauguration of the civilian government by saying that it marked the end of the era of presidents with a military background that existed for the past 30 years, and pushed forward with a comprehensive reform as part of its drive to rectify the country's history, thereby ending the past authoritarian era for good. The civilian government, whose inauguration marked the conclusion of the era of military governments, laid out the key vision of its government administration as the "creation of a New Korea through change and reform" (presidential inaugural address, February 26, 1993). In accordance with this vision, the administration proposed the following five objectives of its government administration: a clean government, a strong economy, a healthy society, a unified Korea, and globalization.

On August 12, 1993, the real-name financial transaction system began to be enforced promptly in accordance with the "Emergency Economic/Financial Order on Real-Name Financial Transactions and Confidentiality Guarantee," which was a decreed by President Kim Young Sam. The president strove to gain the support of the farmers by pledging that "[he] would bet [his] presidency that [he] would never open the domestic market for rice," and by publishing "My Idea on a New Agricultural Policy," which contained his 10 key pledges and 200 policy initiatives. The administration concentrated on introducing new policies in the areas of the treasury, industry, land construction, transportation, and maritime and fisheries. The key tasks in relation to fiscal and tax reform included the gradual increase of the taxation rates, the expansion of the "burden on a beneficiary" principle, the strengthening of the fiscal response capability to changing environment by reducing the fixed and ordinary fiscal expenditure, and the restructuring of the fiscal operation and financing institutions to ensure productivity and transparency in the budgetary management. The administration also strove to grow small and medium-sized businesses as the foundation of the country's economy by taking care of them as the key target of the government policy. Also, in a move to expand the social overhead capital through land construction, the administration laid the foundation for the attraction of private capital, and announced a measure to promote such. In addition, the Ministry of Maritime Affairs and Fisheries was installed by consolidating the hydrographic bureau and by transferring the maritime functions to the ministry.

The key policy direction in the social/cultural/welfare area was the "globalization of living quality." The administration established five key principles: minimum living standard guarantee, productive welfare, community-based welfare, more efficient informatization, and safety-first policy. It also proposed the vision for the 21st-century welfare system and established the mid- and long-term welfare promotion plans. The administration also exerted efforts to spread the new labor - management culture by announcing the new labor - management relations in 1996. With the enactment of the Basic Act on Women Development, the administration aimed to promote gender equality, expand the social participation of women, and promote the welfare of women. With regard to the cultural policy, the administration established the Five-Year Plan to Promote Culture following the reshuffling of the Ministry of Sports and Culture. It also aimed to establish a small but strong government in the area of safety administration, including public safety for everyday living, disaster prevention system, and local self-governing system.

The vision for the new education system was established and announced until the 4th stage of the project (1997), with the goal of establishing an "open education" and "lifelong learning" society. Notable in the info-communication policy was that the Ministry of Info-Communication was inaugurated in 1994. Also, that the informatization strategy for strengthening the national competence unveiled in 1997 was significant in that it laid out the roadmap for the information society. Moreover, the key policy with regard to diplomacy, unification, and defense was the establishment of a foreign policy based on the new foreign policy initiatives and the three-stage unification roadmap for the establishment of the Korean commonwealth.

Section 2

Key Policy Initiatives

1. Real-name financial transaction system

Background

The Kim Young Sam administration was inaugurated amid the great expectations and admiration of the people as it marked the turning point in terms of the abolition of the irrationality and corruption that had accumulated during the 30-year military rule. The South Korean people supported harmony and steady reform based on stability. Economically, the administration was given the mandate to achieve prosperity through the transparent management of the economy. Socially, it was required to resolve the social inequality and the regional conflicts with the assumption of power by the group that led the country's democratization. Against the backdrop of such shifting political environment, President Kim Young Sam's reform drive focused on rooting out the legacy of the past. The success of the reform was largely dependent on how best the administration would overcome the differences within the political alliance under the apparent goal of recreating the government after the three-party merger. The real-name financial transaction system that unveiled as the backdrop of such political environment was one of the key measures pushed forward as part of the administration's reform drive.

The administration focused on "severing the collusive relationship between politics and businesses that provided the resources required to maintain the authoritarian military regime, improving the transparency in the relationship between politics and businesses, and, at the same time, breaking down the monopolistic dominance of politics through the alliance between conglomerates and the political elites." Viewed from this perspective, the administration was required to introduce the real-name financial transaction system as one of the most critical measures that were to be implemented during the early days of the economic-reform drive. The size of the country's underground economy was estimated to have amounted to up to 19 ~ 40% of the country's gross national product in 1991. Given such predicament, the administration's financial or fiscal policy was limited in its capability to achieve the required level of efficiency; the country's current account recorded a deficit amounting to USD 4.528 billion in 1992.

The real-name financial transaction system is the institution that made it mandatory for all the people involved in transactions with financial institutions to use their real names. The age-old practice of using borrowed or pseudo names in financial transactions, which had been entrenched in the South Korean society in the process of implementing the growth-driven economic policy for the past 30 years by increasing the secret transactions of funds, deepened the inequality in the income levels of, or the tax burdens imposed on, different classes and income groups. The real-name financial transaction system made it mandatory to use one's real name in financial transactions, rectifying the injudicious institutions and practices in the past; encouraged the conversion of the financial assets deposited under false names to those deposited under real names; and contained measures aimed at establishing the legal apparatus required to guarantee the absolute secrecy of financial transactions.

Many were convinced that the establishment of the real-name financial transaction system would advance the realization of economic justice and prompt the abolition of corruption. The ultimate goal of the administration in enforcing the real-name financial transaction system, however, was to realize economic justice by ensuring transparency in financial transactions and equality in taxation. The economic justice resulting from the enforcement of the real-name financial transaction system would be realized via the following path: guarantee of equality in taxation → suppression of the inheritance of economic entitlement → all-out banning in principle of unearned income or speculative investment → reduction of the amount of corruption → abolition of money politics and fostering of a clean political environment.

Implementation System

Rather than on the public-consensus-forming process, President Kim Young Sam relied on a few policymakers in making key policy decisions. In the case of the real-name financial transaction system, the president came up with the final decision after secret behind-the-scene discussions with a few policymakers rather than putting up the subject for public debate to draw up a social consensus. The president attempted to minimize the side effects expected in the legislation process by taking an extraordinary approach, which was the "emergency economic/financial order." The president empowered Vice Prime Minister Lee Kyeong Shik and other officials in the Ministry of Finance to play the key role in the establishment of practical policies by making them work on the policy of the real-name financial transaction system in total secrecy. The real-name financial transaction system of President Kim Young Sam was perfected while going through a deliberation process carried out by the following: President Kim Young Sam → Vice Prime Minister Lee Kyeong Shik → KDI doctoral group → Treasury Minister Hong Jae Hyeong → Kim Yong Jin, head of the Department on the Taxation System.

The ruling Democratic Liberal Party was not confident about the eventual enforcement of the real-name financial transaction system. Unlike in the 5th and 6th Republic, the ruling party members did not express their strong opposition to the measure during the decision making process, but they intervened in the implementation of the system by demanding some complimentary measures. Meanwhile, the opposition party had no clear party line on the real-name financial transaction system in the early years of the 5th Republic, but began to demand the immediate implementation of the system by the second half of the 5th Republic. The opposition party also demanded that the real-name financial transaction system be complemented or that any negative side effect that it may have during its implementation process be minimized. Also, it even demanded to take remedial action with regard to the potential unconstitutionality of the president's emergency order.

The overall positive perception of the real-name financial transaction system by the public, which led to their wholehearted embrace of the system, was largely attributable to the consistent "policy campaign" led by activist groups, including the Citizens' Coalition for Economic Justice. The active participation by the activist groups helped the administration considerably in gaining the public support to the eventual implementation of the real-name financial transaction system.

Given that press freedom and free speech were fully guaranteed then, the role of the media in the policy-making process was considerably highlighted compared to that of the past. The media greatly contributed to the eventual implementation of the real-name financial transaction system by faithfully reporting the need for the early implementation of the system in the editorial pages or in news commentaries to open the status of the property and assets owned by the public officials to the public and to ensure the effectiveness of the series of inspections to be performed on them.

Fundamentally, whereas the economic organizations, including the Federation of Korean Industries, expressed their strong opposition to the enforcement of the real-name financial transaction system, both the labor groups and Citizens' Coalition for Economic Justice advocated the implementation of the system. The declaration by the economic organizations, including the Federation of Korean Industries, in September 1992 that they would fully support the implementation of the real-name financial transaction system cleared the last remaining stumbling block on the road to the enforcement of the system.

Implementation Process and Contents

The implementation process of the real-name financial transaction system is very unique compared to those of the country's other policies and those of the policies of other countries. It would have been natural if there were various discussions on the real-name financial transaction system and if various controversies about it arose immediately before its final implementation, but it is unprecedented in any country throughout the world that discussions of the system had continued for 12 years, across three administrations, before its final implementation. Considering that the introduction of the policy had been repeatedly postponed in the 5th and 6th Republic after being challenged by the policy's opponents, the surprise enforcement of the policy by the administration despite the vehement opposition to it by the conglomerates and conservative politicians then can be said to be decisively attributable to the personal will and formidable power of the president himself. In addition, the legitimacy held by the administration as the first "civilian government," and the popular support that the president enjoyed, played an important role in the eventual implementation of the policy.

The lack of a clear goal, however, for the surprise enforcement of the real-name financial transaction system by the administration inevitably caused great confusion. It was not even clear whether the policy intention of the real-name financial transaction system as specified in the emergency decree (Article 3) was "real-name system in ownership" or "real-name system in financial transactions." As a result, numerous violations of the real-name financial transaction system were reported in the process of its implementation. In response, the people and the opposition party demanded the establishment of an alternative law that would replace the original decree to prevent the carrying out of financial transactions under borrowed names, but the ministry governing the policy went ahead and implemented the policy, not being swayed by such proposition. As a result, there were clear discrepancies between the purported and official goals of the real-name financial transaction system.

The potential conflicts inherent in the real-name financial transaction system were as follows. First, a potential conflict was present with regard to the enforcement timing of the policy. The group led by the Democratic Liberal Party, the business community, and the Senior Secretary to the President for Economic Policy took the position that the policy should be introduced after the confirmation of the economic turnaround. On the contrary, since they realized that reform without the implementation of the real-name financial transaction system would be meaningless, the opposition party and a number of activist groups, including the Citizens' Coalition for Economic Justice, argued for the immediate introduction of the system regardless of the economic turnaround.

Second, some conflicts were present with regard to the simultaneous implementation of the system with the consolidated general taxation on financial assets. While one group supported the simultaneous implementation of both policies for the sake of social justice, another group supported asynchronous implementation, in which implementation of the general taxation on financial assets would follow the immediate enforcement of the real-name financial transaction system after a while, when everything is ready. Third, two groups that had conflicting views about the investigation of the sources of funds clashed with each other. One group supported the investigation of the sources of funds deposited under pseudo names. Contrastingly, another group claimed that because investigation of pseudo names would only slow down the conversion of the accounts with pseudo names to those with real names, they argued for the expansion of the target accounts that would be exempted from investigation with regard to their sources. Fourth, there were conflicts with regard to whether only the employees of financial institutions should be included in the group of people required to perform financial transactions with their real names or whether those using banking services should be included in the group as well. Another open question that invited controversy was which comes first: the uncovering of accounts with pseudo names or the protection of privacy.

Many questions were also raised with regard to the Act on the Real-Name Financial Transactions, which was enforced by presidential decree. Many criticized the government for having been negligent in stopping the massive escape of funds deposited with pseudo names as it allowed withdrawal of those funds using pseudo names, even after the enforcement of the real-name financial transaction system. Moreover, the exclusion of some financial assets, such as insurance deposits, from the application target of the real-name financial transaction system raised serious issues, including potentially massive transfers of funds as well as the question of fairness. For these reasons, the amendment of the Act on the Real-Name Financial Transaction System was inevitable. It was feared, however, that a massive escape of funds and the resulting economic confusion would be inevitable, thereby making it impossible to enforce the act, if the policy is to be implemented only after the amendment of the act by the National Assembly. It would be difficult to achieve a sufficient outcome only by banning transactions using pseudo names, which is only one of the many tactics being employed by the underground economy, without considering the fundamental causes of tax evasion and corruption.

The Kim Young Sam administration implemented the real-name financial transaction system in accordance with the "Emergency Economic/Financial Order on Real-Name Financial Transactions and Confidentiality Guarantee" effective at 8:00 p.m. on August 12, 1993. The emergency economic/financial order, which came into effect on August 12, 1993, mainly consisted of three parts: (1) provisions on the mandatory use of one's real name when performing transactions with financial institutions; (2) provisions on the measures to be taken on the existing financial assets deposited with pseudo names, which the public has been notified of; and (3) strengthening of the confidentiality protection on the financial transaction information.

Beginning on August 12, 1993, all people engaging in transactions with financial institutions, including commercial banks, securities firms, insurance firms, investment trust firms, investment banks, local co-ops (including the National Agricultural Cooperative Federation), post offices, saemaul savings banks, and credit association cooperatives, were required to use their real names. The mandatory use of one's real name was applicable, however, only to those transactions performed through financial institutions. Individual account holders were authenticated by checking their resident registration numbers while corporations were authenticated by checking their respective corporate names and business registration numbers, or their corresponding unique serial numbers. In an attempt to enhance the effectiveness of the mandatory use of real names in financial transactions, any employee of a financial institution who violated the act was subject to a fine amounting to KRW 5 million, and it was also specified that a financial institution that violated the act was subject to a matching fine if it was negligent in exercising considerable caution or in performing an oversight role to prevent such violation.

The withdrawal of funds with pseudo names was completely banned, but a two-month mandatory period for changing all accounts to those with real names was offered to all account holders.

It was also stipulated that funds up to KRW 50 million would be exempted from the investigation of the sources of funds, and if anyone is subject to a fine or an administrative penalty as a result of his/her violation of the commercial law, the Act on Securities Exchanges, the Monopoly Regulation and Fair Trade Act, or other law related to the conversion of accounts with pseudo names to those with real names, he/she will be exempted from the imposition of the applicable fine or administrative penalty in accordance with the governing laws if he/she takes remedial action within one year after the violation. Also, if a person carried out a transaction involving financial assets deposited with a borrowed name, and converted such assets to one with his or her real name, such person would be required to pay the differential in the withholding income taxes for the past five years. In addition, any person who converts his/her account to one with his/her real name after the mandatory two-month conversion period shall be charged with a penalty as well as with differentiated tax rates on the income obtained from the interest dividends. Furthermore, the government suppressed the unnecessary fluidization of funds by making it mandatory to report the withdrawal of a high amount of cash to the National Tax Service.

The requirements and procedure through which financial information shall be provided were clearly stipulated in the related laws, and the provision or leaking of information or materials on specific financial transactions without the written request or consent of the account holder was strictly prohibited. Any violation of the duty of confidentiality guarantee shall be penalized in accordance with the newly established provisions. Any employee in a financial institution who leaked such information, or those who demanded the unfair provision to them of such information, or those who leaked the information that they gained in relation to the performance of their business shall be subject to imprisonment for less than three years, or to a fine less than KRW 20 million.

Performance and Assessment

The percentage of account holders who were authenticated with their real names was 98.3% as of end of December 1996, some three years after the enforcement of the real-name financial transaction system. Also the conversion rate to the real name among the accounts with pseudo names was 98.8%. This result confirms that majority of the bank accounts then had either been authenticated or converted to real-name accounts. Another important reason for implementing the real-name financial transaction system was to promote fairness in taxation; after the enforcement of the real-name financial transaction system, the percentage of income tax evasion amounted to 25.7% in 1993 but dropped to 16.3% in 1994, thereby achieving a 9.4% reduction in the cases of income tax evasion.

With regard to the abolition of money politics and the fostering of a clean political environment, notable changes were observed in the four major local elections in June 1995 and the general elections in April 1996. The most prominent change in the elections after the enforcement of the real-name financial transaction system was the growth rate of the total amount of currency in circulation (M2). The judicial disposal of the cases involving the alleged slush funds of two former presidents also became feasible largely due to the introduction of the real-name financial transaction system.

There have been numerous debates and controversies spanning many years with regard to the implementation of the real-name financial transaction system, including several rounds of postponement of the system introduction until its final implementation on August 12, 1993. Touted as the "reform of reforms and the centerpiece of the contemporary reform drive," the implementation of the real-name financial transaction system was the pride of President Kim Young Sam for many years. The real-name financial transaction system, however, had limitations. For instance, it failed to take root as an established institution as it only turned the emergency presidential decree into the general legal system.

Some 20 years have passed since the initial enforcement of the real-name financial transaction system. The introduction of the system enabled the tracking of the sources of illegal funds, thereby improving the transparency in financial transactions and boosting the overall transaction volume, which is assessed to have led to the advancement of the country's banking industry. In addition, the system also helped improve the country's income distribution structure through the introduction of the consolidated general taxation on comprehensive financial incomes. The amendment of the Act on Real-Name Financial Transactions, however, has been an urgent issue for some time, in the wake of the continued uncovering of slush funds of politicians or entrepreneurs who took advantage of bank accounts held under borrowed names, and discussions of how to effectively regulate financial transactions under borrowed names for potentially criminal purposes have continued ever since the implementation of the real-name financial transaction system.

2. Diversified foreign relations ("New Diplomacy")

Background

On May 24, 1993, three months after its inauguration, the administration announced the "Declaration of New Diplomacy," which contained a new policy initiative for diversified foreign relations. The declaration defined the New Diplomacy as "a foreign policy initiative that puts emphasis on the universal values of the human race and on the proactive diplomacy built on the foundation of morality, which focuses on managing the situation with regard to the divided Korea as well as on managing the unified Korea in the future to ensure the prosperity of all the Koreans." In addition, the declaration laid out a three-stage roadmap for the unification of the Korean Peninsula, through which the "two Koreas will be united as one people and one nation by going through an incremental and peaceful unification process starting with reconciliation and cooperation and followed by the union of the two Koreas." Stressing that "the two Koreas should no longer compete with each other but should instead forge a partnership for the good of all the Koreans and for the prosperity of the Asia-Pacific region," the declaration promised that "the South Korean government [would] push forward with the open-door policy and globalization of the country." In particular, the government promised to "improve the sales environment for the foreign companies by softening the regulatory oversight on the investments by foreigners, accelerating the opening of the financial market, and strengthening the protection of intellectual property." It also promised that "the government [would] lay the groundwork for permanent peace in the region by deepening and advancing the mutual security cooperation system led by the United States, and by pushing for security talks within the Asia-Pacific region."

As the first civilian government inaugurated after the democratization of South Korea, the administration exerted efforts to gather and consolidate the opinions of diverse interest groups in the reform process, and comparable consideration and care were also reflected in the area of foreign policy. The unification of Germany in 1990 and the subsequent conclusion of the Cold War brought about a wind of change in South Korean diplomacy. The changing international environment in the wake of the conclusion of the Cold War reduced the country's room for diplomatic activities centered on ideology. As a result, the country's foreign policy, in which it handled most diplomatic issues by relying on Washington, had to face up to considerable challenges. In view of such prospect, the New Diplomacy by the administration pegged its policy directions on five key principles: globalization, diversification, pluralization, regional cooperation, and future-orientedness, and sought to change its foreign policy against the backdrop of the shifting world order. Under the new foreign policy guidelines, the South Korean government put more emphasis on transnational issues, including the spread of democracy, international peace, poverty alleviation/eradication, and environmental protection. Towards these ends, the declaration stressed that South Korea would continue to expand its diplomatic relations with all countries while also playing the role of a mediator that would arbitrate on international issues related to the conflicting interests of the advanced and developing countries of the world. Specifically, the administration exerted efforts to bolster its diplomacy with international organizations like the United Nations in an effort to participate in the new international order and to comply with the international norms, on the strength of the country's much improved status in the international community.

Implementation System

The implementation system of the New Diplomacy by the administration was based on the following five key directions: globalization, diversification, pluralization, regional cooperation, and future-orientedness. Defining the growing interdependence among countries in the 21st century as an expected outcome of globalization, Kim argued that the country would need to respond proactively to the shifting world trends by increasing its contribution to the resolution of global issues like international peace, arms control, poverty alleviation/eradication, and environmental protection and recycling of resources as the process of making valuable contributions to the efforts to make the world a more just and better place to live in.

The administration planned to develop its diplomacy in the following three ways: (1) deepening and advancing its relations with the existing friendly countries, such as the United States and Japan, based on the recognition of the need for diversified diplomacy; (2) advancing its relations with China and Russia into full-scale diplomatic relations; and (3) developing its relations with Southeast Asia, EC, the Middle East, Africa, and Latin America to a new level. Meanwhile, the pluralization of South Korean diplomacy means that the diversification drive shall be applied not only to certain areas, such as the economy, trade, environment, and culture, but also to the actors in each area. Also, regional cooperation was defined as a proactive participation in various activities pertaining to APEC, including the APEC summit, and in the Asia-Pacific regional cooperative system, based on the recognition that Southeast Asia is emerging as the center of the Asia-Pacific region. The inclusion of "future-orientedness" in the key directions for the implementation of the New Diplomacy was an effort to suggest directions for South Korean diplomacy. The main direction of unification diplomacy was set as an effort to persuade Pyongyang to break out of its isolation and to jump on the changing international trend marked by openness and internationalization.

Implementation Process and Contents

In step with the shifting world order, in which peace and cooperation came to be valued more than ever, after the conclusion of the Cold War, President Kim Young Sam stressed that the two Koreas need to cooperate with each other for peace. Saying that "no allied nation is better than the people with a shared ethnicity," the president stressed the importance of close cooperation among the Korean people amidst the new international order. Also, by proposing to hold inter-Korean summit talks, he made it clear that he would strive to unify and realize peace in the Korean Peninsula through close inter-Korean cooperation.

However, the forward-looking policy on North Korea announced at the inauguration of the administration turned its direction abruptly with the declaration by Pyongyang that it would withdraw its membership in the Nuclear Non-Proliferation Treaty. Recognizing that its plan to forge a forward-looking relationship with North Korea at the beginning of the presidency might have to change inevitably, the administration came up with a new basic strategy: pushing for talks with Pyongyang while at the same time putting pressure on the North.

While the Clinton administration was approaching the North Korean nuclear issue from the perspective of nuclear non-proliferation ever since Pyongyang's exit from the NPT framework, the administration considered it a violation of the Inter-Korean Basic Agreement and Joint Declaration on Denuclearization. Also, whereas the Clinton administration put more emphasis on stopping the mass production of nuclear materials by North Korea when the North Korean nuclear crisis was unfolding, the administration argued for the containment of Pyongyang's nuclear ambition from its root.

The Kim Young Sam administration again clashed with Pyongyang in its effort to advance the reunification of two Koreas. In the presidential congratulatory speech of the 49th anniversary of the country's liberation in 1994, the president announced the "Three-Stage Roadmap for the Unification of Korea to Construct the Commonwealth of Korea." Further developed from the existing "Measure to Unify the Korean Community," the roadmap laid out more detailed processes leading up to the ultimate unification of the two Koreas by dividing the unification process into three stages: the "reconciliation-cooperation stage"; the "inter-Korean unity stage"; and the "completion of the one-people-and-one-nation unified state." Since Pyongyang considered such unification goal and method as Seoul's ulterior attempt to realize reunification through absorption, it was inevitable for Pyongyang to maintain confrontational relations with the South's Kim Young Sam administration.

As the Kim Young Sam administration changed the direction of its strategy on North Korea to a two-track strategy alternately employing the tactics of talks and pressure, Pyongyang broke down the inter-Korean channel. As a result, Seoul was forced to rely instead on the Washington-Pyongyang channel. In the process, not only did the administration had to endure constant tension to a certain extent in the inter-Korean relations but also in the ROK - U.S. relations. The key security- and defense-related issues involving the United States during the administration included the suspension and restarting of the Team Spirit Exercise, the ROK - U.S. relations with regard to the transfer of the peacetime operational control authority, and the North Korean nuclear crisis. The Team Spirit Exercise repeatedly went through a process of restarting and holding talks over the potential cancelation of the exercise as part of the strategy to put more pressure on Pyongyang. However, when the North Korean nuclear crisis reached the final resolution stage in the wake of the Carter - Kim Il Sung Nuclear Agreement in June 1994, the exercise did not restart. Meanwhile, the transfer of operational control authority to South Korea had been pushed for a long time, in accordance with the conclusion of the Cold War, the changes in the surrounding environment, and the growth of the overall firepower of the ROK Armed Forces. The South Korean government reclaimed the "peacetime operational control authority" on December 1, 1994. The discussion on the operational control over the ROK Armed Forces started in 1950, when President Syngman Rhee gave up the operational control over the ROK Armed Forces and handed it over to General MacArthur, the Commander of the United Nations Forces. The peacetime operational control authority was reclaimed in 1994, during the presidency of Kim Young Sam, and the discussion on the clawback of the wartime operational control authority has since continued between Seoul and Washington. As of 2006, the operational control authority over the ROK Armed Forces is divided into the peacetime operational control authority and the wartime operational control authority. However, since the agreement on the transfer of peacetime operational control authority to the ROK Armed Forces in the 24th ROK - US Security Consultative

Meeting in 1992, the peacetime operational control authority was officially given back to the ROK Armed Forces on December 1, 1994, the period during the administration.

Critical of the exclusion of Seoul from the direct talks between Washington and Pyongyang, the administration pushed for the policy to strengthen the position of South Korea as the legitimate country to engage in the North Korean nuclear issue. Therefore, the North Korean policy during the administration swung wildly between the hawkish and the dovish lines, which again created considerable tension between Seoul and Washington.

Since the Kim Young Sam administration was deeply interested in the diversification of its diplomacy, it was enthusiastic with the diplomacy with Russia and China. Ever since the establishment of diplomatic relations with Russia in 1990, expectations had been high with regard to the bilateral relations between Seoul and Moscow, but in reality, it was assessed that the bilateral relations between the two countries largely depended on excessive optimism riddled with wishful thinking. Moscow put priority on expanding its trade and economic cooperation with South Korea as well as in maintaining its bilateral relations with Seoul, all of which were aimed at overcoming its economic difficulties. What Seoul considered its utmost priority in its relations with Moscow, however, was political and security benefits, without ever getting out of the confinement of its North Korean policy; the country's economic interests had always taken a backseat in its relation with Russia. As a result, the country's economic cooperation with Russia remained at a state well below the level that was initially hoped for. Neither was Seoul getting the most out of the potential improvement of its relations with Russia. In the wake of the dissolution of the Soviet Union and the subsequent inauguration of the Russian Federation in 1992, Seoul stopped the subsequent payment of the balance of Russia's economic-cooperation loans amounting to US$ 1.53 billion. Seoul's enthusiasm for the Northern policy cooled rapidly as Russia breached the repayment schedule of its debts to South Korea. Therefore, the status of Russia as a legitimate participant in the talks to resolve the Korean crisis was pushed down and stayed low throughout the administration.

The establishment of diplomatic ties with China played the decisive role in opening the floodgate of exchanges and cooperation between the two countries. Since the establishment of diplomatic relations with China, the exchanges between the two countries across nearly all areas, including politics, the economy, the society and culture, as well as those among ordinary people, increased remarkably. The biggest advancement since the establishment of diplomatic ties with China was observed in practical areas, including the economy, trade, and the mutual exchanges of people. The trade between the two countries, which started with small-scale indirect trade in 1989, had since increased twofold, from US$ 4.4 billion in 1991 to US$ 8.2 billion in 1992, and passed the US$ 9 billion mark in 1993, the year when the administration was inaugurated. In 1997, close to the end of the administration, the country's total trade volume with China was inching towards the US$ 24 billion mark after years of remarkable growth, thereby making each country the third largest mutual-trade partner to the other. In addition, China rapidly emerged as South Korea's second largest investment target, after the United States. The number of people visiting the other country exploded as well from 88,000 in 1992, the first year after the establishment of diplomatic ties, to close to 600,000 in 1998.

President Kim Young Sam paid an official state visit to China on March 26～30, 1994 for a summit meeting with Jiang Zemin, then the president of the People's Republic of China. At the summit meeting, the two leaders discussed wide-ranging issues pertaining to the two countries, including the North Korean nuclear issue and economic cooperation. President Kim achieved much in the visit, including the signing of a cultural agreement between the two countries, an industrial agreement, an agreement to install an industrial-cooperation committee, the double-tax avoidance agreement, and an agreement on customs cooperation. Furthermore, President Jiang reciprocated the gesture of President Kim and paid an official state visit to South Korea on November 13~17, 1995 for a summit meeting with President Kim, where the two leaders reaffirmed their commitment to continued mutual cooperation and to the expansion of their countries' relations. The state visit of Jiang to South Korea marked the 4th anniversary of the establishment of diplomatic ties between the two countries. Since the Sino-Korean relations was expanding to other domains as well, including politics, diplomacy, and security, such visit was a historic event that acted as a precursor of the upcoming changes in the order of Northeast Asia.

South Korea's relationship with Japan during the administration can be summed up as being characterized by the pending issues that pertained to the two countries' history and to South Korea's resulting diplomatic conflict with Japan. The historical baggage between the two countries spread to other areas, thereby sparking diplomatic confrontation for an extended period. Japan decided to set up its 200-nautical-mile exclusive economic zone, thereby effectively including Dokdo Island within the zone. To such advancement, President Kim Young Sam responded by proposing that Tokyo deal with the issues of territorial dominium and fisheries agreement separately, a misguided decision that strengthened the position of Tokyo by giving the impression that Dokdo Island is located in disputed territory. Since the move left a room for a potential interpretation that the ROK government, which had stubbornly adhered to the hardline position that Dokdo cannot be treated as the subject of a territorial dispute, or put on the negotiating table, as the island is clearly part of the territory of South Korea, suddenly changed its position and accepted the contrasting position of Tokyo, the diplomatic conflict between Seoul and Tokyo began to show a pattern in which the issue of territorial dominium over Dokdo and the fisheries issue were intertwined during the administration.

One of the key accomplishments of the administration in its diplomacy with international organizations was its participation in the United Nations peacekeeping operations. South Korea had been repeatedly requested by the United Nations to participate in its peacekeeping operations ever since its joining of the United Nations as a member state, which in itself signifies that the country had significantly grown in power and is now ready to contribute to the international community. The government dispatched the Sangroksu (evergreen tree) Company, the ROK Army Corps of Engineers, to Somalia on a PKO mission that lasted from July 1993 to April 1994. The administration also participated in the United Nations PKO mission in Angola beginning in October 1995, based on the experiences it had accumulated in Somalia, thereby expanding the footprints of the Republic of Korea in the international community. The ROK Army Corps of Engineers also participated in the United Nations PKO mission in Angola (UNAVEM III) from October 1995 to December 1996. The South Korean mission contributed to the effective implementation of the United Nations PKO activities by implementing various activities, including the construction of bridges and the carrying out of humanitarian relief efforts.

The New Diplomacy of the administration came to fruition with the country's joining of the Organization for Economic Co-operation and Development (OECD). South Korea became the second country in Asia, after Japan, to join OECD, a club that is considered as the club of advanced economies, as a member state in December 1996. As such, the New Diplomacy of the administration put great emphasis on the diplomacy aimed at realizing the country's globalization. Following the global waves of neoliberalism, the administration set globalization as its key national policy goal and took proactive action to respond to such trend, which can be clearly shown by the administration's great interest in and joining of diverse international organizations. The administration participated in the World Trade Organization (WTO) as a member state since the National Assembly's December 15, 1994 ratification of the motion to join WTO. Amid the rising global trend of free international trade, WTO was inaugurated as an international organization entrusted with the task of monitoring the implementation process of the agreements signed in the Uruguay Round of Multinational Trade Negotiations, all of which were aimed at establishing order in the global free trade by replacing the General Agreement on Tariffs and Trade (GATT) with WTO, and at promoting the opening of the closed domestic market to international trade.

South Korea, however, was embroiled in the foreign currency crunch triggered by the financial crisis that swept East Asia in 1997, and was eventually forced to request IMF to provide bailout funds to it on December 5, 1997. Internally, the country had to deal with a series of bankruptcies, starting with the insolvency of Hanbo Steel in January 1997, and with the serial insolvencies of large conglomerates, including Sammi, Jinro, and Kia Motors. Globally, the exchange rates in Thailand and Indonesia precipitated against the U.S. dollar beginning in the summer of 1997, which was followed by the crash of the stock market in both countries. On November 21, 1997, President Kim Young Sam requested the IMF to provide bailout funds to it to prevent sovereign insolvency, and accepted the draconian measures for economic reform demanded by the IMF in return for the provision of bailout funds. On December 3, Seoul signed the agreement on the provision of bailout funds with Michel Camdessus, then IMF managing director. The signing of the bailout funds was promptly followed by the provision of the first round of emergency bailout funds amounting to US$ 5.6 billion on December 5. As such, South Korea was put under the governance of IMF across a wide range of economic policies.

Performance and Assessment

With the New Diplomacy, the Kim Young Sam administration pushed for globalization in terms of the economy, and strove to deal with the North Korean nuclear crisis in the security area. The globalization and open-door policies in the area of the economy, which were advanced by the administration in the 1990s, took shape in the form of the country's joining of WTO and OECD. Such globalization drive created a passionate following in the country while expanding the horizon of the people's perception. The strategy, however, stopped at simply being a political slogan, without sparking waves of structural changes in the South Korean society or being supported by matching policy implementation. The strategy eventually backfired as South Korea got mired in the Asian financial crisis and was forced to request the IMF to provide it with emergency bailout funds.

In the area of security, the North Korean nuclear crisis triggered by Pyongyang's nuclear ambition was the key policy focus of the administration. The first wave of the North Korean nuclear crisis triggered by Pyongyang's withdrawal from the Non-Nuclear Proliferation Treaty was covered up by the agreement between the former U.S. president Jimmy Carter and President Kim Il Sung in June 1994, and the subsequent establishment of the Korea Energy Development Organization (KEDO). The Agreed Framework that Pyongyang and Washington forged in Geneva, Switzerland, however, was not the ultimate resolution of the North Korean nuclear crisis and had gone through numerous stumbling blocks in its implementation process that depended on the changing diplomatic climate between Pyongyang and Washington. Seen from such perspective, the New Diplomacy of the administration is assessed to have advanced the diplomatic capability of South Korea to a certain extent, amid the globalization trend and the North Korean nuclear crisis, but it ended up having substantial difficulties in effectively responding to the developing crisis owing to the insufficient preparation domestically and to the lack of clear policy directions in its implementation.

The New Diplomacy of the administration provides some meaningful lessons with regard to the overall decision making process on the country's foreign policy: the importance of maintaining sound ROK - U.S. relations in the implementation of the North Korean policy, the lack of democratization and institutionalization in the process of policy formation and implementation that would otherwise have improved the transparency and predictability of the New Diplomacy, and the influence of the domestic politics on the country's foreign policy. It cannot be denied that the formation of the foreign policy was sometimes distorted or changed abruptly due to such domestic political factors, hence damaging the consistency and efficiency of the policy implementation, which again led to a diplomatic confrontation with the partner country. In this regard, the New Diplomacy gives points for the succeeding administrations to reflect on despite some meaningful accomplishments.

3. Re-establishment of the country's legitimate history

Background

Defining the nature of his administration as a "civilian democracy" in his speech marking the 75th anniversary of the March 1st Movement, President Kim Young Sam declared that the country closed the chapter of its tumultuous modern history that began with the Japanese colonial rule with the birth of the "civilian democratic government." The administration was able to justify its political legitimacy and was able to differentiate itself from the past regimes by proclaiming the civilian government as the ultimate fruit of the independence movement launched by the country's patriotic ancestors as well as of the democratization movement that started with the April 19 Revolution. The administration attempted to reclassify various events in the contemporary Korean history and to divide these into two main parts: the independence movement to get out of the grip of the Japanese colonial rule, including the March 1st Movement and the establishment of the Interim Government of Korea; and the democratization movement that started with the April 19 Revolution and continued further with the May 18 Gwangju Democratization Movement and June 1987 Democratic Uprising. In the context of such historical understanding, the administration's initiative to "re-establish the country's legitimate history" can be said to have started with the administration's inauguration.

The key objective of the administration in the reform of the ROK Armed Forces was to eliminate the informal group in the army called "Hana Group," which began as a group of cadets belonging to the military academy's 11th class and later led the protest to support the May 16 military coup d'état under the leadership of Chun Doo Hwan. Now grown as the key informal group within the army, with the support of Park Jung Hee and Yun Phil Yong, Hana Group was effectively controlling the military personnel administration behind the scenes. The elimination of Hana Group started with the replacement of the army chief of staff and the commander of the defense security command in the regular exchange of personnel. Although criticized for having concentrated on human reform rather than on reforming the military institutions, the administration largely succeeded in accomplishing some meaningful achievements, such as eliminating Hana Group, which had grown into a private political group during the military regime, from its core.

On November 1, 1995, former president Roh Tae Woo was summoned to the prosecutor's office for the first time since the foundation of the Republic of Korea, and on November 16, he was imprisoned for the alleged violation of the Additional Punishment Law on Specific Crimes (Acceptance of Bribe). In the investigation by the prosecutors, it was also found that former president Chun Doo Hwan collected illegal funds from various corporations amounting to KRW 950 billion, and spent KRW 700 billion of them as slush funds to finance the party operation and other activities, with the balance amounting KRW 160 billion kept privately for his personal use upon leaving the presidential office in February 1988. That the two former presidents secretly collected and appropriated astronomical amounts of slush funds raised the ire of the Korean people. Specifically, the slush funds of former president Roh Tae Woo sparked the drive for the "re-establishment of the country's legitimate history" campaign in earnest.

Implementation Process and Contents

The "re-establishment of the country's legitimate history" can be considered one of the key reform drives by the administration in that it laid the groundwork for the country to leap forward to the future based on the serious re-evaluation of its history. The administration enshrined the remains of the patriots who gave up their lives for the country's liberation with government financing for the first time since the foundation of the Republic of Korea. It also pushed ahead with the demolition of the erstwhile Japanese Government General Building (Seoul Capitol) in a symbolic gesture to break away with the past colonial rule. In addition, along with the expansion and enshrinement of the April 19 cemetery as a national cemetery, the status of the April 19 Revolution, which had been degraded to a "patriotic uprising," was put back to a "revolution," thereby befitting its historical significance and making it clear that the civilian government imbibed the spirit of the April 19 Revolution. The historical significance of the May 18 Gwangju Democratization Movement was restored as well by defining the movement as the root cause of the establishment of the civilian government, along with the effort to reinstate the honor of the victims by punishing those who had raped the constitutional order through the legislation of the Special Act on May 18.

The "re-establishment of the country's legitimate history" project was first implemented through the personal resolution of President Kim Young Sam, followed by the project's implementation by the governing ministry. However, the process of ascertaining the truth and punishing the perpetrators of the December 12 military coup d'état and the May 18 rebellion was pushed forward with thanks to the bold resolution of President Kim Young Sam, followed by the legislation of the Special Act on May 18 as well as by the formation of the Special Investigation Headquarters in the Prosecutors' Office.

In the case of the inheritance and development of the "spirit of independence" project, however, the commitment of the dedicated government ministry to the project played a relatively greater role, with the project consistently implemented after the presidential approval of the proposed plan in a cabinet meeting. The Ministry of Patriots and Veterans Affairs assumed the leadership in the project, with the task of identifying and rewarding the patriots who contributed to the independence of the country as well as recovering and enshrining the remains of the patriots buried overseas. Also, the Independence Hall and the National Institute of Korean History assumed the leadership in the project involving the collection and publication of historical documents related to the independence movement. The restoration of the Interim Government Building was implemented by the Ministry of Culture and Sports and the Independence Hall, in close collaboration with the Ministry of Foreign Affairs.

With regard to the policy-level decision on the destruction of the erstwhile Japanese Government General Building, the personal resolution of President Kim Young Sam played an important role. The President boldly pushed forward with the destruction of the building, prompted by his personal judgment that the destruction would be difficult to accomplish if it would not be completed within his presidency. The demolition of the erstwhile Japanese Government General Building and the subsequent restoration of Gyeongbokgung Palace were led by the Ministry of Culture and Sports.

The government pushed for the amendment of the laws governing the April 19 Revolution, including the Act on the Respectful Treatment of Men of National Merit, the enforcement act of the said law, and the Act on Establishing an Organization of Men of National Merit led by the Ministry of Patriots and Veterans Affairs and the Ministry of Government Administration. Also, the Ministry of Education fully revised the contents and terms related with the April 19 Revolution through the revision of the education curriculum.

On November 24, 1995, President Kim Young Sam ordered the ruling Democratic Liberal Party to legislate the Special Act on May 18 within the regular session of the National Assembly. The clarification by President Kim Young Sam that the Special Act on May 18 be legislated was made through a surprise announcement, a symbolic gesture suggesting his firm resolution to break through the political upheaval triggered by the slush fund scandal of the former president Roh Tae Woo and to separate from the 5th and 6th Republic forces.

On December 19 of the same year, the National Assembly passed the Special Act on the Statute of Limitations on the Crimes of Destruction of the Constitutional Order with a unanimous vote in the plenary session. The Special Act on the May 18 Democratization Movement was also passed through voting. With the legislation of the Special Act on May 18, which contains the punishment of the people who killed the citizens of Gwangju in May 1980 as well as the regaining of the impaired reputation of the victims, the administration secured the most critical legal grounds for the "re-establishment of the country's legitimate history" project. Also significant was the principle stating that the statute of limitations shall be suspended during the incumbency of the president who seized the power with the December 12 and May 18 rebellions and that the statute of limitations shall no longer be applied to any future rebellion or insurgency.

On May 13, the 322 victims of the May 18 Rebellion, including Jeong Dong Nyeon, the standing chairperson of the Coalition for the Gwangju Democratic Movement, filed a suit at the Seoul District Public Prosecutors' Office, accusing a total of 35 people, including former presidents Chun Doo Hwan and Roh Tae Woo, of "rebellion and homicide for the purpose of rebellion." In November of the same year, the public prosecutors embarked on an "investigation with regard to the prosecution and complaint pertaining to the May 18 Rebellion." After a massive investigation that began with the investigation of the accuser and the prosecutor, including an investigation in writing of the two formers presidents Chun Doo Hwan and Roh Tae Woo, the public prosecutors defined the series of actions carried out by the new military elites from December 12, 1979 until the inauguration of President Chun Doo Hwan on August 27, 1980 as "a political revolutionary process through which Army Security Command Commander Chun Doo Hwan created a new regime and constitutional order on the strength of the military group he dominated." Likewise, they recognized the series of such acts as a coup d'état in all practicality by recognizing the intention of the new military elites to assume the power. The prosecutors concluded, however, that "they have no right of arraignment" on the ground that "the rebellion that succeeded in seizing the power is not subject to judiciary deliberation."

As the National Assembly was pushing for the legislation of the Special Act on May 18, the question of whether the independent special prosecutor system should be adopted emerged as the hottest issue. In order to prevent the introduction of the independent special prosecutor system, the prosecutors installed the Special Investigation Headquarters to investigate the December 12 and May 18 Rebellions on November 30. Also, they reopened the investigation on the two incidents on the ground of the changed situation, including the presidential order by Kim Young Sam to legislate the special act and the slush fund scandal of former president Roh Tae Woo. On December 3, upon the installation of the Special Investigation Headquarters, the prosecutors arrested former president Chun Doo Hwan on "charges of masterminding the rebellion in accordance with the military criminal laws." The prosecutors then pushed on again by summoning those alleged to have been involved in the May 18 rebellion and by visiting Gwangju to listen to the testimony of the surviving May 18 rebellion victims. The Special Investigation Headquarters carried out an investigation on the former presidents Chun Doo Hwan and Roh Tae Woo as part of eight and seven rounds of investigation sessions, respectively, from December 3, 1995 to February 26, 1996. The Special Investigation Headquarters arrested and indicted former president Chun Doo Hwan on charges of masterminding the rebellion on December 21, 1995, and former president Roh Tae Woo on charges of playing the key role in the rebellion.

Performance and Assessment

The Kim Young Sam administration's drive to re-establish the country's legitimate history was pursued along the following three key lines: (1) the revival of the Korean ethnic legitimacy through the eradication of the legacy of the Japanese colonial rule and the restoration of the independence movement, including the demolition of the Japanese Government General Building and the restoration of Gyeongbokgung Palace as well as other projects meant to inherit and advance the spirit of independence movement; (2) the restoration of the history of democratization by highlighting its history and its suppression since the liberation of Korea (specifically, the administration focused on inheriting the democratic spirit of the April 19 Revolution by again highlighting the revolution); and (3) the punishment of the perpetrators of the military coup d'état in a move to break away from the country's history riddled with the unlawful assumption of power. The administration focused on punishing the military elites that led the coup d'état to dissolve the historical perception formed by the military insurgents that led the rebellion by unraveling the truth regarding the December 12 military coup d'état and the May 18 Gwangju Democratization Movement.

The re-establishment of the country's legitimate history, driven by the administration, is significant in that it repositioned the December 12 military coup d'état and the May 18 Gwangju Democratization Movement, which had long been forced to be forgotten and distorted, as a collective historical memory of the country under the state leadership. The re-establishment of the country's legitimate history was the expression of the popular enthusiasm with regard to democratization that started in 1987. In this respect, the re-establishment of the country's legitimate history was driven by the country's democratization, and this again accelerated the country's democratization. Another significance of the re-establishment of the country's legitimate history by the administration was that it was an attempt to heal the national wounds and scars left by the past military dictatorship. Because the May 18 Gwangju Democratization Movement had not received a legitimate historical assessment before the re-establishment of the country's legitimate history, those who had participated in the democratization movement suffered from frustration and a sense of loss for an extended period, leading to amplified regional division within the South Korean society. The series of measures including the legislation of the Special Act on May 18 and the establishment of the national anniversary marking the May 18 Movement played an important role in laying the foundation for the future social integration. The re-establishment of the country's legitimate history embodied the commitment of the administration to abolish the collusive relationship between politics and businesses and that between the corrupt and fraudulent structure.

Specifically, the administration provided an important momentum in rectifying the country's distorted history by sternly punishing those who had raped the constitutional order through the legislation and promulgation of the Special Act on May 18, and by striving to recover the honor of the victims. The administration left an important precedent in the process of democratization: the "punishment of the perpetrators of successful coup d'états" by arresting and subjecting the two former presidents to the tribunal on charges of unlawful assumption of power and of ordering the armed force to open fire at the protesters in Gwangju. The actual legal punishment and the execution of the final court ruling, however, remained merely at the symbolic level. Still, the punishment of state-led violence, such as the unjust assumption of power in the form of a military coup d'état and the subsequent massacre of citizens based on such power bases, is significant in the view of the restoration of the social justice. The re-establishment of the country's legitimate history was a future-oriented policy that laid the groundwork for the "future democracy" by attacking the country's irrational past history head-on.

4. Globalization policy

Background

The globalization drive started in earnest in 1995, when President Kim Young Sam unveiled his plan to globalize the nation in the press conference that was held on November 17, 1994. Following the press conference, the government established the Globalization Promotion Committee on January 21, 1995, which was followed by the announcement of the globalization concept on January 25 of the same year, thereby launching the full-scale globalization drive. In the second year of his presidency, President Kim Young Sam declared that the government would push for globalization as its key policy initiative. The WTO framework inaugurated in January 1995 heralded the tectonic shift in the order of world trade.

The five key directions of globalization declared by President Kim Young Sam were: (1) rising as the key nation in globalized management; (2) developing policy initiatives and training talented professionals capable of harmonizing international competition and cooperation; (3) pushing for the reform of institutions and of the popular perception aimed at promoting globalization; (4) constructing a society where people with creative minds can succeed; and (5) constructing a society where spiritual and personal qualities are valued as much as material prosperity.

The activation of the economy and the governmental reform focused on the liberalization of the South Korean market through the opening of the domestic market to foreign trade depending on the changing economic situation in South Korea and in the rest of the world. Amid the accelerating liberalization and market opening in accordance with the changing economic situation in South Korea and throughout the world, the diverse functions, formerly performed by the country at the comprehensive development state, were scaled back significantly, and the private sectors began assuming such functions. Similar to how it was done during the past government-led economic-development era, the globalization policy pursued by the administration was limited to the simple provision of a policy vision by the government without providing any support. In conclusion, the role of the government was changed to that of fostering a limited-development nation centered on the posterior regulatory system, which was aimed at abolishing various regulations and at encouraging private businesses to proactively participate in the globalization process. In addition, President Kim Young Sam unveiled the following issues across the subsequent six areas to push for reform: (1) construction of an education system capable of fostering top leaders who will be active in the international community; (2) establishment of legal and economic institutions capable of reaching the global levels; (3) pushing for the creation of politics and a press capable of responding to the challenges inherent in globalization; (4) reform of the central and local governments into institutions capable of implementing the globalization policy; (5) pushing for the environmental policy required for the country to participate in the world environmental-protection initiative; and (6) contribution to the world culture by advancing the Korean culture and its unique way of thinking before advancing to the world armed with pride as citizens with cultural sophistication. The government formed the Globalization Promotion Committee, which was composed of high-ranking government officials, scholars, and professionals. The committee then established the strategic reform policy, including 51 projects covering diverse areas across the government administration.

Implementation System

The Globalization Promotion Committee, which was installed in accordance with the pertinent presidential decree was launched as a private - public joint organization that would tap the creativity and expertise of the private sector and allow comprehensive participation by various sectors. The Globalization Promotion Planning Group was installed as a working-level organization that would support the activity of the committee. The Globalization Promotion Planning Group played the role of implementing supporting businesses that would ensure the fluid operation of the committee, including the preparation and drafting of meeting agenda, the adjustment of conflicting opinions on the deliberation agenda among different ministries, and researching on and notifying various meetings.

On the other hand, with the reform businesses, including those carried out by the Globalization Promotion Committee, the Administrative Innovation Committee, and the Education Reform Committee, moving ahead as scheduled, the Government Reform Progress Inspection Group, which was chaired by the head of the Prime Ministerial Administrative Planning and Coordination Office and staffed with grade 1 officials responsible for managing the reform-related committees, was installed to check the reform progress of the committees and to assist them in tackling the difficulties they may be facing.

Each globalization task was implemented through the following process: task selection → collection of the opinions of the related ministries → confirmation of the deliberation on the selected task by the Globalization Promotion Committee → establishment and implementation of a detailed plan by the related ministry. The task selection was carried out by the Globalization Promotion Committee after reviewing the items proposed by the committee members or by the related ministry. Those tasks that were necessary for globalization but were not being pushed for by the government then, or other related tasks across various sectors or multiple ministries, were mainly selected. Once a task was selected, the draft proposal was created by dividing the project into one to be prepared by the related committee members and another to be prepared by the related ministry. Once the draft proposal was prepared, the committee would start to gather opinions on the detailed implementation alternatives from the related ministries. If the selected task was very important, however, or if the opinions on the policy directions were considerably divided, the committee would either invite related external professionals to be involved in the proposal preparation stage in the beginning of the project or draft the proposal jointly or reconcile the conflicting opinions with a separate organization. Once the conflicting opinions were reconciled with the help of the related ministry, the selected globalization task was submitted to the committee and was discussed in a plenary meeting of such committee before going through the deliberation and confirmation phase, where each related ministry was informed of the confirmed task. Then each related ministry drafted and implemented a detailed plan on those issues under its jurisdiction, and a quarterly implementation status report was submitted to the committee. As the globalization tasks were implemented by the government as part of its policy implementation, the Globalization Promotion Committee possessed policy enforcement capacity, albeit indirectly, unlike the other committees. Specifically, the committee was able to raise the interest and incentive of each related ministry by holding a presidential report meeting after each plenary meeting, which again exerted a positive influence on the implementation of the globalization task.

The Globalization Publicity Council, which was composed of the vice minister of the Bureau of Public Information and the grade 1 officials of each related ministry, held a total of 24 meetings. While in the process preparing the publicity plan and setting the publicity directions by ministry on the key issues, including the finalized globalization tasks, the council began with the introductory meeting in February 1995 and established and implemented an effective publicity strategy. Beginning in April of the same year, the council executed the publicity project via an online chatroom or an Internet homepage. The globalization publicity forum and suggestion room were installed in the Chollian online network, where the background, significance, and implementation system of the globalization policy initiative as well as its members and implementation tasks were opened to the public, thereby helping the people better understand globalization while collecting the opinions of the people in the process. The homepage of the Prime Ministerial Office also opened a page on globalization, where information on the globalization progress and other materials were posted.

Implementation Process and Contents

In August 1995, the Globalization Promotion Committee proposed the "Vision and Strategy for Globalization" and prepared a total of 53 globalization tasks. The Vision and Strategy for Globalization was developed from the globalization concept of President Kim Young Sam by coming up with more details on the environment and characteristics of the globalization era, the national development principles in the globalization era, and the globalization implementation strategy.

The deliberation process on the globalization tasks began with the inauguration of the committee. In 1995, a total of 29 tasks were submitted for deliberation, followed by 15 tasks in 1996 and 9 tasks in 1997. They included tasks such as administrative reform in the globalization era, establishment of a unified country, globalization of the economy, establishment of the foundation of scientific and technological advancement, fostering of a first-rate country in terms of knowledge and information, construction of a model country in terms of environmental protection, globalization of the people's living quality, advancement in law and order, construction of a new education system, construction of a cultural-powerhouse country, and key tasks for the implementation strategy of national management in the era of global politics.

Performance and Assessment

It is assessed that it was wise to propose globalization as the key vision and strategy for the establishment of a unified country given the country's internal and external environments at the time. Considering the imbalance caused by the past growth-first policy, it is also assessed that the administration was right in setting a vision and seeking an appropriate strategy and tasks not only in relation to the economy but also in relation to politics, the society, and culture.

The services offered to the people in the area of public administration had been markedly improved, and it is assessed that the people-centric and service-oriented mind spread in the process. The administration not only elevated the status of the country as a central nation in the Asia-Pacific region through proactive diplomatic activities across diverse areas of APEC, but also raised the level of participation of the country in the international community by joining OECD as a member state and by being admitted into the United Nations Security Council as a non-permanent member. On the diplomatic front, diverse efforts to raise the status of the Republic of Korea in the international community, including in the Asia-Pacific region, were made as part of the globalization drive. In the globalization of the country's economy, measures to lay the groundwork for economic growth, such as fostering an environment characterized by fair competition in the domestic market, fostering venture startups, energy conservation, and promotion of technology development, were implemented. At the same time, the administration streamlined the local system, including streamlining and reshuffling the government subsidies and fostering environment-friendly industries.

The Basic Act on Promoting Informatization was legislated to accelerate informatization at the national level; the act formed the Informatization Promotion Committee in an effort to lay the groundwork for the country's future informatization, and is assessed to have steadily implemented the sector-by-sector informatization plan, including the regional informatization plan. In the welfare area, the administration proposed the basic concept of the national welfare system, and steadily pushed for measures aimed at improving the welfare level of the marginalized classes and areas, including the expansion of the living stipends for the low-income class and the expansion of local cultural facilities.

In terms of women's issues, the administration drew the national attention towards the issue by implementing a comprehensive policy package aimed at expanding women's social participation while also providing the momentum for the South Korean women to realize their hidden potentials in the globalization era. Specifically, female cadets were allowed to enter the Army, Air Force, and Naval Academy, which were earlier considered off-limits to women. Likewise, the crumbling of the wall dividing men and women in terms of social activities, as evidenced, can be assessed to have been influenced by the implementation of the series of globalization tasks.

The judicial branch also joined the globalization drive by improving the quality of its legal services and its system of training legal professionals. It also expanded its legal services to the people by substantially increasing the number of available legal professionals while also improving the operation system of the Judicial Research and Training Institute and the bar examination. The administration also strove to improve the communication capabilities of the people in the globalization era by assigning English education to begin in the 3rd grade of elementary schools, a step to globalize the country's education system. Further, while developing local cultural festivals, including Jindo folk dance performances, as the country's key cultural-tour products, the administration also expanded many small-scale museums, libraries, and other regional cultural facilities in an attempt to promote the cultural infiltration of the people's everyday lives and to link the indigenous culture with tourism. Also, measures aimed at promoting social education and at improving leisure culture in the globalization era were implemented, including the strengthening of education under the leadership of civil activist groups. It can be said that such measures also provided an important momentum for activating citizens' movements.

Meanwhile, the implementation of the globalization drive clearly had some limitations and problems: (1) the objective and vision were set without sufficiently considering the realistic limitations; (2) an insufficient number of concrete ideas aimed at overcoming the challenges of the reform were satisfactorily proposed during the reform process; (3) the administration failed to form a sufficient level of national consensus in the selection of the key globalization tasks; and (4) the political will to overcome the challenges in the reform process was not strong enough.

5. Full-scale implementation of the local self-governing system

Background

The history of the country's local self-governing system marked a major milestone in the wake of the inauguration of the administration. The constitutional assembly legislated the Local Self-governing Act on July 4, 1949, which signaled the beginning of the institutional foundation for the country's local self-governing system. As the 2nd National Assembly started to hold the Syngman Rhee administration in check with increasing stringency, President Syngman Rhee introduced the elections for the local councils in an attempt to raise the political forces that would play the role of counterbalancing the National Assembly. In the local assembly elections that were held in two rounds of voting sessions in April and May, those sympathizing with the ruling party won nearly 70% of the total seats on the strength of the full-scale campaign support that President Syngman Rhee provided by mobilizing the administrative capacity. Upon assuming the power in the local councils, those who won in the elections demanded the resignation of those representatives who opposed the adoption of the direct presidential election. President Syngman Rhee amended the indirect presidential election system via the National Assembly into the direct presidential election, by capitalizing on such favorable political climate. In February 1956, President Syngman Rhee amended the Local Government Act, changing the former indirect election system for electing mayors and the heads of towns and villages into the direct election system.

The system was reverted to the appointment system, however, with another amendment in 1958 of the Local Government Act, through which the mayors as well as the town and village heads were appointed by the central government. The Jang Myeon administration of the Democratic Party, which assumed the power after the April 19 Revolution, planned to reintroduce the full-scale local self-governing system to cities, provinces, towns, and villages by amending the Local Government Act in November 1960. In June 1961, the military insurgents led by General Park Jung Hee dissolved the local assembly with Notification No. 4 of the Military Revolution Committee, which was followed by the appointment of governors, mayors, and county heads in accordance with Article 20 of the Emergency Measure Act. The military group made it clear that the heads of local governing bodies shall be government officials appointed by the central government with the legislation of the Temporary Act on the Local Self-governing System in September of the same year.

In the 13th presidential election held in 1987, the ruling party candidate, Roh Tae Woo, cited the reintroduction of the local self-governing system as one of his key campaign pledges. In 1989, after the inauguration of the 6th Republic, the four major parties (Democratic Justice Party, Peace Democratic Party, Democratic Party, and Republican Party) all agreed to elect the representatives of the local councils as well as the heads of the local governing bodies from the cities and provinces down to the counties via direct election by the voters. In 1991, the elections to elect the representatives of the basic local councils and the wide-area local councils were held in accordance with the Local Government Act enacted in 1989. However, the ruling party, which was created through the three-party merger, pushed for the partial amendment of the Local Government Act enacted in 1989 on the premise of economic stability. It proposed and passed the bill to postpone the local elections to elect the heads of local governing bodies until 1995. Therefore, the local self-governing system enforced during the Roh Tae Woo administration remained incomplete, composed only of the local councils, minus the local governing bodies.

President Kim Young Sam pledged to reintroduce the full local self-governing system in the December 1992 presidential election. The full local self-governing system herein signifies the direct election of the local self-governing heads by the voters. After pledging to reintroduce the full local self-governing system in the presidential election, President Kim Young Sam made various policy-level efforts to put the pledge into a reality. However, due to the concentration of the limited administrative resources on the implementation of the other government administration tasks, the full implementation of the local self-governing system was postponed for two years since his inauguration. However, in the second year of the presidency, it was important to ensure the completeness of the institution through the direct election of the local governing heads because the growing demand for the full implementation of the local self-governing system could no longer be ignored and the wide-area and basic local councils had already been composed through direct elections by the voters in terms of the institution of the local self-governing system. In view of such developing situation, the administration announced the holding of local elections in 1995, where the voters could elect their local governing heads.

Implementation System

The various decentralization policies implemented during the administration, including the direct elections of the local governing heads by the voters, did not have their own independent implementation bodies, unlike those of the succeeding administrations. With the exception of the Joint Deliberation Committee for the Transfer of Authority to the Local Governing Bodies, the related policy was established and implemented mainly by the Ministry of Internal Affairs. The country's first institution dedicated to the implementation of the decentralization policy, the Joint Deliberation Committee for the Transfer of Authority to the Local Governing Bodies, was installed in 1991. The Roh Tae Woo administration formed the committee in accordance with the guidelines on government organization management, marking the birth of the local assembly some 30 years after its dissolution in 1961, after the May 16 revolution. However, the Joint Deliberation Committee for the Transfer of Authority to the Local Governing Bodies enjoyed no sufficient institutional support for the decentralization initiative because the committee was not an institution supported by the related laws but a non-standing joint public-private council. The establishment and implementation of each policy initiative aimed at the full-scale enforcement of the local self-governing system were in practice pushed forward by the governing bureaus in the Ministry of Internal Affairs. The local administrative bureau, the local planning bureau, the local finance bureau, and the local taxation bureau played the key role as the governing authority with regard to the full-scale implementation of the local self-governing system.

The administrative procedure that was complied with by the administration in pushing forward with the full-scale decentralization policy was the amendment of the Local Government Act. This was because the Local Government Act covered all the issues related with the country's local self-governing system, and only through the amendment of the said law was it be possible for the government to provide the institutional foundation required for the full-scale implementation of the local self-governing system.

The 11th amendment of the Local Government Act was promulgated by Law No. 4741 on March 16, 1994. The amendment was intended to provide an institutional guarantee to ensure the efficiency of the local-council operation and the fluid activities of the representatives, thereby fostering the stabilization and advancement of the local self-governing system; to ensure the balanced development of the urban and rural areas; and to adjust and supplement the institutional insufficiencies discovered and criticized in the establishment of other local self-governing institutions. The Local Government Act was amended on December 20, 1994 with Law No. 4789. The following are the intention of the amendment and its key contents: (1) the amendment streamlined the related provisions, including the inclusion of the rural county in the metropolitan city as an attempt to strengthen the competitiveness of the local self-governing bodies; (2) the amendment relaxed the oversight and directorship by the central government to go along with the full-scale local self-governing era, which was to begin with the election of the local governing heads; (3) the state public officials working in the local self-governing bodies were to be employed by the governing minister after consultation with the head of the concerned local self-governing body; and (4) any insufficiency discovered in the operation of the other systems currently being enforced then was to be complemented.

The 13th amendment of the Local Government Act was promulgated as Law No. 4877 on January 5, 1995. The amendment specified that all the state public officials over grade 5 had to be employed by the president upon the recommendation of the governing minister after the consultation with the head of the concerned local self-governing body. Also, even though all the public officials lower than grade 6 had so far been employed by the governing minister after the consultation with the head of the concerned local governing body, under the amended act, all the public officials lower than grade 6 had to be employed by the president or by the governing minister upon the recommendation of the head of the concerned local self-governing body.

The 14th amendment of the Local Government Act was promulgated as Law No. 4858 on August 4, 1995. The amendment relaxed the consolidation requirements of the cities with combined rural and urban functions so that those counties with a population of 150,000 and more and that had at least two urbanized towns, each with a population of 20,000 and more within the county, and whose combined total population was over 50,000, could pass for cities, thereby accelerating the speed of regional development and fostering the balanced development of the urban and rural areas.

Implementation Process and Contents

The administration embarked on a massive reshuffling of the local administrative districts before the full-scale implementation of the local self-governing system. Such reshuffling was noted as the largest reshuffling of the local administrative districts since the administrative reshuffling done during the Japanese colonial rule in 1914. The reshuffling was required to readjust the irrational administrative boundaries, to resolve the inconveniences in those districts overflowing with people, and to strengthen the competence of the local regions.

Unlike the practices in the past that focused on improving the administrative efficiency in the urban areas, the reshuffling of the local administrative districts through the consolidation of the rural and urban communities that had been pushed for since 1994 focused on responding nimbly to the changing administrative environment and on strengthening the competence of the local self-governing bodies. The consolidation of the rural and urban communities that was pushed forward with was decided through the process in which the Ministry of Internal Affairs selected the target regions and each local self-governing body decided whether to go ahead with the consolidation by subjecting the matter to a local referendum.

The biggest performance of the administration in relation to the local self-governing system was in the local elections. In the years leading up to the implementation of the local self-governing system, the Act on the Election of Public Officials and the Prevention of Election Malpractice was legislated on March 16, 1994 by consolidating the previous relevant laws, including the Presidential Election Act, the Election of National Assembly Members Act, the Election of Local Assembly Members Act, and the Election of the Heads of the Local Self-governing Bodies Act. In accordance with the newly legislated act, local elections were held on June 27, 1995 for the governors of the provinces and cities, the mayors, the chiefs of counties, the chiefs of districts, and the members of the municipal and provincial councils and of the city, county, and district councils. As to minimize the economic burden brought about by frequent elections and to minimize the waste of national resources, the elections for the National Assembly members, the local-assembly members, and the heads of the local self-governing bodies were to be held alternately every two years. Likewise, the nationwide local elections for the municipal and provincial heads, mayors, and county and district heads as well as the members of the municipal and provincial councils and of the city, county, and self-governing district councils were held at the same time on June 27, 1995.

The participation of the citizens in the self-governing administration had been actively realized either through the official or non-official channel ever since the implementation of the self-governing system by the elected officials. Such implementation of the system established an institutional ground for the resolution of the key local issues by the local governing bodies through local referendums, which would allow the direct participation of the residents. In the case of the comprehensive reshuffling of the administrative boundaries implemented in the wake of the start of the implementation of the full-scale local self-governing system, the opinions of the residents were reflected in the reshuffling of the administrative boundaries by adopting the survey method to determine the collective will of the residents. Moreover, the opening of the information held by the local self-governing bodies and the provision of administrative resources to the residents ensured the active participation of the residents in the local administration and guaranteed transparency in administrative management.

The administration significantly expanded the transfer of the state businesses to the local governments since its inauguration. The transfer project largely focused on handing over the management and development authority to the heads of the local self-governing bodies to allow them to fully demonstrate their creativity and capability. Within the scope and criteria specified by the relevant presidential decree, the quota of administrative institutions and public officials in the local self-governing bodies was decided by the ordinance of the respective local self-governing bodies. On February 4, 1997, the standard quota system and midterm basic human resource management plan were introduced. Then, on August 31, 1998, the abolition of the commonly required organizations that were specified to be installed in all local self-governing bodies on a mandatory basis followed, thereby leaving them to the discretion of the local governments. Further, in an attempt to allow the local units to draft talented professionals that would commit themselves to the advancement of their own hometowns, the local examination was implemented separately from the state examination beginning in 1995.

The nationwide reshuffling of the local administrative organization, which started when the Ministry of Internal Affairs advised all local governments to implement the Efficient Rearrangement of Local Organizations and Workforce in August 1995, and which was implemented until 1996, was intended to foster the formation of a characteristic and resilient local administrative organization robust enough to support the policy intention of the heads of the local self-governing bodies. At the same time, it was to preserve the unique regional characteristics of each local self-governing body in the wake of the opening of the era of the local autonomy system headed by the elected public officials.

Performance and Assessment

The administration successfully implemented the massive reshuffling of the administrative districts, which was aimed at strengthening the competence of the local self-governing bodies, and ran four simultaneous local elections nationwide on June 27, 1995 relatively cleanly and fairly. The direct election in 1995 of the heads of the local self-governing bodies by the residents can be assessed as another remarkable achievement of the administration. Also, although the series of measures, including the transfer of administrative businesses aimed at expanding the function and autonomy of the local administration and at guaranteeing autonomy in organizational and personnel management, mostly belong to the elementary phase of the development of local self-governance, such measures can be assessed to have laid the institutional ground for local self-administration. The identification of creative ideas aimed at securing local finance independently, a critical element for the development of local self-governance that provides a material foundation for it, is also assessed to have provided an impetus for the healthy securing of local finance in the future. The introduction of such various institutions and policies can be regarded highly in that it provided the critical and decisive turning point for the development of the country's local self-governing system.

Meanwhile, it cannot be denied either that the various policies and institutions introduced by the administration in relation to the local self-governing system revealed plenty of limitations in their management, contrary to the original intention of the policy initiative. First, those institutions aimed at expanding the participation of the local residents in the local administration proved to be not so effective in the end. Furthermore, the transfer of state administrative businesses to the local governments, which had been pushed for actively, succeeded in significantly increasing the transfer volume but largely failed to meet the initial expectations. Further, despite the fact that, with the exception of very few local governments, most local governments' fiscal capacity remained at a meager level, they did not work hard to realize a healthy finance. Also, it can be evaluated that the fiscal support from the central government remained at a poor level. For all the contributions or failures in the development of the local self-governing system, the administration can be regarded highly for its bold decision to push forward with the full-scale implementation of the local self-governing system. No one could deny the fact the administration brought the level of the country's local self-governing system one step higher.

Section 3

The Government Reform of the Kim Young Sam Administration

1. Background and direction of the government reform

The 1990s, which coincided with the presidency of Kim Young Sam, was filled with simmering expectations of the people for the government to come up with something different from the past. At the same time, there was a global mega trend of the time that required the country to turn the page in the national reform as to enter the new millennium by the turn of the new century. The fact that it was the first administration that was headed by a civilian president after 32 years of the military regime since the military rebellion that took place on May 16, 1961 raised the general expectations of the people with regard to democratization. Meanwhile, the period was marked by the rising public interest in national competence, with the spread of neoliberalism globally, which again pushed government reform as one of the key global agenda.

Just as the emergence of the civilian government that ended the military regime increased the pressure for change across the South Korean society, the relationship between the political power and the bureaucratic system turned another page. Hidden behind the ideological background of the government reform by the administration was the neoliberalistic reform spirit that signaled the departure from the authoritarian developmentalism that was prevalent during the military regime. As President Kim Young Sam clarified in his inaugural address, the administration pushed for reform under the guiding slogan "Creation of a New Korea" in the early period of its incumbency. "Creation of a New Korea" began as one of the political slogans that the ruling party candidate, Kim Young Sam, adopted for the presidential campaign towards the end of 1992.

The nature of the administrative reform implemented by the administration was basically close to the thesis of neoliberalism and neo-public-management in that the administration flew the flag of a small but strong government, which was to replace the developmental government administration in the past amid the shifting trend of globalization and democratization. The government administration objective of the civilian government was to cure the Korean disease and then to create a new Korea, and government reform objective was to push for the realization of a clean government, a strong economy, and a healthy society. Midstream into the incumbency of President Kim Young Sam, globalization was added to the aforementioned goals. Meanwhile, the basic directions of the administrative renovation included the establishment of a small but strong government, the realization of democratic and efficient administration, and the improvement of the institutional practices focused on people's convenience.

The goals of the administrative reform implemented by the administration were based mainly on two key dimensions: the attainment of legitimacy (cleaning up the authoritarian legacy, re-establishing the country's legitimate history, etc.) and the establishment of a democratic and efficient administrative system. The general reform model of the administration is understood as an "incremental model." It can be assessed that the administration failed to bring about fundamental changes despite such efforts, but it at least strove to realize a paradigm shift in its government administration. The organization responsible for the government reform by the civilian government was the Administrative Renovation Committee, which was directly controlled by the Presidential Office. The committee was inaugurated on April 20, 1993 and, until its dissolution on February 25, 1998, dealt with about 2,500 renovation tasks for five years.

The first-round government reshuffling (March 1993) can be summed up as the consolidation of the Ministry of Youth and Ministry of Culture as well as the abolition of the Ministry of Energy and Resources and the creation of the Ministry of Commerce and Resources, and the second-round government reshuffling (January～November 1994) can be summed up as the voluntary downsizing of the administrative organization and workforce in 28 ministries. Particularly, the third-round government reshuffling seems to have been aimed at realizing a qualitative leap forward in the government administration by graduating from the simple quantitative downsizing. Finally, the fourth-round government reshuffling (June～August 1996) can be summed up as the creation of the Ministry of Maritime Affairs and Fisheries and the Small and Medium Business Administration.

The administrative reform of the administration can be assessed to have been implemented by following the "bottom-up method," which was based on the people's law-abiding spirit and voluntary reform proposals. The administrative reform of the administration can be assessed to have been based on civilian leadership, a competitive spirit, and practicality from its core. In an attempt to push for efficient government reform, the Regulation on the Administrative Renovation Committee was enacted by presidential decree (No. 13878) on April 9, 1993, which was followed by the inauguration of the committee on April 20 of the same year. The committee was formed as a presidential advisory organization and was composed entirely of civilians, including university professors and representatives of economic institutions, the media, and the civil society. The committee is assessed to have played its required roles for five years, during the presidency of Kim Young Sam, as a de-facto deliberation and decision-making organization.

The reform implemented by the civilian government inevitably focused on some big issues, such as the real-name financial transaction system and the reform of the political laws. To realize such gigantic reform goals, President Kim Young Sam frequently employed surprise tactics in the reform process. The very indulgence in such surprise tactics may have helped the early reforms to be perceived as such a great success by the people in the early phase of the reform, but, as such pattern was implemented repeatedly and was overstretched, it was also the very reason that the reform failed beginning in the middle of the incumbency of President Kim Young Sam.

2. Contents of the government reform

Organizational Reshuffling

The administration, which billed itself as a "civilian government" running on the guiding spirit of "globalization," "internationalization," "creation of a new Korea," and "small but strong government," pushed for the reform of the government organization over four rounds of organizational reshuffling. The administration embarked on its first organizational reshuffling in April 1993, during the early years of its incumbency. The first-round organizational reshuffling was implemented on February 23 of the same year, in accordance with the relevant motion submitted on February 21, 1993 by 21 representatives, including Kim Joong Wee of the Democratic Liberal Party. The key contents of the organizational reshuffling were the establishment of the Ministry of Culture and Sports by consolidating the Ministry of Culture and the Ministry of Sports and Youth and the abolishment and the re-establishment of the Ministry of Energy and Resources as the Ministry of Commerce and Resources. As a result, the central administrative organization was reshuffled into 2 boards, 14 ministries, 6 agencies, 15 offices, and 2 external bureaus.

In December 1994, the administration embarked on its second organizational reshuffling, which was much larger and comprehensive in scale than the first-round organizational reshuffling, and was recorded as the biggest throughout the incumbency of the administration. The Administrative Renovation Committee came up with a proposal for innovative administrative organizational reshuffling in the early part of June 1993, after the completion of the first-round organizational reshuffling. The proposal contained the following details: reduction of the number of cabinet members from 22 to 16; abolition of the Economic Planning Board; creation of the Ministry of Social Overhead Capital by consolidating the Ministry of Construction and the Ministry of Transportation; reduction of the power of the institutions, including the Agency for National Security Planning, the Defense Security Command, and the Prosecutors' Office; and downsizing of the part of local administration in the Ministry of Internal Affairs.

The third-round organizational reshuffling was implemented at a smaller scale; it simply changed the Industrial Advancement Administration to the Small and Medium Business Administration. It was followed by the fourth-round reshuffling in August of the same year. The administration eliminated 1 office, 3 bureaus, and 35 departments and reduced the government workforce by 538 until May 1994, via the organizational reshuffling of the central administrative body. In December 1994, a total of 115 departments were eliminated while dismissing 1,002 government workers in its wake by conducting a massive downsizing of the government workforce and amending the organizational system along with the organizational reshuffling earlier explained.

Fiscal Reform

The efforts by the administration aimed at normalizing the government's fiscal function began in 1994 when the administration installed the Ministry of Finance and Economy by consolidating the Ministry of Finance and the Economic Planning Board. The administration's efforts to normalize the government's fiscal function were implemented along two lines; on one hand, the administration strove to expand its financial capability, and on the other hand, it attempted to improve the government's fiscal spending structure. The details of the key reform related with the improvement of the efficiency of the fiscal system included the streamlining of various special accounts and funds, the improvement of the budgetary system, and the activation of the midterm fiscal plan.

The Five-Year New-Economy Plan laid out the reform schedule of the tax system, which was aimed at expanding the government's fiscal capability and enhancing the fairness in taxation. The strengthening of the functions of the income and property tax departments and the improvement of the consumption tax and tariff system can be understood in such context. However, the most important measure was the enforcement of the real-name financial transaction system. The reform of various funds by the administration was aimed at reducing the inefficiency in the administrative operation by boldly reducing the total of 114 funds counted upon the inauguration of the administration. The administration started its efforts to ensure efficiency in the government's fiscal management by introducing the management concept of private businesses, albeit partially.

Personnel Reform

The Administrative Reform Committee improved diverse facets of the personnel system, including the revamp of the public service job classification system (e.g., introduction of the open-type specialist job position system, the public official examination system, the education and training system, and the job performance appraisal system) and the improvement of the wage level and welfare system. The government introduced and implemented job analysis in an attempt to improve the public service job classification system and to introduce the open-type specialist job position system. From 1996 to 1997, the Job Analysis Planning Group in the Ministry of Government Administration, in an effort to enhance the competitiveness of the public service jobs through the improvement of the administrative efficiency and job specialization, attempted to expand the window of job opportunities so that external specialists could enter the domain of public services.

In the examinations for the recruitment of new public officials, the government avoided the unconditional placing of exams on liberal arts that were not directly related with specific jobs through an amendment in 1993 of the Civil Service Examination Decree; replaced the information system theory in the primary test with other subjects, such as the science of public administration, economics, and criminal law; and excluded national ethics in the secondary test. Also, in an attempt to resolve the dilemma associated with the test that relied on rote learning, the pool of questions in the higher civil service examination employing case studies and application-type questions was expanded. In addition, with the revamp of the education and training system, the number of specialized education courses was expanded from 300 courses in 1993 to 450 courses in 1996, and the measure to utilize the government investment institutions and national research centers as specialized education institutions was introduced.

Electronic Government

The full-scale establishment of an electronic government during the administration started to take form beginning with the establishment of the Basic Plan on the Promotion of Informatization, in accordance with the Basic Act on the Promotion of Informatization legislated in 1995. The core principles of the administrative informatization envisioned by the Basic Act on the Promotion of Informatization can be summed up as "free access and utilization of the info-communication infrastructure," "provision of universal roles on an equal footing, without regional or economic discrimination," and "protection of privacy and stabilization of various information resources." In accordance with the global trends, the administration established a national strategy aimed at fostering the development of info-communication technology and informatization.

Beginning with the establishment of the Basic Plan on Constructing a High-Speed Info-Communication Network in March 1994, the government announced the "Comprehensive Plan for the Construction of a High-Speed Info-Communication Infrastructure" in March 1995. The plan proposed to establish a high-speed info-communication network by investing up to KRW 44 trillion by 2015. Moreover, in 1994, the administration installed the Ministry of Info-Communication, which was given the role of comprehensively handling the national policy related with the info-communication technology and informatization. Complete with the list of detailed measures to be taken to realize the vision, the Ministry of Info-Communication unveiled the Comprehensive Plan for the Advancement of the Info-Communication Industry in 1995, in which it clarified the need for the development of the info-communication industry to boost the national competency. The administration pushed for the administrative business automation project to construct the basic infrastructure for the electronic-government project, including document management automation and a consolidated OA system, and a project to link the various administrative computer networks and to expand the comprehensive administrative computer network.

Regulatory Reform

The regulatory reform of the administration was based on the Act on the Special Measure for the Deregulation of Business Activity legislated in 1993, the Basic Act on Administrative Regulation and Civil Service legislated in 1994, and the Basic Act on Administrative Regulation legislated in 1997. Also, a presidential advisory body/committee was installed to push for regulatory reform. Faced with the difficulty of maintaining consistency in the complex regulatory reform, however, the administration installed the Regulatory Reform Promotion Council to push forward with the regulatory reform from the overall perspective of the national economy.

The Kim Young Sam administration implemented a total of 6,000 regulatory improvements during its incumbency based on the aforementioned regulatory reform implementation system and on its legal foundation. As a result, the administration managed to take on a total of 4,447 deregulation tasks, and completed 86.9% (3,918) of them. It was pointed out, however, that they approached deregulation without having an overall perspective, failing to push for sufficient regulatory reform in the core economic sector, and that the public officials were not that enthusiastic in implementing the reform.

Reform and Privatization of Public Corporations

The administration pushed for the privatization of public corporations as part of its reform initiative. Towards this end, the administration established the Detailed Plan for Privatization and Functional Adjustment upon its inauguration. The key targets of the privatization included financial institutions as well as public corporations with strong commercial characteristics, such as Korea Telecom, Korea Tobacco and Ginseng Corporation, Pohang Steel, and Korea Heavy Industry. The discussion on turning the railway business into a public corporation started in the late 1980s, when the National Railway Administration started to see the ballooning of its deficits. In accordance with the Act on Special Cases Related with the Operation of Government Railroads that legislated in 1995, the administration established the Basic Plan to Improve the Management of Government Railroads in the early 2000s. The plan covered such areas as workforce downsizing, facility modernization, and facility improvement projects. The project aimed at privatizing public corporations initially targeted the privatization of 61 of the 133 target public corporations, but it succeeded in completing the privatization of only 16 public corporations during the incumbency of the administration (the total proceeds from the sales amounted to KRW 1.6566 trillion).

Anti-Corruption Reform

The first reform initiative of the administration in line with the anti-corruption reform was the "Clean Upstream Movement," which was implemented in an attempt to demonstrate that the president himself would show leadership in the eradication of corrupt practices. However, it was not fully materialized in the end. The institutional effort to eliminate corruption in the government was the amendment of the Public Servant Ethics Act. In addition, the real-name financial transaction system and the real-name property ownership system were implemented in 1993 and 1995, respectively.

3. Performance and assessment of the government reform

The Kim Young Sam administration, which was the first administration headed by a "civilian president" following the past extended period of authoritarian rule, initially demonstrated a powerful drive for change by suggesting democratization, efficiency, and small government as the goals of administrative reform, based on the reform keyword "administrative renovation." The administration particularly considered the corruption and fraud prevalent at the time as the Korean diseases that should be cured most urgently. It thus considered the eradication of corruption and fraud its most urgent task, which should be carried out if social justice and economic growth were to be realized. The efforts by the administration to root out corrupt and fraudulent practices in the government not only involved individual efforts by high-ranking officials, including the president himself, to clean up corruption in the government, such as the "Clean Upstream Movement," but also encompassed the institutionalization of anti-corruption policies, including the amendment of the Public Servant Ethics Act, the implementation of the real-name financial transaction system and the real-name property ownership system, and the strengthening of the Act on the Election of

Public Officials and the Prevention of Election Malpractice and the Political Fund Act.

The Administrative Renovation Committee, which was born on April 20, 1993, with the inauguration of the civilian government, received a total of 22,917 reform tasks, including a total of 15,870 proposals submitted by the people, and deliberated on and handled 87% (19,942 cases) of these. The administration also established and legislated the Basic Act on Administrative Regulation and Civil Service. The administrative reform implemented by the administration can be summed up as falling under the following four major categories of government administration: (1) transition to civilian rule: audit and inspection of the Yulgok Project, fraud inspection in the Military Personnel Administration, elimination of core informal group in the military, and identification of the political characteristic of the May 16 Rebellion and of other key political events; (2) democratization: measures to suppress human rights infringements, simplification of the civil service, quality improvement of public services, deregulation, and liberalization of the private sector; (3) small government: inclusion of the Ministry of Energy and Resources in the Ministry of Commerce and Industry, consolidation of the Ministry of Sports and the Ministry of Youth; and (4) clean government: opening of property ownership, Act on Service Ethics, real-name financial transaction system, and more stringent audit and inspection,

All of them receiving a relatively favorable assessment. One regrettable fact remains, however: the "small but strong government" of the administration strengthened the core power institutions, such as the Presidential Office, thereby resulting instead in the emergence of a "big and strong government." Moreover, since the committee was left to operate by itself, without the support of a robust legal foundation, the Administrative Renovation Committee is assessed to have failed to live up to the initial expectations due to the limitations in the selection of the administrative reform targets and the fundamental limitation in driving the administrative reform. The political scandal involving the Uruguay Round Talks in late 1993 dealt a devastating blow to the administration. After the president reneged on his campaign pledge that he "would never open the domestic market for rice," and after his public apology to the people for such, the president's will for reform gradually fizzled out. The president's declaration of his globalization initiative in Sydney, Australia in November 1994 was the expression of the president's will to spur government reform, but the declaration failed to garner as much positive response as he did when he announced such bold measures as the real-name financial transaction system and the real-name property ownership system. As such, the opinions are divided over the assessment of the government reform by the civilian government.

What is clear is that, along with President Kim Young Sam's proclamation to cure the "Korean disease" and to "create a new Korea" upon his inauguration, his defining of the eradication of corruption and fraud in the government, of the activation of the economy, and of the re-establishment of national discipline as the three key tasks of the government administration under him was what helped President Kim Young Sam and his civilian government earn their greatest achievement by earning popular support for his powerful reform drive in the early phase of his incumbency. What is regrettable, though, is that the enthusiasm for the reform cooled midstream into President Kim Young Sam's incumbency, which forced him go back to the past, without achieving the performance that he aimed to realize. For all such warts and shortcomings, however, the slogan of the civilian government, "Creation of a New Korea," succeeded in forming a strong undercurrent for the reform ideology as it was elevated to the fundamental value of the government reform activities. This is why the government reform by the administration can comfortably be called the "Movement to Create a New Korea," and why the government reform by the civilian government has been accepted to this date as the gold standard of government reform by the succeeding administrations.

Chapter 6

The Kim Dae Jung Administration

Section 1

Inauguration of the Kim Dae Jung Administration and Foundation of Key Policy Administration

1. Inauguration of the administration and introduction of its organization

The inauguration of the Kim Dae Jung administration, which marked the first horizontal change of power some half century after the foundation of the Republic of Korea, is assessed to have opened a new chapter in the history of South Korean democracy. The transition from the authoritarian regime ruled by a series of military dictators to the democratic political system began in the wake of the June 1987 Democratic Uprising. The Roh Tae Woo administration, however, was an extension of the military regime while the Kim Young Sam administration failed to earn recognition as a genuine democratic administration due to its process of assuming power through a three-party merger with the ruling party. The horizontal exchange of power from the ruling party to the opposition party, true to its definition, was realized in the presidential election in December 1997 for the first time since the foundation of the ROK government. This signifies that South Korean democracy not only "recovered" the past democracy or "transferred" to the democratic system but also started its "transformation" to a new level of democracy.

Specifically, President Kim Dae Jung stressed, "Today, we must start with a rebirth of democracy that promotes freedom, prosperity, and justice both within the country and in the country's relations with other countries, including the less developed ones: a global democracy. A global democracy will recognize the connection between how we treat one another and how we treat nature, and it will pursue policies that will benefit the future generations. Today, we are threatening the survival of our environment through the wholesale destruction and endangerment of all species. Our democracy must become global in the sense that it extends to the sky, the earth, and all things with brotherly affection." President Kim Dae Jung called this democracy "global democracy" or "cosmopolitan democracy."[1)]

1) While conducting studies on subjects of his choice, such as the European Community, democracy, and peace, as a research fellow in the University of Cambridge, President Kim Dae Jung clarified his position on democracy in a talk with Professor Anthony Giddens. President Kim Dae Jung wrote an opinion piece in the "Foreign Affairs" journal (November/December), in which he criticized the position of Lee Kuan Yew, the first prime minister of Singapore, that the democratic values may inevitably be restricted in Asia because of the Asiatic values. In the opinion piece that he wrote for the journal, Kim argued that "any attempt to restrict democracy with the Asiatic values would be a deplorable legacy of Western colonialism. A thorough analysis makes it clear

The overriding mandate of the administration was to eradicate the half-century-old injustice and undemocratic legacy and then to give birth to a new democratic nation that respects human rights and promotes a just society. The period from 1998 to 2002 was marked by major historical milestones and has since been associated with key words such as "overcoming of the Asian financial crisis," the "DJP alliance and the democratic and horizontal exchange of power between the ruling and opposition parties," the "inter-Korean conciliatory and cooperation policy," the "four major social insurances," and an "electronic government."

The imminent task that had to be handled most urgently by the administration was to overcome the foreign currency crisis caused by the failure of the economic policy of the preceding administration. The severity of the economic crisis that the country was facing then can be summed up with the following indicators:

- the foreign currency reserve as of December 18, 1997 was US$ 3.9 billion whereas the total foreign loans that had to be paid back immediately amounted to US$ 25 billion
- the exchange rate shot up to KRW 2,000=US$ 1 while the interest rate soared to 30% levels
- the country's sovereign credit ratings were downgraded to "non-investment" grade
- the yearly factory utilization rate (1998) reached the 67% level and
- the number of insolvent companies (1998) was about 22,800 (67 new bankruptcies on average per day).

Another factors that are attributable to the outbreak of a sovereign crisis would be incompetency and the corrupt political system. The structure of formative and procedural democracy spread continuously through a series of reforms of the political system in the wake of the democratization in 1987, but a host of impediments, including the political system driven by regional factionalism, the inefficient party structure, the costly election structure, the authoritarian political practices, the collusion between politics and businesses, and the government-controlled financial industry, not only corrupted politics but also made the South Korean economy grow on a shaky and corrupt foundation. Also, the rapidly weakening control of the authoritarian regime, owing to the democratization process, opened the pressure valve for the voices of diverse interest groups to be heard, but such groups were never reorganized into democratic forms. These newfound voices served only the special interests of the select few rather than promoting public values, thereby undermining social integration. Such development explains why the extraordinary activation of citizen activism failed to fuel a new reform drive in the society. This means that the democratization during the Kim Young Sam administration failed to spread across the society while the ghosts of the past undemocratic practices continued to be prevalent throughout the society.

Inaugurated with the mandate to push forward with social reform, including overcoming the impending financial crisis, in such an unfavorable internal and external environment, the

---

that Asia has a rich heritage of democracy-oriented philosophies and traditions, if not identical to those of the West. A native religion of Korea, Tonghak, even went further, advocating that 'man is heaven' and that one must serve man as one serves heaven. Clearly, Asia has democratic philosophies as profound as those of the West." He concluded, "Our democracy must become global in the sense that it extends to the skies, the earth, and all things with brotherly affection."

administration named itself the "People's Government" and suggested the following goals for its government administration: democracy, simultaneous development of democracy and a market economy (democratic market economy), and productive welfare. The overriding governing spirits of the administration included the establishment of democracy and of a nation state that values human rights, realization of South Korea's dream of becoming an info-communication powerhouse and of having an advanced economy, realization of productive welfare and improvement of the standard of living of the middle-class and ordinary people, national development on the strength of education and culture, construction of a national foundation for peaceful unification through reconciliation and cooperation, and rise as a global core country on the strength of a robust security base and autonomous diplomacy.

The Kim Dae Jung administration pushed for reform in four major areas: the public sector (including the government), businesses, the financial sector, and labor-management relations, while also pushing for a powerful drive to reform the conglomerates based on the 5+3 principle. The "5" of the 5+3 principle signified enhancement of management transparency, elimination of the mutual-payment guarantee, improvement of the country's existing financial structure, business area specialization, and more stringent management accountability, and the "3" signified prevention of the assumption of the financial industry by the conglomerates, discouragement of the circular form of cross-share holding and insider transaction, and blocking of the irregular inheritance of businesses. However, the reform drive to overhaul conglomerates started to lose steam towards the end of the administration owing to various reasons, chief of which were the elaborate efforts by those in the government who sympathized with the conglomerates and chaebols to sabotage the government reform.

The fact that the productive welfare policy, one of the top three governing principles laid out by the administration, encompassed the provision of national basic living security, the pursuit of a cultural-welfare policy aimed at improving the quality of life of the people, and the provision of compulsory education until the third year in middle school shows that the administration considered the welfare of the people not in light of charity benefits but as basic rights of the people based on human rights. The administration, however, faced oppositions from various parts of the society while pushing ahead with the implementation of the aforementioned welfare policies. The national basic living security and the completion of the compulsory education system were met with opposition by the officials in the government's economic ministries while the introduction of the four major social insurances (medical, pension, unemployment, and occupational health and safety insurance) were met with opposition not only from the businesses but also from the government officials. Particularly, the separation of drug prescribing and dispensing was realized or finally enforced only after going through massive nationwide strikes, due to the collective selfishness of the doctors and pharmacists. Many social welfare specialists and researchers in the related academic fields believe, however, that the administration succeeded in laying the groundwork for an advanced welfare state by unflinchingly pushing ahead with the policy.

The Kim Dae Jung administration pushed for reform as its key task across all areas, including in overcoming the foreign currency crisis, eradicating the legacy of the past military dictatorship, innovating the government, and pushing for socio democratic changes that would enable the country to quickly and effectively respond to the changing trends. The reform drive of the administration did not stop at reducing the administrative apparatus and workforce through simple restructuring; it instead pushed for a qualitative systemic reform based on three key principles: reengineering of the operating system, replacement, and restructuring. Also, the reform was aimed at realizing innovations in perception and culture as well, along with structural reform.

The administration was made up of 18 ministries, 4 agencies, and 16 offices at its inauguration, but has since gone through three rounds of organizational reshuffling. Upon its inauguration, the Board of Finance and Economy was changed to the Ministry of Finance and Economy, with its budgetary functions spun off and assigned to the Budgetary Office. Also, the Planning and Budget Committee was newly installed to assume the role of implementing governmental and regulatory reform. The Financial Supervisory Commission was also newly installed and put under the direct control of the Prime Minister's Office to push for the reform of the financial industry, and the Office of Government Coordination was installed to bolster the coordination function of the Administrative Coordination Office in the Prime Minister's Office, with its office head promoted from the vice-ministerial to the ministerial level.

With the installation of the Office of Trade in the Ministry of Foreign Affairs, the ministry was renamed "Ministry of Foreign Affairs and Trade," and the Ministry of Internal Affairs and Ministry of Government Administration were consolidated to form the Ministry of Government Administration and Home Affairs. The Bureau of Public Information as well as the First and Second State Minister for Political Affairs were abolished while some ministerial-level heads of government institutions were demoted to the vice-ministerial level, and the Minister of Finance and Economy and Minister of National Unification, who were also vice prime ministers, were changed to the ministerial level. Also, with the installation of the Office of the Minister for Trade, the Ministry of Trade and Industry was changed to the Ministry of Commerce, Industry, and Energy, a move aimed at bolstering the reliable securing of global resources. Additionally, in an attempt to grow culture and tourism as the key national strategic industries in the era of culture, the Ministry of Culture and Sports was renamed the "Ministry of Culture and Tourism." As a result of this government reshuffling, the number of cabinet members was reduced from 21 to 17.

The key changes that were made in the second government reshuffling (May 1999) include the consolidation of the National Budget Administration and Planning and Budget Committee into the Ministry of Planning and Budget, the changing of the Press Office in the Prime Minister's Office to the Government Information Agency, and the removal of the personnel administration function from the Ministry of Government Administration and Home Affairs and its assignment to the Central Personnel Committee in an attempt to ensure the modernization and fairness of the personnel administration policy. Especially, the second government organizational reshuffling was the first such government reform implemented through management consultation. In the third government organizational reshuffling (January 2001), the Ministry of Finance and Economy and the Ministry of Education and Human Resources were newly installed as vice-prime-ministerial ministries, a move aimed at pushing for government-wide national human resource development in the knowledge and information society, and at incorporating the changes in the global economy and industrial environment in the era of knowledge economy. Further, the Presidential Commission on Women's Affairs was changed and expanded to the Ministry of Gender Equality.

2. Objectives and directions of the government administration

The Kim Dae Jung administration was the first administration that greeted the 21st century after having successfully achieved a horizontal exchange of power from the ruling party to the opposition party amidst the unprecedented national upheaval caused by the Asian financial crisis. Such historical background of the inauguration of the administration was also reflected in the objectives of the government administration.

In the area of politics, the administration set the following goals: expansion of the participatory democracy through political reform, eradication of corruption and fraud, prohibition of political retaliation, abolition of regional discrimination, and advancement of the local self-governing system. In the area of economy, the administration set the early termination of the oversight and control by the International Monetary Fund (IMF) as its short-term goal and proposed the creation of a new springboard for economic rebound through the improvement of the inherent qualities of the national economy as the objective of its government administration.

In the area of society, the administration aimed to deepen democracy by bolstering the rights of the social constituents who had so far been alienated with detailed goals, including guaranteeing the rights of and benefits for women and workers, educational innovation to grow creative talents, economic stabilization of the middle class, and realization of productive welfare. In the area of culture, the administration aimed to promote the culture industry through the globalization of its traditional cultural assets, a policy that jibes well with the global spread of Hallyu (Korean Wave), which is said to be one of the hottest topics today.

With regard to the government administration in the area of diplomacy, security, and unification, the administration prioritized responding proactively to the shifting international order after the end of the Cold War from a more practical perspective and ditching the Cold War era mentality that damaged the national interest owing to its excessive indulgence in political ideology. To realize this vision, the administration proposed the following objectives: to realize inter-Korean reconciliation and cooperation, to dismantle the Cold War structure and establish a self-reliant collective security framework, and to strengthen the country's economic and cultural diplomacy that puts weight on the national interest.

It can be said that the administration established the following key governing principles and tasks to realize the aforementioned government administration goals. These principles are understood as the underlying philosophy and guiding principles of the Kim Dae Jung administration: "participatory democracy," "simultaneous development of democracy and the market economy," "productive welfare," and "reconciliation and cooperation with North Korea (the so-called "Sunshine Policy")."

The participatory democracy was founded on the personal experience and belief of President Kim Dae Jung. It was only natural that the administration opted to adopt such governing principles in its government administration given that it billed itself as the "People's Government." Such move was the manifestation of its will to expand the horizon of democratic participation by the people through political reform and to create a responsible government that lives up to the demands of the people. In addition, the administration adopted the following as its key governing principles: (1) decentralization by departing from centralized authoritarian rule and (2) fostering of national reconciliation by overcoming the conflicts between different regions and classes.

The "simultaneous development of democracy and the market economy," another governing principle of the Kim Dae Jung administration that was also called "DJnomics," provided the basic guidelines for the administration's economic policy. Well before he was elected president, Kim argued for the necessity of democracy for sustainable economic development in an opinion piece that he wrote for the "Foreign Affairs" journal in 1994. In a similar line of thought, Kim stressed that democracy and the market economy should not necessarily be considered having a mutually exclusive relationship because the two systems share such principles as freedom, competition, and responsibility, and only when the two systems are appropriately reconciled can equality and efficiency be guaranteed, leading to simultaneous growth of the two systems. Even though Kim believed that government-controlled economy operating through excessive government intervention should be abolished, he basically assumed the position that the government should provide the basic framework of order through which the market and free competition can work adequately on the principle of individual responsibility. Likewise, the administration left room for governmental intervention in the market.

Productive welfare was another key pillar of the administration's governing principles. The restructuring of the South Korean economy and the IMF's provision of bailout funds conditional on the compliance with the proposed demands presumed the immense sacrifices of the middle-class and ordinary people, which therefore necessitated the urgent establishment of social safety nets. President Kim Dae Jung proposed "productive welfare" as a core principle in the country's social policy in the congratulatory message that he delivered in 1999 to mark the 44th anniversary of the country's liberation. Productive welfare signifies that the government would push for a welfare policy "centered on human development, with the goal of growing the middle class and of improving the living standard of ordinary people," with its key policy measures including guaranteeing the basic living standard of the people, providing proactive job matching support through occupational training and lifelong education, and practical improvement of the medical, employment, occupational health, and safety insurance and national pension system.

Lastly, the "reconciliation and cooperation" policy, also known as the "Sunshine Policy," provided the basis for the administration's North Korean and foreign policy initiatives. President Kim Dae Jung summed up the key directions of the Sunshine Policy with the following three principles in his inaugural address: (1) the intolerance policy, which signifies that the administration would assume a zero-tolerance approach towards any armed provocation by Pyongyang; (2) South Korea has no ulterior intention to inflict harm on the North or to merge the country with itself through absorption; and (3) the reconciliation and cooperation principle, in which the administration would push for reconciliation and cooperation with Pyongyang beginning with whatever area that is reasonably possible. Further, the administration planned to deconstruct the Cold War structure in the Korean Peninsula through close collaboration with the international community and to build a permanent peace structure in the Korean Peninsula and in Northeast Asia.

To help realize the government administration goals of the administration, the Presidential Transition Committee announced the "100 Policy Tasks for Quality Innovation of the People's Government" on February 12, 1998 as the package of detailed tasks to be implemented by the administration. The 100 policy tasks were distributed to the matching ministries throughout the government, but some practical questions were raised as to whether such policy tasks could be successfully implemented without active participation by the people as they were mostly concerned with institutional reform and public awakening. Others argued for a gradual and phased implementation of the 100 tasks over time, claiming that such approach would be more realistic compared to the simultaneous implementation of all the tasks. Specifically, some proposed to come up with an institutional apparatus that would guarantee presidential intervention because some of the reform agenda would not succeed without the special interest of and oversight by the president.

The 2nd Nation Building Movement, planned by the 2nd Nation Building Committee, was initiated within such context. The committee embarked on the formation of a nationwide organization that would work as a grassroots implementation organization, while elevating the status of the movement to one pushing for the "comprehensive reform of government administration jointly implemented by the public and private sectors to complete the establishment of democracy and of the market economy" Furthermore, the 100 policy tasks selected by the Presidential Transition Committee boiled down to 21 key tasks spanning seven areas, and the implementation priority by segment was also clarified. The key policy tasks in the seven key areas are shown below.

In the area of participatory democracy, governmental innovation was selected as the task with utmost importance. Then, other tasks, such as expansion of citizen participation and overcoming of regional conflicts, followed. In the area of the autonomous market economy, "economic revival" and creation of one million jobs were selected as the key tasks, and the establishment of a credit economy to activate the financial industry and the fostering of a competitive environment through the institutionalization of fair trade were selected as following key tasks. In the area of the realization of social justice, eradication of corruption and fraud was picked out as the task with utmost importance, as expected, along with the establishment of a nation state that values human rights and the establishment of a safe society. In the area of the realization of universal globalism to proactively respond to the challenges posed by the globalization, advancement of enterprises and the banking system up to the global standards was selected as the key task, followed by other tasks, including promotion of international exchanges and cooperation, education of global citizens, and development of South Korea as a cultural powerhouse. In the area of the establishment of a creative knowledge base, development of a creative manpower, construction of an information infrastructure, and promotion and reformation of science, technology, and media industry were selected as the key tasks. In the area of the creation of a new labor - management relations, cooperation and trust building between labor and management emerged as the task with utmost importance, followed by the establishment of a productive welfare system and of social safety nets. Lastly, in the area of inter-Korean reconciliation and promotion, promotion of an inter-Korean conciliatory environment, strengthening of inter-Korean exchanges and cooperation, and construction of a comprehensive security framework were selected as the utmost important tasks that would thus be planned ahead.

Likewise, through the Presidential Transition Committee and the 2nd Nation Building Committee, the administration set the contents of and prioritized the key policy tasks. Specifically, the 2nd Nation Building Committee provided a platform for deliberation on the administration's key policy tasks, which was open for professors, specialists, and activists, thereby incorporating the political philosophy of President Kim Dae Jung: the realization of participatory democracy.

Section 2

Key Policy Initiatives

1. Overcoming of the economic crisis

Background

The Kim Dae Jung administration was inaugurated with a mandate of overcoming the impending economic crisis. The key possible causes of the foreign currency crunch in 1997 include the steady pursuit of external growth that was heavily reliant on exports, the excessive debt ratio of the conglomerates combined with their worsening profitability by the turn of the 1990s, the government-centric economic management and the restrictions of rationalization through free competition, the high-cost and low-efficiency economic structure, and the weakening price competitiveness of the South Korean businesses. The economic crisis started with the serial declarations of insolvency by seven conglomerates, including Hanbo Group, among the top 30 business groups.

The serial bankruptcies of the large conglomerates again resulted in the ballooning amount of non-performing loans held by banks and financial institutions, thereby boosting the amount of distressed loans over twofold, from KRW 16.2 trillion near the end of 1996 to KRW 38.2 trillion by the end of November 1997. Moody's downgraded the sovereign credit ratings of South Korea by six grades (A1 Ca1) for long-term debts, and by two grades (P2 Not prime) for short-term debts, a move replicated by S&P, which downgraded the sovereign ratings of South Korea by 10 grades (CA- B+) for long-term debts and four grades (A1A3) for short-term debts. As a result, the short-term loan interest rates for commercial banks rose rapidly in the overseas financial market, thereby effectively suspending the acquisition of new loans.

Eventually, the debt conversion rates of the seven top commercial banks in South Korea in the overseas financial market deteriorated rapidly from 115.4 points in January 1997 to 32.2 points in December of the same year. The financial institutions in Japan retrieved US$ 13 billion (59%) of their total short-term loans to South Korea amounting to US$ 22 billion in 1997 and an additional US$ 1.3 billion from November 1 to 19, right before Seoul requested IMF to provide bailout funds, and a total of some US$ 9 billion from November to December. Having concluded that it would not be able to resolve the liquidity crunch by itself, South Korea was forced to request IMF to provide a liquidity adjustment fund.

Implementation System

IMF's Board of Governors approved a program on December 4, 1997 to provide South Korea with US$ 21 billion in loans in accordance with the emergency financing mechanism under the stand-by loan agreement with three-year maturity. Also, the Kim administration got deeply involved in the related policy even before the transfer of the administration was completed, and strove to earn the trust of the global financial market by pledging to fully implement the IMF program in compliance with the suggested guidelines while also taking subsequent measures. Such effort was effective in calming down the anxiety in the financial market early on.

What IMF requested the Kim administration to do at the macroeconomic level, along with fiscal and monetary belt-tightening, was to push for a structural reform of the country's financial industry and business sector. IMF made a series of requests to the South Korean companies, including the improvement of the liquidation condition for insolvent companies, the improvement of financial soundness, and guaranteeing management transparency. Towards these ends, IMF requested a revamp of the governance structure of companies, liberalization of the flow of capital and trades, and raise of the flexibility in the labor market. In a move to improve the transparency of the financial statements of corporations, IMF requested the publication of the consolidated financial statements of the conglomerates by the end of 1999, one year earlier than the initial schedule, and also demanded that more universally accepted international accounting principles be applied when preparing the financial statements. In addition, it also requested that the rights of the minor shareholders be strengthened, and that the appointment of non-executive outside directors and auditors be mandatory in an attempt to bolster the apparatus for holding the management in check.

Table 6-1. Structural reform in the corporate sector in accordance with the agreement with IMF

Increase management transparency	- Introducing consolidated financial statements - Raising the accounting standards to the level of the international standards - Strengthening the minority shareholders' rights - Bolstering the apparatus for holding the management in check - Increasing the accountability of the management	- Enforcement of the IMF requirements in 1999, one year earlier than the original schedule - Clarification and internationalization of the accounting principles, adoption of the international standards in bookkeeping - Non-permission of the standalone shareholder right in the representative suit - Lowering of the application threshold of the right to demand the resignation of a board member from 1 to 0.5% of the right for representative suit - Relaxation of the right to read account books and calling for a general meeting of shareholders from 3 to 1% of the total shares - Mandatory appointment of non-executive outside directors and auditors - Designation of the controlling shareholder as a de facto director

Improve the financial structure	- Eliminating the mutual-payment guarantee - Eliminating excessive loans - Abolishing paid-in capital increase	- Banning of the fresh new payment guarantee and complete resolution of the existing payment guarantee by March 2000 - 100% resolution of any amount in excess by March 1998 - Early enforcement of the denial of excessive loans as interest loss - Enforcement in 1998, earlier then the original schedule (2000)
Improve the liquidation requirement for insolvent companies	- Revamping and streamlining the liquidation laws - Activating the M&A market - Simplifying the merger/ acquisition process - Introducing the corporate spinoff system - Defending the right of control over companies	- Early amendment of the Company Reorganization Act, Liquidation Act, and Composition Act - Abolition of the mandatory public takeover bid system - Expansion of the percentage of the pre-approved shares act from 10 to 33.3% in accordance with the Foreign Capital Inducement Act - Early permission in March of a hostile M&A - Abolition of the mandatory approval by the Ministry of Finance and Economy when acquiring companies with total assets exceeding KRW 2 trillion - Statement of the related commercial law - Expansion of the limit of repurchase of treasury stocks from 10 to 33.3% of the total shares
Ensure the flexibility of the labor market	- Ensuring the flexibility of the labor market - Strengthening the employment insurance	- Amendment of the layoff-related laws - Expansion of the employment insurance and unemployment allowance

Implementation Process and Contents

Monetary and fiscal belt-tightening policy

Starting as a liquidity crisis, the South Korean economic crisis soon escalated into a credit panic, further spreading financial woes across all the economy. In the early phase of the crisis, the administration shifted the direction of its macroeconomic policy to that of fiscal and monetary belt-tightening in compliance with the prescription suggested by IMF. As a result of the draconian fiscal belt-tightening, the issue interest rate of corporate bonds jumped from the 12% level before the foreign currency crunch to the 30% level by the end of 1997, while the exchange rate shot up from KRW 800 to KRW 2,000 per US$ 1 by early 1998. Also, in 1998, the economic growth rate, which had always remained at stratospheric levels, plummeted to -6.7%, the largest minus growth ever recorded since the foundation of the Republic of Korea.

However, the fiscal belt-tightening and total demand contraction policy implemented in early 1998 had unwanted negative side effects: the rapid rise of the unemployment rate and social instability. The unemployment rate, which had remained at 2.6% per year, shot up to 7.0% in 1998, while the number of jobless people ballooned from 570,000 in 1997 to 1.49 million in 1998 and to 1.37 million in 1999, thereby becoming near-permanent social woes of the country. As the liquidity crisis seemed to have turned for the worst, the administration strove to realize economic rebound by tolerating interest rate reductions and fiscal deficits while exerting diverse efforts to address the country's unemployment woes, such as through public work projects and the early use of the social overhead capital budget. The number of unemployed people dropped to the below-1-million level in 2000, but for more than 10 years, it had never returned to the level that the country saw before the foreign currency crunch.

Corporate restructuring

On January 13, 1998, President Kim Dae Jung and the chairmen of South Korea's four major conglomerates agreed on the "Five Key Agreements on Corporate Restructuring." Newly inaugurated as the unified financial supervisory body by consolidating similar government functions, the Financial Supervisory Commission ordered the top five conglomerates on March 24 of the same year to sign another loan agreement containing the requirement to lower the debt ratio to 200% by the end of 1999, along with the demand to revamp the loan agreement and to submit supplementary materials. Based on these materials, the Financial Supervisory Commission revised its policy and proposed a renewed restructuring schedule: completion of the due diligence on the assets by the end of September, re-establishment of a financial structure improvement plan based on the due diligence results, and confirmation of the restructuring plan by December 15 of the same year. Any new debt payment guarantee by the top 30 conglomerates was completely banned beginning in April 1998, and the conglomerates were also required to resolve any remaining cross-debt guarantee among their affiliates by the end of March 2000.

Moreover, the top 30 conglomerates were required to prepare consolidated financial statements encompassing their domestic affiliates and overseas subsidiaries on a mandatory basis, beginning in the 1999 fiscal year. The administration announced its plan to allow the establishment of a holding company in an attempt to support the seamless and fluid implementation of corporate restructuring. The plan included highly restrictive regulatory measures: compulsory capital investment exceeding 50% of the total shares of the subsidiary, the debt ratio at the below-100% level, complete resolution of the debt payment guarantee, banning of investment in the other companies of the subsidiary, and banning of the simultaneous investment of financial and non-financial assets.

The liquidation of insolvent companies and the business restructuring of the conglomerates were also actively pushed forward as part of the business portfolio restructuring. The primary creditor bank of each group selected the first batch of 55 companies that would be liquidated on June 18, 1998, and announced the immediate suspension of loan provisions to them. The administration requested the top five conglomerates to draft their own business restructuring plan by the end of August, and to revamp the fiscal structure improvement agreement by the end of September, while the rest of the conglomerates were to be subject to the workout routine led by the top eight commercial banks.

Restructuring of the financial sector

The eight financial groups that had already defaulted on their foreign currency payment were ordered to suspend their foreign currency businesses upon the commencement of the negotiation with IMF in November 1997. In December of the same year, 14 financial groups incapable of carrying out normal business activities due to their insufficient liquidity level, 2 securities firms on the brink of insolvency due to their management failure, and 2 investment trust companies that were having continuous difficulty performing their businesses due to the bank run were all ordered to suspend their business operation.

Further, First Bank and Seoul Bank, two of the 26 commercial banks that were struggling with the worst case of financial difficulty, were ordered to reduce their paid-in capital from KRW 820 billion to KRW 100 billion. Moreover, the gross capital of the two banks was expanded to KRW 1.6 trillion, respectively, with the additional capital investment of KRW 750 billion each by the government and Korea Deposit Insurance Corporation (January 1998). Six of the remaining 24 commercial banks with a ratio of owner's equity hovering below the 6% level when measured based on the BIS standards as of the end of 1997 were ordered to implement management improvement measures, and six other banks with such ratio hovering at the 6-8% level were advised to do the same. The Management Assessment Committee (formed on June 20, 1998), which was composed of experts from the private sector, was given the role of evaluating the feasibility of the management normalization plans submitted by the banks. The liquidation process of those banks with unhealthy financial status was completed by ordering eight outstanding banks (including Kookmin Bank, Housing Bank, Shinhan Bank, Hanmi Bank, and Hana Bank) with a BIS ratio of over 8% to purchase and assume (P&A) the good assets and liabilities of five banks: Daedong Bank, Dongnam Bank, Donghwa Bank, Gyeonggi Bank, and Chungcheong Bank.

Reform of the labor sector

The most important policy of the administration with regard to the labor-management relations was the permanent operation of the Korea Tripartite Commission. Through the commission, the administration successfully enabled the country's labor unions to formulate economic and social policies and to participate in the corporate restructuring process that would exert a significant influence on the country's labor policy and on the workers' employment and working conditions. Inaugurated on January 15, 1998, the commission succeeded in reaching a grand agreement on February 6 of the same year to share the pains associated with the overcoming of the economic crisis on a fair basis, which was followed by the signing of a "social pact" containing 90 agreements on February 9. The social pact included not only a set of agreements associated with the labor issue, such as further enhanced flexibility of the labor market, improvement of the workers' basic labor rights, and expansion of the social safety nets, but also other agreements on the overall reform directions encompassing comprehensive issues of the government administration, including corporate restructuring of businesses, tax reform, and political reform.

In February 1998, along with revamping and streamlining of the country's social security laws, establishment of teachers' unions, unrestricted political activity by labor unions, and joining of labor unions by the unemployed, all of which were required by the labor unions, were realized in accordance with the tripartite agreement and amendment of the related laws. As part of the agreements that would be welcomed by corporations, the laying off of redundant workers and the dispatched labor system were also introduced. However, since both systems had already been widely adopted in practice by businesses, the grand agreement was generally assessed to have been favorable to the labor unions. Meanwhile, the teachers' union was legalized in accordance with the tripartite agreement in February 1998, and the right to organize was guaranteed as well for the government employees (in the form of a workplace council). In addition, the legal status of the

Korean Confederation of Trade Unions, long considered the symbol of the country's restriction of basic labor rights, was also resolved with its legalization in November 1999.

Restructuring of the public sector

With regard to the reform of the central government, the administration pushed for the organizational reshuffling of the government, including the dismantling of the Ministry of Finance and Economy, which was criticized for having brought about the foreign currency crunch and for the establishment of the Financial Supervisory Commission and Planning and Budget Committee. In addition, the administration embarked on the massive privatization and restructuring of public corporations. In accordance with the privatization plan established in 1998, five public corporations (Pohang Steel, Korea Heavy Industries and Construction, Korea Integrated Chemical, Korea Engineering Consultants Corporation, and National Textbook Publishing Corporation) among the 26 mother companies of public corporations were immediately privatized. While six corporations (Korea Telecom Corporation, Korea Tobacco and Ginseng Corporation, Korea Electric Power Corporation, Korea Gas Corporation, Daehan Oil Pipeline Corporation, and Korea District Heating Corporation) were to be privatized on a phased manner, the remaining 12 public corporations were requested to engage in management innovation and business restructuring internally. Moreover, large-scale organizational downsizing and manpower reduction were carried out in numerous other umbrella institutions and government investment corporations under the direct control of the central and local governments.

Measures for addressing the country's unemployment woes, and job welfare policy

The country's institutions associated with the social safety nets remained at a state in which they began to lay down the basic framework based on the public aid system, such as the protection of the minimum living standard system (1961), and on the social insurance system, including the Industrial Accident Compensation Insurance (1964), Medical Insurance (1977), National Pensions (1988), and the Unemployment Insurance (1995). At the time when number of unemployed were increasing in enormous amount due to the shock of the economic crisis, the country's social safety nets had yet incorporated a sufficient institutional cushioning apparatus that would protect the primary victims, most of whom belonged to the vulnerable classes, and the middle-class people.

In the middle of such rapidly developing crisis, the administration prepared comprehensive unemployment measures in March 1998 in a move to quickly and effectively respond to the country's rapidly escalating unemployment woes. The measures included diverse programs spanning four key areas: employment sustenance, job creation, occupational training, and employment security/protection of minimum living standards. In the area of public employment security services, the number of public employment security institutions jumped from 53 (including the regional labor offices in late 1997) to 191 by late 2001 (including 168 employment security centers).

The Unemployment Insurance, which had only been applied to those businesses with over 30 employees on payroll since its introduction in 1995, was expanded to cover any business with one or more employee beginning in October 1998. As a result, the number of employees covered by the Unemployment Insurance jumped from 4.2 million (32.6% of all wage earners in the country) in 1995 to 6.644 million by October 2000, nearly half of all the wage earners in the country. Beginning in 2000, the coverage of the Industrial Accident Compensation Insurance and National Pensions was also extended to include all businesses nationwide. Along with the expansion of the coverage of four key social insurances, the administration ensured that the marginalized classes would be protected and would enjoy the national minimum living standards by implementing the National Basic Living Security System.

Performance and Assessment

Having carried out a series of efforts to overcome the economic crisis, the government succeeded in disposing of some KRW 197.4 trillion of non-performing loans within a period of four years, from March 1998 to March 2002. In particular, the government promptly reduced the non-performing loans held by the financial institutions by KRW 45 trillion within a period of 20 months, from KRW 112 trillion in March 1998 to KRW 66.7 trillion by the end of 1999. With the help of the phased introduction of the "Credit Loan Criteria Lower than FLC Fixed Rate" in March 2000 and the continued corporate restructuring of businesses, the amount of non-performing loans held by the financial institutions dropped to KRW 33.7 trillion after adding up KRW 72.4 trillion in new non-performing loans and deducting KRW 105.4 trillion in disposed-of non-performing loans. The BIS ratio of owner's equity, the key indicator of the management health of financial institutions, improved from 7.0% near the end of 1997 to 10.5% by the end of 2002.

Furthermore, considering that the range of non-performing loans that were subject to the requirement of appropriation of bad/irrecoverable debt was expanded in accordance with the new assets quality classification criteria, the assets quality of the financial institutions can be assessed to have been markedly improved. The liquidity of the stock market, which had contracted substantially since the foreign currency crunch, rebounded by more than fourfold in 2000 compared to its level in 1998 and continued to perform well over the pre-crisis level even in 2001 when the market tanked again. When the restructuring was completed by the end of 2001, the total market capitalization of KOSPI grew to KRW 256 trillion, an about 3.6-fold increase from the KRW 71 trillion level near the end of 1997. The stock market had since grown markedly in terms of overall quantity.

The real economy recovered fast along with the stabilization of the financial market; the short-term cash flow of corporations that had deteriorated significantly in the wake of the foreign currency crunch recovered to its pre-crisis level beginning in 2001. The run-out rate of overdraft, the key indicator of the emergency capital demands by corporations, rose to 33.5% in March 1998 but had continued to show downward trends since 2001, until it recorded 13.4% in April 2002. The number of insolvent companies recorded a total of 22,000 (76 newly insolvent companies per day on average) in 1998 but had since dropped to 6,700 (22 newly insolvent companies per day on average) in 1999, well below the pre-1997 level.

Specifically, the facility investment rate, which had dropped by 38.8% in 1998, soared by 36.3 and 35.3% in 1999 and 2000, respectively, and private consumption recovered as well from an 11.7% decrease in 1999 to a 7.9% growth rate in 2000. As a result, the GDP growth rate recovered rapidly from a minus growth rate in 1998 to 10.9% in 1999 and 9.3% in 2000, while the job market rapidly stabilized as the unemployment rate dropped from 6.8% in 1998 to the 3% level after 2001.

The administration is assessed to have successfully overcome the foreign currency crisis. The objective evidences confirming such observations include the fact that the country's sovereign credit ratings, which had been downgraded to junk status by leading global credit ratings firms, including S&P, Moody's, and Fitch IBCA, near the end of December 1997, were rapidly upgraded until all three rating firms upgraded the sovereign credit ratings of South Korea back to grade A. Furthermore, it is also historically significant that the country graduated from the governance of IMF in 3 years and 8 months on August 23, 2001, three years ahead of the original schedule, by repaying in its entirety the US$ 20 billion in bailout funds that was provided to it by IMF.

Still, many criticize the administration for having lost much in the process of overcoming the economic crisis: as the administration pushed forward with the legal and institutional revamp and business portfolio restructuring, the controversy raged on with regard to the set of principles on which the administration should peg its restructuring process. Moreover, the average share of foreign ownership of the South Korean companies, which remained at the 3.2% level during the crisis, soared to 40%, thereby sparking the criticism that the country's economy was being controlled by speculative foreign capital. Further, the inequality between classes and different industries deteriorated severely with the corresponding worsening of the income distribution structure, thereby making the country pay a hefty price, which made it difficult for it to recover its pre-crisis levels.

2. Inter-Korean reconciliation-cooperation policy (inter-Korean summit meeting for the first time since the division of the Korean Peninsula)

Background

The inter-Korean issue used to be a matter between the two Koreas, but the international influence on the Korean Peninsula grew markedly in the wake of the North Korean nuclear crisis. The internationalization of the Korean issue, which unfolded in the 1990s, had both positive and negative aspects wrapped in a single package. First, KEDO, which was formed to support the North Korean light-water nuclear reactor project, and the four-way talks, which was aimed at establishing a peace structure in the Korean Peninsula, are both considered to have had a positive influence on the Korean issue in that they established the institutional setting for discussing the resolution of the North Korean nuclear issue and the stabilization of the peace structure in the Korean Peninsula. Further, the two initiatives prompted the steady transformation of North Korea through the relations with the U. S. and Japan, and urged North Korea to comply with the norms established by the international community. It was remarkable that the neighboring countries and the international community created an atmosphere to demand that North Korea embark on denuclearization and on transition to a peace structure.

There's one caveat, though: the international community's engagement in and its effort to internationalize the North Korean issue did not lead to deeper inter-Korean relations. Despite the international community's engagement in the North Korean issue and the improvement of the relations between North Korea and the international community, the inter-Korean talks had been shut down since the mid-1990s while the inter-Korean relations remained in limbo. As a result, the international community kept expanding its leverage on the Korean Peninsula whereas the leadership of the two Koreas was weakening significantly because the two Koreas, the parties that can legitimately engage in the issue, were largely excluded from the discussion.

As North Korea succeeded in gaining the support that it wanted from the international community, the need to improve the inter-Korean relations fizzled out, but North Korea needed to advance the inter-Korean relations to guarantee the survival of its regime and to procure economic aid in the wake of the conclusion of the Cold War. In this context, North Korea agreed to hold high-level inter-Korean talks in the early 1990s, and succeeded in concluding the Inter-Korean Basic Agreement and Joint Declaration on Denuclearization. However, since North Korea was wary of the opening of North Korea and of the prospect that South Korea would exert growing influence on the North Korean society should the inter-Korean relations begin to progress at full speed, it never stopped its armed provocation of South Korea, including armed threats directed at Seoul and infiltration of the South Korean territory with submarines, while agreeing to hold the inter-Korean talks for practical purposes, such as the possible procurement of economic aid from South Korea. The inter-Korean relations came to a screeching halt, however, when North Korea's nuclear ambitions began to emerge as the most important issue, and the nuclear issue dwarfed all the other pending issues between the two Koreas.

Amid such shifting environment, the Kim administration recognized the need to establish a peace structure in the Korean Peninsula under the inter-Korean leadership, while also elevating the inter-Korean cooperation to the next level. Given that the Cold War structure at the global level had disappeared long ago, the administration was deeply aware of the need to end the Cold War structure in the Korean Peninsula through reconciliation and cooperation between two Koreas. The administration hoped to instill a virtuous cycle in the Korean Peninsula, where the internationalization of the Korean issue and the development of inter-Korean relations would be locked in a mutually beneficial structure. Furthermore, while the administration intended to change Pyongyang's South Korean strategy by pushing for inter-Korean cooperation wherever feasible, it also maintained rock-solid security preparedness against any armed provocation by North Korea aimed at South Korea. The administration's such reconciliation and cooperation policy with North Korea was based on the functionalism theory, which was applied to the softening of the tension in the integration of Europe. Based on the functionalistic approach, the European states were able to establish a peace structure, thereby succeeding in the integration of Europe, by pushing for incremental and accumulative exchanges and cooperation in non-military and non-political areas such as the economy, society, and culture, after World War II.

Implementation System

The Kim Dae Jung administration partially adopted the national security council system of the U.S. to push forward with its North Korean policy. The existing North Korean policy implementation system was divided into the Office of the Senior Secretary for Foreign Affairs and National Security, which dealt with everyday businesses, and the Coordination Council for Foreign and Security Policies, which dealt with key specific policy issues. Under such dual system, only contrasting positions of the presidential secretaries representing each ministry were consistently put on the table, and not coordinating policies among them. To resolve such dilemma, the standing committee and secretariat of the National Security Council were installed by amending the existing National Security Council Act, thereby enabling the council to assume the role of coordinating the different positions of diverse ministries. The coordination and integration function of NSC was significantly weakened, however, due to its role sharing with the Office of the Senior Secretary for Foreign Affairs and National Security. Meanwhile, the NSC secretariat was a small organization staffed with only 10 officials (5 working-level staff), and with limited influence in terms of its status and workforce. Therefore, the NSC secretariat simply played the role of supporting the NSC steering committee, without possessing sufficient capacity to coordinate the contrasting positions of the different officials dispatched from each ministry.

Meanwhile, the administration exerted diverse efforts to collect the opinions of ordinary people and to gather the expert opinions of related professionals under the leadership of the Ministry of Unification. The public opinions were heard whenever necessary via surveys by professional research firms or via Internet fora. Additionally, the positions and opinions of political, expert, and opinion-leading groups were incorporated in the process throughout different phases from agenda setting to policy making and implementation, policy evaluation, and feedback gathering, by way of unification advisory meetings, expert advisory meetings, a joint public-private council for supporting the North Korean policy, and the National Assembly standing committee for foreign affairs, trade, and unification.

Implementation Process and Contents

The administration's policy for reconciliation and cooperation with North Korea aimed to establish peace in the Korean Peninsula by nudging Pyongyang to change incrementally, thereby realizing the "de facto unification" of the two Koreas. The strategy was intended to open and reform North Korea through inter-Korean reconciliation and cooperation, and to revive the ethnic homogeneity of the Koreans by advancing the inter-Korean relations through peaceful coexistence and inter-Korean exchanges and cooperation, thereby eventually creating a "de facto unified" state.

The first objective of the policy of reconciliation and cooperation with North Korea was based on the three principles below laid out in President Kim Dae Jung's inaugural address. First, the administration would assume a zero-tolerance approach towards any armed provocation. This is because sustained peace in the Korean Peninsula was seen as the very foundation of the reconciliation and cooperation with North Korea and as the basic premise on which the inter-Korean relations could be improved and unification could be realized.

The second principle was to the exclused unification by absorption, which implied never attempt to unify North Korea by absorption. The principle was intended to dispel any fear that North Korea may have of potential regime collapse in light of the collapse of the former socialist bloc and the unification of Germany. Furthermore, the potential conflicts and negative side effects that may arise should the unification be realized with the unilateral leadership of either side were also taken into consideration, given the deepened differences between the two Koreas.

The third principle was the active promotion of inter-Korean reconciliation and cooperation so that North Korea would boldly open itself and change its regime. The administration resolved to keep persuading North Korea that inter-Korean reconciliation and cooperation was best for the two Koreas as it would promote the mutual interests and welfare of the Korean ethnic constituents across the Korean Peninsula, thereby establishing a mutually beneficial inter-Korean relationship.

"Dismantlement of the Cold War structure in the Korean Peninsula"

Beginning in 1999, one year after its inauguration, the Kim administration approached the issue of peace in the Korean Peninsula from the perspective of the dismantlement of the Cold War structure. President Kim Dae Jung suggested the following five tasks for the dismantlement of the Cold War structure in the Korean Peninsula: (1) faithful implementation of the Inter-Korean Basic Agreement and of inter-Korean reconciliation and cooperation; (2) starting the process of normalizing North Korea's relations with the U. S. and Jarpan; (3) promoting the conditions and environment conducive for changes in and the opening of North Korea; (4) realizing arms control, including removal of the threats posed by the North's weapons of mass destruction; and (5) pushing for the realization of the de facto unification of the two Koreas through the transition of the armistice system into the peace structure.

The administration believed that the Korean Peninsula could be transformed from the Cold War system only when the two Koreas would comply with the Inter-Korean Basic Agreement. The agreement covered almost all aspects of the inter-Korean issues, including political reconciliation and trust building, relaxation of the military tension and establishment of peace, exchanges, and cooperation as well as other humanitarian issues. Likewise, the president believed that inter-Korean cooperation could be institutionalized and that the Cold War structure in the Korean Peninsula can be dismantled through the faithful implementation of the agreement. The president was also convinced that the normalization of North Korea's relations with the U.S. and Japan is a prerequisite to the dismantling of the Cold War structure in the Korean Peninsula. He believed that the normalization of North Korea's relations with the U. S. and Japan should be pushed for in view of the fact that the normalization of the Sino-South Korean relations and the USSR - South Korean relations was pushed for after the conclusion of the Cold War.

Berlin Declaration

President Kim Dae Jung unveiled the "Declaration of Inter-Korean Reconciliation and Cooperation for Peace in and the Unification of the Korean Peninsula (Berlin Declaration)" in his special lecture in the Free University of Berlin in March 2000. The declaration touched on wide-ranging issues, including South Korea's comprehensive support of North Korea's economic development, the establishment of peace in the Korean Peninsula, the resolution of the issue of separated families, and inter-Korean talks involving responsible administrative bodies.

The Berlin Declaration had a number of implications. First, the declaration would be considered a Marshall Plan for the Korean Peninsula in that it proposed that South Korea provide support for the economic rehabilitation of North Korea and laid the institutional groundwork for such, including the construction of social overhead capital such as roads, railroads, and ports as well as the preparation of an institutional foundation (e.g., guarantee of investment, prevention of double taxation), and even went further to include a proposal for inter-Korean agricultural cooperation.

Second, the President proposed to end the Cold War between the two Koreas and to establish a platform for peaceful coexistence in the Korean Peninsula. Any unification without the foundation of peaceful inter-Korean coexistence and co-prosperity would put substantial economic burdens and have other social, cultural, and psychological ramifications on the unified Korea. In this perspective, the president stressed in the Berlin Declaration that practical cooperation and efforts to end the Cold War are required, and that a peace structure should be established in the Korean Peninsula.

Third, the President proposed the immediate resolution of the issue of separated families. Since the first generation of the separated families was aging rapidly, the president believed that the resolution of the said issue could no longer be delayed. As the resolution of the issue of separated families requires close cooperation between the governments of the two Koreas, the president urged Pyongyang to take immediate steps to resolve the said issue.

Fourth, the President stressed that government-level talks are essential for the implementation of the Inter-Korean Basic Agreement and for the resolution of the pending related issues. Specifically, the president stressed that the Inter-Korean Basic Agreement should be implemented most urgently as it covers almost all the requirements of the establishment of a peace structure in the Korean Peninsula, and for the improvement of the inter-Korean relations.

With the Berlin Declaration, the administration demonstrated its will to pursue all the practical measures required to realize inter-Korean reconciliation and cooperation, including the provision of support for the recovery of the North Korean economy. The declaration is assessed to have formed a favorable environment for North Korea's eventual agreement to hold the first-ever inter-Korean summit by unveiling the blueprint for the future inter-Korean cooperation, and to have formed an environment conducive for eventual unification.

June 15 inter-Korean summit meeting

The inter-Korean summit meeting provided an important opportunity for the two Koreas to reconfirm the principles that the Korean issue can be handled legitimately only by the Koreans themselves and that the two Koreas can exercise proactive leadership in the resolution of the Korean issues. The hosting of the inter-Korean summit meeting and the June 15 Joint Declaration opened a new chapter for the inter-Korean relationship. The key agreements contained in the June 15 Joint Declaration pertained to the unification principles, unification methods, humanitarian issues, inter-Korean exchange/cooperation, and inter-Korean talks. Below are the joint declaration's unique characteristics.

First, the declaration reclassified the issues associated with the Korean Peninsula into two groups: (1) the problems that may be resolved internally by the Koreans and (2) the problems that can be solved only through international collaboration. The issues of the transition to a peace structure, the North Korean nuclear and missile dilemma, the presence of the U.S. forces in South Korea, military trust building, and arms control are inter-Korean issues as well as issues of international interest that may not be resolved easily and in the short term. The June 15 Joint Declaration excluded the aforementioned issues from the agenda of the inter-Korean talks but singled out the inter-Korean issues contained in the Inter-Korean Basic Agreement that would be relatively easy for the two Koreas to agree on in view of the changed international relations and shifting political environments of two Koreas. The June 15 Joint Declaration had since provided the key frame of reference for the directions of the inter-Korean relations and cooperation projects by area.

Second, unlike the July 4 Joint Statement or the Inter-Korean Basic Agreement which was made in 1972, the June 15 Joint Declaration was signed by the top leaders of the two Koreas after meeting in person. Therefore, it can be said that the declaration demonstrated the will of the top leaders and governments of the two Koreas to implement the agreements. The agreements in the June 15 Joint Declaration mentioned only the basic directions for each principle rather than specifying detailed projects. For this reason, Seoul and Pyongyang put weight on holding a series of talks for the implementation of the agreed principles, and on implementing follow-up actions.

The June 15 Joint Declaration cited the inter-Korean talks as the institutional apparatus required for implementing various forms of inter-Korean cooperation, thereby providing key institutional grounds for holding various talks depending on the functional needs, while pushing ahead with diverse exchanges and cooperation programs. As a result, a series of inter-Korean talks, including the inter-Korean ministerial talks, inter-Korean defense ministerial talks, working-level talks for inter-Korean economic cooperation, special envoy talks, and Red Cross talks, were subsequently held.

Third, the June 15 Joint Declaration also mentioned the unification method as one of the long-term objectives, along with the method of cooperation, which was the short-term goal. In other words, the declaration sought to identify the feasible cooperation methods within the framework of the status quo but also mentioned the goal-oriented unification method required to change the status quo and to bring it to the next level. Article 1 discussed the unification principle. In Article 2, the unification method of the June 15 Joint Declaration laid out the goals and directions of the unification. Lastly, Article 3 and 4 dealt with the humanitarian issues and the issue of exchanges and cooperation, respectively.

Such agreements in the June 15 Joint Declaration can be considered the results of the compromises struck between the two Koreas. Almost all the issues that South Korea wished to put on the inter-Korean agenda were included in the June 15 Joint Declaration, with the exception of the establishment of a peace structure and the removal of the Cold War structure. Among the issues that North Korea wished to include, the basic principle of unification and the unification method were included in the declaration. North Korea put as much priority on the unification issue as on the acquisition of practical economic benefits.

Performance and Assessment

Over 70 inter-Korean talks were held during the incumbency of President Kim Dae Jung, including the summit meeting. Specifically, after the inter-Korean summit meeting, some 60 talks were held to implement the agreed-upon measures, including the inter-Korean ministerial meeting and various other inter-Korean talks. The inter-Korean meeting, the first ever to have been held in the Korean Peninsula since 1995, was held after the inauguration of the administration, and JSA Panmunjom was restored as the meeting venue beginning in 2000, six years after 1994.

The total amount of humanitarian aid given by South Korea to North Korea within the five-year period after the inauguration of the Kim administration was US$ 462.8 million (government aid: US$ 272.08 million), or US$ 92.56 million on average annually (government aid: US$ 54.43 million). The annual aid offered by the ROK government to North Korea slightly dipped during this period compared to the US$ 87.24 million per year on average that was offered during the three-year period before 1998, but the average annual aid offered by the private sector to North Korea jumped more than fivefold, from US$ 7.45 million to US$ 38.14 million, in the same period.

A total of six rounds of reunions of separated families were realized during the incumbency of President Kim Dae Jung, where a combined total of 6,300 people met their loved ones living on the other side of the border. The administration also provided unwavering support to the reunions of the separated families that were held in overseas locations. Beginning in April 1998, the expenses for the reunions of the separated families that had economic difficulties were partially paid by the government. The support for travel expenses of the various activities associated with the reunions, including tracking down the family members, confirming their survival status and current addresses, and arranging the eventual reunions, was expanded, along with the matching increase in the amount of fiscal support. In May 1998, the Council for Exchanges among the Separated Families in South and North Korea, which included 22 organizations associated with the separated families, was launched, thereby significantly strengthening the capability of the private sector to help reunite the separated families.

The inter-Korean human exchanges and trade jumped markedly as well; a combined total of 37,572 (about 7,514 on average annually) South Koreans visited North Korea during the period from 1998 to 2002, 15.6 times the number of people who visited North Korea within the nine-year period from the enforcement of the Basic Guidelines on Inter-Korean Exchanges and Cooperation in June 1989~1997. Inter-Korean economic cooperation was realized during the incumbency of President Kim Dae Jung. The cooperation was centered mainly on three key economic-cooperation projects: (1) the Mt. Kumgang Tourism project; (2) the Kaesong Industrial Complex construction project; and (3) the reconnection of the rails and roads, including the Gyeongui line, the Donghae line, and other roads. Thanks to such projects, the inter-Korean trade added up to US$ 2.02522 billion (US$ 405.04 million per year on average) for the five-year period from 1998 to the end of 2002. The inter-Korean trade volumes contracted due to the foreign currency crunch in 1998, thereby briefly remaining at US$ 221.94 million, but it jumped back to the over-US$ 300-million level in 1999, thanks to the expansion of consigned processing trades boosted by the economic recovery of South Korea, Mt. Kumgang Tourism, and the light-water nuclear reactor project. The inter-Korean trade volumes were at the US$ 400-million level in 2000 and 2001, respectively, but it rose to US$ 640 million in 2002, thanks to the provision of food loans and of the materials and construction equipment required for the project involving the reconnection of the railroads and motorways to the North Korean section.

The booming inter-Korean human contacts and exchanges/cooperation triggered changes in North Korea's South Korean policy as well in the area directly related with the practical economic benefits. North Korea's agreement to hold military talks to discuss Mt. Kumgang tourism, the Kaesong industrial complex construction project, and the reconnection of the railroads and motorways, and to the relaxation of the military tension, can be seen as part of the bigger changes in North Korea's overall South Korean policy. North Korea, however, stuck to its existing policy lines towards South Korea in the areas directly related with the preservation of the North Korean regime, such as security, inter-Korean peace, and politics. Moreover, in the areas of the relaxation of the military tension and the peace structure, Pyongyang pushed for the development of nuclear weapons to warrant the continuity of its regime, and insisted on the signing of the U.S. - North Korean Peace Treaty, all while excluding Seoul.

The Kim Dae Jung administration's reconciliation and cooperation policy towards North Korea led to improve the inter-Korean relations and exerted a positive influence on the international political environment in Northeast Asia. For all such efforts, however, it was not easy to overcome the limitations inherent in the Korean issues imposed by the international community. The defining role of the international community on the Korean issues grew increasingly prominent ever since the emergence of the North Korean nuclear crisis. The administration's reconciliation and cooperation policy towards North Korea could become feasible only upon the completion of the international framework needed to resolve the North Korean nuclear crisis. Given the deteriorating relationship between Washington and Pyongyang after the inauguration of the Bush administration and the subsequent collapse of the U.S. - North Korean Agreed Framework in October 2002, the policy could no longer be expected to become effective.[2)]

Specifically, the adjustment in Washington's policy on the Korean Peninsula after the change of government in the U.S. had a substantial impact on the North Korean policy of the Kim Dae Jung administration. The administration had hoped that the Bush administration would stick to the North Korean policy of the Clinton administration, but the Bush administration condemned North Korea, referring to it as an "axis of evil," and initiated a comprehensive review of the Washington-Pyongyang relations under the Clinton administration. Such shifting environment in international politics highlighted the growing discrepancies between the Kim Dae Jung administration and the Bush administration on the North Korean nuclear issue and on the overall North Korean policy. The growing difference between the Kim Dae Jung administration and the Bush administration on the North Korean policy was one of the reasons that the momentum of the reconciliation and cooperation policy towards North Korea started to weaken near the end of the administration.

3. Nurturing of IT and venture startups (laying the foundation for making South Korea an IT powerhouse)

Background

In 1993, the U.S. accelerated the pace of its info-communication revolution when President Clinton pushed for the formulation of a national information infrastructure plan upon the inauguration of his administration. In South Korea, the Kim Young Sam administration expanded and revamped the Ministry of Postal Service to the Ministry of Info-Communication in December

---

2) The U.S. stopped providing heavy oil to North Korea with the revelation of the North's highly enriched uranium program. In response, Pyongyang declared the termination of the U.S-North Korean Agreed Framework, alleging that Washington had reneged on its last remaining promise in the Agreed Framework. Pyongyang declared its withdrawal from the Nuclear Non-Proliferation Treaty on January 10, 2003 as the situation started to deteriorate further.

1994 and pushed for the construction of a broadband information network as a key national infrastructure policy in preparation for the impending arrival of the knowledge and information society.

The role of the Kim Dae Jung administration in the development of the IT industry in South Korea and in the establishment of an electronic government in the early phase of the info-communication revolution in the country cannot be overemphasized. The much-elevated importance of infomatization and of the info-communication industrial policy during the presidency of Kim Dae Jung is largely attributable to the president's personal knowledge about the information society, as shown in the following quotations from his addresses:

> The Korean people are extraordinarily well suited for the 21st-century information society as they could demonstrate their hidden potential in the changed era. The new government will do its best to help the young generation grow as leaders of the knowledge and information society. The government will make sure that the students would be taught to use computers beginning with the elementary school years, and that they would be able to choose the computer subject in the college entrance exams. The government will make this country the world's best country in terms of the utilization of computers, thereby laying a solid foundation for the country to rise as an information powerhouse in the future (presidential inaugural address, 1998).
>
> In the 1980s, America lost its leadership in the key strategic industries — such as the semiconductor and automotive industries — to Japan, but the country was able to rebound on the strength of the successful development of venture startups mostly in the information industry, which was driven by creativity and innovation. South Korea regards such experiences of America very highly. Given that South Korea desperately needs to recover its competitiveness and to create new jobs, America gives us extremely valuable lessons in this regard. I hope that South Korea would learn from America, the haven of venture startups, where one out of four households is engaged in some form of private business, including a venture startup, because I believe that such venture spirit and startup culture will save South Korea from the economic crisis that it is facing (address delivered in the luncheon meeting hosted by the president of Stanford University, 1998).
>
> We were behind other countries in the industrial revolution, but we will have to do everything to succeed in the information revolution (presidential address marking the opening of the 16th National Assembly).

Three of the top 100 policy tasks recommended by the Presidential Transition Committee of the Kim Dae Jung administration were about the info-communication industry: (1) construction of a broadband info-communication network (the basic social overhead capital required for the transition to the knowledge and information society), the early establishment of a one-computer-per-person culture, standardization of diverse info-communication devices and software, and early activation of the e-commerce industry through the amendment of the related laws and regulations, (2) significant expansion of the investment in the training and education of info-communication professionals, and embarking on the development of core strategic info-communication technologies, including the next-generation mobile communication technologies, digital broadcasting technologies, and multimedia technologies (towards this end, some 440,000 info-communication technology professionals should have been trained by 2002 by investing KRW 650 billion, and the development of info-communication technologies had to be supported with the Informatization Promotion Fund amounting to KRW 6.1 trillion); and (3) granting permission to operate multi-channel satellite broadcasting, and starting digital TV broadcasting, through the early legislation of a consolidated broadcasting act.

Implementation System

The legal and institutional foundation of the informatization promotion system of the administration was specified in the Basic Act on Informatization Promotion. As shown in Figure 18, the Informatization Strategic Council and Informatization Promotion Committee were installed as supreme discussion and legislative organizations, respectively, while the Informatization Planning Office in the Ministry of Info-Communication assumed the role of a secretariat, and the National Computer Agency largely assumed the policy implementation and research function. The informatization strategic council started in May 1998, replacing the Expanded Informatization Briefing Sessions that had been in place and had been run mostly for the purpose of reporting to the president. As the informatization strategic council were chaired by the president himself, they were strengthened in terms of the capacity to engage in practical discussions on and coordination of the key issues associated with informatization and the IT policy.

However, the informatization implementation system headed by the Informatization Promotion Committee, which was chaired by the Prime Minister, was not up to the tasks of promoting informatization and advancing the info-communication industry as it required coordinated management by all the government ministries. Such insufficient planning and coordination capacity of the governmental implementation system resulted in territorial disputes over job jurisdiction, waste of resources due to duplicate investments, lack of information sharing, insufficient links and fragmentation among numerous info-communication plans,and less-than-satisfactory organizational preparedness for the impending fusion of the communication and broadcasting sectors.

Having been inaugurated with a mandate to overcome the impending economic crisis and to reform the government and the public sector, the administration was able to push for the knowledge-informatization and IT industry policy with greater momentum and in an integrated and systematic fashion by making the knowledge informatization policy a higher priority. Among the prime proofs of the presidential office's excellent coordination capability are the top 11 electronic-government projects that were pushed for by the presidential Informatization Promotion Committee. G2C, the administration service innovation project for citizen through informatization G2B, the project involving the innovation of e-commerce between the government and businesses and G2G and the electronic-government infrastructure project spanning multiple government ministries are all examples of the informatization projects that would not have succeeded without fluid policy coordination by different government ministries. Delayed for years due to the broken coordination and collaboration system between the related ministries despite the importance of such government-led projects, these projects were all finally opened to the public in November 2002.

The Ministry of Communication, the governing ministry for the informatization policy, was

Figure 6-1. Informatization implementation system

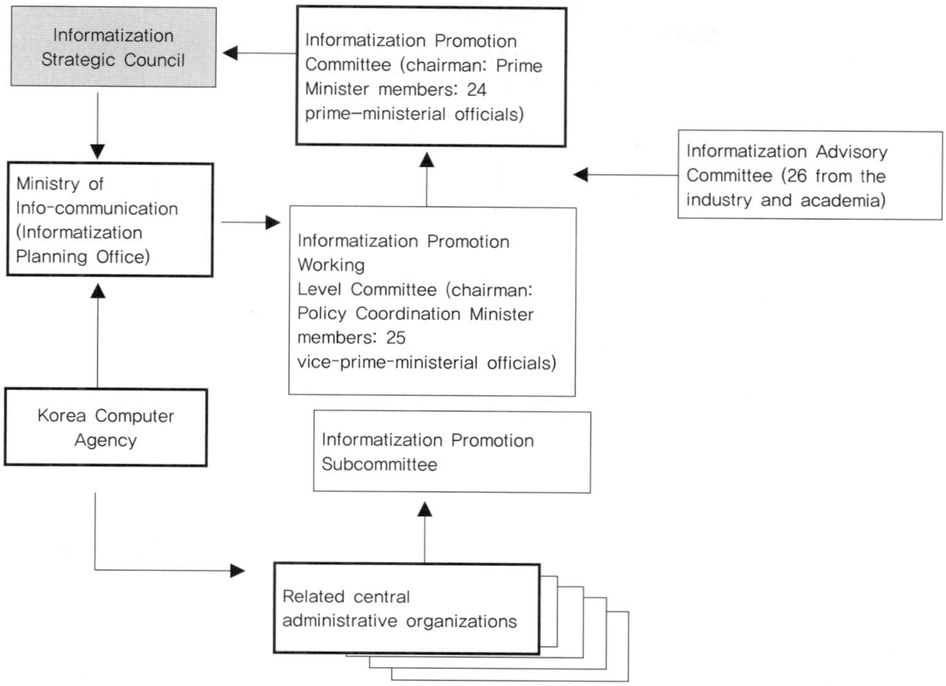

established in the Kim Young Sam administration by consolidating the related functions scattered across the Ministry of Postal Service, Ministry of Commerce, Industry, and Resources, Ministry of Science and Technology, and Bureau of Public Info-communication. The Deliberation Committee on Government Organization Reshuffling of the Kim Dae Jung administration briefly considered abolishing the Ministry of Info-Communication and transferring the businesses in the info-communication industry to the Ministry of Industry and Resources on the premise of "a small but strong government," but the proposal was scrapped based on the committee's conclusion that the abolition of the Ministry of Info-Communication would not be appropriate considering that the administration was striving to overcome the economic crisis by promoting the IT industry and to evolve into an electronic government.

Implementation Process and Contents

Cyber Korea 21

The key structure of the country's national and social informatization policy was completed with the establishment of the Comprehensive Plan to Construct a Broadband Info-Communication Network (March 1994) and with the legislation of the Basic Act on Informatization Promotion (August 1995). The administration developed and expanded the policy even further by unveiling a series of plans, including the "Cyber Korea 21" initiative.

The Kim Dae Jung administration established the Cyber Korea 21 initiative by advancing the contents of the Basic Act on Informatization Promotion (1996~2000), along with the extension of the project period until 2002. With Cyber Korea 21, the administration laid out its vision to raise the share of the knowledge-based industry in the GDP to that of the advanced economies and to make South Korea the 10th knowledge-informatization powerhouse in the world. Towards this end, the plan proposed 159 detailed tasks spanning three key areas: laying the foundation for the country's informatization (63 tasks), general productivity improvement through informatization (58 tasks), and the policy of creating new industries (38 policies). For the informatization initiative, the plan proposed the establishment of an info-communication infrastructure including a broadband info-communication network, raising of the market penetration of the Internet, support for the informatization of the public sector, the establishment of an electronic government, the spreading of e-commerce, the establishment/implementation of a general plan to narrow the information gap (2001~2005), and support for measures to prevent the negative side effects of informatization. In the area of IT industry development as a new growth engine, the plan proposed the training of IT professionals, the development of key future IT technologies (6 key technologies, 2 strategic technologies, and 2 infrastructural technologies), the activation of info-communication venture startups, and the development of the software industry.

To conclude, Cyber Korea 21 was the key IT policy initiative that lived up to the lofty standards expected of a national and social informatization plan encompassing the three key elements required to realize an information society: establishment of an info-communication infrastructure (establishment of an info-communication foundation by establishing IT infrastructure and by informatizing the people); informatization (productivity improvement in the government and private sector through the application of the info-communication technology); and the info-communication industry (provision of the IT hardware and software required for informatization).

Development of venture startups

The Kim Dae Jung administration stressed the importance of growing venture startups as the most effective means to advance the country's industrial structure to a more sophisticated one and to create new jobs. While highlighting the importance of venture startups by naming them the "flowers of industries," The President pushed for the full-scale venture support policy as one of the key policy tasks of the administration (presidential inaugral address, 1998).

Venture startups signify newly incorporated companies that attempt to turn a new technology development idea with a high profitability potential (once it succeeds in the market) into a business. The government drafted and established a host of policies, as shown in Table 15, in an attempt to minimize the management risks associated with venture startups owing to their unique characteristics, such as the novelty of the technology and products, rapid revenue growth, development of a new market, management by founders with an engineering background, and lack of initial capital, thereby activating the creation of new venture startups.

The development of the knowledge-information society is effectively and largely driven by the development of the IT industry, the transition of the government and businesses to knowledge-information-based organizations, and the corresponding increase in the demand of the people for knowledge-information products. The administration aimed to promote the advancement of the IT industry through an IT venture startup support program, including the IT Promotion Fund, and pushed for the informatization of the country by implementing the electronicgovernment project

Table 6-2. Venture startup support system of the Ministry of Info-Communication

<table>
<tr><th>Risk associated with venture startups</th><th colspan="2">Related policy</th><th>Detailed policy</th></tr>
<tr><td>Business risk</td><td colspan="2">Standardization support</td><td>- Activation of standardization fora in the IT industry</td></tr>
<tr><td rowspan="3">Management risk</td><td colspan="2">Venture incubation</td><td>- University IT venture startup support center-software support center-ASIC support center</td></tr>
<tr><td colspan="2">Management support</td><td>- Management support group</td></tr>
<tr><td colspan="2">Export support</td><td>- Overseas IT cooperation center</td></tr>
<tr><td rowspan="3">Financial risk</td><td colspan="2">Indirect support</td><td>- Investment clubs specializing in IT investment-investment firms specializing in IT investment</td></tr>
<tr><td rowspan="2">Direct support</td><td>Capital investment</td><td>- Industrial-technology development project - designation of excellent new technologies-support project-leading foundation technology development projects</td></tr>
<tr><td>Loan provision</td><td>- Industrial-technology development project-designation of excellent new technologies-support project-leading foundation technology development projects</td></tr>
</table>

and adopting an electronic-signature and public certificate system. The administration also pushed for the policies aimed at promoting the informatization of the people and narrowing the information gap among them.

As a part of its policy initiative to alleviate the information inequality and to realize the universal acceptance of the information society, the administration established the "10 Million-People Information Education Plan" in 2000 and embarked on a collaborative information education program by 10 ministries targeted at farmers, fishermen, workers, teachers, students, juveniles and grownups under custody, soldiers, and other local residents. The massive informatization drive for the people greatly contributed to the growth of the number of Internet users, narrowing the information gap among social classes.

Performance and Assessment

Thanks to the proactive informatization policy of the administration, South Korea's Internet penetration rate is currently among the world's highest. The number of Internet users in South Korea, which was 3.1 million in 1998, had jumped to 24.38 million by 2001, 52% of the entire population. The country's broadband Internet penetration rate also rose to 17.16% in 2001, over six-folds higher than the average penetration rate (2.9%) of OECD countries. South Korea embarked on the construction of a broadband Internet network when the country's national informatization index was below that of Japan and Taiwan, but the number of broadband subscribers had jumped past the 10 million mark to 14.5 million by 2002, 69% of the entire population. Certainly, such remarkable achievements would not have been attained with the government's efforts alone, but it can be said that the establishment of the physical and institutional infrastructure for the broadband info-communication network, the narrowing of the information gap, and the government support for IT venture startups that were pushed for by the administration provided the necessary preconditions required for the transition of the country to a knowledge-information powerhouse.

Not only the quantitative dissemination of the Internet but also the qualitative aspect of Internet usage have greatly improved in Korea. The example of such growth can be found from online financial transactions. The number of registered Internet banking accounts soared from 120,000 in 1999 to 11.31 million in 2001. The rapid growth of online financial transactions cannot be explained by the growth of Internet usage penetration alone. Specifically, such unprecedented activation of online financial transactions is largely attributable to the opening of the era of electronic document certification, which was realized thanks to the government's push for the spread of electronic commerce, including the legislation by the end of 1998 of the Basic Act on Electronic Transactions and the Electronic Signature Act.

Table 6-3. Growth of Internet users and online financial transactions

Criteria	1998	1999	2000	2001
Number of Internet users (× 10,000 people)	310	1,086	1,904	2,438
Number of Internet banking registrants (× 10,000 people)	-	12	409	1,131
Share of online stock trading (%)	2.9	25.4	55.9	69.3

The country's IT industry recorded remarkable growth as well during the incumbency of President Kim Dae Jung. The total output of the South Korean IT industry jumped more than twofold, from KRW 75.5 trillion in 1997 to KRW 170 trillion in 2002. The growth of the IT industry is largely attributable to the government's R&D investments: the Ministry of Info-Communication invested a combined total of KRW 5.0264 trillion for the five-year period from 1998 to 2002 in the form of core IT development, training of IT professionals, and standardization and establishment of an R&D foundation. The R&D investment in the IT industry by the private sector expanded 18% annually on average for the aforementioned five-year period, from KRW 3.98 trillion in 1998 to KRW 8.98 trillion in 2002 (Ministry of Info-Communication, 2003). In particular, the small and medium-sized IT and venture startups recorded remarkable growth during the presidency of Kim Dae Jung: the total number of small and medium-sized IT and venture startups jumped more than twofold within a five-year period, from 10,055 in 1998 to 21,812 in 2002, while the share of the IT industry in the country's GDP nearly doubled, from 9.3% in 1998 to 14.9% in 2002.

4. Introduction of the national basic living security system

Background

Along with the -6.7% growth rates of the South Korean economy in 1998, the unemployment rates spiked as well to 7.1% in the same year, with the total number of jobless people reaching 1.536 million ("Economically Active Population" by the National Statistical Office). If the different types of unemployed people, including frustrated jobless people,[3] the unpaid family workers, and the underemployed people, who were not classified as unemployed in the unemployment survey had been counted in the statistics, it can be about 4 million people who were struggling with their living amid the economic crisis. Of these, the marginalized classes naturally suffered the most. With the negligible drop in the income level of the top upper class and the contrastingly significant drop in the income level of the lowest class, the polarization trends among the classes grew increasingly pronounced.[4] The trend of family dissolution grew among the marginalized classes as the parents or children belonging to such classes were entrusted to the public facilities or to their relatives,[5] or many of them got divorced due to their extreme economic hardships. As a result, the number of children skipping meals and the number of homeless people rapidly increased.[6] The massive unemployment triggered by the foreign currency crisis reminded the South Korean society that anyone could lose his/her job and become poor, spreading the idea that the responsibility of guaranteeing basic living security does not fall on the shoulders of individual people but on the state.

As the policy lines of the Kim Dae Jung administration, which focused on strengthening the state's competency through business restructuring and on increasing the flexibility of the labor

3) This term refers to those people who would otherwise continue their job search efforts but remain in an economically inactive status as they gave up their job search due to the prospect of non-availability of jobs any time soon as the overall economy is contracting significantly. Told again, it means those workers that were classified as economically inactive people because they gave up their job search after prolonged efforts to get re-employed, due to the difficulty of landing a job. Therefore, the "frustrated jobless people" are those who gave up looking for a job. The term refers to those individuals among the economically inactive people (all people aged over 15 who are neither employed nor unemployed, including homemakers, students, aged people, and physically and mentally handicapped people) who have the will to get employed and the capability to work but did not engage in a job search during the survey period for one or more of the following three reasons but engaged in a job search at least once in the last year: (1) it seemed that there was no decent job available; (2) could not find any job even though he or she sought one before the week when the survey was conducted; and (3) he or she is not qualified to work.

4) The Gini's coefficient for the household income of an urban working family did not show any meaningful change in the trends during the early and mid-1990s as it remained within the range of 0.25 - 0.27 but shot up to 0.293 in 1998 and to 0.298 in 1999, in the wake of the foreign currency crisis.

5) According to a news report by *Yonhap News*, the number of total national divorces increased by 16.9%, from 79,700 to 93,200, as recorded in the "1997 Dynamic Statistics of Population." In particular, the share of divorced couples who cited economic issues as their reason for separation rose by 0.6%, from 3.6% of the total divorces in the previous year to 4.2%. According to the National Statistics Office, "Even though some 80% of all divorced couples cited marital discord as the reason for their divorce, majority of them divorced due to economic issues, and the economic crisis that started in earnest in the last year is accelerating the dissolution of families."

6) Some 6,000 unemployed homeless people were estimated to have been added to the nationwide pool by the end of 1998. It was estimated that there were still about 5,800 homeless people in 1999 despite the overall economic recovery.

market, were met with worsening unemployment rates and resulted in the disillusionment of its key supporters, the administration sought to turn the direction of its government administration by beginning to stress the importance of the living conditions of ordinary people, and of welfare support. Specifically, the administration focused on realizing its goals of "healthy people" and "a society where people live together in harmony" by harmonizing the principles of market economy and social equity. The administration guaranteed basic living security for the low-income class, bolstered the welfare payment system but focused on building a welfare system that would encourage the beneficiaries to work harder so as not to be trapped in the state of poverty, streamlined the social safety nets by making the social security system more sound, and implemented a public health system in which the health of all the people would be taken care of in each phase of their life cycle.

The number of jobless people passed the 1.5 million mark in 1999, and despite the host of measures that the government took to address the country's unemployment woes, the government failed to guarantee basic living security for the low-income and jobless people. The budget that was set aside for the relief measures for the unemployed people ballooned to KRW 5.3263 trillion in 1998, excluding other indirect unemployment measures. Of this, the budget set aside for public service employment was KRW 1.0444 trillion, about one-fifth of the entire budget allocated for unemployment countermeasures. However, despite the increase in the associated budgets and the much-expanded social safety nets to cover those areas that had not been covered by the unemployment insurance, the public appraisal of the government's unemployment countermeasures was not positive, suggesting that there were still plenty of blind spots, where the social safety nets were not working as intended. Specifically, some urgent measures needed to be taken for the low-income and jobless people among the marginalized classes who were non-voluntarily unemployed but were excluded from the pool of beneficiaries of the unemployment allowances or were not covered by the basic living security system.

Amidst such political and economic environment, the need for an institutional guarantee of basic living security for all the people emerged as one of the most important issues, and the Solidarity for Basic Living Security, which included labor activists, jumped on the issue. Sensing the growing pressure, the Ministry of Labor started reviewing the possible introduction of the Basic Living Security Act as part of its efforts to respond to the request of activist groups, by summoning working-level department heads from the related government ministries to the office of the Deputy Director General for Social Welfare in the ministry.

Implementation System

The Kim Dae Jung administration installed and operated the Preparatory Group for Promoting the Basic Living Security of the People (henceforth, "the Group)" in an attempt to prepare the detailed implementation measures of the Basic Living Security Act. Launched on October 1, 1999, the Group had 15 members, including the group head, the deputy head, 6 representatives of the different sectors of the society, 3 experts, and 4 government officials from the related ministries. The Deputy Director General for Basic Living Security in the Ministry of Health and Welfare was assigned as an assistant administrator to advise the head of the Group and to support the administration. The head of the Group was allowed to form a separate advisory committee composed of 3 experts if needed for the drafting of the detailed implementation measures of the Basic Living Security Act. The members of the advisory committee were required to provide advice on specific issues by participating in the Group meetings or in the advisory committee meetings. In addition, a support team was installed under the control of the Group to provide support for the research on the implementation of the key tasks, to prepare for the discussion topics, and to implement the voting results. The support team was led by the head of the Living Security Department in the Ministry of Health and Welfare, and was staffed with government officials and social welfare specialists.

A social welfare program will not be feasible if the burden that it puts on the society is beyond the society's financial limits, even if it satisfies the social needs. Therefore, the first thing that has to be considered with regard to a social welfare program would be the size of the fiscal spending. As the preparation of the draft bill of the Basic Living Security Act would take at least one year, the poverty rate in 2001 was projected to be 6.3% assuming that the act is enforced in 2001, with the number of people living below the poverty line estimated to be some 3 million. Since not all of the estimated 3 million people living below the poverty line would eventually become beneficiaries of the Basic Living Security Act, the number was projected to drop to 2.04 million owing to the regulations on the duty to support and to the principle of security provision dependent on the application and on other circumstances. As a result, the total budget for the welfare program was projected to go up to KRW 3.6321 trillion (calculated based on the KRW 56,000 average household income of the basic living security provision targets), with the realistic estimate being KRW 2.7336 trillion (based on the assumed KRW 100,000 average household income of the basic living security provision targets). In addition, the total budgetary requirement in accordance with the legislation of the Basic Living Security Act was projected to be KRW 1.3412 trillion at maximum while the realistic estimate was KRW 444.5 billion.

Some feared that the Basic Living Security Act would cause the number of beneficiaries to explode, along with the ballooning amount of associated spending, as the regulations ruled out demographic factors as requirements to receive benefits. In fact, the budget jumped by 26.2% year-on-year in 2000, the first year of implementation of the Basic Living Security Act, followed by a 39% increase year-on-year in 2001. The budget for the 2002 fiscal year increased by only 4.3% year-on-year, however, suggesting that the rapid rise of the related spending in the early phase of the implementation was just a fleeting phenomenon caused by the change of the implementing institution, with no prospect of its continuation for an extended period.

The two key drivers of the ballooning of the basic living security budget were the living and medical allowances, whose shares in the absolute amount were significant and whose growth speeds were fast as well. Of the two, the living allowances increased by 87.1% (KRW 448.4 billion KRW 838.8 billion) year-on-year in 1999 owing to the temporary implementation of the living security system even before the introduction of the system, and soared by KRW 200 billion in 2000 and 2001, respectively, after the Basic Living Security Act was enforced, thereby increasing the related budget. The upward trend in the budgetary spending, however, was not projected to continue but was expected to drop in the future, thereby making no significant contribution to the budget expansion. As for the medical allowances, they increased by more than 48.3% year-on-year in 1999 and by 54.0% year-on-year in 2001, becoming the leading contributor to the expansion of the basic living security budget in both years. Also, in 2001, the medical allowances surpassed the living allowances in terms of the absolute amount of spending.

Implementation Process and Contents

The social welfare reform was based on the following three principles: (1) welfare guaranteeing the basic living security of the people; (2) welfare realized through popular participation in the productive process; and (3) welfare supporting the marginalized classes. These three principles can be summed up with the slogan "productive welfare." The reform was aimed at realizing income redistribution by the state for the socially weak people who were left behind in the fair market competition and at increasing the social investment so as to provide the marginalized classes equipped with work capability opportunities for rehabilitation, human development, and work engagement. Such concept is very similar to the "workfare" of the U.S., and it also jibes well with the philosophy of Anthony Giddens, who argued for a proactive welfare society and a social investment state.

The administration selected the following nine key tasks for its social welfare reform, under the policy slogan "establishment of a productive welfare foundation": (1) expansion of the social safety nets; (2) strengthening of the welfare policy targeted at the marginalized classes, including the aged and handicapped; (3) pushing for the reform of the tax system and for a tax policy to realize welfare; (4) pushing for the reform of the healthcare system; (5) promoting tripartite cooperation and improvement of basic labor rights; (6) pushing for proactive unemployment countermeasures; (7) establishing a system for protecting the rights of workers; (8) improvement of the living environment; and (9) expansion of the social overhead capital. Among these, the Basic Living Security Act, the commencement of the national pension system, and the expansion of the coverage of the unemployment insurance and the industrial accident insurance further developed the idea that welfare is not the act of dispensing benefits to the people but is the constitutional right of the people to receive welfare benefits from the state, specifically the basic right of all the people to receive the welfare services required to enjoy a life befitting a human being, by expanding the coverage of the social safety nets.

The legislation of the aforementioned act became an irreversible reality when President Kim Dae Jung announced in Ulsan on June 21, 1999 that he would enact the "Basic Living Security Act." The presidential announcement was followed by an emergency working-level meeting on June 22, where a host of issues, including the streamlining of the related laws, interviews with related lawmakers, and opening of public hearings, were decided. Moreover, in the emergency policy committee meeting held on June 23, the committee members agreed to prepare for the streamlining of the related laws and regulations within a range that would not deviate significantly from the draft bill passed through voting by the deliberation subcommittee, so that the bill would be approved first in the provisional session of the National Assembly in July.

A series of preparatory works for the amendment of the laws were done after the emergency policy committee meeting, including the opening of public hearings on the Basic Living Security Act (June 24) the streamlining of the related laws by the policy committee members (June 27) interviews with the related lawmakers, including Lee Bu Young, the floor leader of the Grand National Party, representative Kim Hong Shin, and Jeong Se Kyun, chairman of the third Policy Coordination Committee of the National Council (June 28) "Rally to Urge the Construction of

Social Safety Nets and the Legislation of the Basic Living Security Act" organized by the Solidary for Basic Living Security and meetings with the Senior Secretary to the President for Civil Affairs and the Senior Secretary to the President for Welfare and Labor (July 5). On July 6, a total of 131 representatives, including Kim Hong Shin of the Grand National Party, tabled the bill for the Basic Living Security Act, which was followed by the convening of the National Assembly Standing Committee for Health and Welfare, the submission of the bill for the Basic Living Security Act, the forwarding of the bill to the Legislation and Judiciary Subcommittee (July 12), the final approval of the bill through voting in the 206th provisional session of the National Assembly (August 12), and the legislation of the act on September 7, 1999.

The most prominent aspect of the legislation process of the Basic Living Security Act was the role played by the activist groups. Beginning with the "Movement to Secure a National Minimum Welfare Level" in September 1994, diverse activist groups participated in the legislation campaign, including the filing of a joint petition to legislate the Basic Living Security Act on July 23, 1998 by 19 labor and citizens movement groups, including the Korean Confederation of Trade Unions, the Citizens' Coalition for Economic Justice, the People's Solidarity for Participatory Democracy, the Korean Confederation of Medical Insurance Trade Unions, and the Korean Women's Association United. In addition, the Korean Confederation of Trade Unions and People's Solidarity for Participatory Democracy announced a joint statement on November 11, 1998 in which they demanded the "immediate legislation of the Basic Living Security Act," citing it as "a task with utmost importance in the high-unemployment society." On November 26 of the same year, activists led by 18 groups participating in the "One Year after the Financial Crisis: Citizens Action for Reform" announced the "Declaration of the Right for National Welfare," in which they demanded the legislation of the Basic Living Security Act. As a consensus started to form across the society on the need for the legislation, scores of religious groups and people representing social welfare organizations joined the cause, contributing to the efforts to push for the legislation of the act by gearing up the publicity to promote the issue.

On July 5, 1999, scores of activist groups, including the Association for a Healthy Society, the Headquarters of the National Movement for Eradicating Excessive Consumption, Lawyers for a Democratic Society, the Council for Citizens' Solidarity, the Federation of Korean Trade Unions, and the Korea Association of Social Welfare Workers, formed the Solidarity Council for Promoting the Legislation of the Basic Living Security Act. The act was followed by the announcement of a joint statement in a rally to urge the legislation of the act, and the delivery of the statement to the presidents of the ruling and opposition parties as well as to the chairman of the National Assembly.

The following are the implications of the Basic Living Security Act. First, the state began to guarantee a living standard higher than the minimum cost of living for all low-income people living below the poverty line, regardless of their ability to work. Specifically, the move signifies a resolution of absolute poverty by the state in accordance with the changing perception of poverty, which is based on the premise that "all individuals as well as the society should take responsibility for poverty." The Basic Living Security Act specified that all households with incomes lower than the minimum cost of living should be paid living allowances regardless of their ability to work or age, eliminating the existing classification of resident or self-reliant security beneficiaries. At the same time, the act aimed to stabilize the residence of low-income people and strengthen the support system for the beneficiaries in need of urgent living support through the creation of emergency allowances. The administration also established a self-reliant rehabilitation plan per household, and self-reliant rehabilitation support services.

Second, by providing systematic rehabilitation support services to help the people living in poverty escape from poverty, the administration intended to realize productive welfare through the provision of proactive support rather than simply offering them living allowances. For those with the ability to work, the administration established an institutional apparatus that prevents the slumping of the work drive by installing an incentive system that would encourage such people to work, while also making the calculation criteria of recognized income more realistic and rational by deducting part of the income earned from the person's work.

As poverty was redefined as a social dilemma that emerges along with capitalistic development and industrialization, and as the people's perception of poverty changed, with the people embracing the idea that the state should tackle poverty through social and official policies, the public assistance represented by the Basic Living Security Act had great significance as the last safety net for the people.

Performance and Assessment

After the introduction of the basic living security system, the number of beneficiaries of basic living security increased by about 10%, from 1.41 million in 1997 to 1.55 million in 2002. The number of living allowances, however, the core part of the basic living security, jumped 4.1-fold, from 370,000 in 1997 to 1.55 million in 2002, suggesting that some 1.2 million people in the low-income classes were able to enjoy the practical protection provided by the social safety nets thanks to the implementation of the basic living security system. The basic living security system greatly raised the level and expanded the contents of the allowances, along with the expansion of the beneficiaries. The amounts of individual allowances were to be determined in accordance with the age, household size, residential area, and other living conditions of each beneficiary, but the amount was supposed to be higher than the minimum cost of living by counting in the recognized income of the beneficiaries. As a result, the living and residence allowances paid in cash to the beneficiaries jumped from KRW 330,000 in 1997 to KRW 750,000 in 2000 and increased about 2.6-fold to KRW 870,000 in 2002.

The Basic Living Security Act was a policy aimed at establishing institutional social welfare safety nets that were markedly different from those established by the past public assistance policy. The number of beneficiaries of the living allowances jumped from 370,000 in 1997 to 1.51 million in 2000, in the wake of the implementation of the act, and the introduction and implementation of the conditional living allowances and the labor income deduction system, which were designed to boost the beneficiaries' work drive, were intended to strengthen the support for self-reliant rehabilitation, and to create jobs. Therefore, the enforcement of the act signifies that the country's social welfare policy moved from the residual welfare concept in the past to the institutional public assistance concept.

5. Hosting of the World Cup football games

Background

The successful hosting of the 1986 Seoul Asian Games and the 1988 Seoul Olympic Games helped the country raise the public awareness of and trust in its national competence. The hosting of the 2002 Korea - Japan World Cup (henceforth, "World Cup") can be attributed to not only the aforementioned social factor but also more to the changes in the political and economic situation cited below. First, the country needed to publicize to the world the colorful changes that the South Korean society had gone through in the 1980s, as well as the fresh new capability that the country had attained as a mature democracy. Specifically, the country was then required to change the governance style of its national administration, in which the policy objectives were no longer accomplished by the state leadership alone but through the national competence and spontaneity of the people.

Second, the path dependence of hosting international sports games could contribute to the realization of the external expression of the social atmosphere. The hosting of the 1988 Seoul Summer Olympic Games was one of the critical turning points in the country's modern history, making South Korea known to the world as a newly emerging and dynamic country. Sure enough, the successful hosting of the symbolic Olympic Games, which gathered athletes hailing from the East and West, dramatically changed the international appraisal of the national competence of South Korea. Such internal and external assessments of the country influenced the transformational period in the country's democratic social order, thereby fostering a favorable environment for the hosting of another international sports event.

Third, the successful bid for the hosting of the World Cup, and the successful hosting thereof, can be seen as extensions of the country's pan-global diplomatic horizon, which is best symbolized by "Northern Diplomacy." The normalization of the country's diplomatic relations with the former Communist Bloc countries that had been pushed for beginning in the late 1980s started to bring in diverse palpable results in the wake of the country's successful hosting of the 1988 Seoul Olympic Games. The Northern Policy of the Roh Tae Woo administration demonstrated that South Korea was willing to overcome the ideological limitations imposed on it, and had the corresponding capability and willingness to proactively participate in the shifting world order after the end of the Cold War. Since the World Cup, which is a huge pan-global festival, had a track record for favoring host countries that symbolize such changes throughout history, the changes in South Korea's foreign policy that started to materialize in the late 1980s can be said to have provided the most basic foundation for its hosting of the World Cup.

Lastly, the key political-economic factor in South Korea's successful bid for the hosting of the World Cup, and in its successful hosting thereof, was the implementation of the full-fledged and comprehensive liberalization policy. The establishment of a democratic social order triggered the inevitable creation of the proactive liberalization policy targeted at individuals, businesses, and diverse social organizations. In other words, unlike in the past, individuals, businesses, and social organizations were now equipped with an institutional capability to establish diverse goals in accordance with their own purposes and needs, as well as to mobilize the resources required to accomplish the set goals. Specifically, the operational and management capability, networking, and voluntary participation of the citizens are key to the success of international events such as the World Cup that are run by private organizations, and such capabilities can be formed only with the guarantee of institutional liberalization. Therefore, the push for guaranteeing proactive liberalization can be assessed to have played the key role in the development of the country's capability for successfully hosting the World Cup.

Implementation System

The World Cup is run on an operation structure whereby FIFA oversees the preparations for and management of the games as the game organizer while the organizing committee in the host country takes charge of the practical preparations for and management of the games as a representative of FIFA. In South Korea, the 2002 World Cup Preparation Planning Group was launched on June 25, 1996, under government leadership, and the Planning Group founded the Korea Organizing Committee for the 2002 FIFA World Cup Korea/Japan (KOWOC) on December 30 of the same year, in accordance with Article 32 of the Civil Law. Externally, the Organizing Committee was entrusted with the role of establishing a cooperative relationship with FIFA and with the national football association and federation of the key continents, and to form a close cooperative network with the country's co-hosting partner, specifically with the Japan Football Association and the Japan World Cup Organizing Committee. Internally, the Organizing Committee was to play the key role in the joint management of the games with the 10 host cities (Seoul, Incheon, Suwon, Daejeon, Jeonju, Daegu, Gwangju, Ulsan, Busan, and Jeju) and to promote the active participation of diverse cooperative institutions and organizations as well as the citizens in the games preparation. In other words, the Organizing Committee was organized to work as the network hub of the giant project that was the hosting of the World Cup.

The National Assembly institutionalized the legal status of the Organizing Committee by enacting the 2002 World Cup Support Act as Law No. 5278. Legislated on January 3, 1997, the act stipulated the following provisions as the most pertinent institutional foundations for the successful management of the World Cup:

- the Organizing Committee may receive support and funds from the central government or from the regional self-governing bodies
- the Organizing Committee may engage in profit-making businesses, including sports events or the sale of commemorative coins
- the Organizing Committee may receive support staff on loan from the administrative institutions or from other incorporated organizations
- the heads of the local governing bodies in the host cities may formulate and implement a plan for the installation of games-related facilities; and
- the games-related facilities approved in accordance with the Town Planning and Zoning Act shall be considered to have already been approved by other laws, including the Land Erosion Prevention Act.

Lee Dong Chan, the president of Korea Employers' Federation, was appointed as the first president of the Organizing Committee. The key projects of the Organizing Committee included the following: (1) establishment and implementation of short- and long-term comprehensive plans for the hosting of the World Cup games; (2) management of the preparatory works for the World Cup games, and lining up and execution of the necessary funds; (3) coordination with FIFA, the individual football federations by continent, the individual national football associations, the Japan World Cup Organizing Committee, and the Korea Football Association; (4) business cooperation with the government, the host cities, and other related institutions; (5) establishment of support plans for the games-related facilities (including stadiums), accommodations, and other auxiliary facilities, as well as implementation of joint projects with organizations related with the World Cup; and (6) other projects that may be required to accomplish the goals of the Organizing Committee.

In accordance with the 2002 World Cup Support Act and the enforcement decree and enforcement regulations of the act, the World Cup support system of the ROK government was divided into the three components shown below.

i) Ministerial meeting of the related ministries: As an institution for deliberating on and coordinating with regard to the key policy issues, the meeting was headed by the Prime Minister and was participated in by 10 ministers from related ministries. Also participated in by 27 members, including the heads of the local governing bodies in the 10 host cities, the president of the National Intelligence Service, the head of the Office for Government Policy Coordination, the Senior Secretary to the President for Education and Culture, the president of the Organizing Committee, the head of the Government Information Agency, the president of the Busan Asian Games Organizing Committee, and the chairman of the Central Council for Cultural Citizens Movement, the meeting represented the pan-national support system, true to its name.

ii) Vice-ministerial meeting of the related ministries: An institution installed to facilitate the coordination on the advanced review of the agenda and government support items among the related ministries. It was headed by the head of the Office for Government Policy Coordination and was participated in by the vice ministers of the Ministry of Finance and Economy, the Ministry of Foreign Affairs and Trade, the Ministry of Environment, the Ministry of Construction and Transportation, the Ministry of Planning and Budget, and the Government Information Agency. The other participants included the Secretary to the President for Culture and Tourism, the coordinating officer of the Office of Government Policy Coordination as appointed by the Prime Minister, the officer (vice-ministerial) handling the World Cup businesses from the National Intelligence Service, the secretary general of the Organizing Committee, and the secretary general of the Central Council for Cultural Citizens Movement.

iii) Working-level council: Established to facilitate working-level discussions and cooperation among the related ministries, the council was chaired by the Vice Minister of Culture and Tourism (later replaced by the head of the Office of Government Policy Coordination) and was composed of grade 1 officials dispatched from 13 ministries, the Presidential Secretariat, the Office of Government Policy Coordination, the heads of the related bureaus and offices in the National Intelligence Agency, the secretary generals of the 2002 World Cup Organizing Committee and the Busan Asian Games Organizing Committee, and the vice heads of the local governing bodies in the 10 host cities.

The host cities also formed their respective promotion groups to prepare for the games internally. The roles of the host cities were mainly cooperation with and provision of support to the Organizing Committee as well as fostering an environment conducive to the successful holding of the games, including the preparation and construction of a stadium infrastructural facility, the streamlining of the urban environment, and publicity for and preparation of cultural events. Among these, the construction of stadiums was implemented by forming a dedicated organization from the planning stage. Additionally, a dedicated organization was formed from the games preparation stage to cooperate with and to provide support to the Organizing Committee and to publicize and to prepare cultural events.

The financing scheme of the 2002 World Cup was planned and managed by the Organizing Committee based on the independent profit system borrowed from the management practices of private businesses. The initial budget amounting to some KRW 400 billion was financed primarily with the funds provided by FIFA, the proceeds from the ticket sales, the sponsorship money paid for by the official suppliers, the value-in-kind supplied by the FIFA official sponsors, and the computer solution provided by FIFA.

The Organizing Committee signed agreements with FIFA and the 10 host cities with regard to the principles of financial allotment, specifying that the expenses required for the games preparation and management shall be borne by the Organizing Committee while the infrastructural facilities, such as the stadium, the surrounding environment, and the traffic system, shall be borne by the host country and the host cities. The World Cup football stadiums were built in a total of 10 host cities with the investment fund, which consisted of KRW 271.4 billion from the state coffers, KRW 1,202.5 billon from local governments, KRW 187.9 billion from the subsidies provided by the wide-area local governing bodies, and KRW 78.2 billion from private capital.

To ensure the effective management of the fund, the Organizing Committee established the World Cup Fund. Also, FIFA secured the necessary money by tapping diverse income sources, such as the sales of TV broadcasting rights, official sponsorship projects, and the sales of the games license, with a portion of the proceeds provided to the host country as a grant. The total spending from the fund of the Organizing Committee amounted to KRW 311.8 billion as of the end of September 2002, and eventually rose to a total of KRW 351.8 billion by the end of the games. Based on the total profit (KRW 478 billion) earned by the fund, the 2002 Korea-Japan FIFA World Cup succeeded in recording a KRW 126.2 billion surplus, well over the KRW 66 billion surplus recorded in the 1994 U.S. World Cup and the KRW 88 billion surplus recorded in the 1998 France World Cup.

Implementation Process and Contents

The most important driver of the increased likelihood of South Korea's hosting the World Cup was the mention by FIFA of the potential holding of the World Cup in Asia. Following the hint given by Joao Havelange about the potential holding of the World Cup in Asia in 1986, Harry Cavan, the senior vice president of FIFA at that time, hinted about the possible hosting of the World Cup by South Korea during his visit to Seoul, thereby helping promote the formation of favorable opinions among the South Koreans on the country's hosting of the games. This was followed by Japan's expression of its desire to host the World Cup in December 1989.

Such series of events in the late 1980s awakened the South Korean sports field, which was resting on its laurels after the successful hosting of the 1988 Seoul Olympic Games, from complacency. Heightened energy started to spread to the rest of the society after the potential participation in the bid was mentioned in the business report session of the Korea Sports Promotion Foundation on August 8, 1989. Kim Woo Joong, president of the Korea Football Association, sent an official letter containing the country's intent to participate in the bid for hosting the 2002 World Cup to FIFA on June 1, 1990, to which FIFA reciprocated by sending a reply confirming its receipt of the letter. With the ruling party candidate Kim Young Sam, who pledged to realize the country's dream of hosting the World Cup, emerging victorious in the presidential elections, the speed of the bid preparation for the 2002 World Cup accelerated. On December 13, 1993, Jeong Mong Joon, then the president of the Korea Football Association, made public his intent to push for the country's hosting of the 2002 World Cup, thereby officially kick-starting the race for the country to host the 2002 World Cup.

The activities for hosting the World Cup became official with the formation of the World Cup Bid Committee. The 2002 World Cup Football Games Bid Committee Foundation, which was launched on March 15, 1994, was chaired by Lee Hong Gu, the former prime minister, and intended to accomplish the following objectives: (1) discussion and coordination on the various issues related to the successful bid for hosting the 2002 World Cup, and establishment of the necessary measures; (2) bargaining with the FIFA Executive Committee and FIFA member states; (3) fostering of an environment conducive for the joint hosting of the games by the two Koreas; (4) lining up of the funds required for the bid and the hosting of the games; (5) establishing liaison and cooperation with the government and other governing authorities; and (6) implementation of other projects that are necessary to meet the goal of successfully bidding for hosting the 2002 World Cup.

The full-fledged bid activity was led by the Bid Committee and received working-level support from the Korea Football Association, but the efficiency of the bid activity was maximized with the multi-faceted support of the government. Specifically, despite the fact that South Korea started its bid campaign some 4 years behind Japan, the "Resolution to Support the Hosting of the 2002 World Cup," which was adopted by the National Assembly in its 170th regular session, and the support that tapped the government resources played the critical role in catching up with Japan in terms of the overall competitiveness of the bid activity.

The competition between South Korea and Japan to bid for the hosting of the 2002 World Cup only grew fiercer over time. Japan was trying to solidify its superiority in the race by stressing its early bid activity, some 4 years ahead of the competing candidates, and by demonstrating its economic leadership in the international community. On the other hand, South Korea relied on the personal reputation of Jeong Mong Joon, who was elected as vice chairman of FIFA in 1994, while stressing the country's leadership in sports as the Asian football powerhouse.

On September 29, 1995, well before the FIFA Executive Committee meeting in May 1996 to decide the host country, the South Korean Bid Committee submitted its application to FIFA, which was followed by onsite inspections conducted from October to November 1995. After surveying the respective candidate sites and the local atmosphere in both countries, the inspection team concluded that both South Korea and Japan were qualified to host the 2002 World Games. The fierce race to host the games intensified to unprecedented levels, making the wary FIFA Executive Committee members conclude that the heated race would go against FIFA's founding spirit of contributing to world peace. The argument about the potential co-hosting of the World Cup, which would not make either of the two contenders a loser, began to earn growing support among the members of the FIFA Executive Committee. Finally, on May 30, 1996, FIFA asked South Korea and Japan if they were willing to co-host the World Cup. Both South Korea and Japan responded with near-identical answers, saying, "We want to host the games on our own, but if FIFA votes in favor of the co-hosting of the games, we will duly accept the decision." The next day, the FIFA Executive Committee approved the co-hosting of the World Cup in its Zurich headquarters. With both candidates accepting the decision, South Korea and Japan set sail on uncharted waters: the co-hosting of the World Cup.

Performance and Assessment

The direct and most palpable achievements of the 2002 Korea - Japan World Cup were in the areas of games management and safety and spectator participation and exchanges. The World Cup Organizing Committee and the government jointly established a system for fluid games management spanning the stadium facility, games operation, transportation, accommodations, food, translation support services, and volunteers, in an effort to ensure the maximum convenience of the athletes, the journalists covering the games, the tagged officials, the spectators, and the tourists.

The most striking thing that was seen in all the 2002 Korea - Japan World Cup games was the astonishing level of unity of the South Koreans at the national level, which was evidently more pronounced than that in the country's co-hosting partner, Japan. Whereas Japan focused on the self-reliant and autonomous management of the games by the host cities, South Korea succeeded in accomplishing national unity and harmony because the government, the Organizing Committee, and the private sector were united in mobilizing their respective capabilities and energies for the country's successful hosting of the World Cup. Such successful hosting was seen as a much welcome precedent because the South Korean society, long accustomed to the state-driven governing model, finally came up with a new and effective model for accomplishing its policy goals. The 2002 Korea - Japan World Cup is assessed to have created an entirely new success model in global event administration.

Specifically, the South Korean society demonstrated unprecedented public passion and enthusiasm for cheering for the games and for the country's team for a one-month period, in June. The sight of the South Korean national football team crushing the world football powerhouses one by one with its world-class performance and competitive spirit inspired popular enthusiasm and voluntary cheering on the part of the South Koreans, which led to the unprecedented cheering of millions of people on the streets. Such collective experiences can be understood in the context of the recognition of the social dynamics and the newfound national characteristics of a people eagerly contributing to the attainment of their common goals.

Another important effect of the World Cup on the South Korean society was in the economic aspect of the games. According to a study conducted by Korea Development Institute before South Korea's hosting of the games, the direct economic impact of the country's hosting of the World Cup was estimated at KRW 11.4797 trillion in terms of the effect on production inducement, KRW 5.3357 trillion in terms of the creation of added values, and 350,000 new jobs created as a result of the games. The study also identified the indirect effects of the games, including the improvement of the national brand and of the South Korean corporate brands in the global stage, thereby potentially resulting in the promotion of the domestic industries and the expansion of the country's exports.

The projected economic outcome rose to higher levels, however, as the South Korean national football team went on until it succeeded in clinching a spot in the quarterfinals. According to an analysis by Korea Economic Research Institute, the combined economic effect of the country's successful advancement to the quarterfinals amounted to KRW 26 trillion, including increased consumption, KRW 3.7 trillion promotion of the national brand, KRW 7.7 trillion and enhancement of the overall brand image of the South Korean companies, KRW 14.7 trillion. According to the research conducted by Hyundai Economic Research Institute, the additional domestic consumption owing to the South Korean matches during the World Cup was estimated to add up to KRW 6.58 trillion. When considering that US$ 10 billion (KRW 11.8 trillion) needs be spent to improve the brand image of the top 100 South Korean companies by 1%, the total economic effect on the country of its hosting of the World Cup would add up to a whopping KRW 100 trillion considering the improved brand image of the South Korean companies bolstered by the improved national brand image.

Section 3

The Government Reform of the Kim Dae Jung Administration

1. Background and direction of the government reform

The Kim Dae Jung administration was inaugurated amidst a situation unlike previous administrations: a financial crisis and an acute foreign currency crunch. Given the mandate to overcome what the President described as the country's "gravest national crisis since the Korean War," the administration was forced to embark on a full-scale reform to change the existing governing structure and policy administration system.

For the 50 years preceding the Kim Dae Jung administration, the ROK government have led the national development by consistently maintaining and expanding the solid organization and massive workforce. It is undeniable that the powerful government played a critical role in the remarkable economic growth that was achieved, but it is also proven that the same robustness and tenacity of the government triggered an avalanche that eventually escalated into the foreign currency crisis. The IMF pegged its provision of bailout funds on a comprehensive restructuring across the industries based on the premise of free competition and efficiency. By 1998, all the facets of the society had been mired in the massive turmoil created by the restructuring drive under the thick cloud of unprecedentedly high unemployment rates and low growth rates. The public sector, including the government organization, was not exempted from such turmoil. The government was forced to keep pace with the overall efforts of the society to overcome the crisis, even ready to endure substantial negative repercussions from the restructuring by scaling back its organizational size, budget, and workforce. This meant that any public role with no urgent necessity of being implemented by the public sector had to be boldly eliminated to elevate the overall productivity of the administrative services.

The government reform was not limited to the official government organizations but was required across a much larger area, including the semi-public sector. First, the rigidity and inefficiency long entrenched in the organizational and budget structure of the public sector had to be eliminated for the government to become a more nimble and resilient organization capable of responding to the changing situation effortlessly. The widespread demand for change in the government organization was posed based on the social consensus that the economic crisis would not be surmounted without comprehensive reform across the society. Such reform, if realized, would have incorporated the demands of the time, including the activation of the market economy, through the repositioning of the roles of the government and the private sector and the establishment of a mature democracy.

Amid such environment surrounding the administration, the administration pushed for a comprehensive reform drive focused mainly on the four key areas of businesses, finance, the public sector, and labor while billing itself as the "People's Government." Based on the observation that the overall reform of the society would be feasible only after the reform of the public sector is accomplished by proactively incorporating democracy and the market economy, the reform of the public sector usually has to be implemented well ahead of the reform in other areas. Based on this understanding, the People's Government proposed democracy and the market economy as the two key directions that the administration should stick to in reforming the public sector. Democracy, the market economy, and productive welfare were elevated to the level of the three key pillars in the government administration of the People's Government ever since "productive welfare" was added to the objectives in late 1999. The administration strove to solidify such principles and structure of government administration based on the aforementioned three pillars.

The two primary mandates given to the administration were to scale back the role of the government in activating the market and to strengthen the role of the government in guaranteeing welfare and equality. These somewhat conflicting mandates given to the administration signified that the government was required to push for balanced administrative reform to enable the government to adapt to the changed administrative environment and to successfully integrate its opposing realities. What was highlighted as the role of the government in the process of administrative reform was the establishment of order in the market economy, which again signified that the balance between the public and private sectors should be restored. The balance point here was to be identified and nailed down by minimizing the amount of direct regulatory measures and by restricting the government's role in proposing policies and in fair mediation. This principle was stressed particularly in the area of economic activities, with particular focus on the market economy, which guarantees availability of choices and free competition.

The People's Government also aimed to improve the living quality of the people while implementing its administrative reform, where both democracy and welfare were guaranteed. This signified that a rational policy-making and implementation procedure should be established to ensure the people's participation in the administrative process in accordance with the democratization and diversification trend of the society. And, administrative reform guaranteeing the flexible management of the administrative service provision system should be pushed for so that the government could quickly respond to the changes in the administrative environment. This meant that an administrative procedure incorporating the assessment and demands of the consumers of administrative services should be established. Likewise, the administration aimed to downsize the public sector but to expand the private sector, and to introduce the concept of competition to the public sector while also pushing for results-oriented reform. The downsizing of the public sector and the expansion of the private sector were the natural outcomes of the growing distrust in the inefficient bureaucratic organization and incompetent government, which triggered the continuous economic depression and fiscal deficit in the key Western economies beginning in the mid-1980s. The scaling back of the government domain was inevitable to overcome the maladies of the bureaucracy and to restore the people's trust in the government. Towards this end, administrative reform where the private sector would assume a portion of the public service production functions was pushed for.

In addition, the need to strengthen the competitive structure within the public sector to ensure a more flexible and proactive response to the public issues and to enhance the efficiency of the administrative management was raised. The administration aimed to implement results-oriented reform along with the introduction of the "competitive" element, suggesting that it aimed to implement performance-driven reform assessable with some quantitative indices that had been stressed in some of the key advanced economies by the late 1980s. Therefore, the importance of some microscopic tasks, including performance indices, performance assessment methods, and the publication and assessment of the performance information, was stressed.

The People's Government pushed for the comprehensive reform of the public sector in terms of both hardware and software. The hardware reform was largely implemented by the Planning and Budget Committee (reshuffled into the Ministry of Planning and Budget), the Administrative Reform Committee, the Government Innovation Promotion Committee, the Government Function Mediation Committee, the Regulatory Reform Committee, and the Transfer of Function to Local Governments Promotion Committee. On the other hand, the software reform was largely performed by the Central Personnel Committee. Below are the key characteristics of the public reform implementation system of the People's Government, as differentiated from those of the past governments.

First, the public reform implementation system was stabilized as a regular organization of the government ministries for the first time in the history of the Korean government. The public sector reform was led by the administrative reform group, the fiscal reform group, and the public management group in the Government Reform Office of the Ministry of Planning and Budget, which were responsible for the reform of the administration, fiscal budget, and public corporations, respectively. The Ministry of Government Administration and Home Affairs (management of local self-governing bodies), the Office for Government Policy Coordination (regulatory reform and policy assessment), and the Central Personnel Commission (personnel administration of public officials) also participated in the reform process.

Second, whereas the past governments ran only one or two advisory committees for the government reform as in the case of the Government Innovation Promotion Committee of the Kim Young Sam administration, the administration specialized and diversified the advisory committees by reform target, such as the Government Innovation Promotion Committee, the Regulatory Reform Committee, and the Transfer of Functions to Local Governments Promotion Committee.

Third, the participation of the citizen activist groups and private businesses in the public reform process markedly increased. Scores of citizens' groups participated in a variety of reform processes while scores of South Korean and overseas businesses, including management consulting firms, participated in the management consulting on the government functions. As a result, the organizational reshuffling process was conducted transparently and publicly, thereby completing the democratic reform process.

2. Contents of the government reform

Organizational Reshuffling

Multiple rounds of reshuffling of the central government organization were carried out during the incumbency of the People's Government. The first reshuffling of the government organization was mainly targeted at the ministerial organizations in the central government. The organizational reshuffling of the government was finished before the official inauguration of the People's Government. Therefore, the formal appointment routine of the ministers followed the inauguration of the administration. The first reshuffling of the government organization implemented by the Government Organizational Reshuffling Deliberation Committee was modified during its review by the National Assembly. Some argued for the restoration of the changed plan to what was originally intended. Additionally, to mark the 1st anniversary of the inauguration of the new administration, management consulting, with the participation of 19 private professional organizations, on the government organization was performed on the ministries of the central government for a four-month period, from November 1998 to February 1999, in an attempt to improve the problems raised during the process of government administration. The second reshuffling of the government organization was performed in May 1999, based on the results of the management consulting.

The government embarked on the third reshuffling of the government organization in January 2001, in an attempt to strengthen the policy coordination function among the different ministries. The third reshuffling was performed in an attempt to supplement the deficiencies of the policy coordination function in the economy and society, which had been singled out as vulnerable areas during the administration of the government organization, and to strengthen those areas where the demands for reform were expected to increase in the future. The key contents of the third reshuffling were the promotion of the Ministry of Finance and Economy and the Ministry of Education to vice-prime-ministerial grade in an attempt to strengthen their economic policy coordination and human resource development functions, and the revamp and expansion of the Special Committee for Women to the Ministry of Gender Equality in accordance with the growing roles of women.

The restructuring of the local governments was implemented with the objective to change them into efficient, flexible, and productive organizations capable of quickly and effectively responding to the changing environment by adjusting their similar or duplicate functions, reforming their operational system, outsourcing their simple administrative businesses, and implementing a functional change of towns, villages, and districts.

In 1999, the administration intended to enhance the competitiveness and productivity of the government organization with a series of measures, including the legislation of the Act on the Installation and Operation of an Executive Agency in 1999, which would turn the government institutions possessing executive power into executive agencies, thereby giving them autonomy and independence. The executive agency system is an autonomous organization system with the following characteristics: (1) the head-of-government functions, which will be performed more effectively if the principle of competition will be followed while preserving the public nature of those businesses previously executed by the government, shall be carried out through public employment; (2) the employed heads shall be given full autonomy in their personnel, organizational, and budgetary administration; and (3) the executive agencies will all be guaranteed independence while being held accountable for their operation outcomes.

Fiscal Reform

The administration pushed for the innovation of the fund system through two rounds of amendments (1999 and 2001) of the Framework Act on Fund Management. The amendments specified that the funds shall be reviewed by the National Assembly, as was the case with the annual budget review. Also, the improvement of the fund management system was pushed for to ensure the transparency and effectiveness of the fund management through the elimination of those funds that were no longer deemed necessary because their initial goals had been met or the projects they were earmarked for overlapped with other similar projects and through the installation of the Fund Policy Deliberation Committee and Fund Management Assessment Group to strengthen the assessment system.

The government introduced the preliminary feasibility investigation system in 1999 by amending the Enforcement Decree of the Budget and Account Act in an attempt to ensure transparency and fairness in the decision making process on new investment projects. The decree specified that projects shall be implemented in accordance with the following flow: preliminary feasibility investigation → feasibility investigation → design → compensation → commencement of construction, while the associated budget shall be executed by project phase. It was specified as a result of this amendment that a project shall be pushed for only when its economic- and policy-level feasibility had been proven through an intensive review of the following factors before performing the feasibility study and basic design work: benefit-cost analysis, project priority as compared to other projects, appropriate investment window, and economic-and policy-level feasibility.

Reform of Personnel Administration

The Ministry of Government Administration and Home Affairs had limitations in integrating and coordinating the personnel administration businesses of each ministry. Furthermore, since it was performing other complex functions, including administrative activities and local government support activities, the ministry found itself in a more challenging situation to accumulate expertise in personnel administration compared to the period when it was only the Ministry of Government Administration. To enhance the fairness and expertise of the ministry in personnel administration, and to ensure the consistent implementation of the reform of the government's personnel administration, the Central Personnel Committee was established in 1999 as a result of the second organizational reshuffling of the government.

Even before the introduction of the open-position system, the open-specialist-position system was already in place for those positions requiring highly specialized expertise and special techniques. Through such system, qualified people from within or outside the domain of civil service who met certain performance criteria, such as in terms of education, career, or qualifications, were employed. Based on the results of the government management consulting performed from November 1998 to March 1999, the Planning and Budget Committee, the erstwhile Ministry of Planning and Budget, selected and announced a total of 161 positions that may be opened to talents outside the government domain. Also, the Central Personnel Committee was inaugurated and entrusted with the management of the open-type position system after the establishment of the legal ground for the said system through the May 1999 amendment of the National Public Service Law and the National Government Organization Act. The Central Personnel Committee designated a total of 129 positions spanning 38 ministries as open-type positions on November 15, 1999, after a panel discussion participated in by representatives of the academe, media, activist groups, and related officials, based on the results of the management consulting performed by the Planning and Budget.

The reward system for public officials had so far been based on the seniority rule, in which the salary levels are determined in accordance with the work years rather than the job performance or competence. For this reason, the salary levels were determined by salary class, which automatically went up every year, without considering the work performance in determining the salary level. For this reason, the People's Government pushed for the modification of the reward system for public officials to include the following: (1) the granting of performance-based benefits and annual salaries in an attempt to change the salary system from one based on seniority to one based on performance; (2) enhancing the competency and productivity of the public officials by giving them differentiated salaries after assessing their individual capabilities, performance, and contributions; and (3) providing high-quality administrative services to the people.

Electronic Government

The country's IT infrastructure was assessed as by far the best in the world as the previous governments focused on building such infrastructure. The country's IT services for the people, however, failed to reach the expected level. The People's Government pushed for the policy of realizing an electronic government by selecting the top 11 core projects in an attempt to provide optimized public services to the people and businesses — the customers of the People's Government — to ensure their convenience, and to enhance the administrative transparency. The key objectives of the electronic-government projects pushed for by the administration include the following: (1) to realize a government with maximized administrative productivity and transparency (G2G) through the establishment of a safe and reliable electronic-government infrastructure; (2) to provide top-class administrative services to the people (G2C); and (3) to provide an optimal environment for business activities (G2B).

After the administrative network construction project that was pushed for as part of the two phases of the national basic information system project (1987~1996), the country's full-fledged effort to realize the electronic government was implemented by the Informatization Promotion Committee and the Electronic Government Special Committee. Established in 1995 with the legislation of the Basic Act on Promoting Informatization, the Informatization Promotion Committee was participated in by all the ministers, and oversaw the national informatization projects, with its 24 subcommittees carrying out the planning and deliberation functions required for informatization by key area. As for the Electronic Government Special Committee, it was installed in 2001 under the Government Innovation Promotion Committee, a presidential advisory body. The Electronic Government Special Committee selected the 11 key projects that needed early completion in the areas of public service (G2C and G2B) innovation, improvement of administrative productivity (G2G), and establishment of the electronic-government infrastructure, respectively, which were then implemented by each governing ministry.

Regulatory Reform

In April 1998, the People's Government installed the Regulatory Reform Committee, which was directly controlled by the president, by consolidating the multiple regulatory reform promotion institutions scattered across the government. Co-chaired by the prime minister and by a civilian leader, the Regulatory Reform Committee was composed of 12 civilian members as well as 6 members from the government, including the Minister of Finance and Economy, the Minister of Government Administration and Home Affairs, and the Minister of Industry and Resources.

The Regulatory Reform Committee carried out the following functions: (1) researching on and developing the key directions of the regulatory policy and institutions; (2) deliberating on the establishment and strengthening of the regulations; (3) deliberating on the existing regulations; (4) establishing and implementing a comprehensive plan to streamline the regulations; (5) registering and promulgating the regulations; (6) collecting and processing the opinions on the regulatory improvements; and (7) inspecting and assessing the regulatory improvement status of each administrative institution.

Subcommittees were installed in the Regulatory Reform Committee to ensure the effective execution of its tasks. The subcommittees reviewed and coordinated the items to be submitted to the committee before their submission, performed specialized researches and studies, and handled other issues entrusted to them by the committee. Moreover, to push for comprehensive regulatory reforms across the government, each central and local governing body installed its own regulatory reform promotion apparatus and ran it in close collaboration with the Regulatory Reform Committee.

Anti-Corruption Reform

Based on its belief that corruption was one of the main causes of the 1997 foreign currency crisis, the People's Government announced its comprehensive anti-corruption measures after declaring a "War against Corruption" in 1998. In the early stage of the said "war," the Anti-Corruption Special Committee under the direct control of the president implemented the anti-corruption policies. Installed in September 1999 by Presidential Decree No. 16547 as a presidential institution to advise the president in relation to the anti-corruption policy, the committee carried out diverse functions, including the following: (1) declaration of a "War against Corruption"; (2) preparation of comprehensive anti-corruption measures; (3) discussion of anti-corruption issues with international organizations, including the World Bank; and (4) implementation of the OECD Convention on Combating Bribery of Foreign Public Officials. Given its inherent limitations as a presidential advisory institution, however, the committee was able to carry out only limited functions.

Further, with the legislation of the Corruption Prevention Act in 2001, the Corruption

Prevention Committee was installed as a comprehensive anti-corruption policy implementation institution. As a presidential institution, the Corruption Prevention Committee received and processed the reports on corrupt practices, gave advice on the improvement of the related institutions, established and assessed the government's anti-corruption policy, and performed education and publicity functions. The committee, however, had inherent limitations and vulnerability as it did not have the authority to conduct an investigation of corrupt practices.

Reform of Local Administration

The Joint Deliberation Committee on the Transfer of State Businesses to the Local Governments identified and confirmed a total of 1,174 central government's tasks that shall be transferred to the local governing bodies from 1991 to 1997. The transferred businesses, however, were mostly simple unit-level works, and the transfer was realized in the form of the delegation of business, excluding supervisory rights, rather than realized through complete devolution. Further, the functions of the central government that it hoped would be transferred to the local governments, rather than those that the local governments hoped would be transferred to them, were transferred in the end. To resolve this dilemma, the People's Government promulgated the Act on Promoting the Transfer of the Central Administrative Authority to the Local Governments as an institutional apparatus that would ensure the full-scale transfer of the central administrative authority from the central government to the local governments.

3. Performance and assessment of the government reform

For the 50 years preceding the inauguration of the Kim Dae Jung administration, the ROK government led the entire society while consistently expanding the robust organization and massive workforce. Although it is undeniable that the powerful government played a critical role in realizing the country's remarkable economic growth, the very robustness and tenacity of the government also planted the seeds that eventually escalated into the foreign currency crisis. The People's Government was inaugurated amidst a challenging situation that was unlike any faced by the previous administrations. The sloppy oversight on the foreign currency flow led to the shortage of foreign currency reserves, which escalated into the foreign currency crunch. IMF demanded Seoul to embark on a comprehensive restructuring drive on the premise of free competition and efficiency, in return for its provision to Seoul of bailout loans, and the ROK government had no choice but to accept the demand.

By 1998, virtually all the sectors of the society had gotten mired in the turmoil of massive restructuring amidst the suffocating fears created by the unprecedented high unemployment and low growth rates. The public sector, including the government, was not exempted from such turmoil by downsizing the government organization, budget, and workforce, the government was forced to join the society in the efforts to overcome the national crisis despite the potentially substantial negative side effects of such efforts. This meant that the elimination of roles among those performed by the public sector but with decreasing necessity, which could boost the productivity of the administrative services, rose as the most important issue at the time.

The changes in the government administration, specifically the administrative reform, were not limited to the official government organization but occurred in a much larger area, including the semi-public sector. First, the structure, function, and budgetary and operation system of the public sector organization had to be streamlined from the perspective of productivity, while the personnel administration system in the public sector had be rid of the rigidity and inefficiency inherent in it and had to change itself into a flexible organization capable of quickly and effectively responding to the changing situation. The demand for such government changes was based on the widespread consensus that the economic crisis would not be surmounted without a comprehensive reform spanning the entire society. In conclusion, the demand of the time was the activation of the market economy by re-establishing the role of the private sector and solidifying the democratic system.

Chapter 7

The Roh Moo Hyun Administration

Section 7

Inauguration of the Roh Moo Hyun Administration and Foundation of Key Policy Administration

1. Inauguration of the administration and introduction of its organization

The Roh Moo Hyun administration was called "Participatory Government." The moniker was a nod to the critical role that the people played in the birth of the administration through proactive and spontaneous participation, as well as a manifestation that the people were the masters of the state and that the participatory drive of the people was the very foundation of the government administration. In other words, the central pillar of the Roh Moo Myun administration was participatory democracy built on citizen sovereignty, and the administration strove to live up to such lofty cause by aiming to become a "capable and performing government" rather than a "small government."

Politically, the Roh Moo Hyun administration was born from the ashes of the "Three Kims." The governing spirit of the new administration, which ruled out authoritarian leadership but embraced horizontal social consensus, can be understood in the same context. Specifically, the governing spirit was to be realized through the fostering of the political participation of the people (Internet-enabled participatory democracy), the resolution of the regional imbalance (construction of a new administrative capital, opening of the era of regional leadership), and reform of the political institution (eradication of corruption and the past history, confirmation hearing of high-ranking officials, and independence of the prosecutors in terms of investigation).

Economically, "overcoming of the lingering ramifications of the Asian financial crisis" and "economic activation" were the two leading agenda of the administration. Therefore, as the successor of the Kim Dae Jung administration, the administration pushed for the stabilization of the local economy (more stringent regulatory control on corporations, reduction of the unemployment rate, and eradication of the rampant speculative real estate investments) and improvement of the balance of current accounts (activation of export activity, signing of the ROK - U.S. Free Trade Agreement).

The growing importance of welfare support amidst the lingering shock from the Asian financial crisis meant that economic fairness had to be ensured. Therefore, the government administration was implemented along the following policy lines: prohibition of violence (through the investigation of the country's past history and suspicious deaths), abolition of social alienation or discrimination (installation of the Ministry of Gender Equality and the National Human Rights Commission of Korea, legislation of the Juvenile Protection Act, advocacy of balanced regional development, and amendment of the Private School Act).

On the diplomatic front, the North Korean nuclear crisis (2nd North Korean nuclear crisis, Washington's suspension of its provision of heavy oil) was the most significant issue nagging the administration. In the wake of the September 11 terror attack, the room for the peaceful resolution of the North Korean nuclear brinkmanship was rapidly shrinking. However, domestically, the policy line that the Korean crisis should be resolved peacefully through talks (the Age of Peace and Prosperity in Northeast Asia) had been upheld consistently despite the conflicts with the hawkish groups in Washington. In spite of such conflicting views, the Roh Moo Hyun administration was required to maintain a cooperative relationship with Washington, one that places it on equal footing with the U.S. government (Defense Reform 2020, the balancing power in Northeast Asia and the claw-back of the wartime operational command authority). Furthermore, the public acceptance of the U.S. forces in South Korea had been deteriorating due to the killing of middle school girls in 2002 by a U.S. tank.

The historical significance of the Roh Moo Hyun administration was that the administration was born largely bolstered by the popular online participation of the voters. Roh Moo Hyun, as a politician, was able to win the candidacy for president in the ruling party on the strength of the overwhelming support that he enjoyed in the online space, and Roh Moo Hyun, the ruling party presidential candidate, earned the support of the voters through the effective use of the Internet during the presidential elections. The early fall (some 15% behind Lee Hoi Chang, the opposition candidate, in the opinion polls in March 2002) and the unexpected stumbling block (withdrawal of support by Jeong Mong Joon on the eve of the election) that dogged Roh Moo Hyun were canceled out by the massive support that the candidate enjoyed in the Internet, which proved the waning influence of traditional media and the emerging power of digital media in the 16th presidential election. Such development was described as "online democracy" in that cyberspace contributed substantially to the democratic development of politics then by turning itself into a plaza of horizontal exchanges and communications. The enthusiasm for political participation that was manifested in the online space soon developed into a political movement in the offline space with the creation of fan clubs of politicians. Nosamo, MJ Love, and Changsarang were some of the political fan clubs that were active during the campaign. In particular, Nosamo emerged as a powerful political force, with over 80,000 registered members by the time the voting started on election day.

Rather than being a "small government," the Roh Moo Hyun administration aimed to become a "capable and performing government regardless of its size." As a result, the number of ministerial- and vice-ministerial-level government officials increased to a total of 125, and the total number of ministers reached 81 for the five-year presidency of Roh Moo Hyun. Of the 125 political appointees, 81 (53%) had a bureaucratic background, 17% were from the academe, and 16% were from the political circles. The ministerial-level government officials (81) were mostly selected from the bureaucracy (43%), the academia (32%), and the judicial circles (14%). The average incumbency of the ministers was 15 months, not much different from that in the past administrations. In addition, the mandatory confirmation hearing was institutionalized for those candidates that were to join the cabinet.

The Roh Moo Hyun administration unveiled seven governing spirits with regard to the reshuffling of the Presidential Office: abolition of the authoritarian culture, concentration on presidential agenda, effective division between the political service and policy administration, strengthening of the security and crisis management system, strengthening of the personnel and audit system based on mutual check and control, expansion of the principle of people's participation, and a new strategy and concept of policy publicity. The Presidential Office installed the Office of Policy on top of the existing Presidential Secretariat by dividing the political advisory and policy coordination functions of the Presidential Office. Since the Presidential Office controlled the reform tasks through four implementation committees and three implementation groups, the Presidential Secretariat enjoyed unprecedented power compared to that of any other administration in the past. The Presidential Secretariat was revamped from the one-man system represented by the Chief Presidential Secretary to an organization represented by three key men: the Chief Presidential Secretary (political service function), the head of the Office of Policy (policy coordination among the governing ministries), and the National Security Advisor (crisis management). The National Security Advisor was modeled after the security advisor system of the United States. As a result, the Presidential Secretariat was expanded into an organization unprecedented in terms of size (2 heads, 6 advisors, 5 senior secretaries, and 37 secretaries). Meanwhile, there were enough committees in the government to warrant the administration with the name as the "Republic of Committees" (the number of committees controlled directly by the president increased by 21, and the number of all the committees within the boundaries of the government increased from 319 in the early phase of the presidency to 573 by its end). Also, the share of female committee members in the aforementioned committees increased to 33.7%, a slight increase compared to those of the previous governments.

Since the ruling party was divided into the Woori Party and the New Millennium Party upon the inauguration of the Roh Moo Hyun administration, the National Assembly was dominated by the opposition Grand National Party that enjoyed the majority seats. The Grand National Party, the majority party in the National Assembly, did not support the proposed bills and policies submitted by the administration and even led a successful revolt to impeach the president. The 17th General Elections were held with the executive authority of the president suspended temporarily. Largely supported by the majority of the voters who opposed the presidential impeachment, the Woori Party won the elections with a landslide. Additionally, the Democratic Labor Party running on the progressive party lines secured 10 seats thanks to the party list proportional representation system, thereby helping the reformist groups dominate the National Assembly. As the Grand National Party opposed four key reformist bills (the National Security Law, the Private School Act, the Truth Commission on the Past Acts, and other acts governing the media), the political reform failed to accelerate, forcing the president to even break away from the ruling party.

The Roh Moo Hyun administration intended to eradicate the privileges and sense of entitlement prevalent in the judicial circles then. Likewise, the administration pushed for reform so that the judiciary would guarantee the democratic political system, equality in the law, and basic human rights. A total of 13 reform bills were drafted by the Judicial System Reform Promotion Committee, with 9 of them having been approved with majority votes in the National Assembly. Meanwhile, the administration pushed for reform of the prosecutors' office by guaranteeing its political neutrality and independence in investigation, while at the same time strengthening the participatory judicial aspects by introducing the citizen ombudsman and citizen monitoring.

2. Objectives and directions of the government administration

The Roh Moo Hyun administration proposed the following vision and key directions for its government administration: "democracy that goes in step with the people," "a society with balanced development for shared prosperity," and the "era of peace and prosperity in Northeast Asia." First, the Roh Moo Hyun administration aspired to reinstate the people as the legitimate holders of the sovereign power. As the people had been alienated from politics, simply dismissed as being at the receiving end of the orders sent from above instead of being respected as the legitimate holders of the sovereign power, the administration intended to expand the people's opportunities for political participation, thereby ensuring horizontal government administration. Meanwhile, it also attempted to abolish privileges and favored treatment, the legacy bequeathed from the authoritarian era. As the regional imbalance that resulted from the privilege and favored treatment was exacerbating the conflict and antagonism between different regions and classes, the administration stove to recover the fairness by strengthening the government support to the alienated areas (local regions, farming and fishing towns) and social classes (working people). Finally, the administration valued the importance of peace in the Korean Peninsula and of stability in East Asia as the preconditions for the prosperity of the Republic of Korea. Towards this end, the administration laid out the following sub-principles: balanced and practical diplomacy, cooperative and self-reliant defense, and North Korean policy based on trust and engagement.

The Roh Moo Hyun administration summed up the following four key governing principles: abolition of foul practices and privileges fostering of horizontal social consensus. Based on these principles, 12 policy tasks were identified, which were associated with the governing principles, such as "a corruption-free society and an administration that serves the people," "decentralization and balanced national development," "political reform through participation and unity," "establishment of a free and fair market order," "farming and fishing towns that will open the future," "realization of gender equality," and "labor-management relations that promote social integration," as well as other tasks associated with the government administration, such as "establishment of a peace structure in the Korean Peninsula," "advancement to an economic powerhouse in Northeast Asia," "construction of a society built on science and technology," and "educational reform and transformation into a knowledge/culture powerhouse."

Some of the more controversial subjects in the area of the economy were the real estate policy, the push for the signing of free trade agreements, and the reform of conglomerates. First, the real estate policy of the administration was aimed at tackling the excessive housing loans that led to mounting debts of households and real estate bubbles, which began with the rise of the apartment home prices in Gangnam, followed by the nationwide rise of home prices. The administration struggled to stabilize the real estate prices by unveiling a total of 12 measures during its five-year incumbency (management of the acceptable ratio of housing loans and debt-to-income ratio, more stringent control of possession taxes such as the General Real Estate Tax, and supply of rental houses), but failed to live up to the expectations despite the frequent changes in the associated policy. Diverse claims and criticisms were raised with regard to the policies of the Participatory Government, and the handling of such claims by the administration is assessed to have been less than satisfactory.

As the South Korean economy, which had grown on the strength of multilateral trades, came to a standstill in the aftermath of the Asian financial crisis, the administration attempted to overcome the stalemate with the signing of free trade agreements.[1] The administration pegged its policy goals on economic advancement and on the reform of the agricultural sector by reforming the industries, realizing economies of scale, developing the service industry, and bolstering operational efficiency across all the industries. The ROK - U.S. Free Trade Agreement was finally signed after facing nationwide resistance from farmers.

The conglomerates were guaranteed of their market dominance in return for their collusive relations with the past governments, and the chaebols distorted the ownership and governing structure by turning corporate assets into their private property. The Roh Moo Hyun administration proposed the reform bills on the banning of the monopolistic dominance of the market as well as other reform bills governing the financing and inheritance practices in an attempt to restore the fair market order by reforming the country's economic structure, which had largely been dominated by conglomerates. However, after a series of softening of the regulatory measures on the conglomerates towards the end of the presidency, such as omission of the reformist measures and amendments favoring certain conglomerates, the bills for economic reform began to lose momentum.

In the area of social policy, issues such as balanced regional development, the administrative capital, polarization of the society, low birth rates and aging, and protection of temporary employees emerged as the key issues. The administration decided to build the administrative capital in Chungcheong Province after concluding that the excessive economic concentration in the greater Seoul area was undermining the potential for further national advancement, and established a plan to relocate the wide-ranging public institutions, including the Presidential Office and the central government ministries, to the administrative capital.[2] The construction of the administrative capital was scrapped, however, when the Constitutional Court declared the relocation unconstitutional. The administration instead pushed for the "construction of the administrative complex in the Yeonki - Gongju area," but even this scaled-back project did not materialize as it faced resistance from those who wished to maintain the status quo.

The income distribution, which had been improving since the Asian financial crisis, worsened again during the Roh Moo Hyun administration. To attack this issue head-on, the administration

---

1) The Roh Moo Hyun administration pushed for the singing of the FTA with Singapore, EFTA, India, the United States, EU, Canada, and Mexico, and the ROK - Chile FTA, which had been pushed for since the Kim Dae Jung administration, was concluded and took effect.

2) After the legislation of the Special Act on Balanced National Development, the Balanced National Development Committee was installed in the central government, and the Regional Innovation Council in the local governments. Fiscal support was provided to the local governments by installing the Special Account on Balanced National Development and by increasing the amount of fiscal allowances that could be given at the discretion of the local governments through the adjustment of the tax rates of the local grants. The schedule for the construction of the new administrative capital was fixed, with the "ground-breaking in 2007 and commencement of the construction before 2012," and 176 public institutions were selected as the target institutions for relocation to the new administrative capital. The construction of the "innovation city" that would house the relocated public institutions was set to begin in 2007 and to be completed and be fully ready for the relocation of the public institutions by 2012.

expanded and perfected the social safety nets: expansion of the scope of beneficiaries of the mandatory welfare support to reflect the prevailing realities then, implementation of emergency welfare support programs and provision of medical care assistance to near-poverty groups, strengthening of the existing economic rehabilitation programs, and institutionalization of the taxation system to motivate people to work. Also the government pushed for the implementation of social investment programs and for an increase in the overall welfare budget.

The birth rate started to drop beginning in the 1980s, and hit 1.30 births in 2003. Since the rise of the aging population creates various social and fiscal problems, the Roh Moo Hyun administration sought to raise popular awareness of the issue by social pact on the potential measures to tackle the country's low birth rates and aging population, and implemented a series of policies aimed at fostering a family-friendly work environment.

The polarization of labor structure was also one of the serious issues that plagued the previous administrations. The Roh Moo Hyun administration attempted to solve the dilemma through the legislation of governing laws, such as laws governing contract-based and short-term workers, and laws governing the protection of dispatched workers, but the "principle of regulation of misuse and equal treatment" was not reflected during the legislation process.

On the political front, four different reform bills were pushed for. The administration attempted to abolish the National Security Law, which had been criticized for its potential infringement on human rights and for its unconstitutionality, and legislate the Private School Act to allow teachers and parents to exert influence on school operations, the Truth Commission on Past Acts to investigate those incidents involving civilian victims during the period covering the foundation of the ROK government until the outbreak of the Korean War, and the Media Act to put the media companies with dominant market shares under the regulatory oversight of the Fair Trade Commission, but they were either bogged down or became nominal owing to the fierce opposition by the opposition Grand National Party.

The Roh Moo Hyun administration billed itself as a "working government" or an "effective government" rather than as a "small government," which suggests that the administration intensified the state intervention in the social and economic affairs. As a result, the administration succeeded in obtaining some tangible outcomes, such as an annual average growth rate of 4.3%, a per-capita gross national income surpassing US$ 20,000 and the sustenance of 2~3% inflation rates. The low-interest-rate policy aimed at resolving the polarization dilemma, however, created a new group of people living under the subsistence level, while the public sector grew too large as a result of the expanded government roles, along with the resulting increase in fiscal spending. In the financial sector, the administration stuck to the low-interest-rate policy and attempted to restrict the circular equity investment of corporations by applying more stringent oversight on the financial institutions. Furthermore, the administration pushed for the balanced development of the national territory by streamlining the law governing agriculture, forestry, and fisheries, while also striving to warrant stable energy supply and efficient energy use.

In the area of culture, the administration supported culture and the arts based on the principle of "autonomy, participation, and decentralization" and the principle of "select and concentration" and also ensured that the local regions would enjoy the benefits of culture and the arts. It also exerted efforts to construct infrastructural facilities for culture and the arts in an attempt to strengthen the international competence of the country's culture industry. The focus of the environmental policy shifted from the management of contaminants to the health of the people, along with the implementation of the strategic environmental impact assessment. Despite the criticisms by the environmental activist group, large-scale national projects and urban rehabilitation projects were implemented based on the original schedule, but failed to catch up with the international trends in terms of their response to global warming.

The National Emergency Management Agency was installed to "construct a safe Korea, without disasters," along with the preparation of a crisis management and emergency response manual and the establishment of a basic plan on national safety management. The functions of national disaster control, however, were scattered across the Crisis Management Center in the National Security Council in the Presidential Office, the Safety Management Committee in the Prime Ministerial Office, and the Disaster and Safety Countermeasure Headquarters in the Ministry of Government Administration and Home Affairs, with the inherent problems of such setup exposed by the massive oil spill in Taean in 2007.

In the area of education, the administration focused on realizing the qualitative improvement of the institutional education system in its policy implementation, including the development of basic learning capability in the early stages of life, the strengthening of the after-school programs, the expansion of school loans with their repayment guaranteed by the government, and the expansion of universities' autonomy. The administration also pushed for lifelong learning in the domain of non-institutional education. Meanwhile, the administration promoted the Human Resource Management Bureau in the Ministry of Education and Human Resources to the Human Resource Policy Headquarters, along with the promotion of the Ministry of Education and Human Resources from a ministerial- to a vice-prime-ministerial-level ministry. Moreover, the vice-ministerial-level information science/technology advisor was installed in the Presidential Office and was entrusted with the general supervision of the IT and science/technology policies. Further, the "Broadband IT Korea 2007" initiative was announced in 2003, which specified in its roadmap that the informatization strategy of the Participatory Government was to activate the economy and establish an integrated broadband network by capitalizing on the world's top-class informatization preparedness and the new growth engine IT.

With regard to the foreign policy, the administration came up with the concept of "the key player in Northeast Asia," through which the administration aimed to secure its own room for diplomatic maneuvering between China and the United States by maintaining a distance from Washington rather than actively complying with the international order led by the United States. With regard to the North Korean policy, the administration proposed the "Policy for Peace and Prosperity," in which it stressed the importance of promoting the inter-Korean exchanges based on reconciliation and understanding, and from which the improved inter-Korean relations would lead to military trust-building and relaxation of the tension between the two Koreas. In the area of defense and security, the administration pushed for the transformation of the Ministry of Defense into a civilian organization. The policy was aimed at fostering the build-up of the country's defense policy by strengthening and harmonizing the capabilities of civilian and military professionals within the Ministry of Defense.

Section 2

Key Policy Initiatives

1. Relocation to the new administrative capital and balanced national development

Background

The Roh Moo Hyun administration pushed for diverse projects aimed at innovating the country based on the following principles in its government administration: "democracy that goes in step with the people," "a society that promotes balanced development for shared prosperity," and the "era of peace and prosperity in Northeast Asia." Among these, the decentralization and balanced national development policies were implemented to rectify the imbalance and inequality among the different classes and regions caused by the unbalanced development strategy of the past administrations.

One hundred percent of the central administrative institutions, 85% of the public institutions, and majority of the private sector were concentrated in the greater Seoul area, thereby making the Seoul metropolitan region account for nearly half of the total population, two thirds of the national competitive power, and two thirds of the country's tax receipts. Such result suggested that the country was inching towards the point of "self-destructive hypertrophy," in which the greater Seoul area enjoys monopolistic dominance over the country's population and economy. As a result, majority of the South Korean regions, with the exception of the greater Seoul and Gyeongsang area, were excluded from the blessing of national development for an extended period, thereby crawling in an acute economic slump. Unless this age-old dilemma was resolved once and for all, no further sustainable economic growth or social development could have been hoped for.

The Participatory Government saw through the root cause of such problems and intended to bolster the national competence and promote national integration by resolving the excessive concentration and congestion in the greater Seoul area, by establishing the foundation for self-reliant regional development, and finally, by fostering regional development driven by an innovative spirit. Towards these ends, the administration set up a strategy involving the building of a new administrative capital in one region and the relocation of the central administrative institutions and public institutions to the new capital. Such policies met strong opposition from the

Grand National Party and other establishment groups in the greater Seoul area, but the administration was still able to push for the projects legitimately by successfully reaching agreements with the concerned parties after an extended period of negotiations.

The balanced national development policy of the Roh Moo Hyun administration, which was pushed for to rectify the unbalanced development policy of the past administrations, had the same spirit as the Park Jung Hee administration, which also pushed for the construction of a temporary administrative capital and the relocation of the public institutions. The Park Jung Hee administration considered the unbalanced development policy as the cause of the asymmetric national development, particularly the excessive ballooning of the greater Seoul area, a serious issue in view of the regional imbalance, the snowballing budget required to develop and maintain the greater Seoul area, and the traffic congestion, environmental contamination, and security vulnerability. The past administrations had unveiled a series of measures to tackle this issue, including the "measures to prevent population concentration in the metropolitan area" in 1964, the "policy of dispersing the metropolitan population" in 1972, and the official announcement in 1975 of a plan to "construct a temporary administrative capital." They also pushed for other policies aimed at expanding the social overhead capital and industrial facilities in a phased manner, along with the dispersion of the population. The fact that former president Park Jung Hee was well aware of the potential political and social crisis that would be triggered by the regional imbalance and economic inequality caused by the country's accelerated growth shows the significance of the balanced national development policy pushed forward with by the Participatory Government. The policy was not limited to the economic dimension either, but had political ramifications, as specified in paragraph 3, Article 123 of the Constitution (balanced development of national territory and development of regional economy).

Implementation System

The construction of a new administrative capital and the balanced national development policy by the Participatory Government was the policy initiative with overriding importance, surpassing all other policies in terms of significance. Likewise, the implementation body took the form of an open, integrated, and collaborative matrix structure headed by the president and crisscrossed by associated ministries and by the policy task committees. The key implementation organizations were the policy task committees under the New Administrative Capital Construction Promotion Committee and the Balanced National Development Committee, which were installed in accordance with the Special Act on Administrative Capital Construction and the Special Act on Balanced National Development, respectively. Each committee was composed of government officials (the president, the Office of Policy in the Presidential Office, and the ministers of the related ministries) and civilian professionals.

The policy was established in accordance with the following process: the president and the Office of Policy proposed the basic directions of the policy; the planning group installed in each committee prepared the first draft assisted by the specialist committee members; and the first draft was submitted to the committee meeting, where the finalized policy proposal was confirmed. The finalized policy proposal was then reported to the president in the policy task meeting before its final confirmation by the president after a discussion of the policy. The selected policy was then implemented by the respective governing ministry depending on its contents: the new administrative capital construction and relocation of the public institutions were governed by the Ministry of Construction and Transportation; the local industry support policy by the Ministry of Industry and Resources; the development of local universities by the Ministry of Education; and the development of underdeveloped areas by the Ministry of Government Administration and Home Affairs and the Ministry of Agriculture and Forestry.

Such policy build-up process had a number of advantages. First, the guarantee of civilian participation allowed the committee to listen to diverse voices in the society, and the collaborative operation mode activated discussions among the committee members, thereby preventing any possible conflict among the participating members. Second, the participation of all the government ministries in the policy formulation process was beneficial to the establishment of pan-governmental policy initiatives and improved the efficiency of the decision-making and implementation process as the advanced resolution of conflicting opinions was finished in the policy formulation phase. Third, since the final decision-making was implemented in the meeting chaired by the president, it ensured unity and consistency in the policy coordination and implementation among the concerned ministries. The balanced national development policy, however, faced numerous challenges and conflicts throughout the presidency of Roh Moo Hyun due to its intended nature of redistribution. The implementation of the policy, however, was completed within a relatively short period of 5 years, thanks to the unwavering will of the president and the open and collaborative structure of the policy implementation body.

Implementation Process and Contents

Implementation process

The construction of a new administrative capital and the balanced national development policy both met opposition and protests on numerous fronts due to their intended nature of redistribution. The arguments for or against the construction of a new administrative capital started in 2002, when the then ruling party candidate Roh Moo Hyun announced his campaign pledge to relocate the central government ministries, including the Presidential Office, to somewhere in Chungcheong Province in the inauguration ceremony of the Democratic Party Election Committee. The opposition to the proposed policy was particularly vigorous among the politicians representing the greater Seoul area, the local governing bodies, the interest groups, and the expert groups. Upon the legislation of the Special Act on a New Administrative Capital in December 2003, the groups holding entrenched stakes in the greater Seoul area filed a suit assailing the constitutionality of the Special Act, and on October 21, 2004, the Constitutional Court ruled the act unconstitutional due to its violation of the "common constitution."

The new administrative capital construction project stumbled upon the biggest crisis since its inception due to the aforementioned ruling by the Constitutional Court, but the Participatory Government responded to the ruling by immediately coming up with an alternative bill. The administration submitted three different proposals[3] for review by and further discussion with

3) They were the bill for an "Administrative Special City," which contained a proposition to relocate all the central administrative institutions, with the exception of the Presidential Office another bill for an "Administration-centered City," which contained a proposition to relocate majority of the central administrative

various interest groups and stakeholders in the political circles and the society. As their opinions were closing in on the proposal to build an administrative complex city, the government submitted the Special Act on the Construction of an Administrative Complex City to the National Assembly, which was passed with majority votes on March 2, 2005, supported by the consensus formed between the ruling and opposition parties. The establishment group in the greater Seoul area attempted to scrap the revised bill by filing a suit assailing the constitutionality of the act again. However, with the rejection of the suit by the Constitutional Court, all the political and legal conflicts surrounding the relocation of the public institutions to the new administrative capital that started in the 2002 presidential elections finally concluded, thereby enabling the implementation of the policy without being swayed by any external influence.

The policy on balanced national development was relatively well received by the public compared to the policy on the construction of a new administrative capital. According to a survey performed in 2006, majority of the people believed that balanced national development was critical for the country's development. There were as many differing ideas and conflicting opinions, however, on the relocation of the public institutions and on the softening of the regulations on the greater Seoul area. Specifically, the politicians, local governing bodies, and interest groups in the greater Seoul area demanded the softening of the regulatory measures on the greater Seoul area while opposing the relocation of the public institutions in the region without first taking such advanced measures.

Two methods were sought to prevent the opposition of the greater Seoul area and the potential conflicts between the greater Seoul area and other provinces. The first was the "tripartite collaboration strategy," which included the following three strategies: the "collaborative governance" strategy, in which all the parties involved in the conflict were to take part in the policy formulation and implementation process the "consultation" strategy, in which the opinions of all the stakeholders were to be heard and reflected to the maximum extent in the decision-making process; and the "social compact" strategy, in which the agreement between the government and the concerned parties was to be made the official policy agreement before its joint implementation. These three key strategies allowed the parties to coordinate with one another with regard to various issues and conflicts well before the execution of the policy. As a result, the key conflict factors were resolved almost perfectly, thereby amplifying the effect of the policy execution in the implementation stage.

The second method was the flexible application of the regulatory system limiting the development in the greater Seoul area. While it was not easy to soften the regulatory measure limiting the development in the greater Seoul area owing to the complicated web of stakeholders, the administration could not continually ignore the continuous request for deregulation by the group representing the greater Seoul area to warrant an uneventful construction of the new administrative capital and the relocation of the public institutions to the administrative capital. In the end, the parties agreed on limited deregulation applicable only to some high-tech industries whose establishment in the greater Seoul area was deemed necessary in view of their prospective

institutions, with the exception of the Presidential Office and the foreign affairs and security functions; and lastly, the bill for an "Education/Science/Research City," which contained a proposition to relocate select few ministries governing the education and science domains.

contribution to the national economy, all while maintaining the basic regulatory framework on the development in the greater Seoul area. Further, the administration planned to reflect a more proactive intention in the balanced national development policy by incorporating the global and qualitative aspects in the development strategy, on top of the deregulation measure. The three collaboration strategies and flexible regulations were effective in minimizing the conflicts among different provinces, thereby ensuring the fluid implementation of the balanced national development policy.

Implemented contents

Faced with opposition from the establishment group in the greater Seoul area, the new administrative capital policy as intended by the Participatory Government was modified substantially in the end in terms of its relocation scale, scope of urban development, and the fundamental nature of the city. The biggest among the modifications was the change in the target institutions that were to be relocated. The New Administrative Capital Construction Promotion Committee originally planned to relocate all the 73 central government institutions, including the Presidential Office and the Prime Ministerial Office, to the administrative capital, in accordance with the Special Act on the Construction of a New Administrative Capital. However, the administration enacted the Special Act on an Administrative Complex City in place of the original special act, which was rendered ineffective after the Constitutional Court's ruling on its unconstitutionality, and decided to relocate a total of 49 government institutions to the administrative capital, excluding the Presidential Office, Ministry of Foreign Affairs, and Ministry of Defense, as well as their umbrella institutions. The original plan to construct a political and administrative capital foundered and was scaled back to a plan to construct an administration-centered city.[4] Still, the construction and relocation project was a massive national project, with its total project period set at 26 years (2005~2030), with the total project area covering 464.8km^2, with a projected city capacity of up to 800,000 people, and with total project costs estimated at KRW 8.5 trillion.

The previous relocation plan consisted of three phases. In the first phase, those ministries governing the core administrative businesses, national territory management, and agricultural and fishery administration were to be relocated (Prime Ministerial Office; Ministry of Strategy and Finance; Fair Trade Commission; Ministry of Land, Transport, and Maritime Affairs Ministry of Environment; and Ministry of Agriculture and Fishery). In the second phase, covering the period until 2013, those ministries governing the education and culture, industry and science, and society and welfare functions were to be relocated (Ministry of Education; Ministry of Culture, Sports, and Tourism; Ministry of Knowledge Economy; Ministry of Health and Welfare; Ministry of Employment and Labor; and Ministry of Patriots and Veterans Affairs). In the third phase, covering the period until 2014, those ministries governing the core administrative businesses (Office of Legislation and Anti-Corruption and Civil Rights Commission) as well as the National Tax Service and National Emergency Management Agency were to be relocated.

The key governing principles of the new administrative capital were "co-prosperity" and

4) The number of relocated government institutions was fixed at 36 as a result of the government organization reshuffling by the Lee Myung Bak administration.

"taking a leap forward," which embodied the administration's will to realize the three objectives of government administration: national integration, balanced national development, and transformation into the economic center of Northeast Asia. Based on the core principles, the key characteristics of the new administrative capital were defined as follows: an "administration-centered complex city leading the national integration and balanced development," a "pleasant eco-friendly city that promotes harmony between nature and humans," a "convenient and safe human-centric city," and a "culture information city where culture and high-tech mix together."

Meanwhile, the balanced national development policies were classified into the following three types. The first type was "corrective balance," which aimed to rectify the regional imbalance. It was divided into spatial realignment, which signified the relocation of the central administrative institutions and public institutions to other local provinces, and the regional balance policy, which signified providing financial support to underdeveloped regions via the Special Account on Balanced Development. The key content of the spatial relocation policy was the construction of a new administrative capital. An estimated 44,000 people (roughly 12,000 officials in the central ministries and some 32,000 officials working in the public institutions) were to be relocated to the new administrative capital, thereby relaxing the excessive concentration in the greater Seoul area, and the migration of high-quality professionals was expected to strengthen the innovation capability of the local regions. The policy also aimed to transform the single-polar South Korean society into a multipolar society based on the regional distribution of power and resources.

The number of target public institutions that were to be relocated to other provinces added up to 175, and they were reclassified into 10 functional groups in accordance with the functional and industrial criteria. The 10 functional groups were planned to be redistributed to 11 local governing bodies (3 wide-area cities and 8 provinces). In doing so, the administration sought to nail down some optimal matching between the relocated public institutions and the strategic industries in the host cities while constructing some mid-sized new towns named "innovation cities," to which about 10 to 13 public institutions were to be relocated based on the finalized optimal matching results. Specifically, the policy of relocating the public institutions was aimed at promoting the establishment of a collaborative system between the relocated public institutions and the local universities and industries, thereby helping them develop into dynamic innovation clusters.

The second type of balanced national development policy was the "dynamic balance" policy. The key content of the policy was the promotion of the dynamic and indigenous development of each region by strengthening its internal innovation capability and by growing strategic industries, which were identified in view of the competitive edge of each region. The third type of balanced national development policy was the "inclusive balance" policy. For instance, the administration planned to compensate for the population decline and loss of high-quality talents in the greater Seoul area caused by the construction of the new administrative capital and the relocation of the public institutions by promoting the qualitative development of the greater Seoul area. It also planned to establish super-wide-area economic zones so that economic and industrial activities would be implemented through mutual cooperation with the respective administration districts that had jurisdiction over the respective industries.

Performance and Assessment

Construction of a new administrative capital

The construction of a new administrative capital by the Participatory Government was significant in that it eased the perennial congestion in the greater Seoul area and laid the foundation for balanced future regional development by relocating majority of the central administrative institutions as well as the government officials belonging to those institutions. It would be too early to make a meaningful assessment of the effect of the relocation. In view of the fact, however, that industrial infrastructure is being built continuously and the permanent and floating population is steadily increasing, Sejong City is highly likely to develop in the future in ways that would meet the intended policy goals of the project.

The construction of the new administrative capital is significant not only in terms of the dispersion of the population heavily concentrated in the greater Seoul area but also in terms of the resolution of the single-polar economic development and of its economic and geographic significance. Specifically, given that Sejong City is tightly surrounded by numerous industrial complexes, such as the Daedeok R&D complex in Daejeon, the electronic complex in Cheonan-Asan, and the medical and electronics complex in Osong and Ochang, the city has a potential to evolve as the center of the national cluster supporting new technology and new industries by organically linking with its neighboring industrial complexes. Further, if the other industrial complexes located close to the city fuse together by clustering around Sejong City the third economic zone centered on the future high technology will naturally emerge, followed by the knowledge- and finance-centric economic zone in the greater Seoul area and the heavy-industry-centric economic zone in the Gyeongsang area. Should the country's economic landscape be reshuffled along the top three economic zones by adding the Chungcheong zone on top of the two existing economic zones in the greater Seoul and Gyeongsang area, the country may expect some local synergistic effect arising from the transformation of the formerly alienated region into a high-tech industrial complex, as well as an overall strengthening of the industrial competence at the national level.

Balanced national development

The balanced national development policy is significant in that it succeeded in strengthening the self-reliant development capability of each region through the relocation of the public institutions and the development of the local industries. Specifically, significant improvements were realized during the incumbency of the Participatory Government across wide-ranging areas, including the share of each region in the country's GRDP, in the national R&D, in the exports, and in the number of relocated businesses as well as the share of the added values created by each region in the manufacturing sector.

The balanced national development policy was successful in terms of the construction of a new administrative capital, the relocation of the public institutions, the strengthening of the regional innovation capability, and the development of strategic regional industries. The integrity of the policy was significantly compromised, however, after it endured opposition on numerous fronts. In other words, the Presidential Office, the pinnacle of political power, along with some key administrative institutions, remained in Seoul. The inconvenience and inefficiency created by the compromised outcome are the most serious problems for now. In the short term, the government should look for ways to minimize the negative ramifications of separate location of central government complexes.

Meanwhile, the administration-centric city located in the middle of the country may face unexpected problems in relation with the steady decline of its overall population. If the Seoul - Gyeonggi economic zone and the administration center in the Chungcheong zone, two adjacent areas in the upper part of South Korea, ever become integrated as a result of the robust human and logistical traffic between the two regions, the unified zone will evolve as an ultra-economic zone that would attract even more human and material resources from other regions, thereby triggering “destructive hypertrophy,” which would dwarf the populations and economies of other regions. If the construction of a new administrative capital was intended to resolve the excessive concentration of resources in a certain region and to promote balanced national development, the current policy on the new administrative capital should be reviewed and managed from a more complex perspective amid the deepening trends of low birth rate and aging population.

2. Decentralization policy of the Participatory Government

Background

The decentralization drive was pushed for throughout the world in diverse forms for the past 20 years. In 2007, the United Nations - HABITAT adopted the International Guidelines on the Strengthening of Decentralization and Local Self-Government. A quasi-international norm drafted based on the European Charter of Local Self-Government, the guidelines defined the basic principles of decentralization as an “appropriated fusion of representative democracy and participatory democracy,” “establishment of inter-governmental relations based on the principle of subsidiarity,” and “securing of autonomous taxation authority and local taxes.” The Republic of Korea, however, has failed to satisfactorily implement the decentralization policy recommended by the United Nations since it restored the local assembly in 1991, some 30 years after its suspension. Majority of the administrative businesses (80%) still belonged to the state businesses, the national taxes were collected 4 times larger than the local taxes, and the fiscal independence of the local government plummeted to 44.8% in 2014.

The Participatory Government also regarded the decentralization policy as highly as the previous administrations did. There were four different reasons behind the Participatory Government’s adoption of decentralization as the key policy initiative of its government administration. First, the administration was required to establish a nimble and flexible political system while at the same time ditching the authoritarian and centralized governing structure from the past. Furthermore, the decentralization drive pushed for by the previous government bogged down owing to the interruptions by politicians and administrative ministries. Meanwhile, the random activities by the activists demanding an immediate implementation of the local self-governing system started to develop into a full-fledged campaign for decentralization beginning in the early 2000s. Additionally, the popular pressure on the politicians for the immediate implementation of decentralization intensified even more with the birth of the People's Movement for Decentralization just a few months before the presidential elections. Lastly, President Roh Moo Hyun himself was a staunch proponent of decentralization, so much so that he wanted himself to be remembered as the "President of Decentralization."

Implementation System

In close collaboration with the Office of the Senior Secretary to the President for Innovation Management in the Presidential Office and the Government Innovation Headquarters in the Ministry of Government Administration and Home Affairs, the presidential Government Innovation and Decentralization Committee took leadership in the push for decentralization. In 2003, the Special Act on Decentralization was legislated, along with the announcement of the decentralization roadmap. The said special act specified the principles of the decentralization reform, and the Government Innovation and Decentralization Committee was given the authority to manage the businesses related with the implementation of government innovation and decentralization. In 2004, the Comprehensive Five-Year Plan for Decentralization, the further development of the decentralization plan in the form of a roadmap, was announced. The administration accelerated the government reform by removing the impediments to it while making the Ministry of Government Administration and Home Affairs review the laws and institutions associated with the government reform by installing the Government Reform Headquarters in the ministry. In 2005, entrusted with the role of advising the president in the general oversight and coordination of the decentralization and government reform, the Office of the Senior Secretary for Innovation Management was installed in the Presidential Office.

The Government Reform and Decentralization Committee, the key institution entrusted with the role of pushing for government reform, was formed and dismantled three times in accordance with the implementation phase of the reform policy. The first-phase Government Innovation and Decentralization Committee (April 2003～May 2005) played the role of drafting the blueprint for the policy. As much effort for fluid coordination would be required during the first phase, six expert committees by specialized area and the Assistant Administrator Council were installed in the committee. The second-phase Government Innovation and Decentralization Committee (May 2005～July 2006) was required to focus on the management and assessment of the policy tasks contained in the innovation roadmap. The six expert committees were consolidated into the Innovation and Decentralization Planning Expert Committee, along with the installation of the Innovation and Decentralization Assessment Expert Committee and of the task force councils by area to ensure the fluid implementation of the reform tasks. In the third phase (July 2006～February 2007), the six expert committees that were dismantled earlier were restored to ensure a more airtight management of the reform roadmap, thereby increasing the number of expert committees making up the Innovation and Decentralization Assessment Expert Committee to seven.

Implementation Process and Contents

The autonomy and voluntary participation of the civil society was the cornerstone of the government administration of the Roh Moo Hyun administration. The president's firm dedication to "politics by the people" based on "decentralization and autonomy" was clarified in the president's inaugural address. Based on such governing spirit, the administration billed itself the "Participatory Government" and invited by far the largest number of civilian experts and representatives of activist groups to help in the formulation of policies in the history of the ROK government. The 20 policy goals and 150 core policy tasks in the original proposal were consolidated into 12 policy goals of government administration after the election of the president. The consolidated policy goal was followed by the summoning of associated officials for a meeting to identify the key policy tasks and to thresh out their implementation. Of the total of 83 meetings on the policy task implementation, 50 were held intensively during the 18-month period after the president's inauguration. By subject, the issues concerning the government innovation and decentralization were tackled in 18 meetings, and the issues on balanced national development and another group of issues concerning the country's transformation into an economic powerhouse in Northeast Asia were tackled in 13 meetings. In other words, the government innovation and decentralization were the two most important tasks of the Participatory Government.

The Government Innovation and Decentralization Committee played the central role in the implementation of the key tasks associated with the government innovation and decentralization. The Special Act on Decentralization was legislated to give the committee greater authority and a higher political status compared to other presidential committees. Some 700 working-level meetings were held during the active period of the first-phase Government Innovation and Decentralization Committee, including 50 main sessions and 351 meetings of the expert committees. In addition, 28 public hearings and open forums as well as 34 workshops were held in the same period to gather the opinions of the private sector and the related ministries. The second- and third-phase Government Innovation and Decentralization Committee were each entrusted with the role of implementing the roadmap established by the first-phase committee, and of checking its implementation status.

Three key principles of decentralization

Legislated to provide the legal foundation for the decentralization policy, the Special Act on Decentralization defines the principles of decentralization with the following three principles: the principle of subsidiarity; the principle of decentralization first, reinforcement later; and the principle of inclusiveness.

The principle of subsidiarity signifies that the "principle of the prioritization of the basic local self-governing body" was expanded to encompass the private sector and the basic local self-governing bodies. For such reason, all public functions were considered belonging to the domain of the basic local self-governing bodies, whereby the central governing bodies or wide-area local governing bodies were not allowed to carry out those functions that could be handled legitimately only by the private sector or by the basic local self-governing bodies, which again resulted in a change in the nature of the burden of proof on the functional jurisdiction. Unlike the past when the local self-governing bodies had to demonstrate compelling grounds for transferring the administrative jurisdiction from the central government to the local self-governing bodies as the public functions belonged to the domain of the central government, under the changed framework, the wide-area local governing bodies or the central government had to prove its legitimate jurisdiction over the businesses.

The principle of decentralization first, supplementation later signifies that decentralization shall be enforced first, followed by the necessary institutional supplementation. It was intended to counter the potential opposition preemptively, which insinuates that the insufficient capabilities of the local self-governing bodies make it difficult to push ahead with decentralization. It also implies that the local self-governing bodies' attempt to grow their governing capability through trial and error may better meet the underlying intention of decentralization.

The principle of inclusiveness signifies that a public function shall be transferred in its entirety rather than selectively. The principle suggests that the local self-governing system, as per its definition, shall be considered realized only when individual projects and all other associated tasks are handled by the local self-governing bodies and are already under their exclusive control.

Decentralization roadmap

The decentralization roadmap was prepared to show a more detailed vision of decentralization, which posited the "construction of an advanced decentralized state driven by the energy of the local region." The roadmap contained 7 objectives, 20 discussion topics, and 40 detailed tasks. The 7 key objectives were redistribution of the authority held by the central and local governments, push for a bold decentralization scheme, strengthening of the self-governing capability of the local governments, activation of the local assembly and improvement of the local elections system, increased responsibilities of the local governments, empowering the civil society, and establishment of cooperative inter-governmental relationships. According to their respective contents, these objectives can be reclassified into the following three groups: (1) investing more autonomy in the local government in terms of its legislative, administrative, fiscal, education, and police functions; (2) aimed at strengthening the cooperative inter-governmental framework; and (3) aimed at promoting the proactive political participation of the local civil society.

Performance and Assessment

Resistance by the National Assembly and counterattack of centralization

Decentralization implies the reshuffling of the authority from the central government to the local governments. It was expected that only the establishment group, which exercised the dominant power in the centralized governing system, would assume a hostile attitude towards the decentralization efforts as they were not willing to give up their entrenched advantages. The not-so-favorable attitude of the legislative branch towards the decentralization efforts of the administrative branch can be understood in such political context.

The move in 2005 by the National Assembly to abolish the local administrative unit is a case in point. The representatives of the ruling and opposition parties then were united in their support for the abolition of the wide-area cities and of the municipal, county, district, and provincial administrative districts. Moreover, they supported the replacement of those abolished districts and wide-area cities with about 70 stratified wide-area cities for diverse reasons, including the less-than-satisfactory economies of scale, the non-alignment of the administration center and the living zone, the overlapping administrative functions, and the potential incitement of regional rivalry. Should the basic local governing bodies be stratified and expanded through consolidation to cover wider areas, centralized bureaucratic administration, rather than decentralization, would be reinforced because the provision of more intimate and customized administrative services to the residents, which is the primary duty of the basic local governing bodies, would become even more challenging. Lurking behind such argument was the ulterior plan of the representatives to defend their entrenched rights by dismantling the basic local governing bodies, thereby eliminating their potential political competitors preemptively.

The amendment of the Public Official Election Act in the same year by the National Assembly can be similarly understood. As was clearly demonstrated in the "pledge of allegiance" incident that occurred near the May 31 local elections, the party nomination system was appropriated as a means to maintain the party's oppressive dominance over the nominated political hopefuls. Therefore, the inclusion of the representatives of the basic local assembly in the party nomination system was apparently aimed at advancing party politics, but in reality, it was aimed at dominating the representatives of the basic local assembly by enabling those lawmakers representing the corresponding area in the National Assembly to exercise the nomination rights over the representatives of the local basic council. The forced implementation of the party nomination system on the representatives of the basic local council in such situation can be interpreted as the National Assembly's calculated move to strengthen the dominance of the central party system over the representatives of the local basic council, thereby rendering decentralization obsolete and reinforcing the supremacy of the central party system.

The refusal of the National Assembly to review the Sweeping Transfer of Functions to the Local Government Act and the Local Police Act was also part of its scheme to sabotage the decentralization efforts. The sweeping transfer of the administrative functions to the local governments was aimed at minimizing the potential inefficiency arising from frequent amendments of the related laws owing to the amendment of the related laws whenever any functional transfer happened, and at preventing the passive attitude of the officials in the central government ministries from undermining the implementation of the decentralization policy. The National Assembly, however, neutralized the bill by refusing to accept it on the grounds that there is no standing committee in the National Assembly to deal with the bill. Further, the bill for the Local Police Act was tabled to the National Assembly to transfer those police activities proximate to the local residents — such as crime prevention, patrol, traffic control, and facility maintenance — to the local self-governing bodies, but the National Assembly's Government Administration and Home Affairs Committee delayed the review of the bill on the grounds of conflicting opinions among the concerned ministries and insufficient gathering of public opinions, and forced the bill to be automatically terminated upon the closing of the regular session.

Assessment of the decentralization initiative of the Participatory Government

The administration may score higher points in its performance assessment for its launching of Jeju Island as a special self-governing province and for its introduction of the direct political participation system for residents, such as the resident referendum and recall system. Additionally, the local governments' right to form their administrative organization (right to decide the organizational structure and quota of local government employees) was strengthened, while in the area of local fiscal management, greater fiscal autonomy (increase of the stipulated rates of the local grant taxes, abolition of local grants, establishment of the special account for balanced national development, abolition of the local budgetary guidelines, and limit on the total sum in the issue of local government bonds) was guaranteed for the local governments.

Faced with opposition from many interest groups, however, numerous policies were scaled back from the original bill. Specifically, key policies such as the sweeping transfer of the state businesses to the local governments, the streamlining of the special local administrative institutions, the introduction of the local police agency, the transfer of the national tax to a local tax, and the bolstering of autonomy in taxation were not even implemented as the corresponding bills were scrapped owing to the passive attitude of the governing ministries or to the outright refusal of their legislation by the National Assembly. The Participatory Government insisted on transferring the central administrative authority to the local governments, but in reality, the share of the local administrative businesses dropped to levels even lower than those frequently seen during the time of the previous administrations. All told, the perceived impact of the decentralization policy was not considerable when assessed in the aforementioned context.

Lessons learned on the decentralization policy of the Participatory Government

The less-than-satisfactory outcome of the decentralization policy may be attributable to issues arising from the legislative and administrative branches as well as to issues brought about by the people. The largest stumbling block of all was the resistance by the National Assembly, which feared the potential loss of its vested rights due to the introduction of the decentralization policy. As the decentralization bills could not be passed as long as the National Assembly, which has the exclusive right to pass bills into laws, maintains a hostile attitude towards decentralization, it was necessary to come up with some institutional lever to curtail the abusive exercise of legislation rights by the National Assembly through constitutional amendment.

Another reason that constitutional amendment is necessary is that the current constitution contains an insufficient number of provisions with regard to decentralization, and even these provisions contain some toxic elements. Specifically, Article 117 of the constitution denies the legislation rights of the local self-governing bodies while Article 59 denies the autonomy in taxation of the local self-governing bodies by specifying the principle of no taxation without law. Further, the current constitution fails to protect decentralization as a serious constitutional right despite the gravity and complexity of the issue by simply relegating all the issues associated with decentralization to the domain of laws.

The lukewarm embrace of the decentralization initiative by the public officials of central government was another stumbling block to the successful implementation of the policy. It would be unrealistic to expect the public officials to whole heartedly support the reform policy given the characteristics of the bureaucratic community, but the Ministry of Finance and Economy was particularly intransigent in its opposition to decentralization: the ministry wrecked the planned transfer of the national taxes to the local taxes and the strengthening of the autonomous taxation rights of the local governing bodies on the grounds of limitations in the real economy.

Meanwhile, the political awareness and will of the people to participate in politics have to be bolstered as well. Not many people seem to actively oppose the propositions that are antagonistic in nature to representative democracy, such as the dramatic reduction in the number of representatives and the attempted abolition of the 74 district councils in metropolises. This is nothing short of abandoning their rights and duties as the legitimate holders of sovereign power in the country. Furthermore, some suggest that the introduction of direct democracy would be a premature move considering that the civil society has yet to grow its capabilities. Such argument, however, is no different from the suggestion that the civil society should not be given any opportunity to grow its political competence, which the civil society could earn not by reading books but by gaining valuable relevant experiences through trial and error.

3. Policy on the "Era of Peace and Prosperity in Northeast Asia"

Background

As the only policy initiative on foreign relations among the three key policy tasks of the Participatory Government, the Northeast Asian policy laid out the administration's vision for maintaining the inter-Korean relations and the international politics surrounding the Korean Peninsula. Specifically, the policy is significant in view of the following three strategies: the "regional strategy," which aimed to realize peaceful coexistence and a regional community in Northeast Asia; the "Korean strategy," which aimed to stabilize the peace structure in the Korean Peninsula as a precondition to achieving the said goal; and the "national strategy," which aimed to strengthen the national competence of South Korea and to promote the national welfare on the foundation of the national competence. The policy started to take form partly driven by the president's personal perception of the country's history as well as by the rapid rise of the Northeast Asian region in world politics.

President Roh Moo Hyun frequently singled out the geographic endowment of the Korean Peninsula and the country's foreign policy, which had traditionally been based on the country's toadying attitude towards the surrounding powers, as the primary reasons that the country had to endure numerous ordeals historically. Specifically, the president believed that South Korea's political leaders had often been divided over whose side they should take among the superpowers surrounding the country until they were finally invaded by foreign forces. He believed, however, that Northeast Asia was no longer a peripheral region helplessly floating along the giant stream of world history, and the same can be said about the Korean Peninsula. Therefore, he stressed that South Korea should now end its "history as a peripheral country" that had been dependent on powerful nations and should be reborn as a proactive entity that decides its fate independently. Such understanding of Korean history by the president provided a basis for the key policy initiative of the "Era of Peace and Prosperity in Northeast Asia," which in turn provided the guidelines for the foreign affairs and security policies "balanced and pragmatic diplomacy" and "cooperative and self-reliant defense." The concept of the "Balancer in Northeast Asia" encapsulated the key intention of the country's new diplomatic strategy, in which the administration would ensure the security of South Korea by maintaining a balanced position in the region, without being reliant solely on any single super power amidst the divided interests of super powers in the region.

As was obvious from such line of thinking of the president on the Korean history, the shifting trend in world history, in which Northeast Asia was emerging as the key center of the world, provided another key driver behind the administration's Northeast Asian policy. Specifically, the significance of Northeast Asia in the global economy rose steadily with the rapid growth of the

Chinese economy, while the absolute supremacy of the United States in Asia was eroding fast. Sensing such shifting situation, the Participatory Government strove to make the best use of such changes to promote the national interest. As the memory of the territorial and historical disputes among the three Northeast Asian countries were still vivid then and there continued to exist sharp confrontations between the two Koreas, the environmental change could not easily translate into economic gains. Therefore, the Northeast Asian policy initiative, which was originally pushed for from the economic perspective, was reborn as the "Era of Peace and Prosperity in Northeast Asia."

Implementation System

The Northeast Asian policy was pushed for on the pillars of four principles: simultaneous push for peace and prosperity, multi-level cooperation, open regionalism, and establishment of regional community. The reason that the administration hoped to accomplish regional peace and prosperity at the same time rather than individually and sequentially was that the administration would be able to realize synergy by pushing for the two goals simultaneously as they were inseparably linked with each other. Therefore, the administration stressed the importance of pushing for its goals across the areas of security, the economy, and the society in implementing the Northeast Asian policy. The simultaneous-implementation principle was also applied to the inter-Korean relations. Specifically, the administration intended to create two-directional synergy between the inter-Korean relations and the Northeast Asian policy by linking them in the implementation process.

Multi-level cooperation signifies that the administration planned to maximize the room for regional cooperation and to eventually form a regional community on the foundation of solid regional cooperation. Cooperation here encompasses communications and exchanges with local governments, the business community, and the civil society as well as exchanges among the central governments. In other words, multi-level cooperation shall be founded on the participation of and cooperation by numerous actors hailing from various sectors. Open regionalism signifies that the administration was willing to cooperate not only with the states and institutions in other regions that had stakes in the Northeast Asian issue but also with the states and institutions located in Northeast Asia. The key principles of cooperation was non-discrimination and reciprocity, which was the reason that the United States and Russia were assumed as the key players in the Northeast Asian policy.

Finally, the Northeast Asian policy aspired to establish a regional community. Following the footsteps of the European Union, the administration intended to promote exchanges and cooperation within Northeast Asia and to eventually create transnational cooperative governance, based on which the member states would be able to establish shared values and develop a regional community.

In an effort to push for the Northeast Asian policy based on the said principles, the administration established the Northeast Asian Economic Center Promotion Committee upon its inauguration in 2003, with the further expansion of the committee to the Northeast Asian Era Committee in 2004. The Northeast Asian Economic Center Promotion Committee engaged in the establishment of the framework of the Northeast Asian initiative, including the formation of the policy concept, the establishment of a strategy, and the identification/classification of the policy tasks. The committee was headed by the chairman and was made up of government members as well as civilian members. The Office of Planning and Coordination, headed by the Presidential Secretary, was also installed to provide administrative support to the committee.

The Northeast Asian Era Committee was established by presidential decree and was composed of the chairman and less than 25 committee members. No significant change was made in the composition of the government members and of the Office of Planning and Coordination, but the civilian members, including the economists and specialists from the academe who had been active in the Northeast Asian Economic Center Promotion Committee, were extensively replaced due to the change of the nature of the committee. The first-phase Northeast Asian Era Committee (June 1994～March 2005) focused on streamlining the policy principles, strategy, and key tasks while also implementing the following projects: inducement of foreign capital to the free economic zone, development of Jeju Island as a peace center, establishment of the Northeast Asian financial hub, and execution of logistic hub projects. In the second phase (March 2005～February 2008), the committee divided its activities into four areas: foreign policy and security, inter-Korean cooperation, economic cooperation in Northeast Asia, and cultural exchanges and cooperation in Northeast Asia, with a matching expert committee installed for each area. The tasks associated with the development of the country as a Northeast Asian financial hub were transferred to the subcommittee installed in the National Economic Advisory Committee while all the special committees were abolished, with the exception of the Jeju Special Committee.

The committee reported the status of its activities to the president in the Government Administrative Task Meeting, which was chaired by the president and was participated in by the associated government officials, civilian experts, and the committee members. Since the meeting was chaired by the president, the significance and political heft of the meeting was unlike those of any other. For this reason, countless sublevel issues and policy tasks by ministry were derived from the meeting.

Implementation Process and Contents

Implementation process

The Northeast Asian policy was part of the strategy that looked for new economic breakthroughs in the early phase of the Participatory Government. The key body entrusted with its implementation was the Northeast Asian Economic Center Promotion Committee. The committee's role was expanded in the next year, however, by reflecting the changing political and economic dynamics in Northeast Asia in an attempt to deal with the comprehensive diplomatic and security strategy, and the key implementation body was renamed "Northeast Asian Era Committee."

Upon the announcement of the Northeast Asia Initiative, countless issues were raised by various parties with regard to the question of why Northeast Asia, instead of the Korea Peninsula or East Asia, was selected as the policy target, as well as other questions on the potential changes in the ROK - U.S. relations due to the implementation of the new policy initiative. In response to such questions, the administration summed up the background of the policy as the following: being a part of Northeast Asia, South Korea was then required to shatter the passive and dependent attitude that it had in the past as a peripheral country in the region in the wake of the shifting political and economic status of Northeast Asia, and to take leadership in designing its own future through internal unity.

In greater detail, even though the current state of the Korean Peninsula resulted from the Cold War system, given that the historically confrontational power structure among the three Northeast Asian states had yet to be resolved then, the Korean issue should be reviewed from the greater framework of Northeast Asia based on the understanding that the issue of the Korean Peninsula cannot be limited to the two Koreas but is influenced by the power structure of Northeast Asia. Second, the Southeast Asian states had already formed their own regional community in the form of ASEAN, but no such apparatus for regional reconciliation and cooperation exists in Northeast Asia. Therefore, it would be fitting for the country to concentrate its policy efforts on Northeast Asia because it makes more sense in terms of an international political roadmap for the country to narrow its policy focus on the peace and prosperity in Northeast Asia before expanding its horizons to the entire East Asia. Lastly, the administration stressed that the ROK - U.S. alliance would remain as the basis of South Korean security even after the implementation of the Northeast Asian policy. At the same time, the administration unveiled its vision of creating a transnational crisis management commonwealth within Northeast Asia by forming the Northeast Asia Multilateral Security Council, including the United States. Also, the administration redefined the ROK - U.S. relations as a "dynamic, mutually beneficial, and comprehensive partnership" in the 2005 Gyeongju Declaration.

The Northeast Asia Initiative, however, was not implemented smoothly owing to the shifting international situation surrounding the Korean Peninsula then. The major stumbling blocks included Tokyo's territorial provocation and attempts to distort history, Beijing's attempt to appropriate the Korean history in ways befitting its ulterior motives, and the North Korean nuclear brinkmanship. The series of moves by Japan to distort history, including the designation of Takeshima Day by Japan's Shimane Prefecture, Japan's territorial provocations including the sending of an oceanic expedition ship to the waters near Dokdo, and Japan's various attempts to twist and glamorize history, such as by paying tribute to Yasukuni Shrine, cooled the otherwise uneventful development of the Korea - Japan relations. Further, Seoul clashed with Beijing with regard to China's "Northeast Project," in which China attempted to appropriate the history of the Koguryo Kingdom and of ancient Korea by incorporating them into the history of China's regional regimes. In a move to respond to the attempts by Japan and China to distort the Northeast Asian history, the Roh Moo Hyun administration dismantled the existing Koguryo Foundation and launched the Northeast Asia History Foundation. Also, for the first time since the 1st and 2nd North Korean nuclear crises, Pyongyang pushed ahead with its 1st nuclear experiment in 2006, thereby pushing the Korean Peninsula into dangerous nuclear brinkmanship. As a result, the Participatory Government was battered for having effectively supported Pyongyang in the latter's development of nuclear weapons. For such reason, the Inter-Korean Summit was held only in October 2007, near the end of the presidency.

Implementation contents

The key contents of the Northeast Asia Initiative included the establishment of the long- and mid-term security strategy, the relaxation of the inter-Korean tension, Northeast Asian security cooperation, economic cooperation, and Northeast Asian cooperation for social and cultural exchanges. The implications of each endeavor are presented below. The mid- and long-term security strategy was aimed at realizing the following goals: acquiring self-reliant military power and establishing a self-reliant defense system through defense reform to ensure preparedness for possible military confrontation considering the insecurities surrounding the Korean Peninsula, pushing for balanced and pragmatic diplomacy by establishing an advanced diplomatic system, bolstering the ROK - U.S. alliance based on the solid foundation established for such, and establishing a multilateral security system in Northeast Asia to help attain preventive security via diplomacy based on trust-building.

The strategy to relax the inter-Korean tension was aimed at advancing the previous administration's engagement policy with North Korea to the level of peace and prosperity. Towards this end, six-way talks were proposed based on the principle of the peaceful resolution of the North Korean nuclear issue. In a similar vein, the September 19 Joint Statement was announced in 2005. The statement touched on diverse issues associated with the establishment of a peace system in the Korean Peninsula and in Northeast Asia, including the resolution of the North Korean nuclear issue, the restoration of the North Korean economy, the normalization of the Pyongyang - Tokyo and Pyongyang - Washington diplomatic relations, the construction of the Northeast Asian peace and security structure, and the organization of a forum for establishing a peace system in the Korean Peninsula. In 2007, the "February 13 Agreement on Implementation" was signed to create a three-phase roadmap for the resolution of the North Korean nuclear issue.

The strategy for Northeast Asian security cooperation was aimed at constructing a cooperative system through which the Northeast Asian countries may adjust and coordinate their respective security policies to prevent conventional security threats from escalating into armed disputes, and at jointly responding to non-conventional security threats. In the 4th six-way talks held in September 2005, the six countries specified in a joint statement that they agreed to enhance the security cooperation in Northeast Asia. In the ROK - U.S. summit held in November of the same year, the leaders of the two concerned countries agreed to advance the multilateral security talks and cooperation system in Northeast Asia, and inthe ASEM summit held in September 2006, President Roh Moo Hyun unveiled the initiative for multilateral security cooperation in Northeast Asia.

The strategy for Northeast Asian economic cooperation was aimed at creating synergy for the Northeast Asian economy. The Northeast Asian region had grown to become another major economic zone, standing tall along with EU and NAFTA, but its economic potential has yet to flourish to the fullest due to its failure to form an organic single economic zone. The Northeast Asian economic cooperation can be broken down mainly into the areas of energy development, international rail links, and environmental protection.

The cooperation for social and cultural exchanges in Northeast Asia was aimed at bolstering and supplementing political and economic exchanges and cooperation by building mutual trust and by expanding the shared emotional ground. The task was set to be implemented over three phases. In the first phase (~2010), the basic strategy for social and cultural cooperation shall be completed, exchanges shall be promoted via cooperation among the leading industries, and multilateral relations shall be formed. In the second phase (~2020), South Korea's status as the regional bridge linking the Northeast Asian states shall be realized, and a multilateral cooperation council in Northeast Asia shall be formed. In the third phase (2020~), a cultural community shall be formed, and an identity of region-specific citizenship in Northeast Asia shall be established. For the social and cultural exchanges to be implemented fluidly, the various stumbling blocks, such as the distortion of history, closed nationalism, and the unilateral influx of culture, should first be removed, and the central and local governing bodies should support their respective civil societies, establish a government-level cooperative system, and push for the implementation of lead projects.

Performance and Assessment

The Northeast Asia Initiative that was pushed for by the Participatory Government was significant for the following reasons: (1) true to its definition, it was the first policy in the history of the ROK government to seek to establish a self-reliant defense system by first recognizing that the country's security strategy had been overly reliant on the world's lone superpower; (2) it was a long-winded policy that considered various factors in Northeast Asia, including the inter-Korean relations, the ROK - U.S. alliance, and the rise of China; (3) it was the first strategy of the country that seriously responded to the rapid rise of China; and (4) it unveiled the country's vision for a desirable future for and the promotion of the values of Northeast Asia.

4. Real estate policy

Background

The real estate policy was one of the key policy tasks pushed for by the Roh Moo Hyun administration. The environment surrounding the real estate market at the time can be summed up as the following. First, the number of households without a home was nearly 40% of the total households in the wake of the foreign currency crunch, but public rental houses accounted for only 2% of all the homes because the supply of rental houses by the public sector could not meet the exploding demand. Second, the affluent kept buying luxury homes, and such trend broke out of the greater Seoul area and spread to other regional metropolises. Third, a host of policy measures turning a blind eye to the speculative investments in real estate and the capital gains from them[5] were implemented in the process of overcoming the economic crisis triggered by the foreign currency crunch. Fourth, the massive public funds supplied to activate the economy were flowing into the real estate market. Fifth, low interest rates were maintained to protect some 3 million people with bad credit standing and housing mortgage loans. Finally, the overwhelming public sentiment that had traditionally considered real estate as insurance against elderly life or as a means to increase wealth fueled the speculative real estate investment boom on the foundation of the rock-solid myth that real estate investment would never fail.[6]

Amid such environment, the real estate prices kept rising. Stabilization of the real estate prices was important not only for the national economy but also from the perspective of the administration's governing philosophy, as was obvious from one of the three key governing goals

5) The key measures included the general liberalization of the home sale prices and the abolition of the blackout period (1998), the temporary exemption of the transfer income taxes (1998), and the abolition of the reapplication blackout period for winning privately built apartment homes.

6) This is because real estate accounted for some 83% of the household assets in South Korea, with the homes accounting for some 70% of the household assets.

of the Roh Moo Hyun administration: a "society with balanced development for shared prosperity."

Implementation System

In the early years of Roh Moo Hyun's presidency, the Planning Groups for Narrowing the Gap between the Rich and the Poor and for Rectifying Discrimination were entrusted with the role of handling the real estate issue. Under the leadership of the policy chief in the Presidential Office, the governing secretary played the working-level role of reviewing the strategic tasks associated with the real estate issue, and reported the results in the Policy Task Meeting chaired by the president. The "Participatory Government's Housing Welfare Roadmap," which was announced in May 2003, was the result of such deliberation process.

The real-estate market started to calm down after the implementation of the October 29, 2003 measure. However, with the announcement in 2005 of the Pangyo New Town Housing Lot Development Plan, the market started to overheat again. Therefore, presided over by the president, a real estate policy meeting was held in June 2005 to discuss the comprehensive range of countermeasures that could be taken to cool down the market. In line with the presidential meeting, the Government-Ruling Party Council on the Real Estate Policy, chaired by the prime minister, also held a meeting, where representatives of the ruling party as well as high-ranking officials from the government and the Presidential Office coordinated with one another to arrive at a proper policy decision. In the meeting held every Wednesday for 8 weeks beginning in July 6, six key issues were discussed: (1) reform of the taxation system; (2) housing supply and restitution of development gains; (3) measures to stabilize the residences of ordinary people; (4) expansion of the public housing lot development and development of Pangyo New Town; (5) a policy to stabilize the land market; and (6) expanded supply of new housing lots. The key organization in the formulation of the related policy was the Working-Level Planning Group for Real Estate Policy, which was chaired by the presidential economic aid and was staffed with the grade 1 public officials from the related ministries. All the issues that were discussed in the meetings of such group were reported to the president before they were consolidated in the government-ruling party council and in the related ministries. The outcome of such efforts was the August 31 measure, which mainly dealt with measures to improve the transparency of the real estate market, stabilization of the residences of ordinary people, expansion of home supply, and stabilization of the land market.

The administration collected public opinions via diverse channels: "survey of public opinions" through opinion polls and discussions, opening of the online forum and blog site titled "Establishment of a 100-Year Plan for the Real Estate Policy," and holding of opinion polls and public hearings by an advisory council. As such, the real estate policy of the administration was differentiated from those of the past administrations not only because of its comprehensive nature but also because it was the result of extensive efforts to gather comprehensive public opinions covering diverse stakeholders and parties.

Implementation Process and Contents

Implementation process

The administration's vision for its real estate policy was to "realize a society that is full of hope and is free from housing woes," which was again divided into two key policy goals: "stabilization of the real estate market" and "realization of housing welfare." The policy directions associated with the goal of stabilizing the real estate market were restraining the speculative real estate investment boom to cool down the surging home prices, realizing transparency in the market, and ensuring a steady supply of new homes. Meanwhile, in the long term, "realization of housing welfare" was singled out as another policy goal of the administration, with its corresponding policy direction being the stabilization of the residences for ordinary people and for the middle-income class.

Implemented contents

The Roh Moo Hyun administration announced a total of 30 real estate stabilization policies during its incumbency. Of these, some that were vested with greater significance would be the October 29, 2003 measure, the August 31, 2005 measure, the March 30 and November 15, 2006 measures, and the January 11 and 31, 2007 measures. These measures were aimed at stabilizing the real estate market in the short run but were also aimed at achieving structural innovation in the long run. As these measures would revamp the existing institutions dramatically, they invited either substantial social controversy or political resistance upon their announcement. Moreover, the succeeding administrations (the Lee Myung Bak and Park Geun Hye administrations) either abolished or softened the regulations on the premise of activating or normalizing the real estate market.

The measures announced by the administration can be divided into those concerning the financial aspects of the market and those associated with the real market. The administration expanded the target of the restitution of unearned incomes gained from real estate assets by strengthening the transfer income taxes, and increased the real estate ownership costs either by introducing the Gross Real Estate Tax or by strengthening the property tax system. In particular, the Gross Real Estate Tax, the national tax with higher taxation rates targeted at luxury home owners or multi-home owners, was met with substantial opposition from those groups singled out as the imposition targets, and from the conservative media, with regard to the standard imposition amount and the taxation rates. In real estate financing, the loan-to-value ratio was applied to even the non-banking financial sector through the introduction of "measures to strengthen the management of house mortgage loans risks," and the debt-to-income ratio, which was adopted as a government policy to assess the capability of individuals to pay back their loans, was applied to those districts in the greater Seoul area that were overheated with speculative investment boom.

Next, the administration pushed for the expansion of the housing supply. Since the home prices in Seoul and the greater Seoul area rose because the previous administration did not pay much attention to supplying housing lots and building new homes amidst its drive to overcome the foreign currency crunch, the administration strove to resolve the housing crunch of the low-income classes by building new towns and expanding the supply of public rental houses, thereby establishing the foundation of the future home supply. As a result, the number of public rental houses that were built during the administration was much larger than the combined total of the public rental houses built by all the previous administrations.

Performance and Assessment

The significance of the Roh Moo Hyun administration in the country's real estate policy was that the administration succeeded in laying the groundwork for advancing the real estate institutions. First, the administration succeeded in ensuring transparency in the real estate market through the introduction of the mandatory report and registration in the register of the actual amount of each real estate transaction, and through the construction of a real estate information network. The improvement of the market transparency has received favorable assessment regardless of people's political standing. Second, the real estate taxation system was rationalized. The potential methods for improving the real estate taxes and local taxes that had so far been recommended were realized with the introduction of related institutions, including the alleviation of the tax burdens in accordance with the actual market value, the rationalization of the assessed real estate values and tax rates, the abolition of the double contract practices, and the raising of the possession taxes and the reduction of the transaction taxes. Third, the real estate policy was not appropriated as part of the stimulus package. The administration succeeded in maintaining consistency in its policy implementation by sticking to its earlier declaration that it would never resort to any artificial stimulus package, such as deregulation of the real estate policy, tax breaks, or activation of construction businesses.

Another characteristic of the administration's real estate policy was that it increased the supply of new homes by embarking on housing lot development and new-town projects. The Housing Act was legislated in accordance with the August 31 measure, which again led to the establishment of the Comprehensive Housing Plan. The large-scale housing lot development projects and the new-town development projects were pushed for based on this plan. As a result, over 460,000 new homes were supplied on average annually, by far the largest supply of new homes by any administration throughout the country's history, but the policy sparked an oversupply of new homes that were left unsold in the regional cities.

The provision of over half a million public rental houses was another key characteristic of the administration's housing policy. The policy is significant in that it was aimed at stabilizing the real-estate rental market as well as the residential condition of the low-income households. Among the related policies, the provision of multi-household rental houses purchased from the market was particularly significant in that it was a home supply policy that was customized for the low-income classes.

On the other hand, the following problems were exposed in the process of establishing and implementing the administration's real estate policy. First, the administration failed to earn the universal support of the people as it painted specific areas and luxury home and multi-home owners in a hostile fashion, and as it clashed with the media over the real estate policy. Second, the administration's projects aimed at expanding the supply of new homes raised the real estate prices, contrary to their original intention, thereby polarizing the real estate market into two entirely different markets: the greater Seoul area and the rest of the country. Third, the administration failed to prevent the rapid rise of real estate prices as it failed to consider the fact that the real estate prices are determined not so much by the supply of new homes as by the people's implicit desire for home price rise as well as by housing finance, such as low interest rates and housing mortgage loans. Fourth, the administration introduced the mandatory opening of the housing construction costs and the home sale prices ceiling system, but the policy was not effective in lowering the home prices as it was implemented near the end of the administration's incumbency and as private home builders protested against the move, thereby worsening the confusion in the housing market.

Therefore, despite the administration's enthusiasm for realizing a "society full of hope, freed from housing woes," the administration's real estate policy was less than satisfactory in the following areas. The administration's real estate policy stopped at expanding the housing lot supply and implementing deregulation, without attacking head-on the core issue of the real estate woes, such as the sharing of housing development rights, the saving of housing lots, the compensation for lands, and the restitution of development gains. Meanwhile, the administration failed to introduce other necessary real estate regulatory measures that would protect the rights of tenants, including the housing lease registration system, the right of lease contract renewal, and the rental price ceiling system. Also, it adhered to the houses for installment sale and the public rental houses among the available models of public housing provision, thereby failing to boost the supply of new alternative housing types, such as half-price apartments. Finally, the administration did not pay sufficient attention to renovating the existing homes, and its policy focused only on the supply of new homes. As a result, it failed to establish the necessary institutions associated with home renovation, such as joint development by the residents, repair and expansion of existing homes, and protection of the rights of tenants and low-income merchants.

5. Welfare policy

Background

Welfare for the elderly

In preparation for the elderly's "era of longevity without income," the administration sought to stabilize its financial base by addressing the imbalance between the national pension payment and benefit to ensure a steady income flow after retirement. Moreover, diverse developments surrounding elderly people, including the need to resolve the comprehensive blind spots in the institutional guarantee of income for aged people, the rapid increase of the number of aged people with disability enjoying their daily lives, the poor nursing support by the family members, the excessive nursing costs befalling on individual patients or family members, and the financial instability of the health insurance due to the rapid rise of medical bills for the elderly, prompted the introduction of the welfare policy for the elderly.

Welfare for the handicapped

The necessity of a welfare policy for the handicapped emerged due to the following developments: the poor state of income guarantee for and employment of the disabled, the weak enforcement power of the mandatory employment system of the disabled, the insufficient management system of the jobless handicapped people, and the suspension of the subsidies, and the rising need for providing comprehensive support to the disabled as they were being discriminated against in terms of the guarantee of basic living and social activities despite the rising number of registered disabled people.

Childcare policy

The need to establish a childcare policy emerged as a key issue in the minds of people because the need for supporting the simultaneous sustenance of work and family began to be recognized and stressed. The growing urgency of determining the reasons for the country's low birth rates and of preparing a measure to cope with such also contributed to the formation of a childcare policy.

Gender equality policy

The need to establish a gender equality policy emerged as a key issue in the minds of people as the utilization rate of the female workforce remained low due to the growing number of women with broken career paths and the low utilization of highly educated women. The promotion of women's rights and interests, which was governed by the Ministry of Gender Equality, encompassed the following issues: the policy for eradicating prostitution, sexual violence, and domestic violence; protection of the victims of the deepening social dilemmas, including the growing sexual exploitation and human trafficking, which were prompted by the unfettered growth of the prostitution business; and the issue of immigrant women, which began to escalate into the issue of discrimination and human rights violations.

Implementation System

Welfare for the elderly

The key policies for the welfare of the elderly were the basic old-age pension, the long-term recuperation insurance for the elderly, and the job creation project for the elderly. Whereas the basic old-age pension was pushed for by the Ministry of Health and Welfare via the National Pension Service, the long-term recuperation insurance for the elderly was pushed for by the Ministry of Health and Welfare, with its actual management carried out by the National Health Insurance Corporation. The field-level works, however, such as onsite inspection for qualification check of potential beneficiaries of care services, care classification, and preparation of a care service plan, were performed by the National Institute for Elderly Care Assessment Management. The project of creating jobs for elderly people, which was implemented by the Ministry of Health and Welfare and the local self-governing bodies, can be said to have been pushed for largely prompted by the growing social consensus on the need for creating jobs for the elderly in anticipation of a sustainable aged society. The dedicated institution for the job creation project for the elderly was the Korea Labor Force Development Institute for the Aged.

Welfare for the handicapped

The policy to support the employment of the disabled, one of the key welfare policies for the disabled, was governed by the Ministry of Labor. The guarantee of income for the disabled, another key welfare policy for the disabled, was pushed for jointly by the Ministry of Health and Welfare and the local self-governing bodies.

The prohibition of discrimination against the handicapped and the promotion of social participation of the handicapped can be understood in the context of the legislation of the Act on the Prohibition of Discrimination against the Disabled, the streamlining of the associated laws and institutions, and other projects for supporting and supplementing the activities of the handicapped. The Act on the Prohibition of Discrimination against the Disabled, which was pushed for by the joint private-government planning group, was legislated owing to the growing need for a fresh policy initiative. Such policy initiative was prompted by the disabled people's heightened awareness of their rights as well as by the increase in the absolute number of disabled people and their growing diversification. On the other hand, the project for supporting and supplementing the activities of the handicapped was initiated on account of the growing need for a paradigm shift in the welfare system for the disabled in the wake of the recognition of the need for social integration of the disabled and the non-disabled people.

Childcare and Gender equality policy

Administered by the Ministry of Gender Equality, the childcare policy was aimed at expanding the number of universal public childcare facilities in the country, which was transforming into a knowledge-based society.

The key policies associated with gender equality involved the enhancement of the development of female human resources and their participation in economic activities. The Ministry of Gender Equality was pushing for the enhancement of the female human resource development and participation in economic activities jointly with the Ministry of Labor and the National Human Rights Commission.

Implementation Process and Contents

Welfare for the elderly

The basic old-age pension system was proposed by the Committee for the Resolution of the Blind Spots in the Income Guarantee after Retirement, which was inaugurated in February 2004. The committee unveiled the proposal when it issued an official statement on the expansion of the public assistance system to guarantee income for aged people and to solidify the institution designed to prevent the potential blind spots in the future. In April 2007, the Basic Old-age Pension Act was promulgated with the purpose of promoting the welfare of aged people through the provision of support to the elderly group with living difficulties.

The Long-Term Recuperation Insurance System for the Elderly was introduced in July 2008, after a series of pilot projects conducted on the system beginning with the installation of the Long-Term Recuperation Insurance System for the Elderly in January 2000 and lasting until May 2007. The system covers the people over 65 or those younger than 65 with a geriatric illness who are incapable of performing daily life activities alone for more than six months, and who are classified as beneficiaries by the Long-Term Recuperation Grade Classification Committee. Those classified as beneficiaries shall be offered the costs of staying in a sanatorium, the costs of residence recuperation, or cash payment.

The project of creating jobs for the elderly was included in "Fresh New Greeting Plan 2010," which was proposed by the Committee for the Aged and Future Society in February 2004 as one of the sub-implementation tasks aimed at laying the groundwork for the improvement of the living quality in the aged society. The policy for creating jobs for elderly people started to take form as the importance of recognizing the elderly as legitimate constituents of the society and of strengthening the political competence of elderly people was stressed in the wake of the opening of the Rally for the National Working Elderly People in February 2007.

Welfare for the handicapped

The number of businesses subject to the mandatory employment of elderly workers was expanded, and the exemption from the application of such regulation depending on the industry was abolished after the amendment in January 2004 of the Act on Promoting the Employment of the Disabled and Their Occupational Rehabilitation. Also, a comprehensive measure for supporting the disabled containing the differentiated provision of employment services depending on the extent of physical impediment, work competence, and occupational competence of the disabled person the establishment of a one-stop service delivery system that integrates welfare and employment and the development of an employment model for serious physical impediments was unveiled over two rounds of announcements, the first in June 2006 and the second in April 2007. Also, the guarantee income for the disables, disabled allowance, subsidy to medical cost, and education support for the children of the disabled, were introduced.

With regard to the legislation of relevant act and the streamlining of the associated legal systems, the Act on the Prohibition of Discrimination against the Disabled was legislated in February 2001. Then, the promulgation in April 2007 of the Act on the Prohibition of Discrimination against the Disabled and Provision of Aid to Protect the Rights of the Disabled followed. The act contained regulations on the scope and area of discrimination, an apparatus to rectify the discrimination, and the penalty for the violation of the regulations. In April 2007, the project of assisting the disabled with their daily life activities was pushed for as part of the activity assistance support program. The purpose of the project was to promote self-reliant living and social participation of disabled people by providing activity assistance services to people with difficulties in performing daily activities or in social engagement due to their physical and mental impediments.

Childcare policy

The childcare policy of the Participatory Government started in earnest with the complete amendment of the Infant Care Act in 2004, followed by the announcement in June 2004 of the 1st Childcare Support Policy, which was aimed at raising the future workforce and expanding the economic participation of women. In May 2005, the 2nd Childcare Support Policy was prepared, and the 1st Basic Plan for the Low Birth and Aged Society: Fresh New Greeting Plan 2010, which was unveiled in July 2006, contained the childcare policy. The 1st Mid- and Long-Term Childcare Plan: Sprout Plan, which was unveiled in July 2006, was aimed at resolving the insufficiency of the childcare facilities in the country and the heavy childcare burden imposed on the parents, improving the treatment of nursing teachers and ensuring the public nature of the program. Also, the comprehensive national long-term plan created with the establishment of the "Hope Korea Together Vision 2030" unveiled in August 2006 contained a plan for expanding the childcare service.

Gender equality policy

With regard to the human resource development and economic participation of women, the administration established the 1st National Human Resource Development Basic Plan for 2001～2005, and the Ministry of Gender Equality checked and assessed the plan and tasks for improving the human resource utilization of women every year. With the establishment of the 2nd Basic Plan on Gender Equality Policy, the administration pushed for improvement in the development and utilization of the country's female human resources and in the economic participation of women as well as for gender equality in employment. Further, the Comprehensive Plan for Female Human Resource Development for 2006～2010 was established to promote the economic participation of women, to strengthen the job creation strategy for women, and to ensure the harmonious coexistence of the work and family systems.

With regard to the efforts to eradicate prostitution, sexual violence, and domestic violence in the context of fostering women's rights and interests, the Prostitution Prevention Planning Group was launched in June 2003 under the direct control of the prime minister. Then, the enforcement of the Prostitution Prevention Act in 2004, the establishment of the support system for prostitution victims, and the provision of comprehensive services for prostitution victims in November of the same year followed through the coordination meeting for outstanding governing issues by the Ministry of Gender Equality. In addition, the Comprehensive Plan to Prevent Sexual Violence and to Protect the Victims, which cited sexual violence as one of the five types of violence and established a pan-governmental implementation system headed by the prime minister for the prevention of sexual violence was put in place in July 2006. In October of the same year, the Act on the Prevention of Domestic Violence and the Protection of the Victims was amended to expand the scope of the victims and to prepare a support system for the children of the victims of domestic violence. The Comprehensive Management System for the Prevention of Sexual Harassment was introduced in January 2006 to promote a healthy workplace culture.

The policy for immigrant women associated with the enhancement of women's rights and interests was pushed for in earnest ever since the human rights of the immigrant women emerged as a hot issue after the holding of the Symposium on Immigrant Women by Marriage. The concept of "immigrant women by marriage" started to form after the holding of a survey on immigrant women by international marriage in the same year. Finally, a shelter for foreign prostitution victims was constructed in accordance with the Act on the Prevention of Prostitution and the Protection of Prostitution Victims legislated in March 2004.

Performance and Assessment

Welfare for the elderly

The basic old-age pension system partially succeeded in reducing the blind spots in the guarantee of a universal minimum income for the elderly, but it needed to be linked with other institutions because its position as a basic old-age pension system within the overall income guarantee system was ambiguous due to its intermediate nature between the basic pension and the categorical public assistance system.

The establishment of the Long-Term Recuperation Insurance System for the Elderly is assessed to have achieved some results in that it established a social support system where the universal provision of care service for the elderly is guaranteed. The system, however, was assessed to have the limitations of regional deviation in the quality of the associated infrastructure and oversupply of the residential caregiving institutions. Further, an institutional apparatus that would recognize the caregiving by the family members and that would provide an economic-, emotional-, and social-security-level support system for the family caregivers needs to be established as the establishment of residential caregiving institutions was aimed at minimizing the costs associated with caregiving.

The job creation project for the elderly achieved impressive quantitative growth every year since its introduction in 2004, including an annual achievement rate surpassing the target and a 4.7-fold increase in the target project volumes. It also succeeded in encouraging the elderly to work spontaneously by creating part-time jobs tailored for the capabilities of individual elderly workers. Further, it succeeded in reducing the medical bills of the elderly and in minimizing the blind spots in the welfare system for them. However, due to the low education levels and low work proficiencies of the elderly as well as people's generally negative perception of them, the demands of the employers and the desires of the job-seeking elderly did not match well. Also, since the available jobs were mostly concentrated in the area of social contribution related service, the project failed to raise the income of the elderly substantially.

Welfare for the handicapped

The welfare policy for the handicapped was pushed for actively in the first half of the incumbency of the Roh Moo Hyun administration. However, while the employment rate of handicapped people drifted sideways, from 34.2% in 2000 to 34.1% in 2005, the reduction of the employment incentive, one of the key items included in the amended mandatory employment system, only sparked more controversy. Overall, the criticisms were directed at the insufficient understanding of the changing environment surrounding the policy on the disabled, the absence of the public delivery structure required to guarantee appropriate resource distribution to the disabled, and the failure to respond appropriately to the growing mix of traditional and fresh desires of the disabled. On the contrary, the policy of guaranteeing a minimum income for the disabled is assessed to have achieved some results with the rectification of the distorted distribution structure, which was realized by increasing the number of beneficiaries of the allowances for the disabled as well as the amounts of such allowances.

The legislation of the Act on the Prohibition of Discrimination against the Disabled is significant in that the act was legislated driven largely by grassroots participation. It was also assessed to have reflected the dynamic social atmosphere in which the policy on the disabled was shifting, from the concept of dispensation to that of legitimate rights. Further, the project of providing assistance for the activities of the disabled attained some progress in that it expanded the active radius of the disabled and increased the job opportunities for them, but the service classification system or service provision volumes in the implementation process were criticized for having shown some problems.

Childcare and Gender equality policy

The Participatory Government approached childcare in the bigger picture encompassing the overall childcare support policy, but it remains to be seen if the administration guaranteed high-quality public childcare services in view of the accessibility, the appropriateness of the expenses falling on the shoulders of the parents, the service quality, the diversity in the available services, and the public nature of the childcare policy.

The administration obtained diverse achievements in terms of female human resource development and of bolstering women's economic participation, including the comprehensive implementation of the female human resource development, the national expansion of the employment of women, and the expansion of the scope of businesswomen. The need for cooperation and coordination among relevant ministries and for the strengthening of the organic link with employment was proposed, however, to ensure the consistent development of job opportunities for women.

The policy of promoting the rights and interests of women was assessed to have enhanced the effectiveness of the rehabilitation support for the women who escaped from the clutches of prostitution, thanks to the establishment of a comprehensive support system for the victims of prostitution. As for the measures aimed at promoting the social integration of the families of immigrant women by marriage, however, the government's support measure was assessed to have focused on preventing the deterioration of the country's reputation in the global community rather than on promoting respect for human dignity.

Section 3

The Government Reform of the Roh Moo Hyun Administration

1. Background and direction of the government reform

The background of the government reform of the Roh Moo Hyun administration can be mainly divided into political, economic, and sociocultural reform. The most notable aspects of the local political situation faced by the administration were the domination of the National Assembly by the opposition party, which enjoyed majority seats therein, and the dismissal of the presidential impeachment by the Constitutional Court. Internationally, it was a period filled with the fear of global terrorism in the wake of the September 11 terror attack. The heightened interest in the corrupt practices of public officials was another notable development during the incumbency of the Roh Moo Hyun administration. Among the various elements making up the political background of the Roh Moo Hyun administration, what was most notable, however, was the North Korean nuclear brinkmanship. The international confrontation fueled by the North Korean nuclear ambitions only intensified after Pyongyang's unilateral declaration in January 2003 that it would pull out of the Nuclear Non-Proliferation Treaty. It was amidst the escalating nuclear tension in the Korean Peninsula that Seoul and Pyongyang announced the September 19, 2005 joint statement as well as the February 13 and October 3, 2007 agreements on the implementation of the said joint statement.

Economically, the country's gross national product steadily increased during the incumbency of the Roh Moo Hyun administration. South Korea recorded relatively high growth rates (2004: 4.9%; 2005: 3.9%; 2006: 5.2%; 2007: 5.5%) when most of the advanced economies were struggling with low growth rates. Notable among the foreign economic policies of the administration was the signing of the ROK - U.S. Free Trade Agreement. At the time, when the South Korean economy was plagued by soaring real estate prices, the administration declared a war against the speculative real estate investments and pushed for the implementation of diverse policies aimed at quelling the speculative investment boom.

In sociocultural areas, the South Korean society saw the spread of Internet usage, which by then had become a solid part of the everyday life of the South Koreans. The role of the online space also grew substantially in politics. In fact, the birth of the Roh Moo Hyun administration was largely indebted to the advancement of the online space and to the subsequent rise of the netizens. The gap between the "haves" and the "have nots" kept widening, however, during the incumbency of the administration, along with the sharp display of ideological clashes. The Gini coefficient, the key indicator of economic inequality, also kept rising, and there were sustained conflicts between the liberal and conservative groups.

In the early phase of the government reform, the administration set as its governing goal the realization of a well-functioning government along with the people, and aspired to become a capable, participatory, and trusted government to achieve its governing goals. As for the sublevel goals required to achieve such top-level goals, the administration proposed an efficient, service-oriented, transparent, inclusive, and clean administration. The early system of goals shown above, however, changed slightly after mid-2005, including systemic changes and changes in the top five sub-goals. Halfway into the administration's incumbency, "a government trusted by the people," one of the three upper-level goals, was pushed up to a top-level goal, and the importance of a transparent and well-functioning government was stressed to achieve this goal. Moreover, five new sublevel goals (an efficient, service-oriented, decentralized, transparent, and inclusive administration) were proposed in an attempt to attain the newly revamped upper-level goals.

The government reform of the Roh Moo Hyun administration was markedly different from that of the previous administrations. First of all, the government innovation of the Participatory Government was based on the element of New Public Management (NPM), and the administration aspired to implement good governance practices, which stress the importance of people's participation and the responsibility of the state. Specifically, the Participatory Government pushed for the realization of an efficient government along with administrative transparency, defined the public officials not as the target of the reform but as its implementer, and stressed the importance of the people's trust in the government by focusing on the actual function of the government rather than its size. Second, the administration attempted to differentiate its reform drive by highlighting "innovation" instead of "reform," the term that was used by the previous governments.

Third, unlike the past governments, the administration pushed for administrative reform by equating it with the decentralization drive. The Government Innovation and Decentralization Committee assumed the role of implementing the government reform and decentralization simultaneously in an attempt to implement the two different initiatives on an equal footing and in an interlocked fashion. Fourth, the administration did not set any specific goal with regard to the size of the government, unlike the previous administrations. Although it set a well-functioning government as the ultimate goal of its innovation drive and included efficient administration among its top five implementation objectives, it never included a small government in the official goals of the administrative innovation. Fifth, the administration pushed the public officials, who were considered the target of the reform in the past governments, to the frontline of the government reform, thereby having them play the leading role in the government innovation. Finally, one of the most prominent aspects of the administration's government innovation was that it pushed for the reform of the working system and culture, which would be the software of the government, rather than the reform of the organization, which would be the hardware of the government. To sum up, the government innovation drive was the administration's attempt to instill in the public officials then the innovative spirit and behavior required of them to improve the current administrative process and practices, by making them consistently study and determine the desires of the people.

The implementation system of the government reform of the Roh Moo Hyun administration is unique in that an extremely multi-layered structure and various institutions were interlinked with each other to form a network. The reform drive of the administration is differentiated in that a variety of administrative bodies, such as the Office of the Innovation Secretary to the President, the Government Innovation Headquarters in the Ministry of Government Administration and Home Affairs, and the Government Innovation and Decentralization Committee, as well as the innovation officer in each central ministry and the innovation/decentralization officer in each local self-governing body, assumed roles associated with the government innovation in a stratified fashion. Also, the organizations responsible for the government innovation were interlinked organically to assume roles in the related businesses, and formed an innovation network via various working-level councils.

With regard to the administrative institutions that took leadership in the government innovation, the Government Innovation and Decentralization Committee was first formed to assume the roles of proposing the directions and strategy, preparing an innovation roadmap, and identifying the innovation tasks. The committee had diverse expert committees under its control dedicated to administrative reform, personnel administration reform, decentralization, fiscal and taxation system, electronic government, and archiving management. Further, the Innovation Management Expert Committee was installed to enhance its advisory function on innovation management and planning, and the Office of the Senior Secretary to the President for Innovation Management was installed to play an oversight role over the comprehensive government innovation tasks. The Government Innovation Headquarters in the Ministry of Government Administration and Home Affairs played a key role in the implementation of the government innovation projects, including the establishment of a mid- and long-term innovation strategy and the provision of support to each institution with regard to innovation implementation. The central government ministries and local self-governing bodies also installed their respective innovation-related organizations to establish and implement their internal innovation plan, while also accomplishing the common innovation assignments.

In September 2004, the Government Innovation Promotion Council, which was participated in by the president and key innovation-related institutions, was installed to assume the role of systematically implementing and managing the government innovation and of determining its basic directions and strategy. The network of innovation support ministers was made official in the form of regular meetings to deepen and spread the government innovation drive, and the Innovation Support Ministers Council was established in 2005 to accelerate the innovation drive.

The target of the government innovation of the administration was summed up as a host of innovation tasks that were comprehensive and diverse in nature. The innovation tasks were divided into the common tasks that were to be implemented by all the ministries and three to five tasks unique to and selected by each ministry. Specifically, governing and leading ministries were assigned for the implementation of the common tasks to ensure that such tasks would be implemented more efficiently. Beginning in 2005, 17 common tasks spanning personnel administration innovation, fiscal innovation, and operational guidelines and applicable to all the ministries were selected and implemented.

The key characteristics of the government innovation method of the administration were as follows: (1) a roadmap was utilized mostly by the Government Innovation and Decentralization

Committee to establish a long-term plan and (2) the importance of everyday study and discussions was stressed. As study and discussion by the public officials was highlighted as the key method for implementing the government innovation, each ministry implemented its innovation activities via unofficial organizations such as junior boards, knowledge clubs, and study forums, and many reading clubs, where members would read books on government innovation and would hold a follow-up discussion on the associated topics, were active as well throughout the incumbency of the Roh Moo Hyun administration.

In addition, the administration introduced and utilized the latest innovation methods that were popular among private businesses, such as 6 sigma, implementation community, workout, action learning, and BSC (Balanced Score Card). It also actively utilized the Internet and Intranet in the implementation of innovation, and utilized diverse assessments of innovation performance to internalize government innovation. Further, a 40-member-strong consulting group composed of civilian experts was formed in the Ministry of Government Administration and Home Affairs to provide assistance in resolving the impediments and challenges that they were expected to face in the implementation of innovation.

2. Contents of the government reform

Organizational Reshuffling

The administration redesigned the government organization based on the principles of "an upward approach focused on key issues" and "inter-ministerial functional readjustment first, followed by ministerial integration design." Should any new governmental function be required, the administration attempted to address it through the installation of a committee rather than by resorting to the reshuffling of the entire organization. Second, the "Regulations on Government Business Coordination" was legislated to resolve any problem that was present in the existing policy system; it also utilized the Government Project Committee as a horizontal policy coordination apparatus. The Government Project Committee was significant in that it ensured citizen participation in the government administration. The Government Project Committee was criticized, however, for having reduced the authority of the administrative bodies and for having caused conflicts between the civilian members and the secretariat as well as other issues associated with its legal grounds. In addition, the "Government Organization Management Guidelines 2007" was prepared to ensure the institutional improvement of the other government committees.

Third, in an attempt to promote the autonomy of the administrative organizations, the National Government Organization Act and the General Rules on the Organization and Quota of Administrative Institutions were amended to grant substantial autonomy to each ministry in its organization management, thereby allowing the implementation of responsible administration at the ministry level. Further, the Implementation Manual for Designing a Decentralized Government Organization was prepared, and a copy of it was given to each ministry in early 2005. In March of the same year, the "team system" was introduced to the government organization to maximize the autonomy in the organizational management of each ministry. Fourth, the "executive agency system" was improved in an effort to raise the customer-oriented property of the management as well as the people's satisfaction level. As a result, the term of the heads of government institutions was extended to a minimum of two years, and the total personnel expense ceiling system was adopted by the executive agencies on a trial basis. Also, the number of executive agencies jumped to a total of 41, including the additional 26 new institutions that were designated as executive agencies.

Fiscal Reform

The following were the key reforms in the fiscal sector. First, the Five-Year National Fiscal Operation Plan, which consolidated planning and budgetary function with the key contents of the plan, including fiscal operation performance, future fiscal operation environment, basic and policy-level directions of the fiscal operation, and the fiscal investment plan, was formulated. Second, the National Fiscal Act, which focuses on the strengthening of interlinks through the integrated management of the general budget, special accounts, and funds, was legislated. In addition, the funds that did not require flexibility were abolished, and the funds that were not in urgent need of being maintained as government funds were transferred to private institutions. Third, macro-level fiscal sources analysis was performed based on the national priority, and the top-down autonomous budgetary allocation system was established to ensure the posterior performance management of the fiscal spending. As the requisitions that became necessary after the introduction of the said systems, the reduction of the practice of demanding excessive budget/deep cuts, the efficiency maximization of the ministries, and guaranteeing the autonomy and expertise of each ministry during the budget compilation were proposed. With regard to the limitations of such practices, the difficulty of stabilizing the said institutions due to the discordant opinions among the working-level ministries was singled out.

Fourth, the performance management system was introduced to ensure the accountability of the ministries in their fiscal operations. With the introduction of the said system, the administration succeeded in accomplishing diverse results, including the spread of performance-oriented fiscal operation, transparent fiscal operation, and efficient project implementation. Fifth, the local fiscal support system was revamped. The key reform was the streamlining of the government grants system to remove the unnecessary control of the local governing bodies by the central government as well as the inefficiency and waste in the giving of government grants. As part of the reform, the decentralization grants managed by the Ministry of Government Administration and Home Affairs and the Special Account for Balanced National Development managed by the Ministry of Planning and Budget were newly installed. Also, the government grants to local governing bodies were improved with the revamp of the ordinary grants and special grants as well as the introduction of the decentralization grants.

Reform of Personnel Administration

One of the key reforms in the personnel administration was the consolidation of the national personnel functions through the Central Personnel Committee. The personnel administration, state exams, education and training, and review of the petition function of the Ministry of Government Administration and Home Affairs were all transferred to the Central Personnel Committee through an amendment of the Civil Service Act and the National Government Organization Act, thereby improving the past dual personnel administration system. Second, the classification system of official positions was revamped. The occupational groups and ranks of the public officials were improved and supplemented to enhance the flexibility in the personnel administration by changing the rank-based personnel administration system to a job-based one.

Third, high-ranking public official groups were introduced in July 2006, including office- and bureau-chief-level public officials in the central administrative bodies, public officials in special service, and state public officials assigned to local self-governing bodies. The key reforms included the abolition of the grade 1~3 public official ranks, the practice of personnel administration by job rank, opening of positions, filling of positions via the open recruitment system, and the establishment of a compensation plan based on meritocracy. Fourth, the total personnel expense ceiling system, in which the personnel administration ministry would simply control the ceiling of the total quota as well as the quota of individual ministries while the individual quota for each ministry and the quota per job rank would be determined autonomously by each ministry, was put in place.

Electronic Government

One of the key reforms in the electronic government was the construction of the government business management system and of electronic local governments through the consolidation and interlinking of the government businesses. Designed to enable the systematic and continuous management of government businesses and performances by interlinking the government functions and business activities of each ministry, the government business management system was aimed at enhancing the transparency in the decision-making process and at promoting horizontal and vertical cooperation by establishing a real-time sharing system. The key elements of the electronic local government initiative were the municipal and provincial administration informatization project and the project of advancing the municipal-, county-, and ward-level comprehensive administration information system.

Second, Internet-based civil service, the key element of the electronic government, was expanded and improved, and the national support system for the people was expanded to include a civil service processing status alert service via smartphone and Home Tax services, among others. Third, a portal was established for supporting businesses and improving their competitiveness, including the single-contact service for businesses, which would provide civil services and industrial information services to businesses. Fourth, the online public participation was expanded. The "Regulations on Citizen Propositions" was established, with the following contents: establishment of the participation plaza Shinmungo by consolidating all the existing public participation systems, speedy review of public propositions, and provision of appropriate compensation for excellent propositions. Further, the Act on the Disclosure of Information of Public Institutions was fully amended to stipulate the people's right to demand the disclosure of general information and to strengthen the duty of public institutions to disclose government-held information. The administration information disclosure services of 744 administrative institutions were also consolidated in the form of a one-stop service with the opening of the "Open Government Site."

Regulatory Reform

The key regulatory reforms included the following. First, the Regulatory Reform Planning Group dedicated to streamlining the core regulations among the existing regulations was newly installed, thereby turning it into a dual system along with the Regulatory Reform Committee, which dealt with the streamlining of the newly established or reinforced regulations. Second, the individual regulation streamlining system, which focused on the streamlining of individual regulations on a zero basis, was revamped, and the autonomous streamlining of regulations by each governing ministry was put in place. Third, each and every item of the regulatory impact analysis was streamlined, and its influence on the regulatory deliberations was strengthened through the improvement of the regulatory impact analysis system. Further, the results of the regulatory impact analysis were required to be disclosed. Fourth, in a series of moves to improve the regulation registration system, the system was revamped so as to require regulations to be registered by project unit, while the classification system for revamped and registered regulations was renewed along with the mandatory preparation of a regulation map.

Reform of Public Corporations

With regard to the reform of public corporations, one of the first reform measures was the establishment of the public institutions management system. The Act on the Operation of Public Institutions, which enables the systemization of the management innovation by consolidating public corporations and government-affiliated institutions, was legislated, and the Public Institutions Operation Committee was installed to consolidate the various ownership functions scattered across different institutions. Second, the customer satisfaction management and social contribution activities were expanded. A customer satisfaction survey was carried out in relation to the government-affiliated institutions, with the exception of the public corporations, and the survey results were reflected in the management performance assessment.

In addition, the scope of the social responsibility of the public institutions was expanded, thereby triggering the diversification of the recruitment of new employees, the priority purchase of products/services from small/medium-sized businesses, and service expansion, including in the social welfare domain. Third, "Public Institution Disclosure," the consolidated disclosure system for the management information of public institutions, was launched, and the ethical management system was strengthened, making the budgetary compilation and execution criteria more stringent, expanding the mandatory job transparency and integrity contracts for executives, and strengthening the auditory function. Fourth, the performance-oriented management system took root along with the establishment of the management assessment system of public institutions and the expansion of the target institutions, and the public corporations were subjected to management assessment.

Anti-Corruption Reform

One of the first anti-corruption reforms was the formation of the Council of Authority with Jurisdiction over Anti-Corruption, thereby effectively enabling the coordination and consolidation of the scattered anti-corruption functions. Further, the Integrated Anti-Corruption Information

System was constructed to enable the planning and establishment of national-level anti-corruption strategies. Second, corruption impact assessment was performed to assess the simplicity of compliance and appropriateness of discretion in the administrative process as well as its transparency. Third, the Code of Conduct on the Integrity Assurance of Public Servants, the first legally binding code of conduct for public officials, was legislated along with the production of the Code of Conduct for Public Servants Handbook 2006.

Reform of Local Administration

One of the first reforms in the domain of the local administration was the inauguration of the Jeju Special Self-governing Province. The Special Act on the Installation of Jeju Special Self-governing Province and the Construction of an International Free City, which covers the unified self-governing wide-area and autonomous municipal police system, the revamp of the Board of Education, and the consolidation of seven special administrative institutions and deregulation measures, was enforced. Second, the resident participation system, which covers the expansion of the residence referendum system and the introduction of the recall of elected officials system, was streamlined. Third, the board of education was changed to a standing committee within the municipal and provincial assembly to enable the consolidation and linking of the general and education administration and also to stipulate that the members of the educational committee and the superintendent of education should be directly elected by the residents.

Fourth, the administrative authority of the central government was transferred to the local governments through the transfer of administrative businesses as a result of the activities of the Committee for Promoting Transfer of Administrative Business to Local Governments. Fifth, the self-governing administrative capability of the local governments was strengthened through the introduction of the total personnel expense ceiling system by the local self-governing bodies, the amendment of the laws governing the local personnel committee and the work performance assessment system, and the amendment of the Local Government Employee Act. Sixth, local assemblies were activated and the local assembly election system was improved. In a series of moves to strengthen the parliamentary politics of the local assemblies, the local representatives system was held back, along with the amendment of the provisions of the Local Government Act associated with the local assembly, the improvement of the public-financed electoral management system and the party nomination system, the modification of the electoral college, and the establishment of multi-seat constituency and the proportional representation system.

Privatization

The privatization of Korea Electric Power Corporation and Korea Gas Corporation, which had been discussed since the time of the previous administrations, was scrapped due to the absence of potential bidders and the opposition of the trade union, respectively. Also, the National Railroad Administration was not privatized but was turned into a public corporation.

3. Performance and assessment of government reform

The performance of government reform by the Participatory Government can be divided into three categories. First, it was the reform that the administration succeeded in implementing internationally. Having been rated fifth in the world in terms of its execution in the United Nations Electronic Government Assessment, the electronic government project pushed for by the Roh Moo Hyun administration following a similar attempt by the previous administration was regarded highly globally. For instance, "Nara Market place," the electronic procurement system of the Public Procurement Service, was awarded the UN Public Administration Award in 2005 the government innovation index, a tool for the self-diagnosis of the government innovation level of the government ministries and public institutions, in 2006 and the immigration screening service of the Ministry of Justice in 2007. In addition, the Home Tax system of the National Tax Service and the patent application system of the Korea Intellectual Property Office are currently earning plaudits globally.

The second category of the performance of government reform by the Participatory Government was the performance by government ministry and by sub-indices. As the importance of government innovation had been stressed throughout the incumbency of the Participatory Government, various ministries and public institutions competed with one another in the race to identify and implement model innovation cases, including the advancement of the national property management system by the Ministry of Finance and Economy the integrated education information system by the Ministry of Education and Human Resource Development "Research Manu," the online research management system of the Ministry of Science and Technology and the 24/7 Consular Call Center by the Ministry of Foreign Affairs. When the performance of government innovation is assessed by different indices, the administration raised the ratio of the electronic approval from 89.4 to 97.9%, and of the electronic document circulation rate from 78 to 95.8% while also recording significantly higher incidences of administrative information utilization and a growing number of submissions of civil service requests via the government portal. Notable among those indices are the performances associated with the civil service: the processing period of the complex civil service requests encompassing multiple ministries was reduced from 36.1 days on average in 2005 to 14.9 days after the establishment of the participation plaza Shinmungo. Likewise, the overall average processing period of civil service requests involving difficulties treatment was reduced from 12.0 to 7.8 days.

The third category was the reshuffling of the administrative organization. The least amount of changes was observed in this area the administration never implemented a large-scale reshuffling of the government organization or the consolidation of multiple ministries in the process of implementing government innovation, unlike the past administrations. Much of the organizational reform was limited to small-scale patchworks. The key changes in the government organization were the promotion of the level of ministries, the implementation of the executive prime ministerial and multiple vice-ministerial system, and the introduction of the team system.

The government innovation of the Participatory Government was assessed both positively and negatively. The negative assessments included the following: the reform was not implemented by the public officials but based on the president's personal will, in a top-down fashion the consistent government innovation caused a substantial amount of "innovation fatigue" among the public officials and there were too many reform tasks and agenda associated with government innovation. It was also mentioned that the impact of the government innovation was perceived by the people as quite low. On the other hand, the positive assessments included the following: the government innovation was not realized through surgical operation, as was the case in the past administrations, but through software-centric reform in the form of cultural changes diverse performance management techniques of private businesses were stressed and spread throughout the government and public sector and the administrative reform was not a fleeting reshuffling or change but was implemented through the construction and internalization of the continuous-change system.

Chapter 8

The Lee Myung Bak Administration

Section 1

Inauguration of the Lee Myung Bak Administration and Foundation of Key Policy Administration

1. Inauguration of the administration and introduction of its organization

Korea realized remarkable industrialization on the strength of the compressed and rapid growth in the past. However, since the country's private sector and market functions had yet fully matured near the inauguration of the Lee Myung Bak administration in 2008, the Korean economy was losing its vitality. Companies were still reeling from the aftershock of the Asian financial crisis, and the Korean economy, long accustomed to rapid growth rates, failed to catch up with even the average growth rate of the global economy. Evidenced by the university graduates' avoidance of careers in science and engineering, the falling birth rates, the reduction of the productive population, and the rapid transition to an aging society, the weakening growth potential of the Korean economy was becoming an undeniable fact. Meanwhile, local businesses were looking for ways to relocate their production bases overseas, and the total volume of foreign direct investments in the country was waning.

The power structure of the international community was shifting as well with unprecedented speed. The share in and influence of the so-called "BRIC countries" (Brazil, Russia, India, and China) on the global economy were expanding rapidly. Additionally, with the relative slump of the U.S. economy and the rise of China as an economic superpower, the discussion on the emerging G2 structure in the world order started in earnest. On the diplomatic front, the ROK - U.S. relationship was deteriorating because the Roh Moo Hyun administration adopted equidistance diplomacy based on the "balancer in Northeast Asia" concept in an attempt to escape from its past foreign policy characterized by dependence solely on Washington, which again sparked public unease over security assurance coupled with the pending clawback of the wartime operational authority to Seoul. With regard to the inter-Korean relations, the public distrust and sense of betrayal were growing among the Korean people as Pyongyang pushed ahead with the development of nuclear weapons despite the great efforts exerted and support provided by the Kim Dae Jung and Roh Moo Hyun administrations to improve the inter-Korean relations.

Amid such deteriorating situation, Lee Myung Bak, the opposition party presidential candidate, emerged victorious in the 17th presidential elections. The key supporters of President Lee Myung Bak were of course conservative voters, but he enjoyed substantial support from the moderate constituents as well, making him the first opposition presidential candidate who earned an over

50% approval rating on average in Seoul and the greater Seoul area. Moreover, he earned most of his votes across age groups and was the first presidential candidate in the Republic of Korea who succeeded in winning in 13 municipal and provincial electoral precincts, the largest number of electoral precincts that a successful presidential candidate ever won in. On top of that, he defeated Jeong Dong Young, the liberal and left-leaning runner-up candidate of the ruling United Grand Democratic New Party by a margin of more than 5 million votes, the largest number of vote difference ever recorded in the country's election history. With such election results, the conservative group succeeded in reclaiming power some 10 years after losing it to the democratic group in the 15th presidential elections in 1997.

Born amid the change of government power from the liberal to the conservative forces, the administration was inaugurated on the premise of building an "advanced first-rate country" by graduating from the industrialization and democratization stages. Upon its inauguration, the administration defined the Roh Moo Hyun administration as a leftist government, and the total of 10 years that the country was governed by the Kim Dae Jung and Roh Moo Hyun administrations as "the lost 10 years." The administration singled out economic recovery as the most pressing issue faced by the country then, and pledged to realize the so-called "747 vision": the creation of 3 million new jobs by growing 7% annually, and growth into the top 7 economic power within 10 years by achieving a per-capita income amounting to US$ 40,000.

The neoliberalistic reform drive was expected to be pushed forward with at full speed largely bolstered by the landslide victory of the administration in the 17th presidential elections, but the situation did not develop as hoped for beginning with the inauguration of the administration. The administration was put to a serious test within less than three months after its inauguration. Starting with a nationwide candlelight vigils, an anti-government protest sparked as a show of the widespread objection to the importation of U.S. beef. The administration stressed the economic principles that were rooted in the neoliberalistic philosophy, including competition based on the market principles, the scaling back of the social welfare benefits, and the marketization of public services. However, in the struggle to overcome the political crisis triggered by the nationwide candlelight vigils, the administration changed the direction of its government administration.

On the diplomatic front, the administration significantly improved the international reputation of Korea by successfully hosting a series of key summits, including the G20 Summit in November 2010 and the Nuclear Security Summit in March 2012. Also, the administration put the ROK-U.S. relationship back on a firm ground compared to the confrontational relationship that occurred during the Roh Moo Hyun administration, by strengthening the bilateral relations between Korea and the U.S. Further, the administration strove to improve the reputation of the globalized Korea through active international engagement, including the successful bid for the hosting of the Pyeongchang Winter Olympic Games and the dispatch of ROK forces for a UN PKO mission.

The administration made a favorable assessment of its economic performance during its five-year incumbency despite the numerous crises that plagued the country then, including the global financial crisis, the social unrest over the fear of the spread of the mad cow disease, the sinking of the Cheonan corvette, and the North Korean bombing of Yeonpyeong Island. Such assessment was based on the facts that the country's per-capita GNP passed the US$ 20,000 mark, that the country joined the club of advanced economies with a population of over 50 million, and that the country recorded over 10% economic growth compared to the pre-crisis figures while majority of the advanced economies of the world had yet to recover their pre-crisis-level. Contrary to the self-serving assessment of the administration, however, many activist groups were somewhat skeptical of the administration's purported achievements. They claimed that the administration had much to be criticized for in various areas, including the lack of communication and experience in maintaining the administration's relationship with the opposition party, the economic polarization caused by the economic-growth model focused on the conglomerates (polarization between the conglomerates and the small businesses and between the full-time and temporary employees), and the deterioration of the inter-Korean and unification policy due to the administration's hardline approach.

2. Objectives and directions of the government administration

The key vision of the government administration in the Lee administation can be divided into two: the transformation of the country into an "advanced first-rate country," which is the long-held governing philosophy of President Lee Myung Bak, and "green growth," the vision that the president unveiled in 2008 in his congratulatory address marking the 60th anniversary of the country's liberation from the Japanese colonial rule. Then president-elect Lee Myung Bak, who had long considered it his mandate with overriding importance to advance the Republic of Korea as one of the first-rate countries in the world, was convinced that the republic was already in the stage of evolving into an advanced economy and that the establishment of a new development system fit for the current development stage should be the national goal of the republic. In the meantime, "green growth" can be understood as one of the concepts implied in the president's vision of "an advanced first-rate country."

"Advanced first-rate country," the governing vision of the administration, began to take shape with the following three catch phrases. The first was "people enjoying shared prosperity," which implies that the administrationint ended to push for growth supported by a high-quality living standard equally enjoyed by all people. The administration's drive for economic revival was focused on creating jobs. In pushing for economic revival, the administration assumed a virtuous cycle where entrepreneurship would be revived within the domain of the market economy, which again would rekindle the people's investment spirit, while the investments realized as such would create new jobs.

Second, the administration aspired to transform the society into a compassionate one. Understanding that the market economy alone would not be able to improve the welfare conditions of the people, the administration believed that the government should provide the much-needed welfare support to the socially marginalized classes. The administration believed that it was indispensible to construct a robust social safety net through the provision of universal welfare benefits, of preventive welfare support to those who need assistance, and of welfare support tailored to the welfare customers' needs, which change along their life cycle.

Third, the administration aspired to build a powerful nation state. Based on the belief that the national interest and the security of the people would be determined largely by the country's international status and the roles that the country would play in the international community, it stressed the importance of the global environment upon its inauguration. It also believed that a country's capability to harmonize its national interests with the global interests would arise as one of most critical elements of the national power. Therefore, it follows that a country not only should be powerful in economic or military terms but also should be perceived as a soft or smart power/leader.

Figure 8-1. Goals of government administration and governing spirit of the Lee Myung Bak administration

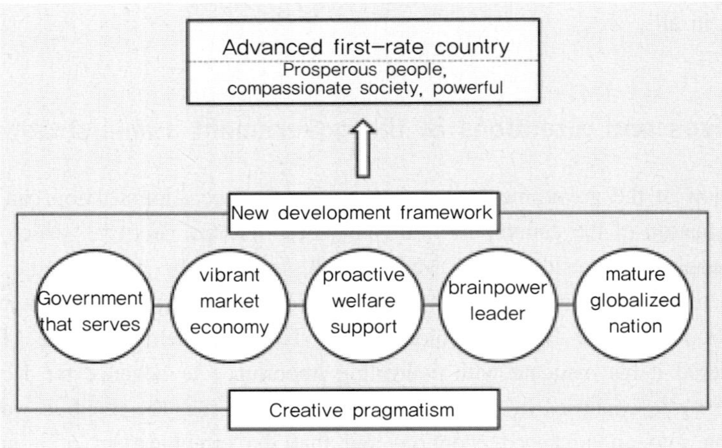

In the process of developing the detailed goals of government administration required for the country's transformation into an "advanced first-rate country," the administration came up with five governing principles: "a government that serves," "a vibrant market economy," "proactive welfare support," "a brainpower leader," and "a mature globalized nation." "A government that serves" reflects the president's will for the government to serve the people by carrying out its duties professionally. The administration originally came up with the phrase "a government that works well" but later changed it to "a government that serves" as the ultimate purpose of "working well" is to serve the people. This principle embodied the solution to the perennial issue of the contemporary country: the bureaucracy's rigidity and slow adaptation to change. It stressed that the government should become more efficient and should respect the autonomy and self-reliance of the private sector. "A vibrant market economy" signified that the autonomy and creativity of the private sector would be valued in the economic management. "Proactive welfare support" originated from the questions of how one can best ensure that welfare support will be provided to those who need it most and how one can best improve the productivity of the overall economy through the provision of welfare support by turning it (welfare support) into a tool for rehabilitation and the development of self-reliance rather than being simply a benefits package.

"A brainpower leader" was proposed in view of the fact that the capability, quality, and competence of each constituent of the country are indispensible for the people's happiness and for the enhancement of the national competence. This principle was based on the understanding that the people are the key elements of the national competence in the knowledge-based economy. The driving force behind the remarkable advancement of the Republic of Korea despite its insufficient natural resources was the overall improvement of the people's capabilities driven by their unrivaled enthusiasm for education. The principle embodied the idea that the country's prosperity in the 21st century could be realized only with high-quality human resources. Finally, "a mature globalized nation" was based on the understanding that considering the new global trends in the 21st century, the fate of a country is inseparably linked with the fate of the world. As the very concept of national sovereignty may change in the globalized era, the administration predicted that the closed concept of national sovereignty based on the conventional nationalism would have no place in the changed world in all practicality. Instead, the administration believed that it would be good for the country to harmonize its national interests with the global interests.

The governing principles or underlying theme of the government administration was formulated based on the leadership style of the president. President Lee Myung Bak focused on the issues in the field or on working-level issues rather than on political ideologies or pretexts. The overriding governing principle of the administration was therefore termed "creative pragmatism," reflecting such leadership style of the president. At the beginning of its incumbency, the administration billed itself as "a business-friendly and pragmatic government" guided by the neoliberalistic principles. The administration unveiled a set of economic concepts based on neoliberalism, including small government, privatization, deregulation, competition in accordance with the market principles, tax reduction, increased labor market flexibility, reduction of social welfare offerings, and marketization, all of which were realized with actual policies: downsizing of government organizations reduction of corporate taxes, comprehensive real estate holding taxes, and transfer taxes abolition of the total investment amount ceiling system applicable to conglomerates softening of the Act on the Separation of Financial and Industrial Capital softening of the regulations on the greater Seoul area privatization of public corporations and privatization of health insurance.

However, in the wake of the political crisis triggered by the nationwide candlelight vigils, the president declared a change of direction of its government administration, from "business-friendly pragmatism" to "people-friendly moderate pragmatism," in his congratulatory address on August 15, 2009. He also laid out his vision of "warming up to the ordinary people and bolstering the foundation of the middle class" and stressing the importance of noblesse oblige on the part of the social-leadership class. The basic policy lines of the administration had since shifted to support economic democratization and the establishment of a fair society while also putting more weight on the people- and small-business-friendly policy. Such sudden shift in policy lines was triggered by the nationwide candlelight vigils, which prompted the administration to rethink neoliberalism, and partly by the growing criticism from the political circles then that the administration took the side of the conglomerates and wealthy people, along with the worsening inequality in the economic structure characterized by the excessive concentration of profits on the conglomerates rather than on the small businesses. To sum up, the administration can be defined as an administration that ran the government for five years under a governing principle based on pragmatism while billing itself as "a moderate administration."

The administration proposed the top 100 policy tasks in an effort to consistently push for the realization of its governing vision (transformation of the country into "an advanced first-rate country") during its incumbency. The structure of the goals of government administration can be subdivided into the top five governing principles, each with four different strategies, and each of such 20 strategies was given five policy tasks. All in all, the administration had a total of 100 government administration goals.

Section 2

Key Policy Initiatives

1. Overcoming the financial crisis

Background

The global financial crisis pertains to the large-scale financial crisis that originated from Wall Street in the late 2000s and that soon spread all over the world. The direct cause of the crisis that spread globally since its outbreak in the United States in 2007 was the subprime mortgage crisis. However, the more widely accepted view is that it broke out when the accumulated structural vulnerability of the macroeconomic system caused by the excessive liquidity and global imbalance was coupled with microscopic factors such as the lax supervision of and regulatory oversight on the financial businesses.

The continued low price structure in the 2000s, which was supported by the massive supply of low-priced manufactured goods from China, lessened the worries over potential inflation in key economies, including the United States. Emboldened by such outlook, Washington wanted to maintain its low-interest policy as long as possible in an attempt to absorb the shock of the depression triggered by the bursting of the IT bubble. As other key economies jumped in and adopted the low-interest policy, the state of excessive global liquidity continued for an extended period. Meanwhile, the global imbalance, where the trade deficits continued to pile up in the United States and other economies while other emerging countries, including China, were enjoying growing trade surplus, persisted. The massive funds in the countries that were enjoying a trade surplus were streaming into the United States and other advanced economies, thereby enabling these states to maintain their low-interest policy. The excessive liquidity and low-interest policy sustained for an extended period at levels well over those required by the real economy prompted diverse participants in the real economy to purchase assets with borrowed funds, which again played a key role in creating asset bubbles, including the irrational rise of real estate prices and excessive investments. As the sell-out stampede of such excessive assets ensued, largely prompted by the falling asset prices owing to the economic recession, the asset bubbles rapidly burst. As the major economic players suffered massive losses due to their possession of such assets, the vicious cycle where the share of the non-performing loans held by the financial institutions spiked ensued.

Adding more woes in relation to such macroeconomic vulnerabilities, other microscopic issues, such as the structural problem inherent in the derivative products, the pro-cyclicality of loans, the highly leveraged state of the financial institutions, the reward system focused on short-term performance, and the lax risk management and regulatory oversight on the financial market, were thrown into the chaotic mix, further worsening the financial crisis.

After the implosion of the Lehman Brothers in September 2008, the country's financial market got quickly mired in the crisis, along with the global spread of the financial woes. In the money market, an acute shortage of foreign currency reserves and a credit crunch were observed for an extended period, chilling down the enthusiasm of the local investors, which again dragged down the stock prices and increased the market volatility. The imbalance in the supply of foreign currency depreciated the value of the Korean won and caused the rapid rise of the CDS premium owing to the massive flight of funds by foreign investors, further worsening the current account balance. In addition, the bond-type domestic funds balance decreased in the local financial market. As most of the bank bonds that soared in volume beginning in 2005 were due to mature in late 2008, the conversion of bank bonds became even more difficult while the supply of call funds was scaled back for some securities firms, thereby triggering a partial credit crunch.

Implementation System

In response to the instability of the local financial market, the authority governing the financial policy streamlined the policy implementation system. First, the Bank of Korea eased the monetary policy in an attempt to supply more foreign currency to the local financial market, a move that coincided with the installation of the government-side joint crisis management system with the Bank of Korea, which was given the role of providing payment guarantee and raising public funds, thereby immediately resolving the urgent foreign currency crunch.

First, the Bank of Korea eased its monetary policy promptly in an attempt to resolve the credit crunch in the local financial market. While the standard interest rate was cut down from 5.25% in August 2008 to 2.0% towards the end of 2009, the interest rate for the total credit line was reduced from 3.5% per year to 1.25%. In addition, the target securities of the RP were expanded to include the bank bonds, some special bonds (the bonds issued by Korea Land Corporation, Korea Housing Corporation, and Small and Medium Business Corporation), and the MBS and corporate bonds issued by Korea Housing Finance Corporation. Also, an additional 12 securities firms were included in the RP target institution. In addition, the Bank of Korea raised the total credit line, which it had continued to reduce from 2002, by KRW 2.5 trillion, from KRW 6.5 trillion to KRW 9.0 trillion, beginning in November 2008, with a further expansion up to KRW 10 trillion in March 2009.

The government and the Bank of Korea joined forces in the effort to stabilize the foreign currency and foreign currency funds market. First, they signed currency swap agreements with the United States, China, and Japan before providing foreign currency liquidity directly to the banks and eased the limit imposed on the use of foreign currency loans. In addition, the government prepared a massive stimulus package in preparation for the prolonged depression of the real economy, with its total budget amounting to KRW 51.3 trillion in 2008 (about 5.01% of the GDP, including KRW 32.6 trillion in reduced tax receipts) and KRW 17.7 trillion in 2009 (about 1.66%

Figure 8-2. Korea's policy response system aimed at stabilizing the financial market

Interest rate reduction & foreign currency supply	Resolution of the KRW credit crunch	Supply of foreign currency	Expansion of the midterm credit line through the expansion of funds
↓	↓	↓	↓
• Lowering of the standard interest rate by 325 bps to 2.00% over six rounds of rate cuts from October 9 • Massive supply of foreign currency through open-market intervention, such as purchase of RP and treasury bonds and premature resale of monetary stabilization bonds	• Increase of the total credit line on October 23 (KRW 6.5 trillion KRW 9.0 trillion) • Expansion of the target securities of the open-market intervention on October 27 through bank bonds and some special bonds • Inclusion of some securities firms in the target institutions of the open-market intervention on December 11 • Payment of the interest for the payment reserves on December 11 (KRW 500.2 billion) • Raising bond market stabilization funds	• Provision of US$ 10 billion to the foreign currency fund market via the foreign exchange equalization funds • Starting competitive-bidding-type swap transactions on October 20 • Starting the approval of foreign currency loans via the ROK - U.S. currency swap on December 2 • Signing of new currency swap agreements with China and the United States effective December 2 • Provision of EXIM financing by the Bank of Korea and the government	• Expansion of the financial support via special banks (Industrial Bank, Small and Medium Industry Bank) • Expansion of the payment guarantee via capital investment in the Trust Guarantee Funds and the Korea Technology Credit Guarantee Fund • Provision of support for the capital expansion of the commercial banks through the Capital Expansion Funds

of the GDP).

In the case of Korea, the vulnerability of the foreign exchange market was singled out as the biggest risk factor. In view of such circumstances, the government opted to control the foreign currency supply by providing foreign currency liquidity to where it was needed, such as the financial institutions and export/import companies. Notable in the process was that the government strove to implement the policy in a market-friendly fashion to the extent that was reasonably possible, including the provision of foreign currency funds priced at the market interest rates via the open competitive bidding format. Also notable was that the payment guarantee to the local commercial banks and the provision of liquidity after the bankruptcy of Lehman Brothers were implemented in a timely manner, thereby helping stabilize the financial market significantly.

Thanks to the proactive responses of the financial authority, the market interest rate as well as the interest rate of the bank and corporate bonds that had been spread fell substantially, thereby rapidly stabilizing the financial market.

Implementation Process and Contents

The measures that the administration took to overcome the financial crisis were the raising of financial market stabilization funds, the provision of foreign currency liquidity, the expansion of the capital of public financial institutions, the provision of financial support to the small and medium-sized businesses, corporate business restructuring, and measures aimed at stabilizing the real estate market. The implementation process and contents of these policies are shown below.

First, the administration raised the financial market stabilization funds. As the global financial crisis triggered by the bankruptcy of Lehman Brothers spread to the Korean financial market, thus making it difficult to issue credit-based bonds (e.g., corporate bonds) and prompting the banks to make the loan provision process more rigorous, the severe credit crunch in the financial market made it difficult for the Korean businesses to line up the needed funds. Meanwhile, the BIS ratio of owner's equity of the domestic banks fell significantly from 12.31% near the end of 2007 to 10.86% by the end of September 2008, which was largely attributable to a host of factors, including the expansion of corporate loans in the first half of the year, the increase in the KRW-converted amount of foreign-currency-denominated assets as a result of the appreciation of the value of the U.S. dollar against the Korean won, and the loss in the valuation of marketable securities owing to the stock market crash. In response to the aforementioned developments, the banks lined up some KRW 16 trillion through an issue of subordinated security bonds and capital increase while the government increased the capital of the national banks through capital investment and expanded the scope of the new variety of equity capital recognizable as the BIS basic capital. In addition, the Bank of Korea supported the capital expansion through interest payment amounting to KRW 500 billion. However, since the aftershock of the global financial crisis was feared to last for an extended period, such measures failed to dispel the fear that the ballooning share of non-performing loans owing to the contraction of the real economy and the corporate business restructuring would deteriorate the capital adequacy of the banks. As part of the preemptive measures aimed at quelling such fear, the government expanded the demand in the direct financial market through an issue of corporate bonds and CP, and raised bond market stabilization funds and bank capital expansion funds in an effort to improve the capital flow to corporations via the indirect financial market.

Second, foreign currency liquidity was provided as the government was required to proactively deal with the significant deterioration of the foreign currency liquidity caused by the acute credit crunch in the international financial market in the wake of the bankruptcy of Lehman Brothers in September 2008 and by the resulting acceleration of fund collection by overseas financial institutions. The ROK government and the Bank of Korea implemented a host of measures aimed at improving the country's foreign currency liquidity. In an effort to prevent the unease prevalent in the local foreign currency market from spreading to other areas owing to the deepening global financial crisis right after the outbreak of the Lehman Brothers crisis, the government provided the payment guarantee for the banks' foreign-currency-denominated debts or signed and expanded the currency swap agreements with the central banks of the United States, China, and Japan. In addition, the commercial banks implemented their own stabilization measures, including the competitive-bidding-style foreign currency swap, the competitive-bidding-style foreign currency loans that rely on the currency swap with the Federal Reserve System of the United States, and the provision of foreign currency liquidity via EXIM Bank. Moreover, in an effort to prevent the possible recurrence of the foreign currency crunch owing to the financial instability in Eastern Europe and the contraction of the global real economy, the government announced on February 26, 2009 a measure for institutional improvement aimed at expanding the country's foreign currency liquidity.[1] Meanwhile, the government successfully issued foreign exchange equalization funds amounting to US$ 3.9 billion on April 9, thereby significantly improving the conditions for local commercial banks' acquisition of foreign loans, and successfully quelling the growing worries over the potential economic crisis in Korea.

Third, the administration expanded the capital of the public financial institutions. The role of the public financial institutions was stressed, with added weight as the government implemented the policy of supporting small businesses by maintaining low interest rates and through collaboration among the economic participants. The midterm fund provision to Industrial Bank and Small and Medium Industry Bank was expanded significantly from KRW 32 trillion (Industrial Bank: KRW 8 trillion.[2] Small and Medium Industry Bank: KRW 24 trillion) in 2008 to KRW 44 trillion (Industrial Bank: KRW 12 trillion Small and Medium Industry Bank: KRW 32 trillion) in 2009. The government, however, invested capital in Industrial Bank and Small and Medium Industry Bank as to prevent possible deterioration of the financial health of the public financial institution due tothe expanded roles of such public financial institutions and as to assure that the payment guarantee power of the guarantee institutions would not deteriorate rapidly as a result of having invested in the Trust Guarantee Funds.

Fourth, the administration provided financial support to the small and medium-sized businesses. In view of the growing difficulty of securing funds for loan provision due to the deepening uncertainty of the domestic and global economic situation beginning in the latter half of 2008, the banks started to apply more stringent rules[3] for the screening of the qualifications of potential borrowers before granting loans. Therefore, the upward trend in the loan provision to small businesses started to go down. The key contents of the loan provision to small businesses included the implementation of the fast-track program, the expansion of the total credit line, the signing of MOUs with banks, and the expansion of the credit guarantee. The fast-track program was established to provide liquidity to the small businesses belonging to classes A and B among those companies that were struggling with a temporary lack of funds but had no clear sign of insolvency. The decision of whether to provide liquidity was made after considering the financial status of the companies upon receiving an application for liquidity provision from them. The

1) The measures for institutional improvement included exemption from paying the withholding tax for the interest incomes when foreign investors invest in Korean bonds; pushing for subscription in WGBI, the leading indicator of the investment in government bonds, as a member state; inducement of the funds held by overseas Koreans; and activation of foreign borrowing by public corporations and local banks.

2) Meanwhile, the Small and Medium Industry Bank originally planned to provide KRW 8 trillion to the small. businesses for the FY 2008 but increased it by KRW 2 trillion, hence pushing up the total to KRW 10 trillion

3) Includes the expansionof the spread and more stringent conditions for loan extension and re-handling.

expansion of the total credit line signifies that the Bank of Korea expanded the total credit line that it had reduced since 2002 by KRW 2.5 trillion, from KRW 6.5 trillion to KRW 9.0 trillion, beginning in November, in an attempt to incentivize the banks to provide more loans to small businesses, and that the bank increased the total credit line by an additional KRW 1 trillion, to KRW 10 trillion, to expand the total amount allowable for the special support program. The expansion of the credit guarantee signifies that the government made an effort to eliminate any impediment to the provision of financial support through the expansion of the guarantee ceiling of the credit guarantee institutions in February 2009, by preparing and implementing a measure to expand the credit guarantee for small and minor companies. The effort was aimed at resolving the financial difficulty of small businesses, which resulted from the deepening credit risk along with the steady rise in the percentage of arrears despite the measures taken to provide funds to small businesses.

Fifth, the administration pushed for corporate restructuring. Economists suggested that the growing instability in the local financial market would undermine the liquidity of the corporations beginning in the latter half of 2008, which would again deepen the downward trends in the real economy. Specifically, the growing number of distressed small construction firms and nascent shipbuilding companies, coupled with the worries over the potential serial bankruptcies due to the credit crunch, was increasing the instability across the economy. Having concluded that prompt and systematic corporate restructuring would be inevitable to quell the anxiety and uncertainty in the market, the government unveiled the basic direction and system of the corporate restructuring drive in December 2008, and started a full-scale implementation of the restructuring plan in 2009. Unlike the wholesale corporate restructuring that was applied to all distressed companies during the Asian financial crisis in the late 1990s, the government focused on rescuing distressed companies from the death knell while swiftly clearing out only those companies with no hope of rehabilitation. Thus, the government pushed ahead with the corporate restructuring by industry only when it was inevitable, based on the principle that the restructuring was to be implemented by company or business group.

Sixth, the administration implemented a measure to stabilize the real estate market. Early in 2009, the real estate market was put under downward pressure amid the instability in the financial market and the growing fears over the possible depression in the real economy in the wake of the global financial crisis. The market shifted again in the latter half of the year, however, largely bolstered by the extremely low interest rates, the sufficient liquidity, and the growing hope for recovery, as well as by the softening of regulations beginning in 2008 and the prospective redevelopment projects, prompting the government to deal with the upward trends in real estate prices. Therefore, the measures for stabilizing the real estate market changed as well in accordance with such shifting price trends in the market: whereas the measures implemented near the end of 2008 were aimed at preventing the free fall of real estate prices, another set of measures prepared and implemented at the end of the year were aimed at preventing the price rise of real estate, specifically those aimed at slowing down the rapid increase in the volume of housing mortgage loans.

Performance and Assessment

The bond market stabilization funds and the bank capital expansion funds both helped soften the credit crunch in the Korean market that started after the implosion of Lehman Brothers and the following spread of the global financial crisis to the Korean market. For the direct results gained from the management of the two funds, the government succeeded in expanding the room for supplying funds to the direct/indirect financial market by expanding the demand for credit-linked financial products and by softening the stringent rules that the banks otherwise might have applied to the loan provision qualification screening process. Indirectly, the measure is assessed to have dispelled the fears in the financial market with the pledge to provide a sufficient amount of funds.

The combined efforts by the government and the Bank of Korea to provide foreign currency liquidity played a decisive role in quelling the acute crunch in the foreign currency fund market that started upon the collapse of Lehman Brothers. It is believed that the provision of foreign currency liquidity by the government and the Bank of Korea, which was realized by tapping the country's foreign currency reserves and the currency swap with the central banks of other economic powers, played a critical role in enabling the local financial institutions to respond to the foreign currency repayment requests of overseas financial institutions.[4] Further, although the actual amount of payment guarantee did not amount to a significant sum, the government's payment guarantee for the local banks' foreign debts is also believed to have bolstered the negotiation power of the Korean banks by providing them with secondary financing means when they sought to line up funds in the global financial market on their own. Meanwhile, the signing of the currency swap agreement with the Federal Reserve System of the United States helped improve Korea's foreign currency status and bolster the credibility of the Korean economy significantly. It dispelled the fears of the overseas financial institutions with regard to Korea's foreign currency liquidity status, and then lowered the CDS premium by more than 200 bp within a week, which was one of the administration's most important achievements in its efforts to overcome the global financial crisis.

The government's capital investment in public financial institutions also played a key role in providing the support needed by small businesses. The move is assessed to have helped stabilize the market significantly by preemptively dispelling the fears that otherwise, the public financial institutions might undermine their own financial integrity while providing support to small businesses. Multi-faceted support was effectively provided by the government, banks, and credit guarantee institutions to small businesses. Specifically, the preemptive measures implemented through close cooperation among the governing ministries are assessed to have provided the critical platform on which to overcome the crisis by softening the shock of the crisis. Further, the diversification of the financing sources was proposed because, should the oversight on the health of the financial industry be tightened, the possibility of providing financing to small businesses would always be present.

---

4) The total foreign currency funds amounting to US$ 46.62 billion provided by the government and the Bank of Korea to financial institutions to help them respond to the collapse of Lehman Brothers was comparable to the net amount of foreign loans repaid by the Korean banks to overseas financial institutions in the 4th quarter of 2008.

2. Signing of the ROK-U.S. Free Trade Agreement

Background

The push for the ROK - U.S. Free Trade Agreement (FTA) by the administration started where the Roh Moo Hyun administration left off: reopening the negotiations and having the approved agreement ratified by the National Assembly and then implemented by the government. The background of the push for the ROK - U.S. FTA, which was initiated by the Roh Moo Hyun administration and completed by the Lee Myung Bak administration, is shown below.

The first multilateral agreement to liberalize the international trade, Doha Development Agenda (DDA), which was attempted at the WTO level largely prompted by the conflicts between the developed and underdeveloped economies, failed to come up with meaningful results since its inauguration in 2001. In an attempt to resolve the gridlock, advanced economies jumped into the race to secure access rights to overseas markets by signing preferential trade agreements with those countries that had shared interests with them, rather than relying on the multilateral free trade system enabled via the WTO. In the process, the ROK government remained relatively faithful to the principle of market opening based on the multilateral structure. Beginning in the early 2000s, however, Seoul has passionately sought opportunities to access the foreign market via the FTA system, based on its understanding that the country was behind other countries in its efforts to secure access rights to overseas markets via preferential trade agreements. Thanks to the relentless efforts of the government, Korea has signed FTAs with 45 countries as of this writing, which were ratified and taken effect successively. The remarkably rapid increase in the number of FTAs of Korea was made possible by the ROK government's adoption of what is called the "simultaneous FTA promotion" strategy.

In 2004, the ROK - Chile FTA, the country's very first FTA, took effect, followed by a series of negotiations for FTAs with countries that had a minimum impact on Korea's international trade, such as Singapore and EFTA (European Free Trade Alliance: Iceland, Norway, Switzerland, Lichtenstein), all of which bore fruit. The FTAs with those countries with relatively limited trade volumes with Korea helped the latter accumulate the FTA negotiation experiences that it needed while minimizing the impact of the free trade, but they were not very effective in expanding the number of markets that the country's industries could actually access. Likewise, the government established the FTA policy direction in which the country would push for negotiations for FTAs with advanced mega markets that would show some practical effects while ditching its early strategy focused on signing FTAs with the country's relatively smaller trade partners which had minimal impact.

The 14-month period from the start of the negotiations on the ROK - U.S. FTA in February 2006 until the reaching of the final agreement was riddled with excessively concentrated social controversy and conflicts that were even more serious than the social conflicts experienced during the period until the ratification of the ROK - U.S. FTA on November 22, 2011. The issue that entailed the deepest social discourse among the key issues that sparked comprehensive social conflicts in relation to the ROK - U.S. FTA was the opening of the domestic rice market via the ROK - U.S. FTA. Even though the percentage of farmers in the Korean society is insignificant, because the opening of the domestic rice market was closely linked with the country's food security, other ordinary citizens who were not directly related with rice farming jumped on the discussion on the ROK - U.S. FTA, which involved the issue regarding the opening of the local rice market, thus joining them in their opposition to the market opening.

As a result, the agreement was finalized on the precondition that Korea would not participate in the U.S. shipbuilding industry and would continue to keep its local market closed to U.S. rice imports. Other issues that were singled out as consistent targets of the ROK - U.S. FTA negotiations were the resumption of Korea's importation of U.S. beef, the abolition of more stringent automobile emission standards, the reduction of the screen quota, and the abolition of the pharmaceutical product price reassessment. The resolution of these issues was requested by Washington as the precondition for the ROK - U.S. FTA negotiations, and majority of the requests were accepted by Seoul. Specifically, the import of U.S. beef later became one of the key issues that would define the national identity of Korea as the fears regarding the safety of U.S. beef spread across the country. Ever since the U.S. beef importation issue became fused with the FTA negotiations, the ROK - U.S. FTA was no longer considered an agreement aimed at maximizing Korea's economic interests through market opening, but escalated into a political issue that would determine the country's national identity. As a result, the opposition to the importation of U.S. beef was equated with the wholesale opposition to the ROK - U.S. FTA, thereby sparking an outpouring of criticisms socially.

The additional social criticism of the ROK - U.S. FTA was the widespread controversy associated with the Investor State Dispute (ISD) clause in the agreement. The key argument associated with the issue of ISD can be explained by the difference between the legal system of the U.S. and Korea's administrative law system, which was based on the European and Anglo-Saxon legal systems. However, the public perception of the ROK - U.S. FTA, which had already been transformed into a political issue, played a significant role in fanning the social controversy on the issue, on top of the aforementioned legal differences. The social costs further ballooned as the critical view suggesting that the ISD system would potentially infringe on the sovereign right of the ROK government was raised in the negotiation process.

The issue continued to be a source of social controversy in the country until well into the final settlement of the ROK - U.S. FTA in 2011. The political background of such unexpected development, in which the political issues involving the ROK - U.S. FTA, rather than the economic benefits of the agreement, became the core of the social discourse, was that the government pushed ahead with the initiation and finalization of the negotiation process without any systematic process to reflect the opinions of the key stakeholders of the ROK - U.S. FTA, including the farmers and the businesses belonging to the related industries. Such unilateral move of the government amplified the suspicion that the government was not pushing for the FTA to maximize the social welfare but to realize some ulterior political agenda.

Implementation System

The administrative implementation system associated with the negotiations for and signing and implementation of the ROK - U.S. FTA is as follows. The implementation system of the ROK - U.S. FTA through which the beginning of the negotiations and the follow-up negotiation strategy for the FTA were decided was established in 2006. According to the implementation system, the

Minister of Trade would prepare the working plan as the working-level department responsible for the FTA negotiations, while the policy coordination and final confirmation would be discussed and decided by the Foreign Economic Policy Committee before the making of the final decision by the president. To establish the FTA negotiation support system, the ministries governing the international trade issues bolstered their working-level workforce, and bi-weekly meetings of the ministers of foreign economies as well as weekly check-up meetings were held to comprehensively monitor the implementation progress of the ROK - U.S. FTA, the key negotiation issues, and the opinions of the internal stakeholders and ministries. Further, the government established the ROK - U.S. FTA Support Committee in August 2006. The roles of the committee were as follows: (1) collect the public opinions on the FTA negotiation swith the United States; (2) provide the public with information on the ROK - U.S. FTA; (3) mediate in the social conflicts related with the ROK - U.S. FTA; (4) support the activities targeting the National Assembly with regard to the ROK - U.S. FTA; and (5) handle all other issues related with the ROK - U.S. FTA.

Headed by a chairman, the committee was made up of 8 civilian members and 6 government members. The former deputy prime minister for economic affairs was appointed as the first chairman of the committee, doubling as the special advisor to the president on the ROK - U.S. FTA. As such, the chairman was empowered to link the trade ministries in the administration and the Presidential Office. For the committee members, the heads of four major economic associations, including the Korea International Trade Association, the press represented by the Korea Newspaper Association, and key figures representing civil associations, including Consumers Korea and the Korean National Council of Women, were commissioned to work as the committee members. The government members were composed of the heads of those ministries and institutions governing the trade and public affairs policies, including the deputy prime minister for economic affairs, the head of the Office for Government Policy Coordination, the head of the Office of the Minister of Trade, the head of the Government Information Agency, the head of the Office of Policy in the Presidential Secretariat, and the Senior Secretary to the President for Public Affairs. The expert members in the committee amounted to 50, with 12 of them dispatched on loan from the central government ministries and 10 from the government-funded research institutes and related organizations, while the professionals in the related field were employed as contractual workers. Further, the ROK - U.S. FTA Settlement Support Team (Settlement Support Team), which was to provide support for the works of the committee, was installed. The support group was headed by a group leader and consisted of 2 bureaus and 8 teams.

On May 15, 2007, right after the finalization of the FTA with the United States, the cabinet decided in a meeting to expand and revamp the ROK - U.S. FTA Support Committee into the FTA Internal Support Committee. While the committee was inaugurated as an administrative institution dedicated to handling the related internal duties, including the ratification of the final FTA by the National Assembly and the establishment of a measure for minimizing the associated damages, the committee was to handle the various FTA support duties, including the provision of information related with the signing and ratification of the FTA to the people, the collection of the public opinions on the matter, the resolution of the related social conflicts, the provision of support to the National Assembly regarding matters related to the FTA, and the provision of internal supplementary measures.

On top of the administrative implementation system, conciliation of the diverse viewpoints of the affected companies, the key internal stakeholders, had to become the core of the implementation system to ensure that the FTA negotiation process would provide the overall industrial restructuring drive, thereby enhancing the competitive edge of the country's industries. Regrets were expressed, however, that the internal negotiation process, which was to conciliate the varying interests of the related businesses and the diverse stakeholders, was not incorporated in the implementation system. The lack of systematic advanced preparations for the internal negotiation process was said to have eventually increased the social costs to a disproportionate level in the process of pushing ahead with the ROK - U.S. FTA negotiations.

Implementation Process and Contents

The implementation process of the ROK - U.S. FTA by the Roh Moo Hyun and Lee Myung Bak administrations can be summed up as follows. First, the administration set the basic policy directions of the ROK - U.S. FTA project in the FTA implementation roadmap prepared in August 2003. According to the roadmap, FTAs shall first be signed with Singapore, EFTA, and other smaller trade partners in the short term, but in the long term, FTAs shall be signed with mega economies such as the United States. Beginning in 2004 and until 2005, three rounds of preliminary working-level check-up meetings on the ROK - U.S. FTA were held, followed by numerous summits of the trade ministers, the visit of the Korean head of the Korean Office of the Minister of Trade to key representatives of the U.S. House and the Senate for persuasion purposes, and efforts to persuade the affected industries to embrace the FTA. In February 2006, the Korean head of the Office of the Minister of Trade and the head of USTR jointly declared the beginning of the ROK - U.S. FTA talks in the U.S. From the commencement of the ROK - U.S. FTA talks and during the negotiations for it, the Korean government commissioned a study on the effect of the ROK - U.S. FTA, in addition to 10 other studies, and held seminars, public hearings, and online polls on the matter. In the online poll conducted jointly with the Korea Federation of Industries, Korea Gallup, and KBIZ, some 80% of the respondents indicated that they favored the signing of the ROK - U.S. FTA.

From the commencement of the ROK - U.S. FTA talks in February 2006 until March 2007, the negotiating teams from Seoul and Washington went through eight rounds of talks. They then declared the success of the talks in April 2007. Such speed and promptness of the negotiation process were unprecedented compared to those of the other FTA talks. There were those who questioned the merit of such speedy finalization of the talks, raising the question of whether such negotiation strategy served the best interests of the country. The motion for the ratification of the ROK - U.S. FTA was submitted to the 17th National Assembly in September 2007, but the ratification process was bumpy as many claimed that the social controversy, especially the opinions of various stakeholders, were not appropriately considered in the negotiation process.

As the controversy over the safety of the imported U.S. beef spread across the society after the inauguration in February 2008 of the administration, the overall public opinion on the ratification of the ROK - U.S. FTA turned sour as it was directly linked with the U.S. beef importation issue. Whereas the negative public opinions played a critical role in the ratification of the ROK - U.S. FTA in Korea, equally critical public opinions were directed at the final agreement with regard to its provisions related to the U.S. automobile and dairy industries. Driven by the disapproval of the FTA provisions from both sides of the Pacific, Washington requested that the negotiations be reopened in 2010, with the talks being finalized in December 2010. The key agreements reached in the additional talks included the following: (1) should the sale of Korean cars soar in the U.S. market after the ROK - U.S. FTA takes effect, Washington shall be allowed to implement an urgent measure to limit the importation of cars from Korea and (2) among the U.S. automobile models imported by Korea, only those that would sell over 25,000 cars per year shall be subjected to the safety inspection requirement. Given that the bestselling U.S. automobile model in Korea sold less than 10,000 units per year at the time, some argued that it would be nothing short of a total abolition of the safety inspection standards for the imported U.S. car.

Following the ratification of the ROK - U.S. FTA Implementation Act in the House of Representatives and in the Senate in October 2010, the motion for the ratification of the ROK-U.S. FTA was approved in the Korean National Assembly in November 2011. The ROK - U.S. FTA finally took effect on March 15, 2012, and the ROK - U.S. FTA Joint Committee, which was established to ensure the effective implementation of the ratified agreement, held meetings in May 2012 and October 2013, respectively. The implementation process of the ROK - U.S. FTA has since been mutually checked by both parties to the agreement, and other supplementary measures have also been implemented.

The contents of the ROK - U.S. FTA can be divided into the key agreements contained in the ROK - U.S. FTA and other supplementary measures for the FTA. The key agreements of the ROK - U.S. FTA are as follows. The ROK - U.S. FTA is a comprehensive package that touches diverse trade-related issues, including products, trade relief, services, investment, competition, intellectual property rights, government procurement, labor, and environment. The two countries agreed to abolish the tariffs on almost all trade items and on most of the manufactured products as early as possible. Meanwhile, the tariffs on agricultural produce shall be immediately abolished for those products that have no impact on the local farming industry or those that are highly dependent on imports. As for the key trade items, the tariffs shall be abolished in a phased manner, including the guarantee of a grace period of over 15 years for some sensitive products. For the service sector, the two countries agreed to allow some leeway for the sector to advance its competence by opening the market in a selective and phased manner, and in the public education and medical industries, the two parties agreed to allow each other discretion in policy-making through the provision of a comprehensive grace period. Finally, in the professional services and financing industries, the two parties agreed to open the market in a phased and limited fashion.

The key countermeasures that the government implemented in response to the ROK - U.S. FTA are as follows. In a move to strengthen the competency of those industries that would bear the brunt of the implementation of the agreement, the administration prepared a comprehensive package in January 2012, which was developed further from the existing countermeasure for the FTA established in November 2007. Newly added to the original package was the investment of some KRW 24.1 trillion in the farming and fisheries industries for 10 years (2008～2017) to improve such industries' competence and to compensate for the direct damages inflicted by the fast-growing importation. In addition, some KRW 29.8 trillion in tax breaks shall be offered through the provision of tax-free oil, zero VAT for agricultural equipment, and the extended application of the sunset regulations. In the manufacturing-service industry, enhancement of the industrial competence through the provision of R&D support as well as provision of loans and consulting via the trade coordination support system shall be sought, while in the pharmaceutical industry, KRW 1 trillion shall be provided for 10 years (2008~2017) as R&D investment and for the construction of infrastructure by preparing a measure to bolster the industrial competence (June 2007). In the area of employment, the administration bolstered the job security through the provision of employment support service tailored for each phase before and after unemployment as well as through the training and education of the top talents.

Performance and Assessment

The key achievements of the ROK - U.S FTA in the product trades are as follows. With regard to the results of the ROK - U.S. FTA in the aspects of the size and structure of the Korea - U.S trade and the trends of the direct investments between the two trade partners for the two years since the FTA became effective on March 15, 2012, the country's exports to the United States jumped remarkably for the two years compared to the growth of the country's exports to the world when analyzed in terms of the trade volumes, and the direct investments from the United States increased as well. Specifically, the growth rate of Korea's exports to (15.7%) and imports from (10.1%) the United States were higher than those to and from the world (6.0%, 5.3%) as of the 2nd year of the implementation of the ROK - U.S. FTA. Furthermore, the direct investments from the United States jumped twofold in the same period.

When analyzed in terms of the direct foreign investments for the 2 years (March 15, 2012 - March 14, 2014) since the ROK - U.S. FTA took effect, the direct foreign investments (as reported) increased by 82.5% during the period compared to the investment amount before the FTA took effect. In 2013, the total foreign investments from the whole world decreased more or less year-on-year, but the investments from the United States dipped by only a small percentage (-3.8%) whereas those from key states, including Japan (-40.7%) and China (-33.8%), fell dramatically. The accumulated total foreign investments from the United States by the end of 2013 was US$ 53.349 billion or some 24.5% of the total FDI in Korea. By investment type, all types of investment increased, not only the M&A-type investment but also the greenfield-type investment, which is excellent for creating new jobs by investing in new plant. By industry, both the manufacturing industry (mainly transport machinery and metal products) and the service industry (mainly finance and insurance) saw an increase in foreign direct investments.

The achievements of the ROK - U.S. FTA in the service sector can be summarized as follows. Regarding the impact of the ROK - U.S. FTA on the service sector two years after it took effect, legal advisors on foreign laws who acquired their license in the United States or American law firms advising on foreign laws entered the local market albeit partially, but other than that, no significant structural change has been seen. In the case of telecommunication service, foreign indirect investment in the basic telecommunication service provider companies, with the exception of KT and SKT, shall be fully permitted beginning in the third year of the implementation of the ROK - U.S. FTA. Also, beginning in the fourth year of the implementation of the agreement, foreign indirect investment in the program provider companies, with the exception of the news, general programming, and home shopping channels, shall be fully permitted, thereby showing no visible movement as of yet.

The policy-level implication of the experience of the finalization of the ROK - U.S. FTA is that the introduction of an efficient internal negotiation process with the concerned industries and stakeholders as well as the delivery of accurate information will be as important as the negotiations with the foreign counterpart in the establishment and implementation of the FTA and the trade policy in the future. Rather than relying on the publicity tactics simply blaring slogans, the administration will be able to effectively communicate the policy signals (e.g., industrial restructuring through the introduction of the FTA) with the concerned parties by delivering to them accurate information on the FTA and by seeking the opinions of the stakeholder sat the same time. Furthermore, such efforts will enable the administration to implement diverse supplementary measures that will effectively bolster the competence of corporations and that will minimize the policy-level shock from the implementation of the FTA.

3. Low-Carbon, Green Growth

Background

One of the key backgrounds behind the push for the future strategy "Low-Carbon, Green Growth" was its historical timing.[5] 2008, the year the Lee Myung Bak administration was inaugurated, marked the 60th anniversary of the foundation of the ROK government. President Lee Myung Bak wished to celebrate August 15, 2008, the 63rd anniversary of the country's liberation from the Japanese colonial rule and the 60th anniversary of the foundation of the ROK government, as the turning point from which the country would leap forward to join the club of advanced first-rate countries. To sum up, the president was convinced that he had been given an once-in-a-lifetime opportunity to look back on the history of the republic and design its future in his first year in office.

In an attempt to have in-house institutions dedicated to the study of the future strategy, the president formed the Future Planning Committee (founding chairman: Ahn Byeong Man) and International Advisory Group (chairman: Dominique Barton) and put them under direct presidential control. Established as an advisory body that would formulate a vision for the republic, the Future Planning Committee, in particular, played the important role of collecting and coordinating expert opinions far and wide on the mid- and long-term vision of the Republic of Korea that were to be incorporated in the special presidential address marking Liberation Day on August 15, 2008. Specifically, the administration ensured that the key agenda identified during the conceptualization process would be reflected in the midterm fiscal plan after close consultation with the related ministries, thereby bolstering the chances that the vision would be realized. Meanwhile, the International Advisory Group, which was composed of foreign members and established as an institution dedicated to advising the administration on the key global trends, pending international issues, and the policy direction and political situation of the key powers, made a substantial contribution in preventing the country from becoming trapped in a myopic path in establishing its future vision and key strategy. The core issues of the republic, which were collected via the

5) For a more comprehensive behind-the-scenes account of the birth of the "green growth" vision, read The Government White Paper on the Lee Myung Bak Administration (February 2008~February 2013), "Green Growth and Future Growth Engine," *The Government of the Republic of Korea*, 2012, pp. 64-75.

Future Planning Committee, the International Advisory Group, and the 60th Anniversary Project Committee, were regrouped as follows: (1) the limitations of quantitative growth; (2) the limitations of the short-term-performance-oriented policy; and (3) the country's weak international standing. Climate change was reinterpreted as the key to overcoming the identified limitations, and was thus encapsulated in the new vision "Low-Carbon, Green Growth."

In the presidential address marking the 63rd anniversary of the country's liberation from the Japanese colonial rule and the 60th anniversary of the foundation of the republic, President Lee Myung Bak proclaimed "Low-Carbon, Green Growth" as the vision of the Republic of Korea:

Today, which marks the 60th year of the foundation of the Republic of Korea, I hereby propose "low-carbon, green growth" as the central part of our new vision. Green growth signifies sustainable growth that reduces greenhouse gases and environmental contamination. This is the new paradigm of national development that would create a new growth engine and jobs.... If we confirm our determination today and push ahead with the action, the country can assume leadership in green growth and can play the leading role in building a new civilization (ahead of other nations). I hereby promise to you today that I will create the key foundation for living of our future generation in the next 10 and 20 years.

The background information behind the administration's surprise appropriation of "climate change," in itself a loaded word, in the positive term and then its elevation to the mainstream agenda that would be pushed forward with under the presidential leadership in the wake of the 60th anniversary of Liberation Day on August 15 is presented below. After reinterpreting the climate change issue as an opportunity to establish the country's vision, the following factors, including "N," "G," and "R," were identified. First, climate change was a "common issue" linked "not just with me but with us" and "not just with the present generation but with the next generation as well" and that has the "characteristic of state leadership (N: noble)" that should be implemented with a bipartisan foundation. Second, climate change also has a global characteristic (G: global) in that it concerns the entire world, and Korea may have room for playing the role of bridging the gap between the advanced and developing nations. Third, climate change embodies a clear and present threat but is no less real (R: real) as a potential opportunity for the country to create jobs by assuming industrial and technological leadership in addressing it. Korea, which saw its average temperature rising two times faster than the global average, was also ranked 7th in the world in terms of the emission of greenhouse gases, thereby being singled out as one of the countries most vulnerable to climate change. The administration took note of the fact that should it respond to the threat, it would not only be able to overcome the energy crunch — the other side of coin — but would also be able to establish the country's next-generation growth engine consisting of the smart grid, energy storage system, and electric vehicles.

Implementation System

The implementation system of the green growth policy can be divided mainly into the pan-governmental and civilian domains. An entirely new and powerful implementation system was essential for the development of the green growth agenda into some concrete policy initiatives. Specifically, many advanced countries tend to maintain a fusion-style interdisciplinary administrative organization in an attempt to facilitate the consolidated handling of the climate change and energy issues, which are closely interlinked.[6)]

It was unrealistic, however, to reshuffle the government organization after the inauguration of the administration. As such, the administration instead opted to install a committee under direct presidential control that would perform pan-governmental policy coordination and deliberation on the key related issues and that would vote on the issues tabled for deliberation. The Green Growth Committee,[7)] which was inaugurated in February 2009 by consolidating the core functions of the Climate Change Committee under the Prime Ministerial Office, the National Energy Committee under the Ministry of Knowledge Economy, and the Sustainable Development Committee under the Ministry of Environment, was the administration's answer to this problem.

Although officially only an advisory body, the committee emerged as a powerful pan-governmental implementation institution controlled by the Presidential Office, co-chaired by the prime minister and a civilian chairperson (Han Seung Soo and Kim Hyeong Kook, respectively), and participated in by 10 ministers of the key ministries as ex-officio members, including the Ministry of Strategy and Finance, Ministry of Foreign Affairs, Ministry of Education, Science, and Technology, and Ministry of Land and Maritime Affairs. Participated in by 29 civilian experts scattered over three subcommittees that dealt with green growth and industries, climate change and energy, and green life and sustainable development, the Green Growth Committee was given the role of establishing the Five-Year Green Growth Implementation Plan, setting the national greenhouse gas reduction goals, and preparing key related bills jointly with the Green Growth Planning Group composed of 50 public officials and working-level members, by collecting the opinions of the related government ministries and diverse stakeholders.

Meanwhile, the Low-Carbon, Green Growth Basic Ordinance was legislated pursuant to the standard ordinance on the local self-governing bodies of the Ministry of Government Administration and Home Affairs to make up for the shortcomings of the top-down administration system of the central government and to push for the serious implementation of the policy, which was firmly rooted in the field.[8)] Further, in a move to strengthen the government-private partnership in

---

6) Denmark established the Ministry of Climate Change & Energy, which was followed by the establishment of the Ministry of Energy & Climate Change in the United Kingdom (2008), the Ministry of Climate Change (2007) in Australia, and the Ministry of Environment, Energy, and Sustainable Land (2007) in France. The Brookings Institution unveiled the top 10 key policy tasks that the president of the United States should push for before the 2009 presidential elections, in which it singled out the green strategy as the second most important issue after the reinforcement of the international financial system, and proposed that the president install the National Energy & Climate Committee in the White House.

7) Established in January 2009 pursuant to the Rules on the Establishment and Operation of the Green Growth Committee, the Green Growth Committee had the Green Growth Planning Group as its working-level organization and was officially inaugurated in February 2009, with the Presidential Secretary for Future Vision as the co-chairperson. The committee was given a legal status in accordance with the Basic Act on Green Growth enacted in December 2009. In September 2011, in the second half of the Lee Myung Bak presidency, the presidential secretary tasked to handle the green growth issue was promoted to a senior-level secretary responsible for planning green growth in an attempt to bolster the implementation speed of the green growth policy.

8) The local governments formed their respective government-private sector joint green growth committees similar to the Green Growth Committee in the central government, but given the absence of a permanent secretariat such as that of the Green Growth Committee in Seoul, the policy formation and coordination activities of such committees were relatively weak. One significant developmentwith regard to the local engagement in the green drive, however, was the 20th Green Growth Committee meeting held on August 31, 2012 in the Kim Dae Jung Convention Center in Gwangju City, with the theme "Green Korea Led by the Local Regions,"where the heads

the push for the green growth policy, the Industrial Council (March 2009), Financial Industry Council (April 2009), Science and Technology Council (April 2009), Green Life Council (October 2009), and Green IT Council (November 2009), all composed of civilian members, started their respective activities.

Implementation Process and Contents

In view of the unique characteristics (N, G, R) of the agenda, green growth is a type of future strategy that would yield a good outcome only when it is implemented consistently on a mid- and long-term basis. Therefore, it was critical to establish a strategy that would focus on constructing a stable foundation and framework for the government's consistent implementation of the policy, even surpassing the limitations of the president's single five-year term, rather than striving to come up with some short-term and tangible results. In view of such assessment, the administration focused on the "institutionalization" of the green growth policy through legislation internally, while externally it focused on the "internalization" of the issue.

Within the administration, the Green Growth Committee, jointly with the private sector, prepared the green growth national strategy and five-year plan in May 2009 and announced the confirmed package after its resolution by the cabinet in a meeting in July of the same year. The confirmed plan contained the vision of joining the club of the world's top 7 green powers by 2020 and of growing into the world's 5th largest green power by 2050 as well as the top three strategies of climate change adaptation and energy independence, establishment of a new growth engine, and improvement of the people's living quality and bolstering of the national status. Along with these strategies, the committee also suggested 10 key policy directions under these three strategies.

The most effective and reliable method of institutionalizing a specific policy is to establish the legal foundation for it. Based on such understanding, the administration established the green growth national strategy and five-year plan, which was then followed by the legislation of the following five acts to provide legal support for the initiative: the Basic Act on Low-Carbon, Green Growth the Act on the Allocation and Transaction of Greenhouse Gas Emission Rights the Act on the Construction and Usage-Promotion of a Smart Grid the Act on the Support for the Construction of Green Buildings; and the Act on the Development of Sustainable Logistics. Key among them were the Basic Act on Low-Carbon, Green Growth (henceforth, the Basic Act on Green Growth) and the Act on the Allocation and Transaction of Greenhouse Gas Emission Rights (henceforth, the Acts on Emission Rights). The administration's green growth policy aimed to introduce a rational regulatory system to reduce the emission of greenhouse gases and to promote the conversion of key energy sources, and set the goal of reducing its emission of greenhouse gases by 30% of the projected emission volumes by 2020.

Meanwhile, the internationalization strategy was implemented with the following process. The legal apparatus alone was not sufficient to warrant the continued implementation of the green growth policy because the existing acts may be modified or discarded when the government and the members of the National Assembly change. The issue here was not the contents of the laws

---

of 16 local self-governing bodies ratified the Gwangju Declaration on Green Growth.

but how to prepare for the damages that could be inflicted by politics on the policy's legal stability. To prepare for such possibility, the administration made the green growth policy go through a screening process by the international community, thereby turning it into an international asset. By employing middle-power diplomacy, the move was also driven by the strategy to overcome the country's lack of soft power, which had been criticized time to time as the soft spot of the country. The first step to achieving such diplomatic roadmap was the OECD Council of Ministers meeting held in June 2009. In the council meeting, all the member states of OECD adopted "green growth" as their new development paradigm in the declaration of the Council of Ministers. In addition, UNEP published the "Overview Report on the Republic of Korea's National Strategy for Green Growth" in 2010 as the first report of the World Green Economy Strategic Project. Following the publication, the G20 Seoul Summit held in November 2010 adopted "green growth" as an official agenda, and in the G20 Summit held in Los Cabos in June 2010, it was elevated as a core agenda. To sum up, the national agenda of the Republic of Korea was turned into an asset in the form of the agenda of the international community.

Furthermore, the administration exerted efforts to establish an international organization that would push for the green growth initiative internationally. In response to such efforts, in 2010, the Global Green Growth Institute was inaugurated as a non-profit civilian organization in Seoul. The institute succeeded in holding a signing ceremony and turned into an international institution in the Rio+ Summit, a summit participated in by 18 advanced and developing nations, held in Brazil in 2012, some two years after its inauguration. Following the ratification of the agreement by the National Assembly in October 2012, the institute was re-launched as an official international organization fully effective pursuant to the international laws. Further, the administration focused on hosting the secretariat of the newly established Green Climate Fund, which would be nicknamed the "World Bank of Climate Change," eventually succeeding in hosting the fund in Songdo, Incheon in October 2012, beating the other contenders hailing from advanced economies like Germany. In addition, the Green Technology Center, which would coordinate the policy directions associated with green technology development and would function as the country's international channel for technology cooperation with the Climate Technology Center & Network (CTCN), was founded and the KAIST Graduate School of Green Growth, which would train the talents who would study the overall green growth topics at the level of higher education, opened. In short, the so-called "green growth architecture" that was to facilitate the implementation of the green growth initiative in a systematic manner both internally and externally was set up.

Performance and Assessment

The green growth initiative of the administration can be deemed a prescient move in that it laid the foundation for the sustained implementation of the green drive through institutionalization and internationalization. Below are the administration's other key related achievements.[9] First, the initiative improved the international competence of the green technology and industry and transformed the industry into the country's new growth engine. According to the interim

9) The 22nd Green Growth Committee meeting, which was the last committee meeting that was held and was chaired by President Lee Myung Bak, compiled and announced a total of 22 key performances of the administration's green drive.

assessment performed in 2011, the country's green technology was assessed to have advanced from a 50.9%-level world-class technology in 2009 to 77.7% in 2011, a remarkable improvement in such a short time. Such trend is assessed to have accelerated even more: the World Wildlife Fund estimated Korea's total revenue in the clean energy industry sector as 5 billion euros in 2011, making it the 8th among the total of 40 surveyed countries, while the growth rate was ranked 3rd, after those of China and the United States.[10)]

Second, the initiative activated the economy and created new jobs. The key objective of "green growth" was to prove that the economy and the environment need not clash with each other but should be in a mutually beneficial relationship. It was necessary in this regard to analyze the impact of the massive "green new deal," which was implemented to stimulate the economy and to facilitate green investments in the wake of the global financial crisis, on the economy. According to an analysis by the World Bank, Korea recorded the fastest economic recovery among all the OECD countries during the period when the massive green new deal was being implemented. Not only that, such fast economic recovery is thought of as the catalyst that helped the country succeed in sustaining growth amidst the fiscal crisis that originated from Europe. Meanwhile, according to an analysis of the job creation effect of the green fiscal investment amounting to KRW 56 trillion from 2009 to 2011, the investment in the green sector created 764,000 new jobs in the green sector. Comparably, whereas if the investment were made in the non-green sector, such investment would have created some 250,000 new jobs, a significantly less number of jobs.[11)]

Third, the green drive demonstrated the possibility of decoupling the GDP growth rate and the greenhouse gas emission trend. According to an analysis by the Greenhouse Gas Inventory & Research Center of Korea, the country's greenhouse gas emission growth rate was recorded as lower than the GDP growth rate in 2012 for the first time since the survey started, a result of the concentrated management of some 400 businesses that were emitting large volumes of greenhouse gases in accordance with the "emission target management system." If such encouraging trend will continue to be upheld in the future, it would be the most important achievement of the green growth drive.

Fourth, the drive enhanced the international reputation of the Republic of Korea. The green growth drive of the administration succeeded in expanding the country's international horizon and elevating the country's international prestige. Many key international figures, including OECD Secretary-General Angel Gurria, joined the cause while praising the green growth of the Republic of Korea as the new paradigm for the international community, an unprecedented development in the history of the country's diplomacy.

Meanwhile, some in the Korean society still had reservations about the green growth policy being pushed for by the administration. These are summed up as follows. First, the initiative was implemented in a top-down manner, thereby failing to sufficiently communicate its details with the civil society. Second, the question on whether the green growth initiative could go hand in hand with the sustainable development issue was raised. Whereas the sustainable development issue

---

10) WWF performed the analysis by commissioning the German consulting firm Roland Berger.

11) The study result, once verified through a positive research rather than through simple calculation, is expected to show more compelling directions for the employment policy.

valued the harmonious relationships among the three key axes (the economy, environment, and society), the green growth drive failed to pay sufficient attention to the eradication of poverty and the resolution of the socioeconomic polarization, and, instead, concentrated on the relationship between the economy and the environment. The green growth initiative, however, could be better understood as an action-oriented strategy that aimed to implement the sustainable development concept to the economic and environment sectors first. Other key criticisms of the green growth initiative were that the drive was a simply a "green wash" designed to advocate the Four Major Rivers Restoration Project, that the total power demand management and greenhouse gas reduction were insufficient, and that green governance is unstable.

The green growth policy began as a vision with the characteristic of a declaration reflecting the demands of the era, but its actual fruits were harvested through a regime that was based on trust in the supporting laws, institutions, norms, and principles as well as on strategic goals and consistent implementation. In this regard, it is still too early to make a final assessment of the green growth initiative.

4. Restoration of the Four Major Rivers

Background

The perennial lack of water is nothing new throughout the world. The supply of fresh water is emerging as a key social issue in many countries. Some estimate that about 3 billion people will be suffering from water shortage by 2025.

Fortunately for Korea, the country's mountains and valleys are sufficiently afforested. However, during the drought season, the situation changes completely. Korea's annual precipitation is 1,283mm on average, some 1.3 times higher than the world's average precipitation, but Korea is one of the countries in the world that are experiencing water shortage, according to an announcement by the United Nations Population Action International. The problem is that the situation is even deteriorating over time. Some estimate that the country's per-capita fresh water supply is expected to drop from 1,470m^3 in 1993 to 1,199m^3 in 2025. According to the government, water was already short in supply by about 2 billion tons in 2012. Meanwhile, the per-capita water usage of the Koreans is 395 liters, the highest among the 29 OECD member states.[12)]

Streams account for over 89% of the country's water supply[13)] with no foreseeable problem expected any time soon via the streams. However, since two-thirds of the rains fall from June to September, the water is in short supply during the drought season, making it difficult to secure sufficient service water or manage the water quality. Comparably, the water overflows during the flood season. The overflows during the flood season create wild fluctuation in the inflow/outflow of the streams, thereby pushing up the coefficient of river regime to 300 - 400, a stark contrast to the European countries' coefficient of river regime, which remains at 10. Such contrasting supply

12) Compared to 296 liters of France, 132 liters of Germany, 246 liters of Denmark, and 393 liters of Japan, the per-capita water usage of the Koreans was surveyed to be ridiculously high.

13) In Korea, 49% of the total service water is being tapped from the streams, and 40% from the dams.

of water puts the country in a challenging situation in terms of water management.

Of the annual precipitation amounting to 127.6 billion tons, only 26% is available in the usual form, and the per-capita precipitation is 2,705 tons, only one-tenth of the global average consumption, amounting to 270 billion tons. The underground fresh water reserve is estimated at 1.5448 trillion tons, and the optimum annual amount that can be reasonably developed is estimated at 13.5 billion tons. However, since massive underwater development is difficult, due to the country's geological structure, only about 3.7 billion tons are being developed annually, thereby limiting the further development potential. The administration pushed forward with the Four Major Rivers Restoration Project in an attempt to overcome such limitations.

Implementation System

The Four Major Rivers Planning Group (installed in February 2009) was jointly expanded and revamped into the Implementation Headquarters in April 2009 by the Ministry of Land and Maritime Affairs, Ministry of Environment, and Ministry of Agriculture, Fisheries, and Food. As the project shifted to full gear on February 4, 2010, the administration pushed for the implementation of the project through an organizational reshuffling, including the installation of the Construction Bureau (renamed and changed to Project Support Bureau in June 2010).

The Government Support Council (chairperson: head of the Prime Ministerial Office; council members: vice ministers of the related ministries) was installed in the Prime Ministerial Office to establish the inter-ministerial cooperation system, and the three related committees — the Regional Development Committee (renamed Balanced National Development Committee in April 2009), the Green Growth Committee, and the National Construction Committee — each played the role of suggesting basic project directions to restore the four major rivers and of advising the government in such regard.

After the confirmation of the Master Plan for the Four Major Rivers Restoration Project, a series of advanced works (streamlining of the legally approved plan, preliminary feasibility study, compensation for right of way, clearing of illegal facilities, disposal of the dredged soil, pre-environmental appraisal, and survey of potential cultural assets) were carried out. After the commissioning and commencement of the project, in-construction environmental impact management andpost-construction maintenance, including the monitoring of the overall issues associated with the project, were performed.

Implementation Process and Contents

The Four Major Rivers Restoration Project began to be implemented in earnest when the Master Plan for the Four Major Rivers Restoration Project was established on June 8, 2009, about half a year after the selection of the Four Major Rivers Restoration Project by the Regional Development Committee on December 15, 2008. The project had been consistently implemented since the first-phase section of the turnkey-based project (16 construction sections in all) was opened for tender on June 29, 2009. The rate of construction was recorded at 90.1% of the total project as of December 22, 2011, and at 96.4% in the main streams.

The key project statuses were as follows. The project budgets that were to be invested in the water system were KRW 3.6 trillion for Han River, KRW 11.7 trillion for Nakdong River, KRW 3.5 trillion for Geum River, and KRW 3.4 trillion for Yeongsan River (including KRW 291.7 billion for Seomjin River). The expected outcomes of the KRW 22.2-trillion project were improved flood control capability, securing of water resources, and water quality improvement.

The key project contents were as follows. The Flood Control Capability Enhancement Project was pushed for in an attempt to minimize the damages by floods in the wake of climate change by dredging the riverbeds deep enough to withstand 200-year floods or bigger ones. Towards this end, reinforcement of the regulating ponds/cistern/aging levee and expansion of the floodgates were pushed for. Graduating from the conventional measures, such as the piling up of levees and the restoration of the damaged sections, a new concept in water control that would block flood damage fundamentally was introduced to dredge the riverbeds. The total project cost for the flood-regulating ponds and the riverside cistern amounted to KRW 610.6 billion. The project for the reinforcement of the aging levees involved the expansion of the cross-section of those levees that were vulnerable to floods because they were built with earth and were being washed away by the streams, and the lowering of the slope of the levees, thereby increasing their overall safety. The project for expanding the floodgates was aimed at bypassing floods fast and at lowering the water levels by increasing the number of floodgates in the estuary banks. The total project cost of the reinforcement of the aging levees (146 sites combined total length: 620km) amounted to KRW 1.6481 trillion, and that of the expansion of the floodgates in the estuary banks (two sites) amounted to KRW 858.9 billion.

The project for securing water resources was pushed for to prepare for the future water shortages and localized droughts by installing multi-purpose dammed pools for irrigation and by piling up the reservoir for agricultural purposes. The total construction cost of the multi-purpose dammed pools for irrigation (16 to regulate the water levels) amounted to KRW 1.5201 trillion that of the new-dam construction, KRW 1.2056 trillion and that of the piling up of the reservoir for agricultural purposes, KRW 2.2986 trillion.

The project for improving the water quality was aimed at pushing up the percentage of the good-quality water enough to allow swimming (Category II water, BOD 3 mg/L), from 75.8% in 2008 to 86.3% by 2012, through the introduction of various means to reduce the waterborne non-point contaminants. The total project cost of the expansion of the basic environmental and contaminant treatment facilities amounted to KRW 3.8837 trillion (2011: 8). In addition, the project for restoring the eco-friendly streams and bicycle roads was pushed for at thesame time. The total project cost of the restoration of the eco-friendly streams and waterfront eco-belt amounted to KRW 3.1143 trillion, and that of the bicycle roads, KRW 194.3 billion.

Performance and Assessment

Unlike many traditional river projects, often with a single purpose, the Four Major Rivers Restoration Project was a multi-purpose project aimed at responding to climate change, promoting regional development, and laying the foundation for green growth by maintaining and reorganizing the main stream of the four major rivers flowing along the length of the Korean Peninsula. The Four Major Rivers Restoration Project should be predictable and objectively assessable even after its conclusion because it is a national project with multiple objectives. However, its performance is hard to predict because its outcome would surface only after a long time, and the opinions are usually divided over its short-, mid-, and long-term performances.

The Ministry of Land and Maritime Affairs, the key implementer of the Four Major Rivers Restoration Project, assessed the project as having shown the country new directions in national land management and as having enabled the country to respond to climate change proactively through its (the project's) uneventful implementation, including the construction of dammed pools for irrigation (16) and dredging (450 million m^3), which lowered the floodwater level (by 2~4m by key point) and secured a rich body of water (1.3 billion m^3). Further, it was mentioned in the 2012 business report of the Ministry of Land and Maritime Affairs that the project was cited as a green growth example through the restoration of the rivers in the 2011 UNEP Green Economy Report. The ministry pointed out, however, that while the project was in progress, the branch streams was vulnerable to the irregular floods occurring in the wake of climate change, thereby flooding the urban areas frequently. The report recommended the adoption of follow-up measures, including the construction of a maintenance system, the streamlining of the branch streams, and the prevention of urban flooding.

It could be determined if the policy assessment by the key governing ministry was reasonable by checking if the Four Major Rivers Restoration Project was pushed for in ways that would meet the policy goals of the project. First, the indices required to assess the performance of the project should be developed, after which the project performance should be assessed using the developed indices. A more precise assessment system should be put in place, however, and the assessment should be made according to the system to implement a more detailed and scientific evaluation of the project that was pushed for on a massive scale.

The assessment of the Four Major Rivers Restoration Project by the academe and the Board of Audit and Inspection in the areas of disaster prevention, securing of water resources, and ensuring good-water quality are shown below. First, the audit report by the Board of Audit and Inspection on the disaster prevention capability of the Four Major Rivers Restoration Project contains a rather unfavorable assessment of the quality management of the key facilities. Key among them were the haphazard patchworks (11, including the Gongju dammed pool) that were applied to the dilapidating facilities without first ensuring the fundamental safety of the facilities. With regard to the reduction of damages from natural disasters, the Ministry of Land and Maritime Affairs revealed that the amount of the damages arising from floods was KRW 2.7 trillion per year on average for the past five years. As it will cost over KRW 4.2 trillion simply to restore the damaged facilities, the ministry argued that it would need to implement some preventive measures. It argued that the Four Major Rivers Restoration Project may be put in a positive light in this regard. It would be better to assess the damages from floods or droughts on a mid- and long-term basis due to the contrasting interpretations of the project, which were sharply divided between those advocating development and those arguing for conservation.

Second, with regard to the performance assessment in terms of securing water resources and improving the water quality, the audit report pointed out the reduced potential in meeting the water quality target due to the arbitrary changing of the water quality target tailored for a given project budget, which again raised the question of whether the water quality improvement target that was originally set was appropriate in the first place. Despite the fact that the National Institute of Environment Research had warned the potential deterioration of the water quality by the Four

Major Rivers Restoration Project, the Ministry of Environment did not adopt comprehensive phased measures such as additional installation of a total phosphorus treatment facility aimed at preventing eutrophication caused by the construction of dammed pools as part of the Four Major Rivers Restoration Project, strengthening of the management of non-point contamination sources and livestock excretion, and elimination of algae. It is thus necessary to consistently follow up the improvement of the water quality when securing water resources.

The project would score points for having reduced the contamination sources by reducing the nitrogen and phosphorous through the elimination of sediments, the reduction of farmlands, and the clearing of the wastes along the rivers. However, the mid- and long-term assessment of the Four Major Rivers Restoration Project will inevitably yield negative results if the following issues will not be properly handled: the algal bloom caused by the reduced water flow speeds after the construction of the 16 dammed pools and the boosting of the sewage treatment rates in the cities scattered along the four major rivers. When the changes in the waterborne ecosystem after the construction of the dammed pools were reviewed, it was confirmed that overall qualitative deterioration of the waterborne ecosystem was occurring. It is therefore assessed that consistent monitoring of the waterborne ecosystem is required as it is feared that the ecosystem would be damaged significantly in accordance with the various environmental changes that occurred in the wake of the construction of the dammed pools.

When the project's performance is assessed in terms of the river environment, the appropriateness of the riverside maintenance plan with regard to the river environment should be checked. Further, no serious discussion has been done on the assessment of the Four Major Rivers Restoration Project in terms of its activation of the regional economy. In the future, it will be necessary to carry out a management-level assessment of the overall impact of the project on the regional economy as well as on the areas surrounding the site of the planned future dammed pools. All told, the Four Major Rivers Restoration Project was successful in improving the country's water resource management efficiency, but it remains to be seen if it improved the sustainability of the environment.

5. Introduction of general programming channels and establishment of a competitive broadcasting channel

Background

The general programming channels refer to those channels that are viewable via cable television or pay television services, and that "contain diverse programming covering news, culture/education, and entertainment in a mutually harmonious way." Specifically, the general programming channels are required to allocate over 50% of their respective total programs to news and culture/education.

The introduction of general programming channels and the bolstering of the competitive system in the broadcast market can be deemed as the most prominent aspect of the administration's media industry policy. Since the introduction of the concept to the Broadcasting Act in 2000, the introduction of the general programming channel as a means to ensure programming diversity and to strengthen the competitiveness of the broadcast contents has been considered several times but to this day has not been turned into a reality. Further, the general programming channel was proposed as the key media policy of the presidential candidate Lee Myung Back in the 2007 presidential elections, which was followed by the adoption of the key policy by the 17th Presidential Transition Committee. With the inclusion of the provisions on softening the regulations on broadcasting in the amended Broadcasting Act among the series of media laws[14] that were passed in July 2009, the general programming channel was introduced, and such introduction became a major milestone. The amendment of the Broadcasting Act, which covers the deregulation of the ownership of broadcast assets, opened the way for newspaper companies to participate in the broadcasting enterprise by allowing conglomerates, foreign capital, daily newspapers, and news agencies to invest not only in the terrestrial channels but also in the general programming channels or in the news channels.

The Broadcasting Act amended in 2009 started to take form with the preparation of the policy of introducing the general programming channel services in 2010. The policy objectives of the introduction of the general programming channels clarified in the Basic Plan on the Approval of Services Using General Programming and Dedicated News Channels in September 2010 were as follows: (1) to proactively respond to the changing media environment; (2) to expand the rights of the viewers so as to bolster the diversity of broadcasting; (3) to activate the content market and to establish a virtuous cycle in the pay broadcasting market; and (4) to secure global competitiveness for the broadcasting industry through the introduction of active. Previously, the newspapers and broadcasting channels were in principle not allowed to be managed by the same owner to prevent the excessive dominance of the public opinion by specific media or capital. Given the global competitive environment where media companies were enhancing their competitiveness through media fusion and cross-entrance to others' turfs, however, the administration concluded that it would no longer be feasible to stick to the rule of strictly separating different media formats, and embarked on the reform to soften the vertical regulations on the media industry. It was expected that new types of channels that would stand shoulder to shoulder with the terrestrial channels in terms of their financing and contents production capabilities would emerge soon with the reform. It was also hoped that the reform would stimulate the broadcast content production practices, which were then overly reliant on the terrestrial channels.

Implementation System

The policy governing the general programming channels was the key media policy of the president, which required the cooperation of the ruling party in the political circle. As the ministry governing the broadcasting policy, the Korea Communication Commission (KCC) took the leadership in the introduction of the general programming channels, from its implementation roadmap to the selection of service providers and until the final approval of the channels. The complicated nature of the general programming channel policy, however, made it extremely

14) Passed by the National Assembly in July 2009, the Media Act is not an official legal term but encompasses diverse laws associated with the media for convenience purposes. In its narrow sense, the Media Act is used to signify the Broadcasting Act, the Newspaper Act, the IPTV Act, the Info-Communication Act, the Media Arbitration Act, and the Digital Conversion Act.

difficult for KCC to push forward with the policy unilaterally further, diverse stakeholders, including the National Assembly, service providers, and civil groups, entered the fray, exposing varying interests and ideological differences in the process.

The key players in the formation of the general programming channel policy included the National Assembly (the ruling and opposition parties) and the governing ministries (KCC, Ministry of Culture, Sports, and Tourism) while the unofficial policy implementers in the private domain included broadcast service providers (general programming channel service providers, terrestrial channel service providers, and small broadcast service providers), newspaper businesses, advertising agencies, and civil groups and those from the academe. Among such players, the Grand National Party, the Ministry of Culture, Sports, and Tourism, KCC, and conservative civil groups were classified as the pro-policy camp. KCC pushed for the implementation of the policy by announcing that it would perform a comprehensive review of the feasibility of the ownership of the broadcasting business and management regulation by daily newspapers and new agencies in its first business report in February 2008. In the presidential report meeting held in September 2008, the commission officially announced the expansion of the concurrent management of media at the government level. Moreover, the Ministry of Culture, Sports, and Tourism proposed the softening of the regulation on the concurrent media ownership/management as well as the abolition of the Newspaper Act and the legislation of its replacement act in the business report session to the Presidential Transition Committee. In addition, in the document submitted in September 2008 to the National Assembly's culture, sports, tourism, broadcasting, and telecommunication sub-committee, the ministry argued for bolstering the competency of the country's media industry through the amendment of the media-related laws, including the Newspaper Act. The Grand National Party also collaborated with the government ministries by establishing the Broadcasting Reform Special Committee in September 2008. Meanwhile, civil groups, including the National Coalition for News Rights, rendered their full support to the approval of the concurrent management of newspapers and broadcasting services and to the approval of the general programming channels and the softening of the approval of the news channels.

Whereas the pro-policy camp gathered around KCC in pushing for the policy, the anti-policy camp pushed for the opposition campaign led primarily by the National Union of Media Workers and activist groups, in close consultation with the opposition party. First, the Democratic Party and the Democratic Labor Party made it clear that they were against the approval of the concurrent ownership/management of newspapers and broadcasting services and the possible privatization of KBS-2TV, and the media activist groups (National Union of Media Workers, Citizens' Solidarity for Media Reform, and Citizens' Coalition for Democratic Media) argued for preserving the Newspaper Act to suppress the chaotic market practices of the newspapers and to ensure diversity in public opinions.

Such concerted efforts of various activist groups led to the inauguration of the "Social Action for the Prevention of Private Ownership of the Media and the Expansion of the Public Nature of the Media (Action for Media)," which was formed with the participation of 54 civil groups in January 2008. The civil groups feared that if the general programming channels participated in by newspapers, then the newspapers' monopolistic dominance over the public opinion would deepen. Likewise, they stressed the need for opposing the cross-ownership and concurrent management to prevent the dominance of the public opinion by massive capital and by the family-owned media group. Further, other civil groups, such as the Forum on the Media's Public Nature, feared the spread of the authoritarian market-centric ideology, and stressed their opposition to the policy based on their understanding that it was upon the inauguration of KCC that the independence of broadcasting began to be threatened and that the media's public nature began to wither. In addition, the Local Broadcasting Council, which sensed a direct threat to their survival with the introduction of the general programming channels, criticized the policy in the following statement: "The government's approval of the ownership of the terrestrial channels, general programming channels, and news channels by conglomerates and capitalists is intended to pave the way for the eventual selling of KBS-2 and MBC."

Implementation Process and Contents

The introduction and implementation process of the general programming channels can be divided into the following phases: legislation of media acts and amendment of the Broadcasting Act and introduction of the competitive system (March 2008~July 2009); selection of general programming channels (July 2009~December 2010); preparation for the opening of the general programming channels (January 2011~November 2011); early phase of the general programming channel businesses (December 2011~August 2013); and re-approval of the general programming channels (March 9, 2013~June 2014). Below is a phase-by-phase look at the process.

In the first phase, where media acts were legislated, the Broadcasting Act was amended and the competitive system was introduced (March 2008~July 2009). As the two opposing camps clashed over the legislation/amendment of media acts, the National Committee on Media Development, whose members consisted of equal numbers representing the ruling and opposition parties, was established in an effort to break through the gridlock but failed to come up with the desired result. The media acts, which were passed amid the pitched confrontation between the ruling and opposition parties, went through two rounds of judicial trials by the Constitutional Court, but the legal controversy was concluded with the rejection of the second request for trial. The passing of the media acts is significant in that it opened the door for newspapers and conglomerates to enter the broadcasting services by softening the regulation on the ceiling of the shares that can be owned by both parties.

In the second phase (July 2009~December 2010), the general programming channels were selected. The selection of the general programming channels shifted to full gear in 2010, after the legislation of the media acts. In the selection process, the parties clashed over the appropriate number of broadcasting service providers and the minimum capital requirement, and in the process, a controversy raged with regard to the potential favors to be given to the general programming channels.

In the third phase (January 2011~November 2011), the general programming channels embarked on preparations for the station opening. After the general programming channels that were selected near the end of 2010 were given final approval in the period from March to May 2011, the key issues associated with the commencement of the practical service were discussed and considered. Chief among them were the issues on the assignment of channel numbers and the potential inclusion of the media representative with regard to the order taking of the advertisement slots.

The fourth phase was the early stage (December 2011~August 2013) of the general programming channel services. The early changes in the broadcasting market in the wake of the introduction of the general programming channels can be summed up as the expansion of the produced contents, the rise of the production costs, and the exploration of new content genres, such as infotainment. First of all, the program production market was expanded significantly as majority of the programs were to be outsourced to external production houses, with the exception of the news, news magazine, and some other genres.

The fifth phase saw the re-approval of the general programing channels (September 2013~June 2014). Attention was paid to the re-approval of the general programming channels scheduled for 2014, some three years after the initial approval of the services in 2011. Specifically, the parties were keen to predict if all the four stations were going to be allowed to offer services again; they were under growing pressure to implement the planned investment in content production while still having to make profit. The other issues that were discussed during the period included the inclusion of the general programming channels in the media representative, the possible independent sales of advertisement slots, and the deferment of the payment for the Broadcasting-Telecommunication Development Fund.

The key schedule associated with the general programming channels is as follows. Although the administration's push for the general programming channels was well predicted, with the inclusion of the policy in the presidential campaign pledge, the practical turning point occurred in the process of legislating and amending the series of media acts in July 2009. Further, in September 2010, the absolute appraisal principle was revealed when the Basic Plan on the Approval of Broadcasting Services Using General Programming Channels and News Channels was announced. According to the selection criteria laid out in the plan, those applicants that succeeded in scoring over 800 points out of the potential 1,000 points across the six subcategories shall be approved of as the service provider. The basic plan also specified the entrance barriers to the service market by making it mandatory to raise at least KRW 300 billion as paid-in capital.

After going through the aforementioned selection process, four out of the six applicants were selected as winning bidders on December 31, 2010. They were JTBC led by *Joong-Ang Ilbo*, CSTV led by Chosun Ilbo (thus renamed "TV Chosun"), Channel A (CHA) led by *Dong-A Ilbo*, and MBN (changed from the namesake news channel to a general programming channel). After finally being approved as the selected service providers during the period from March to May 2011, the four general programming channels commenced their services on December 1 of the same year. The general programming channels sparked a cascade of controversies across a variety of aspects as they were often associated with the Media Rep Act, which coincided with the controversial softening of the deregulation of broadcast advertising, which was aimed at strengthening the competitive system in the media industry, or because they were suspected of having received favors as they failed to make a turnaround in terms of their operational performance. As conditional re-approval was granted to three general programming channels in March 2014 and one in October 2014 and one in October, 2014, the implementation of the early-phase policy with regard to the general programming channels can be deemed to have been concluded.

Performance and Assessment

The performance of the general programming channel policy can be assessed from three different criteria: activation of the competition in the broadcasting market; creation of diverse broadcast contents; and expansion of viewer choices and improved viewer satisfaction with the channels/programs.

First, the activation of the market competition after the introduction of the general programming channels can be viewed from diverse perspectives. The competition among broadcasting channels has intensified since the full-scale introduction of the general programming channels in 2012. As a result, it was assessed that a host of positive developments occurred, including increased welfare of the service users (e.g., general quality improvement of broadcasting services/contents and expanded selections available for broadcasting service consumers and advertisers) as well as alleviation of the excessive concentration of the broadcast advertising market on a few channels. In terms of the competitive setting of the broadcasting market, it was assessed that the increased demand for the outsourced production of contents by non-terrestrial channels resulting from the increased competition among the broadcasting channels reduced the concentration of the production demand on a few terrestrial channels and affiliated PPs(program providers), thereby improving the structure of the outsourced program production market.

In terms of the broadcast advertising market, the market concentration was eased as well, thanks to the entrance of the general programming channels and the improved competency of the key pay television channels, and the entrance of a private media representative formed a real competitive structure in the terrestrial broadcasting market. Another confirmed achievement of the policy is that the welfare of the broadcast service users may be promoted by the increased pressure for investment in contents and facilities owing to the growing competition among different broadcast platforms and channels. Such changes in the key indicators are driving the practical competition in the broadcasting market. The seemingly invincible walls that had protected the entrenched interests of the terrestrial channels for decades have begun crumbling down and transforming in the wake of the transformation of the broadcast market into an arena of unlimited inter-channel competition.

As the average viewing rate of all the general programming channels has risen to over the 1% level, the competition to create high-quality contents will only heat up, and it is the high-quality contents instead of the reputation of the station that will largely give a station a competitive edge. At the same time, the race to produce high-quality contents will also trigger a change in the labor market for broadcast contents production. The increased competition among the broadcast service providers is certainly creating positive changes in the broadcast market, but the increased competition is feared to lower the profit potential of the service providers given the limited financial resources available for contents production and facility investment due to the sluggish growth of the broadcast advertising market. Therefore, close analyses and reviews of the related regulations and institutions will have to be conducted to expand the market and to promote an environment conducive to further investment.

Second, the performance of the general programming channel policy can be assessed from the perspective of the creation of diverse broadcast contents. The emergence of the four new general programming channels in the broadcast market, which had largely been dominated by the terrestrial channels, brought about a sea of change across broadcast programs and contents. The show and entertainment sector, in particular, went through a series of evolutionary cycles as the terrestrial channels and the general programming channels vied for viewership with ever-evolving contents. Specifically, group talk shows kept advancing by incorporating diverse formats and contents in the show. Such evolution was triggered by the efforts of the general programming channels that had difficulty inviting popular show hosts on one hand, but it is significant on the other hand that the group talk shows provided entertainment to and earned the sympathy of the viewers while dealing with diverse topics through the unique perspectives of multiple persons. The niche development strategy that the general programming channels adopted in the culture and documentary sector is also notable. For instance, Channel A's "Special Coverage: North Korean Defectors" showed an experimental spirit hardly found in the terrestrial channels as the team made an in-depth coverage of the entire journey of 15 North Korean defectors as the team followed the defectors' journey from their crossing of Aprok River and their crisscrossing of China and Southeast Asia to their final arrival in Thailand. Channel A's "Special Coverage: North Korean Defectors" was awarded the top prize for the first time as a general programming channel in the 2014 Korea Communication Commission Broadcast Awards, and the grand prize in the documentary segment in the Houston International Film Festival, thereby recording "two firsts" for the general programming channel. Furthermore, the general programming channels experimented with a new news format, which combined the news, talk show, and debate formats, ditching the department-style news assortment of the terrestrial channels.

Third, the performance of the general programming channel policy can be assessed from the perspective of the expansion of the viewer choices and the improved satisfaction with the channels/programs. Whether the general programming channels, which are new to the broadcast market, can satisfy the viewers and expand the range of choices for an extended period in the market largely dominated by the terrestrial channels or will confirm the criticism that they are simply wasting their precious bandwidth after failing to overcome the vast gaps between them and the three terrestrial channels will critically influence the performance assessment of the general programing channels. This question may be answered by reviewing the viewers' satisfaction with the programs produced by the general programming channels as well as by the performance review in the seven key areas of the general programming channels based on KIDSI's 2013 Korea Communications Commission Index Viewer Assessment Report.

With regard to KI, an indication the viewers' program satisfaction, the KI average score was 6.96, the satisfaction index (SI) was 6.99, and the quality index was 6.94. Compared with those of the terrestrial channels in 2013, the KIs of the terrestrial channels were clustered around 7 points whereas those of the general programming channels were clustered around 6.89 - 7.15, with most being centered on the latter half of 6 points. Given that not much time has passed since the inauguration of the general programming channels, it is notable that the programs of Channel A scored higher in terms of satisfaction level than those of MBC, and nearly caught up with those of SBS. Moreover, the fact that there was no significant difference between the general programming channels and the terrestrial channels in terms of programs produced would exert a positive influence on the viewers' selection of the programs produced by the general programming channels. When the channel-by-channel performances were evaluated according to the six key indices (entertainment, diversity, creativity, usefulness, fairness, and public interest), the general programming channels scored over 3 points out of 5 across most of the criteria. By criterion, the general programming channels scored higher in terms of entertainment, diversity, creativity, and usefulness in the 2013 survey while obtaining relatively low points in terms of fairness and public interest. The year-on-year comparison showed that the general programming channels scored higher across nearly all the subcriteria in 2013 than they did in 2012. Compared to the terrestrial channels, the performance indices of the terrestrial channels across the seven key criteria generally scored higher points. As the general programming channels excel in the scores' growth rate, however, the gap may soon narrow.

The future tasks of the general programming channels are improving the quality of their produced contents, boosting their viewership, and resolving their financial deficit. Meanwhile, the key factor that will largely decide the successful landing of the general programming channels on the country's broadcast market in terms of finance is the growth of their revenues and net profits, including those from broadcast advertising. A widening deficit is inevitable due to the massive early investment required for channel operation, but the general programming channels will need to work harder in a sustained way to expand their advertising revenues.

6. Discussion on the relocation of the administrative capital: Development policy for Sejong City

Background

Sejong City is the name of a local governing body as well as another name of the administrative complex city (administrative city). President Roh Moo Hyun pushed for the construction of a new administrative capital in the Gongju - Yeonki region beginning in December 2003 to disperse the population concentrated in the greater Seoul area and to realize balanced national development pursuant to his campaign pledge, but it was ruled unconstitutional by the Constitutional Court. In response to the ruling, the administration instead pushed for the construction of an administrative city (original plan for Sejong City) as a follow-up measure, to which all the government ministries (12 ministries, 4 services, and 2 offices), with the exception of the Presidential Office and the National Assembly, shall be relocated. In November 2009, when the Sejong City construction project was 24% completed, including the establishment of the basic plan for years 2007~2009 and compensation for the lands, the administration pushed for the Sejong City Development Policy (amended plan for Sejong City) in an attempt to address the problems identified in the original plan. There were three problems identified in the original plan for Sejong City, which became the background of the Sejong City Development Policy: lack of self-sufficiency, less-than-satisfactory dispersion effect of the population from the greater Seoul area, and inefficiency in the administration.

First, the lack of self-sufficiency of Sejong City was the key background of the push for the Sejong City Development Policy. According to the measure to develop self-sufficiency for the administrative city, a task that was given to the Ministry of Land (2006), the city would need to grow to become a city of 150,000 people during the early activation stage until 2015, and a city of 300,000 during the self-sufficient and mature stage until 2020, by attracting 150,000 more people. Moreover, the city would add 200,000 more people during the completion stage until 2030, thereby evolving as a mid-sized city. The self-sufficient functions that were discussed then included the central administrative function, the culture-international exchange functions, the university and R&D function, the medical and welfare function, and the high-tech knowledge-based function. Such functions may have helped improve the self-sufficiency of Sejong City, but in the short term, the local economy, which had a direct impact on the fiscal strengthening of the local coffers, had to be bolstered to improve the competitiveness and self-sufficiency of the city. The attraction of a base for self-sufficiency functions with a substantial job creation potential, such as companies and universities, would be critical for the sustainable development of Sejong City. As the area that was allocated for the government buildings was just 410,000m^2 (0.6%) out of the total city area (72.91 million m^2) in the original plan for the Sejong City project, the administration concluded that it would not have sufficient potential to create jobs.

Second, another background of the push for the Sejong City Development Policy was the less-than-satisfactory dispersion effect of the population from the greater Seoul area. The original plan for the Sejong City project anticipated the so-called "government building effect" with the relocation, or that of the attraction of companies and people towards the city in the wake of the relocation of the central government institutions therein, including the Prime Ministerial Office, 9 ministries, and 2 offices. The Sejong City Development Policy argued, however, that the basic assumptions of the original plan were based on a false idea in view of the examples of Gwacheon and Daejeon City. Specifically, the policy report argued that the businesses adjacent to government buildings are usually mom and pop stores such as printing shops and restaurants, which have limited job creation or population-boosting effects. In addition, the report stated that according to the original plan, only 10,000 public officials in the central government ministries at most would be relocating to Sejong City, which would likewise have limited job creation or population-boosting effects.

Third, the most immediate reason behind the push for the Sejong City Development Policy was the potential inefficiency in the government administration due to the relocation. As various forms of administrative inefficiency, such as delay in policy coordination, inconvenience in administrative services, and higher transportation costs, are feared to occur due to the dispersion of the central government ministries, the construction of the administrative capital, including the relocation of the central government ministries, had to be modified according to the proposed policy. The policy also argued that business coordination would become more challenging with the relocation of the administrative ministries to Sejong City, with much inconvenience expected as well in the administration's relations with the National Assembly. Also, the administrative-service users, including companies and ordinary people, would have to shuttle between Seoul and Sejong City multiple times, thereby worsening the overall administrative inefficiency. Should the central government ministries be dispersed, various issues in the quality of the policy can be raised with regard to its timeliness and sensitivity due to the lack of information exchanges.

In the advanced countries such as Japan, the United States, the United Kingdom, and France, with the exception of Germany, majority of the presidential (or prime ministerial) or cabinet institutions as well as the congressional institutions are clustered in a single government mall, and even the dispersed cabinet institutions are located within a 5km radius from the central government mall. Germany, the only exception, saw a total of 66,000 business trips of its public officials, along with travel costs amounting to some 8.8 million euros (about KRW 14 billion), as of 2006 due to the dispersion of the government ministries to Berlin and Bonn. Meanwhile, potential expenditures for relocating the government ministries would be incurred in the reshuffling of the capital for the unified Korea should the two Koreas be united in the future. In the eventual reunification, an entirely new capital for the unified Korea may be constructed anew, or as in the case of Germany, the importance of Pyongyang can be stressed in the interest of balanced national development. In any case, the need to reshuffle the government functions dispersed to Seoul, Daejeon, and Sejong City will be highlighted.

Implementation System

The implementation system for the Sejong City Development Policy in the administration can be summed up as including the Public-Private Joint Committee, the Government Support Council, and the Sejong City Planning Group. The administration installed the Public - Private Joint Committee for Sejong City under the direct control of the Prime Ministerial Office, which was composed of the cabinet members and of civilian experts from diverse fields, in an attempt to collect the public opinions and prepare some effective policy alternatives. The committee had 21 members — 7 government members (the prime minister and 6 ministers) and 16 civilian members (6 from the Chungcheong region, 3 from the Gyeongsang region, 3 from the Jeolla region, and 4 from the greater Seoul area) — and was co-chaired by the prime minister and one civilian member.

The key issues that were deliberated on by the committee included the realization of the self-sufficiency of Sejong City, the improvement of and complementary measure for Sejong City, the establishment and implementation of improvement/complementary measures, the consultation and coordination among the related central government ministries, and the legislation and amendment of the laws associated with the improvement and complementary measures. The committee was convened for a total of 11 meetings in the two-month, 25-day period from November 16, 2009 to January 11, 2010 to prepare ways to develop Sejong City. Then six more meetings followed after the announcement of the revised proposal to further discuss the successive issues.

The Government Support Council was formed to provide work-related support to the government and to coordinate the opinions of different ministries with regard to the activities of the committee. The council was chaired by the head of the Prime Ministerial Office and was made up of the vice ministers of the ministries participating in the committee (Ministry of Strategy and Finance, Ministry of Education, Science, and Technology, Ministry of Government Administration and Home Affairs, Ministry of Knowledge Economy, and Ministry of Land and Maritime Affairs). Further, when it was necessary in relation to the meeting agenda, the related presidential secretaries and the related heads of the Prime Ministerial Office also attended the meeting. The Government Support Council meetings were held on a regular basis right after the vice-ministerial meeting every Monday, where those issues that would be tabled in the committee meeting were reviewed and discussed in advance.

The Sejong City Planning Group was installed to handle the businesses of the committee as well as some working-level issues with regard to the preparation of the revised proposal for

Sejong City. The planning group was headed by the deputy executive director of the Prime Ministerial Office, and the deputy chief of the Administrative Complex City Construction Office assumed the role of the deputy head of the group. Further, the group was staffed with public officials who had been dispatched on loan from related ministries and institutions, including the Administrative Complex City Construction Office, Ministry of Land and Maritime Affairs, Ministry of Strategy and Finance, Ministry of Education, Science, and Technology, and LH Corporation. The group was made up of one bureau and four teams, including the deputy director general for coordination support, the General Planning Team, the Project Assessment Team, the External Cooperation Team, and the Public Relation Support Team.

Implementation Process and Contents

The Sejong City Development Policy began effectively with the installation of the Public-Private Joint Committee on Sejong City. The joint committee discussed the problems associated with the original and revised proposals by holding a total of 11 meetings until they came up with the Sejong City Development Policy (revised version), and after the announcement of the revised version, it discussed the remaining issues in six rounds of meetings. The joint committee perfected the logic and contents of the revised proposal by carrying out a special research project and by holding joint workshops with research institutes as well as seminars and discussions with related experts.

The Sejong City Development Policy set the vision of the city as an economic city focused on education and science, which would be supported with the following sublevel goals: "a self-sufficient city with a million population," "a city that creates a new growth engine for the future," and "a base city in the middle of the country." The Sejong City Development Policy was significantly different from the original proposal in many aspects. The original and revised proposals are compared below by key point.

First, the revised plan is different from the original proposal in that it aims to build an economic city focused on education and science. As such, the relocation of the central government ministries contained in the original proposal was excluded in the revised proposal, but the attraction of companies, educational institutions, and research institutes was included.

Second, the project period was significantly reduced from the phased development until 2030 in the original proposal to the concentrated development until 2020.

Third, the self-sufficient function of the city was extensively complemented. The self-sufficient lots' share of the total area in the original proposal was only 6.7%, but it was expanded to 20.7% in the revised proposal. The central administrative town contained in the original proposal was amended and changed to the lots allocated for science and research, international exchanges, and venture start-ups. Specifically, the revised proposal focused on strengthening the self-sufficient functioning of Sejong City and on establishing five key self-sufficient functions of the city: the formation of a high-tech research base, the development of a high-tech green industry, the invitation of top universities, the promotion of a green city, and the establishment of a global base for attracting foreign investments.

Fourth, the establishment of a fast and convenient urban & wide-area transportation system was included in the revised proposal. The proposal suggested the construction of a convenient and comfortable high-tech transportation system that would be accessible within 2 hours from any other region in the country and within 20 minutes from anywhere else in the city. Specifically, the proposal suggested the advancement of the completion year of the key connecting roads from 2017 to 2015 in the case of the wide-area transportation infrastructure, and from 2030 to 2015 in the case of the beltway.

Upon the unveiling of the Sejong City Development Policy (revised proposal), while the public opinions varied wildly depending on the surveyed period and region, a heated debate ensued between the policy proponents and the opposition group involving the political circles, local governing bodies, and civil groups. The June 2010 local elections was the turning point that had largely decide the fate of the Sejong City Development Policy, and the election result was the landslide defeat of the ruling party. The key positions of the municipal and provincial heads of Incheon City, Gangwon Province, and Gyeongnam Province were all won by the opposition candidates. President Lee Myung Bak said in his 42nd weekly radio address broadcasted on June 14, 2010 that "I can no longer stand by and watch the public opinions being divided and the regional and political gaps continuing to widen. I hereby request the National Assembly to make a final decision on the controversy surrounding Sejong City, and the government will fully respect such decision." The National Assembly voted down the revised bill for the Special Act on the Construction of an Administrative City with 105 "yes" votes, 164 "no" votes, and 6 blank ballots from the total of 275 representatives present in the voting session, thereby discarding the Sejong City Development Policy (revised bill).

On July 12, 2010, the Ministry of Government Administration and Home Affairs announced the changes in the number of government institutions that were to be relocated without delay upon the voting down of the revised bill for Sejong City in 2010. The number of central administrative institutions that were to be relocated was reduced from 26 in the original plan to 16 owing to the organization reshuffling via the consolidation and abolition of ministries. The number of umbrella institutions under the central government ministries was also reduced from 23 to 20.

Performance and Assessment

As the revised bill for the Special Act on the Construction of an Administrative City was voted down in the National Assembly, President Lee Myung Bak immediately retracted the revised bill, respecting the decision of the National Assembly, and then pushed forward with the construction of the government office buildings and the relocation of the government ministries, according to the set schedule. The policy could be deemed a failure as the Sejong City Development Policy was not accepted by the National Assembly, but the policy had a beneficial effect: through the said policy, the administration was able to reconfirm the relocation in the political consensus-building process. The controversy over the relocation is expected to continue, however, based on historical grounds.

Another meaningful achievement of the implementation system and deliberation meetings of the Sejong City Development Policy is the governance system in which the government and the civil society arrived at the final decision jointly. The revised proposal for Sejong City was prepared through a close review of the original plan and deliberation on it by the Public - Private Joint Committee chaired by the prime minister. Three research institutes (Korea Research Institute of Human Settlements, Korea Development Institute, and Korea Institute of Public Administration) were mobilized to come up with objective logics behind the revised policy proposal. Public opinions were gathered far and wide through joint workshops and seminars; the deliberative opinion poll system was utilized (an opinion poll was conducted only after providing sufficient information on the Sejong City development method) and finally, the decision was made through discussions and deliberations by the National Assembly. In this regard, the decision-making process on the Sejong City Development Policy can be said to have gone through the democratic process from its beginning to its conclusion. Accordingly, the achievement here is that the administration changed the rules of the game by shifting from the conventional political game, where the winner and loser are clearly decided, to the win-win game, where both the proponent of the revised bill and the opposition group emerged victorious.

Meanwhile, the reason that the Sejong City Development Policy was not selected despite the introduction of the democratic process and governance-style decision-making process is that it failed to change the people's mentality. In other words, the original plan was pledged to the people time and again.[15)] For this reason, the original proposal was perceived by the people as something that could be modified only if and when some unexpected event, such as a revolution or a natural disaster, occurs.[16)] The Constitutional Court also ruled that the relocation would not seriously undermine the presidential decision-making process because the use of bleeding-edge info-communication technology would help overcome the inconvenience associated with the dispersion of the ministerial functions, which reflected the average thinking.

Even though the revised bill was voted down and the original proposal was pushed for instead, the self-sufficiency of Sejong City, the fundamental task required for the city's future development, remained, and the inefficiency due to the division of the central government ministries still have to be surmounted. In an effort to overcome the different forms of administrative inefficiency, the government plans to establish a video conferencing system (video cabinet meeting system, shared video conferencing system, and video conference system by ministry), realize a smart administration that would enable the mobile processing of businesses on the road, improve the working method (flexible working system, residence-type smart work), and expand the online administrative services. The society is also required to lay the emotional foundation on which the people can communicate and cooperate with one another via the video conferencing system or smart devices. With regard to the relationship between the National Assembly and the civil society, the government is required to ensure efficiency and convenience.

---

15) The president answered in July 2009 that the Sejong City project was being implemented according to the set schedule and could not be canceled or changed at will by the government, but he nonetheless announced the revised proposal in January 2010.

16) If the principle of "change in situation" is applied, the original proposal may not be implemented only if the situation that prompted the legislation of the acts that defined the original proposal went through some substantial change that was not or could not be anticipated.

Section 3

The Government Reform of the Lee Myung Bak Administration

1. Background and direction of the government reform

The government reform signifies a series of intentional and planned efforts to turn a certain object (the government) into something with a better state. Gerald E. Caiden defined the administrative reform that signifies government reform in a wider sense as a deliberate attempt to transform the administration, and stressed the goals of the administrative reform as the simplification of the government organization and businesses, the rationalization of the government institution, the simplification of the administrative procedure and the abolition of the formal businesses contained in diverse regulations, and the reduction of the excessive reliance on the bureaucracy. For the purpose of the discussion herein, government reform shall be used as the same concept as administrative reform, but in a wider sense.

The key environmental analysis behind the administration's push for government reform is as follows. The incumbency of President Lee Myung Bak coincided with an extremely challenging period marked by opportunities like the existence of an international collaborative system, the intensification of global competition, the presence of a vast export market, as well as threats like the hollowing of the domestic industrial base, the falling price competitiveness of export goods, and the country's brain drain. Specifically, the global financial and fiscal crises that hit the world after the inauguration of the administration emerged as the prominent threat and the weakness factor that made it even more challenging for the fledging government to implement its key policy initiatives.

Among the threats that existed, the ballooning social costs caused by the low birth rates, rapid aging, and reduction of the economically active population, coupled with the growing number of multicultural families and the rising living costs in old age due to the expanding expected life span, increased the pressure on the government to raise the fiscal spending on welfare services. On the contrary, the opportunities included the rise of new technology sectors such as IT, BT, and NT as the country's new growth engine, largely prompted by the rapid transformation of the economic structure from an industrial economy to a knowledge-based economy, and the resulting emergence of new business areas through the fusion of different technologies. With such developments, the country required the following: a democratic governance structure and procedure for the management and operation of the country; activation of the people's creativity and of a market economy, which are the roots of national competence; and the state governance system rooted in the increased authority of the civil society as well as in mutual trust and open communication.

The government that the administration aspired to realize to accomplish the national vision, "entrance into the club of first-rate countries through advancement," was a pragmatic government that serves the people. Moreover, the detailed goal of the government reform was to realize the following four visions: a "capable government," a "small government," a "government that serves the people," and a "pragmatic government." Inaugurated amidst rapidly changing times, the administration adopted the three approaches cited below in pushing for government reform aimed at realizing the vision of "entering the club of first-rate countries through advancement" and the four goals of government reform.

The first approach was the reform of the public sector (government organizational reshuffling and reform of the public institutions through advancement). The administration pushed for the consolidation of the government functions as well as the reform and privatization of the public corporations in an attempt to expand the autonomy of the private sector and promote market competition by readjusting the roles of the government as to realize a "government that serves the people." The administration considered the dramatic improvement of the inefficient public sector and services provision to the people as the key policy lever for strengthening the national competence. To realize this goal, the administration reshuffled the government into a capable and lean organization while preparing the roadmap for the solid implementation of the country's advancement plan. The government's roles were reviewed on a zero basis, with the goal of reshuffling the government into a "capable and lean organization as well as a pragmatic government that serves the people." Based on the results of the zero-based review, the tasks that would be performed better by the private sector or local governments were boldly transferred to them while the functions scattered across multiple ministries were consolidated to enable the government to concentrate on what was required of it. Moreover, the unnecessary committees were extensively streamlined to introduce the "greater ministerial principle," which advocates an expanded functional base and organization.

The second approach was the active market economy through regulatory reform. While sticking to the principle of running the economy based on the market-centric approach, the administration reformed the core regulations, which had never been touched by the previous governments, from the zero base, armed with the powerful governing philosophy on regulatory reform and with the systematic and effective regulatory reform implementation system/methods. The administration also pushed for the abolition of the limit imposed on the total investment amount pursuant to the Fair Trade Act in an attempt to promote a business-friendly environment. In addition, the administration streamlined the excessive and irrational regulations applied to the greater Seoul area while preserving the basic framework of the regulatory spirit and ensuring that the benefits of the deregulation would be enjoyed as well by the other regions. It also pushed for other regulatory reforms required for the radical improvement of the investment environment and for the strengthening of the country's industrial competence. Specifically, the regulatory method was changed from the positive system, which assumes the "prohibition in principle, exception allowed" approach, to the negative system, which assumes the "permission in principle, exception prohibited" approach. Meanwhile, the administration strove to promote a management environment that would be on a par with the international levels by adopting the multi-dimensional approach, which utilizes policy levers appropriate for deregulation, fiscal support, and market creation in an attempt to strengthen the competence of the service industry, which has a great job creation potential. Further, it streamlined the regulations on the financial industry to make the industry reach the global standards, by pushing for the reform of the overly rigid and uniform regulations on the separation of banking and commerce.

The third approach was the "fair society" approach (anti-corruption reform). President Lee Myung Bak stressed the importance of realizing a "fair society" as the basic national infrastructure required for Korea to develop into an advanced first-rate country in his presidential congratulatory address marking Liberation Day on August 15, 2010. In a meeting of senior presidential secretaries, the president, with his exertion that "a fair society will be the key principle of the government administration until the last moment of my presidency, as well as something worth passing down to the next administration," urged the secretaries to "identify what constitutes a fair society" from the perspective of each ministry or public institution, and to nail down "what practice would befit the criteria of a fair society, then implement those businesses befitting a fair society."

It is desirable for the government reform implementation organization to establish a powerful control tower, which would push for and perform the consolidated management of the reform process, dedicated to the general coordination of the task implementation and controlled directly by the president. However, no such organization was explicitly established by the administration. Whereas, beginning in the latter half of 2008 until the first half of 2012, individual government ministries, including the Prime Ministerial Office, the Ministry of Government Administration and Home Affairs, the National Tax Service, the Board of Audit and Inspection, and the Anti-Corruption & Civil Rights Commission, each took leadership in implementing their respective reform tasks. In the regulatory reform aimed at accomplishing the government reform goal "active market economy," however, the Presidential Council on National Competitiveness was newly installed on top of the existing Regulatory Reform Committee to push for the regulatory reform and other reform tasks until midway into the administration's incumbency. The government reform implementation organization and system by area are shown below.

Implementation system for the reshuffling of the government organization

Unlike the diverse stratified government innovation promotion organization during the Roh Moo Hyun administration[17] the reshuffling of the government organization by the administration was performed by the Presidential Transition Committee even before the inauguration of the government, with occasional organization reshufflings performed by the Ministry of Government Administration and Home Affairs.

17) Various parties, including the Office of the Innovation Secretary in the Presidential Office, the Government Innovation Headquarters in the Ministry of Government Administration and Home Affairs, the Government Innovation and Decentralization Committee, and the innovation officers in the central government ministries as well as the innovation and decentralization officers in the local governing bodies, took on the role of government innovation.

Fiscal reform

The fiscal reform was performed mainly by the Ministry of Strategy and Finance, whereas the reform tasks tabled in the National Fiscal Strategy Meeting were implemented through the coordination among the Presidential Office, the government, spanning the Ministry of Government Administration and Home Affairs, the Presidential Council on National Competitiveness, and the ruling and opposition parties.

Implementation system for personnel reform

The administration consolidated diverse ministries and committees while billing itself as a small and lean government based on Thatcherism. As a result, the Central Personnel Committee was abolished, with its functions reduced and then transferred to the Personnel Administration Office in the Ministry of Government Administration and Home Affairs, thereby prompting the ministry to take the helm of the reform of personnel administration.

Electronic government implementation system

The administration dismantled the Ministry of Information and Communication as a result of the reshuffling of the government organization, transferring its national informatization function to the Ministry of Government Administration and Home Affairs. As for the informatization policy, the Informatization Promotion Committee, which was controlled by the prime minister and was composed of government officials as members, was promoted and revamped in November 2009 to the Presidential Public - Private Joint Committee, which then performed the general oversight on and coordination of the overall informatization policies.

Regulatory reform implementation system

The administration gave utmost priority to regulatory reform in its government administration. It installed the Presidential Council on National Competitiveness in March 2008, on top of the existing Regulatory Reform Committee, which was put under direct presidential control. The Presidential Council on National Competitiveness was given the role of reforming the core policy-level regulations with huge reverberation potential as well as a cluster of regulations associated with multiple ministries. Its regulatory reform style was also based on the two-track strategy, where the perspective of the administrative consumers rather than that of the public officials was valued while the problems stumbled upon in the field were improved on the spot.

Implementation system for the reform and privatization of the public corporations

The reform and advancement of the public corporations was done through an organic collaborative system formed among the Presidential Office, the Ministry of Strategy and Finance, and the Presidential Council on National Competitiveness. The Presidential Office played the role of harmonizing the conflicting opinions of the associated ministries the Ministry of Strategy and Finance played the role of establishing detailed plans as the ministry performing the oversight role on the public institutions and the Presidential Council on National Competitiveness gathered the opinions of various experts and stakeholders. Installed in each ministry controlling and supervising the public institutions directly was the Public Corporation Advancement Promotion Group. At the same time, the Public Corporation Advancement Promotion Advisory Group was also formed to tap into expert knowledge and collect diverse opinions in the push for the advancement of the public institutions.

Anti-corruption reform implementation system

The administration newly installed the Anti-Corruption and Civil Rights Commission by consolidating the existing Korea Independent Commission against Corruption, the Administrative Trial Committee, and the Ombudsman of Korea, and then pushed for the anti-corruption reform drive.

Local administrative reform implementation system

The reform of the local administration by the administration was pushed forward with by the Decentralization Promotion Committee and the Local Administrative System Restructuring Promotion Committee.

2. Contents of the government reform

Organizational Reshuffling

The key characteristics of the government organization reshuffling implemented during the early years of the incumbency of President Lee Myung Bak can be summed up as follows: First, the administration intended to radically downsize the government organization, thereby improving the organizational efficiency through the adoption of a slim organization, by consolidating the similar or duplicate government functions. Second, it strove to strengthen the functions required to prepare for the future and to improve the administrative services rendered to the public. Third, the administration stove to redefine the roles of the central and local governments as well as those of the central government and the private sector. Fourth, powerful regulatory reform was pushed for from the perspective of the people and business, the very customers of the policy, under the leadership of those ministries formed through consolidation in close association with the regulatory reform drive. The number of staffs dedicated to handling the target regulatory functions in the Ministry of Land and Maritime Affairs, Ministry of Food, Agriculture, Fisheries, the Financial Services Commission, and KCC were downsized in accordance with the size and significance of the respective economic regulations, while the “regulatory reform legal affairs officer” was installed in each ministry in an effort to lay the foundation for pushing for the regulatory reform.

The organizational reshuffling of the central administrative institutions brought forth 2 boards, 15 ministries, 2 agencies, 18 administrations, 3 offices, and 5 committees. Compared with the 2 boards, 18 ministries, 4 agencies, 18 administrations, 4 offices, and 10 committees before the reshuffling, a total of 11 institutions were eliminated based on the criteria of “accounting entities” in the early years of the administration’s incumbency. Furthermore, the respective umbrella organizations of the remaining institutions were reduced by 55 offices and bureaus and 93 departments, totaling 3,427 public officials, through the consolidation of departments performing similar or duplicate functions.

Fiscal Reform

The fiscal reform of the administration changed over time to a more programmatic form. A brief look at the key tasks proposed in the fiscal strategic meeting would reveal that the focus steadily shifted from the "transformation of the country into an advanced first-rate country" (2008) to "economic rebound and preparation for the future" (2009), "sustainable fiscal health" (2010), and "sustainable fiscal management" (2011). After the turning point of the administration's incumbency, it is evident that fiscal health rose as the core task of the government administration. The government pledged to achieve a 7% growth rate under the slogan of "747" in the early years of its incumbency. Sensing its inability to achieve such ambitious goal due to the global financial crisis, however, the government instead pushed ahead with some massive investment projects aimed at stimulating the economy, including the Four Major Rivers Restoration Project, which again aggravated the fiscal imbalance and sovereign debts in the latter half of the administration's incumbency.[18)]

The Lee Myung Bak administration pushed for the following policies to maintain the fiscal health of the government.[19)] First, the administration aimed to revamp the fiscal statistics. This was intended to enhance the credibility and transparency of the national fiscal statistics by streamlining the data through the application of the accrual basis in the fiscal statistics as well as through the application of the latest international statistical standards. Meanwhile, the taxation policy of the administration mostly focused on expanding the fiscal spending and tax breaks to stimulate the economy in the early years of the administration's incumbency. The administration also revamped the taxation system in an attempt to boost the tax revenues, and then to restore the country's fiscal health. Further, the list of institutions with tax exemptions and tax breaks was significantly revamped, and the standard of assessments was modified to reflect the market reality in an effort to identify and capture new sources of tax revenues.

Reform of Personnel Administration

The Lee Myung Bak administration abolished the Central Personnel Committee and transferred its function to the newly installed Ministry of Government Administration and Home Affairs. Excluding the aforementioned organizational reshuffling, the administration did not push for any radical institutional reform of the personnel administration system. The partial changes in the personnel administration system and management of the administration are shown below.

First, the administration intended to strengthen the employment of talents based on the spirit of equal opportunities, including the expansion of the existing employment of handicapped people. It also introduced the "employment quota system for the low-income classes" in 2009. Second, the retirement age of the below-grade-6 public officials were extended in a phased manner beginning

18) The international economic crisis triggered by the European fiscal crisis also contributed to the emergence of fiscal health as a key global agenda.

19) Many international organizations, including the IMF, the World Bank, and the OECD, regarded very highly the four major fiscal reforms (autonomous budgetary planning through the distribution of the total budget, the midterm fiscal planning system, the programmed budget system, and the accrual-based book keeping by double entry in accounting) implemented by the Participatory Government. Until today, the country's healthy fiscal management is seen as the outcome of such reform efforts.

in 2009 to boost the work morale of the working-level public officials. Third, the job ranks of the high-ranking public officials were scaled down from five ranks (A~E) to two ranks (A~B) beginning in 2009 to enhance the flexibility in the personnel administration and to clarify the classification. Fourth, the mandatory percentage of the department-head-level jobs open to all eligible people was expanded, but the entrance to government jobs of the private sector remains at a meager level.

Fifth, the administration bolstered the family-friendly work environment, including encouraging the concerned female employees to use their maternity leave benefits. Sixth, the sweeping exams for employing those equipped with a private sector career as grade 5 public officials was introduced to recruit those equipped with sufficient qualifications for a government post. Seventh, job competency assessment was performed for the department-head-level candidates, followed by the introduction of the job competency certificate system in 2010. Eighth, the right to employ and promote all below-grade-3 public officials was delegated to the minister while the autonomy of each ministry in the management of personnel administration based on duty and performance was expanded. Lastly, the employment of local talents via recommendation was revamped.

Electronic Government

Separate from the national informatization project led by the National Informatization Strategy Committee, the electronic government project led by the Ministry of Government Administration and Home Affairs was implemented during the incumbency of President Lee Myung Bak. The key directions of the electronic government project by the administration are as follows.

First, the administration sought to dramatically improve the quality of administrative services by reducing the number of documents that needed to be submitted by the people by expanding the shared use of administrative information held by the different government ministries, by linking the welfare information respectively run by different ministries, and by simplifying the administrative process for selecting the welfare service beneficiaries, thereby significantly improving the efficiency of the welfare administration.

Second, the administration pushed for the consolidated processing of multi-ministry administration services, including the founding and closure of corporations via a single contact in an effort to stimulate the economy built a sophisticated system capable of processing varying issues of corporations via close collaboration among the associated ministries and sought to expand the integrated national logistic/trade information network by linking various logistic, trade, and customer clearance services.

Third, in an attempt to improve the administrative efficiency, the administration consolidated GIS information by standardizing the related data scattered across multiple ministries, thereby enabling the shared use of the data by the different government institutions; dramatically improved the administrative businesses of the local governments, such as permissions and approvals, by linking the GIS information with the administrative businesses and sought to analyze the civil petitions and popular propositions submitted to "e-People," a unified pan-governmental channel for communicating with the people, and provide feedback on the analysis results for policy formation.

Fourth, the administration linked the support data for missing children and women held by the government and the private domain for the shared use of the information, and sought to realize public services that could be felt by the people by establishing a prompt support structure for the socially weak groups.

Fifth, in an attempt to strengthen the country's informatization base, the administration reduced the informatization project costs, lowered the entrance barriers to new industries for small businesses, and promoted a fair competitive environment through the development and dissemination of the standard framework and the shared components for the electronic government project opened the national information resources that were frequently demanded by the public and private sectors to promote the use of public information by the private sector and sought to create added values through the introduction of new services.

Regulatory Reform

The policy task that was the top priority among those pushed for by the administration was regulatory reform. As the Presidential Council on National Competitiveness was inaugurated when President-Elect Lee Myung Bak was being sworn in as president, massive regulatory reform was performed on the core policies that were hindering the economic development, with its detailed contents presented below.

First, a bold softening of the regulations aimed at preventing excessive economic concentration and realizing economic democracy was realized. Chief among such efforts was the abolition of the regulations on the total investment amount and of the regulations on the cross/circulatory investments pursuant to the Fair Trade Act. Second, the regulation on the separation of banking and commerce, which bans the cross-ownership and concurrent management of the two, was softened. The maximum allowable share of the bank stocks that could be owned by industrial capital was increased from 4 to 9%, thereby making it easier for conglomerates to own banks. Third, the regulation on the greater Seoul area was softened. The regulations on the fresh new construction or expansion of all factory buildings in the industrial complexes located in the overpopulated constrained district were entirely abolished while the environmental regulations applied to the greenbelt district were changed from the limitation of the specific geographic location to the limitation of the total amount and to the regulation of the total emissions. Fourth, the regulations applicable to the military facility protection district were comprehensively softened. Fifth, the regulations governing the broadcasting, communication, and media sectors were singled out as reform targets.

The key characteristic of the regulatory reform pushed for by the administration was the temporary suspension of regulations. The Regulatory Reform Committee selected a total of 280 key tasks and suspended the applicable regulations on a temporary basis in an attempt to overcome the global financial crisis, create jobs, resolve the difficulty in founding new businesses, and reduce the burdens on sales activities. Further, the regulatory sunset system, which was not actively applied in the past, was expanded and applied, and the regulatory management system was complemented by identifying and registering those regulations found in the laws but were never registered. Moreover, the administration enabled the real-time provision of regulatory information by revamping the homepage of the Regulatory Reform Committee to the Regulatory Information Portal.

Reform and Privatization of Public Corporations

The reform of the public corporations by the administration was pushed for along two tracks: hardware advancement and software advancement. The reshuffling of the hardware was realized through privatization, consolidation/liquidation, introduction of competition, functional adjustment, improvement of management efficiency, and advancement of the affiliated invested companies.[20] In terms of the software, the following management improvements were realized: advancement of the labor-management relations, revamp of the payment system, innovation of the personnel administration, simplification of the management performance assessment, and push for the management notification system.

In pushing for the consolidation of government functions and the privatization of the public corporations, the administration sought to increase the autonomy of the private sector and to promote market competition by redefining the role of the government. Privatization, a hardware reform of the public institutions, emerged as a hot topic in association with the improvement of the efficiency in the public sector upon the inauguration in 2008 of the administration. Specifically, the growing need for scaling back the functions of the policy financial institution owing to the activation of the financial market, combined with the return of the financial institutions that were nationalized in the effort to overcome the foreign currency crunch, prompted the administration to push for privatization. Towards this end, the administration prepared the "General Standards on the Sales Process in accordance with the Push for the Advancement of Public Corporations, Including Privatization" and established a plan to privatize 10 affiliated companies, 7 public financial corporations, and Korea Housing Guarantee and to dispose of the government shares in Incheon International Airport Corporation and Korea Airport Corporation. Privatization was sought for a total of 24 public corporations. Among them, 19 shall be completely privatized and 5 shall be partially privatized through the disposal of government shares. As of the end of December 2012, 7 of the 19 privatization targets were finished with the privatization process, and 2 were to be sold via Korea Asset Management Corporation.

When pushing for the privatization option, it is difficult to generate energy for it if no concrete plan is laid out on how, and in what aspect the privatized entity would produce an improved outcome. The privatization of public corporations should not be perceived as an independent task for a specific administration instead, the final decision on privatization should be made by shaping the public opinion on how the status and role of a specific corporation in the national economy shall be redefined from the mid- and long-term perspective. Specifically, the current practice in which the related policy is decided via a closed decision-making process, or in which privatization is treated as one of the reform programs of an administration, should be rectified. Towards this end, some institutional base that would guarantee the continuous and sustainable implementation of privatization should be established.

Anti-Corruption Reform

In his presidential congratulatory message marking Liberation Day on August 15, 2010,

20) The concept of "advancement" can be understood as an act of renaming a reform initiative.

President Lee Myung Bak proposed the realization of a "fair society" as the basic infrastructure required for the country's advancement to a first-rate country. Following the address, the government came up with five key implementation directions (fair judicial and legal operation, a corruption-free society, a society with equal access to opportunities and with no privileged treatment, a healthy market economy, and compassionate treatment of the socially weak) and key policy tasks under the overriding principle of the government administration: "a fair society."

The administration amended the Additional Punishment Law on Specific Crimes in 2008 in an attempt to step up the punishment levels applied to the perpetrators of corruption and sought to strengthen the protection of whistleblowers by legislating the Whistleblower Protection Act in 2011. Further, the administration made it mandatory for the members of the Monetary Policy and Operation Committee, who are appointed by recommendation, to register and open their property status. In addition, the Anti-Corruption & Civil Rights Commission pushed for the legislation of the Act on the Banning of Requests for Favors and of the Pursuit of Personal Interests by Public Officials. It is assessed, however, that the priority status of the anti-corruption policy was pushed down somewhat in view of the fact that the dedicated anti-corruption implementation organization was abolished along with the innovation assessment that was used for assessing various performances.

Reform of Local Administration

The Lee Myung Bak administration demonstrated a strong commitment to balanced national development by adopting decentralization as one of the top 100 policy tasks in relation to the government administration. Among such top 100 policy tasks, those related with regional development were expansion of the power of the local governments, activation of the local economy, fiscal expansion of the local government, construction of a wide-area economic belt, pursuit of co-prosperity with the greater Seoul area, promotion of the development of local small businesses, open-type national land space development, strategic expansion of the investment in science and technology, and expansion of the right to enjoy culture and sports activities. Launched in December 2008, the Decentralization Promotion Committee pushed for a total of 20 policy tasks spanning the four major areas it earlier nailed down. The four key areas were redistribution of the government powers and functions, fiscal expansion of the local governments, strengthening of the self-governing capability, and cooperation and dissemination of sympathy. A brief look at the implementation progress of the 20 tasks spanning the aforementioned four key areas will show that majority of the tasks were completed. Meanwhile, with regard to the separation of the administrative functions into the central government and the local government, the planned abolition of delegated tasks was rolled over to the succeeding administration.

The administration launched the Local Administrative System Reform Committee in February 2011, in accordance with the Special Act on the Reform of the Local Administrative System, which was legislated in 2010. The key tasks required for the reform of the local administrative system were the following: (1) consolidation of cities, counties, and wards; (2) redefining of the status and function of the provinces; (3) reshuffling of the self-governing districts or counties in the special and wide-area cities; (4) self-governance by the residents of the towns and villages (eup, myeon, and dong); (5) allowing of special treatments for the consolidated local self-governing bodies and metropolitan cities; and (6) strengthening of the decentralization drive. The Local Administrative System Reform Committee submitted a proposal for the potential revamp of the status and functions of the special and wide-area cities and of the self-governing districts and counties. Serious efforts to gather the opinions of the members of the National Assembly, government officials, expert groups, local self-governing bodies, and local councils should be made further.

3. Performance and assessment of the government reform

In accordance with the key reform areas (reshuffling of government organizations, fiscal reform, reform of personnel administration, electronic government, regulatory reform, reform and privatization of public corporations, anti-corruption reform, and reform of local administration), the performance of the government reform by the administration can be assessed as shown below.

First, the reshuffling of government organizations by the administration succeeded in responding to the demands of the people and to the changing global environment. As the organizational redesign for a small and lean government, however, was implemented during the short active period of the Presidential Transition Committee and in the early days after the inauguration of the new administration, it was said that the gathering of public opinions was not performed sufficiently. A "small government" signifies the scaling back or redesign of the government functions as well as the resulting downsizing of the workforce, budget, and regulations. However, although the growth rate was lower than that of the Roh Moo Hyun administration, the sizes of the total sovereign debt and the government workforce still increased, with the exception of the deregulation. Other negative aspects, such as the lack of expertise in the policy and the insufficient capability to prepare for the future due to the consolidated ministerial management as well as the lack of chemical fusion inside the organization, and the falling operational efficiency, were also criticized. In an attempt to overcome such problems, the administration pushed for post-merger integration (PMI), in which status analysis and solutions for the organizational culture, personnel administration, and performance of functions would be provided to the consolidated ministries as part of the follow-up measure after the first-phase reshuffling of the government organizations.

Second, the administration is assessed to have responded to the global financial crisis in a timely manner through flexible and nimble fiscal management and to have striven to sustain the country's fiscal health. The administration restructured the tax spending and expanded the tax receipts consistently, thereby succeeding in maintaining the fiscal balance and at keeping the country's sovereign debts at a desirable level compared to the average performance of the OECD states. Thanks to such efforts to improve the country's fiscal health, the three key international credit ratings firms (Fitch, S&P, and Moody's) all upgraded the country's sovereign credit ratingfor its excellent fiscal health, as was evident from the country's consistent fiscal surplus trends and low sovereign debt ratio, while downgrading those of the key economies. Moreover, other international organizations, including the IMF, also regarded highly the ROK government's will and effort to maintain the country's fiscal health. Despite all these, it can still be said that the administration did not meet the expectations in terms of its efforts to push for the fundamental overhaul of the operational framework for the macroscopic and microscopic fiscal management at least in the first half of its incumbency. As the potential risks in terms of fiscal health are believed to still be present, the efforts to improve the country's fiscal health should be further intensified.

Third, the administration reviewed the personnel administration policies of the past governments in a new light and pushed for the selection and concentration approach for those policies that were deemed necessary on the premise of pragmatic government administration. For instance, the high-ranking public official group system was retained after its partial modification because its substantial benefits were recognized in the pro-and-con analysis of the policy. No radical change was made in terms of the reform of the personnel administration, but the administration nonetheless succeeded in reforming the details of the system that were left untouched in the previous governments. Such achievement of the administration in the realm of practical reform is highly regarded.

Fourth, the administration was ranked first among all UN member countries in the United Nations E-Government Survey twice: first in 2010, right after the president's inauguration, and second in 2012. The administration was also ranked first among all countries for two consecutive years in the "online participation index," in which the "electronic government development index" and the online participation in policy-making were assessed.[21)] Specifically, Information Network Village (www.invil.org)[22)] and Administration Service 24 (www.minwon.go.kr)[23)] were awarded the first and second prizes, respectively, in the United Nations Public Service Awards (PSA) held in June 2011. Thanks to the push for the electronic government initiative, the shared use of administrative information and the use of online administration services jumped. The government streamlined and improved the convenience of the administration services and reduced the associated costs by making the related administrative institutions electronically share 92 frequently issued individual administrative data, including the (original) copy of the resident registration, the building register, the tax payment certificate, and the certificate of business registration. The utilization of the electronic government service has steadily increased, but it can be said that it needs to be further activated. This is partly due to the reduced need for the issuance of administrative documents thanks to the information sharing among the administrative institutions, and to the advanced disclosure of information. Still, it would be necessary to identify and push for those measures that would activate the use of the electronic government by reflecting the demands of the people, who are the consumers of the e-government services.

Fifth, the performance of the administration in the regulatory reform can be assessed in terms

---

21) The "electronic government development index" in accordance with the United Nations E-Government Survey, is aimed atmeasuring how countries are utilizing the electronic government, which is an apparatus for the effective delivery of government services. The survey involves the key governmentwebsites that provide fiscal, labor, education, and social welfare services. The "online participation index," on the other hand, focuses on the evaluation of how easily the citizens' participation in policymaking and feedbacking is being realized.

22) Information Network Village was established to resolve the information gaps through the active daily information use of the local residents, and to promote the local economy. The project has great potential and can benefit especially developing countries alienated from information.

23) Administration Service 24, the world's first one-stop administration service project that provides a consolidated offering of administration services that are directly related with the daily lives of the people, such as moving, job search and employment, death, and real estate transactions, over their life cycle.

of the improved satisfaction level, the improved policy-level regulatory measures (including the regulation on conglomerates), the improved regulatory reform performance compared to that of the overseas institutions, the elevation of the regulatory reform to the level of overriding agenda in the government administration, the increased tangibility and effectiveness of the regulatory measure as a result of the introduction of fresh regulatory reform methods such as the regulatory sunset system/temporary suspension of regulation, the improved effectiveness and legality of the regulatory reforms (e.g., the streamlining of the unregistered regulations and of the regulatory management system), and the improved effectiveness and efficiency of the reform of the regulatory information system.

The limitations of the administration's key regulatory reform drive, and its aspects that need further improvement, can be summed as follows: streamlining of the regulatory reform system (improvement of the In-House Review Committee, introduction of the regulatory review system via its legislation by the National Assembly members, and unification of the regulatory reform implementation system) enhancement of the regulatory-reform-mindedness of the public officials the less-than-satisfactory political support the lack of popular participation, expertise, and responsibility demonstrated in the regulatory reform process the mechanism generating irrational regulations precise check-up of the regulations resulting in entrance barriers loss of energy for the regulatory reform drive arising from the change in the direction of the government administration in the latter half of the administration's incumbency the need to analyze the key issues with regard to the selection of the business types that are suitable for small businesses and the regulation on the enterprise-level superstores to ensure shared growth and finally, the confusion in the regulatory reform with the change in the goals of the government administration arising from the excessive reliance on the presidential leadership.

Sixth, the performance of the administration in the reform and privatization of the public corporations (reform to advance the public institutions/corporations) can be summed up as follows. The administration implemented the said policy on the public corporations/institutions by following the plan to "advance the public institutions," which reflected the governing spirit of the president as well as the demand of the time, and realized the goals that it intended to realize with regard to the hardware and software of the public institutions through management rationalization and the consolidation/liquidation of the public institutions, the rationalization of the payment system, and the advancement of the labor-management relations. Specifically, the administration successfully accomplished the tasks that had not been handled properly by the previous governments, such as the merger of Korea Land Corporation and Korea Housing Corporation and the curtailment of the exorbitantly high wages through labor-management agreement. The redefining and improvement of the roles of the public institutions/corporations have to be pushed forward with consistently in accordance with the changing environment.

Seventh, the administration pushed for the anti-corruption reform with the leadership of the Anti-Corruption and Civil Rights Commission. The consolidation of the related works in the commission was deemed positive in terms of collaboration and the potential improvement of the government efficiency owing to the elimination of duplicate functions. With regard to the function and status of the organization, some negative aspects were highlighted, such as the less-than-satisfactory synergistic effect of the consolidation and demotion of status of the institution from one under direct presidential control to one under the control of the prime minister.

Specifically, some suggest that it breached the recommendation by the United Nations Anti-Corruption Convention on the installation of an independent anti-corruption institution. The administration did away with the unfair practices and institutions through institutional improvement, to realize a fair society under the governing spirit for government administration, which was declared in the presidential congratulatory address marking Liberation Day on August 15, 2010: "realization of a fair society," but there are still many issues to be addressed. Whenever any fraudulent behavior by a public official was uncovered, the sincerity of the government was damaged, thereby decreasing the energy required for the realization of a fair society. It is assessed that the administration, concentrating only on legal and institutional improvement, failed to live up to the expectations in terms of innovating the spirit and the culture of the people, which is the fundamental solution to the problem. Therefore, the realization of a fair society should be pushed for based on the cultural and perceptual understanding of fairness, on top of the improvement of the legal system. Specifically, the social leadership will have to show its sincerity by joining the anti-corruption drive and compliance campaign commensurate with the premise of a fair society both in name and content.

Eighth, the issue of decentralization was relatively weakened in the administration, but it was still treated as a key policy goal. The administration pushed for diverse local development policies through the Five-Year Plan for Regional Development or the Wide-Area and Regional Development Special Account, based on the concepts of "wide-area economic zone" and "fiscal decentralization," which also include decentralization or local administrative reform. As a result, it is assessed that the administration succeeded in realizing some tangible performances, such as the development of a local industrial base, job creation, fiscal expansion of the local governments, and establishment of a regional growth base. Specifically, the activation of policy-making participation by the regional areas is significant in that it changed the relationship between the central and local areas into one based on a horizontal and collaborative partnership, and realized decentralized government administration based on collaboration. The administration stressed that the decentralization of the reform of the local administration is one of the requirements for the country to develop into an advanced country. Its policy framework, however, focused on strengthening the local competitiveness rather than on balanced national development, and its will and commitment to regional development was somewhat weakened after it passed the turning point in its incumbency.

Conclusion

Foundation of the Republic of Korea, Miraculous Industrialization and Democratization, and Strategy of Government Administration

Section 1

Foreword: From Foundation to Advancement

1. The past, present, and future of the republic

The Republic of Korea achieved impressive economic growth within a short period, which was so remarkable as to be called the "Miracle of Han River," but it also went through numerous ups and downs. The 60-year history of the republic can be recorded and evaluated from a variety of angles, but this paper records the history focusing mainly on the key policy initiatives and government administration of the past administrations, and analyzes their respective implications.

The Republic of Korea is regarded as one of the few continental nations that have had historical experiences centered on the state. Seen from such perspective, the history of the republic can be understood to have been carved mostly by the state or to have been influenced by the key policy initiatives and contents of the government administration that were ran by the government leadership or the governing group.

2. The government policy and the role of government administration

Depending on the perspective that one takes to interpret the history of the Republic of Korea, the assessment of the government policy as well as of the role that the government played in government administration can vary. Based on the orthodox theory, which puts emphasis on the state, it can be posited that the government will or government administration contents largely decide the past, present, and future of the republic. However, based on the revisionist theory, which puts emphasis on the society, it can be posited that the republic shifted its direction influenced not so much by the government will or policy as by the nature of the social classes in the country or by the dominant factor in the world system.

In the science of public administration, the science of policy, or the traditional state theory, government policy and government administration are treated as independent factors. Majority of this paper's authors also analyzed the key policy initiatives and government administration of the past governments of the Republic of Korea from the perspective of the orthodox theory. Accordingly, majority of this paper's authors described and assessed the nature of the past governments based on identical analytical frameworks, criteria, and items. Although their respective approaches towards each subject are identical in appearance and form, they vary in terms of their emphasis on a particular role or aspect of the past governments. For this reason, this paper analyzes how the respective policy initiatives and government administration of the past governments varied in terms of the formation of the state and the national building as well as of the national development.

3. Nation building, industrialization, democratization, advancement, and unification

The development path of the Republic of Korea can be described in chronological order, without necessarily separating them into individual governments. In such case, however, the development and transformation of the government of the republic may be perceived as an evolutionary continuity rather than as a series of separate periodic segments, giving more importance to the continuity of the different times in the country's history. The republic's past political system, however, had the nature of "politics of turbulence" turning on the axis of the state, and the regime change or power transition was triggered mostly by political upheaval rather than by peaceful elections. Thus, this chapter analyzes the characteristics of each period from the perspective of national development, even though emphasis may inevitably be put on some specific aspects rather than on the continuity of different eras.

If the development path of the past governments of the republic is to be captured with snapshots along the different historical periods, the resulting periods would be the nation-building, industrialization, democratization, advancement periods, and the unfolding of the unification process, in such order. The separation of stage may have been done in accordance with the theory on the stages of national development, but it is also a characterization of the easily captured attributes when the national development process is divided in accordance with the functions and roles of major actors. Such development stages may have unfolded incompletely in some areas, and to some extent, the typical historical periods experienced in other countries may have been significantly shortened in the republic. The detailed accounts of the historical periods may vary depending on the theoretical standing or perspective.

Section 2

Theoretical Framework for Analysis

1. Nation building and the theory on the formation of the state

Orthodox Theory

The theoretical resources available for explaining the foundation of the Republic of Korea differ in construction between the orthodox and revisionist theories. The orthodox theory posits that national development is realized in a phased manner, starting with the formation of a nation and of a people and followed by economic development, political development, and distribution of the accumulated wealth. Assuming that national development is realized along progressively different phases, following the logic of the orthodox theory, the development of the Republic of Korea can be explained based on progressive development, starting with nation building and followed by industrialization, democratization, advancement, and ultimately, unification. Such explanation assumes from the state-centric perspective that a state evolves with its own will and autonomous power.

Revisionist Theory

The revisionist theory does not recognize the state's will or autonomy in the policy contents or government administration; instead, it considers the state as a dependent variable of the greater world system or as an ancillary phenomenon of the social classes within the country, but not as an independent variable. Such school of thought includes the divided and extrapolated state theories, based on which the inauguration of the Republic of Korea can be perceived as a by-product of the world military regime. Other theories that are included are the overdeveloped state theory and the "politics of turbulence" theory, which consider the state an extraordinary case in the context of its relationship with the social classes.

Conclusions

As both the orthodox and revisionist theories have a certain degree of explanatory power, diverse theories and conjectures are being proposed. Therefore, it would be a balanced approach to evaluate the nation-building process by comparing the relationship between diverse theories and the state's will as well as the relationship between the key policy initiatives and government administration.

2. Theories of industrialization

Orthodox Theory

Since the orthodox theory used in explaining the industrialization process considers the industrialization of a state as an interactive process involving multiple independent variables, there are various theories related to it. Diverse theories have been proposed to explain industrialization through the lens of variants of the orthodox theory, such as those in the realm of economics, political economics, international trade, and the science of policy: the theory of national ideology and national policy, the theory of international division of labor in economics and the theory of comparative advantage, the theory of industrialized generation, the theory of the fourth-generation post-late-industrialized states, the theory of state ability, the theory of developing state, the theory of economic/trade (international trade) state, and the theory of the timing of industrialization.

Revisionist Theory

The revisionist theory suggests that in the past, the Republic of Korea had elements that were hardly conducive to achieving self-reliant industrialization, but it still pushed forward with and accomplished self-reliant industrialization for some exceptional reasons not true in the case of other countries. Such theory explains that the country, unlike some of its neighboring countries, was able to realize industrialization through its preservation of its powerful bureaucratic authoritarianism despite its being peripheral to the capitalistic world system. Such line of thinking is adopted by the theory of bureaucratic authoritarianism, the theory of dependent development, and the world system theory.

Conclusions

Depending on different academic disciplines or scholars, 22 different explanatory factors were suggested to explain the republic's successful industrialization. These are the economic aid from the United States, the favorable international environment, the foreign direct investments in the country, the regulations imposed on the country's overseas investments, the export-centric industrialization strategy, the early industrialization strategy focused on the substitution of imports, the contribution of neoclassical economics, the state intervention in and planning of the economy, the roles of entrepreneurs, the collusive relations between the government and businesses, the authoritarian government, the efficient implementation of the key decisions, a ready supply of good-quality labor, low wage levels, the wage disparity between the male and female workers, the lack of natural resources, population control, the homogeneity of the Korean people, the division of the Korean Peninsula, the legacy of the Japanese colonial rule, the cultural heritage of East

Asia, and Confucian ethics. Although these factors may vary in terms of the degree of their influence, the industrialization policy and the government administration contents are understood to have had a direct impact on the performance of industrialization given that the country is assessed (from the perspective of both the orthodox and revisionist theories) to have accomplished industrialization autonomously in accordance with the national interests and will.

The early industrialization focused on the light industries that evolved into one focused on the export-driven heavy industries along with the deepening of the industrialization process, all while the country was overcoming its limited resources with an unbalanced development strategy and accomplishing matching economic, social, and political-economic performances. Such results show that the national will, government policy, and government administration all played important roles in prompting industrialization. With regard to the variables explaining the industrialization of the republic, this chapter considers government policy and government operation independent variables as they are believed to have played the role of consolidating the aforementioned 22 variables.

3. Theory of democratization: The June 1987 democratic uprising

The republic seemed to realize the democratization of its political system in the wake of the April 19, 1960 student revolution, but it failed at it owing to the absence of the political forces and culture that would support the institutionalization of the democratic system. The full-fledged democratization is assessed to have started with the June 1987 democratic uprising. The theories explaining democratization vary as well depending on which schools of thought, the orthodox or the revisionist, they belong to. First, the orthodox school of thought includes the theory of democracy, the theory of democratic institutions, the theory of political culture, the theory of political party, the theory of interest groups, and finally, the Darwinian theory. Meanwhile, the key theories in the revisionist school of thought include the class theory and the revolution theory. In addition, depending on the principal agent and method employed, a revolution can be classified as a "revolution from above," which is led by the military (Germany, Japan, and South Korea after the May 16 military coup d'état) or by the state's bureaucratic elites; a "revolution from below," which is led by workers (Soviet Union) and farmers (China); or a "revolution from beside," which is led by the citizens (Britain, France, the United States, and South Korea after the June 1987 democratic uprising).

4. Theory of advancement: Globalization, advancement, and national competence

The theories explaining the national advancement process include those on the timing of the advancement (1st, 2nd, 3rd, and 4th generations), the theory of national competitiveness, the theory of informatization, the theory of smart evolution, and the theories of neoliberalism and futurology.

5. Theory of unification

Defined as the unification of a divided country, unification can be understood as a part of the complex process from the formation of a state and a people to the state's final integration. As it is the process of establishing a new state through the integration of a divided people, land, and sovereignty, unification is the process of prompting the development of an unfinished nation-building project into a fully completed state. Critical to the unification process is the interactive activities of the divided states, the will of each divided state, and the directions of the respective government administrations amid the hegemony structure of the surrounding powers, including the international politics, the global economic system, and the global security system. The strategy for unification varies as well: the economic approach, the political-militaristic approach, the sociocultural approach, the internal-external approach, and the incremental or radical approach. In the case of the Republic of Korea, the national unification policy and the role of government administration in relation to the United Nations, the United States, Japan, China, and Russia, and the six-party talks, are important on top of the conventional importance of the inter-Korean relationship.

6. Key policy initiatives and government administration of the past governments: An approach based on the orthodox theory

Many theories from the orthodox school of thought that explain the importance of the key policy initiatives and government administration of the past governments with regard to the stages of nation building, industrialization, democratization, advancement, and eventual unification are available for checking out varying perspectives. The relationship between the theories on the stages of national development and the related variables is summed up below using the analytical tool employed in this study.

Figure C-1. Analytical Framework

Presidents of the past ROK governments	Syngman Rhee	Park Jung Hee	Chun Doo Hwan	Roh Tae Woo	Kim Young Sam	Kim Dae Jung	Roh Moo Hyun	Lee Myung Bak
Roles for each period Key policy initiatives Method of government administration	Nation building		→	Industri-alization	→	Democrat-ization	→	Advance-ment/ Unification

Section 3

Foundation of the Republic of Korea: The Syngman Rhee Administration, the Korean War, and the Looming Division of the Korean Peninsula

The foundation of the Republic of Korea, which inherited the provisional government in Shanghai and which is based on the independent spirit of the March 1 Movement, was realized with the liberation of the country on August 15, 1945 and the subsequent establishment of a single government on August 15, 1948. The three-year rule of the U.S. military government can be thought of as the preparatory phase for the eventual establishment of the Republic of Korea. Given the overriding influence of the United States and the Soviet Union owing to their occupation and rule of the divided halves of the Korean Peninsula, the capability of the founding fathers and their close cooperation with the international system were critical to the establishment of the Republic of Korea as the only legitimate state supported by the United Nations. Seen from such perspective, it is significant to analyze the nation-building process of the Republic of Korea centered mainly on the key policy initiatives and government administration of the Syngman Rhee administration, in which President Syngman Rhee and the Korea Democratic Party played the central role.

1. National ideology: Adoption of liberal democracy and market capitalism as the national ideologies

As specified in the Constitution of the Republic of Korea prepared by the Constitutional Assembly, the national ideology of the republic, politically, is liberal democracy, and economically, market capitalism. Considering that other competing ideologies, such as socialism, social democracy, and communism, were comprehensively supported by the public, it is exceptionally significant that liberal democracy and the market economy, then the advanced universal global ideologies, were adopted as the national ideologies of the republic. It can be assessed that the republic was able to accomplish the miraculous feat of advancement from a region peripheral to the capitalistic world system thanks to its prescient adoption of the aforementioned national ideology. Such prescient adoption was done after looking far ahead of the evolutionary path of the international politics and world order during its nation-building process.

2. Establishment of the national organization and legal system

Separation of Powers, Adoption of the Liberal Democratic Legal System, and Formation of Governing Forces

The foundation of the republic is the separation of powers among the legislative, judiciary, and administrative branches as well as the liberal democratic legal system. After extended discussions on whether to adopt the parliamentary system or the presidential system, the Constitutional Assembly eventually ended up adopting the presidential system with an element of the parliamentary system. By doing so, the republic adopted a government system that granted substantial power to the president but also enabled the National Assembly to counterweigh the president's orders with matching clout, rather than granting disproportionate power to any single state institution, thereby succeeding in establishing a constitution that reaffirmed the separation of powers, a rare feat among the states that were born after World War II.

The First Constitution of the Republic dealt mainly with the guarantee of the people's rights or freedom, the separation of powers, the unicameral-chamber system, the presidential system (the dualistic executive branch), and the controlled economic policy-making. The adoption of the presidential system in terms of the power structure in accordance with the will of President Syngman Rhee had a far-reaching influence on the future development of the country's constitutional history. The legislation of the Special Act for the Punishment of Antinational Activity, along with the establishment of the constitution, was intended to exert a critical influence on the formation of the governing forces but ended up with no significant result. As President Syngman Rhee opposed the eradication of the pro-Japanese collaborators, arguing that "the establishment of the republic's foundation holds much more importance than the eradication of the pro-Japanese collaborators," the fledgling new country failed to eradicate the remaining colonial groups. Instead, the resurgent pro-Japanese collaborators were revived on the premise of anti-communism metamorphosed into the Liberal Party, which again suppressed the people, thereby planting the seed of the April 19 student revolution.

Establishment of Armed and Police Forces, and Expansion of the Armed Forces after the Korean War

The Syngman Rhee administration established the armed and police forces as the key institutions supporting the government administration. The ROK Armed Forces began as an 110,000-strong army at its inception, with no sufficient military organization or weapons system, being the forces of a nascent state, although the U.S. Forces in Korea took partial responsibility in defending the country. The U.S. Forces in Korea withdrew from the peninsula in the wake of the introduction of Acheson Line in 1950, which resulted in the outbreak of the Korean War in June 25 of the same year, a war that lasted for three years. During the three-year war, the number of the country's armed forces exploded to some 720,000 through the organizational expansion of the military and the increase in the number of troops. The number of troops had since been maintained at around 600,000 after the ceasefire, which had a variety of decisive influences on the national development.

Along with the military police, the police was an integral part of the Japanese colonial rule. However, they were downsized after the liberation on the premise of the country's being an independent state, while the internal organization of the police was revamped through downsizing. Now that the independent state was established after graduating from the Japanese colonial rule and the U.S. military government, the status and role of the police were downgraded on the pretext of the country's being an independent state. In the first year of the Korean War, however, the police force engaged in combat activities, occupying the front lines, and after the war, they engaged in the clean-up operation of the remaining North Korean armed forces that infiltrated Mt. Jiri and Mt. Taebaek, and suppressed the insurgents as part of their operation to defend the republic. The series of inter-Korean armed confrontations that prompted the build-up of the republic's armed and police forces include the April 3 uprising in Jeju, the Yeosu - Suncheon rebellion, and the Daegu rebellion. The republic's armed forces fortified its military structure while going through the Korean War, and established the foundation of the anti-communist state and reaffirmed the police organization in the process.

3. Demarcation of the national borders and peace line

President Syngman Rhee had to struggle with the limitations of the republic's sovereign land, the core factor in the formation of a state, owing to the division of the Korean Peninsula. Moreover, confronted with a territorial waters dispute with Japan, the president reaffirmed the republic's resolve to defend its territorial waters by declaring a peace line dividing the waters between South Korea and Japan, which made possible by the powerful leadership and international reputation of President Syngman Rhee and the rock-solid diplomatic relations between Seoul and Washington.

4. Institutionalization of the national system: Settlement of the bureaucratic apparatus and government reform

The Syngman Rhee administration strove to establish the republic's personnel administration system by adopting meritocracy and keeping the spoils system in check in an effort to introduce a modern bureaucratic institution. But those officials who were active during the Japanese colonial rule and in the U.S. military government formed the core group of the government officials. The government established the employment and personnel administration of the public officials based on meritocracy. Politically, the government adopted the local self-governing system while also pushing for the eradication of corruption. Contrary to such basic guidelines in the government administration, the administration accelerated the demise of the regime by relying excessively on the special employment of those with a Christian background or those who had studied in the United States. Furthermore, the rampant corruption perpetrated behind the thick cover of a collusive personnel network prompted the final collapse of the regime.

5. Formation of the people: Farmland reform, education reform, and postwar restoration

Upon the foundation of the republic, the Syngman Rhee administration pushed for the establishment of a democratic state that pursued for the people's happiness and that aimed to become a powerful independent, liberal democratic state built on equality. In a move to eradicate the ancient regime represented by the feudalistic social status and the Japanese colonial rule and to establish the liberal democratic system, the administration pushed for the abolition of the distinction between the gentlemen (yangban) and the common people (sangin) as well as of regionalism and the discrimination of men and women. Towards these ends, the administration pushed forward with farmland reform, economic democratization, education reform, and purification of the popular social practices. In particular, based on the principle that all lands confiscated through farmland reform shall be redistributed according to the individual capability of the tiller, the lands held by the Japanese landlords were confiscated while the lands held by large landlords were gathered through force compensation and were then redistributed to the tenant farmers.

Through such process, the foundation of an equal society was established by destroying the economic foundation of the traditional gentleman classes, which again provided a clue as to how the formation of an external state would lead to the internal formation of a people (nation building) with a shared identity. The Syngman Rhee administration laid the foundation for the South Korean education through educational innovation. Given that the key project aimed at forming a people with a shared mind involved propelling ideology, culture, and value sharing, the implementation of mandatory education for all the South Korean people formed the core policy of the fledgling independent state.

6. Capital accumulation and market formation

The core elements of the capital and market build-up during the Syngman Rhee administration were the primary industries, such as farming and fisheries. For this reason, the farmland reform in the early years after the foundation of the state exerted critical influences on the formation of the early economic activities. As the farmland reform was implemented according to the principle of "paid confiscation and paid redistribution," unlike the North's "free confiscation and free redistribution" principle, the government exercised caution not to violate the key principle of capitalism. For all such efforts, however, the transition of the landlord class to the industrial capital did not happen as fluidly as was hoped for, thereby hindering the formation of the people as well as the industrialization process.

The entrepreneurial activities other than farming focused mainly on manufacturing of consumer goods, and the light industries, but their sizes remained at insignificant levels. Overall, as the free market was small and the capital accumulation by businesses remained at insignificant levels, the potential of the market was very low. Further, even the insignificant economic activities were mostly conducted by the enemy business property or by the small-scale light industry businesses.

7. Early efforts at and birth of industrialization: Planning apparatus, Five-Year Economic Development Plan, the Henry Tasca Report, and others

The Syngman Rhee administration installed the Planning Agency in September 1948, pursuant to the constitution, and installed the Budget Bureau, Economic Statistics Bureau, Price Statistics Bureau, and Price Planning Bureau under the agency. The Planning Agency established the Five-Year Material Mobilization Plan and the Five-Year Revival Plan while also resolving the short-term economic issues and handling the budgetary issues. However, since the outbreak of the Korean War made it difficult to implement the economic reconstruction plan, economic stabilization rather than reconstruction emerged as the most urgent task.

The Planning Agency was abolished on February 17, 1955 and was replaced by the Ministry of Reconstruction as it was unable to carry on its intended functions due to the war. The ministry played the role of establishing, implementing, and managing the comprehensive plan on the reconstruction of the country's industry and economy. Some of the early works carried out by the ministry include the Five-Year Material Mobilization Plan (1950~1954: Planning Agency, 1949), the Five-Year Comprehensive Plan (Planning Agency, 1951), the Five-Year Comprehensive Plan (Planning Agency, 1954), the Four-Year Comprehensive Plan (the so-called "Tasca Report," 1954~1957: Henry J. Tasca, 1953), the South Korean Economy Reconstruction Plan (the so-called "Nathan Associates Report," 1954~1958: Delegation led by Nathan Associates, UNKRA Plan, 1954), and the Five-Year Reconstruction Plan (Ministry of Reconstruction, 1957~1961: 1956). The administration's plan in the 1950s to aid the people and reconstruct the economy succeeded in restoring the war-torn country by 1956, and in establishing an economic development plan despite the confusion created by the three-year war.

Second, the creation of the ministry (Ministry of Reconstruction) and apparatus (Industrial Development Committee) for establishing an economic development plan despite the postwar economic confusion laid the key foundation for the industrialization and economic growth beginning in the 1960s. Third, a group of experts (including government officials) capable of establishing and implementing the industrialization and economic policy was formed. Such postwar reconstruction plan and the economic development plans in the early years of the industrialization were prepared with the help of international organizations, including some from the United States. It is significant that in the process of establishing and implementing detailed plans, groups of specialized scholars and bureaucrats trained in the United States, or other international organizations, were formed. As such, the country was able to accumulate a pool of potential talents who would push for the industrialization drive after the 1960s.

8. Rapid development from the embryonic phase in the civil society to the student revolution

Various associations working in concert with government institutions, such as youth and anti-communism organizations, were created during the incumbency of the Syngman Rhee administration, thereby boosting the early stabilization of the national system by supplementing the government activities during the nation-building process. Amid the social confusion experienced in the face of the division of the peninsula, the Korean War, and the postwar recovery, such associations collaborated with the police and armed forces and played key supporting roles. Since majority of the said social associations, however, were those that were working in concert with the government, and since those opposing the government policy were either dismantled or banned entirely from engaging in any activity, the civil society was significantly limited in terms of autonomy or legitimacy. This was the undeniable state of the civil society in the divided country that was formed after going through fierce ideological confrontations and an atrocious war right after state building. For such reasons, the civil society during the incumbency of the Syngman Rhee administration remained at the embryonic stage. However, beginning in the latter half of the administration's incumbency, the civil society centered on the student activists grew rapidly, providing the key driver behind its eventual development into the nationwide student revolution that rose up against the March 15, 1960 rigged elections.

9. Democratization nipped in the bud and early vision of industrialization: The April 19 student revolution and the Jang Myeon administration

The Syngman Rhee administration collapsed in the wake of the April 19 student revolution against the March 15, 1960 rigged elections, and was succeeded by the Jang Myeon administration. The local self-governing system was implemented nationwide to its full potential, and the presidential system was replaced with the parliamentary system via a constitutional amendment, thereby pushing the status of the legislative branch above the administrative branch. The administration experimented with administrative decentralization and with the introduction of the self-governing system until the republic's democratization drive was nipped in the bud in the wake of the outbreak of the May 16 revolution.

10. Assessment of the nation-building process

The foundation of the Republic of Korea was realized as a result of the division of the Korean Peninsula amid the international political order of the time. The country inched towards the formation of the nation and the people in the middle of the Korean War, and started to develop the political elements suggested by the divided, extrapolated, and overdeveloped state theories and by the politics of turbulence theory. The nation-building process of the Republic of Korea conveys the aspects of the general development shared by other states as well as some distinctive characteristics.

Section 4

Industrialization of the Republic of Korea: Development State during the Park Jung Hee, Chun Doo Hwan, and Roh Tae Woo Administrations

1. First phase of the industrialization of the republic: The May 16 revolution and the emergence of the development state of the Park Jung Hee administration

National Ideology: First Priority with regard to Economic Development, Neo-Mercantilism, and Security

The Park Jung Hee administration, which assumed power with the May 16 revolution, pushed for the country's industrialization by progressively accomplishing modernization, economic self-reliance, economic growth, transition from an import-driven economy to an export-driven economy, and the parallel development of farming and industry. The administration unveiled the type of national policy and government administration befitting the unique characteristics of the divided state by putting emphasis on national security along with economic advancement.

National Apparatus and Judiciary System: KCIA, EPB, the National Security Law, and the Anti-Communism Act

The Park Jung Hee administration embarked on a comprehensive reshuffling of the government organization in an attempt to implement the economy-first principle and to ensure national security, the two key principles that the administration assumed as the national ideology. The most prominent among such efforts was the establishment of the Economic Planning Board and the Korea Central Intelligence Agency. The Planning Agency founded in 1961 was revamped and expanded to the Economic Planning Board by assuming some of the functions previously carried out by the Ministry of Finance, Ministry of Construction, and Ministry of Internal Affairs, and the Minister of the Economic Planning Board was promoted to vice prime minister in 1963. The board established and implemented the Five-Year Economic Development Plan. As it was an institution established by consolidating the planning and budgetary functions, the board was designed as the central national institution that would push for the modernization and industrialization policy of the Park Jung Hee administration.

As the head institution supervising the various economic ministries governing the foreign capital inducement, construction, industrial, agricultural, resource management, and science & technology policies, the board was staffed with professional bureaucrats who took responsibility in planning and executing the economic development plan. Following the economic development plans prepared by the board, economic ministries, including the Minister of Commerce and Industry, the Minister of Construction, the Minister of Transportation, and the Minister of Agriculture, carried out their respective tasks associated with land construction, introduction of foreign capital and technologies, exploration of export markets, and industrialization. Further, the Korea Central Intelligence Agency was newly established as a central government institution of the development state that would maintain the authoritarian regime. Along with such institutions, the National Security Law and the Anti-Communism Act provided the key judiciary apparatus central to the sustenance of the development state.

Government Reform of the Park Jung Hee Administration

The government reform that was implemented during the rule of the military regime was pushed for in an attempt to break away from the human and institutional legacy of the 1st and 2nd Republic, to lay a new foundation for nation building, to establish the institutional basis for economic advancement, and to maximize the efficiency of the government administration. Towards these ends, the administration pushed for democratization and for the efficiency enhancement of the administrative process, the separation of the planning and execution functions, the institutionalization of the control function, the consolidation of various departments, the unification and concentration of the administrative system, the reinforcement of the local administrative institution, the strengthening of the control of the project implementation authorities, the promotion of land development projects, and the strengthening of the middle-level management institutions. During that time, the administration established the Korea Central Intelligence Agency and the Economic Planning Board, the foundations and pillars of the development state, which was pushed for by the Park Jung Hee administration. Whereas the economic development plan for industrialization was established and executed by the Economic Planning Board, the Korea Central Intelligence Agency provided the protection required for the uneventful implementation of the plan. This was an institutional attempt to facilitate the union of the professional bureaucratic technocrats specializing in the economy and the elite technocrats dedicated to power maintenance.

The two aforementioned key institutions mobilized the local capital and technologies while the Ministry of Commerce and Industry, National Tax Service, and Korea Customs Service supported the national capability as a government organization. The national capability is made up of the organizing capability, policy levers, market capability, and payment capability. The organizing capability is a state's administrative organizing capability. The installation and operation of the key government organizations, such as the Economic Planning Board, Korea Central Intelligence Agency, Ministry of Commerce and Industry, Ministry of Construction, Ministry of Agriculture, National Tax Service, and Korea Customs Service, are key elements of the organizing capability. The intensity of the power assumption of the organization and the quality of the bureaucratic staff are two of the key aspects of the organizing capability. During this period, the government fully implemented the centralized administrative system and was filled with high-quality technocrats, thereby supplementing the internal capability of the government.

Meanwhile, the government played the role of a development state by improving its implementation capability through the introduction of various new regulatory institutions. The state carried out the functions of capital accumulation, technology inducement, conglomerate development, and financial system streamlining to supplement the underdeveloped market, capital, and financial system in the early years of the country's industrialization. The government reform of the 3rd Republic was realized by deepening the government organization created by the military government into a development state. The government system was changed from the parliamentary system to the presidential system while the National Tax Service, Korea Forest Service, and Fisheries Agency were installed to mobilize the domestic capital. In March 1967, the Ministry of Science and Technology was installed, followed by the installation of the Board of National Unification in 1968 and the Korea Customs Service and Military Manpower Administration in August 1970.

Emergence of the Development State: The May 16 Revolution and the 3rd Republic

Five-Year Economic Development Plan and the Economic Planning Board: The first-phase industrialization strategy of the Park Jung Hee administration was to accumulate capital by inducing foreign capital and technology, and to attract unemployed people en masse as low-wage workers to push for industrialization centered on the light industries. The early focus was on some manufacturing industries, such as the textile, apparel, and toupee manufacturing industries, but things changed by the turn of the 1970s. As the number of low-wage workers exploded, the pressure for organizing the workers and for improving the working conditions exposed the limitations of the industrialization strategy centered on the light industries, thereby putting growing pressure on the existing national strategy.

Normalization of the Korea - Japan diplomatic relations and participation in the Vietnam War - Capital accumulation and security cooperation: The Park Jung Hee administration established the 10-Year National Land Development Plan to push for full-fledged economic development and industrialization. Likewise, the administration constructed the Seoul - Busan Expressway as the national basic trunk line expressway. The construction of the Seoul - Busan Expressway contributed to the integration of the people by accelerating the transport of industrial materials and by promoting inter-regional exchanges. The normalization of the diplomatic relations between Korea and Japan and the dispatch of the ROK Armed Forces to Vietnam played key roles in securing the capital that was necessary for the implementation of the Five-Year Economic Development Plan. Despite the fierce opposition by the opposition party and the students, the government pushed ahead with the normalization of the country's diplomatic relations with Japan and with the troops dispatch to Vietnam in order to secure the necessary industrial capital. The participation of the ROK forces in the Vietnam War also contributed to the reinforcement of the ROK - U.S. security cooperation as the dispatch was implemented in return for the ROK - U.S. military alliance. Furthermore, in return for the troops dispatch, the country enjoyed preferential treatment compared to other countries in exporting its products to the United States, thereby contributing to the successful industrialization of the country in more diverse ways.

Formation of the people and push for the Saemaul Movement for the integration of the people: The Park Jung Hee administration pushed for the Saemaul Movement beginning in the early 1970s in an attempt to narrow the gap between the urban and rural regions, a negative by-product that emerged from industrialization, and to push for regional and national integration. Towards this end, communities were constructed in the urban and rural areas on a healthy foundation, thereby enabling continued national integration based on the autonomous spirit. The Saemaul Movement was built on the following three key spirits: self-help, self-reliance, and cooperation, and was pushed for by the local residents based on the emerging leadership. As the Saemaul Movement and the Seoul - Busan Expressway Construction Project were both conceived and pushed for by the president himself, they both provided the key driving force behind the successful industrialization of the country.

Limitations of the first-phase industrialization strategy and the overcoming of the Yushin regime: The first-phase industrialization strategy of the Park Jung Hee administration focused on the local production of import replacement products and on growing export-driven and light industries. As it relied on the comparative advantage supported by low-wage and low-technology workers, it was feasible only to the extent that the high unemployment rate could justify the low wage levels. However, the comparative advantage supported by the high unemployment rate soon disappeared as the falling unemployment rate prompted a war for scouting for the increasingly scarce labor. Such scarce labor made it inevitable for the administration to shift to the second-phase strategy focused on growing the technology-intensive industries.

In the case of the Latin American states, including Brazil, Mexico, and Argentina, they responded to the same challenge by resorting to bureaucratic authoritarianism. When analyzed from the viewpoint of economic logic, the best way to overcome the limitations of "horizontal expansion" resulting from the imports replacement industrial strategy, as in the Latin American states, would be through the "deepening of industrial sophistication" and "vertical integration." Likewise, it was inevitable for the country to push forward with the strategy of growing the heavy chemical industries. As such industry requires massive capital investment and high technology, however, the country then needed high-wage and high-technology workers. For this reason, the emergence of a politically authoritarian regime was inevitable to suppress the demand for wage raise by the labor movement and popular activists. Furthermore, with the perennial security threats peculiar to the peninsula, the country was forced to adopt the authoritarian Yushin regime to push for the second-phase industrialization strategy.

2. Second-phase industrialization of the republic: The "deepening industrial sophistication" strategy and the Yushin regime of the 4th Republic

Construction of the Yushin Regime of the 4th Republic

The industrialization strategy of the Park Jung Hee administration was implemented over two phases. If the first-phase industrialization drive enabled the country to lay the foundation for industrialization as well as to grow the import replacement and export-driven industries, the second-phase industrialization strategy in the 1970s focused on growing the export-driven industry based on the "vertical integration" of the heavy chemical and light industries through a full-fledged push for the development of the heavy chemical industries for the deepening of the industrial sophistication. For such strategy to work, a powerful administrative system and a control mechanism over the labor sector were needed. Towards this end, the administration constructed diverse legal, institutional, and organizational apparatuses. The state corporatism designed to control the labor and social sectors was realized in the form of the Yushin regime.

The Yushin regime then led to the creation of the generalissimo-style presidential system or the presidential system with permanent power to exercise emergency rule as the regime restricted liberal democracy fundamentally. Since the Political Friends of Yushin, government-sponsored puppet party controlled by the president, occupied a third of the National Assembly seats, the elections were rendered meaningless. Also, the president was indirectly elected by the electoral colleges, thereby undermining the democratic foundation of the republic.

Export-driven Strategy, Heavy and Chemical Industry, Conglomerates, and Labor Policy under the Yushin Regime

The second-phase industrialization strategy of the development state was made up of the following key policies: unbalanced development strategy, increased sophistication of the industrial structure, national development on the foundation of science and technology, supplementation of the social welfare sector, renovation and purification of the officialdom and government reform, pursuit of national harmony and unity as a whole, efficiency maximization, reform of public corporations, regulatory reform, anti-corruption reform, reform of local administration, and reform through privatization.

Second-Phase Industrialization, Government Reform, and Government Administration

The second-phase industrialization of the Park Jung Hee administration can be defined as an institutional construction and streamlining of the development state realized in the form of the Yushin regime. As the economic status of the people improved thanks to the successful implementation of the first-phase industrialization in the 1960s, the capabilities of the labor sector and the civil society improved significantly. As the basic intention of the Yushin regime was to construct an efficient system to mobilize the labor sector and the civil society, the administration expanded its state cooperative-style control while billing itself as the progenitor of the "Korean-style democracy." The domain and influence of the state expanded greatly as a host of measures, including expansion of public corporations, strengthening of the regulatory control over the market, expansion of the financial and credit levers, control of the labor sector, expansion of the security apparatus, strengthening of the National Security Law, and expansion of the Presidential Emergency Order, were pushed for.

Busan & Masan Uprising and the Collapse of the Yushin Regime

As the Yushin regime intensified its suppression of democracy, especially, the labor sector, it soon faced a demand for democratization from the civil society, which had grown on the foundation of industrialization. The suppression of the opposition party along with the expulsion of Kim Young Sam, the president of the Democratic Party who symbolized the opposition to the Yushin regime, from the National Assembly triggered a massive anti-Yushin uprising in Busan and Masan, the political stronghold of Kim Young Sam, in October 1979. The political rivalry within the governing circle between the hawkish figure Cha Ji Cheol, who was the chief officer of the presidential security, and the dovish figure Kim Jae Kyu, who headed the National Security Planning Agency, intensified as the discussion on how to best handle the uprising in the two cities rose up. As the rivalry ended with the assassination of President Park Jung Hee by Kim Jae Kyu, the 4th Republic was finally dismantled. The development state's response to the popular demand for democratization, however, did not lead to the dismantlement of the Yushin regime but ended with a revised form of the development state.

3. Third-phase industrialization of the republic and economic stabilization: The Chun Doo Hwan administration

Democratization Nipped in the Bud and the Subsequent Transformation of the Development State

The Chun Doo Hwan administration was born with the emergence of neo-caudillismo. It assumed control of the military with the December 12 military coup d'état after the collapse of the Yushin regime with the assassination of President Park Jung Hee on October 26, 1979, and while the "Spring of Seoul" in May 1980 was cut short, which then led to the democratic uprising in Gwangju. Economically, the industrialization deepened during the 5th Republic, but politically, the time flew back to the pre-modern age largely dominated by neo-caudillismo. The asynchronism represented by the coexistence of the modernistic industrialization and the pre-modernistic neo-caudillismo was present within the neo-caudillismo structure led by Chun Doo Hwan.

Characteristics of the Chun Doo Hwan Administration

The reasons that the 5th Republic, which was governed by Chun Doo Hwan and the neo-military group, should be understood as a neo-caudillismo are (1) the regime was inaugurated and sustained based on fear and dread; (2) the power was exercised arbitrarily (autocratic control of the head of state, concurrent office of president of the ruling party and head of the administrative branch, and arbitrary control of the legislative and judicial branches); (3) the governing elite group was employed based on its loyalty; and (4) structural corruption and fraud were systematically committed. Chun Doo Hwan and the neo-military group adopted the "seven-year single-term president elected by the electoral-college system" in 1981.

According to the new constitution, Chun Doo Hwan was elected president in the same year while a government with the characteristic of a "soft dictatorship" was launched, with the 11th General Elections held to elect the members of the National Assembly. The general elections played a decisive role in prompting the South Koreans to adopt a strategic path to democratization via institutional reform in the form of elections, which was facilitated by a compromise deal with the authoritarian regime under the political leadership of the opposition party within the political establishment. In fact, the authoritarian regime was destroyed with the elections, which again gave birth to the Kim Young Sam and Kim Dae Jung administrations, during which the democratization of the country was pushed for as the national task with overriding importance.

Economic Stabilization and Liberalization Policy of the Chun Doo Hwan Administration

The Chun Doo Hwan administration, which had the characteristic of a "soft dictatorship," took diverse measures to soften its key characteristic externally. Chief among these were the liberalization policy (liberalization of hairstyles, liberalization of school uniforms, and lifting of the curfew), the purification of social evils, the banning of private education, the economic stabilization policy, and the successful hosting of the 1986 Asian Games and the 1988 Seoul Olympic Games. President Chun Doo Hwan unveiled the four key governing principles of his administration in his presidential inaugural address: "naturalization of democracy," "establishment of a welfare society," "realization of a just society," and "education innovation and culture promotion." Based on such governing goals, the administration pushed for the economic stabilization and liberalization policies at the same time in an effort to overcome the negative side effects of the unbalanced industrialization policy pushed for by the Park Jung Hee administration.

Government Reform of the Chun Doo Hwan Administration

The Chun Doo Hwan administration did not allow checks and balances between the powers and had the characteristic of patrimonialism in that it attempted to monopolize and privatize power. The subordination of the legislative and judicial branches, nepotism, familism, and inheritance of power were rampant throughout the incumbency of the Chun Doo Hwan administration. The key characteristic of the government reform then was that the administration pushed for a small government, in which it reduced the government organization and workforce for the first time in the "October 15 Administrative Reform" on the premise that the government cannot intervene in economic activities. The organization and workforce of the expansion-driven development state maintained during the 1960s~1970s was downsized for the first time while the comprehensive regulatory activity of the government spanning the entire areas of the economy and the society was scaled back radically along with the regulatory reform. Moreover, the five key basic computer networks that were established for the first time by the Chun Doo Hwan administration laid the foundation for the country to rise as a global leader in electronic government. The government reform of the Chun Doo Hwan administration, however, is criticized for having been radical and short-term in nature due to the limitations of its birth as well as its authoritarian nature, which was exposed during its implementation process.

Fall of the Authoritarian Government and Transition to Democratization

The June 1987 democratic uprising opened the door for the country's democratization, which resulted in the first peaceful change of regimes in the republic, in which the president finishes his/her specified incumbency and transfers the power to the succeeding government. Although the presidential candidate nominated within the ruling party assumed the power of the next government, it is still significant that the transition led to the first peaceful transition of power in the history of the republic.

4. Fourth-phase industrialization of the republic and economic democratization

June 1987 Democratic Uprising and Basic Nature of the Roh Tae Woo Administration

The democratization of the republic triggered by the April 19 student revolution was cut short before it came to fruition but took root in the country in the wake of the June 1987 democratic uprising. The Chun Doo Hwan administration attempted to snub the simmering popular demand for democratization, which was centered on the introduction of direct presidential elections with the April 13, 1987 declaration of adherence to the existing constitution, but such measure failed to pacify the political unrest. The hawkish and dovish section in the governing group clashed on this issue for a while until the ruling party presidential candidate Roh Tae Woo accepted the constitutional amendment introducing direct presidential elections in the form of the June 29 declaration. As such, the June 1987 democratic uprising ended through peaceful resolution. As the core leadership of the June 1987 democratic uprising consisted of middle-class people and ordinary citizens, it can be assessed as a successful South Korean citizens' revolution. The June 1987 democratic uprising was institutionalized with the constitutional amendment introducing direct presidential elections in 1987, and presidential elections were held in December of the same year, pursuant to the amended constitution.

However, it did not lead to the creation of a democratic government due to the division of the opposition presidential candidacy. Thanks to the divided candidacy of the opposition, the ruling party candidate Roh Tae Woo, who inherited the power from President Chun Doo Hwan, defeated the opposition candidates Kim Young Sam and Kim Dae Jung with a slim margin. The Roh Tae Woo administration was inaugurated in February 1988, with the National Assembly being dominated by the opposition parties for the first time in the history of the republic. For such reason, the Roh Tae Woo administration started as a minority regime steeped with the characteristic of a soft authoritarian government, in contrast to the political environment at the time, which was dominated by democratic power. Inaugurated as a divided government where the opposition parties were occupying the majority seats in the National Assembly, the administration had to face an unprecedented political environment. As the administration pushed for the holding of public hearings on the "Eradication of the Legacy of the 5th Republic," in which it was forced to deny the very regime that gave birth to it, the administration ended up undermining its own power base.

Dominance of the National Assembly by the Opposition Parties Led by Citizens, and Birth of the Democratic Government

The mandate given to the Roh Tae Woo administration was to accept the popular outcry for democratization and to turn the authoritarian government into a democratic one. However, the series of governments ruled by presidents with a military background preserved the basic nature of the authoritarian regime. The mandate given to the Roh Tae Woo administration at the time, therefore, was to seek how best it could harmonize and arbitrate the clash of powers between the state-centric authoritarian government and the citizen-centric democratic government. The Roh Tae Woo administration was forced to start as a weak government amid a political structure where the opposition parties came to dominate the majority seats in the National Assembly after emerging victorious in the general elections that were held after the start of the presidency. The citizens' demand for democratization was realized with the establishment of a series of national institutions amid the reshuffling of the power structure within the governing group and the subsequent realignment of power between the ruling and opposition parties. The republic had gone through a series of political events, from the introduction of direct presidential elections to its growing control of the National Assembly over the administrative branch and the rise of the dovish faction and the decline of the hawkish faction within the governing group. In such political context, the administration was given the task of rectifying the unbalanced development pushed for by the development state from the Park Jung Hee administration down to the Chun Doo Hwan administration as well as the negative side effects of the export-driven economic growth strategy with an economic policy valuing the daily lives of the ordinary people and welfare support.

Key National Tasks for the Governments with the Mandate to Improve the Living Conditions of the Ordinary People during the Period Marked by a Conflict between Industrialization and Democratization

Situated in a period marked by a conflict between industrialization and democratization, the Roh Tae Woo administration struggled to overcome the crisis in political legitimacy that had been building up for the past 30 years with massive policy tasks focused on improving the living of the ordinary people. For this reason, the administration came to have the characteristics of a post-authoritarian regime, billing itself as a government that valued the daily lives of the people in the democratic era. The mechanisms of the development state had to be eliminated one by one, and the national institutions, policy tasks, and government administration had to be realigned so that the administration would be able to carry out its roles as a democratic government.

The Roh Tae Woo administration pushed ahead with the construction of two million homes for those who did not own a house, the group that was considered the biggest victim of the unbalanced development in the past. Towards this end, the administration pushed for the introduction of a public concept of land ownership as well as for the construction of massive new towns in Bundang, Ilsan, and Pyeongchon. In addition, the administration pushed for a series of massive national projects designed to prepare the country for the upcoming globalized era, such as the construction of a high-speed rail (KTX) and of Incheon International Airport. Although, due to their massive financial requirements, such large-scale projects were inevitably met with opposition from the National Assembly that was dominated by the opposition parties, which again led to delays in the project schedule, they still left a substantial positive impact on the future of the republic in that such massive investments in social infrastructure laid the foundation for the country's globalization and advancement.

Opening of the Globalized Era, Unification, and the Northern Policy

In the wake of the end of the Cold War era, the Roh Tae Woo administration pushed for a proactive approach towards China and the Soviet Union by unveiling the Northern Policy initiative, thereby overcoming the legacy of the development state bequeathed from the Cold War era in accordance with the new security needs. With regard to the unification policy, the administration laid the foundation for the future unification policy of the government by pushing for the ground-breaking inter-Korean unification policy titled "Unification Policy for Global Korean Community" on the foundation of the Northern Policy. Further, the administration's normalization of the country's diplomatic relations with China and the Soviet Union through the proactive implementation of the Northern Policy was assessed to be a new policy initiative aimed at making up for the limitations of the divided state that were left unresolved during the nation-building and industrialization period. The Northern Policy is highly significant in that the Republic of Korea, which had been an export-driven country relying on trade with the United States, Europe, and Asia, made China its no. 1 trade partner through such policy, paving the way for South Korea to evolve as a major trading country by overcoming the legacy of the Cold War. The administration, however, did not make matching progress in the military or political arena, thereby failing to contribute to the inter-Korean unification or to the lessening of the tension in the peninsula.

Government Administration and Government Reform of the Roh Tae Woo Administration

As the inauguration of the Roh Tae Woo administration was based on the political environment that had been formed based on the June 1987 democratic uprising, the administration had to have elements of a democratic government. The administration, however, cannot be said to be a democratic government without reservations since President Roh Tae Woo, the governing group, and the power base itself inherited the legacy of the authoritarian regime led by a leader with a military background. For this reason, the administration would be better defined as a soft authoritarian regime. Contrary to the nature of the regime, the key policy initiatives or governing style of the administration had substantial democratic elements. Its key policies partially adopted economic liberalization and economic democratization by modifying or complementing the traditional industrialization strategy centered on the heavy chemical industries. It also eliminated the authoritarian elements to a certain extent in its government administration, and pushed for a democratic governing style, causing the president to be derided as "Mul Tae Woo (Watered-down Roh Tae Woo)." Further, its government administration was so easygoing that it was described as "indecisive." As such, the Roh Tae Woo administration had substantial democratic characteristics, and its key policy or governing style was also democratic in nature. As the key policies had elements of industrialization, democratization, and welfare, it would be a stretch to simplify their nature. For all such progresses, however, the administration has been classified as belonging to the latter half of the industrialization phase rather than to the democratization phase considering the overall national development stage of the republic.

Section 5

Democratization of the Republic of Korea

1. Democratization and advancement of the republic: The Kim Young Sam administration

Inauguration of the Kim Young Sam Administration and Its Basic Nature

The June 1987 democratic uprising should have given birth to a democratic government, but the divided candidacy of the opposition parties led to their failure to assume power and to the inauguration of the Roh Tae Woo administration. For this reason, the political legitimacy of the Roh Tae Woo administration was challenged throughout its five-year incumbency, and it came under constant pressure to keep its pledge of conducting a midterm referendum on the presidency. Some five years after the June 1987 democratic uprising, which brought democracy to the republic, the Kim Young Sam administration was inaugurated as a truly democratic government. The Kim Young Sam administration was a civilian government inaugurated in accordance with the democratization of the republic. While Park Jung Hee, Chun Doo Hwan, and Roh Tae Woo, who all had a military background, assumed power as the head of a military government, an authoritarian government, and a development state, spanning the past 30 years, Kim Young Sam, who had a civilian background, seized power purely on the strength of democratic forces. As such, the administration is highly regarded for its morality and political legitimacy as a civilian government. To meet such lofty expectations, the Kim Young Sam administration took some bold measures to eradicate the legacy of the authoritarian government and to thereby rise as a truly democratic government. The administration showed a much reduced percentage of cabinet members and power elite with a military background, and a comparatively much higher percentage of officials with a democratic-movement background and with diverse social backgrounds, thereby demonstrating the changing nature of the governing power elite.

Key Policy Initiatives of the Kim Young Sam Administration

The Kim Young Sam administration promoted the slogan "New Korea" in compliance with the changes in the history of civilization as well as with the demand of the times both in South Korea and in the world, and assumed "globalization" and "informatization" as the guiding spirits of its government administration. With the goal of "New Korea," the administration intended to overcome the dark shadows of the past development state while also pushing for a democratized South Korea as well as an open-door policy under the goal of "globalization." In addition, the administration unveiled entirely new policy initiatives aimed at realizing a fully informatized state by graduating from the industrialization phase.

Democratization Policy of the Republic

The Kim Young Sam administration embarked on a powerful drive for the "re-establishment of the country's history" in an attempt to carry out the lofty goal of democratization through the eradication of authoritarianism and the establishment of democracy. Chief among the administration's efforts was the eradication of "Hana Group," a private network in the military. The two former presidents who assumed power and established the 5th and 6th Republic by perpetrating two rounds of military coup d'états (December 12 and May 17) orchestrated by Hana Group were both brought to court and subsequently punished.

Democratization Policy and Government Administration of the Kim Young Sam Administration

The administration tightened the regulatory oversight on the political funds and the underground economy in an effort to institutionalize the democratic government by introducing the property disclosure system for the high-ranking officials while pushing for the adoption of the real-name financial transaction system and the real-name property ownership system in an effort to clean up the underground economy. In particular, the real-name financial transaction system played a decisive role in pushing for political reform, economic reform, and the eradication of corruption as the cornerstone of the social transparency assurance system, which is critical to eradicating political corruption, corporate corruption, and various forms of fraud. The real-name property ownership system, which had been considered for possible introduction by the Roh Tae Woo administration but ended up being adopted only in name, was actually pushed for by the Kim Young Sam administration. It also enforced the full-fledged implementation of the local self-governing system as part of the democratization process, thereby prompting the revolutionary change in which the democratization in the central government was extended to the local governments. The full-scale reintroduction in 30 years of the local self-governing system, which had been implemented right after the April 19 student revolution but was suspended in the wake of the May 16 military coup d'état, facilitated the establishment of the democratic local political system, true to the nature of the civilian government.

Globalization and Advancement of the Kim Young Sam Administration

The globalization policy of the Kim Young Sam administration had two sides: on one hand, the administration strove to revamp the country's legal system, economy, society, and labor system and to upgrade these to the global standard; on the other hand, the administration also pushed for the advancement policy, through which it strove to drive the country to rise as an advanced state by overcoming those characteristics that are unique to the country. Globalization was initially understood as a global phenomenon, but it was soon seen as one of the key policy initiatives of the administration. In an attempt to push for the drive to make it the key national strategy and key policy initiative in the government administration, the Senior Secretary to the President for Globalization was appointed and the Globalization Promotion Committee was inaugurated after the establishment of the "Globalization Blueprint." As part of such efforts, the administration actively responded to the globalization trends in the early years of the drive by joining OECD and ILO as a member state. However, since the National Assembly failed to enact labor laws matching the standards of ILO and OECD, the political and social unrest in the country started to spread even further. The country later fell under the direct stewardship of the International Monetary Fund (IMF), and the Kim Young Sam administration had to weather the crisis.

Government Administration and Government Reform of the Kim Young Sam Administration

As the Kim Young Sam administration took pride in being the first civilian government of South Korea in 30 years, it pushed forward with a series of radical reforms that would live up to the democratization of the republic in the realms of the national ideology, national apparatus, government organization, governing power, power elite recruitment, key policies, and government administration style. The administration, however, lacked the internal capability or support at the level of the political system that was required for the globalization or advancement of the country. As the administration prompted the outbreak of the foreign currency crunch in 1997 after failing to endure the pressure of international capitalism, its pursuit of democratization and of the advancement of the country was cut short before it could come to fruition.

Paradoxical as it may sound, the failure of the Kim Young Sam administration led to the first peaceful regime change in the republic from the ruling party to the opposition party. The identification of the implications of such development requires a deeper and nuanced approach, however, as it was actually the international economic order (global capitalism, neoliberalism) that brought about the foreign currency crunch in the country owing to its vested interests in the country, which led to regime change. Recalling that the United Nations and the country's neighboring powers had overwhelming vested interests and influence in the peninsula when the Syngman Rhee administration founded the republic after the division of the peninsula, the fact that the 1997 Asian financial crisis revived the influence of the global economic system on the domestic politics should prompt soul-searching in the country. Whereas industrialization and democratization were pushed forward with by internal factors such as the state governed by the military elite or the civil society, globalization should be seen as the channel through which the global system could exercise its influence on the country.

2. Democratization, advancement, and unification of the republic: The Kim Dae Jung administration

1997 Asian Financial Crisis, Inauguration and Historical Characteristics of the Kim Dae Jung Administration

The inauguration of the Kim Dae Jung administration signified the birth of the democratic government in accordance with the constitutional order through peaceful regime change from the ruling party to the opposition party for the first time in the republic. Along with President Kim Young Sam, President Kim Dae Jung had been suppressed by the authoritarian regime throughout his long life as an opposition party politician. Whereas President Kim Young Sam inherited the power within the ruling party through a "three-party merger" with the ruling party, President Kim Dae Jung was the first president who succeeded in transferring power from the ruling party to the opposition party by winning in the presidential elections as the opposition party presidential candidate. The inauguration of the Kim Dae Jung administration was the offshoot of the people's choice, which was made amid the deepening economic crisis in 1997, when the Kim Young Sam administration got mired in the foreign currency crunch in the wake of the political upheaval associated with the legislation of the labor law. As South Korea could no longer enjoy the preferential treatment specified in Article 8 of GATT, which it had received on the grounds that the country was the regional security hub guarding global capitalism in East Asia, the country began to receive pressure from the global capitalistic market driven by neoliberalism. The country may have pushed for globalization and joined OECD and ILO as a member state, but as it failed to live up to the global capitalistic order of neoliberalism, the country woke up to the cold and stark reality by being forced to comply with the international order.

Globalization and the Four Key Restructurings of the Kim Dae Jung Administration

The Kim Dae Jung administration was forced to dismantle the development state through a series of reforms aimed at realizing the neoliberalistic "small government," including reform of the public sector, privatization of the public corporations, dismantlement of the conglomerate-centric economy and growing small venture start-ups, institution of flexibility in and reform of the labor market, and restructuring of the financial industry aimed at eradicating the government-controlled financial system. As the IMF received a pledge from all the presidential candidates that they would comply with its policy recommendations, the government had no choice but to push forward with the restructuring. With regard to the restructuring of the labor sector, the government introduced the national basic living security system, and, with regard to the reform of the conglomerates, the government strove to rectify the imbalance between large corporations and small businesses and the distorted economic structure centered on the conglomerates, all of which were the limitations typically found among development states. Moreover, as part of the policy initiatives of growing venture start-ups and of implementing the informatization drive in the economic sector, the government pushed forward with a massive drive to develop IT venture start-ups. Such move was part of the economic restructuring policy aimed at changing the structure and qualitative direction of the economy at the same time.

Unification and Inter-Korean Reconciliation and Cooperation Policy of the Kim Dae Jung Administration

The Kim Dae Jung administration pushed for a conciliatory approach towards Pyongyang by adopting the so-called "Sunshine Policy," in which it attempted to understand and embrace the North. The administration constructed the Kaesong Industrial Complex and granted a business license to a company for tourism businesses on Mt. Keumgang. In addition, President Kim Dae Jung visited Pyongyang for the first inter-Korean summit meeting, where he agreed with Chairman of National Defense Kim Jong Il with regard to the establishment of the first-phase federation for the eventual unification of the two Koreas. In recognition of such achievements, President Kim Dae Jung became the first Korean who was awarded the Nobel Peace Prize.

Government Administration and Government Reform of the Kim Dae Jung Administration

The Kim Dae Jung administration was swayed greatly by neoliberalism owing to the foreign currency crunch that it had to struggle through. Even though he was the proponent of the popular economic movement, President Kim Dae Jung could not but push forward with the four major restructurings policy, which was far detached from his personal convictions. Still, the full-fledged implementation of the local self-governing system and the push for the inter-Korean cooperation and unification policy were significant. The influence of the democratic civil society was greatly strengthened with the expanded participation of the civil organizations, such as the People's Solidarity for Participatory Democracy and the Citizens' Coalition for Economic Justice, in the government administration. As the reform of the public sector was foremost among the four major restructurings that had to be done, the direction of the government reform focused on the implementation of the small government policy or the privatization of public corporations. Such policy faced severe opposition from the labor sector and the civil society, but the neoliberalistic policies were nonetheless pushed forward with amid the foreign currency crunch, thereby prompting the key social forces to be limited by the influence of the global economic system, such as the IMF. The Kim Dae Jung administration reaffirmed the country's international status by successfully hosting the World Cup Soccer Games, which helped the country establish a national status befitting the globalized era, while also responding positively and proactively to the foreign currency crunch.

3. Flinching at the door of national advancement and globalization – the Roh Moo Hyun administration: Balanced regional development and venture into the movement regime

Inauguration and Characteristics of the Roh Moo Hyun Administration

Unlike the Kim Dae Jung administration, the Roh Moo Hyun administration had the characteristic of a movement regime, which was led by the "386 generation" and "Nosamo," and simultaneously pushed for era change, generation change, and reshuffling of the power structure. For the first time as the president of the Republic of Korea, Roh Moo Hyun openly revealed his "anti-American and pro-North-Korean" attitude by asking, "What's wrong with being anti-American?" The president also frequently expressed anti-market remarks in a clear display of the "movement regime" and the "ideological regime." Such raucous remarks soon led to the president's impeachment in the National Assembly in March 2004, which led to an enormous political upheaval. The impeachment of the president backfired, though, as the ruling Uri Party ended up scoring majority seats in the National Assembly in the succeeding general elections. Thanks to such unexpected development, the administration was able to build a robust political base by causing the power structure marked by the dominance of the National Assembly by the opposition party since the Roh Tae Woo administration had crumbled down. Contrary to the populist remarks of the president, however, the administration did not push for left-leaning policies.

Key Policy Initiatives of the Roh Moo Hyun Administration

The key policies of the Roh Moo Hyun administration included the "relocation to the new administrative capital and balanced national development policy," "decentralization policy," "policy on the concept of the Era of Northeast Asia," "real estate policy," and "welfare policy." Specifically, the relocation to the new administrative capital policy was abruptly included in the campaign pledges of the ruling party presidential candidate near the end of the race, and had a direct influence on the ruling party presidential candidate's success in the race, thereby prompting the Roh Moo Hyun administration to push for the policy as a top priority. An act governing the relocation process was passed by the National Assembly after much political haggling, but it received a near-fatal blow when the Constitutional Court ruled it unconstitutional. The administration nevertheless pushed ahead with the policy by legislating another law that would replace the initial act, but the policy remained at the center of political confrontations throughout the administration's incumbency. The administration also pushed for the decentralization and balanced national development policy at the government level by forming respective presidential committees that would handle the policy initiatives. In compliance with the relocation of the central government institutions to Sejong City, the parallel policy of distributing the umbrella institutions and other national institutions from Seoul to other regional cities was also pushed for. The administration intended to improve the daily lives of the ordinary people by implementing the real estate policy and other welfare policies, but it ended up pushing up the real estate prices, triggering other unanticipated negative side effects, thereby failing to carry out its original intention to improve the daily lives of the people.

Passive Response to Globalization and the Concept of the Era of Northeast Asia

Unlike the Kim Dae Jung administration, the Roh Moo Hyun administration maintained a passive and negative attitude towards globalization. While billing itself as the "balancer," the administration shifted the policy on international politics and the economy from one focused on the United States and Japan to one focused on China, Russia, and North Korea, causing its long-time friendly relations with Washington to deteriorate significantly in the process. The administration inherited the "Sunshine Policy" of the Kim Dae Jung administration with regard to the inter-Korean relations, which eventually led to the visit of President Roh Moo Hyun to Pyongyang. However, due to the special prosecutor's investigation of the "illegal provision of funds to Pyongyang by the Kim Dae Jung administration," the administration failed to score substantial achievements on the unification front. Although the administration pushed for the signing of the FTA with the United States, the proposed peace zone on Yellow Sea, which was pushed for with regard to the inter-Korean relations, invited a pitched confrontation in the domestic political scene.

Government Administration and Government Reform of the Roh Moo Hyun Administration

The Roh Moo Hyun administration failed to gain impressive achievements in the realms of national advancement and unification, which were the key mandates of the time. The administration originally attempted to relocate the present capital to the administrative capital for balanced national development, but the original plan was scaled back to the construction of an administrative-centered complex in Sejong City (Happiness City) after the ruling of the Constitutional Court. The administration also made a variety of attempts to change the 50-year history of the republic, but such attempts pushed for by an administration that was unprepared for the presidency and that had an amateurish government administration style only led to a host of unwanted developments, such as the emergence of a conflict with the ruling class, of confrontational relations with the international powers, and of the popular suspicion of the occurrence of behind-the-scene transactions with Pyongyang, which eventually resulted in the shifting of the power to the opposition forces. Contrary to the "imprudence" of President Roh Moo Hyun, however, the government officials and cabinet members who were running the day-to-day government operations as technocrats carried out their roles flawlessly, thereby preventing the aforementioned unwanted developments to wield a significant impact on the government operations. This can be regarded as the result of the successful engagement of path dependency for democratization and national advancement of the ROK government, as well as a clear evidence that a democratic government is not easily swayed by the deviations made by any president. The Roh Moo Hyun administration had a complex governing style as it pushed for democratization, national advancement, and unification as its key policy initiatives but concentrated more on democratization than on national advancement or unification. As the only administration steeped with the characteristic of a movement government among all the past administrations in the history of the republic, it pushed for balanced national development at the government level, which is a clear evidence that the administration put more heft on democratization as its national agenda.

Section 6

Advancement and Unification of the Republic of Korea: Challenge, Frustration, and Renewed Challenge

1. Challenges with regard to national advancement, and the ensuing frustration

Challenges Faced by and Frustration of the Kim Young Sam Administration

The Kim Young Sam administration pushed for a proactive drive for national advancement by forming the Globalization Promotion Committee as a government - private joint committee pursuant to the "Blueprint for a New Korea" and the "Blueprint for Globalization" that it had established. As part of its drive, the administration pushed for the country's joining of OECD and ILO as a member state. Before the administration could embark on a full-scale drive for national advancement, however, its efforts were cut short as the country got mired in the 1997 foreign currency crunch. The administration is therefore assessed to have focused on democratization rather than on national advancement, and it did not score high either in its efforts towards unification.

Challenges Faced by and Frustration of the Kim Dae Jung Administration

The Kim Dae Jung administration contributed to the institutional advancement of the country in that it adopted the neoliberalistic economic order as a global standard by focusing on the four key restructurings policy in an effort to overcome the foreign currency crunch, but it did not gain much economic achievement. On the unification front, however, the administration succeeded in holding the first-ever inter-Korea summit as well as in paying a presidential visit to Pyongyang. Such accomplishments, however, were re-evaluated in the public hearings on the illegal provision of funds to Pyongyang held during the incumbency of the Roh Moo Hyun administration. The Kim Dae Jung administration also faced challenges and met failures in the realms of national advancement and unification, which is probably why the administration focused more on democratization.

Challenges Faced by and Frustration of the Roh Moo Hyun Administration

The Roh Moo Hyun administration also pushed for national advancement and unification. Although the challenges that it faced with regard to these two agenda were not that significant owing to the differentiated national ideology and due to its focus on balanced national development, it did not obtain impressive results either.

2. The Lee Myung Bak administration

Inauguration and Characteristics of the Lee Myung Bak Administration

As the Lee Myung Bak administration adopted a hardline approach in its unification policy with its proposed guideline "resolution of the North Korean nuclear ambition first, then inter-Korean cooperation," it ended up cooling the Sunshine Policy pushed for by the previous administration. The six-way talks for resolving the North Korean nuclear crisis did not go as planned, causing the administration to fail in scoring impressive achievements on the unification front. The integrity of the Kaesong Industrial Complex was not compromised, but the Mt. Kumgang tour program was halted when a tourist died after accidentally being shot by a North Korean guard. The administration, however, succeeded in establishing a precedent in the inter-Korean relations: the holding of "inter-Korean talks on firm principles."

Government Administration and Government Reform of the Lee Myung Bak Administration

The Lee Myung Bak administration succeeded in launching the Global Green Growth Institute, the only international organization that was established as a result of the ROK government's efforts towards national advancement, and secured an important place in the international stage as a host/chairman country of the G20 Summit. The government organization was reshuffled pursuant to the principle of small government, by pushing ahead with the government reform aimed at becoming a small government on the principle of big ministries, big bureaus, and big departments. The government organization became slimmer through organizational reshuffling, including the consolidation of the Ministry of Education and the Ministry of Science and Technology into the Ministry of Education, Science, and Technology. The privatization of the public corporations was pushed forward with on a massive scale; the relocation of the public institutions to local cities, which was initiated by the Roh Moo Hyun administration, was continued during the Lee Myung Bak administration. The administration, however, did not score high in the realms of national advancement and unification, thereby leaving these as the national tasks that had to be handled by the succeeding government.

Section 7

Characteristics of the Key Policy Initiatives and Government Administration of the Past Governments of the Republic of Korea

1. Nation building-industrialization-democratization-advancement-unification: The "Miracle of Han River" made possible by the national ideology and national spirit

The remarkable development of the Republic of Korea could be attributed to the soft power that emerged in it as a combined result of the state spirit, the will of the national leaders, and the aspirations of the people. The nation building of the Republic of Korea was realized thanks to a number of factors — (1) the independent spirit of the March 1 Movement; (2) the volition for independence of the leaders in the provisional government in Shanghai; and (3) the aspiration for liberation and independence of all the South Korean people — which all resulted in the ascendancy of Syngman Rhee and other political leaders. To sum up, the Republic of Korea was built through the establishment of an independent government supported and selected by majority of the people and with the support of the international community.

Industrialization was the national strategy aimed at securing the basic material conditions that were indispensible for postwar restoration and for the survival of the people after the conclusion of the nation-building efforts. The country was able to realize industrialization driven by the energy that was formed when the Saemaul spirit ("can do" and "fight while working" spirit, self-help, self-reliance, and cooperation) and the passion for modernizing the motherland were fused with the leadership of President Park Jung Hee. In conclusion, the economic-development-first principle and the establishment of the nation on the strength of technology and the neo-mercantilism were integrated in the form of spiritual concentration to prompt the cohesion of an ethnic national commonwealth, thereby giving birth to the "Miracle of Han River."

Democratization was the combined result of the great awakening of the citizens to the benefits of democracy, the democratization movement, and the sacrifices of the citizens. The country paid a huge price after the trial-and-error experiments of the April 19 student revolution and the June 1987 democratic uprising, in themselves "citizens' revolutions from beside," prompted the successful democratic revolution of the Republic of Korea.

The foreign currency crunch overwhelmed the country in 1997 as a result of the mixing together "at a wrong time" and "in a wrong place" of democratization, globalization, and informatization, leaving a great conflict and much confusion in its wake. The South Korean people and the government, however, saw an opportunity for the advancement of the republic amid the great confusion by turning the crisis into the nation's zeitgeist: "advancement." The early overcoming of the foreign currency crunch and the ensuing drive for the advancement of the country, contrary to other countries, were attributable to the close collaboration between the people and the corporations. Such people-corporations collaboration also played the key role in preventing the second global financial crisis in 2008 from escalating into another foreign currency crunch, enabling the country to eventually overcome the crisis without paying a hefty price, unlike other countries.

As such, the collective will of the South Korean people and the nation's zeitgeist combined to push the wheels of modern history: establishment of independence and nation building by Syngman Rhee, who fought for the liberation of the country; realization of industrialization by President Park Jung Hee and Chun Doo Hwan, both with a military background; realization of democratization by President Kim Young Sam and Kim Dae Jung, the leaders of the democratization movement; and national advancement and the overcoming of the financial crisis by President Lee Myung Bak, who used to be the CEO of a global company. Such fusion of the powerful will of the people and of outstanding national leadership gave birth to the Miracle of Han River and facilitated the successful harmonization of industrialization and democratization. Seen as such, it was the people's will power, the nation's zeitgeist, the national leadership, the development strategies, and the governing styles that the people selected that made the Republic of Korea what it is today.

2. State leadership, national development strategy, and government administration

The past governments adopted different national development strategies depending on the president and on the nature of the government. First, the Syngman Rhee administration, which opened the 1st Republic, could not afford to find time to establish a systematic strategy for economic development as it concentrated its efforts on nation building. If anything, its strategy focused on exporting primary goods and on building an industrial base that would produce replacement goods for imported products. Busy with building a national system and with promoting national integration, the administration could hardly find time to mull over economic policies and concentrated on its imminent military tasks. The administration pushed for postwar recovery and for the improvement of the daily lives of the people after the ceasefire; the economic aid from the United States following its military assistance was funneled to the postwar recovery and reconstruction projects, which laid the foundation for the development of the imports replacement industry. The Jang Myeon administration of the 2nd Republic established the Tasca Report and other associated economic development plans in an attempt to accommodate the desire for economic development by building imports replacement industries, and was busy negotiating with Washington to obtain loans from it when its development initiative was cut short with the outbreak of the May 16 revolution. The Jang Myeon administration strove to realize the democratization and economic development of the country in a balanced manner based on the build-up of the imports replacement industries, but it failed to see the realization of its efforts.

Second, the full-fledged industrialization of the republic was pushed for by the Park Jung Hee administration. The first-phase industrialization of the country was pushed for by the Park Jung Hee administration of the 3rd Republic based on the export-driven development strategy. The administration pushed for the unbalanced development strategy, where insufficient capital and technology were induced by the government from foreign countries and were then invested in specific areas. Towards this end, the Economic Planning Board and the Korea Central Intelligence Agency were established and maintained while the administration pushed for several rounds of the Five-Year Economic Development Plan. Such drive prompted the creation of the slogan "Export is the only way to survive" and the resulting creation of the export-driven development state.

The second-phase industrialization was pushed for by the Yushin regime of the Park Jung Hee administration. The full-scale operation of the development state caused severe imbalance and a distorted distribution of the country's economic resources, thereby prompting the introduction of the strategy of deepening the development state. The conglomerate-centric export-driven strategy of the Park Jung Hee administration under the 4th Republic was an inevitable result of such strategy. As the export-driven strategy deepened the economic inequality and distorted the market order, it prompted the need for an even more powerful authoritarian regime in the form of the Yushin regime.

The third-phase industrialization took the form of industrialization and economic stabilization after going through some fundamental adjustments under the Chun Doo Hwan administration of the 5th Republic. Such evolutionary changes enabled the proactive push for the economic stabilization and liberalization strategy by softening the authoritative development state of the Yushin regime. The fourth-phase industrialization took a mixed form of the industrialization and economic democratization strategies after going through another round of adjustments under the Roh Tae Woo administration of the 6th Republic. Third, the democratization of the republic began in earnest in the wake of the June 1987 democratic uprising, but a truly democratic government was realized for the first time with the inauguration of the Kim Young Sam administration, the phase 1 government of the democratization era, after going through an interim state during the Roh Tae Woo administration. The Kim Young Sam administration pushed for the real-name financial transaction system and the real-name property ownership system among the economic democratization strategies for industrialization in an attempt to overcome the negative side effects of the development state.

Phase 2 of the democratization was steered by the Kim Dae Jung administration. The administration succeeded in overcoming the foreign currency crunch by pushing for the four key restructurings policy pursuant to the neoliberalistic economic paradigm shift in an effort to overcome the Asian financial crisis. Phase 3 of the democratization was overseen by the Roh Moo Hyun administration. The administration created substantial conflicts and confusion and slowed down the economic advancement by approaching neoliberalism via a unique ideological viewpoint while sticking to the closed economic policy, but it still made contributions to the democratization and balanced regional development. The advancement of the country was pushed for in earnest beginning with the Lee Myung Bak administration. The administration strove to harmonize the country's growth and environment by pushing for the low-carbon, green-growth strategy not only domestically but also at the global level, but failed to come up with meaningful results.

3. Key mechanisms and variables in the push for national development

The key factors that influenced the national development, and the mechanisms that were employed by the past governments to realize national development, were as follows. For the Syngman Rhee administration, they were the Korean War, diplomacy, and armed and police forces during the nation-building process. For the Jang Myeon administration of the 2nd Republic, they were the cabinet and the police force. For the Park Jung Hee administration, they were the Korea Central Intelligence Agency, the Anti-Communism Law, the Economic Planning Board, and the Five-Year Economic Development Plan. For the Park Jung Hee administration of the 4th Republic, they were the Yushin regime, the Yushin Constitution, the indirect presidential election system, the National Council for Unification, the Korea Central Intelligence Agency, the riot police force, the emergency measure, and the armed forces. For the Chun Doo Hwan administration of the 5th Republic, they were the military, the Army Security Command, the indirect presidential election system, the five-year single-term presidency, and the riot police force. For the Roh Tae Woo administration of the 6th Republic, they were the constitutional amendment introducing the direct presidential election system, the National Assembly dominated by the opposition parties, the ballooning power of the National Assembly, the public hearings on the corruption that transpired in the 5th Republic, and the divided government. For the Kim Young Sam administration, they were the civilian government, the Blueprint for a New Korea, the Blueprint for Globalization, the re-establishment of the country's legitimate history, the eradication of Hana Society, the real-name financial transaction system, the political reform, the full-scale introduction of the local self-governing system, and the globalization policy. For the Kim Dae Jung administration, they were the Sunshine Policy, the National Assembly dominated by the opposition party, the NGOs, the globalization, the economically balanced development policy. For the Roh Moo Hyun administration, they were the NGOs, populism, the movement government, the decentralization, and the balanced regional development policy. For the Lee Myung Bak administration, they were the weak government, the government with shared power structure within the governing group, globalization, green growth, the Four Major Rivers Restoration Project, the response to the global financial crisis and the economic advancement policy.

4. Governing ideology, transition of the governing power, and changes in the key policy initiatives

Changes in the Governing Ideology

The governing ideology of the past governments were anti-communism, capitalism, and liberal democracy for the Syngman Rhee administration; liberal democracy, capitalism, and the welfare-centric ideology for the Jang Myeon administration of the 2nd Republic; the economic-development-first principle, neo-mercantilism, and self-reliant defense for the Park Jung Hee administration; the South-Korean-style democracy, the Yushin regime, and state capitalism for the Park Jung Hee administration of the 4th Republic; soft dictatorship, economic stabilization, and economic liberalization for the Chun Doo Hwan administration of the 5th Republic; economic liberalization, democratization, the welfare state, and unification for the Roh Tae Woo administration of the 6th Republic; civilian democracy, economic democratization, and market capitalism for the Kim Young Sam administration; democracy and neoliberalism for the Kim Dae Jung administration; democracy, the balanced regional development policy, and populism for the Roh Moo Hyun administration; and neoliberalism and market capitalism for the Lee Myung Bak administration.

Governing Power and Changes in the Power Elite

The Syngman Rhee administration of the 1st Republic was swayed by the influence of the world military system; the Jang Myeon administration of the 2nd Republic by the democratic social classes; the 3rd Republic by the security state, which was led by the military group; the Yushin regime of the 4th Republic, particularly the Park Jung Hee administration, by the economic ministries that pushed for the development of the heavy chemical industries and by the trading state system; the 5th Republic by the soft authoritarian state system governed by the military elite; the Roh Tae Woo administration of the 6th Republic by the competitive structure between the military group and the democratic social classes; the Kim Young Sam administration by the democratic civil society that emerged after the June 1987 democratic uprising; the Kim Dae Jung administration by the democratic civil classes and the neoliberalistic global capitalistic system, which competed with each other to strengthen their respective hegemonies in the wake of the 1997 Asian financial crisis; the Roh Moo Hyun administration by democratic social class; and the Lee Myung Bak administration by the market dominated by the South Korean conglomerates and the global financial market in the wake of the 2008 global financial crisis.

Changes in the Key Policy Initiatives

The key policy initiatives of the past governments were the establishment of the state system (including nation building) and of the anti-communism system for the Syngman Rhee administration; the dismantlement of the authoritarian regime and the establishment of a democratic regime for the Jang Myeon administration of the 2nd Republic; export-driven industrialization centered on the export of light industrial goods, economic development, and the establishment of national security for the Park Jung Hee administration of the 3rd Republic; the maximized mobilization of the national power, and the export-driven strategy centered on the heavy chemical industries for the Park Jung Hee administration of the 4th Republic; the economic stabilization and liberalization policy through soft authoritarian rule for the Chun Doo Hwan administration of the 5th Republic; economic liberalization pushed for as an adjustment stage for democratization and industrialization for the Roh Tae Woo administration of the 6th Republic; the economic democratization and globalization policies for the Kim Young Sam administration; the four key restructurings policy based on the neoliberalistic principle for the Kim Dae Jung administration; the balanced regional development policy for the Roh Moo Hyun administration; and the overcoming of the global financial crisis and the push for the green-growth policy for the Lee Myung Bak administration. Such key policy initiatives changed the respective roles of the past governments. The key policy initiatives of the past governments were established and implemented along the development stages of the state (i.e., the nation-building, industrialization (modernization), democratization, and unification stages).

5. Adequacy of the key theories in accordance with the development stage of the state

It is assessed that the adequacy of the diverse theories that were employed to explain the development of the Republic of Korea varies depending on the stage of national development. The theory of the development stage of the state well explains the actual stages of the republic's development (i.e., the nation-building, democratization, advancement, and unification stages). Each theory has an explanation power per development stage.

Nation-Building

The orthodox theory has higher adequacy for explaining the nation-building process of the republic. The establishment of the constitution, armed and police forces, and administrative system as well as the defense of the state by engaging in war are the contents of the nation-building process whereas the mandatory education of the people, farmland reform, education in anti-communism, and unification were the tasks that were required for the formation of the people. The overdeveloped and extrapolated state theories and the whirlwind politics theory are useful in explaining the partial power structure or political phenomena that were observed during the nation-building process. Therefore, the state leadership, governing ideology, and key directions of the government administration of the Syngman Rhee administration are assessed to have exerted critical influences on the formation of the state and the people in the early years of the nation-building stage.

Industrialization

Given that even the proponents of the revisionist theory recognize the industrialization of the republic, the explanatory power of the orthodox theory seems to be compelling herein. The key success factors in the industrialization drive of the 3rd Republic are the assumption of power by presidents with a military background since the May 16 military coup d'état, the laser-sharp concentration of the national resources on the industrialization drive through the realignment of the governing ideology and the national institutions along the lines of industrialization, and the effective implementation of the five-year economic development plans. The fact that even the proponents of the revisionist theory single out South Korea as an exceptional world system or dependence theory case for the reason that the country adopted the export-driven economic development strategy rather than a strategy focused on the domestic economy shows that the explanatory power of the orthodox theory is more compelling than that of the revisionist theory. The dependent development theory, the development state theory, and the industrialization timing theory, however, also have explanatory power, albeit only partial and structural. Therefore, it can be said that all the 22 different theories that were employed to explain the industrialization of the republic have a certain level of adequacy. Furthermore, with regard to the export-driven development strategy centered on the heavy chemical industries in the second-phase industrialization, the bureaucratic authoritarian theory, the state cooperative theory, and the world system theory, along with the orthodox theory, have some explanatory power in macroscopic terms.

Adjustment of Industrialization

With regard to the explanation of the adjustment phase of the country's industrialization, no adequate theory could be found. Thus, one-dimensional descriptions of the state's will, the key policy initiatives, and the government administration style were simply performed. This can be explained by the theory that this was the phase where two different orders (the dismantlement of the development state and the establishment of a new state model) were competing in a chaotic state. Other theories, such as the economic stabilization, economic liberalization, and economic democratization policy theories, have been suggested, but all of them seem to have only partial explanatory power.

Democratization

The theory of Barrington Moore Jr. seems to have compelling adequacy in explaining the republic's democratization process. The June 1987 democratic uprising and the resulting June 29 declaration can be deemed successful examples of the "revolution from beside." In the wake of the democratic uprising, the Roh Tae Woo, Kim Young Sam, and Kim Dae Jung administrations emerged with the corresponding rise of a matching governing ideology, governing group, and civil society, which shows that the changes in the political order triggered by the democratization rather than by the results of the key government policies or government administration prompted the changes in the ROK government. In addition, the theory of democratization institutions, the theory of culture, the theory of interest groups, the theory of political parties, and the theory of elections are assessed to have some adequacy. Therefore, one may be able to get a big picture of the republic's democratization process by taking a comprehensive look at all of them.

Advancement and Unification

As the country's advancement and unification are currently still being pursued, no specific theory can be singled out to explain them. Specifically, the fact that the country has yet to pass the threshold of national advancement for the past 20 years and that no significant progress has been made on the unification front suggests that a theory or policy with substantial adequacy in explaining the country's advancement and unification has yet to be found.

Section 8

Conclusions: The Tasks of National Advancement and Unification for the Republic of Korea in the 21st Century

The Republic of Korea is one of the few countries that have successfully accomplished nation building, industrialization, and democratization. It is presently faced with the tasks of national advancement and unification, which the republic has been struggling to achieve for the past 20 years. The country, however, has yet to achieve a meaningful feat. The country successfully overcame the 1997 Asian financial crisis and the 2008 global financial crisis, but it has yet to realize its advancement by overcoming the barriers to the global market with its own capability. The country is one of the top 10 trading states in the world and is the host/chairman country of the G20 Summit, but it still has to carry out plenty of tasks to realize its national advancement.

Compared to industrialization, whose attainment by the country was adequately explained by the catch-up theory, explaining the country's national advancement is a much more challenging task as it requires a creative theory or strategy. The series of policy initiatives or strategies, such as the "New Korea," "Blueprint for Globalization," "2nd Nation Building" or "Green Growth" strategies, have yet to achieve significant performances. Their results paradoxically suggest how their adequacy in explaining the country's advancement has not yet been recognized.

With regard to the unification policy, diverse models for explaining what the country has attained in such regard, such as the unification by absorption and national federal unification theories, were suggested, but it remains an ongoing issue. As the hard or soft landing of North Korea, the key variable in the North Korean issue, as well as the South's strategy and policy, is relatively critical for unification. It may unfold faster or much slower than expected. Unification is a matter that cannot be influenced independently by the governing ideology, the key policy initiatives, or the government administration. Whether the country will follow the precedents set by Germany, Vietnam, or Yemen in its unification process or it will maintain the status quo, as in the case of the relationship between China and Taiwan, shall be determined by how much influence the choice of South or North Korea will have on the process.

At present, the country needs to establish its own national strategy or a new governance style to successfully accomplish national advancement and unification. The country needs to come up with some creative development strategies well above the past practices marked for emulation and catch-up, and to establish a mechanism and network of new governance in which the country is run through collaboration between the state, the market, and the civil society, while graduating from the era where each of these three key factors has dominant power over the remaining two.

Further, the country needs to establish and push forward with the smart governance and smart unification strategies befitting the globalization and smart era. This is because the country will need to come up with entirely new and creative methods unlike anything it relied on in the past to accomplish the goals of national advancement and unification, the two key national tasks that the world's leading IT powerhouse has yet to realize, having failed to realize it in the past 20 years.

As the preparation for smart governance is being pushed forward with by the National Informatization Strategy Committee and other national institutions as well as by the corporate sector, its coverage is expected to expand in the future. Further, the national strategy and unification policy required for smart unification will have to be pushed for anew. Now is the time to push for the Korean Cyber Commonwealth Unification Method, which is well beyond the scope proposed by the Commonwealth of the Korean Unification Method established by the Roh Tae Woo administration in 1992. If South Korea, a country that has developed and distributed world-class smart devices to the world, can spread these to North Korea, it would not be that difficult to form a cyber commonwealth of the Korean people in the North. Furthermore, the country will be able to unify such cyber commonwealth of the Korean. The recent spread of smartphones and smart electronic devices in the North Korean society is certainly a good signal, suggesting that the "unification of the cyber commonwealth of the Korean" will eventually escalate into the unification of the commonwealth of the Korean without much difficulty.

The Republic of Korea successfully accomplished nation building, industrialization, and democratization in the past 65 years, better than approximately 200 any other states in the world did. The republic is now required to concentrate its capabilities through collaborative governance enabled via cooperation among the government, the businesses, and the civil society to attain national advancement and unification in the 21st century, for national advancement and unification cannot be achieved by the government alone.

Index

[P]

[R]

[S]

[T]

[U]

[V]

[W]

[Y]

The Korean Government:
Policies and Administration
1948~2013

Compilation Committee and Participating Members

Publisher
Dr. Yoon-Soo Jung (President of KIPA)

Supervised by
Prof. Dal-Gon Lee (Gachon University)

Advisory Committee
Prof. Suk-Jun Kim (President, Anyang University)
Prof. Young-Hee Park (Honorary Professor, Konkuk University)
Prof. Byong-Man Ahn (Former Minister of Education, Science and Technology)
Prof. Jeong-Gil Yun (Honorary Professor, Konkuk University)
Prof. Dal-Gon Lee (Gachon University)
Prof. Chung-Kil Chung (Chief Director of the Ulsan University Foundation)
Hyeong-Geun Jeong (Former Member of the National Assembly of the Republic of Korea)

Editorial Committee
Prof. Sung-Bae Kim (Soongsil University)
Prof. Yang-Ho Park (Hongik University)
Prof. Dae-Hee Lee (Kwangwoon University)
Prof. Jae-Hyun Joo (Myongji University)
Prof. Heung-Seok Choi (Korea University)
Prof. Mee-Sung Ha (Konkuk University)
Prof. Pyo-Hwan Han (Chungnam National University)

Writing Committee

Foreword: Byong-Man Ahn (Former Minister of Education, Science and Technology)

The Syngman Rhee Administration
Prof. Jong-Cheol Kim (Yonsei University)
Dr. Jeong-Ok Nam (Institute for Military History, MND)
Prof. Tae-Gyun Park (Seoul National University)
Prof. Hee-Bong Park (Chungang University)

Prof. Youn-Chang Shin (Kangwon University)
Prof. Dae-Hee Lee (Kwangwoon University)
Prof. Seo-Hyeng Lee (The Academy of Korean Studies, AKS)
Prof. Ju-Cheon Lee (Wonkwang University)
Prof. Shin-Yung Choe (Sookmyung Women's University)

The Jang Myeon Administraition
Prof. Jung-Yul Kim (Daegu University)
Dr. Hak-Soon Paik (The Sejong Institute)

The Park Jung Hee Administration
Prof. Wook Kang (Korean National Police University)
Prof. Jae-Hoon Kim (Seoul National University of Science & Technology)
Prof. Yong-Su Bae (Kongju National University)
Prof. Soon-Chang So (Konkuk University)
Prof. Jin-Kwang So (Gachon University)
Prof. Won-Hee Lee (Hankyong National University)
Prof. Jong-Soo Lee (Hansung University)
Prof. To-Bin Im (Seoul National University)
Prof. Dong-Jin Lim (Soonchunhyang University)
Prof. Mee-Sung Ha (Konkuk University)

The Chun Doo Hwan Administration
Dr. Il-Gyu Kang (Korea Research Institute for Vocational Education & Training, KRIVET)
Prof. Yong-Soo Kwon (Konkuk University)
Prof. Hyun-Joon Kim (Korea University)
Prof. Jin-Keun Park (Yonsei University)
Prof. Chi-Sung Park (Chungang University)
Prof. Jae-Rok Oh (Jeonju University)
Prof. Tae-Seoung Lim (Hanyang University)
Prof. Hyug-Baeg Im (Korea University)
Prof. Sung-Gul Hong (Kookmin University)

The Roh Tae Woo Administration
Dr. Kyur-Yoon Kim (Korea Institute for National Unification, KINU)
Prof. Keun-Sei Kim (Sungkyungkwan University)
Prof. Tae-Ryong Kim (Sangji University)
Prof. Yang-Ho Park (Hongik University)
Prof. Byung-Seol Byun (Inha University)
Prof. Sang-Yong Sim (National Defense University)
Prof. Soon-Tak Suh (University of Seoul)
Prof. Song Lee (University of Seoul)
Prof. Tae-Soo Ha (Kyonggi University of Seoul)

The Kim Young Sam Administration

Prof. Byung-Moon Kim (Andong University)
Dr. Chang-Ho Geum (Korea Research Institute for Local Administration, KRILA)
Prof. Ik-Sup Shim (Dongguk University)
Prof. Nam-Kuk Lee (Pukyong National University)
Dr. Sang-Rok Lee (National Institute of Korean History, NIKH)
Prof. Chang-Won Lee (Hansung University)
Prof. Jin-Wook Choi (Korea University)
Prof. Pyo-Hwan Han (Chungnam National University)
Prof. Jih-Wan Hwang (University of Seoul)

The Kim Dae Jung Administration

Prof. Byung-Sook Kim (Konkuk University)
Prof. Sung-Jae Kim (Yonsei University)
Prof. Chung-In Moon (Yonsei University)
Dr. Jong-Chul Park (KINU)
Dr. Won-Seok Suh (KIPA)
Prof. Hah-Zoong Song (Kyung Hee University)
Prof. In-Sil Yi (Sogang University)
Prof. Joo-Hun Lee (University of Seoul)
Prof. Heung-Suk Choi (Korea University)

The Roh Moo Hyun Administration

Prof. Seok-Jin Lew (Sogang University)
Prof. Jae-Hyun Joo (Myongji University)
Prof. Chang-Heum Byeon (Sejong University)
Prof. Kyoung-Ryung Seong (Hallym University)
Prof. Seong-Ho Ahn (Daejeon University)
Prof. Su-Hoon Lee (Kyungnam University)
Prof. Ji-Ho Jang (Hankuk University of Foreign Studies)
Dr. Hye-Kyung Chang (Korean Women's Development Institute, KWDI)
Dr. Hie-Shin Hwang (KIPA)

The Lee Myung Bak Administration

Prof. Kwan-Bo Kim (The Catholic University of Korea)
Prof. Dong-Wook Kim (Seoul National University)
Prof. Sang-Hyup Kim (Korea Advanced Institute of Science and Technology, KAIST)
Prof. Sung-Bae Kim (Soongsil University)
Prof. Young-Han Kim (Sungkyungkwan University)
Prof. Jung-Soo Park (Ewha Womans University)
Prof. Chun-Oh Park (Myongji University)
Prof. Hyung-Ki Ahn (Konkuk University)
Dr. Chang-Hyun Yun (Korea Institute of Finance, KIF)

Prof. Hyue-Su Ha (Kyungpook National University)

Conclusions: Prof. Suk-Jun Kim (Anyang University, President)

Director-General of the Project
Dr. Hyun-Mo Yang (KIPA)

Assistant Administrator by the Administration
The Syngman Rhee / Jang Myeon Administration: Se-Hyun Cho (KIPA)
The Park Jung Hee Administration: Dr. Hie-Shin Hwang (KIPA)
The Chun Doo Hwan Administration: Dr. Young-Rok Kim / Sung-Geun Kim (KIPA)
The Roh Tae Woo Administration: Dr. Jong-Seol Yun (KIPA)
The Kim Young Sam Administration: Dr. Sung-Geun Lim (KIPA)
The Kim Dae Jung Administration: Dr. Yoon-Kyung Oh (KIPA)
The Roh Moo Hyun Administration: Dr. Joon-Young Hur (KIPA)
The Lee Myung Bak Administration: Dr. Soon-Young Choi (KIPA)

Assistant to Director-General of the Project
Dr. Gee-Weon Chang (KIPA)

Administration Support (Correction)
Min-Tae Lee (KIPA)